Buy
Wholesale
By
Mail
1999

BUY WHOLESALE BY MAIL 1999

BY THE PRINT PROJECT

Lowell Miller, Executive Producer
Gail Bradney, Executive Editor

Michael Beames, Research Assistant
Joëlle Francis, Editorial Assistant

HarperPerennial
A Division of HarperCollins Publishers

FIRST HARPERPERENNIAL EDITION
ISSN 1049–0116
ISBN 0–06–273633–7
98 99 00 ◆/RRD 4 3 2 1

CONTENTS

HOW TO USE THIS BOOK

Buy Wholesale by Mail 1999 is written to help consumers get good values when buying by mail—or phone, fax, or online. In this book, "wholesale" denotes the savings required as one of the qualifications for a listing—30% or more on list or comparable retail on some of a firm's products or services. Some of the firms will sell to crafters, small businesses, and others on a wholesale basis. Those firms are denoted with a star in the icon line in their listings. For details, see "Buying at Wholesale," page 590.

There are other icons that will help you get the most from the information, so before sending for a catalog or placing an order, please read the key to the symbols in "How to Read the Listings" (from page xi). For more detailed information on mail-order shopping, see "The Complete Guide to Buying by Mail," beginning on page 586.

Following is a guide to several of this book's features that will help you make the best use of the material.

"FIND IT FAST"

This list, right after each chapter's introduction and before the listings (except in chapter sections with only three or four companies), is an at-a-glance guide to different types of products offered by firms listed in that section. For example, if you're looking for companies selling tropical fish supplies, check the "Find It Fast" roster in "Animal and Pet Supplies" instead of reading through all of the listings in that chapter.

"RELATED PRODUCTS/COMPANIES"

Each firm is listed in the chapter that best reflects its business focus, and *cross-referenced* in the "Related Products/Companies" sections at the end of other chapters, as appropriate. For example, Gohn Bros. is listed in the "Clothing" chapter because that's its strong suit. Because Gohn also sells horse blankets, you'll find it cited in the "Related Products/Companies" section at the end of the "Animal and Pet Supplies" chapter.

PATIENCE

Since companies are constantly revising their catalogs and printing new ones, please allow *six to eight weeks* for delivery, unless the listing indicates potential for a longer delay. If the catalog doesn't arrive within the designated period, write or call the company. Please remember that some products, such as flower bulbs and highly perishable foods, can be ordered only at certain times of the year, and catalogs may be mailed during shipping season only.

PRICE QUOTES

Some firms don't issue catalogs at all. Most of these operate under a price-quote system: You tell them the exact make and model number of the item you want, and they give you the price and shipping cost. Price quotes are given by mail, phone, and fax. Businesses that operate this way are clearly indicated in the listings. (Be sure to check the "Special Factors" notes at the end of each listing as well as the core information.) Price-quote firms often have the lowest prices on such goods as appliances, audio and TV components, and furniture; they usually sell well below both the standard manufacturers' suggested list prices and the less-formal minimum prices that some manufacturers try to enforce. Before writing or calling for a price quote or making a purchase in this way, read the "Price Quotes" section of "The Complete Guide to Buying by Mail," page 586.

MINIMUM ORDERS

In a few cases, the best buys are available from firms that require a minimum order in dollars or goods. Minimum requirements are usually flexible, and most firms will accept orders below the minimum, although an extra "handling fee" is often imposed. If you want something that's a real bargain, you may have friends who'll want it as well.

BEFORE SENDING MONEY

If you're unsure of any company, or want to double-check a firm before placing a large order, contact the Better Business Bureau nearest the company (see page 611).

A CAVEAT

Buy Wholesale by Mail 1999 is compiled as a resource for consumers, to help you to find good values available by mail. *Never* order goods directly from this book, even if prices are given in the listing. *Always* contact the company first to get a catalog or a current price quote, and follow specific ordering and payment instructions. *Don't request extra discounts or wholesale prices, unless the listing states they are available. Attempting to bargain with these firms makes the vendors quite unhappy.* All of the information in this book is based on research and fact-checking as of press time, and is subject to change.

Enjoy *Buy Wholesale by Mail 1999,* and please let us know your positive as well as negative experiences with these firms—see "Feedback," page 615, for address information.

HOW TO READ THE LISTINGS

Some of the information in the listings is presented in a simple, coded form at the head of each entry, formatted as follows:

1. **COMPANY/CONTACT INFORMATION:** Company name, mailing address, and phone numbers, including 800, fax, and TDD lines
2. **CATALOG:** Form of literature (catalog, brochure, flyer, leaflet, price list, etc.); the price, followed by "refundable" or "deductible" if you can redeem the cost by placing an order; SASE: send a long (business-size), self-addressed envelope with a first-class stamp (unless more postage is requested); "Information": price quote or information is given over the phone and/or by letter or on the internet (when there is no catalog)
3. **PAY:** Methods of payment accepted for orders (catalog fees should be paid by check or money order unless the listing states otherwise):
   - check: personal check
   - MO: bank or postal money order
   - MC: MasterCard credit card
   - V: VISA credit card
   - AE: American Express credit card
   - CB: Carte Blanche credit card
   - DC: Diners Club credit card
   - Discover: Discover/NOVUS credit card
   - JCB: JCB credit card
   - BRAVO: BRAVO credit card
4. **SELLS:** General type of goods/services sold
5. **STORE:** Location(s), hours, and/or phone number(s) of the firm's retail site or other outlets, if applicable
6. **E-MAIL:** E-mail address
7. **ONLINE:** URL (http) address on the internet or through an online provider, if applicable

♣ THE MAPLE LEAF

This symbol means the firm will ship goods to Canada. Canadian shoppers should ask the vendor about current import restrictions and tariffs before placing an order, and request shipping charges or an estimate before finalizing the order. *Please note:* U.S. firms generally request payment for goods *and* catalogs in U.S. funds, and may stipulate that payment be drawn on a U.S. bank or paid via postal money order.

▦ THE FLAG

A small U.S. flag on the symbol line means the firm will ship goods to APO and FPO (U.S. military) addresses. For more information, see "Shipments Abroad," page 598.

⊕ THE GLOBE

A small globe on the symbol line means the firm has stated that it will ship goods worldwide. Readers having goods delivered abroad should read the listing before sending for a catalog; check with local authorities to make sure products can be imported, what restrictions may apply, and what tariffs may be charged. For more information, see "Shipments Abroad," page 598.

¡Si! SPANISH SPOKEN HERE

This icon means that the firm has Spanish-speaking sales representatives on staff. Before calling a company so indicated, read the listing and the "Special Factors" notes, since the person's availability may be limited to certain hours or days.

ℭ THE TDD SYMBOL

This symbol indicates that the firm can communicate with a TDD (telecommunication device for the deaf). In most cases, the firm uses a separate phone line for the equipment; sometimes, it's combined with a fax line.

★ THE "WHOLESALE" STAR

Firms so marked will sell at wholesale rates to *qualified individuals or other firms*. To sell to you at genuine wholesale, most firms require proof that you're running a company—a business card, letterhead, resale number, or all three—and may impose different minimum orders and sell under terms different from those that apply to retail purchases. Please note that, unless specified, all information in these listings applies to consumer transactions only. For more information, see "Buying at Wholesale," page 590.

THE "INTERNET ONLY" SYMBOL

Firms so marked *do not publish a catalog* and *do not give price quotes over the phone.* They require you to use their websites to access product information and initiate orders. (Note that none requires you to *complete* an order online.) The symbol indicates that you *must* have internet access to do business with the company. Please note that the addresses and phone numbers of such firms are provided solely as references for readers who've placed orders, and to show that the company does have a physical location. *Do not call or write to request catalogs, literature, or prices.*

THE COMPLETE GUIDE TO BUYING BY MAIL

This primer on mail-order shopping, which begins on page 586, can help you with questions on everything from sending for catalogs to interpreting warranties. If a problem arises with a mail-order transaction, look here for help in resolving it.

ANIMAL AND PET SUPPLIES

Livestock and pet supplies and equipment; veterinary instruments and biologicals; pet care and training advice and services

Owning a pet, especially a cat or a dog, has been shown to be beneficial for people suffering from a range of maladies. Having a pet may help prolong your life, lower your blood pressure and cholesterol levels, and reduce your incidence of backaches, headaches, and colds. Pets are now widely used in programs for nursing-home patients, hospitalized children, and psychiatric patients.

If you're thinking about getting a pet, make sure you're picking the best companion for your needs and lifestyle. "The Veterinarian's Way of Selecting a Proper Pet" asks a series of questions to help you define your criteria for the ideal animal. The brochure is available upon request; send a long, stamped, self-addressed envelope with your letter to the American Veterinary Medical Association, Suite 100, 1931 N. Meacham Rd., Schaumburg, IL 60173–4360.

Once you've decided on the kind of animal you want, don't rush to the pet *store:* Seek out pet shelters and animal orphanages, where you can save yourself some money while sparing an animal a questionable fate. Even purebreds can be acquired inexpensively, when a "purebred rescue" group takes in an animal no longer wanted by its owner and holds it for adoption. (After the Disney film *101 Dalmatians,* for example, there were thousands of dalmatian pups orphaned by well-meaning but short-sighted parents.) Ask your local animal shelter to refer you to an organization that performs these services. If the dog of your dreams happens to be a greyhound, you may be able to adopt a former race-track star. For information on the greyhound rescue group nearest you, call the National Greyhound Adoption Network at 800–4–HOUNDS. For additional information on the plight of the greyhound, see the website (http://www.greyhounds.org).

For an all-around great resource that will lead you to humane organizations or concerned individuals who can help you find a shelter or animal hospital in your area, offer more information on pet care, and provide material about specific animal welfare issues, check out ASPCA's website (http://www.aspca.org). You'll find an amazingly comprehensive list of national and state-by-state organizations with websites, as well as links to indices with lots more references and resources. If you're a snail mail enthusiast, you can also call or write ASPCA Public Affairs, 424 E. 92nd St., New York, NY 10128–6804, 212–876–7700, ext. 4650, to request their information packet.

Most of us are unaware of the long-term price of ownership: The typical cat or dog will cost you more than $10,000 over its lifetime. Much of this expense is food and vet bills, but a portion is other pet necessities—leashes, toys, carriers, grooming tools and supplies, beds, etc. Fortunately, there's now an alternative to buying pet products from the grocery store or pet boutique. Based on the successful office and home-improvement models, there are pet-supply discount superstores that offer varying savings on food, grooming products, cages, supplies, and a wide range of pet needs. If there's one near you, check the prices on food and litter against the discounts a local pet store may give on case purchases, and see if they'll deliver.

The companies listed here won't give you great deals on heavy cans of food and bags of litter—the cost of shipping usually offsets the savings. But check the prices of collars and leashes, cages and carriers, feeding dishes and devices, grooming tools, beds, and medications. These firms carry products for a wide range of animals—from hamsters and ferrets to horses and reptiles—and all can save you money.

Mastering the basics of pet care can also save you considerable sums in a variety of ways—in salon costs, the price of obedience school, and sometimes even on vet fees. Hundreds of books and periodicals are available—on breeding, nutrition, training and behavior, grooming, and other aspects of pet care, for every type of animal. The easiest way to get acquainted with what's available is to consult a catalog of current publications. If you own a canine or feline, you'll appreciate the "Dog & Cat Book Catalog" from Direct Book Service. The current issue is 64 pages of books on care, breeds, pet travel, selection, kennel and cattery management, and many other topics, with a special emphasis on dog training, for professionals and pet owners. Standard reference works and encyclopedias are also listed. For a copy of the catalog, call 800–776–2665 or 509–663–9115, e-mail dgctbook@cascade.net, or write to Direct Book Service, P.O. Box 2778, Wenatchee, WA 98807–2778; the website is http://www.dogandcatbooks.com/.

Bird lovers will find that some of the companies in this chapter print separate catalogs for bird owners. Be sure to specify this when ordering your catalog. Some but not all of these carry food and other supplies for wild-bird enthusiasts as well. Check the "Related Products/Companies" section at the end of this chapter for sources in other chapters for wild-bird supplies such as food, feeders, and birdbaths, as well as birdcalls and binoculars for bird-watching.

If you're a fish hobbyist whose interest lies in outdoor goldfish ponds, you'll find that some of the fish-supply firms also carry pond equipment. For other companies that carry pond liners, filters, pumps, etc., scan the "Related Products/Companies" section at the end of this chapter.

Horse fans have a wonderful resource in The Book Stable, a catalog of books, magazines, and videos on all aspects of horse ownership. The Book Stable offers nearly 50 magazine titles alone (and initiates and renews subscriptions), as well as hundreds of books and videos on every aspect of horse ownership and care. You can see the current offerings listed on the website (http://www.bookstable.com/) and order a catalog online, or request the catalog (free, or $2.50 if sent outside the U.S.) by calling 800–274–2665, or by writing to The Book Stable, Dept. WBMC, 210 Division St., Kingston, PA 18704.

Several of the firms listed in this chapter retain veterinarians who can answer questions on products and use, but usually won't give specific medical advice. If your pet is ailing, consult a vet, and always seek professional guidance if you plan to administer any vaccines or medications yourself. To safeguard your pet's well-being, make sure you have the number of a local 24-hour service that handles medical emergencies.

FIND IT FAST

BIRDS • Kennel Vet, KV Vet, Omaha Vaccine, Pet Warehouse, That Fish Place/That Pet Place, Tomahawk Live Trap, UPCO

DOGS AND CATS • Drs. Foster & Smith, J-B Wholesale, Kennel Vet, KV Vet, Pet Warehouse, That Fish Place/That Pet Place, UPCO, Valley Vet Supply

FISH • Daleco, Pet Warehouse, That Fish Place/That Pet Place

HORSES • Dairy Association, Kennel Vet, KV Vet, UPCO, Valley Vet Supply

LIVESTOCK • Dairy Association, KV Vet, Omaha Vaccine, Valley Vet Supply

REPTILES AND SMALL ANIMALS • KV Vet, Pet Warehouse, That Fish Place/That Pet Place, UPCO

TRAPS (HUMANE) • Tomahawk Live Trap
VET, KENNEL, AND GROOMER • Drs. Foster & Smith, J-B Wholesale, Kennel Vet,
KV Vet, Omaha Vaccine, UPCO, Valley Vet Supply

DAIRY ASSOCIATION CO., INC.

P.O. BOX 145, DEPT.
  WBMC
LYNDONVILLE, VT
  05851–0145
802–626–3610
FAX: 802–626–3433

Brochure and Price List: free
Pay: check or MO
Sells: livestock treatments and leather balm
Store: mail order only

Dairy Association Co., Inc., is known to generations of herd farmers for Bag Balm, an unguent formulated to soothe the chapped, sunburned udders of cows. It's also recommended by horse trainers for cracked heels, galls, cuts, hobble burns, and other ailments, and is "great as a sweat" as well. Bag Balm can be used on sheep, goats, dogs, and cats, and is touted as a softener for weather-beaten, chapped hands. A 10-ounce can is $5.55 here; a 4^{1}/2-pound pail costs just over $37. (A 1-ounce size, great for travel, is also offered.) Green Mt. Horse Products, a division of Dairy Association, produces Hoof Softener. Made of petrolatum, lanolin, and vegetable oils, it helps keep hoofs pliable and sound ($4.65 per pint). Tackmaster—a one-step, all-around conditioner, cleaner, and preservative for leather—is cheaper than similar products. Dairy Association has been in business since 1889 and provides product literature free on request.

Canadian readers, please note: Contact Dr. A.D. Daniels Co. Ltd., N. Rock Island, Quebec, for prices and ordering information.

Special Factors: Phone orders are accepted for C.O.D. payment.

DALECO MASTER BREEDER PRODUCTS

**3556 N. 400 EAST
WARSAW, IN 46580–7999
800–987–1120
219–268–6300
FAX: 219–268–6302**

Catalog: free (see text)
Pay: check, MO, MC, V, Discover
Sells: tropical fish and aquarium supplies
Store: mail order only
Online: http://www.dalecombp.com

Daleco, in business since 1966, publishes a 120-page catalog/reference book that's packed with information useful to owners of fresh- and salt-water fish. Daleco discounts tank filters, aquarium heaters, lights, chillers, air and water pumps, foods, water test kits, UV water sterilizers, water conditioners, reef trickle filter systems, and related goods from top-name manufacturers. The catalog is useful to both incidental and serious hobbyists, and Daleco's staff is knowledgeable and helpful. If you're interested in outdoor ponds, Daleco can special-order a kit for you.

International readers, please note: The catalog costs $10 (in U.S. funds) via airmail.

Special Factors: On orders over $50, shipping is included and sent via UPS in the 48 contiguous states; C.O.D. orders are accepted; authorized returns are accepted.

DRS. FOSTER & SMITH, INC.

2253 AIR PARK RD.
P.O. BOX 100
RHINELANDER, WI
  54501–0100
800–826–7206
715–369–2821
FAX: 800–776–8872

Catalog: free
Pay: check, MO, MC, V, AE, Discover
Sells: dog and cat supplies
Store: mail order only
Online: http://www.drsfostersmith.com

As "The Company Owned and Operated by Practicing Veterinarians," Doctors Foster & Smith (the actual people) provide owners of cats and dogs with quality products for health, nutrition, and fun.

The color catalog shows beds and mats, cat perches and scratching posts, nutritional supplements and biologicals, grooming tools and products, lots of toys and rawhide bones and treats, leashes and collars (including a "no-pull humane antitug system" that won't choke your dog, and a cat muzzle), feeding dishes, cages and carriers, and much more. The catalog is clearly written, with complete product descriptions and helpful sidebars on topics of interest (the role of antioxidants in your pet's diet, dental problems, a discussion on the pros and cons of various vaccines, Q & A's about boarding your pet, etc.). Doctors Foster & Smith also sell books, videos, and training audiotapes, and if that's not enough, on Tuesdays and Thursdays you can speak to a staff vet on general pet issues and health care. The special vet hotline number is in the current issue of the catalog.

Special Factors: Satisfaction is guaranteed; returns are accepted.

J-B WHOLESALE PET SUPPLIES, INC.

5 RARITAN RD., DEPT. WB
OAKLAND, NJ 07436
201–405–1111
FAX: 201–405–1706

Catalog: free
Pay: check, MO, MC, V, AE, Discover
Sells: vet, kennel, and pet supplies
Store: 289 Wagaraw Rd., Hawthorne, NJ,
and 347 Ramapo Valley Rd., Oakland, NJ;
Monday to Wednesday 9–6, Thursday and
Friday 9–8, Saturday 10–5, Sunday 11–4
E-mail: jbpet@intac.com
Online: http://www.jbpet.com

J-B Wholesale Pet Supplies, in business since 1981, stocks "over 8,500 different items for showing, grooming, training, breeding," and other animal-related activities. J-B is staffed by professional animal handlers who've kennel-tested all of the products the company sells.

The 72-page catalog features a wide range of goods for cats and dogs, with the emphasis on canines: remedies for common health problems, vitamins and nutritional supplements, repellents and deodorizers, shampoos and grooming products, beds and mats, flea and tick control products, cages, kennels, pet doors, grooming tables and dryers, leashes and leads, feeding devices, rawhide bones, and plush and rubber toys. Every major manufacturer is represented, as well as J-B's own line of grooming aids—shampoo and coat conditioners and tints. Send for the catalog, or call for prices and availability on specific name-brand items.

Special Factors: Satisfaction is guaranteed; C.O.D. orders are accepted; returns are accepted within seven days for exchange, refund, or credit; minimum order is $25.

KENNEL VET

P.O. BOX 523, DEPT.
 WBMC
LAUREL, DE 19956
800–782–0627
302–875–7111
FAX: 302–875–1310

Catalog: $1
Pay: check, MO, MC, V, AE, Discover
Sells: vet, kennel, cattery, and pet supplies
Store: mail order only
E-mail: info@petmarket.com
Online: http://www.kennelvet.com

If you own or raise dogs or cats, you'll find Kennel Vet's compact, 50-page catalog great reading. This firm is price-competitive on products for horses, as well as house pets, and has been family-owned and -run since 1971. The discount prices alongside the regular list prices on all items allow you to readily see the savings.

Kennel Vet offers vaccines, remedies for common health problems, vitamins and nutritional supplements, and other professional products. Kennel Vet also sells stain- and odor-control products, yard tools, stainless steel bowls, shampoos and grooming products, flea- and tick-control products, cages/crates, pet doors, dog and cat beds, grooming tables, dryers, collars, leads, rawhide bones and rubber toys, liver treats, and other goods. Most of the top brands are represented here. The book and video department offers veterinary manuals, books on dog breeds, and a selection on cats, birds, and horses—all at a discount.

Special Factors: Authorized returns are accepted; shipping is not charged on orders of $75 or more (with some exceptions—see the catalog); vaccines are sent where ordinances permit.

KV VET SUPPLY CO., INC.

**3190 N. ROAD
DAVID CITY, NE 68632
800–423–8211
402–367–6047
FAX: 800–269–0093**

Catalog: free
Pay: check, MO, MC, V, AE, Discover
Sells: vet and pet supplies and equipment
Store: South Hwy. 92 and 15, David City, NE; Monday to Friday 8–5, Saturday 9–12 CT

Reader-recommended KV Vet Supply Co. was founded in 1979 to provide pet owners with veterinary supplies, and the firm has since added equine and livestock needs. KV publishes a 275-page catalog with over 4,000 different products for animal health care, grooming, training, working, showing, and other equipment to serve the needs of all of your animals—dogs, cats, horses, cattle, hogs, sheep, goats, llamas, ferrets, birds, and rabbits—at wholesale prices. You'll find vaccines, nutritional supplements, insecticides, wormers, antibiotics, topicals, shampoos, prescription drugs, tack, books and videos, and much more. KV Vet Supply has nearly 40,000 square feet of inventory, so most items can be shipped immediately. The firm has a "dedicated staff of over 60 employees," who "understand the needs of animal owners"—and prices up to 70% below list!

Special Factors: Shipping is included (except on "FOB" items); minimum order is $40.

OMAHA VACCINE COMPANY, INC.

P.O. BOX 7228
3030 L. ST.
OMAHA, NE 68107
800–367–4444
402–731–9600
FAX: 800–242–9447
FAX: 402–731–9829

Catalog: free
Pay: check, MO, MC, V, Discover
Sells: dog, cat, bird, reptile, small animal, horse, and livestock supplies
Store: several locations in NE, SD, MO, and MN; call for addresses and hours
Online: http://www.omahavaccine.com

Omaha Vaccine Company was established in 1965 to serve the needs of livestock producers, breeders, and veterinarians. Since then, the firm has expanded to include horses and companion animals. Omaha's three specialty catalogs feature vaccines, antibiotics, topical treatments, surgical instruments, grooming tools, dewormers, carriers, leads, collars, saddles, tack, blankets, and pet apparel. Prescription products are available (the original prescription, written by the attending veterinarian, must be mailed to Omaha with the accompanying order and payment). Omaha Vaccine is dedicated to providing whatever you need for the health of your livestock, horse, or pet, and veterinary consultation services can be arranged. You can use the 800 number to request "Best Care Pet Catalog," "First Place Equine Catalog," or "Professional Livestock Producer Catalog." Whether you're looking for flea treatments for your dog or are needing supplies for opening a llama farm, you'll appreciate Omaha's 20,000 products and wholesale pricing.

Special Factors: Some pharmaceutical products are available by prescription only (shipment is subject to local ordinances).

PET WAREHOUSE

915 TRUMBULL ST.,
DEPT. BMC 99
XENIA, OH 45385
800–443–1160
937–374–9800
FAX: 800–513–1913
FAX: 937–374–2524

Catalog: free (see text)
Pay: check, MO, MC, V, AE, Discover
Sells: pet supplies
Store: mail order only
E-mail: petwhse@erinet.com
Online: http://www.petwhse.com

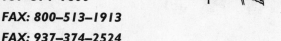

The polished color catalogs from Pet Warehouse are among the best around for the typical pet owner and the advanced enthusiast, who want good prices on basics and cool pet stuff. The firm has been in business since 1986, and sells supplies for cats, dogs, birds, fish, small animals, reptiles, and ponds. The inventory has been split into five catalogs—one for fish, the second for dogs and cats, the third for small animals and reptiles, the fourth for birds, and the fifth for ponds; please specify which one you want when you call or write.

Whether you have a freshwater or marine aquarium, or even a pond, Pet Warehouse can supply you with filters, air pumps, heaters, feeders, lighting, maintenance equipment and water conditioners, tank decorations and plants, fish medication, food, and other fish goods—but no tanks. Bird owners can choose cages, perches and play structures, cage accessories, bird toys, nests, feeders, bird food, dietary supplements and medication, and more. For dogs and cats, there are beds, collars and leashes, a variety of treats, feeding devices, grooming supplies and implements, flea and tick repellents, nutritional supplements, cages and carriers, pet doors, litter boxes and scoopers, toys, and novelty items—even pet costumes! And the reptile/small animal catalog shows rabbit hutches, supplies that run from lizard litter to hamster dragsters, and a range of other products. If you want to read up on pet care or breeds, Pet Warehouse can provide Barrons and T.F.H. titles on a wide range of topics, and manuals on caring for your reptile, snake, amphibian, invertebrate, or bird—as well as for King and Fluffy.

Canadian readers, please note: Trade restrictions prohibit shipment of certain brands.

Special Factors: Specify catalog desired (aquatic, reptile/small animal, dog and cat, bird, or pond); price quote by phone or letter.

THAT FISH PLACE/ THAT PET PLACE

237 CENTERVILLE RD.
LANCASTER, PA 17603
800–786–3829

Catalog: free
Pay: check, MO, MC, V, AE, Discover
Sells: supplies for aquariums, reptiles, birds, dogs, cats, and ponds
Store: same address; Monday to Saturday 10–9, Sunday 11–6
Online: http://www.thatpetplace.com

That Fish Place/That Pet Place calls itself "The World's Largest Discount Pet Care Supply Center" and has been serving the needs of fish and pet owners since 1973 with supplies for aquariums, ponds, dogs, cats, birds, reptiles, and other small animals.

The 96-page color "Complete Aquarist Catalog" is packed with everything a fish lover could need—filters and pumps, heaters and lighting, nets, plastic plants, vitamins, CD-ROMs, books, videos, and more—and is filled with useful information and tips on maintaining a healthy aquarium. The 96-page "Dog & Cat" catalog can save you money on all the basics, including rawhide amusements for the dog and catnip playthings for the feline, as well as grooming supplies, leashes, beds, and much more. Bird lovers will find hundreds of items in the 40-page "Bird Book," including all of the top lines of premium bird food, toys, cages, and health supplies. Love reptiles? "Reptile & Small Animal" is the catalog for you, with 48 pages of equipment, food, and supplies for reptiles of every kind, as well as cages that range from basic to elaborate—for rabbits, gerbils, ferrets, hamsters, and other small mammals. (I loved the tiny fur-lined beds for ferrets and hamsters.) Finally, TFP/TPP offers a fifth catalog, "Ponds and Water Gardens," for those who enjoy outdoor fish, and here you'll find pond and fountain kits, pond liners, filters, ornaments, koi and goldfish food and supplements, and more. There's also a small selection of food and feeders for wild birds.

The good pricing and quantity discounts can yield savings of up to 70%, and the company has a "meet or beat" policy on the advertised prices of other mail-order sellers. Anyone with a pet question can call Dr. Jeszenka, the on-staff veterinarian, Tuesdays 3–6 and Thursdays 5–8, at 717–299–5691 ET. These consultations are free!

Please note: Request the Dog & Cat, Fish, Bird, Reptile & Small Animal, or Pond catalog when you call or write—and be sure to mention BWBM.

Special Factors: Authorized, unused returns are accepted (a 15% restocking fee may be charged).

TOMAHAWK LIVE TRAP CO.

**P.O. BOX 323
TOMAHAWK, WI 54487
715–453–3550
FAX: 715–453–4326**

Catalog: free (see text)
Pay: check, MO, MC, V, Discover
Sells: humane animal traps and animal handling equipment
Store: Tomahawk, WI; Monday to Friday 8–5
E-mail: trapem@livetrap.com
Online: http://www.livetrap.com

Q: What is this company doing in the "animal supplies" chapter? A: These are *humane* traps. Tomahawk's box traps are used all over the world, by state and federal conservation departments, dog wardens, universities, and others who want to trap animals without harming them. (Give that lettuce-eating varmint a lift over to your favorite cousin's down the road!)

Tomahawk, established in 1925, manufactures over 80 different traps and cages, for just about any animal and any size: fish, turtle, beaver, grackle, pigeon, raccoon, opossom, skunk, muskrat, cat, dog, rat, mouse, squirrel, chipmunk, armadillo, badger—and many more. In addition to their standard line of rigid box traps, Tomahawk also manufactures traps with rear transfer doors, collapsible traps that fold to 1" in height, double-door traps that capture the animal entering from either direction, and others models, as well as animal cages, including squeeze and restraint. Tomahawk also manufactures animal-control equipment ranging from cat graspers and snake tongs to heavy-duty gloves and handling nets.

If you wish to receive some free literature and pricing on Tomahawk's products, call, write, or send an e-mail, and be sure to identify yourself as a BWBM reader.

Special Factors: Quantity discounts of 50% are available on orders of six or more of the same trap.

UPCO

P.O. BOX 969, DEPT.
 WBM99
ST. JOSEPH, MO
 64502–0969
800–444–8651
FAX: 816–233–9696

Catalog: free
Pay: check, MO, MC, V, AE, Discover
Sells: supplies for dogs, cats, horses, birds, and small animals
Store: 3705 Pear St., St. Joseph, MO; Monday to Friday 7:30–6, Saturday 7:30–5
E-mail: upco2@aol.com
Online: http://www.upco.com

United Pharmacal Company, better known as UPCO, offers thousands of products for dogs, cats, birds, horses, reptiles, and small animals in a 192-page catalog that runs from "Barker Breakers" (high-frequency, bark-activated sound machines to modify your dog's bad barking habits) to iguana harnesses. UPCO's veterinary line includes antibiotics, wormers, medical instruments, nutritional supplements, skin treatments, insecticides, grooming aids, and related goods. Horse owners should check the dozen pages of medications and supplements, farrier supplies, and tack. Dog and cat owners will appreciate the savings on leashes and leads, collars, feeders, books, toys, feeding dishes and stations, pet doors, and other goods. Professional groomers should note the selection of grooming products for show dogs. UPCO also has a selection of supplies and products for hamsters, gerbils, guinea pigs, ferrets, and rabbits. This company offers hundreds of books and manuals that cover the care, training, and breeding of a wide range of animals. UPCO has a separate catalog devoted to birds, which you can specifically ask for when requesting a catalog.

Canadian readers, please note: Payment must be made in U.S. funds, and vaccines are not shipped to Canada.

Special Factors: Quantity discounts are available; C.O.D. orders are accepted; returns are accepted within 20 days; minimum order is $10. Most orders within continental U.S. qualify for free shipping.

VALLEY VET SUPPLY

1118 PONY EXPRESS HWY.
P.O. BOX 504
MARYSVILLE, KS
  66508–0504
800–360–4838
785–562–5106
FAX: 800–446–5597

Catalog: free
Pay: check, MO, MC, V, AE, Discover
Sells: vet and pet supplies for dogs and cats
Store: mail order only
E-mail: valleyv@midusa.net
Online: http://www.valleyvet.com

Valley Vet's color catalog offers the latest goodies for dogs and cats—from vegetarian dog bones to state-of-the-art litter-box solutions. You'll find dozens of pages of toys and other playthings, feeding equipment, beds and mats, flea and tick products, grooming tools and preparations, training equipment, barriers and cages, leashes, collars, nutritional supplements, vaccines, and related products, from well-known manufacturers. Both books and videos are offered, on everything from obedience and health care to vacationing with your furry companion. Dogs and cats are the featured players, but the review catalog included a page of supplements and drugs for birds and fish as well. Prices are competitive; most items are discounted about 25% from list or regular retail, including the "human" gifts—mugs, tee shirts, key rings, etc.

Please note: Some medications require a prescription, but most can be purchased by anyone.

Special Factors: Satisfaction is guaranteed; returns (except special orders, vaccines, books, and videos) are accepted for exchange, refund, or credit. Orders under $50 incur a processing fee. Shipping is free on most items.

RELATED PRODUCTS/COMPANIES

Birdcalls • Weston Bowl Mill
Bird-watching binoculars • Scope City, Orion Telescope Center, Mardiron Optics, Ewald-Clark
Fly traps • Mellinger's
Horse blankets • Gohn Bros.
Natural products for livestock • Ohio Earth Food
Pet life preservers • Defender Industries
Pond liners and pond supplies • Bob's Superstrong Greenhouse Plastic

Saddlery • *Weaver Leather*

Wild-bird birdseed, feeders, and birdbaths • *Weston Bowl Mill, Terry's Village, Gurney's Seed & Nursery Co., Jackson & Perkins*

ART, ANTIQUES, AND COLLECTIBLES

Fine art, limited editions, antiques, and nostalgia/memorabilia collectibles

The firms listed here offer an eclectic selection of the rare and unusual, from World War II pin-up calendars to fruit crate labels. Although buying from "dealer" sources means you're usually getting the piece at a lower price than you'd pay at retail, don't buy with the expectation of reselling at a profit unless you're sure of what you're doing. Make certain you're buying from firms that have liberal return policies.

Getting to know the market is one of the pleasures of collecting, and there are hundreds of reference books available to give you the necessary grounding. The guides to prevailing market prices for antiques and collectibles are especially helpful in determining whether you're overpaying—or getting a real buy. Ralph and Terry Kovel have been publishing price indexes and collectors' guides for decades, and are best known for the annual *Kovels' Antiques and Collectibles Price List.* The Kovels also help you get the best price on what you buy—or sell—with *Kovels' Guide to Selling, Buying and Fixing Your Antiques and Collectibles* (both titles from Crown). If you check out Amazon.com (http://www.amazon.com), you'll find these and other Kovels' books—as well as many other books about collecting art, antiques, and memorabilia—at a discount, no less!

There's no substitute for old-fashioned legwork when it comes to learning about your field of interest. Visit flea markets, antique shops, art galleries, museums, and auction previews, and don't just look—ask questions. Dealers enjoy an appreciative customer and will usually share valuable tips on what to look for if you demonstrate interest in their wares.

If you like the feel of a Sunday-morning country auction, your heart racing as you bid $5 on a dusty box full of junk from somebody's attic, you'll love Hake's Americana & Collectibles in this chapter, and Ebay, in the "General Merchandise and Surplus Goods" chapter. Both companies require that you bid for their merchandise, and both carry an eclectic assortment of collectibles, some valuable, some not. Hake's operates as a phone/fax/mail auction, while Ebay is strictly online. (Ebay sells new merchandise as well, which is why they're not in this chapter.)

A collection of any merit usually requires the protection of archival quality materials. University Products, Inc., is an excellent source for display binders, albums, boxes, and restoration materials for artworks, books, manuscripts, photographs, textiles, posters, and postcards (see listing in the "Office, Business, Professional" chapter). The firm's archival products catalog includes goods for mounting, display, and storage, and a number of reference works to help do it right, including Jill Snyder's *Caring for Your Art: A Guide for Artists, Collectors, Galleries, and Art Institutions*. See *Kovels' Antiques and Collectibles Price List* for other resources.

FIND IT FAST

AD AND POSTER REPRODUCTIONS • Desperate Enterprises
LABELS • Miscellaneous Man, Original Paper Collectibles
MILITARIA • John W. Poling
PHONES • Phoneco
POLITICAL MEMORABILIA • John W. Poling
POP-CULTURE NOSTALGIA • Hake's Americana, John W. Poling
RARE/VINTAGE POSTERS • Cinema City, Hake's Americana, Miscellaneous Man

---

CINEMA CITY

P.O. BOX 1012-W
MUSKEGON, MI 49443
616–739–8303
FAX: 616–733–7234

Catalog: $3, refundable
Pay: check, MO, MC, V, Discover
Sells: movie posters and ephemera
Store: mail order only
E-mail: info@cinema-city.com
Online: http://www.cinema-city.com

Movie posters circa 1975 and later are the specialty at Cinema City, which has been selling to collectors and dealers since 1976. Thousands of movies are listed in the 64-page catalog, from *A Bridge Too Far* ($15 for a set of 12 stills) to *Ziggy Stardust* (27" by 41" poster, $25). Press kits, scripts, and lobby cards are available for some of the titles. The catalog is arranged alphabetically by movie title and includes a glossary of terms and a guide to the poster sizes. Cinema City adds to its gigantic inventory with each new movie release, and once you're on the mailing list, you'll receive periodic updates—including offerings of autographed posters and photos. Cinema City also handles materials for foreign films and limited-release items. You can send inquiries about these, as well as queries about films made before 1975; include a self-addressed, stamped envelope for a reply.

Canadian readers, please note: Only U.S. funds are accepted.

Special Factors: Posters are sent rolled if Cinema City received them "flat"; folded materials are stiffened to minimize damage and are shipped that way.

DESPERATE ENTERPRISES

DEPT. WBMC
620 E. SMITH RD., #E-8
MEDINA, OH 44256
800-732-4859
FAX: 330-725-0150

Catalog: free
Pay: check, MO, MC, V, AE, Discover
Sells: tin ad and poster reproductions, nostalgic light-switch plates
Store: mail order only
E-mail: tinsigns@apk.net
Online: http://www.desperate.com

Desperate Enterprises takes its name from an observation made by Thoreau, not from the nature of its industry. The firm began business in 1987, selling two reproductions of tin advertising signs, and then expanded to a line of over 680 different images. Desperate Enterprises uses two production processes—four-color photolithography and silk-screen printing—to approximate the detail and depth of color in the originals.

Most of the examples shown in the 64-page color catalog are from the late 1800s through the 1950s, chiefly endorsements by famous people, ads for gas and oil companies, seeds and vegetables, soft drinks, baseball-related advertising, food, ammunition, fishing, tobacco, transportation, highway, liquor, postage stamps, and African-American images. You can find Lucille Ball boosting Royal Crown Cola, a number of images from Remington, wonderful art-deco ads, images for Cracker

Jack, Hershey's, Heinz pickles, Sunbeam bread, and Dewar's, among others. The ads, which average 11" by 16", begin at $12 and go down to about $4 each, depending on how many you buy. Miniatures of 112 of the ads are offered as refrigerator magnets ($14 to about $8 per set of six). Real vintage soda-bottle caps are also available as refrigerator magnets. Sepia-toned photo assortments in broad categories (movies and westerns, sports, motorcycle, etc.) are sold for $54 per hundred, and 20" by 30" posters, light-switch plates in 67 images, and tee shirts are also available. Desperate Enterprises is constantly adding products and images, and is a great resource for gifts.

Special Factors: Satisfaction is guaranteed; C.O.D. orders are accepted.

HAKE'S AMERICANA & COLLECTIBLES

P.O. BOX 1444
YORK, PA 17405–1444
717–848–1333
FAX: 717–852–0344

Catalog: $4 and up (see text)
Pay: check, MO, MC, V, Discover
Sells: pop culture/nostalgia collectibles via auction by phone/fax/mail
Store: mail order only
Online: http://www.hakes.com

Ted Hake is known as "the grandfather of collectibles." Since 1967 he's been running a wildly popular worldwide mail-and-phone auction of pop culture and nostalgia collectibles—from action figures to watches, and everything in between. The 168-page catalog comes out five times a year, and you can order a onetime sample catalog for $4, or subscribe to a year's worth for $30 (U.S. and Canada, or $45 if you live overseas).

This is really fun stuff. Hake's offers original, one-of-a-kind collectibles that are *affordable*—as little as $5, and as much as $4,000. Each item is photographed in black and white, described in minute detail, and coded as to "Estimated Value." The Estimated Value represents that item's current retail value. Bids placed prior to closing days may be higher or lower than the Estimated Value, and the highest bidder gets it (bids below the Estimated Value are accepted at the discretion of the seller). The bidding is done by mail, by phone, or by fax. In the catalog you'll find the complete terms of the auction, including the closing time and date, rules and suggested procedures, as well as a bidding sheet.

On first glance it looks complicated, but Hake's times and rules are clearly and carefully spelled out and explained. Hake's Americana & Collectibles is well-known and -revered among collectors around the world. You'll have lots of fun imagining having your very own Mickey Mouse egg cups, silent movie posters, Li'l Abner and Daisy Mae juice glasses, tin toys, '50s lunch boxes, and more.

Check out the website for more about Hake's. There you'll find a complete explanation of the bidding process, links to related sites, a wonderful biography of Ted Hake (described as "Santa Claus and the Wizard of Oz combined"), and thousands of items priced for immediate sale (not for bidding). Why shop the ordinary way when you can get caught up in a global mail/phone/fax frenzy and land yourself a deal on some great stuff to jazz up your house or office?

Special Factors: Layaway plans are available on purchases of $75 or more. See catalog or website for terms-of-sale details and auction schedules. Auction is not conducted online; mail, phone, and fax bids are accepted.

MISCELLANEOUS MAN

P.O. BOX 1776–W9
NEW FREEDOM, PA
   17349–0191
717–235–4766
FAX: 717–235–2853

Catalog: $7
Pay: check, MO, MC, V
Sells: rare and vintage posters and labels
Store: mail order only; phone hours Monday to Friday 10–6

George Theofiles, ephemerologist extraordinaire, is the moving force behind Miscellaneous Man. He founded his firm in 1970, trading in vintage posters, handbills, graphics, labels, brochures, and other memorabilia, all of which are original—he sells no reproductions or reprints. This is a great source for gifts if you know someone into James Dean, Americana art, war movies, old-time circuses, dogs—or any one of thousands of categories.

Each Miscellaneous Man catalog offers about 3,000 items, including posters, theater and movie publicity materials, product labels and stamps, pin-ups and pin-up calendars, and broadsides. Posters are the strong suit, representing everything from aviation to weaponry: patriotic themes (including both World Wars, other conflicts, and related topics), sports of all sorts, wines and spirits, food advertising, circuses, labor, publishing, fashion, African-Americana, movies, the performing arts, and travel, among other subjects. Some of the posters are offered mounted on linen or conservation paper, and Mr. Theofiles can provide references for other firms that can mount your poster after purchase (proper backing helps to preserve the poster, and doesn't detract from its value). Collections of unused broom handle labels, luggage stickers, cigar box labels, and other ephemera have appeared in previous catalogs. The catalog entries note size and condition, and small black-and-white photos of the items are included; larger shots of individual items may be purchased for $2.

Miscellaneous Man's prices are usually at least 30% below the going rate, and regular customers receive sale catalogs with further reductions. If you're in the market for a vintage poster, call Miscellaneous Man before you buy elsewhere. Although his prices are sometimes comparable (especially on scarce or rare posters), Miscellaneous Man can and has charged 30% to 75% less than New York City sources—and his selection is invariably better. Miscellaneous Man also buys vintage posters and ephemera, in case you have some old beauties in your attic.

Special Factors: Layaways are accepted; returns are accepted within three days; minimum order is $50 with credit cards.

ORIGINAL PAPER COLLECTIBLES

700-W WEST CLIPPER GAP RD.
AUBURN, CA 95603

Brochure, Sample Label: free with SASE
Pay: check or MO
Sells: original, vintage product labels
Store: mail order only

William Wauters began his business in 1970, when fruit crate labels were among the hot collectibles in antique and curio shops nationwide. Snail mail is plenty fast for him, so he and his customers interact by mail. Original Paper Collectibles has thrived over the years, attesting to the enduring appeal of the label designs. At this writing, Mr. Wauters offers labels originally intended for brooms, soda pop, canned fruits and vegetables, and produce crates. Collectors of "Negro Americana" will find a selection of 10 labels depicting black characters.

The collections offer the best per-label prices, and Mr. Wauters says that dealers routinely double his prices when they resell. The price list describes the most popular collection of fruit and vegetable crate labels, which include orange, apple, asparagus, lemon, pear, lettuce, cherry, grape, and carrot varieties—150 for $29, postpaid. (A vintage poster gallery in New York City charges nearly that for a single label.) Sliding discounts of 10% to 35% are given on orders of $100, $250, and $500. If you're searching for a specific label, you may find it among the listings of individual labels, which are grouped by size and type. If you're looking for something out of the ordinary to decorate with, ask here—the labels can framed as art, or even used to cover walls and tabletops.

Please note: Payment for orders should be made to William Wauters, not Original Paper Collectibles, and requests for brochures must include a long, stamped, self-addressed envelope.

Canadian and non-U.S.-based readers, please note: Send a long, self-addressed envelope with an International Reply Coupon, available at your local post office (do not include a stamp, unless it's U.S. postage).

Special Factors: Satisfaction is guaranteed; price quote by letter with SASE; quantity discounts are available. Wholesalers, please inquire about terms.

PHONECO, INC.

P.O. BOX 70, DEPT. WBMC
GALESVILLE, WI 54630
608–582–4124
FAX: 608–582–4593

Catalog: $3
Pay: check, MO, MC, V, AE, Discover
Sells: vintage telephones and accessories
Store: 19813 E. Mill Rd., Galesville, WI;
Monday to Friday 9–5
E-mail: phonecoinc@aol.com
Online: http://members.aol.com/phonecoinc

Communicate through the instruments of the predigital age—literally—with a vintage telephone from Phoneco. This firm has been repairing and restoring old phones since 1971, and sells both refurbished models and hard-to-find components through a 28-page catalog. The current edition features phones from the fifties through the seventies—"Hollywood" styles of the kind one might see in old Hitchcock thrillers; Snoopy and "Princess" models (your first teenage phone); and heavy-duty desk rotary phones (I still have mine!). There are also phones from the thirties, twenties, and earlier, including old pay phones, candlestick phones, art deco phones, European crank models, and many more.

Most of the phones are fully operational, but if you can repair the old ones, you can save by buying "as-is" models and refurbishing them yourself. Here Phoneco can help as well, with a great selection of cords (including the old cloth-covered style), magnetos and ringer boxes, dials and touch pads, receiver parts, line jacks and adapters, and even the decals and brass nameplates that identified the originals. Phone posters, original GTE Communications Handbooks, vintage phone books, and books on collecting and repairing old phones are also available, as well as old keyphones, cable, substations, and even antique oak phone booths.

Price checks on two of the models in Phoneco's catalog revealed savings of 38% (on the Ericofone) and over 50% (on a Bakelite Oslo phone), compared to a local phone boutique. The terms of the sales policy are given in the catalog ($3), but if you have a specific vintage phone or part in mind, you can call or write to inquire about availability and prices.

Special Factors: Price quote by phone or letter; authorized returns are accepted within 30 days for exchange, refund, or credit.

JOHN W. POLING: MILITARY COLLECTIBLES

5998 S. RIDGEVIEW RD.,
DEPT. WBMC
ANDERSON, IN 46013
765–778–2714

Catalog: $2 each (see text)
Pay: check or MO
Sells: military and political collectibles and used books
Store: mail order only

Wars, political slugfests, governmental chicanery—apart from anything else, they all leave a trail of souvenirs in their wake. John Poling sells political memorabilia, chiefly campaign buttons, and an extensive collection of militaria from the U.S. and abroad, as well as "miscellaneous" collectibles. There is a black-and-white catalog devoted to each of the three, full of items at very low prices.

A recent review catalog of political collectibles opened with a group of Alaska election buttons and concluded with an insipid postcard of Richard Nixon and his family posed at the piano. Were you rooting for Charlie Beaver for sheriff (his slogan: "Leave it to Beaver")? Is your outfit lacking a JFK-caricature tie clip? You'll find it here, and chances are you'll get change back from your ten, even if you buy several items. There are also political used books at rock-bottom prices.

Mr. Poling's forte is militaria—clothing, accessories, headgear, insignias and emblems, patches, field equipment, and much more, including an extensive listing of used books, some rare, and a range of printed material (magazines, manuals, broadsides, and newspapers).

This is a collector's gold mine—among the helmets and liners alone there are specimens from the French, British, East German, South African, Spanish, and Italian armies, as well as several branches of the U.S. armed forces. A sample of stock from the current catalog includes a German WWI mess kit, a Japanese Malaysian Occupation dollar, and a Soviet May Day pin.

The Miscellaneous catalog features Boy Scout themes, Elvis, Olympics, Walt Disney, and bills and coins from around the globe, to name a few.

Mr. Poling allows you to review your purchases for 10 days, and accepts returns (in the same condition sent) for a full refund, not including shipping. Please note that each catalog costs $2, payable in U.S. funds. All items are "guaranteed to be genuine" and described accurately; some reproductions were listed in the review catalog, but they were clearly marked as such.

Special Factors: Satisfaction is guaranteed; returns are accepted within 10 days for exchange or refund.

RELATED PRODUCTS/COMPANIES

Antique/rare books • *Editions, Strand Book Store*
Archival-quality storage and mounting materials • *University Products*
Fine art books • *Hacker Art Books, Strand Book Store*
Heirloom/estate silver pieces • *Beverly Bremer Silver Shop, The Silver Queen*
Miscellaneous collectibles • *Ebay*
Rare and vintage film/TV (video-recorded) • *Video Yesteryear*
Vintage fountain pens • *Fountain Pen Hospital*
Vintage fretted instruments • *Elderly Instruments, Mandolin Brothers*
Vintage LPs and 45s • *Berkshire Record Outlet, Record-Rama Sound Archives, Harvard Square Records*

AUTO, MARINE, AND AVIATION EQUIPMENT

Parts, supplies, maintenance products, and services

For auto-related goods, you'll find in this chapter a range of parts and supplies for cars, motorcycles, RVs, trucks, vans, and all-terrain vehicles—mufflers, shocks, tires, batteries, and much more. You can buy salvaged parts through several of the firms listed here, priced as much as 70% less than the same parts if new. You can also buy cars, trucks, and vans through services offered by American Automobile Brokers (listed in this chapter).

The internet offers consumers a whole new way to approach car buying. There are now a half-dozen or more top-rated sites that serve consumers in a number of ways. You can get prices on new and used cars, read reviews, and check out model specifications through a free service provided by the Automotive Information Center (AIC) at their AutoSite (http://www.autosite.com). This excellent clearinghouse for automobile information is a great place to start since it is constantly updated; the people at AutoSite pride themselves on being at the head of their class.

One of the oldest web auto sales operations is Auto-by-Tel (http://www.autobytel.com), which uses about 1,500 dealers who have paid a fee to be part of Auto-by-Tel. These dealers can offer automobiles at lower prices because they're saving money on marketing costs. Auto-Vantage (http://www.autovantage.com) is another nifty site. Here you'll get the best pricing with detailed information on every make and model, accessory and option. Armed with a "preferred AutoVantage price," you're referred to a local dealer, who then completes the deal.

For a good overview of virtual auto dealers and their relative merit, see Internet Shopper's "In the Driver's Seat," a report of online car buying that's archived in their "library." You'll find Internet Shopper at http://www.internetshopper.com/. Here are some additional information sources to help you make the best selection when buying a car:

• *Consumer Reports* publishes reliable vehicle ratings each year and offers price comparisons and reliability ratings of new and used cars. The "Consumer Reports Auto Price Service" provides a computer printout showing both list price and dealer's cost for the model you specify, information on rebates and recommended options, and guidelines for negotiating the lowest possible price. At this writing, one report costs $12, and additional reports ordered at the same time are $10 each. Call toll-free 800–888–8275 for this service. The "Consumer Reports Used Car Price Service" gives current prices, in your region, on models as far back as 1988. To get a price, you answer questions about a specific model—condition, mileage, year, number of cylinders, major options, etc.—to which the computer adds other facts and calculates a price. The service is terrific for someone who wants to negotiate a better deal on a used car, or set a price when they sell. The 900 number costs $1.75 per minute, and a typical call is five minutes. Touch-tone is required; call 900–226–5050 for this service.

• Perhaps the best known reference for used car pricing is the *Kelley Blue Book Used Car Guide.* The latest consumer edition, which covers cars vintage 1983 to 1997, is less than $10. Or check your local library, which will probably have the book or can get it for you. This company also has a fantastic website (http://www.kbb.com) where you can find out the value of your used car for free.

• *The Car Book,* an annual by Jack Gillis (HarperCollins), rates current domestic and imported models on crash-test performance, as well as fuel economy, preventive-maintenance costs, repair costs, and insurance rates. This annual also includes valuable information on evaluating warranties, service contracts, insurance, tires, children's car seats, and used cars. A comprehensive, easy-to-understand "Complaint" chapter can help you to resolve difficulties, and the "Checklist" will help you ask the right questions while shopping.

• *The National Highway Administration Auto Safety Hotline* can help you check safety factors when you're shopping for a new or used car. In addition to crash-test reports and guidelines to buying a safer car, the Hotline has recall information on autos and related products, such as infants' car seats. And you can report safety problems here, too. Call 800–424–9393 for more information, or visit the website at http://www.nhtsa.dot.gov/.

• The Better Business Bureau publishes booklets on subjects including buying used and new cars, leasing cars, car repair, automatic transmissions, and more, for $2 each. See the website (http://www.bbb.org) for a list of these and other consumer publications, and for details on how to order. The Bureau also administers the BBB AUTO LINE, a program to resolve disputes between individual consumers and auto manufacturers over perceived manufacturing defects. Thirty manufacturers are involved, on a national or state-by-state basis, at this writing. Note that the AUTO LINE does not handle complaints about auto dealers, repair services, or insurers—just manufacturers. For more information, call 800–955–5100, or see the website at http://www.bbb.org/complaints/BBBautoLine.html/.

Preventive maintenance notwithstanding, your car will need some kind of repair eventually. Mark Eskeldson, a car mechanic himself, tells all in *What Auto Mechanics Don't Want You to Know* (published by Tech News Corp., available at regular or online bookstores). It will help you identify good repair shops and to recognize deceptive trade practices.

If your interest is boating, you already know about the expenses—insurance, dock fees, upkeep, and new equipment. You can save 30% routinely on the cost of maintenance products, gear, and electronics by buying from the marine suppliers listed here, who sell every type of coating, tool, and device you'll need to keep your vessel afloat. You'll find exhaustive selections of electronics, hardware, and instruments, as well as galley accoutrements and foul-weather clothing. Even landlubbers should see these catalogs for the well-designed slickers and oiled sweaters. And the reference sections of the biggest catalogs have a full range of books and videos on boat maintenance and other marine topics.

If you're a private pilot who'd like to save on some of the gear and electronics you need while flying high, see the aviation discounters. Like the marine suppliers, these firms also sell goods of interest to those on terra firma, at savings of up to 50%.

FIND IT FAST

AVIATION • *Aircraft Spruce, Wag-Aero*
BOATING SUPPLIES AND EQUIPMENT • *Defender, Freeport, M & E Marine, West Marine*
CAR PARTS AND ACCESSORIES • *Car Racks Direct, Cherry Auto, Mill Supply, WorldWide Auto*
FARM/CONSTRUCTION EQUIPMENT PARTS • *Central Michigan*
NEW VEHICLES • *American Automobile Brokers*
RACING EQUIPMENT • *Racer Wholesale*
RV EQUIPMENT AND SUPPLIES • *RV Direct*
TIRES • *Discount Tire, The Tire Rack*

AIRCRAFT SPRUCE & SPECIALTY CO.

**225 AIRPORT CIRCLE
CORONA, CA 91720
800–824–1930 (WEST
COAST)
800–831–2949 (EAST
COAST)
FAX: 909–372–0555 (WEST)
FAX: 770–229–2329 (EAST)**

Catalog: $5, refundable (see text)
Pay: check, MO, MC, V, AE, Discover
Sells: small aircraft and pilot equipment
Store: West, same address; East, 900 S. Pine Hill Road, Griffin, GA; call for hours
E-mail: info@aircraft-spruce.com
Online: http://www.aircraft-spruce.com

Aircraft Spruce & Specialty Co. has been selling aircraft parts and equipment since 1965 and is the source to call for aircraft plywood, flight seats, tubing and sheeting, cable, wire, circuit breakers, AN-MS hardware, headsets, and all kinds of avionics. In addition to an exhaustive inventory of supplies, equipment, and electronics for plane and pilot, there are neat things for the nonflyer: Dahon folding bicycles, propeller wall clocks, and a pedal plane kit for kids. Savings are comparable to those offered by other major aircraft supply discounters, and the firm has a "lowest price" policy. Call for a quote if you know what you want, or send $5 for the 506-page catalog ($20 for overseas orders, U.S. funds only); it's refundable with a $50 purchase.

Special Factors: Satisfaction is guaranteed.

AMERICAN AUTO-MOBILE BROKERS, INC.

24001 SOUTHFIELD RD.,
SUITE 110
SOUTHFIELD, MI 48075
248–569–5900
FAX: 248–569–2022

Information: see text
Pay: check or MO (see text)
Sells: new vehicles
Store: same address; Monday to Friday 10–6

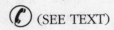 (SEE TEXT)

If you're buying a new vehicle, American Automobile Brokers offers you an alternative to the showroom experience. The firm, in business since 1972, brokers the sale: Prices include dealer prep, all factory rebates, and delivery directly from the factory to a dealership near you by train or truck (for domestic vehicles). Savings depend on the prices in your area. All cars come with a full factory warranty.

If you're looking for a domestic make, you can buy vehicles by General Motors, Ford/Lincoln-Mercury, and Chrysler/Jeep/Eagle. The foreign models include Acura, Audi, BMW, Honda, Infiniti, Jaguar, Mazda, Mercedes, Nissan, Porsche, Saab, and Toyota, among others. (American Automobile Brokers doesn't sell imports to residents of California.) To get a quote, call or write with complete details about the make, model, and a list of the extras you desire. Send a self-addressed stamped envelope when making the request by mail. You get one free quote; extra quotes cost $5 each. You can shop your local dealers, then get a quote here and see what you'll save by buying through American Automobile Brokers.

TDD callers: American Automobile Brokers has worked with operators who assisted incoming calls on TDD equipment, and has successfully completed transactions—but the firm doesn't have its own TDD.

Special Factors: Price quote by phone, letter, or American Automobile Brokers quote form with SASE; checks and money orders are accepted for deposit only, balance payable by certified check, cashier's check, or wire transfer.

CAR RACKS DIRECT

**80 DANBURY RD.
WILTON, CT 06897
800-722-5734
FAX: 203-761-0812**

Catalog: free
Pay: check, MO, MC, V, AE
Sells: vehicle racks
Store: same address; Monday to Friday 10–6
Online: http://www.outdoorsports.com

Car Racks Direct sells just that—Thule and Yakima car racks, to secure bicycles, kayaks, canoes, skis, surfboards, and less playful items such as lumber and furniture. In addition to basic racks, Car Racks Direct carries security cables, locks, straps, crossbars, fairings, brackets, and even cases and boxes engineered to fit the racking systems. Discounts vary on individual items, generally running from 12% to 18% off suggested retail—not deep, but better than paying list. Car Racks Direct has been in business since 1987 and will give you a price quote over the phone, or send you the Thule and Yakima catalogs on request. The Thule catalog includes guidelines for care and maintenance of the racks and accessories, and terms of the limited warranty.

Special Factors: Price quote by phone or letter; authorized returns are accepted.

CENTRAL MICHIGAN TRACTOR & PARTS

**2713 N. U.S. 27
ST. JOHNS, MI 48879
517-224-6802
FAX: 517-224-6682**

Catalog: free
Pay: check, MO, MC, V
Sells: used, new, and rebuilt parts for tractors, combines, and construction equipment
Store: mail order only; phone hours Monday to Friday 8–5:30, Saturday 8–3

Central Michigan can save you up to 50% on parts for tractors and combines. The company stocks new, used, reconditioned, and rebuilt parts, all of which are backed by a 30-day guarantee. The 220-page catalog gives you access to everything from starters to cylinder blocks for machines made by almost every major manufacturer. The rebuilt parts are overhauled completely, so they should function as well and for as long as new ones. Central Michigan, one of 13 firms that make up the

"Parts Express Network," maintains customers' want lists for parts not in stock.

Special Factors: Price quote by phone or letter; C.O.D. orders are accepted.

CHERRY AUTO PARTS

5650 N. DETROIT AVE.
TOLEDO, OH 43612
419–476–7222
FAX: 419–470–6388

Information: price quote
Pay: check, MO, V, MC
Sells: used and rebuilt parts for imports and Chrysler-Jeep-Eagle cars and trucks
Store: same address; Monday to Friday 8:30–5, Saturday 8:30–12; also 25425 John R Rd., Madison Heights, MI (Detroit area); Monday to Friday 8:30–5
Online: http://www.cherry-auto.com

Why pay top dollar for new car parts if you can get perfectly good ones, used, for up to 70% less? Cherry Auto Parts can supply you with the same sizable savings they've been offering auto repair professionals and do-it-yourselfers for over 50 years with new, used, and rebuilt parts. Their expertise is with late-model import and Chrysler-Jeep-Eagle drive-train components such as engines, transmissions, axles, and steering gears, as well as electrical (alternators, radios, computers), glass (headlamps, door and quarter glass), and body parts (wheels, door mirrors, taillights, and bumpers). The savings are great for such models as Acura, Audi, BMW, all of the Chrysler imports (Colts, Raiders, Vistas, etc.), Honda, Hyundai, Isuzu, Jaguar, Land Rover, Lexus, Mazda, Mercedes, Mitsubishi, Nissan, Porsche, Saab, Sterling, Subaru, Toyota, Volkswagen, and Volvo. They also have a complete machine shop for rebuilt engines and cylinder heads, and computerized-parts locating, and extended warranties are available.

Please note: There is no retail brochure or literature.

Special Factors: Price quote by e-mail, phone (preferred), or letter; "All parts are guaranteed in stock at the time of quotation, guaranteed to be the correct part, and in good condition as described"; minimum order is $20.

DEFENDER INDUSTRIES, INC.

**42 GREAT NECK RD.
WATERFORD, CT 06385
800–435–7180
FAX: 800–654–1616**

Catalog: free (see text)
Pay: check, MO, MC, V, Discover
Sells: marine supplies, gear, equipment, and clothing
Store: same address; also Defender Marine Supply NY, 321 Main St., New Rochelle, NY; Monday to Friday 9–5:45, Thursday 9–8:45, Saturday 9–4:45 (call 914–632–2318 for hours, October to February)
E-mail: customerservice@defenderus.com
Online: http://www.defenderus.com

Defender has been selling marine hardware and equipment since 1938, and backs its claim of "the largest selection in the USA at the very lowest prices" with a 400-plus-page catalog that runs from anchors to zippers. It features page after page of boat maintenance supplies, resins and coatings, winches, windlasses, cordage, communications devices, foul-weather gear, books, tools and hardware, optics, galley fittings, navigation equipment, and electronics. You'll find sailboat hardware, outboard engines, and lines of marine electronics from the top companies. Also available: Shakespeare antennae; Pioneer and Sony radios; optics from Fujinon, Minolta, Nikon, and Steiner; inflatable boats and life rafts by Avon, Zodiac, and over a dozen other lines; Henri Lloyd, Musto, and Douglas Gill boating wear; Sebago and Timberland shoes; Force 10 cookers; and Hurricane boat tops and covers—among other items. Defender also sells computers and peripherals by Apple, Compaq, IBM, Toshiba, and other makers. In addition to equipment, Defender is a national leader in boat-building supplies: fiberglass, xynole, epoxy and polyester resins, and other boat construction and maintenance materials are stocked in depth. Defender also offers a range of custom services, such as life raft repacking and repair, rigging services, and canvas goods to order (seat covers, pool covers, car covers, etc.).

Defender's wholesale affiliate, Atlantic Main Corp., specializes in small boat marine hardware and safety gear. Atlantic Main is also the U.S. agent for Blake heads, Taylor heaters, Dynous and Force 4 inflatable boats, and Ibberson yachting knives, XM Yachting inflatables, and safety gear. For details, contact Atlantic Main at 42 Great Neck Rd., Waterford, CT 06385.

Overseas customers, please note: Defender will send the catalog for the cost of postage—write to request the catalog, and you'll receive a quote. The firm has customer sales representatives who speak French, German, Spanish, Dutch, Cantonese, and Portuguese.

Special Factors: Price quote by phone, fax, or letter; returns are accepted within 20 days (a restocking fee may be charged); minimum order is $25.

DISCOUNT TIRE DIRECT

7333 E. HELM DR.
SCOTTSDALE, AZ 85024
800–589–6789
FAX: 602–483–9230

Information: price quote
Pay: check, MO, MC, V, AE, Discover
Sells: tires, wheels, and suspension
Store: mail order only
Online: http://www.tires.com

 ¡Si!

Discount Tire Direct entered the mail-order arena several years ago, and is now a major direct marketer of tires—all-season, high-performance, snow, and light truck. The manufacturers represented include Continental, Dunlop, B.F. Goodrich, Goodyear, Michelin, Nitto, Pirelli, and Yokohama. You'll find wheels here by Antera, Concord, Dial, Enkei, Konig, Momo, TSW, and other makers. You can call or write for a price quote on specific models, or visit the website for more information on their current inventory and special offerings. Discount Tire Direct also runs ads in major auto magazines, which will show you the latest specials.

Special Factors: Satisfaction is guaranteed; returns are accepted within 30 days for exchange, refund, or credit.

FREEPORT MARINE SUPPLY CO., INC.

**47 WEST MERRICK RD.
FREEPORT, NY 11520
516–379–2610
FAX: 516–379–2909**

Catalog: free
Pay: check, MO, MC, V, AE, DC, Discover
Sells: boating and marine supplies and equipment
Store: same address; Monday to Saturday 8:30–6 (Friday till 9 April to Labor Day, Sunday 9–3 April to July 4)
E-mail: sales@freeportmarine.com
Online: http://www.freeportmarine.com

Freeport Marine has been in business, owned by the same family, since 1939, and publishes a 264-page catalog of marine hardware, maintenance products, and electronics for sailboats and powerboats. The stock includes epoxies and finishes, rope, anchors, windlasses, buoys, horns, seacocks, winches, VHF radios, global positioning systems, navigation instruments, safety equipment, radar, marine optics, inflatable boats, and a complete line of marine hardware. Among the manufacturers represented are Apelco, Avon, Barr, Garelick, Icom, Interlux, ITT Night Vision, Jabsco, Magellan, Marinco, Perko, Raritan, Raytheon, Si-Tex, Standard, Stearns, Steiner, and Teleflex. Savings run up to 60%, and if you don't see what you're looking for, call and ask.

Special Factors: Satisfaction is guaranteed; minimum order is $25 with credit cards.

M & E MARINE SUPPLY COMPANY, INC.

**P.O. BOX 601
CAMDEN, NJ 08101–0601
800–541–6501
FAX: 609–757–9175**

Catalog: free
Pay: check, MO, MC, V, AE, Discover
Sells: boating supplies and equipment
Store: Glascow, DE; also Collingwood and Trenton, NJ; call for addresses and hours
E-mail: catalog@memarine.com
Online: http://www.memarine.com

M & E has been serving boaters since 1946 with good prices on everything needed to set sail and stay afloat. The 328-page catalog gives you access to over 30,000 products from anchors to zippers, from well-known manufacturers such as Apelco, Barient, Garmin, Harken, Magellan, Maxxima, Schaefer, Si-Tex, Tasco, and Weems & Plath. If you have a boat or enjoy sailing, you'll appreciate the savings, which average 25% but can reach 80%. A recent sale catalog included navigation equipment, lighting, pumps, electronics, safety equipment, hull repair compounds and finishes, ladders, rope, inflatables (dinghies), horns, bells, and other equipment and supplies. There are lots of products useful on land, such as the Sperry Top-Siders, teak boat accessories, acrylic glassware, watches, fishing equipment, and flags. Both list and M & E's discount prices are given, and everything is covered by the blanket guarantee of satisfaction. You can also order right off their website.

Special Factors: Satisfaction is guaranteed; returns are accepted within 30 days for exchange, refund, or credit; C.O.D. orders are accepted from established customers.

MILL SUPPLY

19801 MILES RD., DEPT.
  WBMC
CLEVELAND, OH 44128
800–888–5072
216–518–5072
FAX: 216–518–2700

Catalog: $4, $8 outside U.S.
Pay: check, MO, MC, V, Discover
Sells: automotive restoration parts and supplies
Store: same address; Monday to Friday 8–5
E-mail: msinfo@millsupply.com
Online: http://www.millsupply.com

Whether you're a weekend grease monkey or you own a body shop, you'll want Mill Supply's 192-page catalog on your shelf. Mill Supply has been selling car parts since 1944 and specializes in replacement panels and supplies for collision and rust repairs for American and foreign vehicles. The index runs from Alfa Romeo to Volvo, with all the hardware, tools, finishes, and other shop equipment you need to do installations. You have to have the know-how to do certain types of jobs, but even driveway mechanics can install rubber mud flaps and replacement side mirrors, or use the professional brushes and car-washing equipment.

Special Factors: Quantity discounts are available; authorized returns are accepted (a 10% restocking fee is charged) within 60 days for exchange, refund, or credit.

RACER WHOLESALE

**1020 SUN VALLEY DR.,
DEPT. WBM
ROSWELL, GA 30076
770–998–7777
FAX: 770–993–4417**

Catalog: free
Pay: check, MO, MC, V, Discover
Sells: auto racing safety equipment
Store: same address; Monday to Friday 9–6
Online: http://www.racerwholesale.com

Racer Wholesale has been serving the serious amateur and professional auto-racing markets since 1985, offering safety equipment and accessories at savings of up to 70% on list prices. The 80-page catalog shows professional driving suits, gloves, boots, helmets, belts, harnesses, window nets, arm restraints, racing seats, fire extinguishers, and other safety products from major manufacturers. Auto equipment is also available, including filters and accessories, mufflers, heavy-duty oil, coolers, hoses and connections, fueling accessories, canopies, towing equipment, wide-view mirrors, battery cutoff switches, rod ends, and related goods. Racer Wholesale has a "guaranteed lowest price" policy—see the catalog for details. For close-outs and other specials, check Racer Wholesale's website.

Special Factors: Authorized, unused returns (except special orders) are accepted within 45 days for exchange, refund, or credit (a restocking fee may be charged). The telephone order line is open 24 hours a day.

RV DIRECT

**P.O. BOX 1499, DEPT.
17032
BURNSVILLE, MN
55337–0499
800–438–5480
FAX: 612–894–0083**

Catalog: free
Pay: check, MO, MC, V, AE, Discover
Sells: RV equipment and accessories
Store: mail order only
Online: http://www.northern-online.com

Make the most of the time you spend in your RV or camper with the right furnishings, equipment, and accessories. RV Direct dedicates 52 color pages to answering your needs, with everything from air-conditioning units to water pumps, hoses, and water-delivery equipment. There's an extensive selection of covers and tarps, awnings and screen rooms for sun and bug protection, steps and mounts, chairs and tables, lighting, galley gear, outdoor cooking equipment, heating units, plumbing and sanitation equipment, pressure-washing equipment, air compressors, RV storage units, directional electronics, generators and power supplies, trailer accessories, towing gear, jacks, chocks, ramps, levels, and much more. Prices are competitive, but just one "value" price is given in the catalog, so shop around to be sure you're getting the best deal. If you find a lower price in a national ad, send RV a copy, and they'll "meet or beat it."

Special Factors: Authorized returns are accepted within 30 days for exchange, refund, or credit. RV Direct has an "EZ Pay" program: Pay off your purchases in four payments, interest free.

THE TIRE RACK

**771 W. CHIPPEWA AVE.
SOUTH BEND, IN
46614–3729
800–428–8355
219–287–2345
FAX: 219–236–7707**

Catalog: free
Pay: check, MO, MC, V, AE, Discover
Sells: tires, wheels, and packages
Store: same address; Monday to Friday 9–4, Saturday 9–3
E-mail: sales@tirerack.com
Online: http://www.tirerack.com

The Tire Rack moved its sales focus to the mail-order market nearly 15 years ago and has found it the ideal way to deliver the best values in the latest models to customers around the world. The staff are serious driving enthusiasts who test the new models as they arrive on the market, and are able to provide informed advice about the best tire for your climate, driving style and conditions, and budget.

The tires available include lines by Bridgestone, Continental, Dunlop, Firestone, General, B.F. Goodrich, Goodyear, Hoosier, Michelin, Pirelli, Sumitomo, and Yokohama. The Tire Rack's specialty is performance tires, but the firm also carries all the others—including models for sport-utility vehicles, minivans, light trucks, and pickups. If you're shopping for wheels, you can call for pricing on models by BBS, Borbet, Fittipaldi, Gara, Kosei, Mille Miglia, Moda, MSW, O.Z. Italy, Sportline, TR Motorsport, and Zagato; tuner wheels for BMW, Mercedes, and Porsche models are available from Alpha, AMG, Breyton, and Carlsson. And if you're in the market for both, you've come to the right place: The Tire Rack assures you that "when you purchase tires and wheels together, they will be expertly mounted and balanced, packaged with all necessary accessories, and will be delivered to you ready to install on your car or light truck." An instruction manual is included with each package.

You can call or write for the catalog, or visit the website, which is very well organized, is continuously updated, and includes a lot of information on selecting tires and wheels. You'll find the online map helpful if you want to pay the firm a visit—if you're in the South Bend area, you can have The Tire Rack install your purchase while you're there. And if you can't make it to Indiana, ask your sales rep to consult the company database of over 900 recommended installation experts nationwide for the one nearest you.

Special Factors: Satisfaction is guaranteed; phone hours are Monday to Friday 8–8, Saturday 9–4 ET; returns of unused merchandise are accepted within 30 days for exchange, refund, or credit.

WAG-AERO GROUP OF AIRCRAFT SERVICES

P.O. BOX 181, DEPT.
  WBM99
LYONS, WI 53148–0181
800–558–6868
414–763–9586
FAX: 414–763–7595

Catalog: free
Pay: check, MO, MC, V, Discover
Sells: aircraft parts, supplies, and aviation accessories
Store: 1216 North Rd., Lyons, WI; Monday to Friday 8:30–4:30
E-mail: wagaero-sales@wagaero.com
Online: http://www.wagaero.com

Wag-Aero is so attuned to the needs of small-aircraft pilots that the catalog includes directions for "fly-in" customers! The firm has been in business for over 38 years, and carries everything from spark plugs and propellers to aircraft decals, aviators' jackets, and manuals. The 148-page catalog features a full range of piloting instruments, windshields, radios, lighting, spinners, engine mounts, wheels, and much more, by some major names—Aeronca, Cessna, Grumman, etc. And there are many value-priced products sold under Wag-Aero's own label. Specials and sale items show up in the seasonal tabloid catalogs as well. Whether you're a dedicated pilot maintaining an aircraft or you just dream of taking to the wild blue yonder, you'll find much of interest here.

Special Factors: Satisfaction is guaranteed; authorized returns are accepted within 90 days for exchange, refund, or credit; C.O.D. orders are accepted.

WEST MARINE

500 WESTRIDGE DR.
WATSONVILLE, CA 95076
800–BOATING
800–621–6885
FAX: 800–825–7678
WHOLESALE DIVISION:
800–621–6885

Catalog: free
Pay: check, MO, MC, V, AE, Discover
Sells: marine supplies and equipment
Store: outlets nationwide; call for locations
Online: http://www.westmarine.com

West Marine publishes a 912-page color catalog of marine electronics, hardware, and maintenance products for sailboats and powerboats, as well as related goods, such as foul-weather clothing and plumbing supplies. The comprehensive selection of gear and materials includes epoxies and finishes, rope, anchors, windlasses, buoys, horns, seacocks, winches, VHF radios, global positioning systems, navigation instruments, safety equipment, hardware, kerosene lamps, marine optics, inflatable boats, and a complete line of galley gear. There are scores of manufacturers represented, including Apelco, Barient, Harken, Interphase, Lewmar, Magellan, Marinco, Navico, Patagonia, Ritchie, Schaefer, Stearns, Steiner, Taylor Made, and Weems & Plath, as well as the firm's proprietary label. West Marine also offers rope-splicing services at "a reasonable fee." Savings run up to 50%, and West Marine has over 30,000 items in stock, so call and ask if you don't see what you're looking for.

Spanish-speaking readers, please note: West Marine has operators who speak Spanish on some, but not all, shifts.

Special Factors: Satisfaction is guaranteed; special orders are accepted.

WORLDWIDE AUTO PARTS

RT. 38

MAPLE SHADE, NJ 08052

800–500–PART

Information: price quote
Pay: check, MO, MC, V, Discover
Sells: OEM car parts (see text)
Store: mail order only; phone hours Monday to Friday 8–5 EST
E-mail: sales@wwparts.com
Online: http://www.wwparts.com

Finding genuine factory car parts isn't difficult—it's paying for them that's painful. Enter WorldWide Auto Parts. The firm began life in 1962 as MSO Parts, offering discounts on original equipment manufacturer (OEM) goods for Honda, Acura, and Mazda models. Now doing business as WorldWide, the company has access to nearly two million parts for both foreign and domestic vehicles.

WorldWide can help you beat local dealer prices on parts on foreign cars made after 1980 by Acura, BMW, Honda, Mazda, Nissan, and Toyota; the domestic models include Buick, Cadillac, Chevrolet, Chrysler, Dodge, Ford, GMC, Lincoln, Mercury, Oldsmobile, Plymouth, and Pontiac. You can call or e-mail to ask about availability and prices, or visit the website and search the online database. Even if you're not shopping right now, it's worth an online visit for the Tech Tips and the good collection of car-related links.

Special Factors: Satisfaction is guaranteed; returns are accepted within 30 days for exchange, refund, or credit.

RELATED PRODUCTS/COMPANIES

Airline and auto seat belt extenders • *Amplestuff*
Auto body refinishing supplies • *Red Hill Corporation*
Automotive accessories • *The Sportsman's Guide, Damark*
Automotive repair/maintenance equipment • *Harbor Freight Tools, Camelot Enterprises, Northern Hydraulics*
Battery chargers • *Surplus Center*
Boats and water sports gear/equipment • *Bart's, Overton's, Mohawk Canoes, SOAR Inflatables, Campmor*
Car care products • *Fuller Brush Independent Distributor*
Car security systems • *Crutchfield*
Car stereos/speaker systems • *Crutchfield, Gold Sound*

Cleaning supplies • The Cleaning Center
Dog seat belts • Kennel Vet
Farm equipment • Northern Hydraulics
Fishing equipment • Overton's
Fuel tanks • Overton's
Infant car seats • Bennett Brothers
Marine equipment/accessories • Bart's, Northern Hydraulics, Overton's
Marine optics • Mardiron
Motorcycle, ATV, minibike, and snowmobile parts • Manufacturer's Supply, Northern Hydraulics
Online car buying • Netmarket's AutoVantage
Radar detectors and police scanners • J & R Music World, LVT Price Quote Hotline, Percy's
RV equipment • Northern Hydraulics
Sailboard car racks • The House
Sheepskin seat and steering wheel covers • Arctic Sheepskin
Trailers/trailer parts • Tool Crib of the North, Northern Hydraulics
Truck boxes and van equipment • Holz Tool Supply

BOOKS, AUDIOBOOKS, AND PERIODICALS

Sources for entertainment and educational books, books on tape, and discount magazine subscriptions

If there's one thing you should learn from this book, it's that paying full price for books and magazines is absolutely unnecessary. Every company in this chapter offers deals on books of every kind—from elegant coffee-table art books to encyclopedias to best-sellers. You'll find brand-new books as well as antiques; you can shop online or through old-fashioned booksellers who deal strictly through the mail and are willing to personally answer your questions and offer recommendations. There isn't a book in existence you won't be able to find here for substantially less than you'd spend at your local bookstore.

You won't find every category of book listed in the "Find It Fast" section. For example, children's books are stocked by many, but not all, of the companies—as new books, used books, and unused but "remaindered" books; the same is true for mysteries, science fiction, self-help, and other book categories. Browsing the company descriptions is your best bet.

If you find yourself commuting or traveling a lot, have vision problems, or just love to keep your hands free while improving your mind, you'll enjoy the audiobook offerings, some of which you can rent instead of buy.

Finally, shave dollars off every magazine subscription you're now carrying with the subscription-services firms. If you've a business that subscribes to several magazines, your savings will be substantial.

Please note: Many if not most of the firms in *Buy Wholesale by Mail* carry books, booklets, guides, and even newsletters on subjects relevant to their businesses. Although some are listed in the "Related Products/Companies" section at the end of this chapter, to list every firm that sells one or two books would be impossible. Therefore, use common sense: If your interest is cooking, see the "Food and Beverages" chapter for companies that stock cookbooks; for books on health-related subjects, check out the listings in the "Health, Beauty, and Hygiene" chapter; for how-to and do-it-yourself books, try some of the firms in the "House and Home: Building, Renovation, and Upkeep" section, or the "Tools, Hardware, Shop Machines" chapter, and so on. Happy reading!

FIND IT FAST

ALTERNATIVE CULTURE • Essential Media
AUDIOBOOKS • Bargain Book Warehouse, Blackstone, Books.com, The Family Travel Guides Catalogue, Reader's Digest
COMICS • Essential Media
CONSUMER PUBLICATIONS • Consumer Information Center, U.S. Gov't Superintendent of Documents
COOKBOOKS • Jessica's Biscuit, Reader's Digest, Storey Communications
COUNTRY WISDOM MANUALS • Storey Communications
DO-IT-YOURSELF BOOKS • Reader's Digest, Woodworkers' Discount
ENCYCLOPEDIAS • Amazon.com, Reference Book Center
FAMILY TRAVEL GUIDES • The Family Travel Guides Catalogue
FINE/APPLIED ARTS BOOKS • Hacker, The Potters Shop
GRAPHIC ARTS BOOKS, MANUALS • Print Bookstore
GENERAL • Amazon.com, Books.com
HARDCOVER BOOKS • Edward R. Hamilton, Tartan
LARGE-PRINT BOOKS/MAGAZINES • Editions, Reader's Digest, Tartan
MAGAZINE SUBSCRIPTIONS • Below Wholesale Magazines, Delta Publishing Group
OLD, RARE, USED BOOKS • Editions, Strand, Tartan
PUBLISHERS OVERSTOCK/CLEARANCE/REMAINDERED • Bargain Book Warehouse, Barnes & Noble, Bear Mountain, Daedalus, Edward R. Hamilton, Tartan
UNIVERSITY PRESS/SCHOLARLY PUBLICATIONS • Daedalus, The Scholar's Bookshelf

AMAZON.COM

P.O. BOX 80387
SEATTLE, WA 98108–0387
800–201–7575 (NOT FOR
   ORDERS)
206–346–2992
FAX: 206–346–2950

Information: internet website, no catalog
Pay: check, MO, MC, V, AE, Discover
Sells: books
Store: online only; phone hours Monday to
Friday 8–7 PT
E-mail: info@amazon.com
Online: http://www.amazon.com

Amazon.com figured out early on that many of us busy consumers would rather shop in our pajamas. This virtual bookstore has 2.5 million titles, a wealth of reviews, personal recommendations, author interviews, excerpts, and much more. Plus you'll enjoy savings of 20% to 40% on 400,000 titles at Amazon.com. The "Gift Center" offers recommendations for readers of all tastes and ages, as well as Amazon.com accessories such as mousepads, tee shirts, and hats. I recently bought three books at Amazon.com. They were in my mailbox two days later! Not only is this a good place to buy books at a discount, but it's a godsend for writers and others who are looking to find references and sources on any subject, since you can search by author, title, subject, or keywords. For those of you who are wary about shopping on the web, Amazon.com guarantees that every credit card purchase is 100% safe. But if you prefer, you can complete the order form except for the credit card information and then call that number in, or fax or mail the order form the old-fashioned way. The website has an extensive FAQ section and customer service information, but unlike other web-only shopping sites, you can also call the Amazon.com staff to have a real human being answer your questions.

Special Factors: Satisfaction is guaranteed; returns are accepted within 15 days for exchange, refund, or credit.

BARGAIN BOOK WAREHOUSE

SODA CREEK PRESS
P.O. BOX 8515
UKIAH, CA 95482-8515
800-301-7567
707-463-1351
FAX: 800-949-4946
FAX: 707-463-2072

Catalog: free
Pay: check, MO, MC, V, AE, Discover
Sells: clearance and publisher's overstock
Store: mail order only
E-mail: scp@sodacreekpress.com
Online: http://www.sodacreekpress.com

The "Bargain Book Warehouse" catalog from Soda Creek Press brings you 88 pages of current and out-of-print titles in a number of categories—history and biography, romance, fantasy and science fiction, and horror and mystery. The last category is especially strong here—you'll find "proper British mysteries," historical intrigues, detective stories, and espionage. The romances run from Regencies (and romantic suspense) to love stories in contemporary settings: Barbara Cartland to Danielle Steel. The horror titles include some gothics, and you'll also find a number of stories for children.

The copy summarizes the plot lines of each title, and both the publisher's and Soda Creek's discount prices are given. And the discounts are great—you can find books by Herman Wouk, originally $24.95, for under $8, a collection of three books by Ray Bradbury for $6.99, and children's books for as little as $1.99. Soda Creek Press also offers the "Book Lover's Surprise Package," with four books of the firm's choosing for as little as $6.99. Bargain Book Warehouse also offers selected books on cassette and videos. Visit the website and find "Internet Specials" with even greater savings, or search the online catalog for the titles of your choice. The generous returns policy makes this a "can't go wrong" resource for your recreational reading.

For mystery and romance lovers out there, Soda Creek offers two other catalogs—"Mysteries by Mail" and "Manderley." While the savings are not as great as those in Bargain Books Warehouse, there are a number of ways the avid reader can still save. You'll still get 10% off all hardcovers, and 20% off best-sellers. And a "Baker Street Dozen" will get you a thirteenth book free if you order a dozen romance or mystery novels. You'll find these two catalogs on Soda Creek's website alongside Bargain Books Warehouse. Check it out.

Special Factors: Satisfaction is guaranteed; returns are accepted for exchange, refund, or credit.

BARNES & NOBLE BOOKS BY MAIL

ONE POND RD.
ROCKLEIGH, NJ 07647
800–THE BOOK
FAX: 201–767–9169

Catalog: free
Pay: check, MO, MC, V, AE, DC, JCB
Sells: books, audio- and videotapes, gifts, etc.
Store: call main number for location nearest you
Online: http://www.barnesandnoble.com

For more than 20 years, book lovers and bargain hunters alike have come to know the Barnes & Noble Books by Mail catalog as America's largest source of publisher's overstocks—all offered at savings of up to 80% off list price. Most of the titles in the catalog are sold exclusively through Barnes & Noble—they are not available in retail stores. Each issue is packed with hundreds of unique and hard-to-find bargains in books, music, videos, and other merchandise. There are no membership requirements or obligations to fulfill, just great books at great prices. Subjects include history, mystery, the arts, science, literature, film, medicine, biographies, satire, juvenilia, current fiction, linguistics, religion, reference, crafts, self-help, and photography. In video, subjects include classics, family favorites, documentaries, BBC comedies, travel guides, science, and history. Calendars, bookshelves, book embossers, bookends, calligraphy pens, games, and book lights are also offered in ongoing catalogs. You can also find them on the web or on AOL. And, of course, you can visit any of dozens of Barnes & Noble bookstores around the country for more, albeit different, choices and values.

Canadian and APO/FPO readers, please note: Inquire for shipping charges, and allow extra time for order processing.

Special Factors: Satisfaction is unconditionally guaranteed; returns are accepted; minimum order is $15 with credit cards. Library and school discounts are available.

BEAR MOUNTAIN BOOKS

**WOODBURY COMMON
CENTRAL VALLEY, NY**
10917
914–928–7565
FAX: 914–928–3396

Information: internet website, no catalog
Pay: check, MO, MC, V, AE
Sells: books, music CDs, videos, and CD-ROMs
Store: same address; Sunday to Wednesday 10–6, Thursday to Saturday 10–8
E-mail: bearmtbk@ny.frontiercomm.net
Online: http://www.bargainbooks.com

Bear Mountain Books & Music, which has been in business since 1974, sells all their books at 20% to 70% off, music CDs for $4.99 each, videos at $2.98, and CD-ROMs for as little as $3. The selection is broad but not deep. It only takes a moment to scroll through the website to see what's currently in stock. It's a little bit like shopping your favorite bargain store—sometimes you'll find something you've been desperately wanting, and you'll feel glee at how much you just saved. Other times there may be nothing there that rings your bell. The book categories include Art/Photography, Business/Investing, Children's, Cooking, Computers, Fiction, History/Biography, Self-Enlightenment, and more. USA Today was "stunned and awestruck" by the classical CDs at only $4.99. The music categories run from Dance, Ethnic, and International to Jazz, Blues, and Big Band, with lots in between. The CD-ROM selections included Children's, General, Graphics, Utilities, and Entertainment and Game. If you're into exercise videos, the current site had a long list of available videos for less than $3 each. By the way, if you want the bookstore to order a title not listed on the website, you'll still get a discount: 20% off paperbacks, 30% off hardcovers.

Special Factors: See website for list of foreign countries to which company can ship, as well as other shipping policies and costs. Order by fax, mail, phone, or online.

BELOW WHOLESALE MAGAZINES

Price List: free
Pay: check, MO, MC, V, AE, Discover
Sells: magazine subscriptions
Store: mail order only
E-mail: bwm@accutek.com

1909 PROSPERITY ST.,
   DEPT. WBM
RENO, NV 89502
800–800–0062
FAX: 702–785–7509

Below Wholesale Magazines lives up to its billing with access to over 1,000 magazines at prices that beat the magazine subscription clearinghouses—"the deepest discounts in America. Period." They're so sure about that, that if you order from them and then find a lower authorized price, they'll match it or credit you 125% of the difference. The brochure lists most major magazines, including trade magazines, and prices are up to 90% below newsstand rates (and often 15% to 30% less than the "best" prices you see elsewhere). Below Wholesale Magazines requires a business card for the best rates on about two dozen popular titles, as well as a trade name or business identification for select publications. There are hundreds of titles available that aren't listed in the brochure, so call if you don't see yours mentioned. You can also extend or renew current subscriptions through Below Wholesale Magazines, which has been supplying waiting room subscriptions since 1984, and selling to the public since 1988. The brochure states terms of the sales policy, and usually includes coupons and special offers for extra savings.

Canadian readers, please note: Only U.S. funds are accepted.

Special Factors: Satisfaction is guaranteed; gift service is available; allow 12 weeks for first issue to arrive.

BLACKSTONE AUDIOBOOKS

P.O. BOX 969
ASHLAND, OR 97520
800–729–2665
541–482–9239 (OUTSIDE
   U.S.)
FAX: 541–482–9294

Catalog: free
Pay: check, MO, MC, V, AE, Discover
Sells and Rents: unabridged recordings of great books
Store: mail order only

When my mother, an avid reader, had cataract surgery last fall, she was unable to read for several weeks. I wish I had known about Blackstone Audiobooks, with the guaranteed lowest prices on full-length (unabridged) high-quality audiobooks. The 148-page catalog is closely printed, with hundreds and hundreds of titles. Blackstone's catalog is organized alphabetically by category, including 20th-century fiction, poetry, children's (great for those long car trips or troubled sleepers), science fiction and fantasy, baseball, business, religion, speeches, plays, Civil War, biography, and many others. The cassettes are for purchase or for rent—usually for 30 to 45 days, depending on the book length. The rentals average around $8 to $10 for children's, or $10 to $15 for adults', which isn't much per day. Owner Craig Black says his audiobooks are about 15% to 20% lower than comparable recordings, and he also offers used audiobooks for 50% off. There are quantity discounts for individuals on purchases and rentals (rent three books, get an additional 10% off, for example), monthly specials, and discounts for libraries and wholesalers (inquire). See the catalog for details on shipping and returning rentals. You can also visit the website to view the sale catalog.

Special Factors: Different shipping rates apply outside the contiguous 48 states.

BOOKS.COM

**1300 EAST 9TH ST.,
STE. 1810
CLEVELAND, OH 44114
800–266–5909
216–694–5747
FAX: 216–696–0386**

Information: internet website, no catalog
Pay: MC, V, AE, Discover
Sells: books, audiobooks, calendars
Store: online only
Online: http://www.books.com

Books.com, formerly known as Book Stacks Unlimited, Inc., is, in the company's own words, "an online bookstore and readers' conference system accessible via the internet from anywhere in the world." Books.com lists about half a million titles in its easy-to-use database, and includes the title, author, publisher, date of publication, ISBN, and often a summary or review in each listing. Many titles are discounted from 20% to 40%, and when you buy at Books.com, you also earn "Bookmarks"—points that can be redeemed for free books. Members of NetMarket (www.netmarket.com) and members of Books.com's Frequent Buyer Club receive the deepest discounts, saving 30% to 40% on the majority of their purchases.

Books.com operates exclusively on the internet, and requires you to initiate your order online. You can stop at the point at which you'd otherwise submit credit card information, and either call or fax it to Books.com to complete the transaction. The order form has been set up to facilitate both styles, and there's plenty of information in the "help" section to answer any questions you might have, as well as e-mail addresses of company contacts if you stump the FAQ.

Special Factors: Satisfaction is guaranteed; resellable returns are accepted within 30 days for exchange, refund, or credit; corporate members get a complimentary Frequent Buyer Card.

CONSUMER INFOR-
MATION CENTER

P.O. BOX 100
PUEBLO, CO 81009
888–878–3256
FAX: 719–948–4000

Catalog: free
Pay: check, MO, MC, V
Sells: consumer publications
Store: over 1,300 Federal Depository
Libraries nationwide (see text)
Online: http://www.pueblo.gsa.gov

 ¡Sí!

The government's Consumer Information Center was established in 1970 "to help federal agencies promote and distribute useful consumer information." Many of the pamphlets and manuals in the Center's 16-page quarterly catalog are free, such as the U.S. Government TDD Directory. The topics include cars, children and parenting, employment, federal programs benefits, food and nutrition, health (drugs, mental health, medical problems, etc.), housing, money (credit, financial planning), small business, travel and hobbies, and more. You can subscribe to FDA Consumer through the Consumer Information Center's catalog, and order pamphlets that help you find out about 600 classic children's books published before 1960, U.S. government property that's for sale, lesser-known areas of the National Park system, and how to choose the cheapest local and long-distance phone carriers, among other things.

You can also request the Consumer's Resource Handbook, a guide to effective complaint procedures, from the Department of Consumer Affairs (it's available in its entirety on the website as well). The Handbook lists the best sources of help if you have a problem as a consumer: contact names, addresses, and phone numbers of customer relations departments of hundreds of major corporations, Better Business Bureau offices worldwide, trade associations, consumer protection offices, and federal agencies. . . all at the best possible price—free.

If you'd like to see the literature before buying, you can visit one of the over 1,300 Federal Depository Libraries around the country; they don't do sales, but they have copies of nearly every Federal Government publication (in print or on microfilm) that's designated for use by the general public. Your local library should be able to help you locate one, or you can write to Federal Depository Library Program, Office of the Public Printer, Washington, DC 20401. To locate a U.S. Government Bookstore, see the listing for "U.S. Gov't Superintendent of Documents" in this chapter.

Please note: A Spanish-language catalog of dozens of federal consumer guides is also available.

Special Factors: A handling fee is charged on all orders.

DAEDALUS BOOKS AND MUSIC

**P.O. BOX 9132 (WBM)
HYATTSVILLE, MD
20781–0932
800–395–2665
FAX: 800–866–5578**

Catalog: free
Pay: check, MO, MC, V, AE, Discover
Sells: literary publications, music CDs
Store: mail order only
Online: http://www.daedalus-books.com

Daedalus, founded in 1980, offers fine books from trade publishers and university presses at 50% to 90% off publishers' prices. These remainders have been culled from thousands to appeal to literary readers looking for culture on the cheap. Daedalus isn't just remainders, though —about half the catalog is devoted to current titles that are discounted about 25%. And the witty, clearheaded descriptions of each book are reading pleasures in themselves. The categories include literature and general interest, visual and performing arts, philosophy, history, feminism, politics, children's books, travel, food and wine, and the social sciences. A gift certificate from Daedalus, presented with the latest edition of the catalog, should delight a reader with wide-ranging interests.

Audiophiles have something to celebrate with the latest offering from Daedalus—the music catalog. Here are 48 pages of classical, jazz, and esoteric recordings on CD, including Library of Congress Great Performances, Deutsche Grammophon "Originals" series, nominees for best-of-year by *Gramophone* magazine, and hard-to-find European imports.

Canadian and international readers, please note: Payment must be made by credit card, a money order drawn in U.S. funds, or a check drawn on a U.S. bank.

Special Factors: Institutional accounts are available; returns are accepted within 30 days.

DELTA PUBLISHING GROUP/MAGAZINE WAREHOUSE

Catalog: free
Pay: check, MO, MC, V, AE, Discover
Sells: magazine subscriptions
Store: mail order only
E-mail: deltapub@usa.net

1243 48TH ST.
BROOKLYN, NY 11219
800–SEND–LIST
718–972–0900
FAX: 718–972–4695

Delta Publishing Group, a.k.a. Magazine Warehouse, is the subscription wholesaler we've all been looking for, with over 800 titles at the absolute lowest prices anywhere. It's shocking to see magazine after magazine here at prices that beat the ones offered by the sweepstakes operations by 40% or so. You don't get the chance at $10 million and you can't split the payments over three or four months, but at these prices and with a selection that runs from *A & E Monthly* to *Zoo Books*, you won't miss the perks.

Delta/Magazine Warehouse, founded in 1991, is a major supplier of wholesale subscriptions to corporation and doctors' offices, and extends similar "courtesy" rates to readers of this book. The firm offers many of the titles in subscriptions of up to three years, so you can lock in the rate of a favorite. (All of the terms are for full years.) Delta offers free tracking service on subscriptions bought from other sources, so you can have your renewals picked up seamlessly. And check the price list you receive for specials—bonus subscriptions and free magazine racks have been offered in the past.

Please note that a score of titles require a "trade" address that includes a business name, and a handful ask for a business card or letterhead; the magazines will be mailed to that address only. Be sure to mention BWBM when you call (800–SEND–LIST) or write for the price list.

Special Factors: Lowest subscription rates are guaranteed.

DOVER PUBLICATIONS, INC.

31 EAST 2ND ST.,
  DEPT. MC
MINEOLA, NY 11501–3852
516–294–7000

Catalog: free
Pay: check or MO
Sells: Dover publications
Store: same address; Monday to Friday 8–4;
also 180 Varick St., 9th Floor, New York, NY;
Monday to Friday 9–4:30

Many of the firms listed in this book sell selections of Dover books, but if you deal with the publisher directly you can buy any in-print Dover publication. In over half a century of publishing, Dover has built a reputation for books as notable for their quality construction as they are for their content. Dover's catalogs feature paperbacks on crafts and hobbies, Americana, mathematics and physics, American Indian arts, architecture, cooking, games, travel, music, and many other topics. Dover's "Pictorial Archives," featuring designs and graphics, typography, banners and scrolls, borders, etc., and the "Clip-Art Series" are copyright-free art that can be used in newsletters, ads, menus, and the like. Dover's postcard sets run from NASA shots to Tiffany windows, and there are stickers, coloring books, posters, and even gift wrap. Dover publishes facsimiles and reprints of rare and valuable texts, "Listen & Learn" language tapes, as well as bird song tapes and musical scores by Scriabin, Liszt, Scott Joplin, Couperin, Ravel, Bizet, Brahms, and other greats. The prices are easily up to 50% less than those charged for comparable publications, and there are children's books and literary classics for just $1.

Canadian readers, please note: The shipping surcharge on orders sent to Canada is 20%.

Special Factors: Satisfaction is guaranteed; returns are accepted within 10 days for refund.

EDITIONS

DESK WM
BOICEVILLE, NY 12412
914–657–7000
FAX: 914–657–8849

Catalog: $2
Pay: check, MO, MC, V, Discover
Sells: old, used, and rare books
Store: 2740 Rte. 28, Ashokan, NY; daily 10–5
E-mail: nleditions@aol.com
Online: http://www.nleditions.com

Editions is a great source for used and out-of-print books, which are often priced 30% to 50% less here than elsewhere. Editions has been selling by mail since 1948 and operates a sprawling store that's stocked with a separate book inventory—55,000 at last count—worth a stop if you're in the area. Owner Norman Levine understands old-world bookworms, who could happily spend a rainy day inside his store, when he writes: "If you are comfortable with computers, listings of our inventory can now be examined at our website."

The 64-page monthly catalogs include partial listings from a range of categories. For example, the January catalog may list poetry titles from Eliot to Neruda, and February's issue will run from Powys to Wyse. Each catalog lists about 10,000 titles, most priced under $20, from categories that include fiction, literature, history, the social sciences, natural history, travel, folklore, the law, women, soldiers and war, the Irish, Americana, British history, theater, philosophy and religion, food, labor, espionage, sports, antiques, gardening, animals, publishing, Judaica, and more. And it's always interesting to see what ends up in the "Miscellaneous Subjects & Nonsense" section. The original hardcover titles, in fine condition, are often cheaper here than the paperback editions. Editions also carries large-print books. Collectors and researchers may wish to see the catalogs for the first editions and books from the Heritage Press and Lakeside Press, as well as the occasional listings of regimental histories, genealogies, and books on local history.

Special Factors: Inquiries by letter, fax, or e-mail only; returns are accepted within three days.

ESSENTIAL MEDIA COUNTERCULTURE CATALOG

**P.O. BOX 661245
LOS ANGELES, CA
90066–1245
800–490–5350
310–574–1554
FAX: 310–574–3060**

Catalog: $2
Pay: check, MO, MC, V
Sells: alternative/underground books, comics, videos, music CDs, etc.
Store: mail order only
E-mail: underground@essentialmedia.com
Online: http://www.essentialmedia.com

Essential Media is the catalog equivalent of an extremely independent bookstore, run by caring iconoclasts who discount 99% of what they sell. The firm fulfills its mission of "providing a guide to some of the most significant works of postmodern, alternative, and fringe culture" with a catalog and website showcasing hundreds of well-chosen books, videos, and CDs. Essential Media offers the classics of counterculture— *The Whole Earth Catalog, Re/Search* journals, the collected observations of *Loompanics* and *Utne Reader,* the best of the Beats (Burroughs, Ginsberg, Bukowski, et al.), diverse comics (Fritz the Cat, *Mad,* Feiffer, Art Spiegelman), and the literary theory of Foucault and Chomsky, to cite a few. The connoisseur of underground media will appreciate the more obscure treasures, from the secrets of Schwa and the primary documents of The Church of the Sub-Genius to *Memoirs of a Sword Swallower* and Guy Debord's *Society of the Spectacle.* Performance art, "transgressive" fiction, conspiracies, feminism, punk, anarchy, 'zines, and culture—cocktail, cyber, club, ambient, and gay—are some of the other categories celebrated here. The $2 catalog fee will bring you 44 pages of books, recordings, and ephemera—or you can check EM's scintillating website for the regular stock and new additions to the repertoire. Just about everything ships within 24 hours, and the website offers secure online ordering.

Special Factors: Satisfaction is guaranteed; returns in original, resellable condition are accepted within 30 days for exchange, refund, or credit.

THE FAMILY TRAVEL GUIDES CATALOGUE

CAROUSEL PRESS
P.O. BOX 6038
BERKELEY, CA 94706–0038
510–527–5849

Catalog: free with long SASE, or $1
Pay: check, MO, MC, V
Sells: child/family-related travel guides
Store: mail order only
E-mail: carous4659@aol.com

Traveling with children is like having a broken leg: You don't realize how difficult or inconvenient it is until it happens to you. This is due in large part to the fact that the world isn't geared toward children. Wouldn't it be nice to know all the great places that welcome children with special activities, facilities, and rates? Carousel Press has put together a collection of really helpful, valuable, and inexpensive books geared toward making your family trip a memorable one. A current review catalog had books on family-friendly lodging and activities in fifteen major American cities (the Kidding Around series); books on DisneyWorld and other child-oriented recreation spots; tips for travel in Europe, Japan, and Mexico; game and entertainment books (for car, train, bus, and airplane rides); books on organizing a baby-sitting cooperative; children's books on tape; guides to wilderness hiking with young children; and much more. A half-price flyer (available on request) featured books for as little as a dollar (!), marked down for a variety of reasons. This catalog is a must for anyone looking to survive a family vacation in the near future.

Special Factors: International orders must be made with credit cards.

HACKER ART BOOKS

45 W. 57TH ST.
NEW YORK, NY
10019–3485
212–688–7600
FAX: 212–754–2554

Catalog: free
Pay: check, MO, MC, V
Sells: books on the fine and applied arts and related topics
Store: same address; phone hours Monday to Saturday 9:30–6 ET
Online: http://www.hackerartbooks.com

Seymour Hacker, an avid art scholar and publisher, opened his original store in Greenwich Village in 1947. Hacker offered the same kinds of titles then that form the core of the current collection—books on the fine and applied arts, architecture, archaeology, and related works. Today, both the uptown store and the 64-page catalog reflect the same informed scrutiny and exacting standards. Each title includes a concise summary of the text, page count and number of illustrations or color plates, size, year and place of publication, and the price. Hacker is listed here because so many of the books are impressively discounted. For most titles he lists the price at which the book was published. Hacker's prices are 30% to 60% less, and sometimes the savings are even greater.

Each catalog offers hundreds of titles, some of which are already out of print. The store is believed to have the largest inventory of art books in the world and should be part of every collector's visit to New York City. In fact, *New York Times* art critic John Russell exclaimed about Hacker: "For handmade service and a sense of quality, no museum store can compare." Order books totaling between $200 and $299 and you'll earn a free book from among the Free Book volumes listed in the catalog.

Special Factors: The minimum shipping charge on international orders is $15; the maximum shipping charge on orders sent within the U.S. is $25. Institutional accounts are available.

EDWARD R. HAMILTON BOOKSELLER

DEPT. 5166
FALLS VILLAGE, CT
06031–5005

Catalog: free
Pay: check or MO
Sells: new, close-out, and remaindered books
Store: mail order only

Hamilton's monthly catalog lists thousands of bargain books (mostly hardbound) in every conceivable category, at savings that average 30% to 80% off the publishers' prices. The tabloid catalog appeals to the bargain-hunting bookworm who likes to explore old bookstores—it's the literary equivalent of shelves and stacks of volumes. Art, humor, poetry, fiction, literature, photography, self-help, reference, business, crafts, psychology, history, film, science, cooking, sports, and biography are all featured. Each listing is accompanied by a helpful two- or three-sentence description. Hamilton's offerings are all new—current best-sellers from *The New York Times* lists are offered at 30% off published prices, as well as remainders, close-outs, and publishers' overstock. Past best-sellers show up here frequently, as well as imports and other books no other remainder source seems to have. Hamilton was founded in 1968 and prefers to do business the old-fashioned way: by mail only.

Special Factors: Satisfaction is guaranteed; returns are accepted and fully refunded; prepaid institutional orders are accepted; shipments to U.S. addresses only.

JESSICA'S BISCUIT

THE COOKBOOK PEOPLE
P.O. BOX 301
NEWTONVILLE, MA 02160
800–878–4264
617–965–0530
FAX: 617–244–3376

Catalog: free
Pay: check, MO, MC, V, AE, Discover
Sells: cookbooks and food and wine reference
Store: mail order only
Online: http://www.jessicas.com

Jessica's Biscuit sweetens its luscious catalog with sale books—scores of them are scattered throughout the 72 color pages of over 800 books on cooking, food service, and domestic arts. Jessica's Biscuit is the preeminent catalog for in-print specialty cookbooks and updates on the culinary commandments of the taste dictators. Even the newest cookbooks are sold at a discount, while catalogs featuring titles "on super sale" appear several times a year. In addition to national cuisines, Jessica's Biscuit offers books with recipes for vegetarian, macrobiotic, microwave, diabetic, gluten-free, low-salt, sugar-free, low-cholesterol, wheat-free, fiber-rich, kosher, and low-cost dishes. There are regional books for everything from soul food to Amish fare, as well as volumes devoted to herbs, muffins, tofu, pizza, biscuits, corn, mushrooms, barbecuing, cheesecake, beans, children's food, chili, garlic, and potatoes. Related topics include professional food service, canning and preserving, outfitting a working kitchen, buffets, wines, and entertaining in style, among others. Savings on the sale titles average 45% and run as high as 80%. If you don't see what you're looking for in the catalog, call; Jessica's Biscuit has thousands of other titles in the warehouse.

Special Factors: Satisfaction is guaranteed; returns are accepted.

THE POTTERS SHOP

31 THORPE RD.
NEEDHAM HEIGHTS, MA
  02194
781–449–7687
FAX: 781–449–9098

Catalog: free
Pay: check, MO, MC, V, Discover
Sells: books and videotapes on ceramics and pottery, ceramics tools
Store: same address; Monday to Thursday 9:30–5:30, Friday 9:30–1:30; also by appointment
E-mail: sbranfpots@aol.com

The Potters Shop, established in 1977, sells books and videotapes on ceramics and pottery at discounts of at least 15%, and as much as 75% on sale titles. The brochure lists hundreds of books and tapes, many of them obscure or hard-to-find imports. You'll find works on pottery technique, historical surveys, profiles of individual potters, ceramics of the East, health and business for the potter, and even a selection of books for children. Among the videotapes (all VHS) are workshops on raku, form, and technique, and The Potters Shop also sells Dolan tools as well as hard-to-find tools (call them if you don't find what you're looking for). The firm will search for books, maintains want lists, and buys used books on pottery and related topics. If you find yourself in Needham Heights, stop in at the shop. The books are there, as well as a pottery school and workshop, where you can see member potters at their craft and buy their work.

Wholesale customers, please note: "You must operate a bona fide retail establishment and be buying our products for resale to qualify for our program." The minimum wholesale order is five titles, and the discount is 30%. Request complete terms and price lists on company letterhead.

Special Factors: Price quote by phone, e-mail, or letter.

PRINT BOOKSTORE

3200 TOWER OAKS BLVD.
ROCKVILLE, MD
20852–4216
301–770–2900
FAX: 301–984–3203

Catalog: free
Pay: check, MO, MC, V, AE
Sells: books on the graphic arts
Store: mail order only
E-mail: printcirc@aol.com
Online: http://www.printmag.com

Print Magazine, which serves the graphic-design community, has run a mail-order bookstore since 1962, offering well-chosen manuals, color charts, and other aids and reference materials on a range of design-related topics. All of the books are discounted, typically 20%, but some are tagged at 30% and 50% below their published prices. The 16-page color catalog offers annuals, books on desktop publishing and computer graphics, working with color on computer, advertising, graphic design, corporate logos and trademarks, type and typography, design and layout, illustration, and color, as well as Pantone color manuals and fanfold color guides. You can also subscribe to *Print Magazine* through the catalog.

Canadian readers, please note: Only U.S. funds are accepted.

Special Factors: Satisfaction is guaranteed; undamaged returns are accepted within 15 days for exchange, refund, or credit; institutional accounts are available. Free shipping on orders over $50.

READER'S DIGEST ASSOCIATION, INC.

PLEASANTVILLE, NY
10570–7000
800–310–6261
TDD: 800–735–4327

Information: internet website
Pay: interest-free installments
Sells: magazines, books, audiobooks, CD-ROMs, videos, music CDs
Store: mail order and online ordering only
Online: http://www.readersdigest.com

Reader's Digest is as American as apple pie. But if you think this company is old-fashioned and only fit for killing time at the dentist office, you haven't checked out the Reader's Digest website. What a fun place to visit! Here you'll get a taste of the various Reader's Digest book, magazine, music, video, and CD-ROM offerings. There's a large-print version of Reader's Digest, as well as RDs in Swedish, Czech, Portuguese (Brazil), Dutch, and other languages. You'll find the links here to the international RD websites, as well as information about how you can subscribe to the magazine, get the "All Products Catalog," or find out about other aspects of the company and what it offers.

This company is really strong on cooking, do-it-yourself, and health books. Regular sales, as well as a Great Buys page—at the time of this writing RD was offering gardening and do-it-yourself books for 20% off—are features of the website. But what really makes the site stupendous is all of the free stuff.

For example, click into How-To Library and you'll find 400 creative projects to make your life easier. The "Home Projects" button lets you search by category to find articles about everything from Asphalt Driveway Repair to Choosing Contractors. Click into "Backyard" to see articles such as How to Play Croquet and Creating Window Boxes. "In the Kitchen" offers advice on Low-Fat Ways to Thicken Stews and Making Herbed Ice Cubes, among other subjects. "Your Health" features short articles on topics from Caffeine and Your Health to Beauty and the Heat ("preventing makeup melt-down").

In another section of the website you can list the ingredients in your cupboards, and they'll suggest a recipe to fit what you have! You can also search for any of hundreds of RD recipes, or browse the tools, techniques, and tips of chefs and cooks. For the handyman or -woman, there's more great (free) stuff here. For example, "Ask the Family Handyman" has answers to just about any problem you have on any topic—in the form of short articles—which you can search for by category.

To find out more about this fascinating company and all of what they offer, check out the website. "Bookmark" this site when you do; you'll be visiting it often.

Special Factors: Online ordering available. Any item is returnable. Pay in interest-free installments.

REFERENCE BOOK CENTER, INC.

175 FIFTH AVE.
NEW YORK, NY 10010
212–677–2160
FAX: 212–533–0826

Catalog: $2
Pay: check and MO
Sells: new and used encyclopedias and reference books
Showroom: Monday to Friday 9–5

When it comes time to make that big investment for your youngsters—the family encyclopedia—here's the place to call first. The Reference Book Center is well known to schools and institutions, but few consumers know that this is a great source for current and used encyclopedias and other references at bargain prices. Here you'll be able to purchase new sets at less than normal retail—sometimes considerably less; the used sets are even better deals. The 20-page catalog also includes every other type of reference book: English and foreign language dictionaries; children's history, geography, and other reference books; atlases; Shakespeare collections; the Great Books; Indians; mythology; astronomy; and references on many more subjects. But the best bargains are the encyclopedias. The review catalog at the time of this writing offered a 20-volume 1997 encyclopedia for $750, while the identical set was being sold on a well-known internet bookstore for more than double that. If you're into rare or older references, be sure to see the last pages of the catalog for some interesting deals.

Special Factors: Call for details on return policies and shipping rates. No C.O.D. orders accepted. Wholesale rates to qualified buyers who purchase in quantity (inquire if interested).

THE SCHOLAR'S BOOKSHELF

110 MELRICH RD.
CRANBURY, NJ 08512
609–395–6933
FAX: 609–395–0755

Catalog: free
Pay: check, MO, MC, V
Sells: scholarly and university press books
Store: mail order only
E-mail: books@scholarsbookshelf.com
Online: http://www.scholarsbookshelf.com

University presses still produce highbrow texts for scholars, but many are of interest—and accessible—to nonprofessionals as well. These books sometimes suffer the same fate as their commercial counterparts—remaindering. The Scholar's Bookshelf, in business since 1974, turns publishing misfortune into intellectual excitement 18 times a year with a wide variety of university press and scholarly imprint remainders, and a selection of videos. The books are sold at an average of 30% below published prices, although savings can run up to 75%.

The general sale catalog is packed with concise descriptions of volumes on literature and drama, music, the Civil War and other military history, architecture and urban planning, archaeology, art history (ancient to modern), photography, world history and politics, psychology, philosophy, religion, Judaica, the sciences, and more. Past issues have included Jane's reference works on military ships and aircraft, Page Smith's eight-volume history of the United States, the Atlas of Medieval Europe, and other illuminated manuscripts (reproductions) and special editions. Throughout the year the Scholar's Bookshelf produces themed catalogs as well, including "Fine Arts Books," "Literature," "History," and "Military History."

Special Factors: Returns are accepted within 30 days for exchange, refund, or credit; minimum order is $10, $15 with credit cards.

STOREY COMMUNI-CATIONS, INC.

SCHOOLHOUSE RD.,
P.O. BOX 445
POWNAL, VT 05261
800–441–5700
FAX: 802–823–5449

Catalog: free
Pay: check, MO, MC, V, AE, Discover
Sells: Country Wisdom Bulletins and books
Store: mail order only
E-mail: storey@storey.com
Online: http://www.storey.com

Storey features "books for country living," guides to herbs, gardening, cooking, preserving, home brewing, raising animals, nature appreciation, homesteading, equestrian subjects, and related topics. Storey can help you learn all about hive management, composting, organic pest control in the garden, home brewing beer, raising your own flock of ducks, and outwitting squirrels. The 56-page catalog features the Country Wisdom Bulletins, a collection of over 110 manuals that include "all the how-to information you need to easily master dozens of country living skills in 30 minutes or less." The titles illustrate the possibilities of self-reliance: "Building a Solar-Heated Pit Greenhouse," "Drought Gardening," and "Creating a Wildflower Meadow" are examples. The Bulletins are a good buy even at $2.95 each (they're often sold for as little as $1.50), especially for the person who needs to know the basics but doesn't have to become an authority on the topic. And even if you're the consummate urbanite, you may find some of the Bulletins of interest, as well as other items—cookbooks, houseplant guides, and crafting manuals.

Canadian readers, please note: Only U.S. funds are accepted.

Special Factors: Satisfaction is guaranteed; returns are accepted within one year for exchange, refund, or credit.

STRAND BOOK STORE

828 BROADWAY
NEW YORK, NY
   10003–4805
212–473–1452
FAX: 212–473–2591

Catalog: free
Pay: check, MO, MC, V, AE, Discover
Sells: new, old, rare, and used books
Store: same address; Monday to Saturday
9:30–9:30, Sunday 11–9:30; also Strand Book
Annex, 95 Fulton St., New York, NY
(212–732–6070); Monday to Friday 8:30–8,
Saturday and Sunday 11–8
E-mail: strand@strandbooks.com

   ¡Si!

The Strand Book Store is the largest used bookstore in the world. Legendary in stature, the Strand boasts over 2.5 million volumes on eight miles of shelves. Founded in 1929, Strand publishes a number of catalogs of used, rare, and discounted reviewers' copies at 50% off list price. In addition, a huge selection of quality remainders is available.

Call, write, or fax for any of these free catalogs: the "Specials" catalog, published several times a year, lists thousands of works. This catalog includes books on art, architecture, philosophy, critique and commentary, biographies, literature, politics, food, drama, and other fields of interest. The "Review" catalog, available to institutional accounts, lists new releases at 50% off the publishers' prices. (Request this catalog on your institution's letterhead.) And, in the tradition of British used booksellers, Strand can supply books by the foot for decorators, TV studios, and hotels.

You have to visit the store to do justice to the Strand; if you do, don't miss the Rare Books Department, which has first, fine, and scarce editions, as well as signed and inscribed books.

Special Factors: Satisfaction is guaranteed; want lists are maintained; appraisals are available; libraries are bought; returns are accepted.

TARTAN BOOK SALES

500 ARCH ST., DEPT. 5N
WILLIAMSPORT, PA 17705
800–233–8467, EXT. 507
FAX: 800–999–6799

Catalog and Brochure: free
Pay: check, MO, MC, V
Sells: used books
Store: same address (Brodart Outlet Bookstore); Monday to Wednesday 11–5, Thursday and Friday 10–6, Saturday 10–4
Online: http://www.brodart.com

Tartan Book Sales, a direct-mail division of Brodart Co., sells recent hardcover titles, including best-selling authors, "Oprah's Picks," and other popular contemporary titles, at discounts of up to 75% on the published prices. All of Tartan's books have seen limited circulation in libraries across the country and are inspected prior to shipping.

Hardcover titles by such popular authors as John Grisham, Stephen King, Tom Clancy, Danielle Steel, Dick Francis, and Patricia Cornwell are listed in the current catalog, which also features biographies, books on business and finance, crime, sports and entertainment, health and self-help, politics, current affairs, mysteries, romance novels, books in large print, and much more. Tartan has been in business since 1960 and offers an excellent opportunity for readers to buy hardcover popular reading at paperback prices. As the company puts it, "Tartan books make good reading cents."

If you're purchasing for resale or for an institution, see the catalog for sales terms, and contact Tartan for pricing.

Special Factors: Quantity discounts are available; institutional and retail accounts are available.

U.S. GOV'T SUPERINTENDENT OF DOCUMENTS

U.S. GOVERNMENT PRINTING OFFICE
P.O. BOX 371954
PITTSBURGH, PA
15250–7954
202–512–1800
FAX: 202–512–2250

Catalog: free
Pay: check, MO, MC, V, Discover
Sells: federal government publications
Store: 24 U.S. government bookstores in AL, CA, CO, DC, FL, GA, IL, MA, MD, MI, MO, NY, OH, OR, PA, TX, WA, and WI (see catalog for locations)
E-mail: gpoaccess@gpo.gov
Online: http://www.access.gpo.gov/su_docs

Have you heard about the "IRS Audit Technique Guides"—originally written for IRS revenue agents—which outline the books and records you must maintain in your industry, and business practices you should follow to avoid a nasty audit? This is just one of the offerings in the current catalog from the U.S. Government Superintendent of Documents. The list of CD-ROMs, periodicals, pamphlets, and books available from the U.S. government is fascinating. The 28-page catalog offers everything from the "Americans With Disabilities Handbook" to the 420-page *Alternative Medicines: Expanding Medical Horizons.* There are handbooks about the history and natural beauty of about four dozen U. S. vacation destinations; books on business, health, education, family issues, history, government and public affairs, environment, science, and defense. This a great source for research materials (for example, the *Census Catalog and Guide),* government information (with an $8 annual subscription to *Consumer Product Safety Review* brings you the latest federal safety actions, studies, and standards involving consumer products), and more. None of the books or pamphlets are free, but many cost under $10 and are real treasure troves of useful information. (Quantity discounts of 25% on orders of 100 of the same title—with some exceptions—are available.) Subscriptions to consumer magazines published by the government can be ordered through the catalog, and there are calendars and a number of posters of American artists' work as well as space shots and maps. The catalog also lists the various website addresses where you can access free government information.

Special Factors: Quantity discounts are available; authorized returns due to government error are accepted within six months for exchange or credit; institutional accounts are available.

WOODWORKERS' DISCOUNT BOOKS

**735 SUNRISE CIRCLE
WOODLAND PARK, CO
  80863
800–378–4060
719–686–0756
FAX: 719–686–0757**

Catalog: free
Pay: check, MO, MC, V, AE
Sells: woodworking books, videos, and plans
Store: mail order only
E-mail: orders@discount-books.com
Online: http://www.discount-books.com

Why fool around with bookstores that only offer a few titles and charge high prices for woodworking books when you can choose from a huge selection and save money, too, with Woodworkers' Discount Books? The 64 well-annotated pages of this catalog list over 400 books, videos, and furniture plans. There are several pages devoted to furniture-making and cabinetry (including plans), joinery and veneering, carving and turning, woodworking machines and hand tools, miniatures and toys, box making, tool techniques, wood finishing, and more, including projects to test and develop your skills. The Fine Woodworking videos are available, as well as text classics such as Tolpin's *Measure Twice, Cut Once.* Check here for books and videos from Fine Homebuilding, including the series of practical single-topic manuals that cover everything from roofing to flooring.

The prices are discounted up to 20% (with deeper discounts on website-only specials), but the strength of this catalog is the selection—these books have been chosen by experts for serious woodworkers—and the excellent summaries of each title. Call or write for the catalog, or visit the website—the catalog is available online and for download.

Special Factors: Satisfaction is guaranteed; returns (except nondefective videos) are accepted in new condition within 30 days for exchange, refund, or credit; shipping is free on orders of three or more items within the 48 contiguous states.

RELATED PRODUCTS/COMPANIES

Art-related books and manuals • *Art Express, Cheap Joe's Art Stuff, A.I. Friedman, Jerry's Artarama, Daniel Smith, Utrecht*

Aviation manuals • Wag-Aero Group

Beekeeping books • Brushy Mountain Bee Farm

Bicycle repair manuals • Bike Nashbar

Boating books • Defender Industries, M & E Marine

Books on billiards, darts, pool, etc. • Mueller Sporting Goods

Books on knife use and collecting • The Cutlery Shoppe

Books on pets of all kinds • Daleco Master Breeder Products, Kennel Vet, KV Vet Supply, Pet Warehouse, That Fish Place/That Pet Place, UPCO, Drs. Foster & Smith, Valley Vet

Build-it-yourself machines and power tools handbooks • Poor Man's Catalog

Ceramics/pottery/sculpture books • Ceramic Supply of New York & New Jersey, Bailey Ceramic Supply, Axner Pottery Supply

Cleaning manuals • The Cleaning Center

Computer-related books • H & R Company

Cookbooks and cooking-related books • ChuckWagon Outfitters, The CMC Company, Gohn Bros., E.C. Kraus Home Wine & Beermaking Supplies, New England Cheesemaking Supply, Professional Cutlery Direct, Rafal Spice, Sultan's Delight, Mountain Ark

Field guides, survival and outdoor guides • Campmor, Mass. Army & Navy

Floral and bridal design, dried-flower and herb craft books • Caprilands Herb Farm, Billiann's, Floral Supply Syndicate

Gardening, herbs, and farming books • Butterbrooke Farm, Caprilands Herb Farm, Fedco Seeds, Johnny's Selected Seeds, Mellinger's, Turner Greenhouses

Graphic arts books/references • A.I. Friedman

Hatmaking books • Manny's Millinery

Health-related topical books • Essential Products, Mountain Ark, American Health Food

Hunting books • Deer Shack

Kites and kitesmithing books • BFK Sports

Large-print books and reading aids for the visually impaired • The New Vision Store, Independent Living Aids

Library marking tools • Hot Tools

Logging books, manuals on chain-saw use, etc. • Bailey's

Maternity-related topical books • Bosom Buddies

Military and political topical books • John W. Poling

Miscellaneous craft and hobby books • Circle Craft Supply, National Artcraft, Warner-Crivellaro Stained Glass Supplies, Glass Crafters, Micro-Mark, The Artist's Club

Music-related books • Elderly Instruments, Giardinelli Band Instrument Co., Mandolin Brothers, Metropolitan Music Co., Musician's Friend, Weinkrantz Musical Supply, West Manor

Photography references • B & H Photo-Video—Pro Audio, Porter's Camera Store, Solar Cine Products, Poor Man's Catalog

Preservation supplies for old-book collections • University Products

Resources for special-needs children • Special Clothes

Resources related to the size-acceptance movement • Amplestuff

Science and astronomy books • Orion Telescope Center, Scope City, The Astronomical Society of the Pacific

Seat-weaving, basketry, upholstery books • The Caning Shop, Frank's Cane and Rush Supply

Shop, construction, contractor manuals and books • Tool Crib of the North, Tools on Sale, Wholesale Tool Co., Poor Man's Catalog, Fidelity Products

Teaching aids for playing bridge • Baron Barclay Bridge Supplies

Textile arts—related books/manuals • Atlanta Thread & Supply, Dharma Trading, The Fiber Studio, Gohn Bros., Great Northern Weaving, Newark Dressmaker Supply, Sewing Machine Super Store, Sewin' in Vermont, Connecting Threads, Webs

Water sports—related books • The House, Overton's Sports Center, World Wide Aquatics

Woodworking, woodcraft reference texts • William Alden Company, Tool Crib of the North, Tools on Sale, Poor Man's Catalog

CAMERAS, PHOTOGRAPHIC EQUIPMENT/SERVICES, AND OPTICS

Cameras and darkroom equipment, photo supplies, film and film-processing services, optical instruments

In this section you'll find companies that sell cameras, bulbs, and film, lighting equipment, screens, film editors, splicers, batteries, projection tables, lenses, filters, adapters, cases, darkroom outfits and chemicals, and custom film processing and digital imaging services—at discounts averaging 40%. Even if you don't need custom work done, you can have your film processed, enlargements made, slides duplicated, and other services done by a discount mail-order lab for half the price often charged by a drugstore or retail outlet.

Take care of your pictures: Keep them out of "magnetic" photo albums, which are made with polyvinyl-film that gives off vinyl chloride gas, and cardboard pages that exude peroxide vapors. Both can cause deterioration of slides and prints. (Photographs should be kept in temperate, relatively dry areas, out of light as much as possible.) To preserve your pictures, use archival-quality materials—acid-free albums and storage boxes, Mylar sheet protectors, "safe" slide sheets, etc. These and other conservation materials are available from University Products (see listing in the "Office, Business, Professional" chapter).

THE GRAY MARKET AND OTHER CONCERNS

Some years ago, the camera and electronics industries were plagued with problems caused by the gray market—a market that legally circumvents authorized channels of distribution to sell goods at prices lower than those intended by the manufacturer (the trademark owner); these gray-market goods were originally produced to be sold in other countries. Gray-market goods are usually less expensive than their "authorized" counterparts, and although they may be just as good, they may be produced under different quality-control standards, contain ingredients not approved for use in the United States, or have a warranty that is not honored in the United States.

Gray-marketers who sell goods not intended for the U.S. market are not knowingly listed in this edition of BWBM. But because companies can change selling policies, if you want to be sure a firm is an authorized distributor of a product, call the manufacturer. Ask the mail-order company whether the warranty is honored by the service centers of the U.S. manufacturer, and make your purchase by credit card, which gives you certain protections under the Fair Credit Billing Act.

Gray-market activity has abated, but another form has become prevalent—"diversions" of goods from the authorized path, often by a wholesaler or mass merchant. In this case, the product was intended for the domestic market, but not for the store in which it's sold. Often, the consumer benefits, as when major department stores buy enormous inventory (to get the lowest possible price) and resell the surplus "out the back door" to other stores and discounters. If it's a product that should be used at the direction of a professional, the manufacturer may assume no liability for poor performance unless the product is sold by an authorized dealer. This may not matter much when the product is shampoo, but it does if it's an enlarger or a microscope.

Before you buy, whether it's from a local store or mail-order firm, you might want to heed the advice of the owner of a buying service, who knows all the "tricks" used by the vendors. He urges you to take the time to contact the manufacturer about the model you've chosen (most manufacturers have toll-free numbers or websites) and find out what the manufacturer includes with the camera—case, lens, cap, strap, manual, coupons, etc. He suggests that, when you're examining the camera, you check the markings on the lenses to make sure the original hasn't been swapped for a lesser model. As he puts it, "You have to do the legwork or you won't get the best deal, and you can be ripped off. The bad businesses shouldn't be there, but they are."

For video cameras, videotape, VCRs, and other video-related goods, see the "Music, Audio, and Video" chapter.

FIND IT FAST

BINOCULARS, TELESCOPES, MICROSCOPES • Ewald-Clark, Mardiron, Orion, Scope City
CAMERAS AND PHOTOGRAPHY/DARKROOM EQUIPMENT • B & H, Ewald-Clark, Mystic, Porter's, Solar Cine
DIGITAL IMAGING EQUIPMENT • B & H, Porter's
FILM AND SLIDE PROCESSING • ABC Photo, Ewald-Clark, Mystic, Owl Photo, Solar Cine

---

ABC PHOTO & IMAGING SERVICES, INC.

9016 PRINCE WILLIAM ST.,
   DEPT. WBMC
MANASSAS, VA 22110
703–369–1906
FAX: 703–631–8064

Catalog: $3, refundable
Pay: check, MO, MC, V, AE
Sells: film processing
Store: same address; Monday to Friday 9–6, Saturday 8–2

 ¡Si!

ABC Photo & Imaging, whose parent firm has been in business since 1945, is a full-service professional and commercial mail-order lab that offers film and slide processing, negative duplication and slide copying, prints, photographic packages (portraits and weddings), high-tech retouching, and scanning—all at competitive prices. Understand that the kinds of services they offer don't come cheap—but ABC offers them at prices that beat what you'd pay at many metro-area photo labs, and if you buy in larger quantities, the savings grow. Formerly known as Skyline Color Lab, ABC has a 28-page catalog that lists the available services and prices, includes directions for cropping, and features a helpful glossary of terms such as "internegative," "dodging," and "push/pull processing." ABC will process your color or black-and-white film (roll or sheet), produce contact sheets, make prints and enlargements (from 3½" by 5" to 48" by 144"), and create murals and photographic displays (from 40" square to 48" by 96"; larger sizes are available on a custom basis). Custom services are offered, including "push" processing to compensate for underexposed film, glass mounts for slides, slide remounting, duplicate negatives and negatives made from slides or transparencies (internegatives), a choice of finishes for enlargements (canvas, pebble, matte, or luster), dry mounting of prints (on art board, foam core, or "gator" foam), mounting on canvas panels or canvas stretchers, printing for backlit display, and "beautifying" digital services for such things as removing acne from skin and braces from teeth. ABC has also put together a "relative's special" perfect for sending to friends and family—as well as wedding album packages. Complete details of the firm's sales policy and guarantees are given in the catalog.

Special Factors: Liability for damaged or lost film is limited to replacement with unexposed film; minimum order is $25; C.O.D. orders are accepted (for delivery within the continental United States); rush services are available.

B & H PHOTO-VIDEO– PRO AUDIO

420 NINTH AVE.
NEW YORK, NY 10001
800–947–9950
212–444–6600
FAX: 800–947–7008
FAX: 212–239–7770

Catalog: free
Pay: check, MO, MC, V, AE, Discover
Sells: equipment and supplies for photography and imaging, video and pro-audio
Store: same address; Monday and Tuesday 9–6, Wednesday and Thursday 9–7, Friday 9–1, Sunday 10–4:45, closed Saturday
Online: http://www.bhphotovideo.com

 ¡Si!

B & H has been serving New York City photographers for over two decades with the latest in professional equipment, accessories, and supplies, all at discount prices. Over the years, the company has expanded its product line and now carries a range of pro-audio, video, and digital imaging (computer) components. The inventory is extensive—80,000 products and counting, with over 100 manufacturers represented in the video department alone. To see what's currently available, you can send for the monthly "flyer," a 104-page catalog sampling all the departments, or see the regular multipage ads in *Popular Photography* and other industry magazines. B & H also plans to publish *The Professional Photo Source-Book,* to complement the edition for the video pro that's now in its second edition. And you can find a wealth of information on the B & H website, including one of the best collections of photography-related links around. In New York, stop by their newly designed 35,000-square-foot store with every major piece of equipment on display.

Special Factors: Satisfaction is guaranteed; authorized returns are accepted for exchange, refund, or credit (see catalog or website for stipulations); C.O.D. orders are accepted.

EWALD-CLARK

17 W. CHURCH AVE.
ROANOKE, VA 24011
540–342–1829
FAX: 540–345–9943

Information: price quote only
Pay: MO, MC, V, AE, Discover
Sells: cameras, darkroom equipment, optics, services, and repairs
Store: same address; Monday to Friday 8:30–5:30; also Bedford, Blacksburg, and Salem, VA

Ewald-Clark is a full-service photography center that's been in business since 1949, but it doesn't publish a catalog—call or write for a price quote on specific models. In addition to cameras (including digital models), lenses, camera accessories, darkroom equipment, and finishing services, Ewald-Clark sells binoculars, all at discounts of 20% to 40%, or an average of 30% off list prices.

Among the available brands are Amphoto, Beseler, Bogen, Bronica, Canon, Fuji, Gitzo, Gossen, Gralab, Ilford, Kodak, Logan, LowePro, Mamiya, Minolta, Nikon, Novatron, Olympus, Pelican, Pentax, Polaroid, Quantum, Ricoh, Samyang, Tamrac, Tamron, Tiffen, Varta, and Vivitar. You can also inquire for rates and specifications on custom photofinishing services.

Please note: Shipments to non-U.S. destinations are subject to hazardous materials regulations.

Special Factors: Price quote by phone or letter with SASE.

MARDIRON OPTICS

THE BINOCULAR PLACE
4 SPARTAN CIRCLE, DEPT.
WBMC
STONEHAM, MA
02180–3230
781–938–8339

Manufacturer's Catalogs, Brochures, and Price List: $1, refundable with first order
Pay: check or MO
Sells: binoculars, telescopes, microscopes, etc.
Store: mail order only

Mardiron, in business since 1983, sells binoculars, spotting scopes, astronomical telescopes, microscopes, riflescopes, theater glasses, range finders, global positioning sensors, and chess and casino game computers—at savings of up to 45% on list prices. Mardiron features goods from Nikon, Leica, Kowa, Minolta, Bausch & Lomb, Canon, Pentax, Parks, Fujinon, Swift, Copitar, Zeiss, Swarovski, Bushnell, Selsi, Tasco, Jason, Simmons, Doctor Optics, Aus Jena, Leupold, Burris, Redfield, and the Steiner military, hunting, and fully integrated compass binoculars, developed especially for eyeglass wearers. There are also chess and casino game computers, teaching blackjack, bridge, backgammon, and craps, by Kasparov, Olympiad, Virtuoso, Mephisto, Milano Pro, Exclusive V1, and others. Write down any item or brand of interest to you, and send $1 to Mardiron; they'll mail you full-color catalogs, brochures, and price lists. (Your dollar is deducted from your first order.)

Special Factors: Price quote by phone; no charge for shipping within the contiguous U.S.

MYSTIC COLOR LAB

MASON'S ISLAND RD.
P.O. BOX 144
MYSTIC, CT 06355–9987
800–367–6061
860–536–4291
FAX: 860–536–6418

Catalog and Mailers: free
Pay: check, MO, MC, V, AE, Discover
Sells: film-processing and enlargement services
Store: same address; Monday to Friday 9:30–5:30
Online: http://www.mysticcolorlab.com

Mail-order film labs abound, but Mystic is one that's gotten good marks in quality comparisons with other labs. Mystic has been in business since 1969 and offers free shipping in postpaid mailers with no handling charges. Mystic Color Lab's prices on processing film, for one set of standard-size prints, are up to 30% below those of other mail-order labs—and considerably less than the one-hour minilabs. But the firm does its best to come close to the minilab turnaround time, by pledging to get your processed film and prints in the mail to you within 24 hours of receipt.

Mystic develops 110, 35mm color print, and slide film, along with one-time-use cameras. The firm makes enlargements (up to 20" by 30" posters) and offers their own film at great prices—a three-pack of 24-exposure, 200 ASA film is only $8.95 at this writing. If you're looking for great ways to enjoy your photos, Mystic offers a variety of options, from photo mugs and mousepads to photo greeting cards and calendars. Cameras and albums are also available. A new service: Mystic can save your pictures on disk or e-mail them to you. Call for the latest catalog and film mailers, or order through the website.

Special Factors: Free shipping.

ORION TELESCOPE CENTER

P.O. BOX 1815, DEPT. WBM

SANTA CRUZ, CA

95061–1815

408–763–7000

FAX: 408–763–7017

Catalog: free, $5 outside U.S. and Canada
Pay: check, MO, MC, V, Discover
Sells: telescopes, binoculars, and accessories
Store: 89 Hangar Way, Watsonville, CA; also Cupertino and San Francisco, CA
E-mail: sales@oriontel.com
Online: http://www.oriontel.com

If you're into stargazing, bird-watching, nature study, sightseeing, or spectator sports, Orion is your source. In business since 1975, Orion is the largest direct-to-consumer dealer of outdoor optics in North America, offering a comprehensive selection of top-quality astronomical telescopes, binoculars, spotting scopes, and related accessories at discount prices. The 100-page color catalog shows a wide variety of popular brands, including Bausch & Lomb, Bushnell, Canon, Celestron, Fujinon, Leica, Nikon, Orion, Pentax, Swarovski, Swift, TeleVue, and Zeiss. In addition to optical goods, Orion carries star atlases, observing guides, astronomy software, tee shirts, books and software, telescope-making parts and books, and gift items. They also have an extensive website, featuring a full online catalog of more than 1,000 products as well as a monthly sky-events calendar and information on how to choose a telescope or binoculars.

Special Factors: Satisfaction is guaranteed; price quote by phone or letter for institutional orders.

OWL PHOTO CORP.

701 E. MAIN ST.
WEATHERFORD, OK 73096
580–722–3353
FAX: 580–722–5804

Mailers: free
Pay: check, MO, MC, V
Sells: film processing and reprinting services
Store: same address; Monday to Friday 7:30–5, Saturday 9–1

Owl Photo has been in business since 1934 and offers reasonably priced film processing services by mail, and will send you self-mailers on request. Owl will develop your color and black-and-white film at prices that are competitive with discount drugstore processing, and you can also order reprints and fresh film—a price list comes with the mailer. Owl processes 110, 135, and advantage (APS) film; reprint sizes run up to 11" by 14". Owl uses Kodak paper and chemicals, and guarantees your satisfaction or your processing costs and postage will be refunded.

Special Factors: Satisfaction is guaranteed; returns are accepted for refund or credit.

PORTER'S CAMERA STORE, INC.

P.O. BOX 628
CEDAR FALLS, IA 50613
800–553–2001
319–268–0104
FAX: 319–277–5254

Catalog: free (see text)
Pay: check, MO, MC, V, Discover
Sells: photographic, darkroom, video, and digital imaging equipment and supplies
Store: 323 Viking Rd., Cedar Falls, IA; Monday to Saturday 9:30–5:30
Online: http://www.porters.com

Porter's has been selling photographic and darkroom equipment since 1914 and publishes a 128-page tabloid catalog packed with an enormous range of photographic products, at prices up to 67% below list. Both amateurs and professionals will appreciate the buys on 35mm cameras, lenses, filters, film, batteries, bags and cases, darkroom equipment and supplies, as well as video accessories and digital cameras. Porter's is famous for its wide selection of hard-to-find items. Popular brands from all the leading manufacturers are represented here, but if you're not sure what's what, Porter's has a staff person to answer all of your questions about equipment. If you're in Cedar Falls, drop by the warehouse outlet store where you'll find everything tagged at catalog prices—a welcome departure from the two-tier policies prevailing at most discount stores.

Canadian readers, please note: The catalog costs $3 in Canadian funds, but orders must be paid in U.S. funds. The catalog describes purchasing procedures and includes a shipping rate chart.

Please note: The catalog costs $10 in U.S. funds if sent to an address without a U.S. or Canadian postal code.

Special Factors: Price quote by phone or fax; authorized returns are accepted; institutional accounts are available; orders are shipped worldwide, subject to a $100 minimum order.

SCOPE CITY, INC.

730 EASY ST.
SIMI VALLEY, CA 93065
805–522–6646
FAX: 805–582–0292

Price List: free
Pay: check, MO, MC, V, Discover
Sells: telescopes, binoculars, microscopes, and other optics
Store: same address; Monday to Friday 9–6, Saturday 10–6; also Costa Mesa, San Diego, and Sherman Oaks, CA; Monday to Friday 10–7

Scope City has been selling telescopes, binoculars, spotting scopes, and other optics since 1977. Telescopes and accessories by Bushnell, Celestron, Edmund Scientific, Meade, Parks, Questar, and TeleVue are available, as well as field and specialty binoculars and scopes by Bausch & Lomb, Dr. Optics, Fujinon, JMI, Kowa, Leica, Minolta, Parks, Steiner, Swarovski, Swift, Zeiss, and other manufacturers. Scope City also offers lenses, eyepieces, adapters, mirrors, star charts, manuals, and other reference tools, and telescope-building components. Most of the prices are discounted, and savings of up to 45% are possible on selected items. If you know the model you want, you can call for a price quote, or request the free price list.

Special Factors: Satisfaction is guaranteed; returns are accepted within 15 days for exchange, refund, or credit; minimum order is $25.

SOLAR CINE PRODUCTS, INC.

**4247 SOUTH KEDZIE AVE.
CHICAGO, IL 60632
800–621–8796
773–254–8310
FAX: 773–254–4124**

Catalog: free
Pay: check, MO, MC, V, AE, DC, Discover
Sells: photo equipment, supplies, and services
Store: same address, Monday to Friday 8:30–5, Saturday 9–1

 ¡Sí!

Solar Cine's 24-page catalog gives a sample of the thousands of items carried by the company—a full range of photographic equipment and accessories from a large number of manufacturers. Solar Cine has been supplying professionals and serious amateurs since 1937, and stocks a full range of still and movie equipment, including videotapes and video batteries. Range Finder cameras, lenses, studio lights, light meters, tripods, and darkroom materials are available from Canon, Kalt/Brandess, Kodak, Pentax, Polaroid, and Vivitar, among others. Scores of books on photography for beginners and professionals are available, as well as electronics and processing services (movies, slides, reprints, and prints). The services are described in the catalog; for more information on cameras and equipment, call or write for a price quote.

Special Factors: Returns (except defective goods) are subject to a restocking fee.

RELATED PRODUCTS/COMPANIES

Archival-quality storage materials for photographs, slides, film, negatives, microfiche, etc. • University Products
Binoculars and marine optics • Defender Industries, West Marine, Hidalgo, Freeport Marine, Damark
Cameras • J & R Music World, Bennett Brothers, Damark
Film • Beach Sales
Handbooks on building your own cameras and photographic equipment • Poor Man's Catalog
Hunting optics and binoculars • The Sportsman's Guide, Wiley Outdoor Sports
Lightboxes • A. I. Friedman
Microscopes • American Science & Surplus
Photo storage sheets and albums • 20th Century Plastics
Surplus optics • H & R Company, Ruvel & Co.
Telescopes • Astronomical Society of the Pacific, Damark
Underwater cameras • Berry Scuba, Central Skindivers

CLOTHING, HATS, FURS, AND ACCESSORIES

Underwear, clothing for all occasions,

and outerwear for women, men,

and children

The firms listed here sell a wide range of clothing for men, women, and children—Amish clothing from Indiana, lingerie from New York City's Lower East Side, Italian silk ties over the internet, custom-made deerskin coats and jackets, and much more—at good savings.

If you're looking for children's clothing, clothes and accessories for nursing mothers, or footwear, you'll find some here. But companies that specialize in these items are grouped together in the two subchapters that follow—"Children and Mothers," page 109, and "Shoes and Boots," page 117. If you're looking for uniforms (e.g., chef's whites, hospital scrubs, janitorial jumpsuits) or everyday clothing such as tee shirts and caps on which to silk-screen or embroider your company slogan, see the "Professional Uniforms and Promotional Products" section of the "Office, Business, Professional" chapter. As always, check out this section's "Related Products/Companies" listings to find many more firms that sell clothing of all kinds.

Finding discount sources for bridal attire isn't easy (see Discount Bridal Service in this chapter), and anyone facing the challenge of planning a wedding today will find *Bridal Bargains: Secrets to Throwing a Fantastic Wedding on a Realistic Budget* an absolute necessity. Written by the intrepid Alan and Denise Fields, the book describes the mechanics of the entire industry and gives the best strategies for everything from booking the site, buying the dress, and ordering food and flowers to hiring the photographer and covering all of the details—without getting burned. The Fields are so confident you'll benefit from their research that they offer a complete refund on the cost of the book if it doesn't save you at least $500 on your wedding expenses. Check out the "Related Products/Companies" section for firms in other chapters that sell bridal supplies, from unadorned headpieces and hats with all the jewels, trim, and satin flowers to decorate them, to sequined wristlets and fans.

Ladies: Do you go through pounds of hosiery each month? No problem. There are sources in this chapter where you can actually buy pantyhose by the pound! And there's no need to spend a fortune on career clothing, either. You'll find companies here from which you can buy business suits, blouses, and coordinated skirts and blazers at prices that allow you to get yourself a week's worth of clothing for the cost of a single item at a local ladies' boutique.

But don't think everything in this chapter is practical. You can dress up your look with inexpensive hats (decorate them yourself or buy a whole collection of them) or a famous designer scarf for less.

There are great deals for men, too, from all-cotton business-attire shirts to casual and sports clothing at amazing discounts.

Please note: If you're a tee shirt fanatic, you're in luck. Many of the companies in this book sell tee shirts imprinted with their logo or a theme. For instance, if you're crazy about cats, look in the "Animal and Pet Supplies" chapter for companies that carry feline-themed gift and novelty items. If you have a soccer or golf fanatic in your house, try the companies in "Sports, Fitness, and Recreation" that sell soccer or golf gear. It would not be space-efficient, in the "Related Products/Companies" section at the end of this chapter, to list all of the firms that sell tee shirts.

FIND IT FAST

BRIDAL ATTIRE • Discount Bridal Service, Manny's Millinery
DANCEWEAR • Dance Distributors
HATS • Manny's Millinery, Paula's Hatbox
MEN'S BUSINESS ATTIRE • America's Shirt and Tie, DesignerOutlet, Huntington, Quinn's Shirt Shop, Ultimate Outlet
MEN'S CASUAL CLOTHING • Bridgewater, Cahall's, DesignerOutlet, Gohn Bros., Mass. Army & Navy, Sportswear Clearinghouse, Ultimate Outlet, WearGuard
MEN'S UNDERWEAR • Chock, Gohn Bros., Huntington, Ultimate Outlet, WearGuard
SHEEPSKIN, DEERSKIN, AND FUR • Arctic Sheepskin, Deerskin Place

SLEEPWEAR, MEN'S AND WOMEN'S • Chock, Gohn Bros., Huntington, Lady Grace

SOCKS AND HOSIERY, MEN'S AND WOMEN'S • Asiatic Hosiery, Chock, Gohn Bros., Huntington, Landmark, No Nonsense Direct, One Hanes Place

WARM- AND FOUL-WEATHER GEAR • Arctic Sheepskin, Cahall's, Deerskin Place, DesignerOutlet, Gohn Bros., Mass. Army & Navy, Ultimate Outlet, WearGuard

WOMEN'S CLOTHING • Bridgewater, Chadwick's of Boston, DesignerOutlet, One Hanes Place, Ultimate Outlet, Willow Ridge/Bedford Fair

WOMEN'S LINGERIE • Chock, Lady Grace, Landmark, One Hanes Place, The Smart Saver, Ultimate Outlet

WOMEN'S SWIMWEAR • Lady Grace, Ultimate Outlet

WORK CLOTHING • Cahall's, Gohn Bros., WearGuard

AMERICA'S SHIRT AND TIE

546 S. MERIDIEN ST.,
   STE. 205
INDIANAPOLIS, IN 46225
800–259–7283
317–321–9999
FAX: 317–639–2029

Information: internet website, no catalog
Pay: check, MO, MC, V
Sells: shirts and ties
Store: online only
E-mail: carl@indy.net
Online: http://www.cottonshirt.com/new/

America's Shirt and Tie is a remarkable company. Carl Levinson, president, began his internet-only store after the longtime family clothier business closed. He started America's Shirt and Tie in 1994 with the idea of creating a company that would sell extremely high-quality shirts and ties for men at the lowest possible prices. Without advertising, print catalogs, and a huge staff, he's been able to do it successfully. In fact, this company has been written up in the *Wall Street Journal* and gets regular television and internet reviews for its excellent selection, fantastic prices, and ethical business practices.

Here you'll save 40% to 50% on shirts made in the U.S., and ties made in Italy. The website is informative and direct. Drop-down charts help you make selections as to size, collar style, brand, cuff style, fit, etc., after which you push a search button and a page of virtual fabric swatches comes up representing shirts available within your choices, at varying prices. (Size choices are vast—great for guys who have a hard time finding the right combination of sizes to fit their measurements—and include big/tall sizes; collar, fit, and cuff styles are pictured and explained; fabric types are described; brands are named and described.) You simply write down your selections and then order online.

Because all orders are processed electronically in four to five minutes—you're providing name, address, credit card information, etc., instead of an employee taking down this information—America's Shirt and Tie can keep their costs very low. They have over 25,000 shirts in stock, starting as low as $17.50 on the current site for white and solid-colored broadcloth and Oxford cloth shirts. The tie section will dazzle you with its low prices and nice selections as well. If you order in units of 12 or more (you can mix and match to reach this number) the prices go down even further. (Corporate and office/group buyers: Call 317–321–9999 for details on quantity discounts and incentive programs.)

Incidentally, if you love what you see here, you might want to check out the brother company (http://www.hugestore.com), which has an expanded inventory that includes tee shirts, boxers, golf shirts, suits, sport coats, casual and dress pants—as well as shirts and ties. The brand selection is wider, and some but not all of the inventory is deeply discounted.

Special Factors: 100% satisfaction guaranteed ("We love our customers 100%"); all items returned for any reason will be refunded.

ARCTIC SHEEPSKIN OUTLET

I–94 & CO. RD. T, BOX WB
HAMMOND, WI 54015
800–428–9276
715–796–2292
FAX: 715–796–2295

Brochure: $2, refundable
Pay: check, MO, MC, V, Discover
Sells: sheepskin clothing and accessories
Store: 30 miles east of St. Paul on I–94 at the Hammond exit; also 3015 E. Hamilton Ave., Eau Claire, WI; Monday to Thursday 8–8, Friday 8–5, Saturday 9–5

Arctic Sheepskin Outlet was founded in 1980 by the energetic Joseph Bacon, whose family has been sheep-raising since 1973. What began as personal gifts to friends and relatives grew into a full-scale outlet for sheepskin items from other tanneries. His Arctic Sheepskin Outlet features slippers, mittens, hats, car seat covers, rugs, bicycle seats, and more. Savings vary from item to item; rubber-soled sheepskin moccasins sell here for $44.95, about $5 less than elsewhere, and the car seat covers are buys at $39 (two for $75), as are mittens for $16.95. Deep-pile sheepskin rugs are $59.95—about a third less than the going rate. There are also hats with earflaps, sheepskin headbands, steering wheel covers, and seat belt strap covers (a welcome item for any woman who's had to endure a long drive with those designed-for-males over-the-shoulder belts). All purchases are covered by Arctic's "money-back guarantee," and you can call for the current specials.

Special Factors: Satisfaction is guaranteed; returns are accepted for exchange, refund, or credit; minimum order is $10.

ASIATIC HOSIERY CO.

P.O. BOX 31
LITTLE FALLS, NJ
  07424–0031
973–872–2111
FAX: 973–872–2114

Catalog: $2, ($4 outside U.S.), refundable
Pay: check, MO, MC, AE, DC, Discover
Sells: hosiery for men, women, and children
Store: mail order only
E-mail: sock1@ix.netcom.com
Online: http://pw2.netcom.com/~sock1/asi-atic.html

If you're willing to buy a dozen of the same color, size, and style of hosiery, Asiatic Hosiery will reward you with amazing savings on a full selection of socks, pantyhose, and other legwear for the whole family.

The prices range from women's sheer knee-highs at $4 per dozen ($6, queen), to pantyhose from under 84 cents a pair to $1.67 for a sheer support style in 9 colors and sizes up to queen. A gross of nylon "shoe try-ons," which can be used as footlets, cost just $7. In addition, Asiatic Hosiery sells opaque tights, knee-high and over-the-knee socks, anklets, slouch socks, and athletic socks for both women and girls, and dress and athletic socks for men and boys.

The eight-page catalog from Asiatic has no pictures or color charts, so you have to correlate the descriptions to products you're familiar with. The company has its own brand name, so if you're unsure about comparable sizing, see the descriptions under each product, which give height and weight guidelines, or call the toll-free number for assistance. Some color selections will include "assortments," which will be the company's choice. You're really buying at wholesale here, so place a small order to begin with to make sure you'll be happy.

Special Factors: Minimum order is one dozen of a style or color.

BRIDGEWATER

BOX 1600
BROCKTON, MA
  02403–1600
800–525–4420
508–583–7200
FAX: 800–448–5767
TDD: 800–978–8798

Catalog: free
Pay: check, MO, MC, V, AE, Discover
Sells: women's, men's, and children's clothing and accessories
Store: mail order only

Bridgewater is a catalog from Chadwick's of Boston (also listed in this chapter). It's "a classic collection for the entire family" and differs from the regular Chadwick's catalog in that it offers fashions for men and children in addition to its women's apparel line. Bridgewater has good choices in women's attire for the office and professional settings—linen blazers, unadorned white cotton shirts, linen skirts in two lengths, a silk jacket dress, and other wardrobe basics. The men's section opens with a linen/cotton blend blazer ($49) and includes sports shirts, all-season gabardine trousers ($25), and a great selection of polo shirts, twill pants, and other pieces that are well suited to after-work and weekend activities. Bridgewater's children's clothing in the current catalog includes 100% cotton twill pants and shorts for boys, 100% cotton pastel-patterned knit dresses, tee shirts/bike shorts outfits for girls, and solid-colored cotton overalls. The overall pricing, as with the parent company, is good, although the best deals here are in the adults', not the children's, clothing.

Special Factors: Satisfaction is guaranteed; returns are accepted for exchange, refund, or credit.

CAHALL'S WORK WEAR

P.O. BOX 450-WM
MOUNT ORAB, OH 45154
937–444–2094
FAX: 937–444–6813

Brochure: free
Pay: check, MO, MC, V, AE, Discover
Sells: work clothing and footwear
Store: Cahall's Work Wear Store; 112 S. High St., Mount Orab, OH; Monday to Saturday 9–6

The Cahall family opened its department store in 1946 and took the leap into mail order nearly 30 years later with heavy-duty apparel and footwear. I love the 4-page brochure, which has an old-timey feeling with pictures and descriptions of no-nonsense work items. Cahall's can supply your favorites—jeans, shirts, jackets, two-piece rainsuits, union suits, hats, lined snap-on hoods, overalls, and more—at savings of up to 30% on suggested list or retail prices. Popular lines from Carhartt, Hanes, Key, Levi's, and other well-known manufacturers are available. Cahall's also offers an excellent selection of work shoes and boots for men and women from Carolina, Danner, LaCrosse, Wolverine, and other names, in hard-to-find sizes. Hush Puppies and Rocky Boot sport boots are also stocked, as well as heavy-duty socks, work gloves, bandannas, tee shirts, and even nail aprons. If you don't find what you're looking for in the brochure, call them and Cahall's may stock it or be able to get it.

Special Factors: Satisfaction is guaranteed; returns are accepted for exchange, refund, or credit.

CHADWICK'S OF BOSTON, LTD.

BOX 1600
BROCKTON, MA
  02403–1600
800–525–4420
FAX: 800–448–5767
TDD: 800–978–8798

Catalog: free
Pay: check, MO, MC, V, Discover, JCB
Sells: women's clothing and accessories
Store: mail order only

Chadwick's publishes "The Original Off-Price Fashion Catalog," full of pretty, professional outfits for office, great dresses for evenings and special occasions, weekend and casual separates, and shoes and accessories. Chadwick's has been in business since 1983 and features labels such as Ellen Ashley, Averroe, Harvé Bernard, Pierre Cardin, Herman Geist, J.G. Hook, Carol Horn, Mootsies Tootsies, Giorgio Sant' Angelo, and Savannah. The styles run from basic casual to career, the sizing from 2P to 26W (although not in every item). The catalog descriptions include care information, and skirt length and pant inseams. Pricing is terrific—many office-worthy dresses are priced at under $50, and just about every edition of the catalog features a seasonable blazer or jacket in a great choice of colors, at a special price—$39 for linen, merino for $49, cashmere blend for $79—with blouses or sweaters to match. And the catalogs often offer no-strings deferred billing, which can give your budget another assist.

Special Factors: Satisfaction is guaranteed; returns are accepted for exchange or refund.

CHOCK CATALOG CORP.

74 ORCHARD ST., DEPT. WBMC
NEW YORK, NY
10002–4594
212–473–1929
FAX: 212–473–6273

Catalog: $2, $5 outside U.S.
Pay: check, MO, MC, V, Discover, JCB
Sells: hosiery, underwear, sleepwear, and infants' layettes
Store: same address; Sunday to Thursday 9:30–5:30, Friday 9–1
E-mail: chock1@juno.com
Online: http://www.chockcatalog.com

 ¡Si!

Chock, known to generations of New Yorkers as Louis Chock, is a family operation that's been selling unmentionables since 1921. Chock's 66-page catalog is packed with good values on name-brand underthings for men, women, children, and infants. The women's department features underpants by Hanes Her Way, Jockey for Her, Lollipop, and Vanity Fair; hosiery by Berkshire, Hanes, Mayer, and PrimaSport; and well-priced smocks, aprons, slips, pajamas, and nightgowns. (For those with special needs, there are two pages of nightgowns and slips that snap up the back.) Men are offered underwear by BVD, Chock's private label, Duofold, Hanes, Jockey, Calvin Klein, Manshape, and Munsingwear; socks by Burlington, Chock's own line, Doré Doré, Thorlo, and Wigwam; and pajamas and robes from Knothe, Munsingwear, and Oscar de la Renta. Men's sizes run up to XXXL (58 to 60).

Chock's has a good choice of basics for babies and children, running from cloth diapers and complete layettes by Carters and Gerber, creepers and sleepers, underwear and sleepwear for boys and girls by Carters and Hanes, socks by Buster Brown and Tic-Tac-Toe, to toys by Montgomery Schoolhouse, bathing accessories, sheets, blankets, and more.

Chock's catalogs usually offer well-priced accessories that make great gifts—typically gloves and Totes umbrellas. How wonderful to find a choice of Caswell-Massey soaps and creams, at nifty discounts of about 25%!

Special Factors: Satisfaction is guaranteed; unopened returns with manufacturer's packaging intact are accepted within 30 days.

DANCE DISTRIBUTORS

P.O. BOX 11440, DEPT. WBMC
HARRISBURG, PA 17108
800–333–2623
FAX: 717–234–1465

Catalog: free
Pay: check, MO, MC, V, AE, Discover
Sells: dancewear and accessories
Store: mail order only
E-mail: dancedstr@aol.com

Both aspiring amateurs and professional dancers can trim at least 25% or more from the cost of their next pair of pointe shoes, leotards, or tights by buying from Dance Distributors. The 32-page catalog lists shoes for ballet, pointe, jazz, tap, modern, and folk dance. Dance Distributors also offer a complete line of bodywear for women, men, and children, including leotards, dance skirts, tights, trunks, and warm-ups. The manufacturers include Baryshnikov, Bloch, Body Wrappers, Capezio, Chacott, Freed, Grishko, Harmonie, Mirella, Prima Soft, Sade, and Sansha. Dance Distributors also sell their own line of leotards, tights, and legwarmers. Prices are generally 25% to 30% below list, but sale offerings can double the discounts. Special orders are accepted on items not listed in the catalog. The catalog has helpful size conversion charts for street shoes to dance styles, and for Continental sizing to inches.

Special Factors: Satisfaction is guaranteed; price quote by phone or letter; returns (except special orders) are accepted within 30 days for exchange, refund, or credit.

THE DEERSKIN PLACE

283 AKRON RD.
EPHRATA, PA 17522
717–733–7624

Catalog: $1, refundable (see text)
Pay: check, MO, MC, V
Sells: deerskin clothing and accessories
Store: same address; Monday to Saturday 9–9, Sunday (December to January) 12–5

The Deerskin Place, in business since 1969, features clothing and accessories made of deerskin, cowhide, and sheepskin, at prices up to 50% less than those charged elsewhere for comparable goods. Among the offerings are fingertip-length shearling jackets for about $400, fringed buckskin-suede jackets for under $200, bomber jackets under $150, motorcycle jackets at $99, and sporty deerskin handbags for about $70. The Deerskin Place offers moccasins and casual shoes, knee-high suede boots, and crepe-soled slip-ons for men and women (from $17), deerskin wallets, clutches, coin purses, and keycases (from about $6), mittens and gloves for the whole family, beaded belts (under $6), and many other accessories.

Special Factors: Satisfaction is guaranteed; inquire before ordering if unsure of color, size, etc.; returns are accepted; C.O.D. orders are accepted.

DESIGNEROUTLET

800–923–9915
212–989–0778
FAX: 212–367–7679

Information: internet website, no catalog
Pay: MC, V, AE, Discover
Sells: designers' overstocks (women's, men's, and children's clothing, footwear, jewelry, accessories, etc.)
Store: website only
E-mail: doutlet@aol.com
Online: http://www.designeroutlet.com

Once you discover this site you'll never want to shop anywhere else. If you're a boutique shopper, you've now died and gone to heaven, because DesignerOutlet has ingeniously come up with a way to buy top designer overstocks and sell them to you at greatly reduced prices. This internet-only store, started by a 15-year fashion industry veteran, can avoid incurring high overhead costs of real estate, catalog printing, and personnel, so the savings are real—to the tune of 35% to 75% off retail. The site is updated every two weeks with new merchandise, new designers, and new categories. Quantities are limited, so if you see something you love, you'd better buy it right away before it disappears into the ether. All items are first quality and guaranteed, and all merchandise is current season.

The site is really easy to use. You can either browse the impressive list of designers to see what they're offering, or you can search in Men, Women, or Children. For example, a recent visit to DesignerOutlet yielded deeply discounted leather accessories, watches, cufflinks, belts, suspenders, socks, and sportswear for men by such designers as Pierre Cardin, Geoffrey Beene, Fendi, and Movado, to name a few. In the women's section there were amazing buys—sportswear, dresses, jewelry, hats, silk scarves, jackets, suits, and more—from top designers who currently sell the same goods at Lord & Taylor, Bloomingdales, and Barney's. Shaneen Huxham NY chenille tweed gloves were selling for $24 (they retail for $36); Longchamp French silk scarves were selling for $90 (down from $140 retail); and Robert Rose silver and crystal earrings were $9.75 a pair (retail for $15). If you want to wear designer clothes because of their longevity and quality, but can't ordinarily afford them, you'll love this site. There were wonderful selections in children's wear too, as well as darling designer animal backpacks from Kreative Kids for $14 (normally $22). This site has real people on the phone who can answer questions for you. And if you're looking for a specific designer, e-mail your request. DesignerOutlet wants to be your personal shopper!

Special Factors: Order by phone, internet, or fax. Company will gladly exchange or credit any purchase that doesn't satisfy you completely. Returns must be made within two weeks; see site for details.

DISCOUNT BRIDAL SERVICE, INC.

144145 NORTH 73RD ST., SUITE 115
SCOTTSDALE, AZ 85260
800–874–8794
FAX: 602–998–3092

Information: call for referral (see text)
Pay: varies (see text)
Sells: women's bridal attire
Store: see text
E-mail: gown@ix.netcom.com
Online:
http://www.discountbridalservice.com

How would you like to carve 20% to 40% off one of the biggest single expenses of your wedding—The Dress? Discount Bridal Service (DBS), a network of hundreds of authorized bridal dealers across the United States and Japan, can refer you to the representative nearest you. You'll work with her directly, ordering your gown at savings that average 20% to 40%, and you can also order the dresses and accessories for the bridesmaids, mother of the bride, the flower girl, and others, at similar savings. DBS does not have their own catalog; the company's "catalogs" are the nationally advertised bridal magazines.

Here's how it works: Simply choose the gown of your dreams from the advertising and editorial in *Bride's, Modern Bride, For the Bride, Elegant Bride, Bridal Guide, Wedding Day Magazine*—or any other source showing current bridal styles. All of the merchandise is first-quality—no seconds or copies are sold. DBS deals with the same manufacturers and resources as do conventional bridal retailers. You'll be responsible for alterations (if they're needed), and if you don't know a good seamstress who specializes in bridal fittings, the DBS rep can give you local references. In addition to saving hundreds of dollars on the gown (and possibly thousands if you outfit the bridal party through DBS), the rep can accommodate you with invitations, accessory items, tuxedos, and many other bridal-related services.

DBS can perform miracles for your wedding budget, but it can't change time: It's still going to take at least 10 weeks, or as many as six months, from the time your order is submitted to when you receive your gown. (The differences depend on the manufacturer and the complexity of the dress; your rep will tell you the time frame for your choice.) And note that you'll have to prepay the entire cost of the gown when you place the order. Even with savings, that requires confidence in your rep (not to mention your spouse-to-be!), but DBS couldn't have survived in this highly competitive business since 1985 unless it had a great reputation and thoroughly reliable salespeople.

Special Factors: Consult with your DBS rep for terms of the sales policy; many accept credit cards.

GOHN BROS. MFG. CO.

105 S. MAIN
P.O. BOX 111
MIDDLEBURY, IN
   46540–0111
219–825–2400

Catalog: $1
Pay: check or MO
Sells: general merchandise and Amish specialties
Store: same address; Monday to Saturday 8–5:30

While other firms add fax machines and websites, Gohn Bros. remains firmly rooted in a world where bonnet board and work coats were stock items in the general store. Gohn has been in business since 1904 and sells practical goods at prices up to 40% below comparable retail.

Home sewers appreciate Gohn for yard goods, staples, and notions, such as the all-cotton Sanforized blue denim ($5.98/yard), muslin (as low as $1.69/yard), heavyweight 72" blanket flannel, pillow ticking, quilting thread, cotton percale and quilting prints, all-cotton sheeting, tailor's canvas, haircloth, mosquito netting, Coats & Clark embroidery floss (25 cents per skein), and wool overcoating (under $14 per yard, in navy, black, and "Confederate gray").

At least half of Gohn's closely printed 12-page stock lists are devoted to work-tailored, sturdy Amish clothing, including men's cotton chambray work shirts ($16.98), cotton denim broadfall work pants ($21.98), men's underwear, including old-fashioned cotton nightshirts, rubber galoshes and footwear by LaCrosse and Tingley, work gloves, felt and straw hats, and handkerchiefs. Much of the clothing is available in large sizes, and many of the items in the men's department are also offered in boys' sizes. If you're assembling a layette, see the catalog for good buys on the basics—diapers, receiving blankets, sleepers, pacifiers, baby pants, and other goods by Curity and Gerber. Nursing bras are available, and women's underwear and hosiery are offered at low prices. Gohn Bros. also carries some "hard-to-find" items such as hairpins, brown leather belting, fitted horse blankets, and bonnet boards (good for quilt patterns and templates). And the "book and game" department has some interesting recipe books, card games, and quilting primers.

Special Factors: Satisfaction is guaranteed; C.O.D. orders are accepted.

HUNTINGTON CLOTHIERS

1285 ALUM CREEK DR.
COLUMBUS, OH
43209–2797
800–848–6203
614–252–4422
FAX: 614–252–3855
FAX: 800–848–0644
(INTERNATIONAL)

Catalog: free, $3 outside U.S.
Pay: check, MO, MC, V, AE, DC, Discover, JCB
Sells: traditional menswear
Store: same address; Monday to Friday 10–6, Saturday 10–5
E-mail: shirts@hclothiers.com
Online: http://www.hclothiers.com

The 68-page catalog from Huntington Clothiers illustrates all the basics of a classic, conservative wardrobe, at prices that are competitive with those of old-line haberdashers; some items cost up to twice as much elsewhere.

Huntington's own line of shirts are offered in Oxford cloth, pima cotton solids, Sea Island cotton, Egyptian cotton broadcloth, and cotton/poly blends. (Monogramming is available for $5.) Huntington also sells neckwear of Italian and English silk—ties and bow ties in tasteful regimental stripes, patterns, and "conversationals." Cotton polo shirts are shown as well as cotton and wool sweaters, kimonos and bathrobes, dress hosiery, leather travel kits, leather wallets, and manicure sets, belts, suspenders, underwear, shoes, and more. The catalog features color photos, a departure from the old hand-drawn color illustrations that were one of the catalog's trademarks.

Special Factors: Satisfaction is guaranteed; returns (except monogrammed goods) are accepted for exchange, refund, or credit.

LADY GRACE INTIMATE APPAREL

P.O. BOX 128, DEPT. 74
MALDEN, MA 02148
800–922–0504
781–322–1721
FAX: 781–321–8476

Catalog: free, $2 outside U.S.
Pay: check, MO, MC, V, Discover
Sells: women's intimate apparel
Store: 14 stores in MA, ME, and NH (see catalog for locations)
Online: http://www.ladygrace.com

The Lady Grace catalog offers women's intimate apparel and is especially strong in large and hard-to-find sizes. They run semi-annual sales that will save you up to 25% on many of their products, including bras, body shapers, girdles, control briefs, slips, panties, nursing bras, breast enhancers, and post–breast surgery needs from top makers such as Bali, Carnival, Flexees, Glamorise, Goddess, Leading Lady, Lilyette, Maidenform, Magic Lady, Playtex, Vanity Fair, and Warners, among others. Lady Grace also sells a wide assortment of sleepwear, loungewear, and swimwear from top sources. Bra sizes run to 54, cup sizes up to J. Bottoms are available up to 9X. If you have a hard time finding quality intimate apparel in your size, you'll appreciate this collection. Lady Grace has been "serving the needs of America's women" since 1937.

Special Factors: Satisfaction is guaranteed; price quote by phone; returns of resellable goods are accepted within 30 days for exchange, refund, or credit.

LANDMARK ENTERPRISES, INC.

HOSIERY DIVISION
P.O. BOX 43506
BROOKLYN PARK, MN
    55443–0506
FAX: 612–502–0715

Catalog: $2, $5 outside U.S.; refundable with first order
Pay: check, MO, MC, V
Sells: women's hosiery and intimate apparel, socks for women, men, and children
Store: mail order only

Landmark Enterprises sells hosiery for women in regular and plus sizes—ultra-sheer pantyhose, control-top pantyhose, body stockings, thigh highs, knee highs, fishnets, colored pantyhose, glitter pantyhose, back-seamed versions, stockings, teddies, socks, panty girdles, and underwear for ladies from 90 to 450 pounds. They also carry men's and boys' socks and girls' socks and tights. You'll pay 30% to 50% less here than at a store. The 28-page black-and-white catalog is fairly straightforward, devoid of photos or brand names. This is new, brand-name merchandise, but since the brands carried change constantly, you won't find them listed. If you don't mind buying a style rather than a label, you'll find some good buys here. There is no minimum order.

Special Factors: Unopened, unused merchandise is returnable; C.O.D. orders not accepted; fax or write for catalog.

MANNY'S MILLINERY SUPPLY CENTER

26 W. 38TH ST.
NEW YORK, NY 10018
212–840–2235/2236
FAX: 212–944–0178

Catalog: $5
Pay: check, MO, MC, V, AE
Sells: hats, millinery supplies, gloves, bridal trimmings
Store: same address; Monday to Friday 9:30–5:30, Saturday 10–4:30

Manny's is nestled among the shops in New York City's "trimmings" district, which has more sequins, tassels, and decorative add-ons per square foot than a Las Vegas floor show. Manny's offers some of that glitter, but the company's specialty is women's hats, millinery supplies, and bridal accessories.

Manny's has two catalogs. (Your $5 with catalog request will get you both.) The "Basic Supply Catalog" was not ready for review at press time, but offers millinery items such as straw, felt, hat pins, beading, feathers, tapes, sizing, veiling, ribbons, and other professional millinery supplies and equipment, including horsehair braid, hat stretchers, display heads and racks, hatboxes and travel cases, and cleaning products. The 62-page "Hat" catalog is fabulous and features 400-plus photographed hats—with and without trim. The styles are many, in materials including pari sisol, chenille, velour, felt (both fur felt and wool felt), twisted toyo, and others. Scores of "frames," or fabric-covered hat forms, are offered. The satin frames are suitable for bridal outfits, and the buckram frames provide a base for limitless flights of fancy.

In addition, Manny's hat catalog offers a variety of jeweled, feather, and beaded hat pins; flower hat pins of every conceivable type; trimmings in a dazzling variety, including cording, wired ribbon, wired mesh, lace, and pleated stretch velvet in many designs, colors, and textures; beaded, sequin, and rhinestone trimmings; wooden hat blocks and basic crowns; oversize hat forms; and hat trees. Savings vary from item to item, but average 33% below regular retail. By the way, if you're into hatmaking or other crafts projects, check out Manny's five "Surprise Grab Bags" (Rounding Assortment, Feather Surprise, Millinery Madness Surprise, Flower Surprise, Triple Flower Surprise). These are 19"–by–19" plastic bags crammed full of one-of-a-kinds, remnants, flawed, seconds, or shopworn items, and worth "5 to 10 times the face value of what's in them." They vary in price and are described in detail in the catalog. You can buy them individually, or get three for $35. Manny's also sells two, at this writing, very excellent books on hatmaking.

Please note: If you're buying hats only, the minimum order is three; if you buy one or two hats, you must also buy $15 in assorted items (frames, trims, etc.); if you're buying assorted items only, the minimum order is $25. There is no minimum book order.

Special Factors: Price quote by phone; minimum order on certain items (see text).

MASS. ARMY & NAVY STORE

15 FORDHAM RD.,
   DEPT. WBMC
BOSTON, MA 02134
800–343–7749
617–783–1250
FAX: 617–254–6607

Catalog: free
Pay: check, MO, MC, V, AE, Discover
Sells: government surplus apparel and accessories
Store: 895 Boylston St., Boston; Monday to Friday 9:30–8, Saturday 12–8, Sunday 12–6; also 1436 Massachusetts Ave., Cambridge, MA; Monday to Saturday 10–9, Sunday 12–8

Mass. Army & Navy offers both reproduction and genuine government surplus, presented as a fashion statement. The 64-page color catalog features camouflage clothing, French and Spanish army raincoats, U.S. and European battle dress uniforms, field and flight jackets, East German guards' boots, U.S. Air Force sunglasses, survival manuals, Yukon hats, and similar surplus. Mass. Army & Navy also offers casual footwear, bandannas, gloves, Levi's jeans, Dockers, bomber jackets, peacoats, knapsacks, sleeping bags, air mattresses, backpacks, duffel bags, tents, mess kits, security products, and insignias and patches, among other useful items. This is a great resource for surplus chic, or the place to turn when you want a gas mask (East German) or WWII-issue grenade (defused, three styles).

Special Factors: Satisfaction is guaranteed; returns are accepted for exchange, refund, or credit.

NO NONSENSE DIRECT

P.O. BOX 26095
GREENSBORO, NC
  27420–6095
800–677–5995
FAX: 910–275–9329

Catalog: free
Pay: check, MO, MC, V, AE, Discover
Sells: hosiery
Store: mail order only
Online: http://www.legwear.com

¡Si!

If you wear No Nonsense, Burlington, or Easy Spirit legwear, you can save up to 60% on the price of your favorite styles through No Nonsense Direct. This mail-order factory outlet of Kayser Roth has been delivering great buys on pantyhose, socks, and other items since 1985. You'll save the most on 12 pairs or more of "Practically Perfect" No Nonsense, Burlington, and Easy Spirit pantyhose, including Sheer & Silky, Control Top, Light Support, Regular, Custom Full Figure, and other lines. The "Practically Perfect" goods have "minor, virtually undetectable imperfections that do not affect looks or wear" and are covered by the No Nonsense Direct guarantee of satisfaction. In addition to saving you money, you get a full choice of sizes and colors when you buy from the catalog—and that means that unless you're under 4' 11", 85 lb., or over 6', 280 lb., you should find a good fit.

Please note: Most items are sold in minimum quantities of three.

Special Factors: Satisfaction is guaranteed; quantity discounts are available; returns are accepted for exchange, refund, or credit.

ONE HANES PLACE CATALOG

P.O. BOX 748
RURAL HALL, NC
27098–0748
800–300–2600
FAX: 800–545–5613
TDD: 800–816–4833

Catalog: free
Pay: check, MO, MC, V, AE, Discover
Sells: first-quality and "slightly imperfect" women's hosiery and underwear
Store: mail order only
Online: http://www.onehanesplace.com

 (SEE TEXT)

The 84-page color catalog from One Hanes Place brings you savings of up to 50% on your favorite pantyhose, activewear, and lingerie from Bali, Champion, Hanes Her Way, Jogbra, Isotoner, and Playtex. The best buys are on the "slightly imperfect" irregulars, and the whole range of L'eggs is available, as well as Hanes hosiery, Bali and Playtex foundation garments and slips, the famous Wonderbra, and Hanes socks, underwear, tee shirts, cotton and cotton-blend casual women's shirts, pants, and dresses, and sweats for the whole family. There are also close-out catalogs where the savings run up to 70%. See the detailed sizing guide in the catalog to be sure of the best fit. Or check out the website, where you can order directly online.

Special Factors: Satisfaction is guaranteed; "slightly imperfect" goods are clearly identified; returns are accepted; TDD service is available Monday to Friday, 8 A.M. to midnight.

PAULA'S HATBOX

P.O. BOX 935
SOUTH EASTON, MA
02375
800–748–6908
FAX: 508–238–1965

Catalog: free
Pay: check, MO, MC, V, Discover
Sells: hats
Store: mail order only

Here's where you'll find the year's most popular hats at the best prices. The 32-page color catalog offers 100% wool berets, velvet crush hats, pillbox hats, faux-leopard caps, fake-fur "cuddlers" (hooded wrappable scarves), Sunday-best and evening-wear styles with veils, feathers, sequins, and metallic finishes, and much more, including casual styles for beach, sports, and other outdoorsy occasions. All of the hats are competitively priced, and there are some good deals when you buy two of the same hat, in different colors, such as the cotton crushers and berets. But the twice-a-year sale catalog is the real bargain here. The review copy at the time of this writing had a wide selection of hats for as much as 50% off! Expert consultants are on call 24 hours a day to answer your questions about styles and fit. If you're a "hat gal," you're bound to find something you like here at a price that can't be beat.

Special Factors: C.O.D. orders not accepted. Returns for exchange or credit accepted; see catalog for details.

QUINN'S SHIRT SHOP

RTE. 12, P.O. BOX 383
N. GROSVENORDALE, CT
  06255
508–943–7183

Price List: $2 with SASE, refundable (see text)
Pay: check or MO
Sells: Arrow shirts
Store: 245 W. Main St., Dudley, MA; Monday to Saturday 10–5

Quinn's, a factory outlet for the Arrow Shirt company, offers slightly irregular shirts at up to 60% below the price of first-quality goods. The firm has been in business since 1956 and will send you a price list for $2 and a stamped, self-addressed envelope (the $2 charge is refundable with your first order). You can also call or write for a price quote on your favorite Arrow shirt (Bradstreet, Dover B.D., Kent Collection, Fairfield, etc.—you must have the style name or line). Quinn's carries shirts in regular, big, and tall sizes, $14^1/2$" to 20" neck, 32" to 38" sleeve. When you order, note whether you want short sleeves or long, and specify the length if long. The shirts may be exchanged if the flaws are too apparent.

Special Factors: Satisfaction is guaranteed; price quote by phone or letter with SASE; returns are accepted for exchange; minimum is four shirts per order; only C.O.D. orders are accepted.

THE SMART SAVER

P.O. BOX 105
WASCO, IL 60183
800–554–4453

Catalog: free
Pay: check, MO, MC, V
Sells: bras, girdles, shapers, and panties
Store: mail order only

We get attached to our brand and style of bra, and we're loyal for life. Right, ladies? If The Smart Saver carries the intimate apparel you love the best, you're in luck. This company has first-quality, fine intimates at 35% off (no seconds, no irregulars). Their catalog calls these "styles for the forgotten lady." These aren't racy numbers worn by Janet Jackson and Madonna. The bras you'll find pictured in Smart Saver's 20-page black-and-white catalog are the classics by Playtex, Exquisite Form, Crown-ette, Bestform, Glamorise, Vanity Fair, Venus, Perfect Comfort, Goddess, and Lollipop. You'll find girdles, bras, and panties in real women's sizes—ranging from S to 9XL. There are girdles and shapers for bottoms, thighs, midriffs, and full leg; bras for women who need extra support and room; good, old-fashioned 100% cotton waist-high briefs; and more. There are also bras for nursing mothers and for women who've had mastectomies. You'll see the suggested retail price alongside Smart Saver's, a feature I always appreciate. The owner, who's had the business for 16 years, says her customers are "very loyal."

Special Factors: 100% satisfaction guaranteed. Will ship to all 50 states, Canada, and locations with postal zip codes (e.g., Guam, U.S. Virgin Islands, etc.).

SPORTSWEAR CLEARINGHOUSE

P.O. BOX 317746–99
CINCINNATI, OH
45231–7746
513–522–3511

Brochure: free with SASE
Pay: check, MO, MC, V, Discover
Sells: printed sportswear overruns
Store: mail order only

Forget about Day-Glo cycling shorts and $200 court shoes—you won't find these at Sportswear Clearinghouse. The fare is sportswear basics—tee shirts in sizes from youth XS to adult XXXL, golf shirts, sweatshirts, shorts, night shirts, and hats, already printed or embroidered with corporate or institutional logos. If you succumb to the brochure, you can wind up wearing a tee shirt printed for the American Embassy at Sanaa, Notre Dame running shorts, and a hat emblazoned with an advertising message from a local welding shop. The Clearinghouse, which has been in business since 1976, also offers tee shirts bearing the names of colleges, sports themes, and slogans in foreign languages. Prices are hard to beat; tee shirts and shorts cost a few dollars each, and hats and visors are priced under $2 apiece. Most of these items are sold at retail in lots of three or more, and the Clearinghouse selects the colors, logos, and slogans. First-quality undecorated athletic socks and baseball hats embroidered with the replica logos of all 30 major league baseball teams and other pro sports (NFL, NBA, NHL), as well as colleges of your choice, are also available. Adjustable baseball/golf hats without logos, in many themes and colors, are also offered.

Special Factors: Satisfaction is guaranteed; unused returns are accepted within 30 days for exchange, refund, or credit; C.O.D. orders are accepted (UPS delivery only).

THE ULTIMATE OUTLET

A SPIEGEL COMPANY

P.O. BOX 182557

COLUMBUS, OH

  43218–2557

800–332–6000

781–871–4100

FAX: 800–422–6697

TDD: 800–322–1231

Information: internet website and catalog (free)

Pay: check, MO, MC, V, AE, Spiegel charge card

Sells: clothing for men, women, and children, and department store goods

Store: Spiegel Ultimate Outlet Stores in CO, FL, GA, IL, IN, MI, MN, MO, NV, OH, PA, TX, and VA; call 800–645–7467 for addresses and hours

Online: http://www.ultimate-outlet.com

What a great company and website! The Ultimate Outlet, a division of Spiegel, sells just about everything you'd expect to find in a department store, with an emphasis on name-brand fashion apparel. The Ultimate Outlet stands out by offering a high level of style and quality at competitive prices. The website is one of the nicest around. You can click on a category (women's dresses, e.g.) and you're transferred to a page of offerings with photographs, was-vs.-now prices, brand names, and descriptions. If you'd like to see the item better, a click on the photo enlarges it and gives you even more information. The clothing for women spans from intimates and swimwear to sportswear, career, and eveningwear. The men's selections are just as great, and the savings are fantastic—up to 50% on many items. There's a small selection of children's clothing here, too. Best of all, Ultimate has one of the best returns policies I've seen anywhere, including the option to return the item to any one of 4,000 supermarkets nationwide. After you've filled up your closet, spend some time browsing the home section for deals on bedding, rugs, window treatments, and more.

Special Factors: Satisfaction is guaranteed. Returns are accepted for refund or credit. Deliveries to Alaska, Hawaii, and APO/FPO addresses are made by the postal service, not UPS. Secure online ordering.

WEARGUARD CORP.

LONGWATER DR.
NORWELL, MA 02061
800–388–3300
781–871–4100
FAX: 800–436–3132

Catalog: free
Pay: check, MO, MC, V, AE, Discover
Sells: work clothing, outerwear, and accessories
Store: mail order only
Online: http://www.wearguard.com

WearGuard, which was founded in 1952, supplies more than a million U.S. companies and consumers with work clothing and outerwear, at prices up to 30% below comparable retail. The 60-page color catalogs show jackets and parkas, work shirts, heavy-duty pants, tee shirts, knit shirts, jeans, gloves, baseball caps, thermal underwear, rainwear, and coveralls. In addition to WearGuard's own label, WearGuard's footwear includes Timberland and Wolverine boots and work shoes. A few jackets and boots are offered in women's styles.

WearGuard's Custom Logo department provides designs on jackets, knit shirts, tee shirts, and work shirts; stock logos and lettering are also available. The screen printing and direct embroidery are done "in house," which means WearGuard should be able to get your custom job to you faster.

Special Factors: Satisfaction is guaranteed; returns are accepted.

WILLOW RIDGE/ BEDFORD FAIR LIFESTYLES

Catalog: free
Pay: check, MO, MC, V, AE, Discover
Sells: career and casual women's apparel
Store: mail order only

421 LANDMARK DR.
WILMINGTON, NC 28410
800–388–8555, DEPT. WBM
  (WILLOW RIDGE)
800–964–1000, DEPT. WBM
  (BEDFORD FAIR)
FAX: 910–343–6859
TDD: 800–945–1118

Finally—a source for attractive business and casual wear for misses, petites, and women—at cash-conserving prices. Willow Ridge and Bedford Fair Lifestyles are shared by the same owner, and both offer great values. Willow Ridge does it with great jackets, shirts, pants, sweaters, dresses, suits, and other pieces, in 6 to 20 misses sizes, 4 to 16 in petites, and 18W to 28W in women's. (Some talls are also available.) The Willow Ridge look is classy but not stuffy, strong on good, flattering color choices and washable fabrics. The prices will please your budget, with belted gabardine trousers under $25, pretty summer dresses under $40, poly shells for $10, and linen-blend jackets for under $30.

The Bedford Fair Lifestyles catalog caters to a slightly different demographic. The emphasis is on easy-care clothing for younger women, perhaps a bit "hipper" and more active. There are some great party dresses (my favorite was only $34), lined silk blazers ($48), crocheted sweaters with coordinating skirts, and more—all at very modest prices. The sizing guide in both catalogs helps ensure a proper fit (be sure to double-check your measurements), and everything is covered by a guarantee of satisfaction.

Special Factors: Satisfaction is guaranteed; returns are accepted for exchange, refund, or credit. Deferred payment is available.

RELATED PRODUCTS/COMPANIES

For baby clothes, diapering needs, children's clothing, and maternity wear, see "Children and Mothers," page 109

For men's and women's footwear, see "Shoes and Boots," page 117

Auto-racing suits • Racer Wholesale

Aviator clothing and headwear • Wag-Aero Group

Bathrobes • Clothcrafters

Bicycling and other sports apparel • Bike Nashbar, Performance Bicycle, Spike Nashbar

Bridal supplies • Billiann's Floral and Bridal, Floral Supply Syndicate, Newark Dressmaker Supply

Costumes • Oriental Trading Company

Extra-large clothing hangers • Amplestuff

Extra-wide socks • Amplestuff

Feather marabous, boas, and fans • Gettinger

Government surplus and vintage military clothing • John W. Poling, Ruvel

Hats and headwear • Paula Young Fashion Wigs, Especially Yours, Beauty by Spector, Billiann's Floral and Bridal

Hunting and camouflage clothing • Wiley Outdoor Sports, Bowhunter's Warehouse, The Sportsman's Guide

Lingerie • Thai Silks, Beauty Boutique, Gold Medal Hair Products

Men's underwear • Marshall Domestics

Outdoor wear • Bailey's, Campmor, Defender, M & E Marine, Ruvel, Sierra Trading Post, West Marine, The Sportsman's Guide, Justin Discount Boots

Plain, undyed cotton and silk clothing, scarves, and baseball caps • Dharma Trading Co., Clothcrafters

Sheepskin mittens and hats • Leather Unlimited

Special-needs clothing for adults • Special Clothes

Stain remover • Solo Slide Fasteners, The Cleaning Center

Support hosiery, socks • Essentials, Support Plus

Swimming and other water sports clothing • Bart's, The House, Overton's, World Wide Aquatics

Uniforms for restaurant, medical, sanitation, and other industry professionals • Tafford, Cotton Scrubs, Cheap Aprons/Allstates Uniform, Clothcrafters, Marshall Domestics

Western clothing and hats • Justin Discount Boots

Women's apparel • Thai Silks, Utex Trading

Work clothing • Tool Crib of the North, Marshall Domestics, Northern Hydraulics, Omaha Vaccine

Children and Mothers

Clothing and accessories for babies, children, and nursing mothers; and related goods

The firms in this section sell clothing for babies, children, and nursing mothers—all at savings of up to 60%. If you're a parent, you know how much the little darlings cost—a lot! Forget about the things over which you have no control—the private school tuition, the endless doctor and dentist bills, and the never-ceasing stream of birthday presents you have to buy for the almost weekly parties of his friends and classmates. Thankfully, you can cut down on diapering and clothing costs if you're a savvy shopper.

One of the best all-around sources for discount baby supplies and buying strategies is *Baby Bargains: Secrets to Saving 20% to 50% on Baby Furniture, Equipment, Clothes, Toys, Maternity Wear and Much, Much More!* by Denise and Alan Fields (Windsor Peak Press, 1997), who wrote an equally valuable guide to saving money on wedding expenses (see the introduction to "Clothing, Hats, Furs, and Accessories"). *Baby Bargains* describes the market for baby-related products, covers some of the issues, such as breast-feeding and paper vs. cloth diapers, and gives source after source for information and products. The Fields guarantee that you'll save $250 on the cost of your baby expenses, or they'll refund the cost of the book. You'll find many other parenting manuals as well as children's books in the "Books, Audio-books, and Periodicals" chapter.

For a wealth of companies that offer children's and maternity clothing and accessories, browse the "Related Products/Companies" section at the end of this section. There are also numerous firms in other chapters that carry various and sundry child-related goods—from children's crafts projects to games and toys to tiny-sized protective beekeeping suits to kids' vitamins. It would be impossible to list them all here, so be sure and browse the relevant chapter if there's something specific you seek (e.g., for children's computer software, see the companies listed in the "Computer Hardware and Software" section of "Office, Business, Professional"; for children's furniture, see the "Furnishings" section of the "House and Home" chapter).

FIND IT FAST

BABY SLINGS AND CARRIERS • Baby Bunz, Natural Baby, Snugglebundle
CLOTH DIAPERS AND COVERS • After the Stork, As a Little Child, Baby Bunz, Natural Baby, Snugglebundle
DISPOSABLE DIAPERS • Diaper Warehouse
INFANTS' CLOTHING • Baby Bunz, Natural Baby, Rubens Baby Wear, Snugglebundle
NURSING BRAS, NURSING CLOTHING, AND ACCESSORIES • Bosom Buddies, Natural Baby, Snugglebundle
TODDLERS' AND CHILDREN'S CLOTHING • After the Stork, Natural Baby, Snugglebundle
TODDLERS' AND CHILDREN'S SHOES • After the Stork

AFTER THE STORK

P.O. BOX 44321
RIO RANCHO, NM
  87174–4321
800–441–4775
FAX: 505–867–7101
TDD: 800–505–1095

Catalog: free
Pay: check, MO, MC, V, AE, Discovery, JCB
Sells: children's clothing
Store: mail order only
E-mail: storkmail@afterthestork.com

At After the Stork, cotton is king and prices are a friendly 25% to 40% below comparable retail. The 52-page color catalogs show playwear and sleepwear in happy prints and vibrant colors, so your kids can look hip without breaking your budget. The company has been price-shopped by pros who've found that you can assemble outfits that look like the upmarket Swedish brand for less than half the cost. After the Stork has lots of tee shirts, sweats, long johns, pull-on pants, coveralls, dresses, rompers, and outerwear, as well as shoes, socks, sneakers, slippers, tights, underwear, and a choice bear or two. Check the size chart before you order—note that After the Stork sizes its clothing after shrinkage, so you don't have to order large.

Wholesale customers, call for requirements.

Special Factors: Satisfaction is guaranteed; returns are accepted.

AS A LITTLE CHILD

**10701 W. 80TH AVE.,
   DEPT. W
ARVADA, CO 80005
303–456–1880**

Brochure: free
Pay: check or MO
Sells: diaper covers and cloth diapers
Store: mail order only

As a Little Child celebrates children as one of life's great blessings, making baby's health and happiness its first order of business with a selection of environmentally positive diapering products that are kind to family budgets. The featured item is the Wabby, the only diaper cover made with Gore-Tex fabric, so it's both waterproof and "breathable." Since air can flow through the cover, baby's bottom stays cooler, which helps to prevent diaper rash. Wabbies are constructed to last, wash and dry quickly, and they have newly designed closures that are strong and durable. The covers are offered in white, blue, pink, and navy blue check, sized from newborn to XL; they work well with Wabby diapers, which team all-cotton flannel with terry cloth for comfort and absorbency. Washcloths and miniwipes are also available.

Special Factors: Quantity discounts are available.

BABY BUNZ & CO.

**P.O. BOX 113–WB99
LYNDEN, WA 98264–0113**

Catalog: $1
Pay: check, MO, MC, V
Sells: cloth diapering supplies, layette items, toys, books, etc., for young children
Store: mail order only

If you use cloth diapers instead of disposables, you may be overwhelmed by all the prefolded diapers and diaper "systems" on the market. One of the most popular diapering duos among the cloth set is a standard or fitted diaper with a natural-fiber cover. Baby Bunz & Co.

has been selling the best-known covers, Nikkys, since 1982. Nikkys are made in soft lamb's wool, waterproof cotton, "breathable" poly, and poly-lined cotton, and are available in sizes from newborn to three years (up to 34 pounds). Budget-priced nylon waterproof diaper wraps and pull-ons are also available. Nikkys are priced at up to 35% below retail.

The Baby Bunz 20-page color catalog also offers a variety of diaper styles—contour, prefolded, flat, and diaper doublers. The catalog includes guides to folding diapers and how to use Nikkys. Adorable layette wear, colorful cotton playsuits, baby buntings, organic cotton items, Egyptian cotton and Merino wool blankets, and a crib-sized lambskin are also featured. The natural theme is carried on with Aromatherapy for Kids, natural baby shampoo, Weleda baby-care products, bath sponges, and natural bristle baby brushes. You'll also find wooden rattles, natural-fiber soft toys, and an ideal "First Doll." Many other useful items are available, including a comfortable baby carrier, a "Boppy" baby pillow, and classic storybooks for children up to three years. These and other new additions to the latest Baby Bunz catalog include several guides on rearing healthy and happy children.

Canadian readers, please note: Only U.S. funds are accepted.

Special Factors: No wholesale orders, please. Baby Bunz offers a "best price" guarantee if you find identical items in other current catalogs with a regular retail price lower than Baby Bunz's. Satisfaction is guaranteed; unused returns are accepted within 30 days for replacement, refund, or credit.

BOSOM BUDDIES

212 BROADWAY, DEPT.
WBM
P.O. BOX 1250
PORT EWEN, NY 12466
914–338–2038

Catalog: free
Pay: check, MO, MC, V, AE, Discover
Sells: nursing bras and clothing
Store: Wednesday to Friday 11–5, and by appointment

Bosom Buddies was founded in 1983 by a nursing mother who saw a market for "breast-feeding fashions." Nursing bras by Leading Lady and Fancee Free are offered, including many all-cotton styles. This is a great source for hard-to-find sizes—some bras run up to size 46J. Nightgowns and other clothing designed to make nursing easy are sold as well. Bosom Buddies also carries nursing pads and a full line of equipment for expressing and storing breast milk, and a number of helpful books. The 12-page catalog includes a guide to taking your measurements, so you're sure to order the right size. Not every item is discounted, but prices are reasonable, and savings run up to 50% on sale items.

Special Factors: Order sale merchandise promptly, since quantities may be limited.

DIAPER WAREHOUSE, INC.

5635 S. MINGO
TULSA, OK 74146
888–791–2229
918–249–8888
FAX: 918–249–8889

Brochure: free
Pay: check, MO, MC, V
Sells: disposable diapers
Store: same address; Monday to Friday 10–6, Saturday 10–2
E-mail: diaper@webzone.net
Online: http://www.diaperwhse.com

Here's a company that came up with a great idea: inexpensive diapers by the case. If you're a frugal parent with infants and toddlers, or maybe run a day-care center, you know how quickly a case of diapers disappears. And when you're toting a sleeping baby in your arms while pushing a fussy toddler in a stroller, the last thing you need is a trip to the supermarket to buy one of those suitcase-size packs of diapers. The folks at Diaper Warehouse imagined such a scenario when they figured out a way to sell diapers at 35% to 50% less than what you pay at discount stores. These are first- and second-quality name-brand diapers produced by leading manufacturers of disposable diapers. Tests have shown that these diapers are just as absorbent as the leading brands. The minimum order is one case (that's 240 diapers in the smallest size, or 120 in X-large). You can call or write for a brochure, or get the exact same information off the website. Whether your child is 7 pounds or 37 pounds, you won't be paying much here. Shipping is a flat rate of $8, so if you have the storage space, buy several cases. Order by phone, fax, or online.

Special Factors: Diaper Warehouse unconditionally guarantees their diapers. Wholesale orders possible; inquire. Shipping within the continental U.S. only.

THE NATURAL BABY CO., INC.

7835 FREEDOM AVE. NW,
   SUITE 2
NORTH CANTON, OH
   44720
800–388-BABY (ORDERS)
330–492–8090
FAX: 330–492–8290

Catalog: free
Pay: check, MO, MC, V, AE, Discover
Sells: diapers, baby and children's clothing, nursing clothing, toys, remedies, etc.
Store: mail order only

Everything in The Natural Baby catalog has been chosen with an eye to making children comfortable and keeping them healthy, without costing Mom and Dad a bundle. The Natural Baby Co. was established in 1983 and has a policy of supporting home-based businesses—so the quilt you buy here for your own baby may have been made by a mother of nine, and the wood cradles and toys crafted by carpenters "in between pouring out the Cheerios"!

The Natural Baby has built its business on cloth diapers and covers, beginning with the firm's own "Rainbow" diaper, a fitted cloth style (pinless, foldless) made of flannel-lined terry cloth ($33 per dozen). If you're on a tight budget, you can get the "Natural Baby Diapers" of bird's-eye, from $20.35 a dozen. Diaper covers from Nikkys and The Natural Baby are available, as well as diaper pads and conventional cloth diapers. Past catalogs have included helpful sidebars on diapering with pinless covers, the cloth vs. disposables debate, and tips on preventing diaper rash.

There's much more for baby: a line of baby clothing from organically grown cotton, baby carriers, sheepskin rugs and play balls, woolen crib blankets, flannel creepers, and Storkenworks shoes. The catalog offers some clothing for kids up to five years, including long johns, Nikkys substantial underpants (in sizes to fit children up to 65 pounds), socks, sweaters, turtlenecks, and other goods, while mothers are treated to Leading Lady bras. Among the offerings are natural and homeopathic remedies, as well as a splendid selection of wooden toys, dolls, rattles, balls, cradles, and other safe and nontoxic diversions.

Special Factors: For wholesale prices and policies, please inquire.

RUBENS & MARBLE, INC.

P.O. BOX 14900-A
CHICAGO, IL 60614–0900
773–348–6200

Brochure: free with SASE
Pay: check or MO
Sells: infants' clothing
Store: mail order only

Rubens & Marble, Inc., has been supplying hospitals with baby clothes since 1890 (!) and sells the same goods to consumers at up to 60% below regular retail prices. The babywear basics include undershirts in sizes from newborn to 36 months, with short, long, and mitten-cuff sleeves; they're offered in snap, tie, and double-breasted slipover styles (many are seconds, with small knitting flaws). First-quality cotton/wool blend and preemie-size cotton undershirts are available as well. Rubens also offers fitted bassinet and crib sheets, training and waterproof pants, kimonos, drawstring-bottom baby gowns, and terry bibs.

Special Factors: You must send a self-addressed, stamped envelope to receive the price list; seconds are clearly indicated; minimum order is one package (varying number depending on type of item).

SNUGGLEBUNDLE

444A N. MAIN ST., #165,
DEPT. WBM
E. LONGMEADOW, MA
01028
TEL/FAX: 413–525–1972

Catalog: $1
Pay: check, MO, MC, V
Sells: cloth diapers, covers, children's clothing, nursing pads, etc.
Store: mail order only
E-mail: snugbdl@aol.com

Mother-owned and -operated Snugglebundle specializes in bundle, bottom, and layette products "for the environmentally friendly baby." This is a great source for those of us who choose to go the cloth-diaper route. A wide selection of cloth diapers including "green" and organic cotton are available. Diaper accessories include diaper covers in several styles and fastener options, cotton wipes, soakers, diaper clips, and pull-on pants. Snugglebundle also carries organic bedding items, such as flannel crib sheets, baby blankets, and cotton crib and cradle bumpers. You'll also find Baby Slings, breast pads, layette items, kimonos, snap tees, bibs, and more—all made of earth-friendly materials (great for allergy prevention). Product samplers and gift sets are available, and free Uses and Care guidelines are included with each diaper purchase.

Mothers of twins, please note: Snugglebundle offers a special discount to mothers who have twins, triplets—even septuplets!

Special Factors: Satisfaction is guaranteed.

RELATED PRODUCTS/COMPANIES

Children's bedding • Chock, Clothcrafters, Gohn Bros.
Children's cowboy boots • Justin Discount Boots
Children's deerskin mittens • The Deerskin Place, Arctic Sheepskin
Children's sweatsuits • One Hanes Place
Cloth diapers • Gohn Bros., Chock
Designer children's clothing • DesignerOutlet
Diaper-changer baby backpack • Campmor
Layettes and infant clothing • Gohn Bros., Lady Grace, Chock
Maternity clothing for health professionals • Tafford, Cotton Scrubs
Maternity hosiery • One Hanes Place
Nursing bras and accessories • Gohn Bros., Lady Grace, The Smart Saver
Special-needs clothing for children • Special Clothes
Toddlers' and children's clothing • Bridgewater, Chock, DesignerOutlet, Gohn Bros.
Toddlers' and children's socks • Asiatic Hosiery, Landmark
Undyed baby clothing • Dharma Trading

Shoes and Boots

Footwear of every kind for men, women, and children

These firms offer everything from arctic boots to moccasins to nurses' shoes, at savings of up to 40%. But there's still the problem of fit, unless you're ordering more of the same model you've worn before. Here are some tips to improve the odds, and to make returns—if necessary—as easy as possible:

- Have your feet measured at least once a year, and order your true size. (Feet continue to grow and change as you age.)
- Buy from firms with liberal return policies, preferably an unconditional guarantee of satisfaction with a 30-day return period.
- Buy styles and shapes that you know fit your foot.
- If the shoes you're buying are also available in a local store, try on a pair before ordering them.
- When the shoes arrive, unwrap them carefully and save the packaging.
- Try them on in the late afternoon, when your feet have swollen slightly.
- Walk around in a carpeted area to avoid scratching the soles.
- Leave the shoes on for at least half an hour, checking for rubbing and pinching after 20 minutes.
- If they fit, consider ordering a second pair now, while they're still in stock.
- If the shoes don't fit, return them according to the firm's instructions, indicating whether you want another size or a refund or credit.

A brochure with fitting guidelines and information on foot problems is available from the American Orthopedic Foot and Ankle Society. Send a long, stamped, self-addressed envelope to AOFAS, 1216 Pine St., Suite 201, Seattle, WA 98101; request the "Ten Points of Proper Shoe Fit" brochure.

Good maintenance is critical in preserving the looks and longevity of your shoes and boots. Some of the firms listed in "Luggage and Leather Accessories" sell leather-care products, as do a number of companies listed in the "Related Products/Companies" listings of that chapter. If your shoes and boots need professional help and you don't have a good repair service nearby, contact the Houston Shoe Hospital, 5215 Kirby Dr., Houston, TX 77098; 713–528–6268. This firm overhauls worn footwear and handles mail-order repairs.

GENE'S SHOES DISCOUNT CATALOG

126 N. MAIN ST., DEPT. WBM99
ST. CHARLES, MO 63301
800–807–4637
314–946–0804
FAX: 314–946–0804

Catalog: $1
Pay: check, MO, MC, V, Discover
Sells: dress, casual, and athletic shoes
Store: same address; Monday to Saturday 9–5:30

Gene's Discount "specialty size" catalog offers women's footwear by Soft Spots, manufactured by Lowell Shoe Company, a New Hampshire establishment that's been crafting women's shoes for almost 70 years. The sizes start at 4 in some styles, go up to 13 in others, and come in four or five widths. The 16-page color catalog walks you through the design and philosophy behind the doctor-designed footwear, and there are around 17 styles from which to choose, from casual to dressy. The regular catalog is a 12-pager in black and white that offers men's and women's shoes and boots discounted about 20%, but savings run to over 30% on some styles. The manufacturers represented in the recent catalog include Trotters, Easy Spirit, Selby, New Balance, and Rockport. You're in luck if you're hard to fit; Gene's offers the women's shoes in AAAA to EEE widths, sizes 3 to 13, and the men's in 2A to 5E widths, from size 5 to 18.

Please note: The prices in the catalog are good on mail orders only, not on in-store purchases.

Special Factors: Satisfaction is guaranteed; unworn, salable returns are accepted within 30 days for exchange, refund, or credit.

JUSTIN DISCOUNT BOOTS & COWBOY OUTFITTERS

**P.O. BOX 67
JUSTIN, TX 76247
800–677–BOOT
FAX: 817–648–3282**

Catalog: free
Pay: check, MO, MC, V
Sells: Western boots and clothing
Store: 101 W. Hwy. 156, Justin, TX; Monday to Saturday 9–6

This firm, although not owned by the Justin Boot Co., sells a number of the Justin boot lines in men's and women's styles at discounted prices. The footwear choices shown in the 32-page color catalog run from work boots and "ropers," comparatively plain, thick-soled boots with Western vamps that rise to mid-calf (about $90), to artful creations in exotic skins—ostrich, shark, lizard, and bull hide. "Lace-Rs" lace-up models are also offered. The catalog shows dozens of women's styles, including lizard Western boots, and "fashion" ropers in a range of colors. Children can get their Justin Juniors in red, navy, brown, and other colors, for under $60 a pair. Coordinating belts are available. Justin Discount Boots, in business since 1978, also sells Stetson Western hats, German silver buckles and belt tips, leather-care products, Wrangler shirts and jeans for men, women, and boys, and Comfy and Tempco goose down jackets. This is a great outfitter for you rodeo gals and guys and boot scooters.

Special Factors: Satisfaction is guaranteed; unworn, unscuffed, unaltered returns are accepted for exchange, refund, or credit; C.O.D. orders are accepted.

KNAPP BOOTS & SHOES

ONE KEUKA BUSINESS
  PARK, STE. 300
PENN YAN, NY 14527
800–869–9955
FAX: 800–276–1070

Catalog: free
Pay: check, MO, MC, V, AE, Discover
Sells: work shoes for men and women
Store: 20 locations in CA, MI, NY, NJ, GA, IL, ME, MA, NC, and AL; see catalog for addresses

 ¡Sí!

Knapp has been keeping America in shoes since 1921, and although only a few discounts top 30% (most are between 18% and 25%), there are shoes in the Knapp catalog that aren't easy to find at any savings. The 48-page color catalog shows work shoes and boots for men and women, from such manufacturers as Dexter, Dunham, Florsheim, Iron Age, and Soft Spots, as well as Knapp. The men's boot selection includes plain-toe boots, steel-toed boots, farm, lineman's, engineer's, hiking, casual, waterproof, rubber, knee, Western, and many more styles. The women's selection is smaller, but there are nice boot and shoe styles for work and casual wear. If you live near one of the Knapp stores, drop by and try them on; otherwise, anything you buy by mail that doesn't fit can be returned, unworn, for an exchange or refund.

Special Factors: Satisfaction is guaranteed; returns of unworn or defective shoes are accepted for exchange, refund, or credit.

RELATED PRODUCTS/COMPANIES

Army surplus shoes and boots • Mass. Army & Navy
Bicycle shoes • Performance Bicycle
Comfort footwear • Support Plus
Dance shoes • Dance Distributors
Deerskin moccasins • The Deerskin Place, Arctic Sheepskin
Designer shoes and boots for men and women • DesignerOutlet
Extra-long shoe horns • Amplestuff
Golf shoes • Golf Haus
Medical professional clogs and shoes • Tafford, Cotton Scrubs
Men's dress and business shoes • Huntington
Outdoor footwear and hiking boots • Sierra Trading, The Sportsman's Guide, Bailey's, WearGuard, Defender Industries

Running shoes • Sierra Trading
Snowshoes • The Sportsman's Guide
Soccer shoes • Acme Soccer, Soccer International
Tennis shoes • Holabird
Volleyball shoes • Spike Nashbar
Water shoes • The House
Work shoes and boots • Gohn Bros., WearGuard, Cahall's, Omaha Vaccine

CRAFTS AND HOBBIES

Materials, supplies, tools, and equipment for craftworkers and hobbyists

These firms can provide the materials for nearly any craft or hobby— miniatures, stenciling, basketry, clock making, stained glass, tole, decoy painting, jewelry making, doll making, music boxes, lamp making, candle making, woodworking, and much more. Some of these companies have been in business for generations and specialize in avocations that your local crafts shop may not even know exist. If you have a problem with a material or technique, most can provide assistance by phone. Ordering from a firm usually assures you a place on the mailing list, which means you'll probably receive the sales flyers, with savings of up to 70%. Save your catalogs, both for comparison shopping and as sources of technical information.

I got a big kick out of thumbing through some of these craft catalogs. If I had nothing but time on my hands, I would braid my own rugs, stencil my entire house, make heirloom Teddy bears and music boxes for my son, design and make all of the clocks in the house, throw my own pots and dishes, hand-dip my own candles to place in my hand-made candlesticks, paint my own picture frames, turn my windows into stained glass masterpieces, make a gorgeous quilt, fill my drawers with sachets, and generally have a house full of homemade crafty knick-knacks. Every couple of months I'd have to change all of the decor to conform with the right season or holiday. Fortunately for my child, I don't have this much time! But you're sure to agree that many of the general craft catalogs are as valuable for the ideas they give you as for the goods they sell.

The firms listed in the first part of this chapter are either general crafts suppliers with a very broad selection or firms specializing in one item or type of goods—feathers, parts for stuffed bears, stained glass supplies, basketry and caning, etc. For help in locating a particular item, see "Find It Fast," below. If you're looking for ceramics, pottery, or sculpture supplies, you'll find some here. But for companies that specialize in ceramics, see "Ceramics," page 142. If you do dried flower arrangements, potpourris, or other floral work, see "Floral and Potpourri," page 146. And if you're looking for fiber, fabric, quilting, knitting, or weaving supplies, or related products, see "Textile Arts," page 151. You'll also find useful and related products in the "Fine Arts and Graphics Arts Supplies" chapter.

If your craft or hobby involves the use of hazardous materials, find out about safety precautions; see the introduction to "Fine Arts and Graphic Arts Supplies" for more information. For additional sources selling wooden toy parts, see the listings in the "Tools, Hardware, Shop Machines" chapter. For lapidary equipment and findings, see the firms listed in "Jewelry and Gems."

FIND IT FAST

CANING, BASKETRY, GOURD CRAFT • The Caning Shop, Frank's Cane and Rush Supply

CLOCK-MAKING SUPPLIES • Creative Clock, National Artcraft, Turncraft Clocks

CRAFT KITS • The Artist's Club, The Caning Shop, Craft Resources, CR's Bear and Doll Supply, Frank's Cane and Rush Supply, Gramma's Graphics, Vanguard, Warner-Crivellaro Stained Glass

DOLL- AND BEAR-MAKING SUPPLIES • CR's Bear and Doll Supply, National Artcraft

FEATHERS • Gettinger

GENERAL CRAFTS SUPPLIES • Circle Craft, Craft Catalog, National Artcraft, Sunshine Discount Crafts, Vanguard

GLASS CRAFTS • Glass Crafters, Warner-Crivellaro Stained Glass

LEATHER CRAFT • Weaver Leather

"SUN-PRINTING" SUPPLIES • Gramma's Graphics

THERMOGRAPHY AND EMBOSSING • Think Ink

TOLE AND DECORATIVE PAINTING • The Artist's Club

WOOD-BURNING AND WOODWORKING • Hot Tools

THE ARTIST'S CLUB

P.O. BOX 8930
VANCOUVER, WA
  98668–8930
800–845–6507
FAX: 360–260–8877

Catalog: free
Pay: check, MO, MC, V, AE, Discover, JCB
Sells: tole and decorative painting supplies
Store: mail order only

 ¡Si!

The Artist's Club is devoted to artisans whose painting skills are applied to surfaces other than canvas, creating what might be called contemporary folk art—also known as tole. Half of the firm's business is done in books, and their predominance in the 88-page catalog reflects that. There are books on painting flowers, decorating in the Victorian modes, Christmas and other holiday themes, creating clocks, decorating with gardening themes, painting jewelry, angel motifs, working with crackle medium, fabric painting, Americana, and more. Many of the complete project kits employ cute country designs done on wood forms, including eggs, clock blanks (which accept "fit up" clock works), and useful household items—napkin holders, keepsake boxes, step stools, tissue boxes, quilt racks, lap desks, menu boards, etc. Also available are papier-mâché forms and boxes, lovely handblown glass Christmas ornaments awaiting decoration, unpainted canvas items, woodenware, and ready-to-paint tinware. The Club also offers a great selection of DecoArt, Delta, and Jo Sonja paints, and many brush choices and styles by Bette Byrd, Langnickel, Loew Cornell, Robert Simmons, and Royal Golden. Prices are discounted an average of 20%, and ten flyers throughout the year offer specials at 30% to 40% off.

Japanese readers, please note: The Artist's Club now puts out a Japanese-language catalog. The store in Japan is open Monday to Saturday 9–5; phone 045–510–4221, fax 045–510–4065.

Special Factors: Satisfaction is guaranteed; returns are accepted within 30 days for exchange, refund, or credit.

THE CANING SHOP

926 GILMAN ST., DEPT. WBM
BERKELEY, CA 94710–1494
800–544–3373
510–527–5010
FAX: 510–527–7718

Catalog: $1, refundable
Pay: check, MO, MC, V, Discover
Sells: seat-reweaving, gourd-crafting, and basketry supplies
Store: same address; Tuesday to Friday 10–6, Saturday 10–2
E-mail: wbm@caning.com
Online: http://www.caning.com

   ¡Si!

The Caning Shop stocks the materials, tools, and instructions you'll need to restore your woven-seat chairs—or weave a basket from scratch. The firm was established in 1969 by Jim Widess, one of the authors of *The Caner's Handbook*. His more recent interest in gourds, an ancient craft, has culminated in *The Complete Book of Gourd Craft* (co-authored with Ginger Summit). Other texts are available, as well as a line of gourd-related tools and supplies.

The 40-page catalog shows 15 kinds of prewoven cane webbing, which is used in modern and mass-produced seating. For older chairs, The Caning Shop offers hanks of cane in a full range of sizes, including binder cane, and also sells Danish seat cord, rawhide lacing, fiber rush, Hong Kong grass (sea grass), ash splint, Shaker tape, whole reed (for wicker), wicker braid, rattan, pressed fiber (imitation leather) seats, and tools. Basket makers should look here for kits, materials, hoops, and handles. And there are 20 pages of books and videos on both subjects. If you live in or near Berkeley, check the schedule of classes: "Pine Needle Basketry," "Gourd Masks," and "Miniature Rustic Furniture" are typical of the fascinating topics.

Canadian readers, please note: All payments must be in U.S. funds.

Special Factors: Satisfaction is guaranteed; C.O.D. orders are accepted.

CIRCLE CRAFT SUPPLY

P.O. BOX 3000, DEPT. WBMC
DOVER, FL 33527–3000
813–659–0992
FAX: 813–659–0017

Catalog: $1
Pay: check, MO, MC, V, Discover
Sells: general crafts supplies
Store: 13295 U.S. Hwy. 92, Dover, FL; Monday to Saturday 9–5

The 96-page catalog from Circle Craft Supply lists everything—from "abaca shapes" to zip-lock bags—that you'll need for scores of arts, crafts, and hobby projects. Circle Craft was founded in 1982 and sells at discounts that average 30%, and reach 40% on some items. There are tools and materials here for a wide range of crafts and pastimes—beading, jewelry making, basketry, flower making, quick-count plastic canvas crafts, doll making, lamp making, clock making, Christmas ornaments, macramé, chenille crafts, and much more.

Special Factors: Authorized returns are accepted within 10 days; C.O.D. orders are accepted.

CRAFT CATALOG

P.O. BOX 1069
REYNOLDSBURG, OH 43068
800–777–1442
FAX: 800–955–5915
FAX: 740–964–6212

Catalog: $2
Pay: check, MO, MC, V, Discover
Sells: general craft supplies
Store: 2087-K Rt. 256; Monday to Friday 10–9, Saturday till 6, Sunday noon to 5

Here's a catalog that will get you thinking about all the projects you wish you had time for. This would be a great resource for camp counselors, people who work with the elderly, and others looking for a one-stop craft supply source. The 188 pages are filled with supplies and equipment for virtually every kind of crafts discipline: woodworking, miniatures, clocks, dolls, sewing, tole, fabric painting and dyeing, wood antiquing, glass crafts, papier-mâché, box making and decorating, ornament making, stenciling, needlework, quilting, candle making, floral design, decoupage, jewelry making, potpourri, lamp making, rub-on art, and more. And there are scores of books peppered throughout on everything from window design to foil finishing. The catalog is well-indexed and -organized, and the prices here are excellent, about 20% to 50% less than normal retail. You'll find coupons for certain items that bring greater savings, and if your order is over $30, Craft Catalog will send you a free surprise gift of their choosing.

Special Factors: Free shipping on orders of $60 or more; no C.O.D. orders accepted; quantity discounts available.

CRAFT RESOURCES, INC.

Catalog: $1
Pay: check, MO, MC, V
Sells: craft kits for education, rehab use, etc.
Store: mail order only

BOX 828
FAIRFIELD, CT 06430–0828
203–259–4473

Craft Resources, founded in 1972, specializes in crafts projects in kit form and offers "the largest selection of latch-hook kits available for schools, hospitals, and other institutions." The 16-page color catalog shows kits for projects in latch hooking, stamped and counted cross-stitch, embroidery, crewel, wood crafts, rubber stamp art, and cut-and-copy clip art. The kits range from very basic designs for the beginner to more complex patterns, but a patient novice should be able to tackle any of these projects, with reasonable to impressive results. Craft Resources also sells yarn, embroidery floss, needlepoint and embroidery tools, knitting needles and crochet hooks, and embroidery hoops and frames. Therapists and instructors will find great values, and the kits provide an ideal way for the rest of us to "try out" a craft without investing much money.

Special Factors: Satisfaction is guaranteed; unused returns are accepted within 60 days; minimum order is $20 with credit cards.

CREATIVE CLOCK

BOX 565
357 HIGH STREET
HANSON, MA 02341
800–293–2856
781–293–2855
FAX: 781–293–0057

Catalog: $1, refundable
Pay: check, MO, MC, V
Sells: battery-operated quartz clock movements, dials, and clock-making tools and supplies
Store: mail order only

Creative Clock is a small, personable company whose main objective is to keep its customers happy. The company issues a 14-page catalog at wholesale prices that's for everybody—from do-it-yourself hobbyists and schools to clock and craft shops. The only requirement is a minimum order of $15. The prices at Creative Clock are already good, and if you buy in quantity, the discounts deepen. Additionally, Creative Clock says if you can find someone else selling the same item for less, they'll try to meet or beat that price. Here you'll find a variety of movements (mini-quartz, thermometer, high torque quartz clock, 24-hour—even specialty movements that operate in reverse!); clock hands and sweeps of all shapes and sizes in black, white, red, and brass; weather instruments; fit-ups; clock faces and painted clock dials; clock face components ranging from old-fashioned Arabic numerals to minimalist dots; and accessories and supplies galore—bits, hex nut drivers, magnets, saw-tooth picture hangers, corner ornaments, clock stands, polymer coating and brushes, dial templates, and much more.

Special Factors: Unconditional lifetime guarantee on all clock movements; C.O.D. orders add $4.75; some shipping restrictions apply; see catalog for details.

CR'S BEAR AND DOLL SUPPLY CATALOG

BOX 8–WM91
LELAND, IA 50453
515–567–3652
FAX: 515–567–3071

Catalog: $2 (see text)
Pay: check, MO, MC, V, Discover
Sells: doll- and bear-making supplies
Store: 109 5th Ave., Leland, IA; Monday to Friday 8:30–3:30
Online: http://www.crscraft.com

Never considered trying your hand at making a doll or Teddy bear? Then you haven't seen the catalog from CR's Bear and Doll Supply, also known as CR's Crafts. It's 148 pages of patterns, kits, parts, and the related miscellany that go into making some of the most adorable, collector-quality dolls and furry friends you'll find anywhere. If you don't fall in love with Tyler, Brewster Bear, or Cotton Tail, you're made of pretty stern stuff.

CR's Crafts sells everything you need to make any of hundreds of delightful creatures, including the fabric and fur, bodies and limbs, heads and faces, voice boxes and squeakers, armatures, wigs and hair, teeth, eyelashes, stuffing, music boxes, stands, books and manuals, and much more. Prices are competitive with other toy-making supply catalogs, and very low compared with finished products purchased elsewhere. CR's is also a good place to pick up parts and materials for repairing damaged dolls and stuffed toys, and a source for well-priced clothing, accessories, and furnishings for toys and dolls—with a large selection of items for popular 18" dolls. CR's Crafts has been in business since 1981, and if you're in Leland during showroom hours, you're invited to drop in and see the stock of 4,500-plus items.

Please note: The catalog for consumers costs $2 if sent within the U.S., $4 if sent to Canada, $7 if sent elsewhere outside the U.S.; the wholesale catalog costs $5 (U.S. funds only).

Special Factors: Orders shipped outside the contiguous 48 United States are sent via U.S. Parcel Post.

FRANK'S CANE AND RUSH SUPPLY

7252 HEIL AVE., DEPT. WBMC
HUNTINGTON BEACH, CA 92647
714–847–0707
FAX: 714–843–5645

Catalog: free
Pay: check, MO, MC, V, AE, Discover
Sells: seat-reweaving supplies, furniture, kits, books, natural fiber matting, grasses, tropical fencing, etc.
Store: same address; Monday to Friday 8–5
Online: http://www.franksupply.com

Frank's has been in business since 1975, and the firm's comprehensive 40-page catalog of seat replacement materials includes over a dozen weaves of cane webbing as well as strand and binding cane, spline, fiber and wire-fiber rush, fiber wicker, Danish cord, oak and ash splints, round and flat reed, and fiber and real reed braid (often used as trim on wicker furniture). Frank's also sells rattan, basketry materials, raffia, sea grass, "tissue flex" (for rag coil baskets), wood hoops and handles, brass hardware, upholstery tools and supplies, dowels and woodcrafts parts, and spindles and finials. The catalog also has six pages of books on seat reweaving, woodworking, basketry, and upholstery. Prices are competitive on these goods, and there are some bargains—Frank's sells the same decorative upholstery nails that cost $5.25 per hundred locally, for just $3.25. The furniture kits include hardwood Shaker-style arm and side chairs, rocking chairs, and stools. Prices are reasonable: $13.95 for a stool kit, $34.50 for a child's ladder-back chair kit, and $73 for an adult's chair. (The furniture comes with enough fiber rush or flat fiber—your choice—to complete the seat.)

Frank's now has a second, new, "tropical" catalog that includes such exotica as raincape thatching, raffia fabric, Chinese and Japanese fencing panels and gates, palm leaf matting, sugar palm fiber, and much more—to give your sun room or barbecue patio the feel of a tropical paradise. You can also buy bamboo poles of various types, diameters, and lengths, as well as the bamboo splitters you'll need to build with this amazing stuff. Frank's recommends that you order samples first (at 50 cents per sample plus shipping) if you're unsure of the product. Due to their exotic nature and handcraftedness, some of the materials in the tropical catalog are not inexpensive. But if you have your heart set on Pakistan grass or rattan poles with skin, it may be hard to comparison shop.

GETTINGER FEATHER CORP.

**16 W. 36TH ST.
NEW YORK, NY 10018
212–695–9470
FAX: 212–695–9471**

Price List and Samples: $2
Pay: bank check or MO
Sells: feathers
Store: same address (8th floor); Monday to Thursday 8:30–5:30, Friday 8:30–3

Gettinger has been serving New York City's milliners and craftspeople since 1915 with a marvelous stock of exotic and common feathers. Even if you're not a creative type, you can add cachet to a tired hat with a few guinea hen feathers, and Gettinger's feather boas are a dashing alternative to furs for gala occasions.

Ostrich, pheasant, guinea hen, turkey, and peacock feathers are available here, as well as dyed fluffs and strung natural feathers. Pheasant tail feathers, 6" to 8" long, cost $15 per 100; yard-long peacock feathers are priced at $25 per hundred; and pheasant hides cost $9 and up per skin. Feather boas are available, sold by the yard, as well as ostrich and marabou fans. And if you're reviving old feather pillows, you may be interested in the bedding feathers, which cost $10 to $45 per pound, depending on the quality (minimum 5 pounds).

Special Factors: Minimum order is $20.

GLASS CRAFTERS

**398 INTERSTATE CT.
SARASOTA, FL 34240
800–422–4552
FAX: 941–379–8827**

Catalog: free
Pay: check, MO, MC, V, AE, Discover
Sells: stained glass and other glass craft supplies
Store: mail order only
Online: http://www.glasscrafters.com

Whether you're new at stained glass or a professional craftsperson, Glass Crafters is a godsend. In business since 1975, Glass Crafters offers a wide selection of instructional videotapes, pattern books, projects, tools, supplies, and, of course, stained glass. Their 66-page catalog lists a unit price for most items, and a discount price even if you buy in small quantity, which usually nets a 15% savings or more. On many of the items, you can "mix and match" and still get the quantity discount. Bimonthly 8-page sales flyers offer specials that will save 30% to 50% on selected items (these flyers can be viewed on the company's website). But even the routine prices are better than most everyone else's—some as much as 50% better—this verified by a local glass artist who constantly bargain hunts for the best suppliers.

The catalog features all kinds of glass-crafting equipment and accessories: glass cutters, diamond glass grinders, specialty cutters, soldering tools, copper foil and tools, lead and brass came, glass mosaics, and more. There are sections devoted to lamp making, bead making, clock making, and box and frame making, with all the tools, parts, and hardware you'll need. You'll find cast figures, etching stencils, paints, markers, jewels, and a wide selection of patterns and pattern books for projects ranging from mosaics to quick-and-easy lamps to distinctive vases.

Special Factors: Satisfaction guaranteed. Returns within 14 days of receipt, not including glass, lead came, or videotapes, unless defective. Airmail postage is $2 for Canada, $4 for Europe, $5 for Asia/Pacific Rim.

GRAMMA'S GRAPHICS, INC.

**20 BIRLING GAP,
    DEPT. TWBM-P9
FAIRPORT, NY 14450–3916
716–223–4832, 4309
FAX: 716–223–4789**

Brochure: long SASE and $1 (see text)
Pay: check or MO
Sells: blueprint cloth-imaging materials and Sun Print diazo paper
Store: mail order only
E-mail: 70671.321@compuserve.com
Online: http://www.frontiernet.net/~bub-blink and http://www.grandloving.com

Can't draw, paint, or appliqué? You can still create original designs with Sun Prints, which "blueprint" an image on prepared fabric, creating a photographic representation in shades of blue (which can be toned to brown, charcoal, tan, amethyst, or green). The fabric must be untreated, 100% cotton or natural fiber, since the imaging solution will bead up and roll off synthetics, sizing, or resin. Gramma's Graphics sells all of the ingredients, from the imaging solution to the fabric, as well as instructions for creating the prints, assembling a pillow, and making an heirloom portrait quilt. The brochure suggests a number of subjects for projects—family portraits, wedding invitations, certificates and degrees, photographs—and other applications, including banners, dolls, place mats, tote bags, etc.

Gramma's Graphics also sells the Sun Silhouette dry-process paper "sun"-printing materials, in a notecard kit with 12 cards and envelopes, and the economical "classroom" kit, which has five times the amount of paper (although no envelopes) but costs less than $1 more at this writing. The paper is offered in blue, brown, or black, and all of the kits and components are unconditionally guaranteed. For the last word in Gramma-approved activities with the little ones, see her book, *Grandloving: Making Memories with Your Grandchildren*. It's packed with ideas for low-cost fun, as well as guides to favorite children's books, good programming, and other helpful resources.

Overseas readers, please note: The catalog costs $3 if sent outside the U.S.

Wholesale buyers, please note: The minimum order for wholesale pricing is 24 kits.

Special Factors: Satisfaction is guaranteed; quantity discounts are available.

HOT TOOLS

24 TIOGA WAY
P.O. BOX 615
MARBLEHEAD, MA 01945
781–631–7100
FAX: 781–631–8887

Flyers: free
Pay: check, MO, MC, V
Sells: wood-burning tools and accessories
Store: mail order only
Online: http://www.mmnewman.com

If you're a sail maker, kite smith, bird carver, or woodworking hobbyist, you're caught between a rock and a hard place when it comes to wood-burning tools and hot knives. You can go for the really cheap, hand-held junkers that are available in craft shops, inexpensive but not made for heavy-duty use; or you can spring for the second tier—the sophisticated, professional versions that will set you back several hundred dollars. M.M. Newman, the parent company of Hot Tools, has solved this problem by creating and manufacturing affordable, high-quality wood-burners and passing the savings directly to the consumer without a middleman. Unlike the hobby-shop models, the Hot Tool has a generous 64" cord and slim design, is lightweight, has a handle that stays cool, and features a heat shield, slide-on changeable tips, and heating elements under the tip. When you call or fax Hot Tools (or contact them through their website), they'll send you several pages of flyers with photographs and detailed descriptions of their products. The Hot Tool with standard tip is priced at $28.95. You'll also find #8 needle tips, reshapable blank tips, feather tips, multigroove tips, and buttons tips, as well as circle and round tips from $1/16"$ to $3/16"$—all for $4.75 each, except for the two multigroove tips ($10.44 each). The helpful text gives step-by-step instructions on how to carve realistic feathers and do other fine work.

Other offerings include a heavy-duty wood-burner that heats up to 1,050 degrees and sells for $44.95; a hot knife tip, blank tip, and standard tip for the heavy-duty model are $9.39 each. You'll also find the Hot Knife, intended for cutting and melting synthetic materials such as sailcloth, spinnaker cloth, indoor/outdoor carpeting, etc. It's $44.95, and its three tips (Hot Knife, blank, or standard) are $9.39 each. You'll find wood-burner stands, the Dial-Temp precision temperature controller, stencil makers, a Lacquer Burn-In Knife ($29.95), library marking tools, metallic marking foils, and other items here. These tools are good values, great quality, and will last a long time. Wholesale prices are offered on purchases of 12 or more items; resale number is required for wholesale.

Special Factors: Hot Tools will gladly replace any defective product; C.O.D. orders are accepted.

NATIONAL ARTCRAFT CO.

7996 DARROW RD.
TWINSBURG, OH 44087
800–526–7419
FAX: 800–292–4916

Catalogs: $3 for "Main"; $2 for "Doll"; $1 for others (see text); $5 for any combination without "Doll"
Pay: check, MO, MC, V, Discover
Sells: musical movements, lighting and electrical parts, doll-making, ceramics/sculpture, clock-making supplies, and general craft supplies
Store: mail order only
E-mail: nationalartcraft@worldnet.att.net
Online: http://www.nationalartcraft.com

If you're a hobbyist or craftsperson, or you have your own craft business, get yourself a three-ring binder, 'cause National Artcraft has a main catalog as well as five satellite catalogs designed to bind for easy reference again and again. National Artcraft is a wonderful find if you love to make dolls, lamps, clocks, music boxes or carousels, ceramic and pottery items, and just about anything else. You can buy any item singly at a good price, but the prices are really great—up to 50% less— when you buy in larger quantity. Price breaks vary for each item, and unit prices are listed under each quantity, so you can calculate the discounts. National Artcraft sells "wholesale direct"—they ship directly from their warehouse—but anyone can buy here as long as you meet the $25 minimum.

The 112-page "Main" catalog has an eclectic selection that includes all types of craft accessories: embroidered angel wings, beveled glass mirrors, ballpoint desk pen sets (you make the base), flatware parts (you design the handles), lotion pumps, teapot handles, oil lamp and candle accessories, doll components, decorative egg stands, fountain pumps, jewelry parts, gold leaf, blank china ready to decorate, brushes of all kinds, special scissors for greeting card edges, and much, much more. If you specialize in ceramics, pottery, or sculpture, request the comprehensive 64-page "Ceramic & Pottery" catalog. There you'll find supplies and equipment (including kilns) for almost any related medium, at great prices. The "Music & Sound" catalog is 32 pages of wind-up and electric musical movements in over 400 melodies and sound effects (voices, animal noises, laughing ghosts, etc.) with parts that rotate, spin, seesaw, fly, throw, twirl, rock, nod, and wave. You'll find all the components here to create an heirloom music maker for that special loved one. If you're wired into lamps and lights, you'll find what you need in the 32-page "Electrical & Lighting" catalog's collection of components and accessories. The 12-page "Clocks" catalog serves clock makers with a good selection of movements, clock components, and accessories. Finally, the "Doll-making Supplies" catalog is 48 color pages of eyes, hair, teeth, and other body parts, as well as head and body molds, armatures, and frames, footwear, hosiery, eyewear, hats, clothes, parasols, movements, tools, and supplies for making dolls of every kind. There are also doll-making books here. You can order off the website, but you won't find the full inventory there.

Special Factors: Satisfaction guaranteed; returns made within 30 days will be fully refunded; quantity discounts available; C.O.D. orders add $4.75; shipping within 24 hours.

SUNSHINE DISCOUNT CRAFTS

P.O. BOX 301, DEPT. WBM
LARGO, FL 33779–0301
813–538–2878
FAX: 813–531–2739

Catalog: $2, $4 for Canada (see text)
Pay: check, MO, MC, V, AE, Discover
Sells: general crafts and hobby supplies
Store: mail order only
Online: http://www.sunshinecrafts.com

Leafing through Sunshine Craft's 176-page, closely printed catalog gave me the feeling of being in a giant warehouse, where one might find buckets of plastic animal eyes, barrels of colorful beads, aisles of paints, and cases of polymer clays and mosaic tiles. In fact, this catalog boasts over 14,000 products for the craftsperson and hobbyist, and you won't be disappointed by the prices—25% to 35% below regular list, with better prices on some items when you order in small quantity. There are supplies here for doll makers, clock makers, jewelry crafters, home decorators, glass artists, woodworkers, tole fanatics, and more. There's also plenty here for the kids—rubber stamps, memory scrapbook kits, beading, glitter, feathers, barrettes, baskets, and on and on. Whether you're making a stuffed animal, creating Easter ornaments, or decorating your own bridal headpiece, you'll find what you need here.

Express catalogs are $5, refundable with your first order. International customers: Catalogs are $10.

Wholesale orders: Please inquire about price lists and policies.

Special Factors: See catalog for returns policy. Orders under $20 require an additional $2.50. C.O.D. orders: cash only, and add $5. Quantity discounts are available on some items.

THINK INK

7526 OLYMPIC VIEW DR.,
   SUITE E-W
EDMONDS, WA
   98026–5556
425–778–1935
FAX: 425–776–2997

Catalog: $2, refundable with first order
Pay: check, MO, MC, V, Discover
Sells: thermography/embossing powders, GOCCO printers, supplies, etc.
Store: same address; Monday to Friday 9:30–5:30
Online: http://www.thinkink.com

Think Ink features Print GOCCO's printing press silk-screen devices and embossing powders, which provide crafters with a great way to get custom prints inexpensively. Use clip-art designs, or if you can draw, GOC-COs will enable you to custom-color and print flyers, bulletins, cards, tote bags, tee shirts, and nearly anything else made of paper, fabric, wood, or leather. There are two Print GOCCO presses, the B6 model (with a 4" x 5³⁄₄" image area) for $99, and the B5 (with a 6" x 9" image area) for $360. Both models work by creating a master of your design that can be inked like a silk screen and printed.

The GOCCO Printer inks are offered in a wide range of colors and types, including 40cc tubes of textile ink, metallics, fluorescents, pastels, pearlescents, and basics, as well as enamel inks for nonporous surfaces. One application of the ink yields 80 to 100 prints. If you send $2 (refundable with a purchase), Think Ink will send you GOCCO-printed samples, a price list, and a brochure on the Print GOCCO printers. Rubber-stamp artists should check the prices they're currently paying for embossing powders. Think Ink's powders do the same job, but are sold at bulk discount prices—as much as 60% to 70% less, compared with the prices charged by rubber-stamp supply firms. The selection of 120 powders includes many unique powders: Luscious Lips, Rose Gold, Ultra Chocolate, and Black Confetti, to name a few.

Among the other goods offered here are *The New GOCCO Guide*, a 245-page guide to your GOCCO printer with ideas and projects; printer supplies such as bulbs and filters; fabric stampers; tote bag blanks; glue pens; assorted foil sheets, including gold; and videos. Wholesale customers, please note: Send a copy of your business license to receive the wholesale terms and pricing.

Special Factors: C.O.D. orders are accepted.

TURNCRAFT CLOCKS, INC.

P.O. BOX 100–WBM
MOUND, MN 55364–0100
800–544–1711
FAX: 612–471–8579

Catalog: $2
Pay: check, MO, MC, V, Discover
Sells: clock plans and movements
Store: 4310 Shoreline Dr., Spring Park, MN;
Monday to Friday 8–5

Clock makers and woodworkers will enjoy Turncraft's full-color 32-page catalog of clock plans, movements, and hardware components. Turncraft is celebrating nearly a quarter of a century of supplying home hobbyists with materials at savings of up to 30%.

You'll find over 150 clock projects in the catalog, as well as clock dials, time rings, bezels, mini-quartz movements, pendulum movements, chime and strike movements, clock hands, knobs and hinges, hangers, latches, brass decorations, weight shells, and quartz fit-ups. Paint and stains, glue, drill bits, plywood, walnut letters, numbers, and symbols are offered, making this a good source for both clock makers and woodworkers.

Special Factors: Satisfaction is guaranteed; minimum order is $15 with credit cards.

VANGUARD CRAFTS

DEPT. WMC, P.O. BOX
340170
BROOKLYN, NY
11234–0003
718–377–5188
FAX: 718–692–0056

Catalog: $1, refundable
Pay: check, MO, MC, V, Discover
Sells: crafts, kits, and materials
Store: 1081 E. 48th St., Brooklyn, NY; Monday to Saturday 10–5

Vanguard has been selling fun since 1959 through a 72-page color catalog of crafts kits and projects. Vanguard is geared to educators and others buying for classroom use, but it's a great source for rainy-day projects at home.

You'll find kits and supplies for hundreds of crafts, including shrink art, foil pictures, grapevine wreaths, mosaic tiling, basic woodworking crafts, suncatchers, Styrofoam crafts, leather working, fabric flowers, decoupage, copper enameling, pompom crafts, stenciling, string art, crafts-sticks projects, Indian crafts, clothespin dolls, calligraphy, rug hooking, and other diversions. Vanguard also features a line of kits inspired by the "spirit of the Southwest"—Santa Fe picture frames, "Pueblo" pottery, concho accessories, dream catchers, worry dolls, bead looms, and more. Basic art supplies and tools—adhesives, scissors, paper, paint, pastels, hammers, craft knives, etc.—are also available. The prices are very reasonable, and the large selection makes it easy to meet the $25 minimum order.

Special Factors: Minimum order is $25.

WARNER-CRIVELLARO STAINED GLASS SUPPLIES, INC.

1855 WEAVERSVILLE RD.
ALLENTOWN, PA 18103
800–523–4242
FAX: 800–523–5012

Catalog: $2 (see text)
Pay: check, MO, MC, V, AE, Discover
Sells: stained-glass tools and supplies
Store: same address; Monday to Saturday 9–5 ET
Online: http://www.warner-criv.com

Warner-Crivellaro serves the old art of stained glass with an 80-page catalog of glass sheets, bevels, glass-cutting tools and machines, grinders, foil and foiling equipment, strips and spools of lead came, soldering tools and irons, patinas, flux, etching acid, finishing compound, cutting oil, and several pages of books and manuals. If you're new to the craft, see the starter kits, which begin at under $46 and include everything you need to begin a project. Once you've mastered a suncatcher or one of the beautiful bevel ornaments, you may be ready to tackle a lampshade.

Warner-Crivellaro also publishes a 200-plus-page catalog (free with your first $50 order) of materials and supplies for more complex projects. But even the general catalog ($2) includes nearly four dozen lamp bases, most with a bronze-look or antique brass finish. The bases are fully wired and harped, and begin at under $9 for minis. Since reproduction lamps made in these styles usually fetch much more when they're sold in stores, consider saving by buying the base here and the shade elsewhere. The catalog shows other lamp and shade parts, including harps, vase caps, spiders, brass channel and bead edging, and two pages of solid bronze reproduction Tiffany lamp bases, which run from $140 to $775. Even the red oak frames sold here, which are designed to encase stained glass panels, can be employed by nonartisans to frame and finish other works of a similar thickness.

Please note: Orders sent to Alaska, Canada, and overseas must be paid in U.S. dollars or by credit card.

Special Factors: Authorized returns are accepted; minimum order is $25; C.O.D. orders are accepted.

WEAVER LEATHER

P.O. BOX 68
MT. HOPE, OH 44660
800–932–8371
330–674–1782
FAX: 800–693–2837
FAX: 330–674–0330

Catalog: free
Pay: check, MO, MC, V
Sells: leather and leather-working and saddlery supplies, parts, and tools
Store: mail order only; phone hours Monday to Friday 7:30–7 ET

Weaver Leather is a supplier to professional leather workers and saddlery shops, but if you can meet the $50 minimum order, you can buy here, too—and take advantage of Weaver's great stock, selection, and prices.

The 109-page color catalog opens with a range of leather—apron split, bellies, bridle, premium English bridle, chrome oil tanned, deer, garment, harness, lace, latigo, strap, tooling, molding, nubuck, patent, rawhide, saddle skirting, shearlings, shoulders, sole bends, suede, upholstery, and veg chrome retanned. The well-designed "Leather Shopper" describes the texture, thickness, and applications of each type, and refers you to the relevant section of the catalog. There's lots of information for the leather worker here, including a visual guide and helpful facts on selecting leather and minimizing waste, and if you're not sure about what you want, you can get assistance from customer service. There are quantity price breaks, and goods are sold by the pound, side, or foot, depending on the product. You'll find a range of leather-working tools and equipment here, too, many made by Weaver, from hand tools for cutting and stamping to heavy equipment for production work (Adler sewing machines and shoe-repair equipment, strap cutters, riveters, edge finishers, etc.). Thread, glue, dye, oil, conditioner, and cleaners are also offered, both Fiebing's and Weaver's own line.

You'll also find a line of Montana silver hardware, such as belt buckles, saddle trim, and conchos.

Much of the catalog is devoted to saddlery and harness making. Here are wooden and rawhide stirrups, harness and saddle hardware (bits, chain, buckles, snaps, loops, harness and saddle ornaments), and leather and nylon billets and cinch straps. If you'd like to learn to repair or build saddles, you'll find help in *Saddlemaking,* a 110-minute video that teaches you how to build, finish, and repair saddles.

The pricing here is competitive on single items, but even better if you can buy in quantity. Weaver makes it easy to save, too, by allowing you to mix and match leather, hardware, and stirrups to meet the minimums. Some products are offered in case lots, and these count toward the volume discounts as well.

Special Factors: Satisfaction is guaranteed; authorized returns are accepted for exchange, refund, or credit; minimum order is $50 ($15 service charge for orders below minimum); C.O.D. orders are accepted.

RELATED PRODUCTS/COMPANIES

For pottery and ceramic supplies and equipment, see "Ceramics," page 142
For floral and herb crafts, see "Floral and Potpourri," page 146
For textile arts and crafts (weaving, quilting, sewing, knitting, etc.), see "Textile Arts," page 151

Books on country crafts • Storey Communications
Candle-making supplies • Brushy Mountain Bee Farm, Ott's Discount
Doll making • Home-Sew, Newark Dressmaker Supply, Oppenheim's
Feathers and trim • Manny's Millinery
General craft supplies • Axner Pottery, Ceramic Supply of NY & NJ, Oppenheim's, Ott's Discount, Pearl Paint, Texas Art
Jewelry craft • House of Onyx, Eloxite, Hong Kong Lapidaries
Kite-building • BFK Sports
Leather craft • Leather Unlimited
Model-building tools, supplies, plans • Micro-Mark, Poor Man's Catalog
New and surplus tools and machine/gizmo parts • H & R Company
Soap-making supplies • Brushy Mountain Bee Farm
Stencils • Stencil House of N.H.
U-Build power tool plans • Poor Man's Catalog
Unfinished wooden boxes • Weston Bowl Mill
Woodworking books • Woodworkers' Discount Books
Woodworking tools, hardware, and supplies • Ott's Discount, Tools on Sale, Northern Hydraulics, Tool Crib of the North, Econ-Abrasives, Camelot Enterprises, Woodworker's Supply

Ceramics

Materials, supplies, tools, and equipment for pottery, sculpture, and other ceramic crafts

Most people think of mugs, pots, and bowls when they think of ceramics. But people who love to work with clay also make lamps, clocks, jewelry, mirrors, ornaments, sculptures, candlesticks—the list is as endless as the craftsperson's imagination. You'll find ceramics supplies, tools, and even heavy equipment such as kilns carried by the companies in this section.

AFTOSA

1034 OHIO AVE.
RICHMOND, CA 94804
800–231–0397
510–233–0334
FAX: 510–233–3569

Catalog: free
Pay: check, MO, MC, V, AE, Discover
Sells: pottery accessories and craft supplies
Store: mail order only
E-mail: aftosa@worldnet.att.net
Online: http://www.aftosa.com

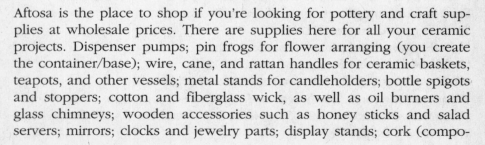

Aftosa is the place to shop if you're looking for pottery and craft supplies at wholesale prices. There are supplies here for all your ceramic projects. Dispenser pumps; pin frogs for flower arranging (you create the container/base); wire, cane, and rattan handles for ceramic baskets, teapots, and other vessels; metal stands for candleholders; bottle spigots and stoppers; cotton and fiberglass wick, as well as oil burners and glass chimneys; wooden accessories such as honey sticks and salad servers; mirrors; clocks and jewelry parts; display stands; cork (composition, bark-top, and natural); metal and glass shades; wooden trivet boxes; and, of course, potter's tools and supplies can all be found here at prices that are 35% to 50% less than retail. There's no minimum, but if your order is under $50, there's a $5 surcharge. Shipping is free!

Special Factors: Orders to Hawaii, Alaska, and Canada add 15%; other international orders, see catalog for details. Returns are subject to a 10% restock fee; see catalog for complete returns policy.

AXNER POTTERY SUPPLY

◼◼◼◼◼◼◼◼

P.O. BOX 621484
OVIEDO, FL 32762–1484
800–843–7057
407–365–2600
FAX: 407–365–5573

Catalog: free
Pay: check, MO, MC, V
Sells: pottery supplies, books, and videos
Warehouse/Showroom: 804-A Eyrie Dr., Oviedo, FL; Monday to Friday 9–5, Thursday till 7, Saturday 9–2
E-mail: axner@attmail.com
Online: http://www.axner.com

 ¡Si! ★

A professional potter recommended Axner Pottery Supply as a good source with reasonable prices. Axner's goods average about 20% less that what you'd find in a ceramic supply shop—if you're lucky enough to live near one. The 192-page newsprint catalog has a lot of explanatory text alongside the photographs of products, which makes it a good resource. Quantity price breaks are included for many items, and suggested retail prices versus Axner's prices are also listed on some, but not all, products. Here you'll find equipment, tools, and supplies for making tile, jewelry, pots and dishes, lamps, clocks, and more. You'll find the big equipment here—kilns, wheels, and mixers, for example— as well as clay and glazes of all types. (There's an 8-page color insert for the glazes.) Axner claims to have the largest supply of pottery supplies and equipment "in the known universe," so just about any tool, finishing supply, or other pottery-related item you seek will be here. Be sure to leaf through the pottery/ceramics books and videos section, for which Axner is renowned.

Special Factors: Satisfaction guaranteed; 30-day return policy; wholesale orders accepted; no C.O.D.'s.

BAILEY CERAMIC SUPPLY

P.O. BOX 1577
KINGSTON, NY 12402
800–431–6067
914–339–3721
FAX: 914–339–5530

Catalog: free
Pay: check, MO, MC, V
Sells: professional ceramic supplies and equipment
Showroom: 62 Ten Broeck Ave., Kingston, NY; Monday to Friday 9–12, 3–4:30; call beforehand. Mail-order phone hours: Monday to Friday 8:30–5:30 ET

Jim Bailey and his wife Anne Shattuck Bailey are dedicated ceramists. Since 1984, Bailey has been supplying professional potters with great products that are up to 25% less than retail when you buy in quantity, and major name-brand pottery equipment at "the lowest prices in the USA." Bailey also manufactures many of its own products, such as extruders, slab rollers and wheels, and kilns, and sells them at factory-direct prices. The 188-page black-and-white catalog offers chemicals, clays, and glazes; small tools and accessories; hand-building equipment; wheels and wheel accessories; mixing equipment; kilns; safety, production, storage, and spray equipment; packing materials; display and accessory items; lamp and jewelry accessories; an extensive video and book library; and much more.

Special Factors: Satisfaction guaranteed on every order; five professional potters on staff to answer questions; most orders shipped within 48 hours.

CERAMIC SUPPLY OF NEW YORK & NEW JERSEY, INC.

7 RTE. 46 W.
LODI, NJ 07644
973–340–3005
FAX: 973–340–0089

Catalog: $4
Pay: check, MO, MC, V
Sells: sculpture, pottery, glazing, and crafts supplies and equipment
Store: same address; Monday to Friday 9–5, Thursday 9–9
E-mail: cersupnynj@aol.com

   ¡Si!

Ceramic Supply of New York & New Jersey serves both of its name states with free delivery (in many areas) on orders of $125 or more. The company has been doing business since 1981 and offers good values on glazes, brushes, and a wide range of lightweight ceramics supplies that can be shipped worldwide at nominal expense. The 212-page catalog devotes most of its space to ceramics supplies and equipment: gas and electric kilns (including some that run on household current), raku and fiber kilns, glazes, resists, mediums, brushes, airbrushing tools, slip-casting equipment, potters' wheels, armatures, grinders, and related goods, with a new section on ceramic bisqueware. The manufacturers include Alpine, Amaco, Brent, Kemper, Kimple, North Star, Shimpo, and Skutt, among others. The catalog includes color charts of glazes, underglazes, and other finishes by Duncan and Mayco, bisque dinnerware and assorted pieces, and dozens of types of clay, from white Grolleg porcelain to water-based to "economy" clay made of odds and ends of other clays. And there are lots of other modeling materials—Sculpey, plasters, and wax—as well.

Even if you're not a potter or sculptor, the catalog may interest you for the music box parts and movements in scores of tunes, lights and accessories for ceramic Christmas trees, hard-to-find lamp parts, clock movements and parts, jewelry findings, studio furniture, or safety equipment. Don't overlook the reference section, which features books on sculpture, ceramics, art hazards, and related topics, and videotapes and filmstrips.

Special Factors: Returns are accepted within 10 days (a restocking fee may be charged).

RELATED PRODUCTS/COMPANIES

Books and videotapes on ceramics and pottery, ceramics tools • The Potters Shop
Clay and kilns • Ott's Discount, Texas Art Supply

Floral and Potpourri

Supplies for live, dried, silk, and satin flower arrangements and craft, wreaths, potpourris, sachets, etc.

"Send me dead flowers by the mail"—when Mick Jagger sang these lyrics, maybe he was thinking to spend some of his off time making cute, fanciful wreaths to cheer up the Rolling Stones tour bus decor. If so, the companies in this section could have availed him of anything his heart desired. Whether you're decorating an entire banquet hall with flowers plus all the elaborate trimmings, making a personal, herb-filled "dream pillow" for your beloved, or designing a bridal headpiece, you'll find what you need here—at up to 50% less than you'll pay elsewhere.

ATLANTIC SPICE CO.

P.O. BOX 205
NORTH TRURO, MA 02652
800–316–7965
508–487–6100
FAX: 508–487–2550

Catalog with Potpourri Recipes: free
Pay: check, MO, MC, V, Discover
Sells: ingredients for potpourri and spices, teas, and herbs
Store: same address; Monday to Friday 9–5, Saturday 10–2
Online: http://www.atlanticspice.com

If potpourri, pomanders, and wreaths are your specialty, Atlantic Spice Co. can supply you with many of the botanicals and fragrance oils you need, at savings of 50% and more. Atlantic Spice also sells culinary herbs and spices (the smallest size is one pound), organic botanicals, and even tea, dehydrated vegetables, seeds for sprouting, baking products (powdered lemon juice, bee pollen, vanilla extract, etc.), and shelled seeds and nuts.

The potpourri ingredients run from whole Jamaican allspice to yellow yarrow flowers, and the botanicals begin with alfalfa and end with yucca root. Looking for a source for the freeze-dried fruits that are used so extensively in wall decorations and wreaths? They're here—apple slices, artichokes, orange peel and slices, pieces of peach, and pomegranates—as well as whole nutmeg, bay leaves, three-inch chili peppers, cinnamon sticks, pine cones, hibiscus pods, oak moss, rosebuds, and other natural materials. The fragrance oils are offered in 1-ounce bottles, the botanicals in 1-pound units. Rounding out the map-size, one-page catalog are related supplies and equipment—sachet bags, potpourri jars, self-seal tea bags—and a number of recipes for jar and simmering potpourri, sachets, and pomanders. There are no illustrations, but the listings are flagged to note items that shouldn't be used in food or drink, and others that are especially well suited for "wreaths, centerpieces, topiaries & garlands." Atlantic's very low prices drop 15% on orders of 25 or more pounds of the same item (based on the 1-pound rate), and shipping is free on orders over $200 (subject to some restrictions).

Special Factors: Satisfaction is guaranteed; quantity discounts are available; minimum order is $30.

BILLIANN'S FLORAL AND BRIDAL SUPPLY

P.O. BOX 35
ATLANTA, IN 46031
765–292–6388

Catalog: $4 (see text)
Pay: check, MO, MC, V
Sells: floral and bridal supplies
Store: 125 W. Main, Atlanta, IN; Tuesday, Thursday, Friday 9–5, Wednesday 1–8, Saturday by appointment

Here's a great source of silk and satin flowers, bridal accessories, and floral supplies at wholesale prices—about 30% or more below what you'd pay in a retail store. Billiann's sells satin and silk flowers that are so lifelike in the photos, I had to call and verify that they weren't real. Roses and rosebuds, carnations, lilies, daisies, orchids, spider mums, calla lilies, gardenias, and other romantic delights are all available in one of 39 colors, or they can be custom-dyed to match your gown.

There is also "greenery" here: ferns and ivy of many kinds, plants and bushes among them, in addition to assembled cascades and nosegays with greenery and lace.

Besides flowers and greenery, Billiann's sells jeweled and flowered bridal wreaths, caplets, headbands, unadorned hats, fans, wristlets, baskets, and parasols, as well as all the floral supplies and accessories to decorate your own wedding: pearl strands, sequined flowers, laces, wire door wreath hangers, Styrofoam cones and wreaths, floral adhesive, tape, wire, wood wire picks, and more. If you're saving money on your wedding by doing the flowers and decorations yourself, be sure to check out Billiann's collection of wedding and floral-design books. There's no minimum order on merchandise, and the price of the catalog is refundable with your purchase.

Special Factors: No minimum order; C.O.D. orders add $4.50.

FLORAL SUPPLY SYNDICATE

P.O. BOX 1305
CAMARILLO, CA 93011
800–347–9994
FAX: 805–389–1232

Catalog: upon request
Pay: business check, MO, MC, V, AE, Discover
Sells: florist supplies, decorative packaging, and events accessories
Store: 16 locations in UT, CA, NV, AZ, WA, MO; call for locations and hours
E-mail: camarillo@fss.com
Online: http://www.fss.com

Floral Supply Syndicate sells wholesale hard goods to the florist, gift store, and events-planning industries. If you have a resale card for any type of business you're in, large or small, get this catalog. There are so many great products here for any number of uses, and you'll save up to 50% on these products. The bargains are endless; for example, a dozen $7^1/_2$" glass vases come out to about $1.25 each, which is great if you're setting up a Bar Mitzvah or wedding reception on a tight budget. The 150-page color catalog has everything you'll need if you have a flower craft business, decorate shop windows, do catering, are planning a wedding or holiday event, do craft fairs, or run a small business where decorative packaging is important.

The well-organized catalog begins with satin ribbon in 46 dazzling colors and ends with vases and flower stands. Ribbons, bows, roping, netting, and lace of every description; every kind of basket imaginable;

gift wrap; small decorating novelties in holiday themes, musical themes, Teddy bears, angels, and more; bells, ornaments, and beads; sprays and swags from flowers to fruit; candles and candleholders; balloons; floral moss, silk and dried flowers, preserved greens, wheat, etc.; wedding decorations and accessories; vases galore—this is just a sampling of what's available. Be sure to check out Floral Supply's selection of design and other books, in subjects that include flower drying, floral arrangements, and wedding floral designs. The entire inventory is now online, and you can view the products and order directly off the website.

Special Factors: Satisfaction guaranteed; customers must have a resale card.

TOM THUMB
WORKSHOPS

14100 LANKFORD HWY.
P.O. BOX 357-WBMC
MAPPSVILLE, VA 23407
757–824–3507
FAX: 757–824–4465

Price List: free with a long SASE
Pay: check, MO, MC, V
Sells: potpourri, spices, herbs, oils, etc.
Store: same address (Rt. 13); Monday to Friday 9–5

Although they're both called potpourri, there's a world of difference between an artificially scented pile of dried things and dyed wood shavings, and a blend of flowers, herbs, spices, essential oils, and natural fixatives. Tom Thumb sells the ingredients and directions for making the real thing, from premixed blends such as "English Country Garden" and "Lavender Tranquillity" to a list of hundreds of herbs, spices, dried flowers, cones, peels, and pods. The eight-page price list also shows a range of botanicals perfect for wreaths and arrangements—artemisia, eucalyptus, dried pomegranates, wheat, and lotus pods among them. Dozens of essential oils and blends are available in $\frac{1}{8}$-ounce vials for $3.25, and the blended potpourri costs $7.50 for four ounces, or $19.95 per pound. These prices are 20% to 45% below those charged elsewhere for "house blends" of potpourri, and you can deduct 25% from the cost of the goods (with some exceptions) if your order is over $100. Tom Thumb, in business since 1975, also sells materials and equipment for drying flowers, as well as pressed flowers; spice jars and other containers, gifts; kits, patterns and how-tos; crafting accessories; and a number of guides on subjects such as perfumery, papermaking, and marbleizing.

Wholesale buyers, please request the bulk price list and include a long, stamped, self-addressed envelope.

Special Factors: Satisfaction is guaranteed; returns are accepted within 30 days; minimum order is $15, $30 with credit cards.

RELATED PRODUCTS/COMPANIES

Flower-drying equipment • *Johnny's Selected Seeds*
Wreaths, pomanders, sachets, essential oils, herbs, etc. • *Grandma's Spice Shop, San Francisco Herb, Caprilands Herb Farm, Taylor's Cutaways and Stuff*

Textile Arts

Supplies and equipment for sewing, knitting, weaving, quilting, needlework, and other crafts using textiles

Sewing it yourself—clothing, home accessories, and crafts—not only saves you money but also gives you a custom job with the fabric and details you want. The sources here can help you find the right tools and materials for your project.

There are lots of companies in other chapters of the book that sell related supplies and equipment. Be sure to check out "Related Products/Companies" at the end of the company listings in this section.

If you do needlework and use DMC floss, you'll want the DMC Embroidery Floss Card in your files. This reference includes samples of each DMC floss color and a guide to which colors are available in pearl cotton in sizes 3, 5, and 8. (Most discount sources carry DMC floss, but not all offer color guides.) The American Needlewoman sells the DMC Floss Card; request the free catalog from The American Needlewoman, P.O. Box 6472–WBMC, Fort Worth, TX 76115.

FIND IT FAST

BATTING, PILLOW INSERTS, FIBERFILL • Buffalo Batt & Felt, Connecting Threads, Monterey, Oppenheim's
CUSTOM-MADE ZIPPERS • The Button Shop, A. Feibusch
DOLL-MAKING SUPPLIES • The Fiber Studio, Home-Sew, Newark Dressmaker Supply, Oppenheim's, Taylor's Cutaways and Stuff
DRAPERY HARDWARE • Atlanta Thread

FABRIC • Connecting Threads, Fashion Fabrics, Oppenheim's, Taylor's Cutaways and Stuff, Thai Silks, Utex Trading
FABRIC DYES • Dharma Trading
FAKE FUR • Monterey, Oppenheim's, Taylor's Cutaways and Stuff
LOOMS • The Fiber Studio, Great Northern Weaving, Webs
QUILTING PATTERNS • Connecting Threads
RUG-MAKING SUPPLIES • Great Northern Weaving
SEWING AND PRESSING MACHINES, SERGERS, DRY-CLEANING EQUIPMENT • Atlanta Thread, The Button Shop, Solo Slide Fasteners, Thread Discount Sales
SEWING NOTIONS AND TOOLS • Atlanta Thread, The Button Shop, A. Feibusch, Home-Sew, Newark Dressmaker Supply, Solo Slide Fasteners, Thread Discount Sales
UNDYED FABRIC AND CLOTHING BLANKS FOR DYEING • Dharma Trading, Thai Silks
YARNS • The Fiber Studio, Smiley's Yarns, Bonnie Triola, Webs

---

ATLANTA THREAD & SUPPLY

695 RED OAK RD., DEPT.
  WBMC 99
STOCKBRIDGE, GA 30281
800–847–1001
770–389–9115
FAX: 800–298–0403

Catalog: $1
Pay: check, MO, MC, V, AE, Discover
Sells: sewing tools, notions, and pressing equipment
Store: mail order only

Atlanta Thread, a division of a major distributor of sewing equipment, has been doing business since 1948 and boasts the lowest prices around on Gingher shears, Gosling drapery tapes, Kirsch drapery hardware, YKK zippers, and many other goods. This is where even professionals go to find quality supplies and equipment: coned thread, zippers and parts, custom-tailoring linings and pads, buttons, Singer's sewing guides and professional tailoring manuals, cords, crinoline stiffening bands, fringe, hook-and-loop tape, professional pressing equipment—tables, boards, and irons—and commercial-quality sewing machines, sergers, and parts. The 64-page catalog is illustrated, but if you need more information on a product, call and ask.

Special Factors: Satisfaction is guaranteed; returns are accepted within 30 days for exchange, refund, or credit; C.O.D. orders are accepted.

BUFFALO BATT & FELT CORP.

3307 WALDEN AVE., DEPT. WBMC
DEPEW, NY 14043
716–683–4100, EXT. 130
FAX: 716–683–8928

Brochure and Samples: $1, refundable
Pay: check, MO, MC, V
Sells: fiberfill, quilt batts, and pillow inserts
Store: mail order only

Buffalo Batt's "Super Fluff" polyester stuffing is so springy and resilient, the snowy-white samples nearly bounce out of the brochure. The firm has been in business since 1913 and sells this craft and upholstery stuffing by the case at savings of 40% or more on regular retail prices.

Super Fluff is manufactured in rolls 27" wide by 20 yards long and is the ideal filler for upholstery and crafts in which support and a down-like feel are desired. In addition to having high loft and nonallergenic properties, Super Fluff is machine washable and dryable, mildew-resistant, and easy to sew. Buffalo Batt also sells Super Fluff in 12-ounce and 2-pound bags, bulk rolls, pillow inserts (from 14" square to 30" square, 12" by 16" and 14" by 18" rectangles, and neckrolls), and both "traditional" and 2-inch-thick "comforter-style" quilt batts. Ultra Fluff, a slick, premium fiberfill that gives a softer hand, was recently introduced; it's also available in 10-ounce bags and in bulk. Another new product, "thermobonded" quilt batt, is soft, dense, and flame-retardant; it's available on 20-yard rolls. Buffalo Batt also sells "Soft Heart" Quallofil pillow inserts, in sizes from 14" to 26" square, as well as the popular rectangles, and in bulk rolls.

The only negative is the minimum order of any two cases, which may be more than most single projects require. But it's a manageable amount for a home-based crafts business, quilting circle, cooperative, or major decorating project—or store the surplus for future use, or share with crafty friends!

Please note: Orders are shipped via UPS within the continental United States only.

Special Factors: Quantity discounts are available; minimum order is any two cases; C.O.D. orders are accepted.

THE BUTTON SHOP

P.O. BOX 1065-HM
OAK PARK, IL 60304
TEL/FAX: 708-795-1234

Catalog: free
Pay: check, MO, MC, V
Sells: buttons and sewing supplies
Store: 7023 Roosevelt Rd., Berwyn, IL; Monday to Friday 9–4, Saturday 10–2
E-mail: basicsew@aol.com

The Button Shop, founded in 1900, stocks closures of all kinds, as well as trims, sewing machine parts, scissors, and other sewing tools and notions at savings of up to 50% on list prices or regular retail. Several pages of the 18-page catalog are devoted to buttons—anonymous white shirt buttons, clear waistband buttons, tiny buttons for doll clothes, classic four-hole coat and suit buttons, gilt heraldic buttons for blazers, designs for dressy clothing, Navy peacoat buttons, braided leather buttons for tweeds, and dozens of others, including baseball gloves and other novelty designs for children's clothing. If you want to custom-cover buttons with your own fabric, you'll find Maxant and Prym kits, as well as make-your-own fabric belt and buckle materials, gripper snaps and grommet sets, hooks and eyes of all types, zippers (including odd sizes to 108"), and Velcro by the inch and by the yard.

The Button Shop sells all kinds of rickrack, bias tape, cording, white and black elastic (from 1/8" to 3"), replacement jacket cuffs, elbow patches, trouser pockets, shoulder pads, and other notions and supplies. Thread in cotton, cotton-covered polyester, and polyester is offered from major manufacturers.

The Button Shop's comparatively deep inventory of sewing machine supplies and parts includes needles, presser feet, bobbins, bobbin cases, needle plates, motors, foot controls, lightbulbs, and belts. The catalog descriptions are brief, and line drawings are the only illustrations. If you're not sure an item is the right one and need more information, call or write before ordering. You may also send a fabric swatch for the best color match if you're buying trim, thread, or buttons, and The Button Shop custom-makes zippers in lengths up to 120".

Special Factors: Returns are accepted within 30 days for exchange, refund, or credit; minimum order is $5, $10 with credit cards; C.O.D. orders are accepted.

CONNECTING THREADS

P.O. BOX 8940
VANCOUVER, WA
  98668–8940
800–574–6454
FAX: 360–260–8877

Catalog: free
Pay: check, MO, MC, V, AE, Discover, JCB
Sells: quilting patterns, materials, and supplies
Store: mail order only

   ¡Si!

Connecting Threads answers the needs of "the busy quilter" with 64 pages of pattern and reference books, fabrics and batts, project plans, cutting and sewing tools, stencils, and equipment. If you haven't worked on a quilt in years, you may be surprised by the complexity and sophistication of the designs: Seminole patchwork, Amish miniatures, Sashiko (Japanese quilting), "photo" keepsake quilts, reverse appliqué, and Jewish quilting may be new to you. In addition to books, Connecting Threads offers stencils for both hand and machine quilting (top-stitching through the batt) and lots of other tools and sewing helpers. There are also books on related crafts—fabric painting, ribbon work, dolls, fabric ornaments, and "art" clothing. Savings average 25%, and both retail and discount prices are listed.

Special Factors: Satisfaction is guaranteed; returns are accepted for exchange, refund, or credit.

DHARMA TRADING CO.

P.O. BOX 150916
SAN RAFAEL, CA
  94915–0916
415–456–7657
FAX: 415–456–8747

Catalog: free
Pay: check, MO, MC, V, Discover
Sells: textile craft supplies and clothing "blanks"
Store: 1604 Fourth St., San Rafael, CA; Monday to Saturday 10–6
E-mail: catalog@dharmatrading.com
Online: http://www.dharmatrading.com

    ¡Si! ★

The "whole earth" movement may have peaked in 1969, the year this firm was founded, but Dharma Trading has survived—and prospered. The firm sells tools and materials for the textile arts—dyes, paints, resists, fabrics, and clothing "blanks"—and declares, "We are the source for the tie-dye dyes used by most tie-dyers." The informative 120-page catalog provides helpful tips on the features of the dyes and paints, application techniques and suggested fabrics, and even metric conversion charts and a shrinkage "estimator." Prices are good, running up to 50% off list or comparable retail.

Coloring agents by top manufacturers are offered, as well as color remover, soda ash, urea, Synthrapol, gutta serti, and other resists. The tools include bottles and droppers for dye mixing and application, textile pens, brushes (flat, foam, sumi), and steamers for setting dyes. Nearly half of Dharma Trading's catalog is devoted to silk and cotton clothing blanks—everything from silk fan, baseball cap, and earring blanks to cotton skirts, jackets, sweats, baby rompers, and more are shown in the current catalog. A list of cotton, rayon, and silk fabrics that have yielded good results with dyeing and painting is included in the catalog; samples (silk or cotton/rayon) are available for 25 cents each. Selected books dealing with fabric design, painting, screening, stamping, direct dyeing, batiking, tie-dyeing, and other techniques are also sold.

Special Factors: Quantity discounts are available; institutional accounts are available; C.O.D. orders are accepted.

FASHION FABRICS CLUB

10490 BAUR BLVD.
ST. LOUIS, MO 63132
800–468–0602
FAX: 314–993–5802

Membership: $10 (see text)
Pay: check, MO, MC, V
Sells: dress fabric
Store: 10512 Baur Blvd., St. Louis, MO; Tuesday to Saturday 10–5, Sunday 12–5

Fashion Fabrics Club speaks to the needs of home sewers who make their own clothing but don't have the time to comb fabric stores for the perfect selection. Each month, Fashion Fabrics Club sends its members a brochure with over a dozen coordinated fabric swatches, discount coupons, and other offers. The fabrics are chosen to allow you to create coordinated outfits; a recent mailing featured selections from Curio, Endeavor, Jade Jacquard, Kelly, and others at $4.99 to $9.99 a yard. Care recommendations and "usual" selling prices are noted for each selection, and the savings are significant, often 50% or more less per yard than you'd pay elsewhere.

Write to Fashion Fabrics Club to buy an introductory membership for $4.95; a $5 gift certificate will be included in your first mailing. All purchases are covered by the Club's pledge of satisfaction, and you'll receive discount coupons with each order you place, entitling you to savings on future orders.

Please note: Membership is available only to individuals living in the United States or its possessions.

Special Factors: Satisfaction is guaranteed; returns are accepted for exchange, refund, or credit; minimum order is $5; shipping and handling is $6.95 per order.

A. FEIBUSCH

27 ALLEN ST.
NEW YORK, NY 10002
212–226–3964
FAX: 212–226–5844

Information: price quote
Pay: check or MO
Sells: zippers, thread, notions, and garment supplies
Store: same address; Monday to Friday 9:30–5, Sunday 10–5

Feibusch has been helping New Yorkers zip up since 1941, handling requests from the mundane to the exotic. Zippers of every conceivable size, color, and type are sold here—from minuscule dolls' zippers to heavy-duty closures for tents, luggage, and similar applications. If your requirements aren't met by the existing stock, Feibusch can have your zipper made to order. Talon and YKK zippers are available, and Feibusch also carries all-cotton and polyester thread in a full range of colors. There is no catalog, so write with your requirements. Describe what you're looking for or send a sample, specifying length desired, nylon or metal teeth, open or closed end, and other details. Enclose a scrap of fabric, if possible, to assure a good color match. Be sure to include a self-addressed, stamped envelope with your correspondence if you want to receive a reply. If you'd prefer to call with general information questions, note that Feibusch has salespeople who speak Chinese, French, and German, as well as Spanish!

Special Factors: Price quote by letter.

THE FIBER STUDIO

9 FOSTER HILL RD., DEPT. WBMC

P.O. BOX 637

HENNIKER, NH 03242

603–428–7830

Book and Equipment Catalog: $1 (see text)
Pay: check, MO, MC, V
Sells: knitting, spinning, and weaving equipment and supplies, doll hair fiber, skins, etc.
Store: same address; Tuesday to Saturday 10–4, Sunday by chance
E-mail: fiberstudio@conknet.com
Online: http://www.conknet.com/fiberstudio

The Fiber Studio has been serving the needs of knitters, spinners, weavers, and doll makers since 1975 with a well-chosen line of tools and supplies, and great prices on yarn. The catalog lists looms, including children's, spinning equipment, and accessories by Ashford, Harrisville Designs, Leclerc, Louet, Norwood, Schacht, and others. The prices on these aren't discounted, but shipping is free on some models (see "Special Factors," below). Natural dyes, mordants, and a good selection of spinning fibers—from mohair tops to silk roving—are offered at competitive prices. (The sample card of current spinning fibers costs $4.) And scores of texts on knitting, spinning, and weaving are available.

The bargains here are on yarns, which are sold in two ways: through the stock shown in the yarn sample set ($5), and through the yarn close-outs. The stock yarns include rug wools, natural yarns, Emu Guernsey wool, Norwegian wool, cotton, silk, mercerized cotton, and more, priced up to 35% less at The Fiber Studio than at other sources. Quantity discounts on these yarns run from 10% on orders over $100 to 20% on orders over $200. If you can get to Henniker, you have a treat: The shop offers an extensive selection of beads from around the world, made of semiprecious stones, wood, bone, glass, horn, clay, and other materials, as well as unusual findings. The Fiber Studio also sells Tibetan lambskins, of special interest to doll makers. These items aren't listed in the catalog, but you can make inquiries and order by phone.

Canadian readers, please note: Only U.S. funds are accepted.

Special Factors: Specify the spinning fibers ($4) or yarns ($5) sample set; shipping is not charged on most models of Harrisville Design, Leclerc, and Schacht looms; quantity discounts are available; minimum order is $15 with credit cards; C.O.D. orders are accepted.

GREAT NORTHERN WEAVING

451 EAST D. AVE.

P.O. BOX 462

KALAMAZOO, MI

49004–0462

800–370–7235

616–341–9752

FAX: 616–341–9525

Catalog and Samples: $2.50
Pay: check, MO, MC, V
Sells: rug-making supplies and tools
Store: same address; Monday to Friday 9–4

The homey crafts of weaving, crocheting, and braiding rugs are served at Great Northern Weaving, which has been in business since 1985 and prices most items competitively—rags and filler cost up to 50% less here than elsewhere.

The 12-page catalog lists tools and materials for rug weaving and rug braiding. Braid-Aids, Braidkins, Braid-Klamps, Fraser rag cutters, reed and heddle hooks, shuttles, and warping tools are all available. The materials include coned cotton warp (8/4 ply) in over two dozen colors, and the same gauge cotton/poly warp in colors and "natural"; all-cotton rug filler in 15 shades; 16-ply rug roping; new cotton "rags" on rolls; color loopers; and loopers in bulk. Great Northern Weaving is introducing a two-harness folding rug loom, designed by Kessineck Looms. You don't have to commit to full-scale rug weaving, though—see the small frame looms, pot-holder looms, and even "inch worm kits," recommended as child pleasers. Reference books are also available.

Canadian readers, please note: Payment must be made in U.S. funds.

Special Factors: Handling fee on orders under $40; C.O.D. orders are accepted.

HOME-SEW

P.O. BOX 4099, DEPT.
  WM9
BETHLEHEM, PA
  18018–0099
610–867–3833
FAX: 610–867–9717

Catalog: 50 cents
Pay: check, MO, MC, V, Discover
Sells: sewing and crafts supplies and notions
Store: mail order only

Home-Sew, which has been in business since 1960, offers savings of up to 70% on assorted laces and trims, as well as a wide range of sewing and crafts supplies. Home-Sew's 32-page catalog is well organized and easy to use, with clear photographs of the trims and notions.

In addition to scores of laces (Cluny, Venice, nylon, poly, eyelet, etc.), Home-Sew offers elastic, satin ribbon, rickrack, tape, lace doilies, felt packages, and appliqués. Specialty thread—for general sewing, overlock machines, carpets, and quilting—is available on cones and on spools, including metallic threads. There are zippers, snaps, hooks and eyes, buttons, Velcro dots, belts and buckles, pins, needles, and scissors, as well as floss, adhesives, spangles, beads, animal and doll parts, a 10" porcelain baby doll, interfacings, and related items. You'll also find handy gadgets such as "Turn-It-Around," for turning tubes inside out, and needle threaders. If you're making your own curtains or slipcovers, check the prices on shirring and pleater tape, tasseled and moss fringe, cording, and related goods. Home-Sew makes it easy to see the trims before you buy—just join the Sample Club (50 cents, order through the catalog) and you'll receive three mailings of lace, trim, ribbon, and elastics samples per year.

Wholesale customers, deduct 25% on all orders over $100.

Special Factors: Satisfaction is guaranteed; returns are accepted for exchange, refund, or credit; quantity discounts are available; shipping is not charged on orders over $50 that are paid by check or money order.

MONTEREY INCORPORATED

1725 E. DELAVAN DR.
JANESVILLE, WI 53547
800–432–9959
608–754–8309
FAX: 608–757–3312

Price List: free with SASE
Pay: check, MO, MC, V
Sells: fake-fur fabric
Store: same address; Monday to Friday
8–4:30; Saturday 8–12 (April to September),
8–4:30 (October to March)

Monterey Inc. has been manufacturing deep-pile fur fabrics for a quarter of a century and sells them at prices up to 50% below the usual retail. The brochure describes the fiber content of the different "fun" furs and lists the available colors, pile height, and ounces per yard. In addition to basic plush, "kurl," and shag, you'll find patterns and colors simulating the pelts of bear, seal, calf, tiger, and cheetah. Prices are given per cut yard, per yard on the roll (there are 15 to 20 yards per roll), and for quantity orders. Cut yards run from between about $11 and $19 per yard, and prices drop from there. You can buy the fabric in remnants (the mill will choose the fur type) for $4.50 a pound, or $4 per pound by the carton (35 to 40 pounds). Stuffing for craft projects is available as well, at 85 cents a pound and up.

Please note: A set of samples is offered for $5 ($10 to addresses in Canada), a worthwhile investment unless you're buying only remnants.

Special Factors: Minimum yardage order is one yard; minimum order is $25, $100 on orders shipped C.O.D.

NEWARK DRESSMAKER SUPPLY INC.

6473 RUCH RD. DEPT.
WMJ
P.O. BOX 20730
LEHIGH, PA 18002–0730
610–837–7500
800–736–6783
FAX: 610–837–9115

Catalog: free
Pay: check, MO, MC, V, Discover
Sells: sewing notions, crafts, and needlework supplies
Store: mail order only

Searching for specialty patterns, smocking guides, bear joints, alphabet beads, silk thread, or toy squeakers? Such requests are routine at Newark Dressmaker Supply, which offers trims, appliqués, scissors, piping, ribbon (including wire-edged), lace, braid, twill, zippers, sewing gadgets, bridal supplies, knitting supplies, name tapes and woven labels, interfacing, buttons, thread, floss, bias tape, rhinestones, wreath-decorating materials, supplies for making dolls and stuffed bears, fabric, upholstery materials, books and manuals, and much more. "Sew Little" patterns for infants' and children's clothing are stocked, as well as doll patterns to fit Barbie dolls, dolls from the American Girl Doll Collection, and the 18" Goetz dolls.

Newark Dressmaker has been in business since 1950 and is a great mail-order source for home sewers, since it offers a huge array of notions and other supplies, from glass-headed pins to yard goods, through the 60-page catalog. The prices are very competitive—up to 50% below regular retail on some items—and that doesn't count the 10% discount you get if your order totals $50 or more. There are also coupons in the back of the catalog that you can clip out and use for additional savings on some items.

Wholesale customers, request the wholesale order form with the catalog; the minimum order is $125, and no specials, bonuses, or other offers apply to wholesale sales.

Canadian readers, please note: Only U.S. funds are accepted.

Special Factors: Satisfaction is guaranteed.

OPPENHEIM'S

P.O. BOX 29
120 E. MAIN ST.
NORTH MANCHESTER, IN
  46962–0029
800–461–6728
219–982–6848
FAX: 219–982–6557

Catalog: free
Pay: check, MO, MC, V, Discover
Sells: yard goods, notions, crafts materials
Store: mail order only

The venerable Oppenheim's has been in business since 1875 and publishes a 64-page newsprint catalog of all kinds of crafts staples and specials. The firm's strength is fabrics, sold in cutaways, remnants, and by-the-yard cuts. The catalog includes collections of calico, broadcloth, rib knits, Pendleton woolens, fun fur, denim, and other fabrics, in remnants and cutaways (sold by the lot or the pound). The yard goods will appeal to anyone looking for great prices on fabrics for crafts, plain clothing, and home decorating: shirting, sheeting, chambray, flannel, pillow ticking, cheesecloth, cotton tablecloth check, bridal satin, terry cloth, Rembrandt rug canvas and needlepoint canvas, ripstop nylon, and stretch fabric for exercisewear are all offered in the lists of "staple" fabrics. Some of the fabrics are irregular; Oppenheim's will send you swatches (include a SASE with your request), and returns are accepted.

The catalog also includes an extensive roundup of notions—laces, ribbon, facings, cording, buckles, hook-and-loop tape, and more. Sewing tools, from seam rippers to sleeve boards, are featured, and there are lots of pillow tops and stuffed toy kits, appliqués, preprinted quilt tops, pillow forms, patterns for Christmas stockings, aprons, and much more. If you're long on ideas and imagination but short on funds, Oppenheim's will be a welcome addition to your list of sources. By the way, Oppenheim's catalog features six pages of reader classified in the back if there's something you're wanting to buy or sell at a great price.

Special Factors: Satisfaction is guaranteed; returns (exceptions noted in catalog) are accepted within 10 days for exchange, refund, or credit.

SMILEY'S YARNS

92–06 JAMAICA AVE.,
  DEPT. W
WOODHAVEN, NY 11421
718–847–2185 (MAIL
  ORDER)
718–849–9873 (STORE)

Brochure: free with SASE
Pay: check or MO
Sells: yarn for hand knitting and crocheting
Store: same address; Monday to Saturday
10–5:30 (closed Wednesdays)
Online: http://www.smileysyarns.com

Smiley's, where "Yarn Bargains Are Our Business," has been selling first-quality yarns at a discount since 1935. Each month, Smiley's offers a different "Yarn of the Month" selection at discounts from 30% to as much as 80% off list prices. Among the manufacturers represented are Bernat, Emu, Grignasco, Hayfield, Lion Brand, Patons, Phildar, Pingouin, Plymouth, Reynolds, Schachenmayr, Schaffhauser, Unger, and Wendy. You can call or write for a price quote on goods by these firms, or inquire about knitting and crocheting yarns by other manufacturers—they may be available. For samples of the current "Yarn of the Month" offering, send a long, stamped, self-addressed envelope. Requests without envelopes can't be honored.

Wholesale customers, inquire for terms.

Special Factors: Price quote by phone or letter with SASE; quantity discounts are available; store is closed Wednesday and Sunday.

SOLO SLIDE FASTENERS, INC.

8 SPRING BROOK RD.,
  DEPT. WB
P.O. BOX 378
FOXBOROUGH, MA 02035
800–343–9670
FAX: 800–547–4775

Catalog: free
Pay: check, MO, MC, V, AE, Discover
Sells: dressmaking and dry-cleaning equipment, sewing and alteration supplies
Store: mail or phone order only
E-mail: solozip@tiac.net

Solo Slide is a family-run business that's been supplying dressmakers, dry cleaners, tailors, and other clothing-care professionals with tools and equipment since 1954. Among the offerings in the firm's 66-page catalog are a number of items found in the "hard-to-find" sections of notions catalogs, at prices as much as 50% less.

Solo offers an extensive selection of zippers, zipper parts (slides and stops), straight pins in several sizes, snaps, hooks and eyes, machine and hand needles, buttons (dress, suit, metal, leather, etc.), thread on cones and spools, knit collars and cuffs for jackets, shoulder pads, elbow patches, belting, elastic, and other notions. Fine-quality linings are stocked, as well as pocket material. There are scissors in the most useful models, pressing boards for sleeves and other specialty tasks, pressing pads and other hams and rolls, and professional irons, pressers, and steamers—all from top-name manufacturers. The catalog also shows commercial/industrial sewing machines (blind stitch and lockstitch) and overlock machines. And don't miss the stain removers (including one for Magic Marker) that can save you trips to the dry cleaner.

Please note: Solo Slide has Korean-speaking sales reps on staff.

Special Factors: Authorized, unused returns (except custom-ordered or cut goods) are accepted within 30 days for credit; minimum order is $30; C.O.D. orders are accepted.

TAYLOR'S CUTAWAYS AND STUFF

2802 E. WASHINGTON ST.,
DEPT. WBMC–99
URBANA, IL 61802–4660

Catalog: $1
Pay: check, MO, MC, V
Sells: cutaways and patterns
Store: mail order only
E-mail: tcutaway@sprynet.com
Online:
http://www.home.sprynet.com/sprynet/
tcutaway

"Cutaways" are what's left when the pieces of a garment are cut from material. These scraps, sometimes running to a yard long, are perfect for doll clothing, piecework, quilting, and other crafts. Taylor's Cutaways, in business since 1977, offers bundles of polyesters, cottons, blends, calicos, and other assortments, as well as silk, satin, velvet, velour, felt, and fake fur cutaways. The catalog (available for $1) lists a wide variety of patterns and project designs for such items as draft stoppers, puppets, dolls, Teddy bears, pigs, ducks, and other animals. (Teddy bears seem to be a specialty; there are precut Teddies, mini sachet Teddies, velvet Teddies, Teddies made of cotton flannel, and

Teddy bear adoption certificates sold in packs of 15.) Crocheting patterns for toys and novelties, iron-on transfer patterns, button and trim assortments, and toy eyes and joints are available.

The completely unskilled will appreciate Taylor's for the potpourri, already blended and scented, and "Potpourri Magic" fixative, essential oils, and satin squares for making sachets. Prices of these and most of the other goods average 50% below comparable retail, and savings can reach as high as 75%. This seems an especially good source for anyone who makes sachets and potpourris, dolls, toys, pieced quilts, and bazaar items.

On the practical side, Taylor's sells "tea baglets," little fiber bags you fill with the tea of your choice and heat-seal with a household iron. (This is a great way to take a favorite loose tea with you when you travel.)

Special Factors: Quantity discounts are available.

THAI SILKS

252 STATE ST.
LOS ALTOS, CA 94022
650–948–8611
FAX: 650–948–3426

Brochure: free
Pay: check, MO, MC, V, AE
Sells: silk and other all-natural fabrics, silk scarves, silk clothing, etc.
Store: same address; Monday to Saturday 9–5:30

Beautiful, comfortable silk is also affordable at Thai Silks, where the home sewer, decorator, and artist can save up to 50% on yardage and piece goods (compared to average retail prices). The large selection includes habotai, or China silk, silk crepe, charmeuse, chiffon, noil, shantung silk, heavy- and suit-weight silk, a silk/wool blend, and more—in many variant weaves, textures, patterns, colors, etc. Thai Silks also sells rayon/silk velvet, 100% rayon, 100% cotton, 100% hemp, and 100% ramie at good prices. A complete set of samples is available for $30, and you'll get $10 off your order if placed within 30 days of receiving the samples, or you can return the samples at a later date for a $10 refund. Hemmed white and colored silk scarves and neckties for painting and batiking; Chinese embroidered handkerchiefs; silk kimonos, pants, sarongs, vests, capes, and other garments are also available, as well as small silk bags in three styles.

If you're a serious sewer or textile artist, consider joining Thai Silk's "Silk Fabric Club." For $20 a year you'll receive four swatched mailings of new silks, and samples of close-outs. Thai Silks has been in business since 1964 and can answer your questions about fabric suitability for dyeing and specific uses.

Wholesale customers, the minimum order is 15 to 17 yards (if fabric); $100 in goods. Request the "wholesale" price list.

Special Factors: Satisfaction is guaranteed; samples are available (details are given in the brochure); authorized returns are accepted; minimum order is ½ yard of fabric; C.O.D. orders are accepted.

THREAD DISCOUNT SALES

**P.O. BOX 571597, DEPT. W
TARZANA, CA 91357
TEL/FAX: 818–348–2969**

Price Sheets: free with long SASE
Pay: check, MO, MC, V, AE, Discover
Sells: coned thread, sewing machines, and sergers
Store: mail order only; phone hours are Monday to Saturday 10–6

This firm sells machines and supplies for the serious sewer—sewing machines, sergers, overlock machines, and "coned" thread—at savings of up to 50% on list prices. Thread Discount Sales, in business since 1962, offers a batch of photocopied sheets as its catalog; they feature White and Singer sewing and overlock machines at an average 50% discount on list or original prices.

Among the coned thread available is all-purpose polyester thread, 6,000 yards of overlock at under $3 a cone in black and white ($3.49 in any of the 200 colors), and "super rayon" embroidery thread in 1,000-yard cones, in 500 colors, for $2.89 each. Most of the thread is offered in a full range of colors, which are listed by name and number (color charts are available for $1.50). In addition, Thread Discount Sales carries novelty metallics in a variety of colors, two sizes of nylon filament thread for "invisible" work, and "woolly" nylon in 200 colors at $3.49, regularly $5.99.

Please note: A shipping surcharge is added to orders sent to Alaska, Hawaii, Puerto Rico, and Canada.

Special Factors: Minimum order is 6 cones of thread (on thread orders; colors may be mixed).

BONNIE TRIOLA YARNS

343 E. GORE RD.
ERIE, PA 16509–3723
814–825–7821
FAX: 814–824–5418

Catalog and Samples: $10 (see text)
Pay: check, MO, MC, V
Sells: yarns
Store: mail order only
E-mail: btriola@moose.erie.net
Online: http://moose.erie.net/~btriola

For those of you who love to use knitting machines, looms, and even embroidery machines, you should know about Bonnie Triola. She tests and works with all of her yarns and will happily answer any of your questions regarding their use. For $10 you receive a year's worth of mailings with yarn samples, price lists with special close-out sales, and newsletters full of helpful hints, resources, seminar notices, and new product reports and reviews. On top of Bonnie's already discounted prices, many of her yarns are eligible for quantity discounts where you can save up to 25% additionally. She also has a wholesale catalog (no minimums) for qualified buyers, with deep discounts on everything. She carries her own lines of natural and synthetic fibers, overruns from New York designers, and yarns by Tamm, Millor, and Sunray. (Samples and color cards on these latter three are not included with the $10 catalog; inquire for prices.) Her metallic yarns are popular with people who use embroidery machines, but almost any textile artist or craftsperson will find great choices and buys here. Most of Bonnie's yarns are sold as full cones only, and many of the markdowns are close to 75% less than retail.

Special Factors: C.O.D. accepted; net 30 billing for qualified wholesalers (request the wholesale price list).

UTEX TRADING ENTERPRISES

826 PINE AVE.
NIAGARA FALLS, NY 14301
TEL/FAX: 716–282–8211

Price List: free with SASE
Pay: check, MO, MC, V
Sells: imported silk fabric
Store: same address; by appointment only
E-mail: utextrade@aol.com

 (SEE TEXT)

Utex was established in 1980 and offers textiles to artists, decorators, designers, and home sewers—over 200 weights of silk fabrics in different colors, weaves, and widths. The enormous inventory includes silk shantung, pongee, taffeta, tussah, crepe de chine, brocade, twill, habotai, peau de soie, lamé, and suiting. Most of the fabrics are 100% silk, and the price list includes a guide that recommends appropriate fabrics for specific purposes. Scarves and ties, silk thread, yarns, and dyes for silk-painting are also stocked.

Canadian readers, please note: Utex's Canadian address is 111 Peter St., Suite 212, Toronto, Ontario, M5V 2H1; the phone number is 416–596–7565.

Special Factors: Volume discounts are available; C.O.D. orders are accepted.

WEBS

P.O. BOX 147, DEPT.
WBMC
NORTHAMPTON, MA
01061–0147
413–584–2225
FAX: 413–584–1603

Price Lists and Samples: $2 (see text)
Pay: check, MO, MC, V, Discover
Sells: yarns, and spinning and weaving equipment and books
Store: Service Center Rd. (half a mile off I–91), Northampton, MA; Monday to Saturday 10–5:30
E-mail: webs@yarn.com
Online: http://www.yarn.com

Knitters and weavers of all types—production, hand, and machine—will find inspiration in the yarns from Webs, which has been selling natural-fiber yarn for up to 80% below the original prices since 1974. Webs' mailings offer conventional and novelty yarns of cotton, wool, linen, silk, rayon, and blends, sold in bags, coned, wound off, sometimes in balls, and in packs. (The packs come in assortments of 25, 50, and 100 pounds, at outstandingly low prices.)

Each set of samples is folded into a descriptive price sheet, which notes special considerations concerning supply, suitability for knitting or weaving, gauge, length per unit (e.g., yards per ball, cone, or pound), and prices and minimums. There are usually great buys, such as mohair in choice colors, ribbon yarn in several hues, fine-quality cotton yarns in different weights and fashion colors, and novelty yarns. The stock features Webs' own private label yarns, including mohair, rayon chenille, cottons, wools, silks, and linens, in solid and variegated colors, as well as mill-ends, discontinued lines, and yarn overstock from well-known manufacturers. Savings can be boosted with an extra 20% discount if your yarn order totals $60 or more, or 25% on orders over $120. (Take note of the exceptions, marked "no further discount" or "NFD" in the price sheets.) Looms, spinning wheels, and drum carders are available at nondiscounted prices, although shipping is free on these items (which can be worth $25 to even $100, depending on where you live and the weight of the article). Webs also sells books. Webs' website is friendly and easy to read if you want more information on current specials and inventory.

Please note: State your craft—hand knitter, machine knitter, or weaver —when sending $2 for the price list and samples.

Special Factors: Shipping is not charged on looms, spinning wheels, or drum carders; quantity discounts are available; authorized returns are accepted within 30 days (a 15% restocking fee may be charged); minimum order is $20 with credit cards.

RELATED PRODUCTS/COMPANIES

All-cotton woven fabric for upholstery, linens, draperies, etc. • Home-spun Fabrics
Blank textile goods for dyeing and decorating • Clothcrafters, Texas Art Supply
Decorator fabric, trim • Silk Surplus, Fabric Center, Hancock's of Paducah, Shama Imports
Doll-making supplies • CR's Bear and Doll, National Artcraft
Fabric • Gohn Bros., Campmor
Feathers and trim • Manny's Millinery, Gettinger Feather
Needlepoint/embroidery supplies and kits • Craft Resources, Sewin' in Vermont
Quilting supplies • Hancock's of Paducah, Gohn Bros.

Sewing machines • Sewin' in Vermont, Sewing Machine Super Store, Discount Appliance Centers

Sewing notions • Gohn Bros., Sewin' in Vermont, Sewing Machine Super Store

Silk-screening/fabric painting supplies • Jerry's Artarama, Ott's Discount Art Supply, Pearl Paint, Texas Art Supply

"Sun-printing supplies" • Gramma's Graphics

Thermography/embossing supplies • Think Ink

FINE ARTS AND GRAPHIC ARTS SUPPLIES

Materials and equipment for fine artists and graphic designers

You don't have to starve to be an artist, but the cost of good tools and supplies almost guarantees it—unless you buy them discount. Small art stores seldom knock more than 10% off list prices, except on quantity purchases. But mail-order discounters routinely offer savings of at least twice that. The firms listed here sell supplies and materials for fine arts and some crafts: pigments, paper, brushes, canvas, frames, stretchers, pads, studio furniture, vehicles and solvents, silk-screening supplies, carving tools, and much more.

Concern about the safety of art materials led to the Art Materials Labeling Act of 1988, and Congress has also asked the Consumer Products Safety Commission to create standards for the art materials industry, and banned the use of hazardous materials by children in the sixth grade or younger. This is important legislation, since the list of substances found in widely used materials has included toluene, asbestos, chloroform, xylene, n-hexane, carbolic acid, trichlorethylene, lead, and benzene, to note just a few. Even with reformulation and warnings, art materials can still pose some hazards.

Good studio protocol can minimize much of the exposure:

- Select the least toxic and hazardous products available.
- If your work creates dust or fumes, use a quality, OSHA-approved respirator suitable to the task—there are masks to filter organic vapors, ammonia, asbestos, toxic dusts, mists and fumes, and paint spray.

- Use other protective gear as applicable: gloves to reduce the absorption of chemicals through the skin, earplugs to protect against hearing damage from loud machinery, and safety goggles to avoid eye damage from accidents.
- A good window-exhaust system is essential to reducing inhaled vapors. Create a real airflow when working with fume-producing materials—the breeze from an open window isn't enough.
- Keep children and animals out of the workplace, because chemicals reach higher levels of concentration in their systems.
- Keep appropriate safety equipment on hand to deal with emergencies: an eyewash station if caustics are being used, a first-aid kit, a fire extinguisher if combustible materials are present, etc.
- Ask your school board to make sure the least toxic and hazardous products are used in the classroom.

For more information about art materials in general, as well as toxicity issues, pick up a copy of *The Artists' Handbook of Materials and Techniques,* by Mayer and Sheehan (Viking Press). Another book, Michael McCann's *Health Hazards Manual for Artists,* has become something of a classic and is a must for every artist's studio library. The fully revised edition has the most current information on safety, labeling, and new chemicals. It outlines the dangers for artists in such fields as painting, photography, ceramics, sculpture, printmaking, woodworking, textiles, and many others, and has a special section on health hazards for children working with art materials. Both of these titles are available from many of the bookstores listed in this book.

You'll also find materials, equipment, and furniture for artists and art studios, as well as graphic design–related software and computer goods, in the "Office, Business, Professional" chapter. The firms listed in the "Crafts and Hobbies" chapter carry supplies for fine artists and graphic artists as well. See "Related Products/Companies" at the end of this chapter for relevant company listings found in various other chapters of the book.

FIND IT FAST

ART AND GRAPHIC DESIGN BOOKS/VIDEOS • Art Express, Cheap Joe's, A.I. Friedman, Jerry's Artarama, Daniel Smith, Utrecht
COMPUTER GRAPHICS SUPPLIES • A.I. Friedman, Utrecht
FRAMING SUPPLIES • American Frame Corporation, Art Express, Dick Blick, Frame Fit, Graphik Dimensions, The Italian Art Store, Jerry's Artarama, Pearl Paint, Daniel Smith, Stu-Art, Utrecht
GENERAL ART/GRAPHICS SUPPLIES, TOOLS, AND EQUIPMENT • Art Express,

Dick Blick, Cheap Joe's, A.I. Friedman, The Italian Art Store, Jerry's Artarama, Ott's Discount, Pearl Paint, Texas Art Supply, Utrecht
SPECIALTY PAPERS • Daniel Smith
STUDIO FURNITURE • Art Express, A.I. Friedman, Pearl Paint, Daniel Smith

---

AMERICAN FRAME CORPORATION

400 TOMAHAWK DR.
MAUMEE, OH 43537–1695
800–537–0944
FAX: 800–893–3898

Catalog: free
Pay: check, MO, MC, V, AE, Discover
Sells: preassembled and sectional frames and supplies
Store: same address; Monday to Friday 9–4:30
E-mail: info@americanframe.com

American Frame, in business since 1973, sells assembled wood frames —a great way to get the look of a custom framing job, at do-it-yourself prices—as well as metal sectional frames in a wonderful selection of colors. American Frame's prices are 35% to 50% lower than those charged by other art-supply firms.

The 36-page catalog features frame sections in basswood, maple, poplar, oak, and cherry, in a variety of stains and treatments, many of which are gilded. Each wood frame includes spring clips to hold the mounted artwork securely in place, hangers, and wall protectors. (Assembly requires screwing the spring clips and hangers; the joints are preassembled.) The metal frames are offered in dozens of colors and a choice of 12 profiles, to accommodate ordinary flat work and extra-deep canvases.

Bainbridge board—acid-free mat, perfect-mount, and foam core—is sold in groups of 10 or more sheets, depending on the item. The mat board is offered in over 100 colors in the 32" by 40" size or cut to order (custom-cut mats can be ordered individually); foam core and perfect-mount boards are cut to order in dimensions up to 24" by 30". Rolls of polyester film are available, as well as acid-free acrylic picture "glass" (cut to order in dimensions up to 24" by 30").

Special Factors: Measure carefully before ordering; restocking fee applies to returns; phone hours are 8:30 A.M. to 6 P.M. ET.

ART EXPRESS

P.O. BOX 21662, DEPT. C
COLUMBIA, SC 29212
800–535–5908
FAX: 888–278–3977

Catalog: $3.50
Pay: check, MO, MC, V, AE, Discover
Sells: art supplies and equipment
Store: mail order only
E-mail: artexpress@artxpress.com
Online: http://www.artxpress.com

Art Express publishes an 80-page catalog featuring a well-chosen selection of art tools and equipment at discounts averaging 40%, with each suggested retail price listed alongside Art Express' so that you can compare. The inventory includes papers and board, canvas, brushes, mediums and solvents, pens, portfolios, paint (including casein), Art Bin artists' cases, folding stools, art racks, inks, pastels, pencils, airbrushing equipment, easels by Anco, Best, Julian, Stanrite, and Trident, light boxes, Logan mat cutters, and Artograph opaque projectors. Many other top-name brands are represented here. Several pages list available books and videotapes on art technique, history, and related topics. If you don't see what you're looking for, write or fax Art Express with product information—the item might be in stock. It's promised that the website will have the full catalog on it by press time, so check it out.

Special Factors: Quantity discounts are available; institutional accounts are available; minimum order is $25 on stock paper.

DICK BLICK ART MATERIALS

P.O. BOX 1267
GALESBURG, IL
 61402–1267
800–828–4548
FAX: 800–621–8293

Catalog Supplements: free
Pay: check, MO, MC, V, AE, Discover
Sells: fine art materials and supplies
Store: 34 retail stores in CT, GA, IN, IL, KS, IA, MI, MO, MN, NV, NE, OH, PA; see flyer for addresses
E-mail: info@dickblick.com
Online: http://www.dickblick.com

  ¡Si!

Dick Blick was established in 1911 and issues three sales supplements per year (they're really 60-page color catalogs) with savings up to 60% on all kinds of art materials for the fine artist. A recent review copy included Winsor & Newton oils discounted 40%, Raphaël Kolinsky red sable brushes at 50% off, 40% off Rembrandt pastels, and 40% off Prismacolor marker sets, to name but a few. List and sale prices are side by side, so you can see where the best deals are, but just about everything in Dick Blick's sales flyers is a real bargain, from airbrushes and easels to mat cutters, frames, and much more.

Special Factors: Full refund, credit, or exchange on returns made within 30 days; satisfaction guaranteed. C.O.D. orders not accepted.

CHEAP JOE'S ART STUFF

374 INDUSTRIAL PARK RD.
BOONE, NC 28607
800–227–2788
704–262–0793
FAX: 800–257–0874
FAX: 704–262–0795

Catalog: free
Pay: check, MO, MC, V, Discover
Sells: art supplies and equipment
Store: Boone Drug Co., 617 E. King St., Boone, NC; Monday to Saturday 8–6
E-mail: cheapjoe@aol.com
Online: http://www.artscape.com

There's a real Joe here at Cheap Joe's, the driving force behind the 128-page full-color catalog that's full of tips on how to make the most of your tools and materials. Cheap Joe's dream of keeping his company small may be confounded by his great prices—savings of 30% are routine, and quantity pricing deepens the discounts to 60% on at least a few items.

The catalog features papers by Arches, Bockingford, Canson, Fabriano, Lana, and Waterford; paint from Da Vinci, Daler Rowney, Holbein, Rembrandt, Sennelier, and Winsor & Newton; paintbrushes from Robert Simmons and Winsor & Newton, as well as Cheap Joe's own line. New this year are watercolors and watercolor papers by Cheap Joe at excellent savings. You'll also find easels, shrink-wrap systems, Logan mat cutters, adhesives, foam core, Artograph projection equipment, Fredrix canvas, print racks, and books and videotapes on painting and art theory. Cheap Joe set up shop in 1986, and he wants to keep his company from getting too big so that he can stay in touch with his artist customers. He's a serious watercolorist, and welcomes your questions and suggestions about materials and equipment.

Special Factors: Satisfaction is guaranteed; shipping is not charged on brushes; institutional accounts are available.

FRAME FIT CO.

**P.O. BOX 8926, DEPT.
  WBMC
PHILADELPHIA, PA 19135
800–523–3693
FAX: 800–344–7010**

Brochures and Price List: free
Pay: check, MO, MC, V, Discover
Sells: aluminum, wood, and composite sectional picture frames
Store: mail order only
Online: http://www.framefit.com

Frame Fit sells aluminum, wood, and composite picture frames and hardware at wholesale prices. The aluminum series is offered in five profiles, for both stretched canvas and other works of art, and comes in 22 vibrant colors with a choice of finishes—polished face and brushed sides, satin finish with brushed sides, or polished or satin finished face and sides. Even sizes and fractional sizes are available from 4" to 90". Corner assembly hardware is included, with screw hangers and springs sold separately. The wood series features premium ash molding in four profiles and six hand-stained finishes, and is available in sections, assembled, or in 10-foot lengths, all assembly hardware included. The Evolutions series is made of composite molding, which resembles wood, but its core is made up partially from recycled plastic. This series features the more ornate and decorative styles—38 choices in all—and is available in sections, assembled, or 10-foot lengths.

Frame Fit has been in business since 1977, and the firm's prices beat those of discounted frames sold elsewhere by 20% and more. If you can use 50 pairs of the same color, size, and profile, you can save from 15% to 25% more, depending on the color you choose. And if your order totals $300 plus, shipping is free (except on bulk chop goods and 10-foot lengths).

Special Factors: Shipping is not charged on most orders over $300 (see above) sent within the continental United States; C.O.D. orders are accepted.

A.I. FRIEDMAN

44 W. 18TH ST., DEPT.
  WBMC
NEW YORK, NY 10011
212–337–8600
FAX: 212–929–7320

Catalog: $5 (see text)
Pay: check, MO, MC, V, AE
Sells: graphic arts supplies and tools
Store: same address; Monday to Friday 9–6;
also 431 Boston Post Rd., Port Chester, NY,
914–937–7351; open daily

If you're a professional graphic designer or artist, you'll want to add A.I. Friedman to your short list of suppliers. The firm, which has been in business since 1929, serves the creative community with the best in tools and equipment. You can send $5 for the well-organized loose-leaf catalog, but it's free to design professionals requesting it on letterhead.

The catalog itself is an object lesson in good design, making it easy to find what you want. It is divided into four categories: computer graphics, presentation materials, studio furniture, and traditional art materials. You'll find drawing instruments, markers, paint, brushes, paper and board, airbrushing supplies, audiovisual equipment, frames, and reference books here. Friedman offers goods not found in every art supply catalog: light boxes, dry-mounting presses, the complete Pantone line, precision drawing and drafting tools, a large selection of templates, and complete Photostat systems. Among the manufacturers represented are Agfa, Apple, Bainbridge, Canson, Chartpak, D'Arches, Dr. Ph. Martin's, Grumbacher, Hewlett-Packard, Iris, Iwata, Koh-I-Noor, Letraset, Liquitex, Luxo (lamps), Mayline, Mont Blanc, Osmiroid, Paasche, Pelikan, Staedler-Mars, Strathmore, 3M, Tektronix, and Winsor & Newton. The catalog prices are not discounted, but if your order totals $50 or more, discounts of 20% to 40% are given. (Some items aren't discounted, including the Agfa products.) Call or write for a quote on specific items.

Special Factors: Price quote by phone or letter; institutional accounts are available; minimum order is $50 (see text).

GRAPHIK DIMENSIONS LTD.

2103 BRENTWOOD ST.
HIGH POINT, NC 27263
800–221–0262
910–887–3700
FAX: 910–887–3773

Catalog: free
Pay: check, MO, MC, V, Discover
Sells: sectional and custom-made frames and accessories
Store: same address
Online: http://www.graphikdimensions.com

You can get the frame you want with frame sections from Graphik Dimensions—or you can have it custom-made by the firm's expert crafters. Graphik Dimensions is run by an artist and photographer who have firsthand experience in selecting the right frame for the piece, and finding the best price. Their 36-page color catalog offers the "classic" metal sectional frames often sold in art supply stores, in both standard depths, for use with glass, and "canvas" depth, for oil paintings, in metallics and enamels. The selection also includes wooden gallery frames in plain, gilded, embossed, rustic, and natural finishes. Graphik Dimensions' custom line features wood moldings, some of which include linen liners at no extra charge. If the prospect of putting a frame together seems overwhelming, there's help: Graphik Dimensions also sells preassembled and custom-made assembled frames in several different styles, and offers custom-cut mats.

Framing kits are available in your choice of wood frames, and include the glass (or acrylic), backing board, retainer clips, hanging screws, and wire—no tools necessary. Before you order a frame, order the sample set of corners. These are actual pieces of the frame that show color, depth, and corner joinery style. The cost of the sample sets ($5 to $30, depending on the line) is repaid in the trouble you save if the frame wasn't right for the work. (Individual pieces of framing are available free on request.) And all wood frames come with hangers, retainer clips, and wire.

Special Factors: Satisfaction is guaranteed; quantity discounts are available; authorized returns (except custom frames) are accepted (a 15% restocking fee may be charged); C.O.D. orders are accepted.

THE ITALIAN ART STORE

84 MAPLE AVE.
MORRISTOWN, NJ 07960
800–643–6440
973–644–2717
FAX: 973–644–5074

Catalog: free
Pay: check, MO, MC, V, Discover
Sells: fine art supplies
Store: same address; Monday to Friday 9–5

The Italian Art Store began business paying homage to the epicenter of the Renaissance, selling mainly Italian art supplies. Raphael watercolor brushes, Maimeri Restoration Colors, Fabriano papers, and Sennelier pastels—all among the finest of their type—are still offered today. The Italian Art Store has since expanded the selection, with oils from Blockx, Old Holland, Schmincke, and others; acrylics from Golden; canvas from Fredrix, Stretch Art, and others; watercolors from Winsor & Newton and Schmincke; and on and on. You'll find top-quality brushes, sketchbooks, pastels, mat cutters, and more in the 60-page catalog. The Italian Art Store's own line includes pigments, brushes, canvas, and easels. Discounts average 50% on list prices, but specials and close-outs run up to 75% off.

Special Factors: Unused goods in their original wrapping are accepted within 45 days for exchange, refund, or credit. Free shipping on all orders of $100 or more.

JERRY'S ARTARAMA, INC.

P.O. BOX 58638, DEPT.
WBMC
RALEIGH, NC 27658
919–878–6782
FAX: 919–873–9565

Catalog: $2
Pay: check, MO, MC, V, AE, Discover
Sells: art supplies, picture frames, etc.
Store: stores in West Hartford, CT; Bellerose and Rochester, NY; Deerfield Beach, FL; and Fort Collins, CO (call for hours and addresses)
E-mail: uartist@aol.com
Online: http://www.jerryscatalog.com

Jerry's Artarama, in business since 1968, publishes a 108-page compendium of materials, tools, and equipment for commercial and fine arts that includes both basics and specialty goods seldom discounted elsewhere. Here you'll find some items discounted as much as 50%.

The catalog offers pigments, brushes, vehicles and solvents, airbrushes and compressors, studio furniture, lighting, visual equipment, canvas and framing supplies, papers, and other goods, and features an extensive section of supplies for oil, watercolor, and acrylic painting. Jerry's also sells supplies for drawing, graphic arts, drafting, calligraphy, printmaking, sumi-e, airbrushing, fabric painting, marbleizing, and professional framing. There are some "generic" brands, but most are familiar names. Don't miss the dozen pages of publications, including technique manuals, color guides, and workshop videotapes—all at terrific prices.

Special Factors: Satisfaction is unconditionally guaranteed; color charts and product specifications are available on request; quantity discounts are available; minimum order is $20, $50 with phone orders.

OTT'S DISCOUNT ART SUPPLY

102 HUNGATE DR.,
DEPT. WBMC
GREENVILLE, NC
27858–8045
800–356–3289
919–756–9565
FAX: 919–756–2397

Catalog: free
Pay: check, MO, MC, V
Sells: art, graphics, and craft supplies
Store: mail order only
Online: http://www.otts.com

Painters, sculptors, and artists of all types can get great prices on all of their needs from Ott's, a family-run firm that also serves schools and institutions. In the 64-page catalog you'll find top-brand oils and tempera paints, acrylics, watercolors, pastels, stretchers, canvas, pencils and charcoal, paper, airbrush and silk-screening equipment, easels, projection equipment, craft paints, clay and kilns, Styrofoam, candle-making and wood-burning supplies, adhesives, craft knives and brushes, and more. There's a good selection of instructional materials, including guides from North Light Books, and great rainy-day projects such as the Deluxe Volcano and Solar System Kits. Ott's has been in business since 1972, and will special-order items not in the catalog.

Special Factors: Satisfaction is guaranteed; returns are accepted within 30 days for exchange, refund, or credit; institutional orders are accepted; orders under $30 are charged shipping, handling, and a small-order fee.

PEARL PAINT CO., INC.

308 CANAL ST.,
  DEPT. WBM
NEW YORK, NY
  10013–2572
800–221–6845
212–431–7932
FAX: 212–274–2290

Catalog: $1.50
Pay: check, MO, MC, V, AE, Discover
Sells: art, craft, and graphics supplies, studio furniture, etc.
Store: same address, also 16 other locations in CA, FL, GA, IL, MA, MD, NJ, NY, TX, and VA; call for locations
Online: http://www.pearlpaint.com

 ¡Si! ★

Gotham artists have been flocking to Pearl Paint since 1933 for good prices on fine paints, tools, and supplies, and since then Pearl has opened stores in nine other states as well (locations are listed in the catalog). Since the 144-page catalog represents a fraction of the available stock (fine art materials), call, fax, or write if you're looking for something that's not listed. In addition to tools and supplies for the fine arts, Pearl sells materials and equipment for all kinds of crafts: pigments, brushes, stretchers, papers, canvas, manuals, studio furniture, children's supplies, and much more. Pearl also stocks fine writing instruments, house paint, frames and framing supplies, and gilding and faux-finishing supplies.

Special Factors: Quantity discounts are available; weekly specials are run on selected items; minimum order is $50.

DANIEL SMITH

P.O. BOX 84268
SEATTLE, WA 98124–5568
800–426–6740
206–223–9599
FAX: 800–238–4065

Catalog: $5 with rebate; supplements free
Pay: check, MO, MC, V, AE
Sells: fine-art supplies and equipment
Store: 4150 First Ave. South, Seattle, WA; Monday to Saturday 9–6, Wednesday 9–8, Sunday 10–6
E-mail: dsartmtrl@aol.com

Daniel Smith's catalogs are designed by artists, for artists, and are appreciated as much for their book reviews, technical discussions, and visual appeal as for their offerings. Daniel Smith has been recommended by artists impressed by the company's line of materials and responsive service department; the firm features competitive pricing and regular sales.

The annual "Reference Catalog" presents an extensive collection of paper from Arches, Canson, Fabriano, Lana, Magnani, Rising, Strathmore, and other makers, for watercolors, printmaking, drawing, bookmaking, and other applications. This catalog also features uncommon specialty papers, including banana paper from the Philippines, Mexican bark paper, genuine papyrus, and Japanese "fantasy" paper embedded with maple leaves.

Daniel Smith has been manufacturing etching, relief, and lithographic inks and artists' paints for more than 20 years, and features the Daniel Smith Original Oils, Autograph Series Oils, and the very popular Daniel Smith Extra Fine Watercolors—paints notable for their quality, rich formulation, and unique color range—including luminescent and metallic colors. Daniel Smith sells acrylics, oils, watercolors, egg tempera, and gouache from such companies as Golden, Grumbacher, Sennelier, Schmincke, Talens, and Winsor & Newton. The brush line covers all painting media, and includes Daniel Smith's own line, as well as brushes from Isabey, Strathmore, and Winsor & Newton. Canvas, custom-cut wood frames and Nielsen sectional metal frames, solvents, pastels, colored pencils, calligraphy pens, printmaking materials, and other tools and supplies are available, rounded out by a fine collection of studio furniture, portfolios, easels, and reference books.

Canadian readers, please note: Only U.S. funds are accepted.

Special Factors: Satisfaction is guaranteed; authorized returns are accepted for exchange, refund, or credit; minimum order of paper is 10 sheets.

STU-ART

2045 GRAND AVE.,
  DEPT. WBMC
BALDWIN, NY 11510–2999
516–546–5151
FAX: 516–377–3512

Catalog: free
Pay: check, MO, MC, V, Discover
Sells: mats, frames, and framing supplies
Store: same address; Monday to Saturday 9–5

Stu-Art sells sectional frames and framing materials—everything you'll need to do a professional job. The firm has been supplying galleries and institutions since 1970, and it offers the best materials, a range of sizes, and savings of up to 50% on list prices.

Nielsen metal frames are offered in nine profiles, for flat, stretched canvas and dimensional art (deep) mounting, in a stunning array of brushed metallic finishes, soft pastels, and deep decorator colors. Sectional wood frames are also available, in different profiles and a variety of finishes. Acid-free single and double mats are sold in rectangles and ovals. The catalog includes precise specifications of the frames, and samples of the mats. Stu-Art also sells nonglare and clear plastic (which can be used in place of picture glass), and shrink film and dispensers. If you have to get work framed, see the catalog before handing it over to a professional—you may decide you can do the job yourself.

Special Factors: Shipping is not charged on UPS-delivered orders over $300 net; authorized returns are accepted (a restocking fee may be charged); minimum order is $15 on sectional frames, $25 on other goods.

TEXAS ART SUPPLY

2001 MONTROSE BLVD.
HOUSTON, TX 77006
800–888–9278
713–526–5221
FAX: 713–526–4062

Catalog: $3; $2.50 for catalog on CD-ROM
Pay: check, MO, MC, V, AE, Discover
Sells: fine arts, graphics, and craft supplies
Store: same address; two other TX stores, call for locations
E-mail: info@texasart.com
Online: http://www.texasart.com

Texas Art Supply, in business for over half a century, packs the 400-plus pages of its catalog with a wide range of products for fine arts, graphics and design, ceramics, and other crafts. The brands include the trusted standards—Berol, Bienfang, Chartpak, Conte, Crescent, D'Arches, Duncan, Grumbacher, Koh-I-Noor, Liquitex, NuPastel, Pantone, Paragon, Robert Simmons, Speedball, Strathmore, Winsor & Newton, and X-Acto, among many others. Basics for silk-screening, airbrushing, block printing, scratch art, clay and stone sculpture, stenciling, fabric painting and batiking, and other crafts are also available, as well as products with broad appeal: Lettering and sign supplies, glue guns and refills, bronzing powders and metal leaf, projectors, office supplies, lamp parts, music-box works, cotton "blanks," crayons, and educational supplies and teaching aids are all offered.

The price list shows the list and discounted prices, and the terms of sale are stated clearly in the catalog, in English and Spanish. The catalog is available in print or on CD-ROM, and you can also call directly for a quote. Note that Texas Art Supply lists only a portion of the stock in the catalog anyway, so if you don't see what you want, ask.

Special Factors: Price quote by phone or letter; quantity discounts are available; shipping is included on orders over $100 sent to the 48 contiguous states; authorized returns are accepted in original, unopened packaging within 30 days for exchange, refund, or credit.

UTRECHT

33 35TH ST.
BROOKLYN, NY 11232
800–223–9132
718–768–2525
FAX: 718–499–8815

Catalog: free
Pay: check, MO, MC, V
Sells: general art supplies
Store: 9 locations in NY, MA, CA, DC, MI, IL, and PA; see catalog for addresses and phone numbers
Online: http://www.utrechtart.com

 ¡Si!

Utrecht has been selling supplies and equipment for painting, sculpture, and printmaking since 1949, and manufactures some of the best values in oil and acrylic paints on the market. The 52-page catalog describes the manufacturing process and quality controls used to produce Utrecht's paint, and features Utrecht acrylics, oils, watercolors, gesso, and other mediums and solvents. The firm also sells a full line of professional artists' materials and equipment, including canvas, stretchers, frames, pads, paper, brushes, books, easels, flat files, taborets, pencils, drafting tools, and much more. In addition to the Utrecht label, goods by Arches, Bainbridge, Bienfang, Canson, Chartpak, Claessens, D'Arches, Deka, Eberhard Faber, Grumbacher, Koh-I-Noor, Kolinsky, Liquitex, Niji, Pentel, Rembrandt, Speedball, Strathmore, Vermeer, Winsor & Newton, and other manufacturers are available. Utrecht's prices are competitive, and the best buys are on the house brand and quantity purchases.

Special Factors: Institutional accounts are available; quantity discounts are available; minimum order is $40.

RELATED PRODUCTS/COMPANIES

Cardboard tubes for storing and shipping art • *Yazoo Mills*
Clip art • *Dover Publications*

Commercial and fine arts books and manuals • Print Bookstore, Hacker Art Books

Computer graphics hardware and software • Dartek, Computer Discount Warehouse

Studio furniture and equipment • Fidelity Products

FOOD AND BEVERAGES

Bulk foods, health foods, ethnic foods; coffee, tea, and other beverages

Sales of mail-order food are in the billions of dollars annually, reflecting an increase in the demand for good foods not available locally, and hard-to-find cooking ingredients. The dominant mail-order foodstuffs are cheese, fruit, and nuts, as well as preserves and condiments, coffee, tea, and seasonings. The listings that follow are representative: You'll find caviar and wild mushrooms, Japanese and Lebanese foods, giant pistachio nuts, Vermont maple syrup, and more from the firms listed here—at savings that run to 80%.

Food makes the perfect gift. If you want to maximize your savings, choose something like tea or dried fruit, buy it in bulk, and repackage it yourself in gift tins. You can save a lot of money by going in on an order with friends and buying in large quantities. Dry goods like grains and beans keep almost indefinitely if tightly sealed, as do dried fruits. Nuts should be kept in a sealed container or zipper-lock bag, and refrigerated at all times; their high oil content makes them susceptible to rancidity.

If you're seeking out companies that primarily sell herbs, spices, condiments, and flavorings, see the section after this one, "Spices, Condiments, and Flavorings," page 204.

If you'd like to improve your diet and cut food costs, a food co-op may be the answer. To find out who's running a food co-op near you, call or write Co-op News Network, Box 57, Randolph, VT 05060, 802–234–9293. The nice folks there can look up your area in the National Co-Op Directory to locate the one closest to you.

There are a couple of helpful websites as well. You can access the Directory of U.S. and Canadian Food Cooperatives at http://www.

prairienet.org/co-op/directory.html/. To click into the world of online food co-ops, go to http://www.columbia.edu/~jw157/food.coop.html/. Both of these sites have wonderful links to other kinds of co-ops (e.g., banking), nutrition newsletters and information, agriculture sites, and much more.

By now everyone has heard of the famous "Food Pyramid," the U.S. government's guide to sensible eating. In brief, the bulkiest foods are the ones that should constitute most of our diet—fruits, vegetables, grains, beans, and legumes—with animal products, fat, and sugar making up a small portion of our overall diet. Eating this way is not only healthiest, but cheapest, too.

As simple as the food pyramid seems, changes in the government's food labeling regulations are not. Some of the best ongoing sources of information that sort food facts from fallacies are newsletters. *Nutrition Action Healthletter,* published by the Center for Science in the Public Interest (CSPI), broke the stories about the high-fat content of Chinese and Mexican restaurant food. It's a fearless champion of truth in advertising, which is what you'd expect of a Ralph Nader publication. Subscriptions are currently $24 per 10-issue year; write to CSPI-Circulation, 1875 Connecticut Ave. NW, Suite 300, Washington, DC 20009–5728, or call 202–332–9110 for a subscription. The e-mail address is cspi@cspi. net.org.

With Deepak Chopra and Dr. Andrew Weil occupying the best-seller lists, it's clear that people across America are looking for ways to enhance their own body's ability to heal itself and to stay healthy. Even if you're not particularly New Age-y or spiritual, there's a great book out there that even my mother loved. It's called *Food—Your Miracle Medicine,* by Jean Carper (HarperCollins). Here you'll find out the results of the most recent scientific studies on different foods, and how they can help cure or prevent particular health problems. Most of the companies in the "Books, Audiobooks, and Periodicals" chapter will carry this book or be able to get it for you.

In addition to nutrition, food safety is a big concern among consumers. Warm weather gives rise to "picnic anxiety," and the fall brings "stuffing fears," common concerns about handling troublesome foods properly. Help is just a call or letter away:

- The American Dietetic Association answers questions on all aspects of food safety; 800–366–1655; Monday to Friday 8 A.M. to 8 P.M. CT, for a registered dietitian.
- USDA Meat and Poultry Hotline answers your questions on the safe handling of meat and poultry; 800–535–4555, in DC 202–720–3333 (both TDD); Monday to Friday 10 A.M. to 4 P.M.; November 1–30

and the weekend before Thanksgiving; 9 A.M. to 5 P.M.; Thanksgiving Day 8 A.M. to 2 P.M., all ET. Or check out their website at http://www.usda.gov/fsis/.

- "A Quick Guide to Safe Food Handling," a USDA publication, gives guidelines on food handling and charts of cooking requirements for different meats and egg dishes—plus one that gives the projected shelf life of refrigerated and frozen foods. Send a long, stamped, self-addressed envelope to the USDA, with your request for HG–248, to Human Nutrition Information Service, 6505 Belcrest Rd., Hyattsville, MD 20782.

- "How to Help Avoid Foodborne Illness in the Home," published by the FDA, covers risks and safety precautions for buying, handling, storing, and preparing food. A copy can be ordered from the Consumer Information Center, listed in this book.

- The FDA's Seafood Hotline dispenses answers to your specific questions on fish-related safety issues; call 800–FDA–4010, Monday to Friday 12 noon to 4 P.M. ET. If you have internet access, the FDA website is extremely user-friendly—even fun. There you can look up articles on all kinds of food- and health-related issues. The online address is http://www.fda.gov/.

- When you're ordering food by mail, keep food safety in mind. Don't purchase highly perishable or temperature-sensitive items such as chocolate, soft cheese, fruits, vegetables, and uncured meats during the summer, unless you have them shipped by an express service and plan to eat them immediately.

FIND IT FAST

CANDIES • Bates Bros., Bulkfoods.com, Durey-Libby
CHEESE • Deer Valley Farm, Gibbsville Cheese, New England Cheesemaking Supply
COFFEE AND TEA • Northwestern Coffee Mills
DRIED NUTS AND FRUIT • Bates Bros., Bulkfoods.com, Deer Valley Farm, Durey-Libby, Festive Foods, Jaffe Bros., Maples Fruit Farm, Mountain Ark
GOURMET FOODS • Caviarteria, Deer Valley Farm, Festive Foods, Maples Fruit Farm, Mountain Ark, Red Hill Mushrooms, Sultan's Delight
GRAINS, BEANS, CEREALS • Bulkfoods.com, Deer Valley Farm, Jaffe Bros., Mountain Ark
HERBS AND SPICES • Bulkfoods.com, Deer Valley Farm, Festive Foods, Jaffe Bros., Mountain Ark, Sultan's Delight
MEAT AND FISH • Caviarteria, Deer Valley Farm, Gibbsville Cheese
SUGAR-FREE CANDY/CONFECTIONS • Bulkfoods.com, Mountain Ark
WINE- AND BEER-MAKING SUPPLIES • E.C. Kraus

BATES BROS. NUT FARM, INC.

15954 WOODS VALLEY RD.
VALLEY CENTER, CA 92082
760–749–3333
FAX: 760–749–9499

Catalog: free
Pay: check, MO, MC, V, Discover
Sells: nuts, dried fruits, and candy
Store: same address; daily 9–5; also Terra Nova Plaza, 358 E. H St., #604, Chula Vista, CA; daily 10–7:30

Nuts are the featured item at Bates, which was founded in 1971 and grows some of what it sells. Price checks routinely show savings of almost 40% on selected items, compared to the competition. Bates' 8-page brochure lists the standard almonds, walnuts, peanuts, cashews, pecans, and mixes, as well as macadamia nuts, filberts, pignolis, pumpkin seeds, sunflower seeds, and pistachios. You can buy them raw, roasted and salted, smoked, and saltless. The dried fruits include apricots, raisins, dates, papaya, figs, banana chips, pineapple, and coconut, as well as other sweets. These are the ingredients for trail mix, which Bates also sells ready-made, as well as granola, wheat germ snacks, popcorn, and old-fashioned candy—malted milk balls, English toffee, yogurt pretzels, nut brittle, saltwater taffy, gummy bears and worms, and candy corn, among others. And look here for good prices on glacé fruit: fruitcake mix, cherries, colored pineapple wedges, orange and lemon peel, and citron. Gift packs are available year-round.

Special Factors: C.O.D. orders not accepted.

BULKFOODS.COM

FAX: 888-BULK-COM

Information: internet website, no catalog
Pay: MC, V, AE, Discover
Sells: nuts, grains, cereals, sugar-free candy, penny candy, etc.
Store: mail order only
Online: http://www.bulkfoods.com

It's hard to imagine when one might need 33 pounds of M&M's. But if you did, Bulkfoods.com would gladly fill your order. This internet-only store sells health-food items such as rolled oats, 12-grain cereal, and beans; great candy including "Gummies" in every conceivable shape, chocolate-covered raisins and peanuts, lollipops, licorice, etc.; an unusual selection of sugar-free candies, including such items as sugar-free chocolate-covered peanut butter cups; dried fruit, including unsulphured bananas and apricots; a large selection of nuts—roasted and raw, salted and not; herbs, spices, and baking goods such as sprinkles, milk chocolate drops, and cherry bits. If you order here, be ready to order in huge quantities—5- to 33-pound bags. And you'll pay shipping based on weight (via UPS ground in the 48 contiguous United States; this is not a good source if you live in Hawaii or Alaska), the amount of which is clearly shown at the bottom of your order form before you have to commit to buying. But even with the shipping cost added, the prices here checked out to be at least 20% less than supermarket prices, and some sale items on the "Specials List" page were 40% less than the local health food store prices. This would be a good source for a church or school fund-raising event.

Special Factors: Credit cards only; no check or money orders accepted.

CAVIARTERIA, INC.

502 PARK AVE., DEPT. WBMC
NEW YORK, NY 10022
800–4-CAVIAR
212–759–7410 (WITHIN NY)
FAX: 718–482–8985

Catalog: free
Pay: MO, MC, V, AE
Sells: caviar and gourmet foods
Store: same address (store and tasting bar); Monday to Saturday 9–8; other locations in CA and NV
Online: http://www.caviarteria.com

 ¡Si!

Caviarteria, established in 1950, brings its line of caviar to the world through a 12-page catalog. This family-run business stocks every grade of fresh Caspian Beluga, Oscetra, and Sevruga caviar, plus American sturgeon, whitefish, trout, and salmon caviar. What Caviarteria believes is the "world's most exquisite Caspian Beluga caviar costs $725 for 14 ounces"—but is available as "partly broken grains" for half that. Prices begin a bit more affordably at about $18.95 per ounce for Kamchatka bottom-of-the-barrel vacuum-packed, and run up to $285 for 3½ ounces of "Ultra" Beluga. Price comparisons of Caviarteria's Beluga Malassol to those of another caviar-by-mail firm show you can save as much as 40% here, and even the caviar servers—spoons and bowls—are already priced lower than usual retail.

The catalog lists other gourmet treats: whole sides and "center cut" packages of smoked Scottish salmon, Icelandic gravlax, fresh foie gras from the U.S. and France, game meats, and other delicacies. If you're in New York City, stop by Caviarteria's tasting bar on Park Avenue for a glass of champagne or a caviar sampler with toast points. Caviarteria will send caviar, foie gras, and other delights for next-day delivery anywhere.

Special Factors: Satisfaction is guaranteed; minimum order is $25 with credit cards.

DEER VALLEY FARM

R.D. 1, BOX 173
GUILFORD, NY 13780
607–764–8556

Catalog: $1
Pay: check, MO, MC, V
Sells: organic and natural foods
Store: Rt. 37, Guilford, NY; Monday to Friday 8–5; two other locations in Oneonta and Cortland, NY; call for hours

Deer Valley Farm, which has been in operation since 1947 and is certified organic by New York State Natural Food Associates, sells a full line of foods—from baked bread and cookies to wheat middlings. Whole grains, flours, cereals, nut butters, crackers, fruits, pasta, herbs and spices, tea, soy milk, preserves, and yeast and other baking ingredients are usually available. You can buy "organically grown" meats here at substantial savings: Hamburger, typically priced at $4.50 to $6 per pound in health food stores, costs $3.49 per pound, and the trimmed sirloin is $6.29 a pound; veal, pork, lamb, and even fish are also available. Deer Valley sells raw milk cheese, and the cheddar is only $3.29 to $4.89 per pound, less than some of the supermarket varieties. The only drawback here is the minimum order, $150, necessary to reap savings of 25% to 40% on the prices you'd pay if buying the same goods from your local health food store. But if you get your friends together, you can meet that amount easily with a combined order—just be prepared for an impromptu feast when the cartons arrive!

Special Factors: Deliveries are made by Deer Valley truck in the New York City area (elsewhere by UPS); minimum order is $15, $150 for wholesale prices.

DUREY-LIBBY EDIBLE NUTS, INC.

**100 INDUSTRIAL RD.
CARLSTADT, NJ 07072
201–939–2775
FAX: 201–939–0386**

Catalog: free
Pay: check or MO
Sells: nuts, edible seeds, candy, dried fruit
Store: same address; Monday to Friday 10–5, Saturday 10–3

Durey-Libby, established in 1950, picks and processes "delicious fresh nuts you don't have to shell out a fortune for," as well as edible seeds, snacks, candies, and dried fruits. You can't eat fancy tins, stoneware crocks, and rattan baskets, so if you're buying nuts, why not pay for nuts—and nothing but. Durey-Libby's no-frills price list features walnuts, pecans, cashews, almonds, macadamia nuts, pistachios, cocktail mixes, and more (roasted and unroasted, salted and unsalted, etc.), packed in bags and vacuum tins. You can buy broken milk chocolate here at $1.75 per half pound; dime-store candy such as gummy worms and sour patch kids by the pound or 5-pound bag; dried fruits in many varieties; and snack mixes such as Jamaican mix and M&M gorp. The prices are up to 50% less than those charged by gourmet shops and many food catalogs, and most items are available in 1-, 2-, and 5-pound amounts.

Special Factors: Satisfaction is guaranteed; shipping is not charged on orders within the contiguous United States.

FESTIVE FOODS OF THE ROCKIES

**P.O. BOX 49172, DEPT.
WBMC–99
COLORADO SPRINGS, CO
80949–9172
719–594–6768
FAX: 719–522–1672**

Catalog: $2
Pay: check, MO, MC, V, AE
Sells: baking ingredients, fancy foods, herbs and spices, etc.
Store: mail order only
Online: http://www.delve.com/festive.html

Festive Foods of the Rockies has been supplying serious home cooks and bakers with fine ingredients since 1984, and offers a number of items not often seen in other fancy foods catalogs. There are 20 pages of temptations, from pure Belgian chocolate to fine dried fruits. Festive Food's per-ounce prices of the bulk-packed herbs are much lower than those charged at the supermarket: 8 ounces of pure vanilla extract cost $8.25 here, while just 2 ounces of extract cost $5.39 locally. The 12-ounce pack of Old Bay seasoning is $3.95 here, compared to $3.13 for 6 ounces. Savings on the other goods vary, depending on the item and amount ordered.

Festive Foods offers a wide range of products, including pastry and baking ingredients, chocolate and cocoa, extracts, essential oils of plants and spices, a wide variety of herbs and spices in spice-jar "refill" packs as well as the more economical bulk sizes, seasoning blends, tea (black, green, herbal, and flavored), dried mushrooms (porcini, morels, shiitake, chanterelles), maple syrup, sun-dried tomatoes, flavored vinegars, dried fruits, gourmet beans, rice, and grains. Among notable products are French coffee extract, Tahitian vanilla beans, pine nuts, asafetida powder, horseradish powder, fine sea salt, Chaat Masala, chutneys, and mushroom powder. If you enjoy cooking and eating, stock up—Festive Foods will pay shipping if your order totals $150 or more.

Special Factors: Satisfaction is guaranteed; shipping is not charged on orders over $150; returns are accepted for exchange, refund, or credit.

GIBBSVILLE CHEESE SALES

W–2663 CTH–00
SHEBOYGAN FALLS, WI
  53085–2971
920–564–3242
FAX: 920–564–6129

Price List: free
Pay: check or MO
Sells: Wisconsin cheese and summer sausage
Store: same address (5 miles south of Sheboygan Falls on Hwy. 32); Monday to Friday 7:30–5, Saturday 7:30–4

Gibbsville Cheese Sales is a standout even in Wisconsin, the Dairy State, where everyone produces cheese. The company's prices are appetizingly low—as little as $2.80 a pound for mild cheddar in 5-pound bulk packaging. Several types of Old Wisconsin summer sausage and beef sticks are also offered, in addition to well-priced economy and gift boxes for a variety of budgets and tastes.

Gibbsville has been in business since 1933 and produces the most popular kinds of cheese, including cheddar (mild, medium, aged, super-sharp white, garlic, and caraway), Monterey jack (including jacks flavored with salami and hot pepper), and colby (including a reduced-fat version). Five pounds of rindless colby cost $2.80 a pound, and prices of other cheeses are just as reasonable. If you can get to the store in Gibbsville, you can even watch the production process through a viewing window. In addition to the cheeses of its own manufacture, Gibbsville Cheese sells swiss (baby, medium, aged, and lace), provolone, muenster, Parmesan, Romano, mozzarella, gouda, Pine River Cold-Pack Cheese Spreads (including Sharp Cheddar, Swiss Almond, Port Wine, Smoked, etc.), and blue, Limburger, and string cheeses. The price list indicates which cheeses are "lower in fat" and includes several "lite" versions of favorites.

Please note: Shipments are not made during summer months (approximately June to September).

Special Factors: Price quote by letter with SASE.

JAFFE BROS. NATURAL FOODS

P.O. BOX 636-W
VALLEY CENTER, CA
92082–0636
760–749–1133
FAX: 760–749–1282

Catalog: free
Pay: check, MO, MC, V, Discover
Sells: organically grown food
Warehouse: (call first) 28560 Lilac Rd., Valley Center, CA; Sunday to Thursday 8–5, Friday 8–3
E-mail: jb54@worldnet.att.net

Jaffe Bros., established in 1948, sells organically and naturally grown dried fruit, nuts, seeds, beans, grains, nut butters, honey, and many other organically grown items, through the 22-page catalog. Prices average 30% below comparable retail, but there are greater savings on certain items, and quantity discounts are offered on many goods. Jaffe's products are marketed under the Jaybee label, and virtually all of them are grown "organically" (without fumigants or poisonous sprays and with "nonchemical" fertilizers) or "naturally" (similarly treated but not fertilized).

You'll save on wholesome foods here—dried peaches, Black Mission figs, Monukka raisins, papaya, dates of several types, almonds, pine nuts, macadamias, nut butters, brown rice, flours and grains, seeds for eating and sprouting, 15 kinds of peas and beans, unheated honey, coconut, jams, juices, carob powder, salad oil, olives, herb teas, and much more. (Most of the produce is packed in 2-, 5-, 25-, and 50-pound units.) The catalog also lists dehydrated mushrooms, sun-dried tomatoes, canned olives, organic spaghetti sauce, low-salt dill pickles and sauerkraut, organic whole wheat pasta, kosher maple syrup, organic applesauce, and Organica cleaning products. If you'd like to bestow goodness upon a friend, be sure to see the group of gift assortments—nicely packaged selections of favorites, at reasonable prices.

Wholesale customers, please request the "wholesale" catalog on your company letterhead; minimums (pounds or number of items) apply.

Special Factors: Quantity discounts are available; problems should be reported to Jaffe within 10 days of receipt of goods; warehouse is closed Saturdays; C.O.D. orders are accepted.

E.C. KRAUS HOME WINE AND BEER-MAKING EQUIPMENT AND SUPPLIES

P.O. BOX 7850-WC
INDEPENDENCE, MO
  64054
816–254–7448
FAX: 816–254–7051

Catalog: free
Pay: check, MO, MC, V
Sells: wine- and beer-making supplies
Store: 733 S. Northern Blvd., Independence, MO; Monday to Friday 8–5:30, Saturday 9–1

E.C. Kraus, founded in 1967, can help you save up to half on the cost of wine, beer, and liqueurs by producing them yourself. The firm's 24-page illustrated catalog features supplies and equipment for the home vintner and brewer, beginner or experienced: malt and hops, fruit and grape concentrates, yeasts, additives, clarifiers, purifiers and preservatives, fruit acids, acidity indicators, hydrometers, bottle caps, rubber stoppers, corks and corkscrews, barrel spigots and liners, tubing and siphons, steam juicers, fermenters, fruit presses, dried botanicals, and much more. The T. Noirot extracts can be used to create low-priced liqueurs, and there are books and manuals to provide help if you want to learn more. If you're just getting started, you may find the Kraus "Necessities Box"—equipment and supplies for making 5 gallons of wine or 4 gallons of beer—just what you need.

Special Factors: Local ordinances may regulate production of alcoholic beverages; C.O.D. accepted.

THE MAPLES FRUIT FARM, INC.

P.O. BOX 167
CHEWSVILLE, MD 21721
TEL/FAX: 301–733–0777

Catalog: $1
Pay: check, MO, MC, V, Discover
Sells: dried fruit, nuts, coffee, gift baskets, etc.
Store: 13144 Pennsylvania Ave., Hagerstown, MD; Monday to Thursday 9–6, Friday 9–7, Saturday 8–5

The 16-page catalog of dried fruits, nuts, coffee, tea, and sweets from Maples Fruit Farm pictures an early view of the Farm, which has been operated by the same family for 200 years. The prices here are mouth-watering—savings of 25% to 50% were found on selected items. The dried fruits include apricots, dates, pears, peaches, and pineapple. (Fruits prepared with sulphur dioxide are clearly indicated in the catalog.) Raw and roasted (salted and unsalted) nuts are offered, including cashews, almonds, peanuts, pecans, macadamia nuts, filberts, black walnuts, and a number of others, including trail mix. Two pounds of raw pecans from Maples are half as expensive as those from a specialty pecan source, and the roasted macadamia nuts, honey-roasted peanuts, and cashews are all better buys here. Among sweets, Maryland grade-A amber maple syrup costs less than the syrup offered by competitors (who sell Canadian and New York state products). Maples Fruit Farm also sells 38 kinds of gourmet coffee, roasted fresh at the firm's gourmet shop daily.

Reasonably priced gift baskets are available, and if you can stock up or share orders, check the wholesale prices on cases. Don't miss the store if you're in the Hagerstown area—drop in to smell the coffee roasting, and sample some of the 5,000 gourmet treats on the shelves.

Special Factors: Satisfaction is guaranteed; minimum order is $25 (excluding shipping).

MOUNTAIN ARK TRADING CO.

799 OLD LEICESTER HWY.
ASHEVILLE, NC 28806
800–643–8909
FAX: 704–252–9479

Catalog: free
Pay: check, MO, MC, V, Discover
Sells: Japanese natural foods
Store: same address; Monday to Friday 9–5:30
Online: http://www.mountainark.com

This is a great source for persons who are on macrobiotic diets or who love to cook Japanese-style. Mountain Ark was recommended by a reader who regularly orders her grains, seaweed, and nuts in bulk from this company. The 38-page black-and-white catalog has a reader-friendly table of contents that will guide you from aduki beans to yuku vinegar. Beans, seeds, and grains of every kind, Chinese herbs and Taoist tonic herbal formulas, teas, vinegars, seaweeds, noodles, flours and cereals, and lentils; sugar-free candies, cookies, and syrups; an array of miso, dried fruits, soy and other sauces, and cooking oils are among the fine foods listed here. There are plenty of obscure and hard-to-find items, such as dried daikon, spelt pasta, and mugwort mochi. Mountain Ark also has cookware and kitchen items such as steamers, tempura pots, sushi-making kits, and Japanese knives. A full line of Weleda personal care products (sage deodorant, salt toothpaste, calendula baby soap, green clay powder, etc.) are available, as well as a number of intriguing books about healing, alternative approaches to diet and health, and Japanese and macrobiotic cooking. The prices are excellent, about 20% to 25% less than you'd find at stores, but are dependent to some degree on the dollar's strength against the yen and other foreign currencies. The minimum order is $35. Japanese is spoken here, as well as English.

Special Factors: Returns are accepted, but see catalog for terms; quantity discounts and wholesale orders available; C.O.D. orders are accepted; Canadian orders must be made in U.S. funds.

NEW ENGLAND CHEESEMAKING SUPPLY CO.

P.O. BOX 85, DEPT. WBM
ASHFIELD, MA 01330–0085
413–628–3808
FAX: 413–628–4061

Catalog: $1
Pay: check, MO, MC, V
Sells: cheese-making supplies and equipment
Store: same address; Monday to Friday 8–4 (call first)
E-mail: info@cheesemaking.com
Online: http://www.cheesemaking.com

Making cheese at home is one of the few do-it-yourself endeavors with a nominal price tag that doesn't require significant skills or time investment. New England Cheesemaking Supply, in business since 1978, can provide you with all the tools and materials you'll need to produce hard, soft, and semi-soft cheeses, at savings of up to 80% on the prices charged by supermarkets and specialty stores for the same kinds of cheeses.

Soft cheese is the easiest to make, and may be the cheapest, since you can get as much as two pounds of cheese from a gallon of milk. Milk sells for $1.30 a half gallon in some parts of the country, and flavored soft cheeses often cost $4.50 to $7.00 per pound, or as much as $2.80 for packaged, four-ounce varieties. So, by using the "Gourmet Soft Cheese Kit," you can recoup the $16.95 cost, plus the price of the milk, after making as little as two pounds of soft cheese. This kit is designed for the beginner and comes with cheese starter, cheesecloth, a dairy thermometer, and recipes. It can be used to make crème fraîche as well as fromage blanc—generic soft cheese—in as little as ten minutes. (If you use skim milk, you can produce low-calorie, low-cholesterol cheese, and omit the salt for sodium-restricted diets.)

New England Cheesemaking Supply also sells a "basic" cheese kit (for ricotta, gouda, Monterey jack, cheddar, etc.), and others for making mozzarella and goat cheese. Rennet (animal and vegetable), a large selection of starter and direct-set cultures, lipase powders, mold powder, cheese wax, cheesecloth, thermometers, molds for shaping hard and soft cheese, and several books on cheese production are offered. Experienced cheese producers should see the 16-page catalog for the machinery as well: a home milk pasteurizer and Wheeler's hard cheese press are available. The woman who runs this firm is an experienced cheese producer and can answer your questions by phone or letter.

Special Factors: Price quote by phone, e-mail, or letter (with SASE); minimum order is $20 with credit cards; C.O.D. orders are accepted.

NORTHWESTERN COFFEE MILLS

MIDDLE RD., BOX 370
LA POINTE, WI 54850
800–243–5283
715–747–5825
FAX: 715–747–5405

Catalog: free, $2 outside U.S.
Pay: check, MO, MC, V, AE
Sells: coffee, tea, herbs, spices, coffee filters, coffee flavors, and syrups
Store: same address, and 217 North Broadway, 2nd Floor, Milwaukee, WI; Monday to Friday 10–5:30, Saturday 10–4
E-mail: nwcoftsp@win.bright.net

If coffee is America's drink, Wisconsin may be harboring a national treasure. It's the home of Northwestern Coffee Mills, which set up shop in 1875 in a town better known for a different sort of brew. Northwestern begins with top-quality Arabica, and roasts each type of bean separately to develop its optimum flavor. The "Midwest" or European Roast is the specialty here; it's lighter than the "West Coast" coffees best characterized by the famous Seattle beanery.

The 16-page catalog describes each of the blends, straights, dark roasts, and decaffeinated coffees, noting relative strength, body, aroma, and flavor. Among the blends are American Breakfast, North Coast Blend (a strong, after-dinner coffee), Mocha Java, a New Orleans chicory blend, and Island Blend, a favorite of local restaurateurs that "stands up well when heated for hours on end." There are fancy straights, including Brazil Santos, Costa Rica Tarrazu, Kenya AA, Colombia Excelso, and Sumatra Lintong. Puerto Rico Yauco Selecto is available, as well as estate-grown Java and Hawaiian Kona, Yemen Mocha (the real mocha from Yemen), and other rare straight coffees. Decaf drinkers can choose from water-processed blends and straights. Northwestern Coffee anticipates a good supply of organic beans, which it offers in regular and dark roasts, plain and decaffeinated. Coffee filters for all types of drip and percolator systems are sold, including Chemex and Wisconsin-made "Natural Brew" unbleached filters.

Northwestern also maintains a premium tea department. The catalog describes how tea is grown and processed, tea grading, and the types of teas Northwestern sells—flavored, black, green, oolong, and decaffeinated. The varieties include rare estate teas and top-grade Ceylon, India Assam, Darjeeling, Irish Breakfast, Russian Caravan, Japan Sencha, "China Dragon Well Panfired Leaf," and Orange Spiced tea, among others. Northwestern's prices on single pounds of coffee or four-ounce packages of tea are market-rate, but the firm will sell both to consumers at bulk rates, saving you up to 30%. There are price breaks at 5, 10, and 25 pounds, and since coffee in whole-bean form will keep well for several months in the freezer, it makes sense to order as much as you can store. Northwestern is also introducing a coffee subscription plan to save you money on shipping charges—see the current catalog for details.

Last but not least, Northwestern publishes a separate price list that features herbs, spices, and other flavorings, in supermarket sizes and in bulk. Several capsicums (peppers) are offered, and dried vegetables (garlic granules, horseradish powder, mushrooms, etc.), blended salt-free and salted seasonings, coffee syrups, and natural extracts (vanilla, almond, cocoa, cinnamon, orange, etc.) are also listed.

Special Factors: Satisfaction is guaranteed; quantity discounts are available; returns are accepted within 90 days for exchange, refund, or credit.

RED HILL MUSHROOMS

P.O. BOX 4234
GETTYSBURG, PA 17325
800–822–4003
717–337–3038
FAX: 717–337–3936

Price List: free
Pay: check, MO, MC, V
Sells: fresh mushrooms and growing kits
Store: 1540 Biglerville Rd., Gettysburg, PA; Monday to Friday 8–5:30, Saturday by appointment
E-mail: info@supergrit.com

¡Si!

Shiitake and oyster mushrooms enjoyed a great vogue in fashionable food several years ago and have subsequently found a permanent home in the dishes of many good cooks. Red Hill Mushrooms sells oyster mushrooms, which have a fine, delicate flavor, and the slightly nutty shiitake, which is crunchy when raw. The price at this writing is competitive, depending on where you live and how available these mushrooms are to you—$10 a pound for shiitake, $8 for oyster mushrooms—and they're offered in 3- and 5-pound boxes. Red Hill is also home to the "Shiitake Log Kit" ($25), a compressed sawdust log enriched with wheat germ and millet and infused with shiitake spawn. Follow the care directions given in the literature, and you should be rewarded with as many as four crops of shiitake. When the log ceases to produce, you can crumble it up and use it as mulch in your garden!

Special Factors: Minimum order is $25.

SULTAN'S DELIGHT

P.O. BOX 090302
FORT HAMILTON
  STATION
BROOKLYN, NY
  11209–0302
800–852–5046
718–745–2121
FAX: 718–745–2563

Catalog: free with SASE
Pay: check, MO, MC, V, AE, Discover
Sells: Middle Eastern and Mediterranean foods and gifts
Store: mail order only
Online: http://www.sultansdelight.com

Sultan's Delight specializes in authentic Middle Eastern food specialties, sold at excellent prices—up to 50% below comparable goods in gourmet shops. The firm was established in 1980 and offers both raw ingredients and prepared specialties. See the catalog if you're looking for canned tahini, couscous, tabouleh, fig and apricot jams, stuffed grapevine leaves, bulghur, orzo, fava beans, ground sumac, or Turkish figs. You'll also find olives, herbs and spices, jumbo pistachios and other nuts, roasted chickpeas, halvah, Turkish delight, marzipan paste, olive oil, Turkish coffee, fruit leather, filo, feta cheese, and other specialties. Cookbooks for Greek, Lebanese, Indian, and Middle Eastern cuisine are available, as well as Turkish coffeepots, inlaid backgammon sets, and other intriguing items.

Special Factors: Minimum order is $20.

RELATED PRODUCTS/COMPANIES

For other mail-order food companies, see "Spices, Condiments, and Flavorings," next section.
Cookbooks • Jessica's Biscuit
Discount coupons to local restaurants and food stores • Hot Coupons
Gourmet foods • Zabar's, Le Jardin du Gourmet
Guides to preserving, home brewing, canning, etc. • Storey Communications
Honey products and mead-making supplies • Brushy Mountain Bee Farm
What's-in-your-cabinet recipe ideas • Reader's Digest

Spices, Condiments, and Flavorings

Herbs and spices, condiments, flavoring oils and extracts

The companies in this section carry all the little items that jazz up our palates, whether it's exotic and unusual oils for flavoring, Cajun spices, Indian chutneys, or Vermont maple cream. These are some of the best items to buy mail order, since they're often sold in bulk—which can mean up to 90% savings. Just be sure that you store your herbs and spices in airtight bottles or jars, away from heat and light.

Also see the listings in the previous section for other firms that sell gourmet condiments, spices, and herbs.

FIND IT FAST

CONDIMENTS • The CMC Company, Grandma's, Palmer's Maple Products, Spices Etc., Wood's Cider Mill
ETHNIC SEASONINGS, SAUCES, CONDIMENTS • The CMC Company, Pendery's, Spices Etc.
FLAVORINGS, ESSENTIAL OILS, EXTRACTS • Bickford, Rafal, San Francisco Herb
HERBS AND SPICES • Grandma's, Pendery's, Rafal, San Francisco Herb, Spices Etc.
TEA AND COFFEE • Grandma's, Rafal, San Francisco Herb, Spices Etc.

BICKFORD FLAVORS

19007 ST. CLAIR AVE.
CLEVELAND, OH
44117–1001
800–283–8322
216–531–6006
FAX: 216–531–2006

Price List: free
Pay: check, MO, MC, V
Sells: flavorings
Store: same address; Monday to Friday 9–5

Bickford, established in 1914, makes and sells its own concentrated flavorings, from naturally derived oils, leaving out the usual alcohol and sugar that you'll find in other "pure" essences. Over 100 flavorings are offered, from almond to onion to watermelon. Vanilla is sold here in white, dark, and regular versions. (The white vanilla won't tint your angel food cake or meringues.) All of Bickford's flavorings are sold in 1-ounce bottles for $2.39, which is competitive pricing, but the good buys are pints ($20.75) and larger sizes. (Vanilla is also sold in bottles of 2, 4, and 8 ounces.) In addition to an unparalleled selection of flavorings, Bickford also sells about 100 exotically flavored oils (ginger, peach, caramel, and sherry oil are all available), food colorings, and carob syrup.

Special Factors: Flavorings are free of alcohol and sugar. If you order $1,000 worth of merchandise in one year, you'll qualify for their wholesale rates thereafter.

THE CMC COMPANY

P.O. DRAWER 322
AVALON, NJ 08202
800-CMC–2780
609–861–3062
FAX: 609–861–3065

Catalog: $1, refundable with first order
Pay: check, MO, MC, V, AE, Discover
Sells: gourmet seasonings and ethnic specialties
Store: mail order only
Online: http://clever.net/wwwmall/cmc

If you're one of the legion of home cooks who'd love to replicate the great flavors of Mexican and Asian restaurant cuisine, you've just found the source for the flavorings that make the dishes authentic. CMC has been in business since 1990 with a seasonings line that features Mexican chilis (dried, powdered, canned, etc.), hot sauces, and moles (rojo, verde, poblano, pepian), as well as such specialties as Mexican dried shrimp, chorizos, masa harina, and cooking utensils for Mexican dishes. CMC's Thai food selection includes curry pastes, tamarind paste, trassi (dried shrimp paste), Kaffir lime leaves, jasmine rice, and all of the sauces—fish, mushroom soy, satay, sriracha, etc.—that make Thai food transcendental. Your efforts at inspired Indian food will be improved by tandoori paste and Patak chutneys, black cumin seed, chapati flour, a great selection of individual curry spices, ghee (clarified butter), and the other ingredients sold here. And there are Szechuan spices, Japanese seasonings and ingredients, and Busha Browne's Jamaican Specialties (pukka hot sauce, hot pepper sherry, jerk sauce and seasoning, etc.). Many of the spices and flavorings listed in the 32-page catalog are hard to find elsewhere, and therefore hard to comparison-price, but several products—garam masala, basmati rice, and lemon grass powder, for example—were found to be 10% to 50% less expensive here than at other gourmet sources.

Wholesale customers, please note that discounts are given to resellers and food-service professionals.

Special Factors: Keep the catalog, since it's updated with inserts from printing to printing.

GRANDMA'S SPICE SHOP

Catalog: $1, refundable
Pay: check, MO, MC, V
Sells: herbs, spices, coffee, tea, etc.
Store: mail order only

HC 62, BOX 65-D
UPPER TRACT, WV 26866
TEL/FAX: 304–358–2346

Once upon a time, a real Grandma—rocking chair and all—ran this gourmet emporium. Since its sale several years ago, the firm has expanded the range and depth of the stock to include such items as Hawaiian and Cuban coffee, Linzer Torte coffee (flavored with raspberry and chocolate), raspberry leaves, and herbal Worcestershire sauce, among other items. The 26-page catalog includes coffees (regular, flavored, and decaffeinated), loose teas (green, black, flavored, decaffeinated), special rare estate teas, Benchley tea bags, a large herb and spice selection, dehydrated vegetables, bean soup blends, powdered vitamin C, herbal vinegars and honeys, massage oils, and much more.

Spice racks, mortar and pestle sets, gift baskets, pepper mills, and a smattering of other nonfood items are also available. The herbs and spices afford the best savings, up to 60% if bought in bulk (half or full pounds). Coffee and tea connoisseurs should see the catalog for the unusual and rare varieties (which are not sold at a discount).

Several catalog pages are devoted to potpourri, sachets, and related ingredients—simmering spice blends, cedar moth mixes, bath herbs, pomander rolling mixes, pinecones, dried flowers, potpourri oils, and bath oils (stock scents and custom blends are available). Prices of the smaller sizes are competitive with bath and gift shops; as with the herbs, you'll save the most on the potpourri and ingredients when you buy by the pound.

Please note: Grandma's Spice Shop offers a recorded (audio) version of the catalog and can supply labels for spices and other purposes in Braille, at no extra charge.

Special Factors: Minimum order is $15.

PALMER'S MAPLE PRODUCTS

BOX 240 R.D.
WAITSFIELD, VT
05673–9710
TEL/FAX: 802–496–3696

Brochure and Price List: free with long SASE
Pay: check, MO, MC, V
Sells: maple syrup, cream, candy, and jelly
Store: Mehuron's Market and Bisbee's Hardware, Waitsfield, VT

Delbert Palmer has been sugaring since he was 10 years old, and in early spring he heads for the woods to draw the sap that will be transformed into a season's worth of maple syrup. He's still using the sugar house that his great-grandfather built 180 years ago! The Palmers' brochure describes the entire process, including grading and canning.

The Palmers are nice when it comes to the price, which at this writing is $11.40 a quart, compared with $16.95 for the same grade of Vermont syrup sold through another gourmet foods catalog. Even the Palmers' highest per-ounce price, for half pints, is lower by a third than what other mail-order firms are charging. The Palmers sell three grades of syrup—light amber (Fancy), medium amber (A), and dark amber (B)—at the same price. If you like a very delicate flavor, try the Fancy grade; grade B has a strong "mapley" flavor that suits some palates and purposes (cooking and baking) more than the other two grades. Maple cream, maple jelly, and candies may also be available; see the price list for information.

Special Factors: Send long, stamped, self-addressed envelope for brochure and price list.

PENDERY'S INC.

1221 MANUFACTURING ST.

DALLAS, TX 75207

800–533–1870

214–741–1870

FAX: 214–761–1966

Catalog: $2, $3.50 outside U.S.
Pay: check, MO, MC, V, AE, Discover
Sells: herbs, spices, Mexican seasonings, hot sauces, and cooking accessories
Store: 304 E. Belknap St., Fort Worth, TX

 ¡Si! ★

Pendery's has been spicing up drab dishes since 1870 and can add the authentic touch of real, full-strength chilies to your Tex-Mex cuisine for a fraction of the prices charged by gourmet shops. The firm's 96-page catalog describes the origins of the company and its contributions to the development of Tex-Mex chili seasonings. It's not a coincidence that "those captivating capsicums" occupy several catalog pages and include whole and ground pods, blends, and salsas, over 200 hot sauces, and chili memorabilia. Scores of general and specialty seasonings and flavorings are offered, including fajita seasoning, jalapeño peppers, and spice-rack standards from allspice to white pepper. Among the unusual or hard-to-find ingredients available here are masa harina, Mexican chocolate, annatto, horseradish powder, Worcestershire powder, dehydrated cilantro, corn shucks for tamales, and Mexican vanilla. Pendery's catalog also offers cookbooks, mortars, mills, decorative tableware, and handsome kitchen accessories.

Special Factors: No C.O.D. orders.

RAFAL SPICE COMPANY

2521 RUSSELL ST.
DETROIT, MI 48207–2632
313–259–6373
FAX: 313–259–6220

Catalog: free
Pay: check, MO, MC, V, AE, Discover
Sells: spices, herbs, coffee, tea, flavorings, cookbooks, etc.
Store: same address; Monday to Saturday 7–4

If you have a weakness for Cajun and Creole dishes, you'll love Rafal Spice, which charges up to 57% less than a New Orleans mail-order firm selling the identical foods. Rafal Spice also sells coffee and tea in a range of blends and flavors, and well-priced herbs and spices, from alfalfa leaves to za'atar powder. Rafal offers a number of very uncommon ingredients, such as bladder wrack, devil's claw tuber powder, hawthorn berries, sanicle, skunk cabbage root, and powdered soy sauce.

Among the food and flavorings brands you'll find in the 72-page catalog are Angostura, Bell's, Clancy's, Crystal, Gaylord Hauser, Jamaican Hellfire, Konriko, Lawry's, Mrs. Dash, Mrs. Wages, Old Bay, Trappey, Wright's, and Zatarain's. Liquid Spice by Dilijan, Lorann flavorings and extracts, food coloring, kitchen tools, spice grinders, labels, storage jars, coffee filters, tea infusers, and six pages of cookbooks wrap up the catalog. The shipping is computed fairly (on weight and distance), and the catalog even includes a few recipes.

Please note that botanicals not intended for consumption are indicated in the catalog with an asterisk.

Special Factors: Satisfaction is guaranteed; allow three weeks for delivery of order.

SAN FRANCISCO HERB CO.

**250 14TH ST., DEPT.
WBMC
SAN FRANCISCO, CA
94103
800–227–4530
415–861–7174
FAX: 415–861–4440**

Catalog: free
Pay: check, MO, MC, V, Discover
Sells: culinary herbs, teas, spices, essential oils, and potpourri ingredients
Wholesale Outlet: same address; Monday to Friday 10–4, Saturday 10–2
Online: http://www.sfherb.com

Reader-recommended San Francisco Herb Co. is known for excellent prices and a great selection of herbs, spices, potpourri ingredients, essential and fragrance oils, flavorings, botanicals, and teas. San Francisco Herb was founded in 1973 and sells to the public at wholesale prices.

The culinary herbs and spices range from the routine—allspice, cinnamon, garlic, saffron—to such uncommon seasonings as spice blends for Greek foods and cilantro leaf. Among the botanicals are St.-John's-wort, goldenseal powder, psyllium, pau d'arco, and echinacea. Some of the botanicals for beverage use are chamomile, peppermint, and spearmint.

The catalog also features dozens of recipes for sachets, and simmering and jar potpourris. The "Holiday Fruit and Nut" recipe is a festive combination of apple slices, cinnamon sticks, nuts, and pinecones with a delectable cider spice fragrance. "Orchard Peach" is a lazy summer blend of peachy fruit slices, pods, and soft white blossoms. If you are not experienced in making potpourri, try some of the recipes to become more familiar with blending colors and fragrances.

The spices and botanicals are sold by the 4-ounce unit and by the pound, with quantity discounts of 10% on purchases of 5 pounds or more of the same item. San Francisco Herb also sells glass vials, spice jars, flavored teas in bulk, dehydrated vegetables, shelled nuts, sprouting seeds, and such foods as lemon powder, arrowroot powder, bacon bits, pine nuts, and roasted chicory root.

Special Factors: Satisfaction is guaranteed; volume discounts are available; authorized returns are accepted within 15 days (a 15% restocking fee may be charged); minimum order is $30; C.O.D. orders are accepted.

SPICES ETC.

P.O. BOX 5266
CHARLOTTESVILLE, VA
22905–5266
800–827–6373
804–293–9410
FAX: 800–827–0145
FAX: 804–293–4655

Catalog: free (see text)
Pay: check, MO, MC, V, Discover
Sells: herbs, spices, tea, etc.
Store: mail order only
E-mail: spices@spicesetc.com
Online: http://www.spicesetc.com

"For everything there is a seasoning"—so goes the motto of Spices Etc., which has been in business since 1991. They offer a wealth of seasonings through a 48-page catalog, including straight bulk-packaged herbs and spices at savings of up to 75%. The spice blends cover a wide culinary range, from celery salt and apple pie seasonings to garam masala, pesto, and exotic specialty blends. Chilis, snack seasonings, dehydrated vegetables, natural seasonings, bulk-packaged teas, hot pepper sauces, mustards, and other edibles are available, and there are lots of creative seasoning blends to substitute for plain salt to enliven your popcorn, salad dressings, and homemade chips. There are pages of grinders (including a battery-powered pepper mill), mortar-and-pestle sets, spice racks, and empty jars in several sizes. Gift assortments and seasoning collections are also offered.

Please note: The catalog, regularly $2, is free if you mention BWBM.

Special Factors: Spices and seasonings are available in one-gallon quantities.

WOOD'S CIDER MILL

R.D. 2, BOX 477
SPRINGFIELD, VT 05156
802–263–5547

Brochure: free with SASE
Pay: check, MO, MC, V
Sells: cider jelly and syrups
Farm: call for appointment

The Wood family has maintained a farm in Vermont since 1798 and today produces wonderful, cider-based treats for mail-order customers. The prices here are better than reasonable—in fact, Wood's cider jelly can be found selling in other catalogs at prices nearly twice as high as those charged by the Woods themselves! And another firm's cider jelly is double the price for the same amount.

The Cider Mill is best known for its jelly, which is made of evaporated apple cider. From 30 to 50 apples are needed to make the cider that's concentrated in just 1 pound of jelly, but you'll understand why when you taste it on toast or muffins, or try it with pork and other meats as a condiment. Boiled cider is also available; it's a less-concentrated essence that is recommended as a base for a hot drink, as a ham glaze, and as a topping for ice cream and pancakes. For pancakes, however, try the cider syrup, a blend of boiled cider and maple syrup. (It's also outstanding as a basting sauce for Thanksgiving turkeys and even roast chicken.) Straight maple syrup is also produced on the farm, and look for the Woods' newest—cinnamon cider syrup.

Special Factors: Satisfaction is guaranteed; returns are accepted for exchange or refund; quantity discounts are available; minimum order is four 8-ounce jars.

RELATED PRODUCTS/COMPANIES

Condiments • Jaffe Bros., Mountain Ark, Zabar's, Le Jardin du Gourmet, EDGE Distributing
Ethnic seasonings, sauces, and condiments • Mountain Ark, Sultan's Delight
Flavorings, extracts • Northwestern Coffee Mills
Spices and herbs • Bulkfoods.com, Deer Valley Farm, Festive Foods, Mountain Ark, Northwestern Coffee Mills, Caprilands Herb Farm, Atlantic Spice, EDGE Distributing

GARDEN, FARM, AND LAWN

Seeds, bulbs, live plants, supplies, tools, and equipment for gardening, farming, lawn care, and landscaping

The earliest mail-order catalog in this country is believed to have been a seed list, and if you're one of the nearly 70 million Americans who gardens, you probably use catalogs extensively to plan your garden. So you know that the mail (or UPS truck) can bring you a fantastic selection of bulbs, plants, flowers, herbs, and other growing things, as well as tools and equipment—often at considerable savings, compared to farm and garden centers.

Choosing what to grow depends on what you want. An apple orchard, a little alyssum edging the walkways, a crop of asparagus, a windbreak at the property line, all require completely different kinds of resources. And they yield different benefits, from aesthetic (flowers) to nutritional (vegetables) to financial (market crops, property enhancement, etc.). Before you buy a single seed, make sure what you're planting is suitable for your climate or home environment. In addition to evaluating the light and drainage, test the soil. Ohio Earth Food, listed in this chapter, will test your soil for $17, which is less than half the price of the best-known home gardener kits.

After you decide what you're going to do with your land or growing space, hit the books—horticultural literature is rich with masterworks on every aspect of the "whats" to grow and the "hows" of doing it.

If you need farm machinery, see the listing of Central Michigan Tractor & Parts in "Auto, Marine, and Aviation Equipment." If you're building your own greenhouse or cold frames, see Arctic Glass & Window Outlet in "House and Home: Building, Renovation, and Upkeep" for thermopane panels. Other lawn- and garden-related products are sold by some of the companies listed in the "Tools, Hardware, Shop Machines" chapter. You'll also find lawn and garden furniture in the "Furnishings" section of "House and Home."

FIND IT FAST

BEEKEEPING SUPPLIES • Brushy Mountain Bee Farm

BULBS • Breck's, Daylily Discounters, Dutch Gardens, Jackson & Perkins, Mellinger's, J.E. Miller, Pinetree Garden, John Scheepers, R. H. Shumway, Van Bourgondien, Van Dyck's, Van Engelen

FLOWER, VEGETABLE, HERB SEEDS • Burrell's, Butterbrooke Farm, Caprilands, Fedco, Gurney's, Johnny's, Le Jardin du Gourmet, Mellinger's, J.E. Miller, Pinetree Garden, Rohrer's Seeds, Seymour's, R.H. Shumway

GARDEN AND LAWN DECOR AND FURNITURE • Caprilands, Florist Products, Jackson & Perkins, Turner Greenhouses

GARDENING BOOKS • Burrell's, Butterbrooke Farm, Caprilands, Daylily Discounters, Fedco, Johnny's, Le Jardin du Gourmet, Mellinger's, Pinetree Garden, John Scheepers, Turner Greenhouses

GREENHOUSES • Bob's Superstrong Greenhouse Plastic, Burrell's, Florist Products, Mellinger's, Turner Greenhouses

LIVE PLANTS • Brittingham, Carino Nurseries, Fedco, Gurney's, Jackson & Perkins, Le Jardin du Gourmet, Mellinger's, J.E. Miller, Nor'East Miniature Roses, Pinetree Garden, Prentiss Court, R.H. Shumway

POND LINERS AND POND EQUIPMENT • Bob's Superstrong Greenhouse Plastic

TOOLS AND SUPPLIES • Burrell's, Daylily Discounters, EON Industries, Fedco, Florist Products, Johnny's, Mellinger's, Ohio Earth Food, Pinetree Garden, Rohrer's Seeds, Van Bourgondien

BOB'S SUPERSTRONG GREENHOUSE PLASTIC

BOX 42-WM, NECHE, ND
   58265
BOX 1450-WM, ALTONA,
   MB R0G OB0 CANADA
204-327-5540
FAX: 204-327-5527

Brochure: $1 or two first-class stamps
Pay: check or MO
Sells: greenhouse plastic and fastening systems, and pond liners
Showrooms: Neche, ND, and Altona, Manitoba, Canada (by appointment)
E-mail: northerngreenhouse@mb.sympatico.ca

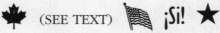 (SEE TEXT) ¡Si! ★

Bob Davis and his wife, Margaret Smith-Davis, are resourceful gardeners who experimented with different materials while trying to create an inexpensive greenhouse and discovered that woven polyethylene makes an ideal greenhouse skin, even in harsh climes. Their experiences with the material were so successful that they decided to market it themselves. In 1979, they founded Bob's Superstrong Greenhouse Plastic (also known as Northern Greenhouse Sales), which has become a great source for other resourceful gardeners who want to design their own greenhouses.

The Davises offer "superstrong" woven poly and two anchoring systems. One is "Cinchstrap," a bright-white, flat, flexible poly strapping material that can be used for permanent anchoring and abrasion reduction in installation, and as a replacement for wood lathing in greenhouse assembly. The other, "Poly-Fastener," is a channel-system anchor that uses a flat spline to secure the poly. Prices for the woven poly run from 18 cents to 25 cents per square foot, depending on the quantity ordered; the standard width is 10 feet, but Bob can heat-seal additional widths together to create a wider swath. The Poly-Fastener runs between 53 cents and 58 cents a linear foot in 300' and 100' rolls (or $1 per foot for cut pieces), and the Cinchstrap costs 11 cents a linear foot on 100' rolls.

The 32-page catalog also includes several pages devoted to money-saving ideas and problem-solving tips from other customers. The poly applications aren't limited to greenhouses: solar collectors, vapor barriers, storm windows, pool covers, and tent floors are other possibilities. For more information and a copy of the catalog, send $1 or two first-class stamps. Call if you have questions, but please note the phone hours, below.

Canadian readers, please write to Canadian address for literature.

Special Factors: Calls are taken daily between 6 A.M. and 8 P.M., CST; C.O.D. orders are accepted.

BRECK'S DUTCH BULBS

6523 N. GALENA RD.,
  DEPT. CA 9610 A1
U.S. RESERVATION
  CENTER
PEORIA, IL 61632
800–854–4699
FAX: 309–589–2096

Catalog: free
Pay: check, MO, MC, V, AE, Discover
Sells: Dutch flower bulbs
Store: mail order only
Online: http://www.gardensolutions.com

Breck's has been "serving American gardeners since 1818" with a fine selection of flower bulbs, imported directly from Holland. The 52-page catalog is bursting with tulips, crocuses, daffodils, hyacinths, irises, jonquils, anemones, and wildflowers. Blooming period, height, color and markings, petal formation, and scent are all described in the text. Each order is shipped with the Breck's "Dutch Bulb Handbook," which covers naturalizing, planting, indoor growing, bulb care, and related topics. Discounts of up to 50% are offered on orders placed by July 31 for fall delivery and planting, and there are special savings on "samplers" and bulb collections.

Special Factors: Satisfaction is guaranteed; early-order discounts are available; returns are accepted for exchange, replacement, or refund.

BRITTINGHAM PLANT FARMS, INC.

P.O. BOX 2538, DEPT.
 WBM9
SALISBURY, MD 21802
410–749–5153
FAX: 800–749–5148

Catalog: free
Pay: check, MO, MC, V
Sells: berry plants
Store: Rte. 346 and Philip Morris Dr., Salisbury, MD; Monday to Friday 8–4:30, Saturday 8:30–12

Brittingham, a family business established in 1945, specializes in berries. The firm's 32-page color catalog is packed with cultivation tips and handling guidelines, and details on Brittingham's participation in Maryland's strawberry certification program. (The strict standards assure you virus-free strawberry plants.) Strawberries dominate the offerings, with over two dozen varieties in the current catalog, for early through late yields. Prices begin at $10.50 for 25 plants, and top at $83 per thousand for 25,000 plants (you may mix up to four varieties; new and patented varieties cost more). In addition to strawberries, Brittingham sells blackberries, raspberries, grapes, blueberries, asparagus, and rhubarb; quantity pricing also applies to these offerings.

Please note: Plants are not shipped to AK, CA, HI, NM, or outside the continental United States.

Special Factors: Satisfaction is guaranteed; replacements, refunds, or credits are offered within a specified date (see catalog); minimum orders vary, depending on the item; C.O.D. orders are accepted.

BRUSHY MOUNTAIN BEE FARM

610 BETHANY CHURCH
RD.
MORAVIAN FALLS, NC
28654–9600
800–233–7929
336–921–3640
FAX: 336–921–2681

Catalog: free
Pay: check, MO, MC, V, Discover
Sells: supplies for beekeeping, candle making, soap making, etc.
Store: same address; Monday to Friday 8:30–5
E-mail: sforrest@wilkes.net
Online: http://www.beeequipment.com

You'll like this company, whether you're a seasoned beekeeper or merely interested in the subject. The 72-page catalog printed on newsprint makes for a great read. Did you know that queen-marking colors are internationally standardized so that any queen's age can be easily determined? (1998's color: yellow.) The catalog is jam-packed with articles, calendars, suggested references, product descriptions, personal anecdotes, checklists, and advice. If you didn't know much about beekeeping before, you'll be tempted to buy the "Brushy Mountain Bee-Ginners Kit" with video here for $139.95. The prices at Brushy Mountain are about 20% to 30% below retail, and the owners, who've been in business since 1978, have a friendly attitude toward their customers. You'll find beekeeping supplies and equipment aplenty, from complete hives to all the necessary components, tools, and accessories; protective clothing for adults and children; mite treatments; queens and package bees; bee food; queen-marking kits; honey-producing presses, extractors, and other equipment; honey jars, bears, and bottles in every size and style; honey and beeswax products; mead-making books and equipment; candle molds and supplies; soap-making supplies; children's bee-related books, games, and puppets; and books and videos in many subjects, from instructional videos to a natural cosmetics primer. There's so much more, but you'll want to discover all the goodies in this catalog yourself.

Special Factors: Wholesale orders available to qualified buyers (inquire); satisfaction guaranteed; unused merchandise must be returned within 30 days (see catalog for details).

BURRELL'S BETTER SEEDS

P.O. BOX 150-WBMC
ROCKY FORD, CO 81067
719–254–3318
FAX: 719–254–3319

Catalog: free
Pay: check, MO, MC, V
Sells: flower and vegetable seeds, and growing supplies
Store: 405 North Main, Rocky Ford, CO; Monday to Friday 8–5

The home gardener who muses on the possibilities of turning a hobby into an income-producer should know about Burrell's Better Seeds, which has been serving commercial growers and florists since 1900. Burrell's also offers the home gardener modestly priced seed packets, but the professional grower will appreciate the quarter and half ounces and pounds—with price breaks at 1, 5, 25, 50, and 100 pounds. (You can combine orders with friends and neighbors to consolidate shipping costs on the larger sizes.)

Burrell's understands its mission: "No seedsman can hope to survive the critical judgment of the trade unless his product consistently delivers satisfaction." The varieties are chosen for a combination of marketability (appearance, disease resistance, longevity, and durability) and sensory pleasure. Burrell's treats some of its seeds, but you can request untreated. The catalog includes cultivation tips and typical yields for hundreds of varieties of vegetables and melons, from Mary Washington asparagus to Crimson Sweet watermelon. A few herbs—basil, chives, sweet marjoram, sage, etc.—are offered, as well as nearly 20 pages of flowers, including alyssum, asters, candytuft, digitalis, the "world's finest hybrid" petunias, sweet William, viola Johnny jump-up, wildflower seed blends (in dry and moist mixtures for different climates and soil types), and zinnias. Burrell's also sells a mechanical seeder, heater cables for out-of-season cultivation, weeders, sprayers, insecticides, peat pellet starter pots, 42" greenhouse "umbrellas" for under $17 each, portable greenhouses, and other cultivation tools, as well as several books helpful to the small commercial grower.

Customers outside the United States, please note: Catalogs cost $5 (in U.S. funds), and orders must be paid by postal money order or checks (drawn on U.S. banks) in U.S. currency.

Special Factors: Shipping is included on certain items; quantity discounts are available; institutional accounts are available; handling is $1 per order.

BUTTERBROOKE FARM SEED CO-OP

Price List: free with long SASE
Pay: check or MO
Sells: seeds
Store: mail order only

78 BARRY RD.
OXFORD, CT 06478–1529
203–888–2000

"Only pure, open-pollinated seeds will produce plants from which you can save seeds for planting another year." So says the straightforward price list from Butterbrooke Farm Seed Co-Op, where becoming "seed self-reliant" is one of several gardening objectives. Butterbrooke's members include organic farmers and seed savers, and the co-op has been in business since 1978. For just $15 per year, co-op members receive a 33% seed order discount, the quarterly Farm newsletter, *Germinations,* advisory services, the opportunity to buy rare or heirloom seeds, and other benefits. This is no-frills gardening at its sensible best, from the selection of scores of seeds (a well-rounded kitchen-garden full) to the Farm's own "Home Garden Collection" for first-time planters—a group of vegetable favorites. The packets are measured to reduce waste: The standard size (65 cents) will plant one to two 20-foot rows, and the large size ($1.50), three to four times that. All of the seeds are fresh, and they've been selected for short growing seasons. Butterbrooke also offers booklets on related topics—mulching, making compost, saving seeds—at nominal sums. You don't have to be a co-op member to buy from Butterbrooke, but the price of membership is low, and the advice service alone should justify the expense.

Special Factors: C.O.D. orders are accepted.

CAPRILANDS HERB FARM

**534 SILVER ST.
COVENTRY, CT 06238
860–742–7244**

Brochure: free
Pay: check, MO, MC, V, Discover
Sells: live herbs, dried herbs, seeds, spices, and gifts
Store: same address; daily 9–5 except holidays
E-mail: webmaster@caprilands.com
Online: http://www.caprilands.com

Caprilands offers live and dried culinary and medicinal herbs and a potpourri of herbaceous gifts, seasonings, and rite materials. The Farm is run by Mrs. Simmons, a herbalist of 60 years' standing, who provides a legendary luncheon program for visitors to her 18th-century farmhouse. (Reservations are essential; details on the program are given in the brochure.) In the years since its founding in 1929, Caprilands has become a respected source among collectors of hard-to-find herbs and those who dabble in "natural magic." Over 300 kinds of standard culinary herbs and less common plants are available, including Egyptian onions, rue, wormwood, mugwort, monardas, artemisia, santolinas, germander, lamb's ears, nepetas, ajuga, chamomile, woodruff, and many varieties of thyme ($2 to $3 per plant). Scented geraniums, roses, and flowers are also offered. (The plants are available at the Farm only, not by mail.) Packets of seeds for herbs and herbal flowers are available by mail for $1.25 each. Mrs. Simmons' own guides to the cultivation and use of herbs, including one of the bibles of herbal horticulture—*Herb Gardening in Five Seasons*—are sold through the brochure.

Caprilands offers a marvelous array of related goods: bronze sundials, wooden "good luck crows" for the garden, kitchen witches and costumed collectors' dolls, pomanders and sachet pillows, spice necklaces, wreaths, herbal hot pads, stoneware, note paper and calendars, and much more. Amid this olfactory plenty are two other great buys—rose petals and buds and lavender flowers for $12 per pound, compared with $15 and $22 in other catalogs; essential oils are also sold. Check out Caprilands' new website if you're browsing the net.

Wholesale customers, Caprilands Press books alone are sold at wholesale to resalers with a minimum order of 6 or 12 of the same title, discounted 20% to 40%; and to herb societies and garden clubs at 10% off. Orders to Caprilands Press can be made at the same address and numbers above.

Special Factors: Certain goods listed in the catalog are available only at the Farm.

CARINO NURSERIES

P.O. BOX 538, DEPT.
  WBMC
INDIANA, PA 15701
800–223–7075
724–463–3350
FAX: 724–463–3050

Catalog: free
Pay: check, MO, MC, V, Discover
Sells: evergreen seedlings and transplants
Store: mail order and nursery pickup only
E-mail: carino@mail.microserve.net
Online: http://www.carinonurseries.com

Carino Nurseries has been supplying Christmas tree farmers, nursery owners, and other planters with evergreen seedlings since 1945, and its prices and selection are excellent—savings of 60% are routine. The 36-page color catalog lists varieties of pine (Scotch, white, Mugho, Ponderosa, Japanese black, American red, and Austrian), fir (Douglas, Balsam, Canaan, Fraser, and Concolor), spruce (Colorado blue, white, Englemann, Black Hills, Norwegian, and Serbian), and white birch, dogwood, olive, black walnut, Chinese chestnut, Canadian hemlock, arborvitae, and other deciduous shrubs and trees.

Each entry in the catalog includes a description of the variety, age, and approximate height of the plants, and the number of years spent in original and transplant beds. There are specials on 10-plant collections, but most of the seedlings are sold in lots of 100 at prices up to 65% below those of other nurseries. If you're buying 500 or more, Carino's prices drop 50%. Recommendations on selecting, planting, and shearing (for later harvest as Christmas trees) are given, and the shipping methods and schedule policies are detailed in the catalog as well.

Special Factors: Shipments are made by UPS; minimum order is 10 or 100 plants (see text).

DAYLILY DISCOUNTERS INTERNATIONAL

ONE DAYLILY PLAZA
ALACHUA, FL 32615
904–462–1539
FAX: 904–462–5111

Catalog: $2
Pay: check, MO, MC, V, AE, Discover
Sells: daylilies
Store: mail order only
Online: http://www.daylilydiscounters.com

If you think that there are three kinds of daylilies—orange, yellow, and pink-and-white—Daylily Discounters will enlighten you. Between the voluminous text and the color photos, the firm's catalog covers 80 pages and includes details on the plant anatomy (including bracts and scapes), cultivation and division, and the hundreds of flowers themselves. Companion perennials are available, as well as soil enrichers, plant tags, and reference books. If you're not familiar with daylilies, you'll find them quite varied in color, markings, and formation; many bear a resemblance to orchids, but they're much less tricky to cultivate. Daylilies are less expensive, and more modestly priced yet at Daylily Discounters. And once you're on the mailing list, watch for flyers on clearance sales, with further savings of up to 50%.

Non-U.S. readers, please note: Before ordering, obtain import permits (if required), as indicated in the catalog.

Special Factors: Quantity discounts are available; minimum order is $25.

DUTCH GARDENS

P.O. BOX 200, DEPT.
  WMC9
ADELPHIA, NJ 07710–0200
800–818–3861
FAX: 732–780–7720

Catalog: free
Pay: check, MO, MC, V, AE, Discover
Sells: Dutch flower bulbs and perennials
Store: mail order only

Dutch Gardens publishes one of the most beautiful bulb catalogs around—over 200 varieties shown in breathtaking flower "head shots" that approximate perfection. Dutch Gardens has been in business since 1961, and its prices on flower bulbs are solidly below other mail-order firms and garden supply houses—30% less on average, and up to 50% on some bulbs and collections.

The fall planting catalog offers tulip, hyacinth, daffodil, narcissus, crocus, anemone, iris, snowdrop, allium, amaryllis, and other flower bulbs. The tulip selection alone includes single, double, fringed, parrot, lily, and peony types. The spring planting catalog showcases a dazzling array of lilies, begonias, dahlias, gladioli, peonies, tuberoses, anemones, freesia, hostas, and other flowers; and onions and shallots (for planting) are also available. Each Dutch Gardens catalog lists the size of the bulbs and the common and botanical names, height, planting zones, blooming period, and appropriate growing situations of each variety. A zone chart, guide to planting depth and bulb grouping, sun requirements, and hints on naturalizing, rock gardening, terrace planting, indoor growing, and forcing are included.

Special Factors: Bulbs are guaranteed to bloom (conditions are stated in the catalog); bulb bonuses are available on quantity orders.

EON INDUSTRIES, INC.

Brochure: free
Pay: check or MO
Sells: metal garden markers
Store: mail order only

DEPT. WBM
107 W. MAPLE ST., P.O.
  BOX 11
LIBERTY CENTER, OH
  43532–0011
419–533–4961

EON Industries specializes in a useful garden item: metal plant markers. EON has been manufacturing markers since 1936 and currently offers four styles in several sizes, at prices that begin at under $20 (plus shipping) for 100 10" Rose markers and run up to $29 per hundred (plus shipping) for the 20" Nursery style. There are two styles of Mini Marker for about $15 and $16 per hundred—these are ideal for miniature roses, rock gardens, or wherever an understated marker is appropriate. (Volume pricing is available on large orders; inquire.) The markers create the impression of serious horticultural doings when staked among even common specimens, which is why upmarket garden catalogs carry them—at nearly twice the price! The brochure has several columns of text explaining the whats and hows of marking and "unmarking" your labels.

Wholesale buyers, please send your inquiry on wholesale pricing on company letterhead, or fax to 419–533–6015.

Special Factors: Satisfaction is guaranteed; minimum order is 25 markers at retail, 100 markers at wholesale.

FEDCO SEEDS, INC.

P.O. BOX 520-WBM
WATERVILLE, ME
04903–0520
TEL/FAX: 207–873–7333

Catalog: $1 (see text)
Pay: check, MO, MC, V
Sells: seeds, trees, seed-starting and cultivation tools, etc.
Store: mail order only

In 1978 the Fedco garden seed cooperative was formed, working with the now-defunct Maine Federation of Cooperatives and the still-thriving Maine Organic Farmers and Gardeners Association. Now, 20 years later, Fedco is going strong, providing high-quality seeds at the lowest possible prices (20% to 70% less than you'll pay elsewhere).

This is not your ordinary seed catalog. Fedco does not have an individual owner or beneficiary: "Profit is not our primary goal." Consumers own 60% of the cooperative, and workers 40%. About half of Fedco's customers are individuals, and the other half are cooperatives. The inside spread of their catalog explains how you can form a buying cooperative with friends, neighbors, and family, and indeed the savings when you order in bulk are substantial. There are separate order forms for individuals and groups, and a strict schedule by which you must place your order. Once you've read all the fine print, it makes a lot of sense to buy this way, and you'll get a good feeling that you're participating in keeping prices low by doing some of the work normally handled by a team of employees on the other end of the phone line. Once you've filled out the form (and double-checked it for errors), you can either mail or fax it (no phone orders).

One of three catalogs—"Fall Bulbs," "Trees and Spring Bulbs," and "Seeds, Organic Growers Supply, and Moose Tubers"—will come to you at the appropriate time of year with an ordering deadline. Each of these catalogs is a labor of love and intelligence, chock full of standard and interesting varieties, some heirloom, with valuable descriptions, historical sidelights, instructions for growing, plenty of witty and wise philosophy, and good, sound advice. There are books, mostly of the "politically green" variety, about medicinal herbs, organic gardening, earth-friendly insect management, coloring and comic books, and more; tee shirts; and tools, supplies, and accessories, particularly for the organic gardener. You get a year of mailings for the $1 fee, which is usually $2, so be sure to mention BWBM when you order.

Canadian readers, please note: Only seeds are shipped outside the United States (no live plants), and payment is required in U.S. dollars.

Special Factors: Satisfaction is guaranteed; handling is included on orders over $50; quantity discounts are available.

FLORIST PRODUCTS

P.O. BOX 3190
BARRINGTON, IL 60011
800–828–2242
FAX: 800–252–4022

Catalog: free
Pay: check, MO, MC, V, AE
Sells: greenhouse and nursery supplies
Store: mail order only

You'll save up to 40% on your gardening supplies by shopping with Florist Products. The 42-page "Hobby & Homegrower Catalog" offers a wide selection of equipment, tools, and supplies for professional growing at home. Among the 4,500 items available are hanging baskets, flats, and pots; fertilizers and injectors; greenhouse structures, benches, and heating and ventilation systems; labels; pesticides; plant supports; safety equipment; soil testers; sprayers; thermostats; gardening tools; and watering and irrigation supplies. Florist Products runs frequent specials and offers quantity discounts as well, where the savings are greatest.

Wholesalers should request the Commercial Price List.

Special Factors: Satisfaction is guaranteed.

GURNEY'S SEED & NURSERY CO.

---

110 CAPITAL ST.
YANKTON, SD 57079
605–665–1671
FAX: 605–665–9718

Catalog: free
Pay: check, MO, MC, V, AE, Discover
Sells: general garden and nursery stock, tools and supplies
Store: same address; Monday to Friday 8–5:30, Saturday 8–5 (extended hours March 15 to June 15)

The oversize, 64-page color catalog from Gurney's is a welcome arrival in the dead of winter, with its promise of great spring planting at great prices. The catalog shows annuals and perennials, roses, vegetables, berries, fruit and nut trees, landscape trees, shrubbery, ground cover, grasses, and even houseplants. You'll also find lots of equipment and supplies, from "seed-starting helpers" to birdseed and feeders to pest control to the kitchen equipment you'll need to make the most of your edible harvest—dehydrators, slaw-cutters, canning tools, etc. Quantity pricing is offered on everything, and the catalog is peppered with special offers that translate into real bargains. Gurney's also provides a great deal of gardening information, including "How to Choose" sidebars, a zone chart, a vegetable seed-planting chart, a key to tree shapes and mature heights, and a guide to planting windbreaks and shrubs. If you're new to gardening and easily overwhelmed, this catalog can give you a manageable amount of information and help you get started at a very reasonable cost.

Special Factors: Satisfaction is guaranteed; returns are accepted for exchange, refund, or credit; seeds, plants, and nursery stock are guaranteed one year from shipping date.

JACKSON & PERKINS

Catalog: free
Pay: check, MO, MC, V, AE, Discover
Sells: roses, bulbs, perennials, gifts, etc.
Store: mail order only
Online: http://www.jacksonandperkins.com

1 ROSE LANE, DEPT. 83B
MEDFORD, OR 97501
800–854–6200
FAX: 800–242–0329
TDD: 800–348–3222

¡Sí! Ⓒ

The subject is roses at Jackson & Perkins, which has been supplying gardeners nationwide since 1872. The horticultural classic absorbs three-fourths of the 56-page catalog—from miniatures and patio roses to classic hybrid teas, floribundas, and grandifloras. Jackson & Perkins is prominent in variety development and has taken a number of "rose of the year" awards from All-American Rose Selections, an independent organization that ranks entries on how well they grow in diverse settings (they're tested in gardens all over the country).

Unlike many other catalogs, Jackson & Perkins notes the type of fragrance and the bud shapes of the roses, as well as plant height range, blossom size, number of petals, color, variety, patent notes, awards, and other data. In addition to a stunning collection of hybrid tea roses, Jackson & Perkins sells classic and striated floribundas, grandifloras, hedge roses, tree roses, patio roses (2' to 4' tall), and climbers. There are roses selected for their fragrance, exhibition roses, varieties from Germany and Denmark, David Austin's English roses, bush roses, and miniatures. If you buy in small quantities, you'll get discounts that will make your roses smell even sweeter.

Jackson & Perkins also sells daylilies and hybrid lilies, "garden classics"—hydrangeas, phlox, wisteria, lavender, astilbes, etc.—and begonias, ranunculus, and more. The catalog is peppered throughout with birdbaths, stem-cutters, single blossom holders, wind chimes, wrought-iron garden furniture, and more. And "The Basics," a guide to planting and enjoying your roses, is included with every order. Follow the planting directions and you should enjoy show-worthy blooms—all roses are 100% guaranteed to grow.

Special Factors: Satisfaction is guaranteed; returns are accepted for exchange, refund, or credit.

JOHNNY'S SELECTED SEEDS, INC.

R.R. 1, BOX 2580
ALBION, ME 04910
207–437–4301
207–437–9294
FAX: 800–437–4290

Catalog: free
Pay: check, MO, MC, V, AE, Discover
Sells: seeds, roots, tubers, seed cultivation supplies
Store: Monday to Saturday 8:30–5; phone hours June to December, Monday to Friday 8:30–5; January to May, Monday to Friday 8–7, Saturday 8–5
E-mail: homegarden@johnnyseeds.com
Online: http://www.johnnyseeds.com

   ¡Si!

Johnny's Selected Seeds received a high recommendation from a reader who appreciates the firm's clear catalog, low shipping fees, and the impressive germination rate of the seeds. It was a pleasure to discover that Johnny's packets were priced consistently lower than those from firms selling the same varieties. Johnny's holds an open house each summer at the farm in Albion, Maine, where trials are run and stock is raised. (The store is open year-round, and workshops are held seasonally.)

The 144-page color catalog shows photos of the farm, the staff, and the stock—anticipated yields from the seeds for vegetables, flowers, and culinary and medicinal herb seeds. The descriptions include seed counts on the mini-packets, and you can calculate the counts on larger amounts. There are price breaks at fractions of an ounce and pound, and on 1, 5, 25, 50, and 100 pounds (the last for corn). The catalog, half of which is devoted to vegetable seeds, opens with Globe artichokes and ends with zinnias. Everlastings, vines and trailing flowers, a variety of farm seed (legumes and grasses), seed-starting supplies and equipment, pest control, hand tools, garden carts, watering equipment, food mills and dehydrators, flower-drying materials, and books are also sold, and everything has been chosen to make the most of your time and money. Johnny's, in business since 1973, also offers one of the most generous guarantees of satisfaction in the industry, marking it as a genuinely consumer-friendly company.

Special Factors: Satisfaction is guaranteed; shipping is included on orders over $100 within the 48 contiguous United States; quantity/volume discounts are available; returns are accepted for exchange, refund, or credit.

LE JARDIN DU GOURMET

P.O. BOX 75-WC
ST. JOHNSBURY CENTER,
 VT 05863
802–748–1446
FAX: 802–748–9592

Catalog: 50 cents
Pay: check, MO, MC, V, AE, DC, Discover
Sells: seeds, plants, and gourmet foods
Store: mail order only
E-mail: flowers.herbs@kingcon.com
Online: http://www.kingcon.com/agljdg

If you like to cook, and if you have even a small patch of land on which you can grow things, you'll appreciate Le Jardin du Gourmet. Founded by a transplanted New York City chef who developed a business from growing his own shallots, Le Jardin is now run by his daughter and her husband. They share an appreciation for fine food; chestnut spread, chutney, fancy mustards, and Pompadour herbal teas are a few of the catalog offerings. The prices of some of these food items are very good, but the firm is listed here for one of the last great mail-order buys—the 25-cent seed packet.

Le Jardin du Gourmet sells seeds for hundreds of herbs, vegetables, peas, beans, and even some flowers: angelica, bok choi, pennyroyal, milk thistle, kohlrabi, dwarf corn, French endive, mache, salsify, German "beer garden" radishes, African pumpkins, Vidalia onions, fava beans, and forget-me-nots are all here. The 16-page catalog has a few line drawings and horticultural tips, as well as a recipe for scotched chestnut-bacon appetizers and a guide to making popcorn-on-the-cob in a microwave oven. If you're a novice gardener, invest a few quarters and test a number of "sample" packs of seeds, or play it safe with the live herbs and perennials also available from Le Jardin. The plants are sold in 2¼" pots, and suggestions for herb use and growth conditions are given in the catalog. Don't overlook the books on herbs and preserving food (canning, pickling, etc.) and good prices on plain and decorated balsam wreaths, roping, and small cut trees at Christmastime.

Canadian readers, please note: Only U.S. funds are accepted, and plants and bulbs are not shipped to Canada.

Special Factors: Minimum order is $15 with credit cards.

MELLINGER'S

W. SOUTH RANGE RD.,
DEPT. WBMC
NORTH LIMA, OH
44452–9731
330–549–9861
FAX: 330–549–3716

Catalog: free
Pay: check, MO, MC, V, Discover
Sells: seeds, bulbs, live plants, and home and garden supplies
Store: same address; Monday to Saturday 8:30–5 (June 16–April); 8–6 (April to June)
E-mail: mellgarden@aol.com
Online: http://www.mellingers.com

Mellinger's publishes "the garden catalog for year-round country living," 96 pages of seeds, bulbs, live plants, reference books, greenhouses, garden supplies, and tools. Mellinger's, in business since 1927, has outstandingly low prices on some items and nominal savings on others. The offerings include flower seeds and bulbs, potted trees and shrubs, shade tree and evergreen seedlings, herb plants, fruit trees, vegetable seeds and vines, tropical plants, and seeds for rare and unusual plants. Everything you'll need for successful cultivation is available, from seed flats to greenhouses. You'll find insect and animal repellents, plant fertilizers, soil additives, pruning and grafting tools, spades, cultivators, hoes, seeders, watering systems, cold frames, starter pots, planters and flower boxes, and related goods. In addition to chemical fungicides and insecticides, Mellinger's sells ladybugs, praying mantis egg cases, and other "natural" predators and beneficial parasites. Birdseed and feeders are also stocked.

Mellinger's has poly-skin greenhouses in small and commercial sizes, polyethylene, and ventilation equipment, heaters, and thermostats. Books on topics from plant propagation and gardening to Bonsai and cooking are also available. The catalog includes a guide to hardiness zones and a statement of the terms of the warranty covering plant orders.

Special Factors: Plants are warrantied for 13 months (see the catalog for terms); authorized returns are accepted (a 10% restocking fee may be charged); $1 service fee on credit card orders under $10.

J.E. MILLER NURSERIES, INC.

5060 W. LAKE RD., DEPT.
WBM
CANANDAIGUA, NY 14424
800–836–9630
716–396–2647
FAX: 716–396–2154

Catalog: free
Pay: check, MO, MC, V, AE, Discover
Sells: plants, shrubs, trees, and nursery stock
Store: same address; Monday to Friday 8–4:30 (daily during the spring)
Online: http://www.millernurseries.com

Miller's spring and fall catalogs offer a full range of plants, seeds, bulbs, shrubs, and trees, at savings of up to 50%, compared to prices charged at garden centers. Miller Nurseries has been in business since 1936 and features a fall selection that includes russet apple, golden plum, grapes (including seedless varieties), red raspberry, blueberry, cherry, strawberry, and dozens of other fruit and nut trees, plants, and vines. Shade trees are offered, including poplar, locust, maple, and ash; there are ornamental grasses and plants for the vegetable garden and some common flower bulbs as well. Garden supplies and equipment, including pruners, animal repellent, soil additives, wheelbarrows, mulch sheeting, etc., are also offered. The 60-page catalog includes horticultural tips, and each order is sent with Miller's 32-page planting guide. This firm has gotten rave reviews from several readers of this book, who've praised Miller's service and prices.

Please note: Orders are shipped to U.S. addresses only (not APO/FPO).

Special Factors: Trees and shrubs are sent as plants, guaranteed to grow; minimum order is $10 with credit cards.

NOR'EAST MINIATURE ROSES, INC.

P.O. BOX 307-WB
ROWLEY, MA 01969
978-948-7964
FAX: 978-948-5487

Catalog: free
Pay: check, MO, MC, V
Sells: miniature roses
Store: 58 Hammond St., Rowley, MA; also
955 W. Phillips St., Ontario, CA; Monday to
Friday 8–4, both locations

Nor'East publishes a 32-page catalog of its specialty, miniature roses, which are priced at $5.25 each, compared to over $7 for the same varieties sold elsewhere. (Nor'East doesn't tack on a per-plant handling fee, as do some of its competitors.) Dozens of types of miniature bush roses are available, including micro-minis (4" to 8" tall at maturity), climbers, and tree roses (miniatures budded to understocks). The varieties are grouped by colors, which include reds, pinks, yellows, oranges, apricots, whites, mauves, and blends. Among the fancifully named specimens are old favorites and new entries: Good Morning America, Cupcake, Party Girl, Scentsational, and Ice Queen, to name a few. The catalog descriptions include height of the mature plant, blooming pattern and coloring, scent, suitable growth situations, and other information.

Nor'East offers quantity discounts and specially priced bonuses for large orders. "We pick 'em" collections are also offered—prices drop if you let the firm make the selection. Nor'East offers other collections, including easy-to-cultivate choices, fragrant types, and a beginners' kit that includes pots and potting mix. Planting and care directions are sent with each order. And a selection of small vases, Ortho's Guide to *Enjoying Roses,* and gifts are available.

Special Factors: Returns of plants that fail to perform are accepted within 90 days for replacement.

OHIO EARTH FOOD

5488 SWAMP ST., NE
HARTVILLE, OH 44632
330–877–9356
FAX: 330–877–4237

Catalog: free
Pay: check, MO, MC, V, Discover
Sells: natural fertilizers and natural pest controls
Store: same address; Monday, Tuesday, Thursday, Friday 8–5; additional days and hours between March 30 and June 6

Ohio Earth Food has been serving gardeners and farmers since 1972 with natural fertilizers and pest control products. The 16-page catalog offers dozens of products certifiable for organic crop production by Ohio Standards at the time of this printing. If you have a summer roadside vegetable stand, participate in farmer's markets, have a large garden, or even own a full-scale farm, Ohio Earth Food has great prices when you buy in bulk. (Growers' price breaks include ton lots.) You'll find natural fertilizers such as Re-Vita Compost Plus, Jersey greensand, cottonseed meal, diatomaceous earth (made of ground fossil shell), liquefied seaweed, fish products, rock phosphate, and others; insect and disease controllers such as rotenone and milky spore powder—great for Japanese beetles; herbicides for killing weeds and grass; natural products for livestock; growing supplies such as potting soil, compost makers, soil test kits, and powdermill dust applicators; and a small selection of books about bio-friendly growing. Detailed contents and descriptions accompany each product listing, as well as quantity price breaks. Send in a soil sample and Ohio Earth Food will analyze it for $17 with the base exchange capacity of your soil, organic matter content, levels of nitrogen, potassium, phosphorous, calcium, magnesium, and sulfur, and the amount of lime needed, if any.

Wholesalers: Ask for the grower price list with your catalog.

Special Factors: Shipments over 500 pounds are generally shipped by commercial truck; see catalog for all shipping rates and requirements.

PINETREE GARDEN SEEDS

P.O. BOX 300
NEW GLOUCESTER, ME
   04260
207–926–3400
FAX: 888–52-SEEDS

Catalog: free, $1.50 outside U.S.
Pay: check, MO, MC, V, AE, Discover
Sells: seeds, bulbs, plants, garden equipment, and books
Store: mail order only
E-mail: superseeds@worldnet.att.net
Online: http://www.superseeds.com

Pinetree Garden Seeds was established in 1979 to provide home gardeners with seeds in small packets, suitable for backyard gardens or horticultural experiments. The firm has far exceeded this mandate, with a 152-page catalog packed with well-chosen kitchen gadgets, gardening tools and supplies, books and other useful goods. But Pinetree's strength is the stock that built the business—over 800 varieties of vegetable and flower seeds, just a handful of which are treated. Of special interest are the "vegetable favorites from around the world," including radicchio, fava beans, snow peas, entsai, epazotes, and chilis. You'll also find plants and tubers for shallots, asparagus, berries, and potatoes. The flower section features seeds, tubers, and bulbs for annuals, perennials, everlastings, and wildflowers.

The tools and equipment run from kitchen and canning helps to hand tools. Fertilizers, netting, and related goods are offered. Over 30 pages of the catalog are devoted to books, including a number of gardening literature classics, cookbooks, garden planners, and many other well-priced titles. Prices are quite competitive, and even the seed packets are backed by Pinetree's ironclad guarantee of satisfaction.

Special Factors: Satisfaction is guaranteed; returns are accepted for exchange, refund, or credit.

PRENTISS COURT GROUND COVERS

Brochure: $1
Pay: check, MO, MC, V
Sells: live ground-cover plants
Store: mail order only

P.O. BOX 8662,
  DEPT. WBM
GREENVILLE, SC
  29604–8662
864–277–4037
FAX: 864–299–5015

Prentiss Court, in business since 1978, offers a wide range of plants at up to 50% below nursery prices and gives spacing and planting guides in the brochure. The current crop includes varieties of Cotoneaster, crown vetch, daylilies, Euonymus fortunei, fig vine, Hedera canariensis and helix, honeysuckle, hosta, jasmine, hypericum, Ophiopogon japonicus, Pachysandra terminalis, Parthenocissus, Trumpet creeper, and Vinca major and minor. In English, there are over 70 kinds of plants, including many types of ivy and flowering and berry-bearing ground cover. The plants are sold bare-root and/or potted, at prices that run from 41 cents for "Green Muscari," a liriope, to $5.70 for a large-blossomed hosta; most are under $1.

Ground cover provides an attractive, labor-efficient alternative to a conventional lawn—which may have to be "limed, aerated, re-seeded, fertilized, weed-treated, mowed, and raked," to quote the admittedly partisan but accurate president of Prentiss Court. Ground cover, on the other hand, should be mulched, not fertilized, and it seems to discourage weeds and pests all by itself. Follow the light and soil guidelines when selecting and planting and you should be able to enjoy lush, low-maintenance grounds without chemical intervention.

Special Factors: Minimum order is 50 plants of the same variety.

ROHRER'S SEEDS

P.O. BOX 250
SMOKETOWN, PA 17576
717–299–2571
FAX: 717–299–5347

Catalog: free
Pay: check, MO, MC, V, Discover
Sells: flower and vegetable seeds, gardening supplies, lawn seed, forage, crop seed, etc.
Store: 2472 Old Philadelphia Pike, Smoketown, PA; call or see the catalog for directions and hours

Pennsylvania's Lancaster County boasts some of the best farmland in this country. For the past 75 years, P.L. Rohrer & Bro. Inc. has been supplying the farmers who work it, with corn, soybeans, pasture mixture, legumes, grazing and haying mixtures, and other grasses and crop seed. You'll find several pages of this stock in the catalog, as well as herbicides, insecticides, fungicides, and soil enrichment. But most of the 60-page catalog is devoted to home gardening needs, with a good selection of perennials and annuals, vegetables, legumes, herbs (seed), potatoes (seed), berries, and bulbs. There's also a good roundup of tools and supplies, including seed-starting supplies, watering equipment, and both organic/natural and conventional insect and fungus control. Houseplant treatments are also offered. And Rohrer's sells both lawn seed blends and treatments.

In addition to the company's magnanimous commitment to your happiness—"Every Seed You Buy Must Satisfy You—or Your Money Back"—Rohrer's prices are much, much lower than those of several other firms selling the same varieties of seed, in the same amount. "Autumn Beauty" sunflower seed are under $2 a half ounce here, $3 elsewhere. Bachelor's Buttons run $3.25 an ounce at Rohrer's, but $6 for three-quarters of an ounce from another firm. A packet of Walla Walla Sweet onion seed is 99 cents here, $1.80 in another catalog, and so on. You won't find a lot of color in the catalog, but if you know your varieties and the prices others are charging, you won't miss the pictures.

Special Factors: Satisfaction is guaranteed (see the catalog for terms of warranty); returns are accepted for exchange, refund, or credit.

JOHN SCHEEPERS, INC.

23 TULIP DR., DEPT. WBM
BANTAM, CT 06750
860–567–0838
FAX: 860–567–5323

Catalog: free
Pay: check, MO, MC, V
Sells: Dutch flower bulbs
Store: mail order only
E-mail: catalog@johnscheepers.com
Online: http://www.johnscheepers.com

John Scheepers has been in business since 1910, serving gardeners with premium, exhibition-quality Dutch bulbs of cultivated stock, at very good prices. Scheepers is affiliated with Van Engelen, which offers wholesale pricing on large orders (see that listing if you buy in 100-bulb lots). Scheepers's own prices are lower than market price, but the bulbs themselves—and the plants and blossoms—are significantly bigger.

The 68-page color catalog from Scheepers, "Beauty from Bulbs," with over 600 bulb varieties, is heavy on tulips and narcissi: early-flowering Fosterianas, tulips from Asia Minor, trumpet narcissi, peonylike tulips, Giant Darwins, parrot tulips, and more. Like Van Engelen, Scheepers has a good selection of crocus, allium, fritillaria, iris, lilies, and other spring flower bulbs, as well as a number for shady, woodsy areas, and for holiday forcing, such as paperwhites and amaryllis. Bulb food, gifts, and books are available, and cultivating instructions are packed with each order. Most of the bulbs are sold in lots of 10, and the per-bulb price drops the more you order. The sales policy is similar to Van Engelen's, except the minimum order is just $25.

Wholesale customers, please call or write about placing large orders.

Special Factors: Quantity discounts are available; minimum order is $25 per address.

SEYMOUR'S SELECTED SEEDS

Catalog: free
Pay: check, MO, MC, V, Discover
Sells: "English garden" flower seeds
Store: mail order only

P.O. BOX 1346
SUSSEX, VA 23884–0346
803–663–3084
FAX: 888–SEYMOUR

"Lady Sarah Seymour" opens the catalog with a letter to her "American Gardening Friends," detailing her efforts to bring the blooms of the classic English country garden to the yards of the United States. She explains that the key to success is variety; that "Americans rightfully appreciate the sparkling jewels of impish impatiens or the billowing sails of bouncing petunias, but very few indeed have experienced the grace and charm of climbing asarinas or the sinister beauty of devilish nemophilas."

What follows is over 80 pages of the kinds of flowers that create the English country look: convolvulus, geraniums, alyssum, papaver, lavender, pansies, lobelia, nasturtium, tropaeolum, sweet peas, lathyrus (the Matucana is said to be the original sweet pea, dating back to 1699), viola, portulaca, primrose, hollyhocks, and many others. The catalog descriptions include the common names of the varieties, origins, general sowing and care tips, mature height, bloom size, and other details. (You'll have to find garden layout suggestions and hardiness zone information from other sources, however.) Germination rates are estimated as 60% to 80%, and the data includes the seed count. The packets themselves are reasonably priced, and savings are considerable if you're buying quantity (750 to 4,000 seeds); there are "Early Bird" offers of bonus packets (terms are subject to change). Seymour's promises a replacement, refund, or credit if you're not completely satisfied with what you buy.

Overseas customers, please note: Seymour's ships only seeds outside the U.S.

Special Factors: Satisfaction is guaranteed; shipping is included; quantity discounts are available.

R.H. SHUMWAY SEEDSMAN

P.O. BOX 1-WBMC
GRANITEVILLE, SC 29829
803–663–9771
FAX: 888–437–2733

Catalog: free
Pay: check, MO, MC, V, Discover
Sells: seeds, bulbs, and nursery stock
Store: Graniteville, SC; Monday to Friday
8:30–4 (open Saturday 8:30–12 in spring season only)

"Good Seeds Cheap" declares the cover of R.H. Shumway's catalog, which is full of old-fashioned engravings of flowers, fruits, and vegetables—there's not a photograph in sight. Shumway has been "The Pioneer American Seedsman" since 1870 and is notable for the number of old, open-pollinated seeds it carries, as well as new varieties.

The 64-page catalog features spring flower bulbs, many pages of berries, vines, beans, vegetable seeds, corn, onions, squash, tomatoes, and Shumway specialties—lawn grasses, grasses for pasturage and hay, millet and other "forage" seed, sorghums, Sudan grasses, clover, legumes, and alfalfa. Another specialty catalog, "Totally Tomatoes," offers over 400 varieties of tomato and pepper seeds, together with all of the supplies you'll need to grow America's favorite crop, at savings of 30% to 40%.

Shumway offers over a dozen types of ornamental gourds—dishcloth gourds, small spoon, birdhouse, dipper, bottle, and more. Herb seeds are available, for both culinary and ornamental plants—angelica, coriander, shiso, burnet, pyrethrum, upland cress, and cardoon, as well as the spice rack standards. Market gardeners and other small commercial growers should check Shumway's wholesale prices on bulk seed orders or get together with gardener friends and combine orders to take advantage of the bulk pricing. Special offers and bonuses are sprinkled liberally throughout the catalog, which also offers a selection of well-priced garden helpers.

Wholesale customers, the 136-page "HPS" catalog offers wholesale prices on flower and vegetable seeds to greenhouse growers and nursery operators. (Request this catalog by name on company letterhead.)

Special Factors: Satisfaction is guaranteed; quantity discounts are available; returns are accepted within 90 days for exchange or replacement; C.O.D. orders are accepted; minimum order is $15 with credit cards.

TURNER GREENHOUSES

Catalog: free
Pay: check, MO, MC, V
Sells: greenhouses and accessories
Store: mail order only
Online: http://www.turnergreenhouses.com

P.O. BOX 1260, DEPT. 131
GOLDSBORO, NC
  27533–1260
800–672–4770
FAX: 919–736–4550

Turner Equipment Company was founded in 1939 and has been producing greenhouses since 1957. Turner currently offers three basic series with a choice of options, or a total of 46 models. Prices average 25% less than the competition, and similar greenhouses in other catalogs sell for 35% more.

The three series include a 7-foot-wide lean-to and two freestanding lines, 8 and 14 feet wide. Each greenhouse comes equipped with a ventilating system and aluminum storm door and can be expanded lengthwise in four-foot increments. You can choose from a 6-mil polyethylene cover or fiberglass (warrantied for 10 years). Turner also sells electric and gas heaters, exhaust fans and air circulators, cooling units, greenhouse benches, thermometers, misters, sprayers, and more. In addition, the 20-page color catalog features well-chosen books on composting, organic gardening, greenhouse growing, herb cultivation, and related topics. Free with every greenhouse is a short video that takes you step-by-step through your greenhouse's assembly process.

Special Factors: Satisfaction is guaranteed; authorized returns in original condition are accepted within 30 days for refund or credit (less freight); minimum order is $10.

VAN BOURGONDIEN BROS.

P.O. BOX 1000
BABYLON, NY 11702
800–622–9997
516–669–3500
FAX: 516–669–1228

Catalog: free
Pay: check, MO, MC, V, AE, Discover
Sells: flower bulbs and perennials
Store: mail order only
E-mail: retail@dutchbulbs.com
Online: http://www.dutchbulbs.com

¡Si!

The 72-page spring and fall catalogs from Van Bourgondien offer a wealth of growing things for home, lawn, and garden at up to 40% less than other suppliers. Van Bourgondien was founded in 1919 and offers early-order discounts, bonuses, and specials on collections.

Both of the catalogs feature hosta and hybrid lilies, ground covers, and a wide range of flowers. Past fall issues have shown tulip, daffodil, hyacinth, iris, crocus, narcissus, anemone, allium, fritillaria, and other bulbs. Geraniums, delphiniums, shasta daisies, tiger lilies, lavender, flowering houseplants, foxtails, black-eyed Susans, native ferns, and other greenery and flowers are usually offered. If you can't wait for the thaw, you can buy prepotted lilies of the valley, Aztec lily, paperwhites, amaryllis varieties, and crocus bulbs, all of which can be forced. The spring catalogs feature begonias, gladiolus, dahlias, caladiums, perennials, hostas, ferns, cannas, ground cover, and similar goods. Bulb planters and plant supplements are offered as well, and orders are shipped to the 48 contiguous United States.

Special Factors: Goods are guaranteed to be "as described" and to be delivered in perfect condition; quantity discounts are available.

VAN DYCK'S

P.O. BOX 430
BRIGHTWATERS, NY
11718-0430
800-248-2852
FAX: 516-669-3518

Catalog: free
Pay: check, MO, MC, V, AE, Discover
Sells: flower bulbs and perennials
Store: mail order only
E-mail: jan@vandycks.com
Online: http://www.vandycks.com

¡Si!

This firm goes back generations in Holland and has been doing business in the United States since 1990.

The Van Dyck's catalog features irises and other favorites—tulips, daffodils, crocuses, narcissi, hyacinths, alliums, fritillaria, ranunculus, and snowdrops. Anemones, crown imperials, daylilies, and other later-blooming flowers are offered. All of Van Dyck's bulbs are commercially cultivated, and the 100-page color catalog includes a hardiness guide and cultivation tips to help maximize the success of your plantings. The pricing structure rewards big buys, and the proprietors recommend combining orders with friends and gardening co-ops to get the best discounts.

Special Factors: Satisfaction is guaranteed; quantity discounts are available.

VAN ENGELEN, INC.

DEPT. WBM, 23 TULIP DR.
BANTAM, CT 06750
860-567-8734
FAX: 860-567-5323

Catalog: free
Pay: check, MO, MC, V
Sells: Dutch flower bulbs
Store: mail order only
E-mail: catalog@vanengelen.com
Online: http://www.vanengelen.com

Van Engelen, in business since 1971, is the wholesale affiliate of John Scheepers, another vendor of Dutch flower bulbs. Scheepers serves the needs of gardeners buying fewer than 50 of the same bulb at the same time, but Van Engelen sells most bulbs in lots of 50 or 100 and requires a $50 minimum order. If you can meet the minimum, you'll have the choice of over 600 different varieties of tulip, narcissus, crocus, daffodil, anemone, allium, freesia, iris, fritillaria, hyacinth, amaryllis, and lily, all of which are shown in the 36-page catalog. In addition to buying bulbs à la carte, you can choose from several collections that are priced below listed wholesale. Each has from 215 to 525 bulbs, and if you like the selection of varieties and colors, they're a real buy.

Special Factors: Quantity discounts are available; minimum order is $50.

RELATED PRODUCTS/COMPANIES

Bamboo and other natural fencing panels and supplies • Frank's Cane and Rush

Birdbaths, birdhouses, and bird feeders • Terry's Village, Weston Bowl Mill, Tender Heart Treasures

Chain saws and logging equipment • Bailey's

Farm and garden equipment • Northern Hydraulics

Gardening books and manuals • Storey Communications, Reader's Digest

Gourd craft books and supplies • The Caning Shop

Lawn and patio furniture and decor • Weston Bowl Mill, Fran's Wicker & Rattan, Wicker Warehouse, Ellenburg's Furniture, Loftin-Black Furniture, Bennett Brothers

Multipocketed aprons for gardening and yard work • Clothcrafters

Outdoor fish and pond supplies • Daleco Master Breeder Products

Planters • Tender Heart Treasures

Porous plastic sheeting for frost protection • Clothcrafters

Posthole diggers • Harbor Freight Tools

Reforestation supplies • Bailey's

Swimming pool equipment and supplies • Water Warehouse

Tires for mowers and wheelbarrows • Manufacturer's Supply

Tractors and farm equipment • Central Michigan Tractor & Parts

Woodpile covers and firewood carriers • Clothcrafters

GENERAL MERCHANDISE AND SURPLUS GOODS

Great values in a wide range of products

Most of the companies listed in this chapter offer such a diverse selection that it might be confusing to put them elsewhere: Everything from electric mattress warmers to cleaning supplies to snowblowers turns up. These are some of my favorite catalogs to browse, the print equivalents of a big Sunday-morning six-family yard sale. Go through the listings carefully since there are some real finds here, and countless answers to the question of what to give for Christmas, birthdays, and other occasions.

There are some interesting internet sites here as well—Ebay, an online real-time auction where you can bid for great steals and deals on everything under the sun, and Andy's Garage Sale, which is exactly as it sounds, only virtual.

The section that follows this one, "Internet Malls," page 259, is where you'll find hundreds of companies selling products at significant discounts, in just about any category you can imagine.

The following three books would make valuable additions to a consumer reference bookshelf. *The Practical Guide to Practically Everything 1998,* "the ultimate consumer annual," is just that, over 1,000 pages on money, health, education, employment, travel, entertainment, consumer issues, and lots of helpful charts that you can never find when you need them—metric converters, anniversary gift lists, perpetual calendars, time-zone maps, and much more. It's edited by Peter Bernstein and Christopher Ma and published by Random House. The suggested retail price is $13.95, but there's no reason to pay that. Check the bookstores in the "Books, Audiobooks, and Periodicals" chapter for better deals on this and all books.

Finding ways to save on all the things you buy—food, clothing, housing, transportation, education, insurance, vacations, and even luxury goods—is covered in *Cut Your Spending in Half: How to Pay the Lowest Price for Everything,* by the editors of Rodale Press (Rodale Books, 1995). It's a mine of information and ideas that can help you buy smarter and cheaper.

And *The Consumer Bible: 1001 Ways to Shop Smart* (Workman Publishing, 1995), by consumer advocate Mark Green, outlines strategies for getting the best buys and will help you avoid problems in the marketplace, whether you're shopping for flu remedies or funeral services.

Be sure to check out "Related Products/Companies" at the end of this section to find other general-merchandise companies elsewhere in the book.

FIND IT FAST

CLEANING SUPPLIES • EDGE Distributing, Fuller Brush, Marshall Domestics
CLOTH GOODS • Clothcrafters, Marshall Domestics
DISCOUNT SERVICES • Hot Coupons
EDUCATIONAL GIFTS • American Science & Surplus, Astronomical Society
FOOD • EDGE Distributing, Hot Coupons
GOVERNMENT SURPLUS • Ruvel
JEWELRY • Bennett Brothers, Ebay
OVERSTOCKS AND CLOSE-OUTS •American Science & Surplus, Andy's Garage Sale
PERSONAL CARE ITEMS • Damark, EDGE Distributing, Fuller Brush
SERVICE-INDUSTRY SUPPLIES • Marshall Domestics
TOOLS, ELECTRONICS, AND GADGETS • American Science & Surplus, Bennett Brothers, Damark

AMERICAN SCIENCE & SURPLUS

3605 HOWARD ST.,
DEPT. WBM–99
SKOKIE, IL 60076
847–982–0870
FAX: 800–934–0722

Catalog: free
Pay: check, MO, MC, V, Discover
Sells: industrial, educational, and scientific surplus goods
Store: Milwaukee Ave. at Foster, Chicago, IL; Rte. 38, East of Kirk Rd., Geneva, IL; 15138 S. LaGrange Rd., Orland Park, IL; and 6901 W. Oklahoma Ave., Milwaukee, WI
E-mail: jarvis@sciplus.com
Online: http://www.sciplus.com

American Science & Surplus offers a wide variety of surplus wares through witty catalogs that are published about six times a year. The firm has been selling surplus since 1937, and offers that blend of the strange and useful that is catnip to fans of surplus goods: everything from talking door mats to vinyl stripes for your car. American Science is also cited on several websites devoted to educational materials as a great source for well-priced tools and supplies for teaching sciences to all grade levels.

Past catalogs have shown small DC motors, staplers, grow-your-own butterfly kits, microscopes, lasers, magnets, pharmaceutical bottles, collections of drive belts, dozens of kinds of tape, whetstones, DPDT switches, pumps, casters, glow-in-the-dark bats, piano hinges, Chinese riffler tools, and magnifying lenses. (Please don't expect to find these particular items in the catalogs you receive—these are surplus goods, and stock is limited.) The descriptions, which are droll and explicit, note the original and possible new uses for the products, as well as technical data when available. Savings on original and if-new prices can reach 95%.

Special Factors: Satisfaction is guaranteed; returns are accepted within 15 days; minimum order is $10 in goods.

ANDY'S GARAGE SALE, INC.

25 MCLELAND RD.
ST. CLOUD, MN
 56395–2007
800–711–ANDY
FAX: 320–654–7565

Information: internet website, no catalog
Pay: check, MO, MC, V, Discover
Sells: manufacturer's overstock, close-outs, etc.
Store: online only; customer service phone hours Monday to Friday 8–8 CT
Online: http://www.andysgarage.com

If the gritty experience of flea-market shopping leaves you cold but you love the bargains, now you can have it both ways. Power up the modem and log onto Andy's Garage Sale (affiliated with Fingerhut), where fantastic buys await. Andy, who may be a mythic figure but delivers real goods, pulls together a "Top 20" every week for your budgetary pleasure. It's a well-rounded list with at least one "gotta-have-it," especially at savings of up to 70% on the original selling price. As with a real garage sale, the items sold at this virtual one change weekly. Here's an example of one week's offerings: The "Top 20" list included a 16-piece set of Bake King bakeware for $13, an electric roaster oven, a set of three Wearever sauté pans, an American Camper queen-size air bed for $24, an Audiovox auto subwoofer, a Nikko radio-controlled racer for $30, packs of four chintz throw pillows ($10) and three standard bed pillows ($13), a gold and diamond pendant, a Magnavox cordless phone, a 15-piece Campbell Hausfeld air tool set for $45, a West Bend coffeemaker, and 220-count all-cotton comforter covers for $16. (A test order placed on this last item arrived promptly and was exactly as represented.) If the "Top 20" aren't enough, there's "Andy's Big Deal of the Day," which was an enormous stuffed animal on one occasion, priced ridiculously low.

Andy's Garage Sale is an internet phenomenon—there is no catalog. But Andy makes it easy to order once you've seen what you want. You can do it online, or over the toll-free line, or by fax or mail. Andy's online "Fax Gizmo" allows you to enter your choices on a form, print it out, and fax it in without sending your credit information over the internet. (If you wish to pay by check or money order, you can mail your order.) The shipping fee is a flat $4.95 per order at this writing, which represents significant savings. If you have questions, consult "Ask Andy" on the website, and if you don't see the answer, you're urged to e-mail your query—as well as jokes and your favorite recipes.

Special Factors: Satisfaction is guaranteed; authorized returns are accepted within 30 days for exchange, refund, or credit.

THE ASTRONOMICAL SOCIETY OF THE PACIFIC

390 ASHTON AVE.
SAN FRANCISCO, CA
  94112
800–962–3412
FAX: 415–337–5205

Catalog: free
Pay: check, MO, MC, V, Discover
Sells: astronomy resources and gifts
Store: mail order only
E-mail: catalog@aspsky.org
Online: http://www.aspsky.org

The Astronomical Society of the Pacific (ASP) is a nonprofit organization that was founded in 1889 to support astronomical research and improve the public's appreciation of science, especially astronomy. To further this end, ASP offers a variety of materials: videotapes, books, posters, charts and maps of the heavens, slides, observing tools, software, CD-ROMs, educational items, and astronomy-related gifts. The 32-page color catalog features an intriguing collection that includes the latest images from the Hubble Space Telescope, a selection of IMAX videotapes, a 3-D spherical earth jigsaw puzzle, and a comprehensive collection of star atlases and maps. There are breathtaking posters of the planets, a moon phase calendar for the whole year, astronomical CD-ROMs, computer programs that simulate travel through the galaxy, and a number of slide sets covering nebulas and galaxies, the solar system, images from the Hubble, and Space Shuttle views of Earth.

ASP's prices are reasonable but don't seem particularly low ($29.95 for videotapes and $8.95 for posters), until you check the catalogs of supplies for educators selling similar products. There are school sources charging an astonishing $300-plus for a single videotape. So even if you're not in the market for ASP's goods yourself, let your school board or PTA know about this source. Proceeds are used to advance the Society's education programs.

Canadian readers, please note: Only U.S. funds are accepted.

Please note: Wholesale discounts, based on volume, are given to organizations and companies.

Special Factors: Satisfaction is guaranteed; returns in "as-new" condition are accepted for exchange, refund, or credit; institutional accounts are available.

BENNETT BROTHERS, INC.

**30 EAST ADAMS ST.
CHICAGO, IL 60603
312–263–4800
FAX: 312–621–1669**

Catalog: free
Pay: check, MO, MC, V, AE, Discover
Sells: jewelry, appliances, electronics, luggage, furnishings, etc.
Store: same address; Monday to Friday 8:15–5 (see catalog for holiday shopping hours); also 211 Island Rd., Mahwah, NJ; Monday to Saturday 9–5:30
E-mail: bennettbros@worldnet.att.net
Online: http://www.bennettbros.com

At the turn of the century, much of Bennett Brothers' business was in jewelry, gems, and watches. These are still a big part of the company's trade, but Bennett's current offerings, shown in the annual "Blue Book," also include furnishings, leather goods, electronics, cameras, sporting goods, and toys.

The "Blue Book" is 144 color pages of name-brand goods, of which jewelry makes up over a third of the offerings—wedding and engagement bands, pearls, pins and bracelets, necklaces, and other pieces featuring all kinds of precious and semiprecious gems, as well as charms, lockets, medallions, anniversary jewelry, Masonic rings, and crosses and religious jewelry. The watch department offers models from Armitron, Bulova, Casio, Citizen, Jules Jurgensen, Pulsar, Seiko, and Timex.

Bennett Brothers offers a fine selection of clocks, timepieces, and weather instruments. Silverware and chests, silver giftware, tea sets, pewterware, and fine china are also sold. The catalog shows kitchen cutlery sets, cookware sets, small kitchen appliances, microwave ovens, vacuum cleaners, air cleaners, exercise equipment, sewing machines, personal-care appliances, bed linens, towels, tablecloths, and luggage. The leather goods department includes briefcases and attaché cases and luggage from American Tourister, Monarch, Samsonite, and Winn.

The "Blue Book" also features a large group of personal electronics and office supplies—clock radios, portable cassette players, stereo systems and components, TVs and video equipment, phones and answering machines, cameras, projectors, telescopes, binoculars, pens, globes, cash registers, calculators, typewriters, files, and office furnishings. Home furnishings are also available, including patio furniture. The catalog includes Bachmann trains, Cox radio-controlled planes, playing cards, and board games. There are also exercise machines, golf clubs, basketballs, fishing rods, and croquet sets. Flashlights, chain saws, and other tools round out the offerings.

Bennett's prices are listed next to "suggested retail" prices throughout the book. Price comparisons of several goods substantiated Bennett's guideline prices (suggested retail) and the savings of 30% to 40%. Corporate buyers should contact Bennett Brothers for details on the firm's corporate gift programs and their employee award and incentive programs at price levels from $16 to $1,000.

Special Factors: Authorized returns are accepted within 10 days for exchange or credit.

CLOTHCRAFTERS, INC.

P.O. BOX 176, DEPT. WM99
ELKHART LAKE, WI 53020
800–876–2009
TEL/FAX: 920–876–2112

Catalog: free
Pay: check, MO, MC, V
Sells: home textiles
Store: mail order only
E-mail: catalog@clothcrafters.com
Online: http://www.clothcrafters.com

This firm, established in 1936, sells "plain vanilla" textile goods of every sort, from cheesecloth by the yard to flannel patches for cleaning guns. The 20-page catalog is packed with inexpensive, useful things: pot holders, chefs' hats, bouquet garni bags (12 for $4), salad greens bags, fabric coffee filters, striped denim place mats, cotton napkins ($12 a dozen), hot pads, aprons, and supermarket produce bags ($9 for 6). Clothcrafters has a great selection of well-priced kitchen tools, including parchment paper, rubber spatulas, spatter lids, radiant heat plates, and other handy utensils.

You'll also find laundry bags, tote bags, flannel shoe bags, woodpile covers and firewood carriers, garment bags, cider-press liners, computer covers, flannel polishing squares, and mosquito netting. The bed and bath department offers cotton duck shower curtains, lightweight cotton terry towels and bath wraps, terry tunics, barbers' capes, flannel sleeping-bag liners, and flannel crib sheets. Textile artists should check this source, since many of these items can be painted, embroidered, dyed, and otherwise embellished.

Gardeners will find the "PlyBan" porous plastic sheeting ideal for protecting newly planted rows from frost and insects ($9 for 4' by 50').

Clothcrafters also sells mosquito-netting helmets, multipocketed aprons, and denim knee pads—add an old shirt and dungarees and you'll be ready to tackle the back forty.

Canadian readers, please note: Only U.S. funds are accepted.

Wholesale customers, please note: Request the wholesale price list on business letterhead.

Special Factors: Satisfaction is guaranteed; returns are accepted for exchange, refund, or credit.

DAMARK INTER-NATIONAL, INC.

7101 WINNETKA AVE. N.
P.O. BOX 9437
MINNEAPOLIS, MN
55440–9437
800–827–6767
FAX: 612–531–0281

Catalog: free
Pay: check, MO, MC, V, AE, Discover
Sells: computers, home/office furniture, home improvement items, sports/fitness equipment, etc.
Store: mail order only
Online: http://www.damark.com

Damark, the catalog and website, is a good source for great deals. In business since 1986, Damark International, Inc., has built a loyal mail-order customer base through its catalog and Preferred Buyers Club, which provides discounts on travel, food and lodging, entertainment, and merchandise purchased through the catalogs or online. If you're a basic club member, which costs $59.99 a year at this writing, you get 10% off all purchases, discount coupons galore, and special deals through the membership-only catalogs. (See catalog or website for more information on other Damark clubs and membership benefits.)

Happily, you don't have to be a member to order through Damark. What's fun about Damark is the eclectic selection—like a modern-day general store with a high-tech slant. The website and catalog—for all shoppers, not just members—offer discounts up to 60% on such items as snow throwers, radar detectors, shredders, stainless steel flatware, electric blankets, portable PCs, telephones, VCRs, industrial garment racks, folding creeper/shop seat (for automotive repair), fog machines, inflatable mattresses, acupressure clips to suppress your appetite, vacuum cleaners, Wonder Forms figure-enhancer bras, televisions, calculators, two-room tents, Lionel train sets, parking meter banks, cappuccino makers, office furniture, magnifying lamps, Cuisinart 13-piece heavy-duty cookware, and more. Some of the best deals on electronics here are the factory refurbished items—not brand new, but they still come with warranties. Damark's website has received good marks from BizRate (see listing in next section), which means that Damark shoppers think highly of the company's products, prices, and service.

Special Factors: "Easy Pay Plan" allows customer to pay over the course of 4 or 6 months (minimum purchase for "Easy Pay" is $99.99 as of this writing; see catalog for details); satisfaction guaranteed; 30-day return policy (see packing slip for complete details).

EBAY

Information: internet website, no catalog
Pay: seller's discretion (see text)
Sells: collectibles, gadgets, jewelry, shoes and clothing, electronics, etc.
Store: online only, 24 hours/day
Online: http://www.ebay.com

This is the largest person-to-person trading area on the internet and functions as an online auction, where you bid for goods and the highest bidder wins—sometimes at significant savings. It is also the longest-running and the most innovative, with over 300 categories divided into easy-to-use subcategories, from antiques, collectibles, and computers to magazines, jewelry, toys, and dolls. A perusal at the time of this writing had the site featuring 316,823 items for sale in 371 categories!

Ebay recommends your making phone or e-mail contact with the seller before you begin bidding. People interested in buying from a vendor can look up the vendor's selling history, a collection of actual buyers' reviews of this vendor. If the vendor turns out to be reliable, get started! Friends who have used this site love it. It's best if you have a general idea of how much an item costs before you catch the bidding bug. For example, a pair of women's suede boots starting at $1 looks promising, but not if the winning bid eventually exceeds the boots' suggested retail price!

Ebay's site map is a table of contents that links to you pages that will explain the whole bidding or selling process, will give you tips on how to have the best experience, will offer hints on how to find what you're looking for, etc. Bidding time spans and starting bids vary for each item. Most items are pictured, which is helpful if not necessary. Credit card payment, shipping requirements and procedures, and warranties and guarantees will vary from seller to seller.

Special Factors: Valid e-mail address is required.

EDGE DISTRIBUTING, INC.

760 BUSSE HWY.
P.O. BOX 307
PARK RIDGE, IL 60068
800–373–3726
847–696–1623
FAX: 847–696–9284

Price List: free
Pay: check, MO, MC, V
Sells: pantry items—spices, prepared foods, cleaning and personal care products
Store: mail order only

Competition for supermarket shelf space is fierce these days, so if some of your favorite products aren't everyone's favorites, they may be bumped for better sellers. What do you do when your tried-and-true cleaner, stain remover, or floor wax disappears from your local mart? If it's one of the brands represented by EDGE Distributing, you can buy it by mail—as long as you're willing to order at least a case of it. EDGE's current 20-page "Product List" includes kitchen- and bathroom-product brand names you'll recognize, among them Lysol, Chore Boy, Easy-Off, Mop & Glo, Old English, Snowy, Woolite, Wizard, Zout, Easy Wash, and others. There are also personal hygiene products from Bidette and Binaca, among others; household necessities such as Rid-X, Cool Blues, and D-Con, and miscellaneous pantry items such as Gulfwax paraffin. The "Spice Catalog" is full of classic pantry items from companies including French's, Durkee, Spice Island, and Dec-a-Cake. Here you'll find everything from shredded coconut to Bacon Bits to candles to rice and bean side dishes.

The lists include the product name, size, number per case, and case weight, but you must call for current prices and shipping costs. Depending on prices and availability in your area, you may be able to save a little money here—spot checks on several products showed per-item prices that were 13% to 20% below supermarket rates. (The calculations don't factor coupons, sales tax, or shipping.) EDGE is listed here not for the discounts, but for availability of a number of products you may not be able to find locally.

Special Factors: Minimum order is one case.

FULLER BRUSH INDEPENDENT DISTRIBUTOR

J&R SYSTEMS INTERNA-
TIONAL
5117 NW WALDEN DR.
KANSAS CITY, MO 64151
800–8–FULLER
816–741–1042

Catalog: $2
Pay: check, MO, MC, V, Discover
Sells: Fuller Brush products
Store: mail order only
E-mail: fullerbrush@gowebway.com

The Fuller Brush Company was founded in 1906 and built its reputation on honest practices and quality products. I can remember, as a child, when the Fuller Brush man came to our home each year with his bag of goodies (he always left little hand lotion samples for us children). So good were those products then and now that the company is still thriving with its cleaning solutions, polishes, laundry products, and toiletries.

J&R Systems International, an independent distributor of the Fuller Brush Company, sells the line by mail through the Fuller Brush catalog. The 44 pages are strong on general cleaning tools—brooms, mops, carpet sweepers, utility brushes, wax applicators, dusters, squeegees, etc.— as well as special-purpose implements, such as jar brushes, refrigerator coil brushes, grill scrubbers, car dusters, metal-polishing brushes, and bathtub swabs. Fuller makes a cleaning solution, wax, shampoo, deodorizer, or polish for every tool, and the most popular products—laundry detergent, degreaser, germicide, etc.—are offered in larger, money-saving sizes. Several pages of the catalog are devoted to personal-care products, including Fuller's famed boar-bristle hairbrushes, comb- and brush-cleaning tools, bath brushes, lint brushes, shampoos, body lotions, foot products, kid's bath foam, and more.

The Fuller Brush catalog prices are suggested retail, but other companies that sell the same products may mark them up—one catalog of household gadgets featured a number of Fuller Brush items at prices 11% to 26% higher than suggested retail. J&R Systems International enhances the savings with regular specials, coupon inserts, and quantity discounts.

Special Factors: Satisfaction is guaranteed; price quote by phone or letter.

HOT COUPONS

Information: internet website, no catalog
Offers: free coupons to your local stores, restaurants, etc.
Online: http://www.hotcoupons.com

Hot Coupons is simple to explain, and even simpler to use. Just log on, enter your zip code, and Hot Coupons brings up coupons that will save you money at various stores and restaurants in your local area. You can then print out these coupons and use them. Period! The current site at the time of this writing was offering deals in the following areas: food, auto, home improvement, services, household, retail, health/beauty, professional, travel, H.O.T. Deals, office, and miscellaneous. For example, a local bagel joint was offering a half-dozen free bagels; an automotive shop was offering a free oil change. I could get six free tanning sessions at a local salon, a free pair of glasses, buy-one-get-one-free brunch at a local restaurant, and much more. This site is regularly updated, so check it out often. And if you're not online, or don't have a printer, get a friend to download local Hot Coupons for you. Incidentally, who says you can't get something for nothing?

Special Factors: Internet access and printer required. Hot Coupons not available in some areas.

MARSHALL DOMESTICS

Catalog: free
Pay: check or MO
Sells: institutional and restaurant textiles and supplies
Store: mail order only

P.O. BOX 107
12 FACTORY ST.
WEST WARWICK, RI 02893
800–556–7440
FAX: 401–821–2230

Marshall Domestics was recommended by a reader who was ecstatic about the great buy he'd gotten there on dishtowels. He was right: Marshall, in business since 1970, serves restaurants and institutions with competitive prices on everything from those dishtowels (heavyweight, under $13 a dozen) to latex exam gloves, and will do business with individuals as well.

Marshall provides the food-service industry with kitchen textiles, chef's coats and toques, shirts and pants for kitchen workers, and table linens and skirting. The hospitality industry shops here for bed and bath linens, pillows, blankets and bedspreads, mattress protectors, shower curtains, and little hotel soaps. The health care industry buys latex gloves, patient gowns, bibs, scrub shirts and pants, lab coats, and incontinence products from Marshall. Everyone cleans up with the janitorial supplies—scrub brushes, mops, dusters, disinfectants, deodorizers, laundry detergent, and more. And Marshall also sells the full line of Dickies work clothing, Fruit of the Loom underwear for men and boys, socks, and tee shirts. Prices are very low, but note that some items are sold only by the dozen or in quantity, and special-order items (including some of the table linens) may not be returned. But a sample order for a dozen kitchen bib aprons was delivered quickly, and the aprons were perfect—good, heavyweight cotton, a great value at the price. Marshall has separate flyers for the Dickies clothing, and a line of uniforms and goods for the health care industry, so inquire specifically if you'd like those as well.

Special Factors: Satisfaction is guaranteed; claims are not honored on laundered goods; notify Marshall of discrepancies in your order within 10 days of receipt; volume discounts are available.

RUVEL & CO., INC.

4128–30 W. BELMONT
AVE., DEPT. WBMC
CHICAGO, IL 60641
773–286–9494
FAX: 773–286–9323

Catalog: $2, $3 outside U.S.
Pay: check, MO, MC, V
Sells: army/navy surplus equipment and supplies
Store: same address; Monday to Friday 9–4, Saturday 9–1:30

Ruvel, established in 1965, is the source to check for good buys on government-surplus camping and field goods. U.S. Army and Navy surplus goods are featured in the 64-page catalog, including G.I. duffel bags, high-powered binoculars, leather flying jackets, mosquito netting, M65 field jackets, U.S. Marine Corps shooting jackets, dummy grenades, U.S. Army technical manuals, rubber 5-buckle overshoes, inflatable river boats, kerosene lanterns, fit-in-your-pocket wing stoves that burn fuel tablets, folding knives, suit bags, and similar items. Past catalogs have offered Israeli and M9 gas masks, Kevlar helmets, hammocks, strobe lights, mess kits, nightsticks, snowshoes, U.S. Army blankets, parade gloves, first-aid kits, packboards, and duffel bags. Ruvel is noteworthy for its low prices and extensive stock of real surplus—there are hundreds of genuine government-issue items available here, and many intriguing, useful surplus things that are increasingly hard to find these days.

Special Factors: Order promptly, since stock moves quickly.

RELATED PRODUCTS/COMPANIES

For additional internet sources of general merchandise, see "Internet Malls," next section.

Appliances, electronics, tools, and gadgets • *Percy's, Coastal Tool, Surplus Center, Poor Man's Catalog, Harbor Freight Tools, All Electronics*
Bags and containers for everything imaginable • *Associated Bag*
General department-store goods • *The Ultimate Outlet, Gohn Bros.*
Surplus and overstocks • *Sportsman's Guide, Surplus Center, Mass. Army & Navy*

Internet Malls

Highly rated virtual malls for online shopping of every kind

If you're like I am, the idea of online shopping is appealing, but the reality may be altogether different. There are too many people out there in cyberspace selling too many products. Some online stores have great sites with an "About Us" page, a customer service phone number where you can actually speak with a human being, and searchable inventory with a shopping and purchasing system that's easy to use and to understand. Other stores I've browsed are slow, confusing, and oblique. (One I visited recently didn't have a company address, phone, fax, or even an e-mail; my only option would have been to submit my credit card information and purchase!)

The internet malls listed here are some of the best, and the shops they "rent space to" are likewise reputable. Each "mall" takes a slightly different approach, which you'll discover when you read the descriptions, but they all have one thing in common: consumer-friendly formats and reviews of the online stores they house. In other words, if you're looking for furniture, you can go to one of these malls and find "their" stores that sell furniture. You'll be able to read a little blurb about each store to decide whether it has the kinds of prices and inventory you're looking for, rather than wasting time visiting each one.

Now that I've "bookmarked" the sites in this section, I find internet shopping to be really fun and convenient. I've also discovered it's a wonderful way to save time and money.

BIZRATE

Information: internet website, no catalog
Features: consumer and staff reviews/ratings of internet shopping sites, with links to internet shops
E-mail: feedback@bizrate.com
Online: http://www.bizrate.com

It's nice to know that someone is looking out for the consumer in the big, anarchical world of web shopping. Luckily, BizRate's practices also help the internet shops themselves, so it's a win-win situation for everyone. If shopping on the internet is intimidating to you, it just got easier. BizRate is dedicated to helping shoppers find quality online merchants by providing a site where you can view the results of consumer and BizRate staff reviews and ratings. This is a free service to both consumers and the businesses that get listed here. (To find out why BizRate does it for free, see their FAQ page.)

Here you'll find the top 25 companies—those that scored highest in overall customer satisfaction—updated weekly. You can also search by category (apparel, computers, food and drink, hobbies and collectibles, to name a few) and see how different internet vendors fared in the ratings. What's good about this site is that it's not just an internet mall, but a living, changing compendium of companies with descriptions of their products and services, as well as links to their home pages.

BizRate makes it simple to find companies offering significant discounts, since you can search by "price" within categories, which then sorts the companies in that category in descending order (highest-scoring companies are those that consumers were most satisfied with vis-à-vis their pricing). There's lots more here, including a nice reference section about consumer rights and company responsibilities. This is a site with which all internet shoppers should become familiar.

INTERNET SHOPPER

Information: internet website and quarterly magazine

Features: online reviews and articles about internet sites offering goods and services, and links to these sites

Online: http://www.internetshopper.com

The internet is vast and overwhelming. So how do you find the great shopping sites? How can you distinguish the good from the dreck? You'll love Internet Shopper. Internet Shopper's stated goal is to serve "consumers who want to get the most out of their internet investment—who want to use the internet to make better purchasing decisions, get better information, and be smarter consumers."

Internet Shopper has a staff of writers who continually search the web for the most interesting sites and then write excellent, comprehensive articles and reviews for the rest of us. For example, at the time of this writing Internet Shopper had features on where and how to buy a PC on the net; perfect gifts for movie buffs; shopping for wine; best ornaments and trinkets; advice for parents looking to buy educational games for their children; the ins and outs of home loans, with good resources on the subject; fitness equipment sites; and best travel bargains to Israel. Eclectic enough for you?

There's more. Internet Shopper has "Store of the Week," where they highlight an internet store and its products, and tell you why that website is good or great. Wherever a website is mentioned in any article or review, there's a link, so you can go directly to the site (or "bookmark" it) after you've read about it. The articles are generally well written and informative. Past issues of the e-zine are indexed and archived, so you can go back and check out articles on internet car buying, book buying, online florists, online return policies, and much more. This is a great site to peruse once a week, both for its reviews and for its good articles on subjects of general consumer interest. Let the professional surfers weed through the chaos for you!

MALL 21

306 W. COLLEGE AVE.
STATE COLLEGE, PA 16801
888–508–5999
FAX: 814–861–3199

Information: internet website, no catalog
Pay: check, MC, V
Features: listings of stores selling merchandise of every kind, and links
Store: mail order only
Online: http://www.mall21.com

So you need to go to the mall, but you only have an hour before you have to pick up the kids? Don't despair. Now you can go malling on the web. Mall 21 is a megasite that houses hundreds of mail-order companies selling brand-name merchandise at wholesale prices and deep discounts. There are similar mega-shopping sites on the web, but this one is great because it's comprehensive and user-friendly. The categories include art, audio/visual/camera, Christian, computer, fashion, garden, health, home, jewelry/watch, personal goods, sporting goods, toy, and travel services. Although you don't have to register to shop here, you're eligible for special member discounts if you do. (Mall 21 guarantees that they will never sell or distribute any of your customer information.)

What I like about this virtual mall is that they run a small description of every shop, synopsizing what each one sells and often the percentage you'll save there. For example, at the time of this writing there was a luggage shop that offered 60% off on American Flyer luggage; another shop offered Canon cameras at 35% off list. You can get tips on how to search for specific items, a detailed description of Mall 21's online security protections, FAQs, and other information by visiting the website. Mall 21 has a customer service number (with a real human being on the other end) if you need additional assistance. Ordering can be done online, by phone, or by fax.

Special Factors: Secure credit card transactions; if paying by check, you must order by phone and allow two weeks for check to clear before merchandise is sent out.

NETMARKET

40 OAKVIEW DR.
TRUMBULL, CT
  06611–4748
  888–466–9420

Information: internet website, no catalog
Pay: check, MO, MC, V, Discover
Features: links to online stores that sell general merchandise, autos, and travel packages
Store: mail order only
E-mail: service@netmarket.com
Online: http://www.netmarket.com

This is a mammoth website shopping mall that proclaims, "Save 10% to 50% off manufacturer's suggested list price!" (And they also offer a "lowest price" guarantee—see website for more details.) Netmarket's parent company has been a pioneer in online shopping since the early 1980s. With 60 million customers, Netmarket connects directly to manufacturers and passes the savings on to you—no warehouse, no middleman. From *Business Week* to *Motor Trend* to television's *20/20,* this site gets high marks if you're shopping for a car (at AutoVantage—www.autovantage.com) and want to shave a couple thousand or more off the usual dealer's price.

Other categories for shopping here are travel, "Complete Home," local discounts, auction, grocery, flea market, and classified. Within each category, the options are vast. Netmarket was offering at the time of this writing a trial membership of three months for $1, and they will send you a "Free Entertainment Savings Book," which has buy-one-get-one offers and coupons for savings of up to 50% at hotels, restaurants, and attractions. Annual membership is $69, which is little when you see the amount of money you'll save by regularly shopping here. Membership itself has many benefits: 5% (and up) Netmarket cash back on each purchase; car-care discounts up to 20% off regular prices; and travel discounts of up to 50% on hotel rooms and 25% on car rentals and vacation packages. Members also receive $10 back on each already low-price airline ticket, as well as members-only specials, monthly newsletters, and a date-reminder service.

When you buy with Netmarket, you automatically receive a 2-year warranty on your purchase (see website for details). On the current site I found a coupon for a free brunch at one of my favorite local restaurants, a Polaroid camera that was $79.72 (suggested retail: $145.99), and some grocery items (Campbell's soup and Bounty paper towels) that were about 30% less than supermarket prices. Perhaps Netmarket and others like it represent the future of shopping in America.

Special Factors: Lowest price guarantee; no shipping outside the U.S.

HEALTH, BEAUTY, AND HYGIENE

Prescription and over-the-counter drugs, vitamins, cosmetics, perfumes, and other health and personal-care products

Consider this section a print version of a trip to the drugstore. Here you'll find companies selling prescription drugs and other drug-store goods by mail, which is not only convenient, but also a great way to save money. Even generic drugs may be cheaper by mail, affording you savings of up to 60% on some commonly prescribed remedies.

You can save a solid 30% on many of your cosmetic and beauty needs and still get the same name brands featured in beauty emporiums and department stores when you buy by mail. Products may be in perfectly good but discontinued colors, promotional sizes or packaging, or have some other attribute that distinguishes them from the full-size, full-price product.

Good discounts on perfumes are somewhat elusive; the savings tend to be closer to 20% off list, and if the discounts are deeper, the scent may be specially packaged, a gray-market product, or counterfeit. You may find a bargain in "copycat" scents (or, said more politely, "fragrance interpretations"); see listing for Essential Products. If you like their version, you'll save up to 90% on the cost of the real thing.

Since they're not regulated as drugs by the FDA, vitamins, minerals, and nutritional supplements are listed here. If you're going to take anything to augment your diet and improve your sense of well-being, be sure to consult your primary-care physician, especially if you're already taking medication or have a health problem. Just because something is "natural" doesn't mean it's good for you! And megadosing has been shown to cause all kinds of medical side effects and complications in otherwise healthy people.

The best way to find out about vitamins and nutritional supplements is to go to your local library or health food store, pick up a book on the subject, and inform yourself. There are hundreds of such books out there.

Refer to "Related Products/Companies" at the end of this section for more firms selling health-related products, such as medicinal herbs, essential oils, fitness equipment, and products for people with limited mobility, impaired hearing or vision, or other health conditions requiring special clothing or aids.

For companies that specialize in wigs, hairpieces, and products for hair, see "Wigs and Hair Care" following this section, page 276. For mail-order firms offering prescription glasses and contacts, as well as sunglasses, see "Eye Care and Eyewear," page 281.

FIND IT FAST

COSMETICS • Beauty Boutique

HEALTH-RELATED BOOKS • American Health Food, PIA Discount Vitamins

PERFUMES • Beauty Boutique, Essential Products, Fragrance International

PRESCRIPTION AND OTC MEDICATIONS • Essentials, Medi-Mail

SENIORS' PRODUCTS • Essentials

SKIN AND HAIR PRODUCTS • American Health Food, Beauty Boutique, Cal Ben, Essentials, Fragrance International, Kettle Care, L&H Vitamins

VITAMINS AND NUTRITIONAL SUPPLEMENTS • American Health Food, Essentials, Freeda Vitamins, L&H Vitamins, PIA Discount Vitamins

AMERICAN HEALTH FOOD

875 W. ROGER RD.
TUCSON, AZ 85705
800–858–2143
520–888–8234
FAX: 800–352–0569
FAX: 520–888–0969

Catalog: free
Pay: check, MO, MC, V, Discover, AE
Sells: vitamins and health supplements
Store: mail order only
Online: http://www.amerhealth.com

 ¡Sí!

Here's a great company for vitamin and health supplement values. American Health Food claims you'll save 20% to 50% off on most items, and a comparison check with two local health food stores bore that out. The 62-page catalog features thousands of vitamins and minerals, herbal formulas, powder mixes, and nutritional supplements, from such companies as All One, American Body Building, Cybergenics, FutureBiotics, Nature's Herbs, Nature's Way, Rainbow Light, Twinlab, Unison, and many more, as well as American Health Food's own brand (where you'll find savings up to 60% on some items). American Health lists the retail price alongside their price, so you can calculate your savings at a glance.

The catalog also has other health-food-store products, including Bach Flower Remedies by Nelson's Homeopathy, essential oils, weight-loss formulas, sunblock, skin- and hair-care products, juicers, and books on subjects ranging from yeast sensitivity to the benefits of echinacea to fighting cancer. Postage/handling is $3.95 regardless of your order size (within the continental U.S. and Canada). With orders over $50 you receive a "free gift." The website, where you can order online, features even more products, particularly the smaller, hard-to-find companies, and runs limited-time manufacturers' offers for even deeper discounts. At American Health Food there is no minimum order, and if you don't see something you're looking for, ask. They might have it in stock or be able to get it for you.

Special Factors: Flat-rate shipping ($3.95) to anywhere in the continental U.S. or Canada.

BEACUTY BOUTIQUE

6836 ENGLE RD.
P.O. BOX 94520
CLEVELAND, OH
44101–4520
440–826–3008

Catalog: free
Pay: check, MO, MC, V, Discover
Sells: cosmetics and treatment products
Store: mail order only

Before you pay top dollar for cosmetics and perfumes, see the 80-page catalog from Beauty Boutique, which can save you as much as 90% on the original or full-size selling prices. You'll find page after page of cosmetics, beauty treatments, perfumes, and accessories, from names such as Almay, Elizabeth Arden, Borghese, Chanel, Coty, Giorgio, Halston, Calvin Klein, Lancôme, Estée Lauder, L'Oréal, Monteil, Prince Matchabelli, Oscar de la Renta, Revlon, Stendhal, and Yves St. Laurent. In addition, the catalogs feature skin treatments, beauty tools, jewelry, a small selection of lingerie, home care products and organizers, and other useful items. Prices are genuinely low, and because some products are packaged in promotional sizes, buying here is a great way to try something out without making a full-size investment.

Special Factors: Satisfaction is guaranteed; returns are accepted for exchange, refund, or credit.

CAL BEN SOAP COMPANY

9828 PEARMAIN ST.,
DEPT. WBMC
OAKLAND, CA 94603
800–340–7091
510–638–7091
FAX: 510–638–7827

Catalog: free
Pay: check, MO, MC, V, AE, Discover
Sells: natural, earth-friendly soaps for bath, hair, laundry, and dishes
Store: mail order only

The Cal Ben Soap Company has been in business for over half a century and employs a curious blend of old-fashioned products and eye-popping futuristic promotional materials. As producers of "Five Star Natural Ecology Pure Soap Products for the Third Planet From the Sun," Cal Ben emphasizes simple ingredients—white vegetable tallow, cocoa butter oils, natural extracts of almond, citrus, and coconut—and environmental safety concerns. You can feel really good about their cruelty-free, environmentally safe products, because they also deliver a good value: The 3-ounce bar of hand soap is offered in packages of 24, 36, 100, and 150 bars, for as little as an average of 70 cents each. Cal Ben also sells triple-concentrated shampoo, liquid cream soap for hand-washables and dishes, dishwasher concentrate granules, and all-temperature laundry soap, most in graduated sizes at varying savings. Free "Data Bulletins" with guidelines for using the products are available upon request, and everything can be bought in sample sizes. If you like everything Cal Ben makes, consider stocking up with one of the four "Super Star" collections, 65 to 290 pounds of bar soap, shampoo, dishwasher granules, liquid cream soap, and laundry soap. The prices of these packages run from $125 to $395, and they're calculated to last the average family one to six years. Anything that could keep a daily necessity off your shopping list for that long is worth checking into. Mention BWBM when you send for the literature and when you order.

Special Factors: Satisfaction is guaranteed; returns are accepted for exchange, refund, or credit.

ESSENTIAL PRODUCTS CO., INC.

**90 WATER ST., DEPT.
  WBM
NEW YORK, NY
  10005–3587
212–344–4288**

Price List and Sample Cards: free with SASE (see text)
Pay: check or MO
Sells: "interpretation" fragrances
Store: same address; Monday to Friday 9–6

"We offer our versions of the world's most treasured and expensive ladies' perfumes and men's colognes, selling them at a small fraction of the original prices"—so states the literature from Essential Products Co., Inc. Ralph Nader, in his *Buyer's Market,* praised this company as being consumer-friendly, with good-quality products and great value. How do they do it? They don't spend a lot of money on fancy packaging, royalties for the couturier's name, or international advertising—which are what contribute to the incredibly high cost of most perfumes.

Essential Products was founded in 1895 and markets its interpretations of famous perfumes under the brand name of "Naudet." The company stocks 50 different copies of such costly perfumes as Beautiful, Boucheron, Chanel #5, Coco, Giorgio, Joy, L'Air du Temps, Opium, Paloma Picasso, Passion, Poison, Shalimar, White Diamonds, and Ysatis, as well as 23 "copycat" colognes for men, including Drakkar Noir, Eternity, Obsession, Polo, and Joop. A 1-ounce bottle of perfume is $20 (½ ounce, $11.50), and 4 ounces of any men's cologne costs $11. When you write to Essential Products, please identify yourself as a BWBM reader, which entitles you to five free "scent cards" of Essential Products' best-selling fragrances. The sample cards give an idea of how closely the Naudet version replicates the original, but you should try the product to evaluate it properly. You must also enclose a long, stamped, self-addressed envelope for the set of samples.

Special Factors: Satisfaction is guaranteed; returns are accepted within 30 days for refund; minimum order is $20.

ESSENTIALS

AARP PHARMACY SERVICE INC.

P.O. BOX 13671, DEPT. WBM

RICHMOND, VA 23286–2616

800–456–2277

800–260–4452 (SPANISH)

FAX: 800–456–7631

TDD: 800–933–4327

Catalog: free
Pay: check, MO, V, MC, Discover
Sells: generic drugstore and pharmaceutical items
Store: mail order only

Retired Persons Services, Inc., is an entity that paid AARP (American Association of Retired Persons) a fee to use AARP's name and logo in its mail-order pharmacy name. It is not affiliated with the well-known seniors' organization. It appears, however, to have some of the same interests—i.e., saving seniors and others money on prescription and over-the-counter drugs and drugstore sundries that are a day-to-day necessity for many of us. "Essentials" is the name of the catalog.

The 80-page catalog specializes in generic products—that is, these items have the same active ingredients as common brands such as Tylenol, Preparation H, and Imodium A-D but are sold for much less, sometimes half—under the AARP Pharmacy label. The catalog offers generic vitamins, nutrition formulas, antacids, face creams, sleep aids, toothpaste, sunglasses—just about anything you'd find in a drugstore. Additionally, the Essentials catalog carries products to assist elderly folk with everyday living, featuring items such as elevated toilet seats, heating pads, cholesterol home test kits, humidifiers, and on and on. AARP Pharmacy functions as a full-service pharmacy and can fill any prescription with brand-name or generic medications. Using the latter will net you 30% to 50% savings. See the catalog for details on prescription and other ordering. There's a full-time pharmacist on duty at the main number—8 A.M. to 8 P.M., Monday through Friday ET, and 8:30 A.M. to 5 P.M. Saturday—to answer all of your prescription drug queries. Ostomy customers: Request the special Ostomy products catalog.

Special Factors: AARP Pharmacy honors most prescription insurance plans. Prescription medications can be labeled in Braille upon request when you order. All shipping is $1, no matter how large the order.

FRAGRANCE INTERNATIONAL, INC.

398 E. RAYEN AVE.
YOUNGSTOWN, OH 44505
800–543–3341
330–747–3341
FAX: 330–747–7200

Information: price quote
Pay: check, MO, MC, V, Discover
Sells: men's and women's fragrances
Store: mail order only
E-mail: fii@cisnet.com

Living well may be the best revenge, but doing it at a discount goes one better. Fragrance International can help you carve an average of 28% to 33% off your next purchase of men's or women's scent, whether you're buying full-strength perfume, eau de parfum, eau de toilette, cologne, after shave, body cream, lotion, dusting powder, or deodorant. Not every scent is offered in every form, but the current list includes hundreds—from Adolfo to Yves Saint Laurent's "Y" for women, and Aramis to Zizanie for men. In addition, a selection of bath salts and shower gels, cosmetic bags, manicure accessories, cosmetic trays, makeup mirrors, and other beauty and bath accessories is available.

Special Factors: Orders under $50 are charged a $5 handling fee.

FREEDA VITAMINS, INC.

36 E. 41ST ST.
NEW YORK, NY
10017–6203
800–777–3737
212–685–4980
FAX: 212–685–7297
TDD: 800–777–3737

Catalog: free
Pay: check, MO, MC, V, AE, Discover
Sells: dietary supplements and prescriptions
Store: Freeda Pharmacy, same address; Monday to Thursday 8:30–6, Friday 8:30–4

   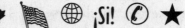

Freeda, a family-run operation, has been manufacturing vitamins and minerals in its own plant since 1928. Freeda is dedicated to providing the purest possible product, and its formulations are free of coal-tar dyes, sulfates, gluten, starch, animal stearates, pesticides, sugar, and artificial flavorings, and are suitable for even the strictest vegetarian or kosher diet—and don't upset sensitive stomachs. The Zimmermans, who run the firm, put an extra tablet in every bottle just to be nice, and their prices represent savings of up to 40% on some of the supplements.

The 36-page catalog lists vitamins, minerals, multivitamins, and nutritional products, which are available in a dizzying choice of combinations and strengths. The vitamin selection includes A and D, B, C, and E; among the minerals are calcium, iron, magnesium, potassium, selenium, and zinc; amino acids, proteins, and other dietary extras are offered. Freeda is listed here not for its megadose formulations, but because of its emphasis on quality production and additive-free goods. It's great to find a source for children's (and adults') natural vitamins. (Freeda's chewable vitamins are naturally flavored, and there is an unflavored version for children on restricted diets. All of the Freeda vitamins are approved by the Feingold Association.) Needless to say, the Freeda catalog is free of the preposterous claims and misleading information often given by supplement sellers. And wonderful as all of this is, it's still important to check with your health-care professional before taking supplements and to avoid megadoses unless they're specifically recommended.

Special Factors: Courtesy discounts are given to health-care professionals; most major health plans are honored; C.O.D. orders are accepted.

KETTLE CARE

710 TRAP RD., DEPT.
WBMC
COLUMBIA FALLS, MT
59912
TEL/FAX: 406–892–3294

Catalog: $1, $2 outside U.S.
Pay: check, MO, MC, V, Discover
Sells: natural skin-care and bath products
Store: mail order only
Online: http://www.kettlecare.com

Every skin-care empire ever built began with someone at the stove, turning improbable ingredients into the stuff of dreams. That's the business of Kettle Care, where natural products and botanicals are combined to create moisturizers, facial creams, facial scrubs, lotions, balms, and other things to soothe your skin and spirit. The 16-page color catalog features lavender liquid castile-based facial soap, botanically scented massage oils, hand-saving Worker's Creme, natural facial scrubs, lotion for normal-to-oily complexions, Essential Facial Creme, and pure essential oils. Herbal sleep and dream pillows, bath herbs, and woodsy herbal sachets are part of the "Herbal Pleasures" section. The prices are very reasonable: Kettle Care's Herbal Aid Creme with cocoa butter and almond oil costs $8.50 for 2 ounces, while Caswell-Massey's Almond Night Cream costs nearly $15 for the same amount. (The offerings here compare favorably to favorite unguents from Weleda and Aubrey Organics, too.) Among the other good buys are quarter ounces of essential and fragrance oils for $5, and jars of naturally flavored lip balm for $2.25. You can buy everything individually, or take advantage of the sample sets and discounted "packs" of four or six of the same kind of item. (Kettle Care offers a 25-cent credit for every container returned; many products are available packaged in glass.) The catalog lists the ingredients of most of the products and includes directions for use. And there's a guide to which skin-care products suit which complexion types, so you can develop your own treatment line and regimen.

Wholesale customers: The wholesale catalog costs $1, the minimum order is $35, and the discounts average 45% to 50% off retail catalog prices.

Special Factors: Satisfaction is guaranteed; returns are accepted for exchange, refund, or credit.

L&H VITAMINS

32–33 47TH AVE.
LONG ISLAND CITY, NY
11101
800–221–1152
FAX: 718–361–1437

Catalog: free
Pay: check, MO, MC, V, Discover
Sells: nutritional supplements and self-treatment products
Store: mail order only
Online: http://www.lhvitamins.com

"Take good care of yourself" means different things to different people, but for many of us, the translation is a good diet, exercise, and nutritional supplements. And when it comes to deciding what to take, the interpretations are even more wide ranging. Enter L&H Vitamins, which offers over 10,000 different items in the closely printed, 84-page catalog and guarantees that you'll save up to 40% off. The listings run from amino acids to zinc and include treatment lines for skin, hair-care products, and pet vitamins. The catalog is organized by brand name and cross-referenced in the alphabetized "Vita-Guide" by category, making it easy to find what you want. L&H represents scores of manufacturers and labels, including American Health, Bach, Doctor's Best, Food Science Laboratories, FutureBiotics, Kyolic, Natrol, Nature's Way, Reviva, Schiff, Synergy Plus, Thompson, Twinlab, and many others. Their prices are a welcome break from those charged at health food stores. Do your homework before picking up the catalog, though, because the limitations of catalog space and the enormous selection don't allow for formulations and ingredients to be listed. Or you can call toll-free and a sales rep will be able to give you the ingredients from the L & H "Vitabank."

Special Factors: Satisfaction is guaranteed; returns are accepted within 30 days for exchange, refund, or credit.

MEDI-MAIL INC.

P.O. BOX 98520
LAS VEGAS, NV 89193–8520
800–793–3548
FAX: 702–361–3422
TDD: 800–423–3724

Brochure: free
Pay: check, MO, MC, V
Sells: prescription drugs and health-care products
Store: mail order only; phone hours Monday to Friday 6–5 PT

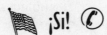 ¡Si! ℂ

Medi-Mail is a national pharmacy-by-mail that offers name-brand and generic prescription medications and over-the-counter health products at competitive prices. You may request the firm's brochure, which answers general questions, as well as a catalog of over-the-counter items. Medi-Mail can provide an itemized receipt with each order, which may be submitted to your insurance carrier or kept for your records—be sure to ask for the receipt when you order.

Special Factors: Price quote by phone; minimum order is $10.

PIA DISCOUNT VITAMINS

**708 SAW MILL RIVER RD.
ARDSLEY, NY 10502
800–662–8144
914–693–3632
FAX: 914–693–3557**

Catalog: free
Pay: check, MO, MC, V, AE, Discover
Sells: supplements, homeopathic remedies, vitamins, herbs, books, etc.
Store: mail order only
E-mail: piavitamins@prodigy.net

There are plenty of companies selling generic lines of vitamins, but the 32-page catalog from PIA offers name-brand vitamins, minerals, and remedies at a minimum savings of "always 20%" on list. Additionally, PIA offers frequent specials, such as those listed in the "Fall Blow-Out" catalog, where prices are 50% off. The formulations are not given, but they're easy to locate when you visit your health food store or pharmacy to price shop. There is a 6-page, A to Z "Vitamin and Mineral Guide," which includes herbs and food supplements, with a helpful and interesting paragraph describing the sources, uses, and benefits of each.

The catalog is organized by manufacturer and alphabetized within each company. PIA offers savings on Bach Flower remedies (hard to find at a discount), FutureBiotics, Good 'N Natural, Klamath, Kyolic, Nature's Herbs, Nature's Way, Gary Null's products, Schiff, Twinlab, and many others. The name of the product, form (caplet, tablet, etc.), potency, and amount are given, with the retail and discounted prices. If you don't see what you're looking for, call PIA to see whether it can be ordered. PIA also carries selected health-related books.

Special Factors: Satisfaction is guaranteed; price quote by phone or letter.

RELATED PRODUCTS/COMPANIES

For companies that specialize in wigs and hair-care products, see "Wigs and Hair Care," page 276
For companies carrying eye-care products, see "Eye Care and Eyewear," page 281
Breast prostheses • B & B Company
Children's and baby-care products • Baby Bunz, The Natural Baby, Fuller Brush Independent Distributor
Health and fitness equipment • Damark, Creative Health Products, Fitness

Factory Outlet, Better Health Fitness

Health-monitoring equipment • Cotton Scrubs, Tafford Manufacturing

Health-related books • Mountain Ark Trading Co., Bosom Buddies

Medicinal herbs • Rafal Spice, San Francisco Herb, Atlantic Spice, Caprilands Herb Farm

Perfume-making supplies and books • Tom Thumb Workshops

Personal-care appliances • Bernie's Discount

Personal-care products • Dairy Association Co., Mountain Ark Trading Co., Grandma's Spice Shop, Fuller Brush Independent Distributor, EDGE Distributing, National Allergy Supply

Products for allergy-sensitive people • National Allergy Supply

Products for people with limited mobility • Comfort House, Amplestuff

Products for the visually impaired • The New Vision Store, Independent Living Aids, Comfort House

Support hosiery and therapeutic footwear • Support Plus

Vitamins and nutritional supplements • Fitness Systems Mfg.

Wigs and Hair Care

Wigs, hairpieces, and hair-care products for women and men

Changing the length, style, or color of your hair for one day with a wig, wiglet, or fall can be lots of fun. But for people who've lost their hair, having a natural-looking wig is a necessary part of regaining self-confidence. The firms in this section offer styles for women as well as men, and there's one company geared to the tastes and preferences of African-American women (see listing for Especially Yours).

All of the wig companies carry hair products. But one, Gold Medal Hair Products, specializes in shampoos, conditioners, and other hair products designed to suit the needs of African Americans.

BEAUTY BY SPECTOR, INC.

1 SPECTOR PLACE,
   DEPT. WBMC–99
MCKEESPORT, PA
   15134–0502
412–673–3259
FAX: 412–678–3978

Catalog: call (see text)
Pay: check or MO (see text)
Sells: wigs, hairpieces, wig accessories
Store: mail order only

Beauty by Spector, Inc., offers the Alan Thomas line of wigs and hairpieces at savings of up to 50% compared with salon-selling prices. The 32-page color catalog features a number of designer styles for women, modeled in gorgeous full-page photographs. The wigs range from neat, softly coifed shorter styles to the magnificent below-shoulder-length drape "Obsession."

The styles are contemporary and fashionable—pretty, relaxed, and well-shaped. Included in the catalog are wiglets, cascades, and extensions that are ideal for everyday wear as well as for dressy occasions (or when you just want to change your image for a night without doing something permanent).

There are men's hairpieces here, too, in several styles. Thermal-conductive monofilament and polyurethane are available in the men's pieces for maximum comfort.

The wigs and hairpieces are available in a wide variety of synthetic fibers as well as human hair and are offered in dozens of colors. For color selection, you may purchase a set of actual hair samples, or if you prefer, send a sample of your hair for color matching. You'll also find shampoos, conditioners, hair accessories (turbans and scarves, for example), brushes and combs, and wig stands and mannequins.

Beauty by Spector has been in business since 1958 and is extremely knowledgeable in the field. Wig specialists are on duty 24 hours a day to answer your questions.

Special to BWBM readers: Be sure to identify yourself as a *Buy Wholesale by Mail* reader and Beauty by Spector will include the "Wholesale Price List," plus other special offers, with your catalog.

Special Factors: Specify men's or women's styles when requesting information, as added material and flyers pertaining to your gender will be enclosed with the catalog; the price of the catalog was not known at press time, so please call to inquire; pay by money order and receive an additional discount; quantity discounts are negotiable.

ESPECIALLY YOURS

P.O. BOX 105
SOUTH EASTON, MA
  02375
800–748–6910
FAX: 508–238–1965

Catalog: free
Pay: check, MO, MC, V, Discover
Sells: wigs and hats for African-American women
Store: mail order only

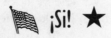 ¡Si! ★

This is America's largest wig catalog for African-American women. Especially Yours has over 85 "wig consultants" ready to answer your questions seven days a week. The 28-page color catalog features wigs starting at $19, and the suggested retail is listed alongside Especially Yours' price, so you can really see the savings—as much as 50% on many items. The current catalog features the Diahann Carroll Wigs collection, which are stylish, contemporary shorter cuts for the most part, and very natural-looking. The catalog also has ponytail falls, braided buns, curly add-on hairpieces, and bangs, as well as other chic wigs in long, shoulder-length, and shorter styles—including curly, hand-braided, and waved examples. There are 21 colors to choose from, from jet black to honey ash blond to frosted blends to dark auburn. Turbans, flapper hats, headwraps, and other headgear are available, as well as wig-care accessories.

Special Factors: Complete satisfaction guaranteed; see catalog for returns policy on unworn wigs, wiglets, etc.; wholesale accounts available.

GOLD MEDAL HAIR PRODUCTS CO.

ONE BENNINGTON
 AVENUE
FREEPORT, NY 11520
800–841–7770, EXT. 408
FAX: 516–378–0168

Catalog: free
Pay: check, MO, MC, V, AE, Discover
Sells: hair and skin products for African Americans; lingerie, music videos, jewelry, etc.
Store: mail order only

Gold Medal Hair Products has been in business for 56 years, catering to the black population with products to fit your different beauty needs and desires. The 36-page color catalog is busy and jam-packed with an eclectic assortment of products, dominated by hair-related products and tools. You'll find tamers, conditioners, shampoos, hair-setting gels, coloring and highlighting agents, perm kits, styling accessories, and hair sprays, as well as wigs, weave sections, and hairpieces—for women, men, and children.

There is also an extensive selection of videos and music cassettes focusing on black culture, from black movies and black history to gospel and comedy. Also available are all kinds of skin products and accessories, figure-controlling (and enhancing) bras, slips, and panties, and even a section on jewelry, vitamins, and cosmetics.

Although the prices are competitive, Gold Medal does offer twofers, specials, and combo items for extra savings. There aren't enough companies like Gold Medal out there, and that's why I'm happy to list them here.

Wholesalers: Minimum order is $250; 40% off. Call for details.

Special Factors: C.O.D. orders require a $10 deposit; satisfaction is guaranteed or you'll be credited or refunded; returned cassettes and videos must remain unopened, and wigs and clothing must be unworn.

PAULA YOUNG FASHION WIGS

P.O. BOX 483
BROCKTON, MA 02403
800–472–4017
FAX: 508–238–1965

Catalog: free
Pay: check, MO, MC, V, Discover
Sells: wigs, headwear, and wig-care accessories
Store: mail order only
E-mail: pywigs!custserv@attmail.com
Online: http://www.paulayoung.com

 (SEE TEXT) ¡Si!

So you want to be a redhead, but maybe only once in a while? Call Paula Young. They've got fabulous wigs at inexpensive prices—up to 50% off list. The current catalog features "super saver" short wigs for only $29 each, with most wigs averaging around $49. The 32-page color catalog has page after page of wigs to fit every mood and lifestyle. (For African-American styles and selections, see their sister company, Especially Yours, also listed this section.) There are short, sophisticated styles, curly cascading styles, and 'dos with long layered waves. You'll also find falls and wiglets, which you can clip on to your shorter hair to create added length, curls, volume, or drama. The available colors are wide ranging, and you'll find a size chart in the catalog to help you choose the right fit, as well as color-choosing tips. Paula Young has a small selection of wigs for men and carries wig accessories and supplies such as turbans, headbands, wig liners, wig stands, carrying cases, and styling brushes and combs, as well as wig shampoos, conditioners, and more.

Canadian readers, please note: There is a special Canadian catalog. Call the main number to have one mailed to you.

Special Factors: Satisfaction guaranteed (see catalog for details on returning unworn wigs for refund or exchange); wholesale customers should call main number for terms and pricing; no C.O.D. orders.

RELATED PRODUCTS/COMPANIES

Children's shampoo • *Baby Bunz*
Hairbrushes • *Fuller Brush Independent Distributor*
Hair-care products • *American Health Food, Cal Ben, Mountain Ark Trading Co., Fuller Brush Independent Distributor*

Eye Care and Eyewear

Contact lenses and supplies, eyeglasses, and sunglasses

If you're a contact lens wearer, you know how much you spend every year on lenses, eye check-ups, cleaning and soaking solution, contact lens insurance, etc. You'll still need to see your doctor once a year, but you can save a great deal of money by using the companies in this section for replacement lenses and contact lens supplies. You'll also find companies here that specialize in eyeglasses and sunglasses at a discount.

FIND IT FAST

CONTACT LENSES • Contact Lens Replacement Center, Lens Express, National Contact Lens Center, Prism Optical
LENS-CARE PRODUCTS • Lens Express
PRESCRIPTION EYEGLASSES • Hidalgo, Prism Optical
SUNGLASSES • Contact Lens Replacement Center, Hidalgo, Lens Express, Prism Optical, Sunglasses U.S.A.

CONTACT LENS REPLACEMENT CENTER

P.O. BOX 1489, DEPT. 99
MELVILLE, NY 11747
800–779–2654
516–491–7763
FAX: 516–643–4009

Price List: free with long SASE
Pay: check, MO, MC, V, AE, Discover
Sells: contact lenses and sunglasses
Store: mail order only
E-mail: info@clrc.com
Online: http://www.clrc.com

Contact Lens Replacement Center, in business since 1986, sells contact lenses of every type at savings of up to 50%. The replacement lenses include hard, soft, planned-replacement, disposable, and gas-permeable types. Toric, bifocal, and aphakic lenses are also available. The brands include Barnes Hind/Hydrocurve, Bausch & Lomb, Boston, Ciba, Cooper-Vision, CSI, Fluorex, Fluoroperm, Hydron/Ocular Sciences, Johnson & Johnson, Paraperm, Sunsoft, and Wesley-Jessen. All soft, planned-replacement, and disposable lenses are shipped in factory-sealed containers. Hard and gas-permeable lenses are made to order.

Please note: This is a replacement service—not for first-time lens wearers—and you must supply a current prescription for the lenses you are now wearing. The prices are so low that it may make sense to discontinue lens insurance and rely on this service if you lose or damage your contacts—the Center's staff can help you determine the least expensive way to replace your prescribed lenses. And there are no membership fees of any kind. Sunglasses by Bollé, Gargoyles, Ray-Ban, Revo, Serengeti, Sun Cloud, and Vuarnet are also available, at discount prices. Call with the specific model name and number for a price quote.

Special Factors: Price quote by phone or letter with a long, stamped, self-addressed envelope.

HIDALGO

45 LA BUENA VISTA,
   DEPT. WM
WIMBERLY, TX 78676
512–847–5571
FAX: 512–847–2393

Catalog: free
Pay: check, MO, MC, V, AE, Discover
Sells: prescription eyeglasses, sunglasses,
binoculars, watches, knives, etc.
Store: Wimberly North Too Shopping Center, Wimberly, TX; Monday to Friday 10–6

Hidalgo's 56-page catalog makes ordering your eyeglasses by mail seem so easy that you'll wonder why you haven't tried it before. Hidalgo has been in business since 1967 and understands the concerns of the person who's buying glasses by mail. The catalog includes detailed descriptions of the frames, lenses, and special coatings and includes a "Consumers' Guide to Sunglasses" that answers just about every question you can think of. There are instructions on taking your "pupil distance" measurements, and a chart that shows the light transmission data on the lenses sold by Hidalgo. The "try-on program" allows you to order up to three frames and try them out before ordering your glasses—a great feature for people who have a hard time finding frames that fit or flatter.

Hidalgo's own frames dominate the selection, including those made of "Memory Metal," and the lens options include a choice of materials (glass, plastic, etc.), colors, coatings, and UV protection. Terms of Hidalgo's warranty are stated clearly in the catalog, as well as details of the try-on program. The prices are as much as 40% less than regular retail on the nonprescription eyewear, and 50% or more below customary charges for prescription glasses. You'll also find an eclectic assortment of nonvision-related items in the black-and-white newsprint catalog, including everything from Simpsons chess sets to coin sorters!

Special Factors: Returns in new, unused condition are accepted within 30 days for exchange, refund, or credit.

LENS EXPRESS, INC.

350 S.W. 12TH AVENUE
DEERFIELD BEACH, FL
33442
800–593–LENS
954–422–8181
FAX: 800–FAX–LENS

Catalog: free
Pay: check, MO, MC, V, AE, CB, DC, Discover
Sells: contact lenses, lens-care products, sunglasses
Store: mail order only
E-mail: customerservice@lensexpress.com
Online: http://www.lensexpress.com and on AOL: keywords LENS EXPRESS

Lens Express sells 80,000 contact lenses a day, which is why they can sell you the same brand-name lenses prescribed by your doctor for much less than you'd pay elsewhere—from about 35% to 45% less—and this includes the "one-hour" discount vision stores at the mall. (Lens Express offers a "lowest price guarantee"; see catalog for details.) You can call the company with your prescription information, order online, or have Lens Express staff call your doctor to get the prescription. The 24-page color catalog offers contacts by Ciba, Bausch & Lomb, Wesley-Jessen, PBH, CooperVision, and Johnson & Johnson, from exotic tinted lenses to bifocal disposables, and every style and type in between. Lens Express also carries a full line of their own brand saline solutions and cleaners at prices that are nearly half what the famous-name-brand items sell for at your local drugstore. If you become a member of the Lens Express Discount Club—$25 for a three-year membership—you'll receive discounts on eye care through a network of national participating providers; eyeglass frames and lenses at savings up to 50%; additional discounts on eye-care products; automatic lens replacement at regular intervals; and more. (See catalog for details.)

Lens Express has another catalog that features sunglasses. Here you'll find all the best manufacturers—Ray-Ban, Revo, Giorgio Armani, Calvin Klein, and Gargoyles among them—in a range of styles, at prices, like their contact lenses, that are up to 45% off list. Swiss Army knives in their various configurations are also available here at good discounts.

Special Factors: Lowest price guarantee; satisfaction guaranteed (see catalog for special conditions on gas permeable and toric lenses); quantity discounts available.

NATIONAL CONTACT LENS CENTER

410 "F" JEREMIAH DR.
SIMI VALLEY, CA 93065
800–326–6352
FAX: 805–583–0121

Brochure: free
Pay: check, MO, MC, V, Discover, JCB
Sells: soft and gas-permeable contact lenses
Store: same address; Monday to Friday 8–5
E-mail: mtalmadg@interserv.com

National Contact Lens Center, established in 1974, can save you up to 75% on your next pair of contact lenses. You must be an experienced lens wearer to buy here, since the firm can't provide through the mail the fitting and monitoring services needed by first-time wearers. No membership fees are ever charged.

National Contact Lens Center sells all the major soft contact lens brands, including lines by American Hydron, Bausch & Lomb, Boston, Ciba, CooperVision, Johnson & Johnson (Acuvue), Ocular Science, Pilkington/Barnes Hind, and Wesley-Jessen. Colored, standard, extended-wear, disposable, planned-replacement, and opaque lenses are offered, as well as toric (for astigmatism) lenses. Hard and gas-permeable lenses are also available. Savings can reach 75%, depending on the lens and manufacturer, and every lens is backed by National Contact Lens Center's 30-day replacement guarantee—honored even if the vials are opened.

Please note: A Japanese-language edition of the price list and order form are available upon request.

Special Factors: Satisfaction is guaranteed; price quote by phone; returns are accepted within 30 days for replacement, exchange, refund, or credit.

PRISM OPTICAL, INC.

10992 NW 7TH AVE., DEPT. WC99
NORTH MIAMI, FL 33168
305–754–5894
FAX: 305–754–7352

Catalog: $2, $5 outside U.S.
Pay: check, MO, MC, V, AE, Discover
Sells: prescription eyeglasses, contact lenses, and sunglasses
Store: same address; Monday to Friday 8:30–5

 ¡Sí!

Prism Optical has been selling prescription eyeglasses by mail since 1959 and publishes a 24-page color catalog that shows over 100 eyeglass frames for men, women, and children, discounted an average of 30% to 50%. Frames (and designer sunglasses) from Armani, Bollé, Carrera, Cazal, Christian Dior, Gucci, Anne Klein, Neostyle, Polo, Ray-Ban, Revo, and Serengeti are available. One of the benefits of ordering from Prism is being able to choose from a number of lens options, including photochromic lenses, polycarbonate (ultra-thin) lenses, permanently tinted lenses, lenses with gray mirror-finish, and UV-filtering coating and scratch-resistant coating. The lens styles include single-vision and bifocal lenses, trifocals, and "invisible" bifocals, among others. Prism guarantees that the glasses will fit correctly, and the catalog provides guides to gauging the correct size of the temple and bridge pieces.

Prism Optical also sells prescription contact lenses at prices up to 70% below those charged elsewhere. The firm sells "all brands," factory-sealed and guaranteed against defects. Call Prism with your prescription information for availability and price information.

Special Factors: Satisfaction is guaranteed; returns are accepted within 30 days for refund or credit; C.O.D. orders are accepted.

SUNGLASSES U.S.A., INC.

469 SUNRISE HWY.
LYNBROOK, NY 11563
800–USA–RAYS
FAX: 516–599–4825

Catalog: free
Pay: check, MO, MC, V, AE, Discover
Sells: Ray-Ban sunglasses
Store: same address; Monday to Friday
10–5:30

Sunglasses U.S.A. sells Ray-Ban sunglasses at 33% to 50% off suggested retail. The catalog includes information on the lens material, color, and protection factors against glare and ultraviolet light. The Ray-Ban lines currently available include Classic Metals, Driving Series, Innerview, Marine Line, Killer Loop (shields), Traditionals and Premier Traditionals, Wayfarers, Leathers, Tortuga, Cats, and Retrospecs. The price list includes sizing and style numbers, so you'll be sure you're buying the right model.

Special Factors: Shipping and handling cost a flat $3 per order.

RELATED PRODUCTS/COMPANIES

Magnifiers and other aids for the visually impaired • Independent Living Aids, The New Vision Store
Sunglasses • Spike Nashbar, Holabird Sports, Mass. Army & Navy

HOUSEHOLD APPLIANCES AND TVS

Large kitchen appliances, small personal-care appliances, vacuum cleaners, sewing machines, televisions, air conditioners, etc.

The companies listed here offer primarily white goods (washers, dryers, refrigerators, and ranges), brown goods (TVs, air conditioners, etc.), personal-care appliances, sewing machines, vacuum cleaners, and floor machines. For an explanation of gray-market goods—what they are and why the companies listed here don't carry them—see page 73.

For companies that specialize in audio and/or video equipment, see the "Music, Audio, and Video" chapter. For office machines and computers, see the "Office, Business, Professional" chapter.

Price is important, but it's just one purchase consideration. One of the best product information resources is *Consumer Reports,* which features monthly reviews of name-brand goods and services; it's supplemented by the annual *Buying Guide,* which summarizes scores of the reviews. In addition to dispassionate assessments of product performance and guides to features, the reviews often include both suggested list and "benchmark" retail selling prices. *Consumer Reports* also publishes news on product recalls, deceptive selling practices, health issues, money management, and related consumer interests.

Most appliance and electronics manufacturers will send brochures on specific models upon request. You can often find the manufacturer's address on product packaging, and the consumer contacts and addresses of hundreds of major corporations are listed in "Consumer's Resource Handbook," which is available from the Consumer Information Center (see the listing in "Books, Audiobooks, and Periodicals").

If you run into trouble with a major appliance and can't get it resolved, you may be able to get help from the Major Appliance Consumer Action Panel (MACAP). MACAP, which is sponsored by the Association of Home Appliance Manufacturers (AHAM), can request action from a manufacturer and make recommendations for resolution of the complaint. (The panel's advice is not binding, but it resolves over 80% of the cases it handles.) You can turn to MACAP with problems about dishwashers, ranges, microwave ovens, washers, dryers, refrigerators, freezers, garbage disposals, trash compactors, air conditioners, water heaters, and dehumidifiers. If your complaint concerns one of these appliances, and your attempts to get the problem resolved with the seller and the manufacturer have been futile, write to Major Appliance Consumer Action Program, 20 N. Wacker Dr., Ste. 1231, Chicago, IL 60606. Your letter should include the manufacturer's name, model number of the appliance, and date purchased, as well as copies of relevant receipts and correspondence. (Call 800–621–0477 for more information.)

For firms in other chapters selling appliances, see "Related Products/Companies" at the end of this section.

FIND IT FAST

AIR CONDITIONERS • Bernie's Discount Center, Dial-a-Brand, LVT Price Quote Hotline, Percy's

CENTRAL VACUUM-CLEANING SYSTEMS • AVAC Corporation

MAJOR APPLIANCES • Beach Sales, Bernie's Discount Center, Cole's Appliance, Dial-a-Brand, EBA Wholesale, Kaplan Bros., LVT Price Quote Hotline, Percy's

SEWING MACHINES AND SERGERS • Discount Appliance Centers, Sewin' in Vermont, Sewing Machine Super Store, Suburban Sew 'N Sweep

SMALL APPLIANCES • Bernie's Discount Center, Sewin' in Vermont, Sewing Machine Super Store

TVs • Bernie's Discount Center, Cole's Appliance, Dial-a-Brand, LVT Price Quote Hotline, Percy's

VACUUM-CLEANER REPAIRS • ABC Vacuum Cleaner Warehouse

VACUUM CLEANERS, RUG SHAMPOOERS, FLOOR POLISHERS • AAA Vacuums, ABC Vacuum Cleaner Warehouse, AVAC Corporation, Discount Appliance Centers, LVT Price Quote Hotline, Suburban Sew 'N Sweep

AAA VACUUMS

1230 NORTH ROAD
ABILENE, TX 79601
800–533–VACS
915–677–1311
FAX: 915–677–9309

Flyer: $2, refundable
Pay: check, MO, MC, V, Discover
Sells: vacuum cleaners, rug shampooers, floor polishers
Store: same address; Monday to Friday 8:30–5
E-mail: aaavacs@aol.com

You can save on some of the best names in the cleaning business at AAA Vacuums, which has been in business since 1975 and offers discounts of up to 50% on list prices. They buy in volume and have a low-key PR approach, which allows them to pass the savings directly to consumers. Canister, upright, convertible, and mini vacuum models are available, from Bissell, Clarke, Kirby, Mastercraft, Oreck, Panasonic, Powr-Flite, Rainbow, Royal, Sanitaire, Sharp, and other names. Both home and commercial lines of vacuum cleaners, floor buffers, and rug shampooers are stocked, and AAA Vacuums also sells reconditioned Kirby and Rainbow machines, and supplies and accessories for a range of floor machines. Since you'll receive just a couple of offset sheets for the $2 fee—and there isn't much product information given—call to discuss your needs or for a price quote. Phone orders are preferred to fax orders.

Canadian readers, please note: Only U.S. funds are accepted.

Special Factors: All merchandise comes with AAA Vacuum's Parts and Service Contract with a product protection plan and/or the original manufacturer's warranty; satisfaction is guaranteed; layaway plan is available; returns are accepted within 10 days; C.O.D. orders are accepted.

ABC VACUUM CLEANER WAREHOUSE

6720 BURNET RD., WM99
AUSTIN, TX 78757
800–285–8145
512–459–7643
FAX: 512–451–2352

Catalog: free
Pay: check, MO, MC, V, AE
Sells: vacuum cleaners
Store: same address; Monday to Friday 9–6, Saturday 9–5
E-mail: discount@abcvacuum.com
Online: http://www.abcvacuum.com

ABC purchases from suppliers who are overstocked or going out of business, and passes the savings—up to 50% on the suggested retail or usual selling price—on to you. Most of the folks who call ABC already know what they're looking for. ABC doesn't spend a lot of time or money on glitzy mail-order catalogs. Their two-page listing of makes, models, and great prices is really for people who already know what they want. If you want to chat with their friendly personnel about the pros and cons of different brands, however, or need brochures on certain lines, they'll gladly accommodate. All machines are new in the original box, unless noted. ABC has been in business since 1977 and sells machines by Bissell Plus, Eureka, Hoover, Oreck, Royal, Sanitaire, and Simplicity. They say, "We want to have the lowest prices in America," and if you can find the same models for less, they'll try to beat that price. See the price list for bags, filters, accessories, and attachments for selected models. ABC also offers repair services by mail—call for information if you're having trouble getting your machine repaired locally.

Canadian readers, please note: Shipments are not made to Canada.

Special Factors: Satisfaction is guaranteed; returns are accepted within 30 days for exchange, refund, or credit; C.O.D. orders are accepted.

AVAC CORPORATION

666 UNIVERSITY AVE.
ST. PAUL, MN 55104–4896
800–328–9430
612–222–0763
FAX: 612–224–2674

Brochure: see text
Pay: check, MO, MC, V, AE, Discover
Sells: vacuum cleaners, related parts, and supplies
Store: 1441 University Ave., St. Paul, MN; two other MN stores—call for locations
E-mail: bojacker@avacorp.com

AVAC Corporation sells the full line of household and commercial vacuum cleaners by Bissell, Jenn-Aire, Panasonic, Sanitaire, and Sharp Electronics. AVAC also sells the Hayden Central Vacuum Cleaning System, for do-it-yourselfers, as well as the parts and supplies needed to keep models of most major brands functioning.

Special Factors: Quantity discounts are available; minimum order is $25.

BEACH SALES

80 VFW PKWY.
REVERE, MA 02151
781–284–0130
800–562–9020
FAX: 781–284–9823

Information: price quote
Pay: check, MO, MC, V
Sells: major appliances, audio and video components, scanners, film, etc.
Store: same address

Beach Sales offers "the best brands at wholesale prices," discounts of up to 50% on everything from watch batteries to major appliances. This firm has been serving the greater Boston area since 1947 and offers the same savings to customers nationwide. There is no catalog, but you can call, fax, or write with the manufacturer's name and model number for a quote on audio and video components, fax machines, major appliances, police scanners and related electronics, and even things such as snow blowers, from Bose, General Electric, Maytag, Mitsubishi, Polaroid, Whirlpool, and scores of other manufacturers. Beach Sales also has great buys on film and tape (audio and video)—inquire about quantity prices.

Special Factors: Price quote by phone, fax, or letter; returns in original packaging are accepted for exchange, refund, or credit.

BERNIE'S DISCOUNT CENTER

821 SIXTH AVE., D–8
NEW YORK, NY
  10001–6305
212–564–8758, 8582, 9431
FAX: 212–564–3894

Catalog: $1, refundable
Pay: check, MO, MC, V, AE (see text)
Sells: appliances, TV and audio components, office machines
Store: same address; Monday to Friday 9:30–6, Saturday (except July and August) 11–4

 ¡Si!

Bernie's has been in business since 1947 and sells "pluggables"—everything from electric brooms to fax machines—at 10% to 15% above dealers' cost, or an average of 30% off list. The catalog is available for $1 (refundable with a purchase), but it shows just a smattering of the stock at Bernie's, and you're better off calling for a price quote. One of the city's best sources for discounted electronics and appliances, Bernie's tries to carry the top-rated goods listed in popular buying guides, and Bernie's does not handle gray-market goods.

Bernie's sells electronics (audio, TV, and video equipment) by Aiwa, AT&T, Brother, Fisher, JVC, Mitsubishi, Panasonic, Quasar, RCA, Sharp, Sony, Toshiba, and Zenith. White goods (shipped in the New York City area only) are available from Amana, Caloric, Frigidaire, General Electric, Jenn-Air, Magic Chef, Maytag, KitchenAid, Whirlpool, White-Westinghouse, and other manufacturers. Bernie's is one of the best sources in the metropolitan area for air conditioners (Airtemp, Carrier, Emerson, Friedrich, General Electric, Gibson, Panasonic, etc.), fans by Duracraft and Lakewood, heaters by Duracraft and Pelonis, and air cleaners and ionizers by Bionaire and Envirocare. Bernie's carries Bionaire and Duracraft humidifiers and a full line of filters and wicks for both brands. Small and personal-care appliances from Black & Decker, Braun, Brita, Clairol, Eureka, Hamilton Beach, Hitachi, Hoover, Interplak, KitchenAid, Krups, Norelco, Oster, Panasonic, Presto, Remington, Sunbeam, Teledyne (Water Pik and Instapure), Toastmaster, Wearever, West Bend, and other brands are available as well.

Please note: Purchases charged to American Express/Optima cards are shipped to billing addresses only, and MasterCard and VISA are accepted for in-store purchases only.

Canadian readers, please note: Orders are shipped to Canada via UPS only.

Special Factors: Store is closed Saturdays in July and August.

COLE'S APPLIANCE & FURNITURE CO.

**4026 LINCOLN AVE.
CHICAGO, IL 60618–3097
773–525–1797**

Information: see text
Pay: check, MO, MC, V, Discover
Sells: appliances and home furnishings
Store: same address; Monday and Thursday
9:30–9, Tuesday, Friday, and Saturday
9:30–5:30 (closed Wednesdays and Sundays)

Cole's, founded in 1957, sells electronics (TV and video), appliances, and home furnishings and bedding at discounts of up to 50%. If you're pricing something from Amana, Asko, Caloric, Dacor, General Electric, Gibson, Hitachi, Hotpoint, Insinkerator, Jenn-Air, KitchenAid, Magic Chef, Maytag, Panasonic, Pioneer, Premier, Speed Queen, Sub-Zero, Thermador, Viking, Whirlpool, Wolf, Zenith, or any other major manufacturer, call Cole's for a price quote. Deliveries are made by Cole's in the greater Chicago area, and via UPS elsewhere.

Special Factors: Price quote by phone or letter.

DIAL-A-BRAND, INC.

**57 S. MAIN ST.
FREEPORT, NY 11520
516–378–9694
FAX: 516–867–3447**

Information: price quote
Pay: check, MO, MC, V, Discover
Sells: appliances, TVs, and video equipment
Store: same address; Monday to Friday 9–6,
Saturday 9–12

¡Sí! ★

Dial-a-Brand, which was founded in 1967, has earned the kudos of institutions and individuals with its wide range of appliances and popular electronics. Dial-a-Brand offers discounts averaging 30% and does not sell gray-market goods. Call or write for prices on air conditioners, TVs, video equipment, microwave ovens, and large appliances. Dial-a-Brand ships chiefly within the New York/New Jersey/Connecticut area, but deliveries (via UPS) are made nationwide. Freight charges may offset savings on outsized or heavy items shipped long distances, so be sure to get a firm quote or estimate before you place your order.

Please note: You must call with the manufacturer's name and model number to receive a price quote.

Special Factors: Returns are accepted for exchange if goods are defective or damaged in transit; minimum order is $99.

DISCOUNT APPLIANCE CENTERS

8426 20TH AVE., STE. 100
ADELPHI, MD 20783
301–559–8932
FAX: 301–559–1335

Information: price quote
Pay: check, MO, MC, V, AE
Sells: vacuum cleaners and sewing machines
Store: mail order only

Discount Appliance Centers sells sewing machines and vacuum cleaners, and accessories and supplies for both, at good discounts. The firm has been in business since 1964 and doesn't have a catalog—you must write for prices and availability information, since quotes are given over the phone as staff time permits. Inquire by model name and number about vacuum cleaners by Airway, Electrolux, Eureka, Filter Queen, Hoover, Kirby, Mastercraft, Oreck, Panasonic, Royal, Sanitaire, Sharp, or Tri-Star. The sewing machines include models by Bernina, Elna, Juki, Necchi, Pfaff, Riccar, Singer, and Viking. If you're trying to find vacuum-cleaner bags, belts, or attachments, note the model and product you need, and write for a price quote. Include a stamped, self-addressed business envelope with your inquiry.

Special Factors: Price quote by letter only with SASE; minimum order is $49.

EBA WHOLESALE

2361 NOSTRAND AVE.
BROOKLYN, NY 11210
800–380–2378
718–252–3400
FAX: 718–253–6002

Flyer: free
Pay: check, MO, MC, V, Discover
Sells: appliances, audio, video, mattresses, etc.
Store: same address; Monday to Friday 9–8, Saturday 9–6, Sunday 10–5

Bargains abound at this Brooklyn discount house, which has been in business since 1970 and sets prices based on its cost plus 5% to 10%—the savings run from 10% to 40% on list or suggested selling prices. EBA Wholesale offers everything from Maytag washers and Amana refrigerators to mattresses and AT&T phones; the lines include Aiwa, Brother, Caloric, Eureka, General Electric, Hotpoint, Jenn-Air, KitchenAid, Magic

Chef, Panasonic, RCA, Sanyo, Sharp, Sony, Toshiba, Whirlpool, White-Westinghouse, and Zenith, among others. EBA's flyer features some of the current specials; you can order from it, or call for a price quote on other models.

Special Factors: Satisfaction is guaranteed; price quote by phone, fax, or letter.

KAPLAN BROS. BLUE FLAME CORP.

523 W. 125TH ST.
NEW YORK, NY
   10027–3498
800–528–6913
212–662–6990
FAX: 212–663–2026

Brochure: free with SASE
Pay: certified check or MO
Sells: commercial restaurant equipment
Store: same address; Monday to Friday 8–4:30

Kaplan Bros. Blue Flame Corp., established in 1953, sells commercial restaurant equipment at discounts of 50% on list prices and will send you manufacturers' brochures on request for a self-addressed, stamped envelope. Blue Flame is best known as a source for Garland commercial stoves and the Dynamic Cooking System.

Please note: Goods are shipped to "mainland U.S.A." only—no orders can be shipped to Alaska, Hawaii, Canada, or APO/FPO addresses.

Special Factors: Request brochures by name of manufacturer; if purchasing a stove for residential installation, have kitchen flooring, wall insulation, and exhaust system evaluated before ordering, and upgrade if necessary.

LVT PRICE QUOTE HOTLINE, INC.

BOX 444–W99
COMMACK, NY
11725–0444
516–234–8884
FAX: 516–234–8808

Brochure: free
Pay: cashier's check or MO
Sells: major appliances, TVs, vacuum cleaners, electronics, office machines, etc.
Store: phone hours Monday to Saturday 9–6
E-mail: calllvt@aol.com
Online: http://members.aol.com/calllvt

LVT, established in 1976, gives you instant access to over 3,000 products from over 40 manufacturers, at savings of up to 30% on suggested list or full retail prices. The brochure includes a roster of available brands, and price quotes are given on individual items. LVT does not sell gray-market goods. For information, read LVT's brochure for the sales and shipping policies, then call with the manufacturer's name and exact model number for a price quote on major appliances, bread-making machines, microwave ovens, air conditioners, vacuum cleaners, washers and dryers, TVs, video equipment, phones and phone machines, calculators, typewriters, fax machines, and word processors.

The brands available include Admiral, Amana, AT&T, Bosch, Broan, Brother, Canon, Carrier, Eagle, Emerson, Eureka, Fedders, Friedrich, Frigidaire, General Electric, Hewlett-Packard, Hitachi, Hoover, Hotpoint, Jenn-Air, JVC, Magic Chef, Maytag, Modern Chef, Panasonic, Quasar, RCA, Rolodex, Roper, Samsung, Sanyo, Sharp, Smith-Corona, Sony, Summit, Tappan, Texas Instruments, Toshiba, Toyatomi, Whirlpool, White-Westinghouse, and Zenith—see the brands list for others.

Special Factors: Shipping (UPS), handling, and insurance charges are included in quotes; all sales are final; all goods are sold with manufacturers' warranties; minimum order is $100; C.O.D. orders are accepted on local deliveries.

PERCY'S, INC.

GOLD STAR BLVD.
WORCESTER, MA 01605
800–922–8194
FAX: 508–797–5578

Information: price quote
Pay: MO, MC, V, Discover
Sells: large appliances, home and car audio, TV components, video, computers, etc.
Store: same address; Monday to Friday 10–9, Saturday 10–6
E-mail: alanl@percys.com
Online: http://www.percys.com

Percy's has been selling appliances since 1926, at prices up to 40% below list. Percy's sells no gray-market goods. Call, write, or e-mail for a price quote on washers, dryers, dishwashers, refrigerators, freezers, ranges, microwave ovens, TVs, video equipment and tapes, audio components, computers, satellite dishes, radar detectors, dehumidifiers, air conditioners, disposals, trash compactors, and other appliances. The brands available at Percy's include Aiwa, Amana, Asko, Bosch, Bose, Caloric, Canon, Compaq, Denon, Eureka, Frigidaire, General Electric, Hitachi, Hewlett-Packard, Hotpoint, IBM, Jenn-Air, JVC, KitchenAid, Magic Chef, Maytag, Mitsubishi, Onkyo, Panasonic, Pioneer, Quasar, Samsung, Sharp, Sony, Sub-Zero, Thermador, Toshiba, Viking, Whirlpool, White-Westinghouse, and Zenith. Please note that Percy's does not sell small appliances and does not publish a catalog.

Special Factors: Price quote by e-mail, fax, or phone.

SEWIN' IN VERMONT

84 CONCORD AVE.
ST. JOHNSBURY, VT
05819–2095
800–451–5124
802–748–3803
FAX: 802–748–2165

Brochure: free
Pay: check, MO, MC, V, Discover
Sells: sewing machines and accessories
Store: same address; Monday to Friday 9:30–5, Saturday 9:30–1

If you're shopping for sewing or embroidery supplies or a sewing machine or serger, call Sewin' in Vermont. The firm carries several of the best brands, including Jaguar, New Home, and Singer. Professional-quality irons and presses by Rowenta, Singer, and Sussman are also carried. The brochure lists selected models, as well as sewing aids—from thread and pins and needles to pressing hams—and Singer dress forms, Johnson ruffling machines, sewing-machine attachments, cabinets and carrying cases, sewing-room furniture, supplies, books, videos, and more.

Sewin' in Vermont has been in business since 1960 (by mail since 1978), and the sales staff can help you choose the right equipment for your needs; call the 800 number for information and price quotes.

Special Factors: Price quote by phone or letter; C.O.D. orders are accepted.

SEWING MACHINE SUPER STORE

9789 FLORIDA BLVD.,
DEPT. WBMC
BATON ROUGE, LA 70815
800–739–7374
504–923–1285
FAX: 800–866–1261
FAX: 504–923–1261

Price List: free
Pay: check, MO, MC, V, AE, Discover
Sells: sewing machines, sergers, and embroidery and knitting equipment, and accessories
Store: same address; Monday to Friday 9–6 CT
E-mail: sewserg@aol.com
Online: http://www.allbrands.com

Sewing Machine Super Store, which also does business as All Brands, offers deep stock on a range of home and industrial sewing machines, sergers, and embroidery and knitting machines. The brands include Babylock, Bernina, Brother, Elna, Jaguar, Johnson, Juki, National, Necchi, Melco, New Home, Passap, Pfaff, Riccar, Simplicity, Singer, Thompson, Viking, and White, among others. The firm has been in business since 1976 and offers an extensive selection of sewing tools as well as machines—Schmetz and Organ needles in bulk; Eastman electric rotary cutters and Gingher shears; Horn & Parsons sewing cabinets; irons by Europro, Rowenta, and Sussman; Singer presses; dress forms and design software; and even Schacht weaving equipment. In addition to new machines, Sewing Machine Super Store sometimes has refurbished, reboxed, and demonstrator models available for sale—see the website for more information. Goods are shipped both from inventory and drop-shipped from manufacturers and distribution points across the U.S. and in Canada. Service and repairs are available on all brands of sewing machines, sergers, and embroidery and knitting machines, and many of the models sold here are sold with instructional videos. Workbooks may be available on selected models as well—inquire. You can send for the closely printed price list, which includes a sample of what's available; visit the 50-page website, which has a complete product list and sales terms; or call for a price on any model made by the manufacturers represented. If you need more information, contact the firm—Sewing Machine Super Store will mail color or fax black-and-white manufacturers' brochures to you.

Special Factors: Layaway plan is available; authorized returns are accepted (a 15% restocking fee may be charged); C.O.D. orders for cash, bank certified check, or money order are accepted for delivery within the 48 contiguous United States.

SUBURBAN SEW 'N SWEEP, INC.

8814 OGDEN AVE.
BROOKFIELD, IL 60513
800–642–4056
708–485–2834
FAX: 708–387–0500

Information: inquire
Pay: check, MO, MC, V, AE, Discover
Sells: sewing machines and vacuum cleaners
Store: same address; Monday to Saturday 9–5

Suburban Sew 'N Sweep has been selling sewing machines since 1975, and although a brochure is available, you can call for a price quote on sewing and overlock machines by Singer, White, and other top brands. Discounts vary but run up to 50%. Suburban Sew 'N Sweep is an authorized dealer for several major sewing machine manufacturers.

Special Factors: Price quote by phone; C.O.D. orders are accepted.

RELATED PRODUCTS/COMPANIES

Appliance parts • Clegg's Handyman Supply
Garbage disposals • CISCO
Humidifiers, air cleaners • Essentials, National Allergy Supply
Major kitchen appliances • Peerless Restaurant Supplies
Personal-care appliances • Bennett Brothers, Damark
Sewing machines, sergers, irons • Atlanta Thread & Supply, Solo Slide Fasteners, Thread Discount Sales, Bennett Brothers

Small kitchen appliances • *American Health Food, Bennett Brothers, Colonial Garden Kitchens, Comfort House, J & R Music*
Televisions • *Crutchfield, J & R Music*
Vacuum cleaners, replacement bags • *The Cleaning Center, Bennett Brothers, Damark, J & R Music*

HOUSE AND HOME
Bed, Bath, and Table Linens

Towels, bedding, and tablecloths; bedroom

and bathroom accessories

The firms in this section carry "soft goods" for your bathroom, bedroom, and dining room, including bath mats, shower curtains, toilet seat covers, towels, sheets, comforters, pillows, bed ruffles, mattress pads, pillow shams, tablecloths, place mats, table pads, and more. For other firms that sell household textiles, such as upholstery fabric and curtains, see "Wall and Window Treatments, Decorator Fabrics," page 378, as well as the "Related Products/Companies" section following the listings below.

ELDRIDGE TEXTILE CO.

**277 GRAND ST., DEPT. L
NEW YORK, NY 10002
212–925–1523
FAX: 212–219–9542**

Catalog: $3, refundable
Pay: check, MO, MC, V, Discover
Sells: bed, bath, and window textiles
Store: same address; Sunday to Friday 9–5:30
Online: http://www.eldridgetextile.com

 ¡Si!

Eldridge has been selling soft goods and housewares since 1940 and offers mail-order customers savings of up to 40% on bed, bath, and window treatments. In fact, they guarantee that their prices are lowest; they'll beat any competitor's prices on identical items in current catalogs. Fully coordinated ensembles are available from Laura Ashley, Bay Linens, Croscill, Crown Crafts, Echo, Faribo, Fieldcrest/Cannon, Martex, Pacific Designs, Phoenix (down products), Revman, Richloom, Royal Sateen, Thomasville, Utica, Wamsutta, and other firms. Some of the best-selling sheet and towel lines are featured in the 32-page color catalog, as well as upholstered headboards, ottomans, and footstools. You'll also find wall sconces, mattress pads, pillows, toilet seats, throw pillows, and other necessary bed and bath items.

Special Factors: Price quote by phone or letter with self-addressed, stamped envelope; returns of unused goods are accepted within 30 days for refund or credit; lowest price guarantee.

HARRIS LEVY, INC.

278 GRAND ST., DEPT. WBM
NEW YORK, NY 10002
800–221–7750
212–226–3102
FAX: 212–334–9360

Catalog: $2, refundable
Pay: check, MO, MC, V, AE
Sells: bed, bath, and table linens; bath, kitchen, and closet accessories
Store: same address; Sunday to Friday 9–5
E-mail: harrislevy@aol.com

Harris Levy, established in 1894, is one of the plums of New York City's Lower East Side—a firm that sells the crème de la crème of bed, bath, and table linens at savings of up to 60%. They search the world over for one-of-a-kind and exclusive items. Custom sewing, embroidery, and custom-sized bedding, tablecloths, and table pads are their specialty, as well as great buys like fine imported bed linens at substantial savings, and heirloom-quality linen tablecloths discounted far below other luxury-linen catalogs. This is a 104-year-old family business still run by the fourth generation of the founding family, a member of which is always on the premises and available. Good old-fashioned care and service abound.

Harris Levy's imports include Egyptian cotton sateen and linen sheets, English kitchen towels, Irish damask tablecloths, and bedding from Switzerland, England, France, and Italy—all worth a trip to the store. Mail-order shoppers can call or write for the catalog, or call for price quotes on bed and bath linens from the major names: Fieldcrest Cannon, Crown Crafts, Frette, Palais Royal, Revman, Sheridan, Wamsutta, and many more. The catalog also gives a sampling of their large selection of towels, pillows, down comforters, tablecloths, place mats, cocktail napkins, decorative pillows, mattress pads, bath and closet accessories, shower curtains, and rugs.

Special Factors: Information and price quote by phone, fax, or letter; swatch and thread color sent by mail when available.

J. SCHACHTER CORP.

**5 COOK ST.
BROOKLYN, NY
11206–4003**
**800–INTO–BED
718–384–2732, 2754
FAX: 718–384–7634**

Catalog: $1, refundable
Pay: check, MO, MC, V, Discover
Sells: down-filled bedding, linens, and custom services
Store: same address; Monday to Thursday 9–5, Friday 9–1:30

 ¡Si! ★

Schachter has been making comforters and pillows for the bedding industry and recovering old comforters for private customers since 1919. Custom work is featured in the firm's 12-page catalog, but stock goods are also available. Schachter specializes in custom jobs: Comforters, coverlets, bed ruffles, pillow shams, duvets, and shower curtains are popular requests, and Schachter will take your sheets and create quilted blanket covers, or lightweight summer quilts, with them. Filling choices for the comforters include lamb's wool, polyester, white goose down, cotton, and a nonallergenic synthetic down alternative. Schachter carries bed and bath linens by the major mills—Bay Linens, Burlington House, Cannon, Croscill, Fieldcrest, Martex, Springs Industries, J.P. Stevens, and Wamsutta, and labels from France, Germany, England, Switzerland, Italy, and Belgium, including Bruna, Palais Royal, Peter Reed, and Sferra. Carter cotton bath rugs, and blankets by Atkinson, Chatham, Early's of Whitney, Faribo, and Hudson Bay are offered, as well as pillows in down, feather/down blend, latex rubber, and poly fill. Schachter's own stock comforters and accessories are all available, and the firm can recover and sterilize old down pillows and comforters.

Special Factors: Store is closed Saturdays and Sundays.

RELATED PRODUCTS/COMPANIES

Acrylic bathroom and household accessories • *Plexi-Craft*

Baby sheets and blankets • *Chock Catalog, Snugglebundle, Baby Bunz, Rubens Baby Wear Factory*

Bath and sleeping aids • *Comfort House*

Bedding feathers • *Gettinger Feather*

Bedspreads • *Shama Imports, BMI Home Decorating*

Cardboard tubes for storing tablecloths wrinkle-free • *Yazoo Mills*

Custom fabric lamination for tablecloths • *Hancock's of Paducah*

Custom-made headboards • *BMI Home Decorating*

Extra-wide blanket flannel • *Gohn Bros.*

Mattresses • *EBA Wholesale, Priba Furniture, Cole's Appliance & Furniture, Quality Furniture Market, Southland Furniture Galleries, Loftin-Black*

Pillow ticking and pillow forms • *Hancock's of Paducah, Gohn Bros., Buffalo Batt & Felt*

Sheets, pillows, blankets, down comforters • *Damark, National Allergy Supply, Marshall Domestics, BMI Home Decorating, Gohn Bros., Clothcrafters*

Shower curtains • *Marshall Domestics*

Table skirting and table linens • *Marshall Domestics, Clothcrafters, Kitchen Etc., Peerless, Shama Imports*

Towels • *Clothcrafters*

Waffle-foam bed pads • *Essentials*

Wooden towel racks, shelves, coat stands, household accessories • *Weston Bowl Mill*

Building, Renovation, and Upkeep

Supplies for designing, constructing, improving, maintaining, and cleaning your home

This section features all kinds of great companies you'll want to know about for saving big-time on the hardware, fixtures, cleaning supplies, raw materials, window and door parts, and other items you need for your home building and improvement projects.

Be sure to refer to this section's "Related Products/Companies" for more firms that sell handyman supplies, such as shop tools, plumbing supplies, woodworking hardware and tools, house paints, fence panels, storage sheds, and more.

If you're thinking of building a home, the Shelter Institute in Bath, Maine, offers a wide variety of classes for individuals and couples who want to do it themselves. (It's a great way to combine learning with a gorgeous summertime getaway.) The Institute leads hands-on courses of varying length on just about every aspect of home design and building. For more information on the Institute, visit their website at http://www.shelterinstitute.com; call them at 207–442–7938; or write to Shelter Institute, 38 Center St., Bath, ME 04530.

After furnishing and decorating your house, there's upkeep. That means maintaining those ills that befall even the finest homes: roof leaks and ice dams, damp basements, peeling paint, insect infestation, and a hundred other problems. Keeping it clean and in good repair can be a never-ending task, so doing it faster, better, and cheaper is a common goal. Reader's Digest publishes *The Family Handyman Helpful Hints: Quick and Easy Solutions, Timesaving Tips, and Tricks of the Trade* (1995), nearly 400 well-organized pages of great ideas for doing everything from setting up a workshop to repairing masonry. (For lots of free articles on every conceivable home-repair question, see also the Reader's Digest website, http://www.readersdigest.com/.)

Other good resources include *50 Simple Ways to Save Your House,* by Bruce Johnson (Ballantine Books, 1995); *500 Terrific Ideas for Home Maintenance and Repair,* by Jack Maguire (Budget Books, 1997); and *Clean and Green: The Complete Guide to Non-Toxic and Environmentally Safe Housekeeping,* by Annie Berthold-Bond (Ceres Press, 1994). All of these books are available at a discount from Amazon.com and other mail-order vendors in the "Books, Audiobooks, and Periodicals" chapter.

FIND IT FAST

BATHROOM AND KITCHEN HARDWARE AND FIXTURES • *Baths from the Past, CISCO, Clegg's Handyman Supply, The Faucet Outlet*
CABINET AND SHELVING HARDWARE AND COMPONENTS • *Clegg's Handyman Supply, Woodworker's Supply*
CLEANING SUPPLIES • *The Cleaning Center*
DOORS, WINDOWS, GLASS PANELS, AND COMPONENTS • *Arctic Glass, Clegg's Handyman Supply, Oregon Wooden Screen Door*
FLOOR-PLAN AND 3-D MODEL KITS FOR BUILDING • *Design Works*
HOUSE SHUTTERS AND SHUTTER SUPPLIES • *Shuttercraft*
WOOD VENEERS, BUTCHER BLOCK, AND FINISHES • *Woodworker's Supply*
WOODWORKING TOOLS • *Woodworker's Supply*

ARCTIC GLASS & WINDOW OUTLET

565 COUNTY RD. T
HAMMOND, WI 54015
800–428–9276
715–796–2291
FAX: 715–796–2295

Catalog: $4, refundable
Pay: MO, MC, V, Discover
Sells: exterior doors, windows, skylights, sunroom glass
Store: I–94 at Hammond Exit, 35 miles east of St. Paul, MN; also 1232 W. Clairemont Ave., Eau Claire, WI; Monday to Thursday 8–8, Friday 8–5, Saturday 9–5

Joseph Bacon began his business after discovering that surplus patio door panes doubled perfectly as passive solar panels in the greenhouse he was building—and cost up to 50% less. Since founding Arctic Glass in 1979, he's watched it outgrow several facilities and increase revenues 2,000%. In fact, Mr. Bacon has shipped to 49 of the 50 states—he's just waiting for that order from Hawaii!

Arctic Glass sells surplus patio door panels from two of the best-known manufacturers in the business. Different types of double panes are available (some with low E coating), most of the glass is ³/₁₆" thick, and all of the panes are double-sealed. The many suitable applications and uses for those panels are listed in the literature. Arctic also stocks Velux skylights and the complete line of Kolbe & Kolbe doors and windows—wood-framed casements, tilts, slider, direct-set, eyebrow, and fanlight windows and a variety of doors. Weather Shield wood and vinyl windows and doors, Therma-Tru doors, and Velux skylights are also available.

Prices average 10% to 50% below list, and all of the panels are guaranteed against leakage or failure for ten years. You'll get a down-home feeling from this company, and the literature is instructive and entertaining. The warranty terms and installation instructions, including retrofitting, are detailed in the literature. If you have any questions, you can talk them over with Mr. Bacon himself.

Special Factors: Quantity discounts are available; minimum crating charge is $50 for mail orders; returns are accepted within 30 days for exchange, refund, or credit; minimum order is $50.

BATHS FROM THE PAST, INC.

83 E. WATER ST.
ROCKLAND, MA 02370
800–697–3871
781–335–2445
FAX: 781–871–8533

Catalog: free
Pay: check, MO, MC, V, Discover
Sells: bathroom and kitchen hardware
Store: same address; Monday to Friday 9–5

Nothing completes a period bathroom like authentic-looking hardware—brass spigots, porcelain shower roses, and telephone-style tub fillers—but nothing breaks a budget faster. Baths from the Past makes it more affordable to buy these, as well as kitchen faucets, shower curtain rods, Victorian porcelain bathroom sinks, and bathroom accessories, at prices up to 30% below other sources (for comparable quality and finish—chrome, polished brass, and polished lacquered brass). Baths from the Past has been in business since 1981 and guarantees the finishes for three years, and the fixtures themselves for life (against failure or defective workmanship).

Special Factors: Satisfaction is guaranteed; minimum order is $50; C.O.D. orders are accepted.

CISCO

CHANUTE IRON & SUPPLY CO.
P.O. DRAWER E
1502 W. CHERRY ST.
CHANUTE, KS 66720–1005
316–431–9289
FAX: 316–431–7354

Information: price quote
Pay: check, MO, MC, V, AE, Discover
Sells: plumbing supplies and fixtures
Store: same address; Monday to Friday 8–5, Saturday 8–12 noon
E-mail: m_becker@computer-services.com

CISCO stocks a full range of fixtures and equipment for plumbing, heating, and air conditioning. CISCO has been selling plumbing supplies, fixtures, and tools since 1941 and offers a portion of the inventory by mail at savings of 25% to 40%. Delta and Moen faucets, In-Sink-Erator garbage disposals, Burnham boilers, NuTone medicine chests and accessories, and whirlpools and fixtures by American Standard, Aqua Glass, Aquatic, Grohe, Jason, and Kohler are available. There are Elkay, Moen, and Swanstone sinks, Crane fixtures, Cal-Spas and saunas, spa and swimming pool accessories and parts (no chemicals), tools by Rigid, and the professional line of tools by Makita. Replacement parts for all types of faucets are also stocked.

Please note: No catalog is available.

Special Factors: Price quote by phone, fax, or letter with self-addressed, stamped envelope; minimum order is $25; CISCO pays freight on UPS-shippable items over $100.

THE CLEANING CENTER

P.O. BOX 39, DEPT. WC
POCATELLO, ID 83204
208–232–6212
FAX: 208–232–6286

Catalog: free
Pay: check, MO, MC, V, Discover
Sells: cleaning tools and products
Store: 311 S. 5th Ave., Pocatello, ID; Monday to Saturday 9–6

When you've been in the cleaning business for a quarter of a century, you develop some strong opinions on the best way to do a job. Don Aslett, "America's #1 Cleaning Expert," used his expertise in speed-cleaning techniques to create *Is There Life After Housework?*—the first of many books on how to do more cleaning in less time and "plan" the dirt out of your house. He brings both the books and his tools of choice to market through the informative "Cleaning Report" catalog, 46 pages of concentrated solutions for general cleaning and windows, wood, bathroom fixtures, waxed floors, and carpets, plus deodorizers, disinfectants, protective acrylic sealer, spot removers, and wax stripper. Mr. Aslett's favorite tools are available—scrub brushes, commercial spray bottles, cleaning cloths, Ettore window scrubbers and squeegees, the "Scrubbee Doo" mop system, professional mop buckets and push brooms, carpet rakes, and walk-off mats. He also sells the Sanitaire upright vacuum cleaner and Eureka's Mighty Mite II, and replacement bags (standard and super-filter) for both models.

The Cleaning Center products represent excellent value on a per-use basis, compared to supermarket brands. In addition, price checks showed good savings compared to other specialty sources: The X-O Odor Neutralizer that pros use to combat serious smells costs 20% to 50% less from the Cleaning Center than from another discounter; the "dry sponge," used to clean unwashable surfaces, costs $3.75 from a popular tool and gadget catalog but just over $2 here, or as little as $1.75 when bought by the dozen. Check the back of the catalog for the seasonal specials—mats and window-cleaning tools seem to go on sale once a year.

Please note: The cleaning solutions are concentrated and must be diluted and used according to directions. Any spray bottles you fill should be clearly labeled and used for refills of the same product only.

Canadian readers, please note: Only U.S. funds are accepted.

Special Factors: Satisfaction is guaranteed; returns are accepted for exchange, refund, or credit; C.O.D. orders are accepted.

CLEGG'S HANDYMAN SUPPLY

P.O. BOX 732, DEPT. W99
OREM, UT 84059–0732
801–221–1772

Information: inquire (see text)
Pay: check or MO
Sells: hardware, home fixtures, etc.
Store: mail order only

Clegg's, a family-run firm dedicated to the "frugal home handyperson," discontinued its catalog in favor of total customer service—special orders. Clegg's has provided readers with products they couldn't find locally, like the motel owner who bought a number of special dead-bolt locks unavailable at his hardware store. Customers who haven't been able to find a certain item at a discount have found it here for less, and those looking for bulk discounts—a houseful of light switches and outlets, for example—have been pleased.

Clegg's says it best: "We carry, or can get, almost anything a typical hardware or home-improvement center has, and more. We don't normally ship anything that can't be sent via UPS or regular U.S. mail, such as a bathtub or snowblower. However, on a hard-to-find item where cost is not such a factor, special arrangements may be made."

Among the products available are plumbing supplies (faucets, faucet repair parts, sinks, drain parts, valves, toilet parts, showerheads, tub spouts, etc.), bathroom accessories (towel racks, vanity kits, medicine cabinets, etc.), electrical accessories (extension cords, lightbulbs, switches, outlets, boxes, light fixtures, ballasts, wire, etc.), appliance parts (thermostats and range elements, dryer vents and door switches, etc.), window and glass components (screening, latches, rollers, storm-door closers), general hardware (hinges, screws, weather stripping, saw blades, screwdriver bits, etc.), hand and power tools, sundries (paintbrushes and roller sleeves, sandpaper, drop cloths, masking tape, caulking, etc.), and much more. Prices average 30% to 50% or more below suggested or regular retail, depending on the item and quantity ordered. Clegg's has been in business since 1992 and prides itself on responding to the needs of its customers. Clegg's has published *How and Where to Buy Handyman Supplies at the Best Possible Price*—a guide to mail-order sources, strategies for getting the best prices locally, and sources of help for business owners. Clegg's doesn't have a catalog but has prepared a free flyer describing the publication—and be sure to mention BWBM when calling or writing for it, since Clegg's is extending a special discount on their report to readers of this book!

Special Factors: Satisfaction is guaranteed; quantity discounts are available; returns are accepted.

DESIGN WORKS, INC.

11 HITCHING POST RD.
AMHERST, MA 01002
413–549–4763

Information and Flyers: free (see text)
Pay: check, MO, MC, V, AE
Sells: peel-and-stick design floor plans and 3-D model kits for home-building
Store: mail order only
Online: http://www.crocker.com/ designworksinc/

  ¡Si!

If you've ever tried to plan a new home, addition, or remodeling project, you know the hardest parts are organizing the floor plans and visualizing your ideas in three dimensions. Design Works has come up with a unique (and inexpensive) solution. In business for 16 years, owner Dan Reif has developed two ingenious products. With the Home Quick Planner, for $19.95, you receive 700 precut, reusable, peel-and-stick furniture and architectural symbols, plus a ¼" floor plan grid, to plan a home up to approximately 2,000 square feet. Go ahead: Knock down walls, move furniture and fixtures, put in too many windows and bathrooms—you can always change your mind later for free. A Deluxe version for $10 more has additional symbols that make the Planner suitable for floor plans up to approximately 4,000 square feet.

There are also separate Quick Planners just for Kitchen, Bathroom, Office, or Interior Design. The 3-D Home Kit ($29.95) lets you visualize your dream house, sunroom, or new wing in three dimensions. You can use the kit's printed posterboard building materials—from brick, stone, siding, roofing, and decking to windows, doors, skylights, kitchen cabinets, and appliances—to construct a detailed ¼" scale model of your own design up to approximately 2,000 square feet. There are also materials for interior walls, stairs, floor plan—even scale people and pets! (The Deluxe version of the 3-D Home Kit has materials for up to 4,000 square feet and costs $39.95.) Both 3-D Home Kits include a "Hands-on Design and Math" booklet to help you solve some common design problems: for example, how to calculate the minimum size for windows, design the roof and calculate its slope, and determine the amount of paint, paneling, or concrete needed. Whether you're teaching architecture to students or daydreaming about how you'll spend that lottery win, this will be a fun and illuminating project.

THE FAUCET OUTLET

P.O. BOX 547
MIDDLETOWN, NY 10940
800–444–5783
FAX: 914–343–1617

Catalog: $4 (see text)
Pay: check, MO, MC, V
Sells: bathroom and kitchen fixtures
Store: mail order only; phone hours Monday to Friday 8–6 ET
E-mail: faucet@faucet.com
Online: http://www.faucet.com

We don't spend much time thinking about those things that deliver water from the pipes into the shower, tub, or sink, so when they need replacing it's a shock to discover how many there are, and how much they cost. Thank goodness for The Faucet Outlet.

This mail-order concern specializes in spigots, spouts, knobs, connections, hot water dispensers, and related items by American Standard, Celcon, Delta, Grohe, Jado, Kohler, Moen, and many other firms. The 32-page catalog features a sampling of products from a number of manufacturers, as well as valuable service information and The Faucet Outlet's lowest price guarantee. Claw-foot tubs, fans, intercoms, security videos, and medicine cabinets are also available. You can order the catalog, or if you know exactly what you want or don't see the model you're looking for, call with the stock or item number for a price quote. Or visit the website to browse the entire inventory, complete with product information. (Check before ordering to make sure your fixtures comply with local codes and are compatible with existing plumbing.) Discounts run up to 50% on manufacturers' list prices at this writing, but are subject to change and may vary from line to line. The catalog fee, usually $4, is $2 to readers of this book, so be sure to mention BWBM when you send for it.

Special Factors: Authorized returns are accepted; price quote by phone or letter.

OREGON WOODEN SCREEN DOOR COMPANY

Brochure and Price List: $3
Pay: check, MO, MC, V
Sells: wooden screen and storm doors
Store: same address

2767 HARRIS ST., DEPT.
  WBMC
EUGENE, OR 97405
541–485–0279
FAX: 541–484–0353

The satisfying *thock* of a wooden screen door closing is one of the many small sounds of a great summer day. Revive this lovely component of a well-tailored home with the help of Oregon Wooden Screen Doors, which sells 30 door styles but allows you to amend the designs with your choice of spandrels, brackets, and other embellishments. The categories break down into "Ornamental," "Classic," "Muscular," and the "Designers Collection." They range in complexity from "Settler," a straightforward, two-panel door, to "Wright's Delight," a tribute to the master architect. Each door is constructed of 1/4"-thick vertical-grain fir, with mortise-and-tenon and dowel joinery, for strength and warp resistance. Wood-framed screen and storm inserts are available, and all of the wood is primed with wood preservative—you provide the final finish. Solid brass hardware can be ordered with your door, or you can obtain it locally.

Prices begin at under $200 for the kit versions of the simplest styles, to several hundred for the most elaborate. Since the doors are made to measure, this approximates a custom job—at a prefab price! If you have questions about any aspect of design or construction, or want a fully customized design, the staff will be pleased to help.

Special Factors: Authorized returns are accepted.

SHUTTERCRAFT, INC.

282 STEPSTONE HILL RD.,
  DEPT. WBM
GUILFORD, CT 06437
203–453–1973
FAX: 203–245–5969

Brochures and Price Lists: free
Pay: check, MO, MC, V
Sells: interior and exterior house shutters and hardware
Store: same address; Monday to Friday 9–5
Online: http://www.galaxymall.com/shops/shuttercraft.html

Authentic, "historic" exterior wood shutters with movable louvers are sold here at prices well below those charged for custom-milled shutters. An added advantage: They look more substantial than the vinyl versions, and the firm's literature points out that "real wood shutters are naturally ventilating and do not cause the wood siding behind them to rot." Shuttercraft's cedar shutters can be bought in widths up to 36", in lengths to 144", and in shapes that include half-circle tops, Gothic arches, and cutouts in the raised panels. (A pine tree and 24 other styles are shown, and Shuttercraft will execute your pattern for $20 per pair of shutters.) Also available are fixed-louver shutters, exterior raised-panel shutters in Western cedar, interior plantation styles, S-shaped holdbacks, and shutter hinges. Shuttercraft will prime, paint, trim, and rabbet your shutters for a fee; details are given in the brochures.

Special Factors: Free shipping on orders totaling $500 or more.

WOODWORKER'S SUPPLY, INC.

5604 ALAMEDA PL. NE
ALBUQUERQUE, NM
  87113
800–645–9292
FAX: 800–853–9663

Catalog: $2
Pay: check, MO, MC, V, Discover
Sells: woodworking tools and equipment
Store: same address; Monday to Friday 8–5:30, Saturday 9–1; also Graham, NC; Casper, WY; and Seabrook, NH; call for addresses and hours

Woodworker's Supply publishes a 156-page color catalog of woodworking tools and hardware, priced up to 30% below comparable goods sold elsewhere. The company has been in business since 1972, selling basics—from abrasives to rolling table shapers—as well as a number of hard-to-find items. Typical offerings include drills (including cordless models), power screwdrivers, routers, saws (circular, jig, orbital, table, band, etc.), sanders (finish, belt, orbital, etc.), laminate trimmers, heat guns, biscuit joiners, power planes, grinders, jointers, drill presses, shapers, and other tools. Drawer slides are carried, as well as hinges, coated-wire fixtures for custom kitchen cabinets, furniture and cabinet levelers, cassette storage tracks, halogen canister lights, wood project parts, veneers, butcher block, locks and latches, glue scrapers and injectors, steel wool-backed sheets for finish sanders, and a complete supply of finishes and finishing supplies. Like the best of such catalogs, Woodworker's Supply can give you as many ideas for new projects as it provides solutions to old woodworking problems.

Special Factors: Satisfaction is guaranteed; returns are accepted; minimum order is $5 ($25 to Canada).

RELATED PRODUCTS/COMPANIES

Bamboo and other tropical fencing • Frank's Cane and Rush
Cabinetry and other hardware • Camelot Enterprises, Surplus Center, H & R Company, William Alden, Tool Crib of the North, Tool Hauz
Central vacuum systems • ABC Vacuum Cleaner Warehouse, AVAC Corporation
Cleaning supplies • EDGE Distributing, Marshall Domestics, Jaffe Bros., National Allergy Supply, Cal Ben Soap Company, Fuller Brush Independent Distributor, Colonial Garden Kitchens, Enco Manufacturing
Cotton and flannel cleaning cloths • Clothcrafters
Do-it-yourself books and manuals • Woodworkers' Discount Books, Poor Man's Catalog, Reader's Digest
Floor-care machines and supplies • AAA Vacuums, ABC Vacuum Cleaner Warehouse, AVAC Corporation, Fuller Brush Independent Distributor
Garbage disposals • Percy's
Greenhouse supplies • Bob's Superstrong Greenhouse Plastic, Turner Greenhouses, Mellinger's
Home safes • Safe Specialties, Value-tique
House paint and supplies • Pearl Paint
Lighting and wiring supplies • All Electronics
Lumber, wood paneling, molding, flooring inlays • Rare Earth Hardwoods, Prestige Carpets
Plastic sheeting for storm windows, pool covers, greenhouses, etc. • Bob's Superstrong Greenhouse Plastic

Professional shop and handyman tools • Holz Tool Supply, William Alden, Harbor Freight Tools, Tool Crib of the North, Tool Hauz, Enco Manufacturing
Replacement parts for chandeliers • King's Chandelier
Screen doors and window screens • Coppa Woodworking
Swimming pool maintenance supplies and equipment • Water Warehouse
Wood-burning furnaces and heaters • Manufacturer's Supply

Flooring

Rugs, carpeting, floor coverings, padding, underlays, tiles, flooring, etc.

Large rugs and wall-to-wall carpeting can represent the biggest single expense in redecorating a room. Saving up to 50% on the cost of the rug and padding is easy through the firms listed here. Most are based in North Carolina and Georgia, close to the carpet mills that turn out millions of miles of broadloom every year.

Before you order wall-to-wall carpeting, make sure you have someone local who can install it. (It's almost impossible for a novice to do a good job, and a poor job leads to shifting, rippling, and uneven wear.) Choice of carpet weave, fiber, and color depend on where it's going, the purpose of the room or area, the anticipated foot traffic, and overall decor. Interior design textbooks usually discuss the difference in fiber and construction, as well as appropriate sites for different types of carpeting. For information on installation, maintenance, and a stain-removal guide, send a long, stamped, self-addressed envelope to The Carpet and Rug Institute, P.O. Box 2048, Dalton, GA 30722, or call them at 706–278–3176.

If you'd like to visit a really good and useful website, check out theirs at http://www.carpet-rug.com/. Not only are there great articles about the care and maintenance of rugs, how to choose carpet, carpet and the environment, and more, but here you'll find the Spot Removal Computer. This is a real find. Type in a stain, or search the alphabetized list of hundreds, and click on it. You'll get a succinct but detailed, step-by-step solution to your particular rug or carpet stain. It's a gold mine of free information.

For more firms selling rugs and carpeting, read "Related Products/ Companies" at the end of this section.

CARPETING AND AREA RUGS • Bearden Bros., Prestige Carpets, Village Carpet, Warehouse Carpets
NEW AND ANTIQUE ORIENTAL RUGS • Charles W. Jacobsen, Wall Rug
VINYL FLOORING • Bearden Bros., Prestige Carpets, Warehouse Carpets
WOOD FLOORING • Prestige Carpets, Rare Earth Hardwoods

BEARDEN BROS. CARPET & TEXTILES CORP.

4109 S. DIXIE HWY., DEPT. WBMC
DALTON, GA 30721
800–433–0074
888–BEARDEN
FAX: 706–277–1754

Catalog: $2 (see text)
Pay: check, MO, MC, V, AE, Discover
Sells: carpeting, rugs, padding, and vinyl flooring
Store: same address; Monday to Friday 8:30–6

Bearden Bros. Carpet & Textiles set up shop in 1989 in Dalton, Georgia, "Carpet Capital of the World," joining hundreds of other companies in the manufacturing and sales of carpeting and flooring. Bearden sells carpeting and flooring lines from scores of mills, including Aladdin, Beaulieu, Cabin Craft, Citation, Cumberland, Evans and Black, Galaxy, Horizon, Interloom, J.P. Stevens, L.D. Brinkman, Lees, Mohawk, Philadelphia, Salem, Shaw, United Carpet, and World—and that's just a few of the many brands available.

You can call with the manufacturer's name, style name, color codes, and number of square yards you plan to buy and ask for a price quote, or send a carpet sample if you don't have that information. Bearden Bros. also sells its own line of flooring and carpet products, as well as reproduction Oriental, Victorian, and contemporary designs, braided rugs, border designs, and even brass stair rods. A catalog of rugs—braided, flat weave, designer, Oriental, etc.—is available for $2 (regularly $4); mention BWBM when you send for it. Bearden Bros. ships carpeting to all 50 states and countries around the world.

Special Factors: Written confirmation of phone orders is required; quantity discounts are available.

CHARLES W. JACOBSEN, INC.

LEARBURY CENTER
401 N. SALINA ST., DEPT.
WBMC
SYRACUSE, NY 13203–1773
315–422–7832
FAX: 315–422–6909

Catalog: free
Pay: check, MO, MC, V
Sells: new and antique Oriental rugs
Store: same address; Monday to Saturday 10–5, Monday and Thursday till 8; also 268 Broadway, Saratoga Springs, NY, Tuesday to Saturday, 10–5, Thursday till 8, Sunday 12–5
E-mail: rugpeople@jacobsenrugs.com
Online: http://www.jacobsenrugs.com

Charles W. Jacobsen, Inc., has over 70 years of experience in the sale of fine Oriental rugs and publishes a 26-page color portfolio that shows a portion of rugs selected from the 8,000 the firm has in inventory. Rug collectors know Jacobsen for the company's stock and good prices, but both are worth considering if you're buying a rug for your home and want something more than run-of-the-mill. Jacobsen buys the rugs directly from the countries where rugs are woven, then imports them directly to Syracuse, so there's no wholesaler's markup. This coupled with large volume allows the firm to "sell better quality rugs for less."

Jacobsen's stock-in-trade is handwoven carpets, of recent vintage, from India, Pakistan, Turkey, Iran, Afghanistan, China, and other countries (subject to trade restrictions and availability). The sizes vary with the type of rug, but most are available from 2' by 3' to 10' by 14', with some available in sizes to 12' by 20'; many of the designs are also made as runners. If you've been shopping for good, machine-made reproductions of Oriental rugs, you'll be familiar with some of the names: Kashan, Herez, Tabriz, Sarouk, Abadeh, Sarabend, Bijar, Ferraghan, Shirvan, and Bokhara are some of the most commonly known. Even if you think your budget relegates you to no more than a good copy of a handmade rug, check here before you buy. In some cases, Jacobsen's prices on the new rugs—made completely by hand, with wool or silk pile, often with some vegetable dyes (which lend a mellow quality to the rug over time)—are not much higher, and are lower than those charged for comparable examples by other rug merchants.

Buying a one-of-a-kind anything by mail can be tricky, but Jacobsen will work with you to get it right. The questionnaire provided with the catalog captures information about your preferences, room requirements, and budget; based on this information, you'll be sent slides of rugs that best suit your needs. When you've settled on a selection, you can have the rug sent on approval to try in the intended setting—the only way to be sure it's the right choice. For more about this marvelous firm, visit their website, which is easy and fun to use, complete with color photographs and interesting consumer information about rugs and rug buying.

Special Factors: Satisfaction is guaranteed.

PRESTIGE CARPETS, INC.

P.O. BOX 516
DALTON, GA 30722
800–887–6807, EXT. 100
706–217–6640
FAX: 706–217–2429

Catalog: free
Pay: check, MO, MC, V, AE, Discover
Sells: carpeting, vinyl and wood flooring, area rugs, and padding
Store: 2301 Shannon Dr., Dalton, GA, Monday to Friday 8–5

Prestige sells its own line of residential and commercial carpeting, guaranteed against wear and stains just like the national brands—all at wholesale prices. Carpet samples are available, showing the range of colors and the specifications (fiber content, guarantees, etc.) of each style. Prestige also works with over 40 carpet mills and flooring makers to get good deals on carpet and vinyl and wood lines from a wide range of manufacturers, at prices up to 80% below those charged by department stores and other retail outlets. If you've decided on your floor covering, call or write for a free quote with the name of the manufacturer, the style name and number, and the square yardage required. Prestige also offers custom area rugs, which can be produced to match wallpaper and furniture. Samples are shown in the free catalog (available upon request). Padding, adhesives, and tack strips for installation are also available.

Special Factors: A deposit is required when you place your order, and final payment must be made before shipment (common carrier is used); both residential and commercial carpeting needs are served here.

RARE EARTH HARDWOODS

6778 E. TRAVERSE HWY.
TRAVERSE CITY, MI
  49684–8364
800–968–0074
616–946–0043
FAX: 800–968–0094
FAX: 616–946–6621

Information: inquire
Pay: check, MO, MC, V, Discover
Sells: lumber, hardwood flooring, inlays, etc.
Store: same address; Monday to Friday 8–5,
Saturday 8–12
E-mail: rare.earth@traverse.com
Online: http://www.rare-earth-hardwoods.com

Rare Earth Hardwoods sells genuine hardwood flooring—not laminate or composition—in woods that run from American cherry to zebrawood. Prices are often better than those of other specialty dealers, though you won't beat the cost of a floor-in-a-box. Rare Earth manufactures stair risers, treads, moldings, paneling, and more, and specializes in custom millwork. You can purchase a set of 30 sample pieces of the lumber for $22 (price includes shipping) and experience the colors firsthand. Price lists for the ¾" tongue-and-groove flooring, Brazilian decking, hardwood plywood, and marine lumber and plywood are available upon request.

    Special Factors: Price quote by phone, fax, or letter with a stamped, self-addressed envelope.

VILLAGE CARPET & INTERIORS

3203 HWY. 70 SE
NEWTON, NC 28658
704–465–6818

Brochure: free
Pay: check or MO
Sells: carpeting and padding
Store: same address; off I–40 near Hickory;
Monday to Friday 8:30–5, Saturday 9–3

Village Carpet & Interiors offers well-known names in carpeting—Aladdin, Beaulieu, Cabin Crafts, Citation, Cumberland, Evans and Black, Galaxy, Milliken, Mohawk, New Visions, Philadelphia, Queen, Salem, and others, at discounts of up to 40%. Padding and underlays are also available. All of the carpeting is first quality, and shipping is made by common carrier. The only drawback is the minimum order, $300, which might be high if you're doing a small job. If you have difficulty getting style information or calculating the amount you need, just ask—the salespeople deal with these problems regularly.

Special Factors: Satisfaction is guaranteed; quantity discounts are available; minimum order is $300.

WALL RUG & CARPETS

4309 WILEY DAVIS RD.
GREENSBORO, NC 27407
800–877–1955
336–852–9573
FAX: 336–292–3601

Information: price quote
Pay: check, MO, MC, V
Sells: rugs
Store: same address (Exit 120 I–85)

Wall Rug & Carpets sells first-quality Karastans, at prices up to 40% below Wall's suggested list, as well as designs by Oriental Weavers, 828 Trading Company, and Mastercraft Imports Ltd. Wall has been in business since 1928 and provides dealer warranties on the rugs it sells. Call or write to Wall if you need advice, or when you're ready to order.

Special Factors: Inquire about returns policy.

WAREHOUSE CARPETS, INC.

P.O. BOX 3233
DALTON, GA 30719
800–526–2229
706–226–2229
FAX: 706–278–1008

Brochure: free
Pay: check or MO
Sells: carpeting, vinyl flooring, and padding
Store: Walnut Ave. and Airport Road, Dalton, GA; Monday to Friday 8–5

Warehouse Carpets began in 1977 as a carpeting wholesaler and has since moved into mail order, offering customers savings of as much as 50% on carpeting and floor coverings. Call or write with the name and style of almost any major brand of carpeting, vinyl flooring, or padding you're interested in, and Warehouse Carpets will give you a price quote. Shipments are made by common carrier.

Special Factors: All goods are first quality; price quote by phone or letter.

RELATED PRODUCTS/COMPANIES

Area rugs and carpeting • Carolina Interiors, The Furniture Patch of Calabash, Priba Furniture, Southland Furniture, Harris Levy, Ellenburg's Furniture
Carpet-stain removers • The Cleaning Center
Floor stencils • Stencil House of N.H.
Sheepskin rugs • Arctic Sheepskin Outlet, The Deerskin Place, Leather Unlimited, The Natural Baby Co.
Steerhide rugs • Steerhides

Furnishings

Furniture and accessories for
home and patio

You can save as much as 50% on suggested retail by ordering your furniture from North Carolina, the manufacturing center of the industry. The discounters don't take the staggering markups that make furnishings and home accessories prohibitively expensive in department and furniture stores. This doesn't endear them to the furniture manufacturers; in fact, it's becoming common for manufacturers to do everything they can to make it difficult for discounters to sell by mail, by forbidding them to trade outside designated "selling areas" and sometimes prohibiting the firms from having 800-number phone lines. (Manufacturers elicit compliance by threatening to refuse to fill the discounters' orders.) This practice has the effect of limiting trade, and raising the prices we all have to pay. To avoid creating problems for the discounters, while giving access to the best buys possible, brand names have been omitted from these listings. So while you're reading the listings, bear in mind that most of the firms listed here can supply catalogs, brochures, and swatches, give decorating advice over the phone, and take orders for furniture and accessories from hundreds of manufacturers.

It's smart to use the "in-home delivery service" when a firm offers it, since your furniture will be uncrated exactly where you want it, and if there are damages, you'll see them right away and can contact the company while the shipper is there to find out what to do. In-home delivery is usually made either by the company's own truck, or with a moving-van service that's accustomed to handling furnishings.

If you have an office or studio in your home, be sure to see the company listings in "Office, Business, Professional: Office Furnishings."

FIND IT FAST

ACRYLIC FURNITURE AND ACCESSORIES • Plexi-Craft

CHILDREN'S FURNITURE AND ACCESSORIES • Coppa Woodworking, Eastern Butcher Block, Fran's Wicker & Rattan, Marion Travis, Wicker Warehouse

COUNTRY-STYLE TABLES, CHAIRS, AND ACCESSORIES • Coppa Woodworking, Eastern Butcher Block, Genada Imports, Marion Travis

HOME ACCESSORIES AND KNICKKNACKS • Tender Heart Treasures, Terry's Village

HOME AND OFFICE FURNITURE • Blackwelder's, Carolina Interiors, Ellenburg's, The Furniture Patch of Calabash, Loftin-Black, Priba Furniture, Quality Furniture, Shaw Furniture, Sobol, Southland

MODERN AND CONTEMPORARY • Genada Imports

RADIATOR ENCLOSURES • ARSCO, Monarch Radiator Enclosures

STEERHIDES AND STEERHIDE PILLOWS • Steerhides

TABLE PADS • Factory Direct Table Pad Co.

UNFINISHED FURNITURE • Marks Sales, Marion Travis

VICTORIAN- AND FRENCH-STYLE FURNITURE AND ACCESSORIES • Heirloom Reproductions

WICKER AND RATTAN FURNITURE AND ACCESSORIES • Ellenburg's, Fran's Wicker & Rattan, Wicker Warehouse

WOODEN BASKETS • West Rindge Baskets

ARSCO MANUFAC-TURING COMPANY, INC.

3564 BLUE ROCK RD.

CINCINNATI, OH 45247

800–543–7040

513–385–0555

FAX: 513–741–6292

Catalog: free
Pay: MO, MC, V, Discover
Sells: radiator enclosures
Store: same address, Monday to Friday 8–4

"Once you own ACE Radiator Enclosures, you won't ever catch yourself staring at those naked radiators." So reads the brochure from ARSCO Manufacturing, which makes enclosures for conventional steam radiators, fan coil units, and fin tube (baseboard) heaters. Putting looks aside for the moment, these enclosures also save fuel by preventing outside wall heat absorption; protect drapes, walls, and ceilings from airborne dust; protect children from contact with hot radiators; and help circulate the air into the room, rather than letting the heat go directly to the ceiling—and they're easy to clean. If you live within 500 miles of Cincinnati, ARSCO will send someone to measure your radiator; farther afield, you can use the guide ARSCO provides and do it yourself.

Standard sizes run up to 42" high and 96" long (larger sizes can be made), and there are 14 stock colors of paint enamel, although custom color matches can be provided for a fee. Other options include special notches, doors, or cutouts for valve access, a built-in humidifier pan, insulated tops, and adjustable legs for uneven floors. Prices are a solid 35% below those charged by local sources for the same kinds of enclosures, and if your unit is measured by ARSCO's personnel, the fit is guaranteed. If you're measuring it yourself, do it twice and then again, since the enclosures are all made to order, and are not returnable.

Special Factors: Enclosures are not returnable.

BLACKWELDER'S INDUSTRIES, INC.

294 TURNERSBURG HWY.
STATESVILLE, NC 28625
800–438–0201 (U.S.)
704–872–8921
FAX: 704–872–4491

Catalog and Price List: $19.45, refundable (see text)
Pay: check, MO, MC, V, AE, Discover
Sells: home and office furniture and accessories
Store: phone hours Monday to Friday 9:30–5:30
E-mail: jblackwelder@blackwelder.com
Online: http://www.homefurnish.com/blackwelders

Blackwelder's Industries, Inc., was founded in 1936 with the aim of giving the customer access to fine furniture at fair prices, with full-service delivery. The firm is well regarded among consumers and offers an "information worksheet" to help you keep track of price quotes and shopping information. The 240-page color catalog showcases home and office furnishings and other goods from a number of the hundreds of manufacturers represented at Blackwelder's, and the price list helps to give you a sense of the possible savings. The catalog with price list costs $19.45—refundable upon return to Blackwelder's within 90 days of receipt—and includes a $30 gift certificate. (You can also purchase a catalog by e-mailing the address above.) The catalog selections have been very carefully selected and represent some of the best values available, but you may also call or write for a price quote on specific items or brands. The shopping worksheet, which is available upon request, lists details of the sales policy, delivery costs, and other options; inquire directly if you need information on contract services and quantity prices on large runs.

Do check out the website. It's really great to browse for classy, well-priced furniture in the comfort of your own home. You'll find an online catalog, with selections not shown in the print version, at Blackwelder's website, complete with gorgeous color photographs.

International readers, please note: Blackwelder's is experienced in shipping to Japan, the Middle East, and other countries around the world. Fax your inquiries to 704–872–4491.

Special Factors: Satisfaction is guaranteed; price quote by phone, fax, e-mail, or letter; shipments are made by van or common carrier; authorized returns are accepted within 30 days (a 25% restocking fee is charged) for exchange, refund, or credit.

CAROLINA INTERIORS

115 OAK AVE.
KANNAPOLIS, NC 28081
704–933–1888
FAX: 704–932–0434

Brochure: free
Pay: check or MO
Sells: home furnishings and accessories
Store: same address (1–85, Exit 63); Monday to Saturday 9–6

Carolina Interiors is run by several veterans of the furnishings trade, whose relationships with over 350 manufacturers help assure discounts of 30% to 60%. If you're traveling through North Carolina near Cannon Village, locate the Fieldcrest Cannon factory outlet store, and you'll find Carolina Interiors next door—over 250,000 square feet of furnishings, wall and floor treatments, rugs, and bedding. You can call or write for a price quote if you know what you want, and to request the brochure that lists a number of the available brands and details the sales policy. Carolina Interiors requires a 30% deposit (protected by surety bond) when you place the order, and features in-home delivery in most areas.

Special Factors: Price quote by phone, fax, or letter.

COPPA WOOD-WORKING, INC.

1231 PARAISO AVE.
SAN PEDRO, CA 90731
310–548–4142
FAX: 310–548–6740

Catalog: $1
Pay: check, MO, MC, V
Sells: Adirondack furniture, screen doors, windows, etc.
Store: same address; Monday to Friday 8–5

¡Si! ★

Coppa Woodworking is a small firm that manufactures Adirondack-style furniture, screen doors, and window screens in a variety of finishes, woods, and other options, at prices up to 40% below those charged elsewhere for comparable products. (You know you're dealing directly with the craftsmen when the catalog itself smells of fresh lumber!) Classic low-slung, slat-back Adirondack chair styles are featured, from the children's model for about $30 to the "fanback" for under $70 to a 51-inch-wide love seat for about $100. All of the seating and complementing footrests and side tables are made of unfinished pine that can be stained (white, blue, or green) for a small fee. Matching footrests, end tables, coffee tables, spindle handle Adirondack magazine baskets, butcher block tables, flowerpot window shelves, picket fence slats, bar stools, and other items are also available here.

The other side of Coppa's business is screen doors, dressing screens, and sidelights (panels); the doors can be produced in over 100 styles to suit every decor. A number of options are available, including wood choice (Douglas fir, sugar pine, red oak, mahogany), stain and varnish, single or double-door fixtures, custom sizes, built-in pet doors, and a choice of fiberglass screening materials (including heavy-duty cat-proof mesh). Prices begin at just $42 for the plainest style in pine, and custom charges are quite reasonable. And if you'd like a feature or detail not mentioned, be sure to ask, since Coppa may be able to provide.

Special Factors: Satisfaction is guaranteed; returns are accepted, except on custom sizes.

EASTERN BUTCHER BLOCK

25 EAGLE ST.
PROVIDENCE, RI 02908
401–273–6330
FAX: 401–274–1811

Eastern Butcher Block specializes in dining tables and chairs, most with butcher-block tops, in country or contemporary styling. The 24-page catalog shows scores of combinations of tops (extension, drop-leaf, rounded, oblong, etc.) and bases (pedestal, trestle, straight-leg, Shaker-style, turned-leg, with and without drawers, etc.) in maple or ash. The hardwood chairs run from Breuer reproductions to Windsor-style side chairs. Swivel-seat stools, rockers, children's chairs, and even office styles are offered. Accessories include chopping blocks, hutches and sideboards, microwave carts, accessories, toy chests, snack tables, folding screens, bookcases, and end tables.

Prices range from nominal to serious, depending on whether the item is on sale, in the "promotional" group (of lower-grade maple or ash), or incorporates customer options in base style and finish. Eastern Butcher Block manufactures the furniture and offers eight stains and four paint colors, with the option of an age-sanded "antique" finish. All of the furniture is finished in a durable two-step catalyzed process and carries a lifetime structural warranty. The butcher block can be ordered as custom-cut countertops, and ordering instructions are given in the literature.

Special Factors: Price quote by phone or letter.

ELLENBURG'S FURNITURE

Catalog: $6.50, refundable
Pay: check, MO, MC, V, Discover
Sells: home furnishings
Store: same address
Online: http://www.ellenburgs.com

I–40 & STAMEY FARM RD.
P.O. BOX 5638
STATESVILLE, NC 28687
704–873–2900
FAX: 704–873–6002

Ellenburg's Furniture is family owned and operated, and the owners say they'll "go the extra mile" in getting you the best for least. It sells some of the country's most popular lines of American-style furniture and rugs, from scores of manufacturers, and is a great source for wicker and rattan furnishings as well. The $6.50 catalog fee (refundable with purchase) brings you a sheaf of brochures from different manufacturers, a price list, details on Ellenburg's sales policy, and current specials. A 25% deposit is required when you place your order, and delivery is available from Ellenburg's own van service, a furniture carrier, or common carrier. Ellenburg's has been in business since 1978 and offers savings of 40% to 50% on retail, and up to 75% on sale items and close-outs.

Special Factors: Price quote by phone or letter; returns of damaged and defective goods only are accepted.

FACTORY DIRECT TABLE PAD CO.

Prices and Samples: $1
Pay: check, MO, MC, V, Discover
Sells: custom-made table pads
Store: mail order only

1501 W. MARKET ST.
INDIANAPOLIS, IN 46222
800–428–4567
FAX: 317–631–2584

Factory Direct's spiffy little color brochure states that about half of the cost of a custom-made table pad is the fee paid to the person who measures the table. For $1, Factory Direct Table Pad will send you a guide to doing this yourself, as well as several sample swatches of the table pad top, which can be made in pebble-grain or smooth finish, in plain colors or in wood grain, in different thicknesses. Factory Direct has been in business since 1982 and warrants its table pads for 7, 15, or 20 years. Complete details of the terms of sale are given in the literature.

Special Factors: Authorized returns are accepted within 15 days.

FRAN'S WICKER & RATTAN FURNITURE, INC.

295 RT. 10E
SUCCASUNNA, NJ 07876
973–584–2230
FAX: 973–584–7446

Catalog: $2
Pay: check, MO, MC, V, AE, Discover
Sells: wicker and rattan furniture and accessories
Store: same address; Monday to Friday 9–5:30, Wednesday and Thursday 9–8:30, Saturday 9–6, Sunday 12–5

Fran's Wicker is in its third generation of family management, having grown from a basket importer to one of the best sources for wicker and rattan furniture. The 64-page color catalog is packed cover to cover with furniture and decorative accessories in natural and painted wicker, and high-quality rattan. If you're looking for a seating and table set for porch or patio, or your living or dining room, you'll find dozens here. The styling runs from Victorian curves to modern shapes. Breakfast sets, bedroom furniture, étagères, rockers, TV carts and entertainment centers, office furniture, trunks, plant stands, bookcases, magazine racks, hampers, mirrors, lamps, and baskets are offered. There are a number of pieces for children, including bassinets, changing tables, chairs and tables, rockers, and toy chests. The catalog details your options in cushion coverings and delivery, and the "lowest price" guarantee.

Special Factors: Satisfaction is guaranteed.

THE FURNITURE PATCH OF CALABASH, INC.

DEPT. WBMC
10283 BEACH DR. SW
P.O. BOX 4970
CALABASH, NC 28467
910–579–2001
FAX: 910–579–2017

Brochure: free
Pay: check or MO
Sells: furniture, lighting, accessories
Store: same address; Monday to Saturday 9–5:30

The Furniture Patch of Calabash invites you to spend some time at their showroom when you're in the area visiting Myrtle Beach, but if you can't make the trip, help is available by phone or mail. The Furniture Patch represents several hundred manufacturers of home (indoor and outdoor) and office furnishings, decorator fabric, lighting, mirrors, rugs, and decorative accessories. The brochure includes a partial listing of some of the best names in home and industrial design, and savings run up to 60%. Details on the sales policy and ordering guidelines are included, and the knowledgeable sales assistants can answer any other questions you may have and give you quotes on specific items you're pricing. The Furniture Patch has been in business since 1990 and provides in-house delivery and setup to all states in the continental United States.

Special Factors: Price quote by phone, fax, or letter; returns of transit-damaged goods are accepted for repair or replacement.

GENADA IMPORTS

P.O. BOX 204, DEPT. W–99
TEANECK, NJ 07666
TEL/FAX: 973–790–7522

Catalog: $1
Pay: check, MO, MC, V
Sells: Danish, modern, and contemporary furniture
Store: mail order only

Genada has been in business since 1968, selling Danish modern furniture in its most American incarnation: low-slung, teak-finished chairs and couches, with loose-cushion backs and seats of tweed-covered foam. The style has weathered fad and fatigue quite well, and the furniture's basic appeal is only enhanced by its low prices. Armchairs begin at under $100, couches at under $170, and armless divans are priced from $120.

Genada isn't limited to Scandinavian design; the catalog shows reproductions of the Eames chair and other modern classics, folding chairs with woven rope seats and backs, knock-down bookcases and cabinets, butcher block tabletops and bases, convertible foam-block chairs and sofas, gate-leg tables with chairs that store in the base, and bentwood chairs. The catalog also features modern chairs by Paoli Chair Co., suitable for home or office, as well as several handsome styles in molded teak, walnut, and rosewood finishes, from about $300 and up. Imported armoires, patio furniture, "country" kitchen furniture, freestanding wall units, computer workstations, desks, VCR carts, and bar stools are all available. If you're shopping for a bridge table with folding hardwood chairs, you'll find several reasonably priced styles here.

Special Factors: Price quote by phone or letter; specify upholstery and finish materials when ordering.

HEIRLOOM REPRODUCTIONS

1834 W. FIFTH ST., DEPT. WBM
MONTGOMERY, AL
36106–1516
800–288–1513
334–263–3511
FAX: 334–263–3313

Catalog: $5, refundable
Pay: check, MO, MC, V
Sells: Victorian and French reproduction furniture, clocks, lamps, etc.
Store: same address; Monday to Friday 10–5 CT
Online: http://www.victoriana.com

If a button-tufted, damask-covered, center-medallion camelback sofa speaks to you, you have a weakness for Victorian decor. But as anyone who's tried to find good examples of the style knows, they're hard to come by at a reasonable price. Enter Heirloom Reproductions, where gooseneck rockers, fainting sofas, and bustle chairs are stock-in-trade. The 28-page color catalog and other literature show classic parlor sets—sofas and marble-topped occasional tables—and curio cabinets, entertainment centers, hall trees, armoires, dining room sets, bedroom furniture, folding screens, and other pieces. The catalog text includes dimensions, some notes on construction features, and prices, which are discounted 40% to 55% from list. You can select the wood finish from several options and specify fabric—damasks, brocades, prints, tapestries, and velvets—if you're not supplying your own. Heirloom Reproductions also offers a collection of reproduction clocks (regulator, anniversary, Westminster chime, cuckoo, etc.) and collectors' cabinets. If you need help in choosing the best pieces for your decorating scheme, consult the staff designer, who can also give you complete details on fabrics, construction, and the firm's sales policy.

Special Factors: Price quote by phone or letter; swatches are available on request; orders are shipped from the factory by insured truck.

LOFTIN-BLACK FURNITURE CO.

III SEDGEHILL DR.
THOMASVILLE, NC 27360
800–334–7398
910–472–6117
FAX: 910–472–2052

Brochure: free
Pay: check, MO, MC, V, Discover
Sells: furnishings, bedding, and accessories
Store: same address; Monday to Friday 8:30–5:30, Saturday 8:30–5; also 214 N. Main St., High Point, NC (910–883–4711)

Loftin-Black, founded in 1948, delivers selection, service, and savings on fine home, office, and patio furniture and accessories from hundreds of companies, including the top names in furnishings. Their discount to you is 35% to 50% less than the manufacturers' suggested prices. Check with Loftin-Black before ordering table pads or mattress sets—they're also available, at sizable savings. Loftin-Black is an authorized factory dealer for hundreds of prominent manufacturers, listed in the free brochure. It also includes the terms of sale (a 50% deposit is required when ordering, and the balance is due upon delivery) and shipping options. Loftin-Black will provide in-home delivery and setup, although you can engage a common carrier if you prefer. If you're in the Thomasville area, drop in and see Loftin-Black's 14,000 square feet of furniture on display.

Special Factors: Price quote by phone or letter; in-home delivery is made by Loftin-Black's van service.

MARKS SALES CO., INC.

Catalog: $3 bulk, $3.75 first class
Pay: check or MO
Sells: unfinished, assembled furniture
Store: mail order only

151–20 88TH ST., DEPT. 2G
HOWARD BEACH, NY
11414
718–835–9319

The Marks Sales catalog is 62 pages of clear photographs of over 100 pieces of reproduction antiques that await your finishing hand. The flavor is Continental—side chairs and armchairs and matching counter and bar stools with graceful legs, rush seats, and cane backs, imposing cane-back "tub" chairs with lion's-head arms, settles with serpentine ladder-backs and carved aprons, Chinese Chippendale styles, bombé chests, and even tables, desks, headboards, and semanieres are among the offerings. Every piece is made in Spain or Italy, carved by hand from beechwood and arrives completely assembled and sanded (these are not kits), ready for paint or stain and finish. Seats are made by hand of rush, cane, or muslin-covered foam. Prices are wholesale, and if you finish your selection yourself (or even have the furniture done professionally), you can create a custom look for 30% to 60% less than you'd pay for the same pieces in local decorator shops.

International readers, please note: Only U.S. funds are accepted.

Special Factors: Satisfaction is guaranteed; authorized returns are accepted within 20 days for full refund, less cost of freight.

MONARCH RADIATOR ENCLOSURES

P.O. BOX 326, DEPT.
  WBMC
111 KERO RD.
CARLSTADT, NJ 07072
201–507–5551
FAX: 201–438–2820

Brochure: $1, refundable
Pay: check, MO, MC, V
Sells: all-steel radiator enclosures
Store: mail order only
Online: http://www.monarchrad.qpg.com

If you're tired of looking at the exposed ribs of the radiators in your home, consider enclosures. They not only render the unsightly heating fixtures more decorative, but also help to direct the heat into the room. Monarch sells radiator enclosures in two dozen styles, from a basic grill-work design to an elaborate enclosure that includes shelves. Monarch's enclosures are constructed of heavy steel, and price comparisons show savings of up to 35%. There is a choice of colors in baked enamel, including wood-grain finishes. Monarch's literature includes a guide to measuring your radiator prior to ordering.

Special Factors: Most enclosures can be shipped by UPS; larger enclosures are shipped via common carrier.

PLEXI-CRAFT QUALITY PRODUCTS CORP.

514 W. 24TH ST., DEPT.
  WBMC
NEW YORK, NY
  10011–1179
800–24–PLEXI
212–924–3244
FAX: 212–924–3508

Catalog: $2
Pay: check, MO, MC, V
Sells: Plexiglas and Lucite home furnishings and accessories
Store: same address; Monday to Friday 9:30–5
E-mail: plexi@escape.com
Online: http://www.escape.com/~plexi

Plexi-Craft manufactures its own line of premium Plexiglas and Lucite goods and gets them to you factory-direct, resulting in prices that are up to 50% less than what department and specialty stores charge for comparable items. The 16-page catalog shows furnishings and accessories of all kinds that give the impression of clean, minimal styling that's very chic. There are a number of tables—dining, cocktail, Parsons, TV, snack, and side—and the models with separate bases may be ordered with glass instead of acrylic tops. Several rolling bars are available, as well as chairs, pedestals, computer stands, vanities and stools, luggage racks, wine racks, magazine units, easels, wastebaskets, place mats, telephone tables, and much more. Desk sets, kitchen organizers and paper towel holders, and bathroom fixtures round out the selection, and there's an anti-static cleaner and a polish formulated for Lucite/Plexiglas to keep everything gleaming. Plexi-Craft, founded in 1972, also accepts orders for custom work.

Special Factors: Price quote by phone, fax, or letter on custom work.

PRIBA FURNITURE SALES & INTERIORS

P.O. BOX 13295
GREENSBORO, NC
27415–3295
336–855–9034
FAX: 336–855–1370

Brochure: free
Pay: check, MO, MC, V, Discover
Sells: furniture, accessories, bedding, rugs, etc.
Store: 210 Stage Coach Trail, Greensboro, NC; Monday to Friday 9–5:30, Saturday 9–5
E-mail: pribafurniture@worldnet.att.net
Online: http://www.pribafurniture.com

Priba's 40,000-square-foot showroom is a must-see if you're in the High Point/Greensboro area, but if you're not planning to travel, Priba will bring the furnishings to you. The firm has been in business since 1972 and represents over 350 manufacturers of home furnishings, including bedroom and dining room suites, leather, patio furniture, lamps and accessories, carpeting, decorator fabrics, wall coverings, and mattresses. The choice of manufacturers tends to the upmarket end of the scale, and a number are usually listed as "to the trade only" in decorator magazines. Send for the brochure for details on Priba's sales policy, and call for price quotes or for assistance in making your selection. Savings run up to nearly 50% on list or regular retail, and Priba uses van-line service, so your furniture will be uncrated and set up within your home.

Special Factors: Credit cards are accepted for deposits only; shipping charge is calculated on a minimum weight of 150 pounds.

QUALITY FURNITURE MARKET

2034 HICKORY BLVD. SW
LENOIR, NC 28645
704–728–2946
FAX: 704–726–0226

Information: price quote
Pay: check, MO, MC, V
Sells: furnishings, bedding, and accessories
Store: same address; Monday to Saturday
8:30–5

Quality Furniture Market, in business since 1955, takes its name seriously: You're invited to check the firm's ratings with Dun and Bradstreet, the Lyons listing, and the Lenoir Chamber of Commerce (800–737–0782) before you buy. The firm's magnificent selection is offered at prices that are 20% over cost, compared with the usual 110% to 125% markups. The company has been recommended as a "great price" store by Oprah Winfrey and *Woman's Day* magazine.

Quality Furniture sells indoor and outdoor furniture, bedding, and home accessories by literally hundreds of firms. The list of brands is given in the brochure, as well as terms of sale and other conditions. Readers have written to say they were very pleased with Quality's prices and the firm's in-home delivery service. If you're traveling near Lenoir, drop by and get lost in the three floors of furniture galleries and display rooms.

Special Factors: Price quote by phone or letter with self-addressed, stamped envelope; all orders must be prepaid before shipment; shipment is made by common carrier or in-home delivery service.

SHAW FURNITURE GALLERIES, INC.

131 W. ACADEMY ST.
RANDLEMAN, NC 27317
336–498–2628
FAX: 336–498–7889

Brochure: free
Pay: check, MO, MC, V
Sells: home and office furnishings
Store: same address; Monday to Friday
9–5:30, Saturday 9–5

Shaw Furniture Galleries is one of the largest discount furniture operations in North Carolina and has been in business since 1940. You can save up to 50% on top-brand furniture here, where customer service is the main priority. When you call, a sales associate will readily discuss your plans and can mail you color brochures of the collections that interest you. If you're in the area, be sure and visit. Many showrooms are housed in the original Randleman School, and the 35,000-square-foot building next door houses beautiful galleries by Thomasville, Century, Hickory White, Hickory Chair, Bernhardt, and Stanley. Shaw's sells and delivers throughout the U.S. and uses Executive Delivery Red Carpet Service to deliver your furniture, with free setup in your home.

Special Factors: Price quote by phone or letter with self-addressed, stamped envelope; Shaw credit cards available.

SOBOL HOUSE

141 RICHARDSON BLVD.
P.O. BOX 219
BLACK MOUNTAIN, NC
 28711
704–669–8031
FAX: 704–669–7969

Brochure: free
Pay: check or MO
Sells: home and office furnishings
Store: same address; Monday to Friday 9–6:30, Saturday 9–5:30, Sunday 12–5 (June to October)

Sobol House has been saving informed consumers 40% to 50% on their quality furniture purchases since 1971, and the firm's low prices have helped build a clientele worldwide over the years. "All we ask is the chance to give you a competitive bid!" Although Sobol carries contemporary furnishings, the firm's specialty is traditional, 18th century, and country styles, from the most prominent names in the business. Sobol can help you make your selection—with advice and manufacturers' catalogs—and gives price quotes on specific items. Both sidewalk and in-house delivery are available, and details of the sales policy are given in the brochure and order form.

Special Factors: Price quote by phone, fax, or letter.

SOUTHLAND FURNITURE GALLERIES

1244 HIGHWAY 17
P.O. BOX 1837
LITTLE RIVER, SC 29566
803–280–9342
FAX: 803–249–4527

Brochure: free
Pay: check or MO
Sells: home furnishings and accessories
Store: same address; Monday to Saturday
9–5:30

The 30,000 square feet of Southland Furniture Galleries is a short jaunt from the attractions of Myrtle Beach, worth a stop between visits to the local beaches and rounds of golf. Southland is run by people who own two other furnishings galleries, and they have many years of experience in selling and shipping to customers out of state. In addition to home furnishings, Southland sells lighting, rugs, mirrors, clocks, and bedding by some of the best names in the business. The brochure lists the hundreds of manufacturers represented here and takes you through the ordering and delivery process. The full-service amenities include a professional interior designer on staff, and in-home delivery with setup. Savings vary depending on the manufacturer and line, but average more than 40% off suggested list.

Special Factors: Sales policy is detailed in the brochure; price quote by phone, fax, or letter.

STEERHIDES

M.C. LIMITED, DEPT.
  WBM
P.O. BOX 17696
WHITEFISH BAY, WI 53217
414–263–5222
FAX: 414–263–5508

Brochure and Price List: free
Pay: check, MO, MC, V
Sells: steerhides and hide pillows
Store: mail order only

I once met an Irish-American living in Woodstock who thought he was a medicine man. His teepee floor was adorned with black-and-white cow skins. Being a cow fanatic, I always wondered where he got them. Imagine my thrill when I opened up M.C. Limited's Steerhides brochure and saw eight color photographs of natural and printed steerhides! The company offers processed skins in full hides (36 square feet on average, 5' to 6' wide by 7' to 8' long) in six natural colors for $235, as well as stenciled animal prints (zebra or leopard) for $345. The natural steerhides are nearly 40% below prices by two New York City leather suppliers for comparable skins. M.C. Limited also makes steerhide pillows with suede backs, which are offered in the six natural colors and stenciled zebra or leopard, plain or with silver beads and fringes on the corners. Sizes range from 12" to 24" square and are priced from $65 to $175. M.C. Limited notes that all of its hides are by-products of the beef industry and are not claimed from animals raised primarily for their skins. A special new tanning process is reputed to render the hides "soft and beautiful" as they age, so they won't stiffen, dry out, and lose hair.

Special Factors: Satisfaction is guaranteed; authorized returns (except pillows) are accepted (a restocking fee is charged) within 30 days.

TENDER HEART TREASURES, LTD.

10525 J ST.
OMAHA, NE 68127–1090
800–443–1367
402–593–1313
FAX: 402–593–1316

Catalog: free
Pay: check, MO, MC, V, AE, Discover
Sells: "country" home decor and gifts
Store: mail order only
Online: http://www.tenderheart.com

Tender Heart Treasures specializes in "country" home accents and seasonal displays and decorations at prices that are a solid 30% to 50% below retail. The 72-page color catalog features hundreds of gifts, display pieces, and seasonal decorations: bears of all types in costume and the buff, "welcome" signs and hospitality plaques, dolls and figurines, angels, electrified kerosene lamps, bent-wire decorations, nesting baskets, picture frames, birdhouses, doll furniture, planters, wooden apples and other fruit, wreaths, miniatures, terra-cotta discs to keep your brown sugar moist, and lots more. In addition to terrific prices, Tender Heart Treasures makes ordering a breeze—there's no minimum, and shipping charges are easy to compute to any destination.

Wholesale inquiries should be made to 800–443–1367; a copy of your resale tax certificate will be required with your first order.

Special Factors: Satisfaction is guaranteed; quantity discounts are available; authorized returns are accepted within 30 days for exchange, refund, or credit; C.O.D. orders are accepted.

TERRY'S VILLAGE

P.O. BOX 2309, DEPT. 826
OMAHA, NE 68103–2309
800–200–4400
402–331–5511
FAX: 800–723–9000
TDD: 800–833–7352
  (RELAY)

Catalog: free
Pay: check, MO, MC, V, AE, Discover
Sells: gifts, home accessories, and crafts
Store: mail order only
Online: http://www.terrysvillage.com

 ¡Si! ℭ

What wonderful catalogs arrive from Terry's Village, full of decorative treats to make your home special for the holidays and to mark the seasons throughout the year. The spring edition is full of bunnies celebrating Easter, shown on tin boxes that can be filled with candy, outside their own miniature village, and on banners, wreathes, and soap dishes. Cherub wall and shelf statues, terra-cotta birdbaths, handpainted mushroom finches, muslin dolls, candles, and vegetable-shaped soup crocks describe the range of gifts and accents. The Christmas edition shows angels of every type, Nativity scenes, beautiful collector dolls, grand Santas in gold with fur trim, winter villages (including a porcelain gingerbread version), ornaments, water globes, and even wrapping paper and ribbon assortments. The prices are so low that it sometimes costs more to make a craft item yourself than it does to buy it as a finished product here. For holiday gifts, favors, hostess presents, home decor, and even resale (depending on the prices prevailing in your area), don't buy elsewhere until you've checked the Terry's Village catalog.

Special Factors: Satisfaction is guaranteed; returns are accepted within 30 days for exchange, credit, or refund.

MARION TRAVIS

**P.O. BOX 1041
STATESVILLE, NC 28687
704–528–4424
FAX: 704–528–3526**

Catalog: $1
Pay: check, MO, MC, V
Sells: country chairs, benches, and tables
Store: 354 S. Eastway Dr., Troutman, NC;
Monday to Thursday 8–3:30, Friday 8–noon

You can pay hundreds of dollars for an oak pedestal table at your local antique shop, and search every tag sale in the state for a matched set of ladderback chairs. Or you can send $1 to Marion Travis for the catalog that shows these and other furnishings made in ash, oak, maple, and other hardwoods. The 12 pages of black-and-white photographs show country furniture, including a good selection of rockers and ladderback chairs with twisted cord, cane rush, or wood slat seats. There are armchair and rocker styles and children's models, beginning at $27. Plain, slat-seat kitchen chairs and a classic oak kitchen table with utility drawer are shown, as well as a porch swing and Kennedy-style rockers with cane rush backs and seats. The prices cited are for unfinished furniture, but Marion Travis will stain and finish your selection in natural, golden oak, or walnut for a surcharge. If you're in the vicinity of Troutman, you can receive a 25% discount on most items by going to the showroom, making a purchase, and taking it with you, unboxed. Special discounts are available on 25 or more pieces.

Wholesale customers: Request the wholesale catalog and price list from Shaver Woodworks, P.O. Box 946, Troutman, NC 28166. The minimum wholesale order is 12 pieces.

Special Factors: Minimum order is 2 pieces of furniture; authorized returns of defective goods are accepted within 30 days.

WEST RINDGE BASKETS, INC.

**47 W. MAIN ST.
RINDGE, NH 03461
TEL/FAX: 603–899–2231**

Brochure: free
Pay: check or money order
Sells: handmade, handwoven wooden baskets
Store: same address; Monday to Thursday 8–4 (all year), Friday to Saturday 10–4 (May 30 to Christmas)

West Rindge has been making baskets from local New Hampshire wood since 1925. The baskets here start as rough-cut, slab-edge white birch or oak from local forests, and are handmade, handwoven, and individually inspected for flaws. Don't be expecting the $5 made-in-Asia basket you'd buy in a dime store. West Rindge baskets are upscale, impeccably made baskets to keep over a lifetime. The color brochure shows the selection—40 in all—which includes baskets for shopping, pie and cake holders (including a double pie holder), picnic baskets, baskets designed for apple picking, wine-toting, planters, wastebaskets, barbecue utensils, French bread, and many more, including ones with swing handles, stiff handles, and hinged lids. The baskets here sell for less than what you'd pay for items of comparable quality in a gourmet shop or decorator store. The prices are very reasonable—averaging around $25. This is a very nice, family-run business.

Wholesale Buyers: West Rindge has a wholesale price list at about 30% less, which you can request if you're a reseller. In New Hampshire, a "reseller" is not required to have a resale number. The only requirement is that you purchase a minimum of $100 on your first wholesale order.

Special Factors: Satisfaction is guaranteed; C.O.D. orders accepted for an additional charge.

WICKER WAREHOUSE INC.

**195 S. RIVER ST.
HACKENSACK, NJ 07601
800–989–4253
201–342–6709
FAX: 201–342–1495**

Catalog: $6, refundable
Pay: check, MO, MC, V, Discover
Sells: wicker furniture and accessories
Store: same address; Monday to Saturday
10–6, Wednesday 10–7
Online: http://www.wickerwarehouse.com

Why comb antique stores and flea markets for vintage wicker furniture when you can find freshly minted versions of the same styles, in pristine condition, at comparable prices? Wicker Warehouse, established in 1978, sells current styles by the top names in the business, including lines treated to withstand the elements—so you don't have to drag everything inside the garage when it starts raining. The 128-page color catalog shows great groupings for sun porch and summer home, and wicker-embellished bedroom furnishings, mirrors, lamps, dining chairs, stools, nursery accoutrements, bathroom accessories, trunks, and even doll buggies. You'll also find teak, wrought-iron aluminum and cast aluminum furniture, sectionals, recliners, sleepers, dining room furniture, and dinettes. Fabric and finish options are shown as well. Prices are 30% to 50% below list, and orders are shipped anywhere within the continental United States.

Special Factors: Satisfaction is guaranteed; price quote by phone; phone hours are 24 hours a day.

RELATED PRODUCTS/COMPANIES

Air conditioners • S&S Sound City, Bernie's, Dial-a-Brand, LVT Price Quote Hotline, Percy's
Books on furniture making and upholstery • Woodworkers' Discount Books, The Caning Shop, Frank's Cane and Rush Supply
Ceiling fans • Main Lamp/Lamp Warehouse, Golden Valley Lighting
Custom fabric lamination for patio furniture • Hancock's of Paducah
Custom-upholstered headboards, ottomans, footstools • Eldridge Textile
Deer-themed decor and home accents • Deer Shack
Furniture kits • Frank's Cane and Rush Supply
Home furnishings • Cole's Appliance & Furniture, Bennett Brothers

Leather-care products • *Leather Unlimited, UPCO, Weaver Leather*
Miscellaneous household accessories • *Damark*
Pool and billiards tables and game-room decor • *Mueller Sporting Goods*
Ready-made chair and cushion covers • *Shama Imports*
Upholstery stain remover • *The Cleaning Center*
Wooden towel racks, shelves, coat stands, household accessories •
Weston Bowl Mill

Kitchen Equipment, Cookware, and Cutlery

Small kitchen appliances, kitchen gadgets, pots, pans, baking accessories, knives, cooking utensils, food storage, etc.

These firms sell everything from measuring spoons to bread-making machines, frequently at 30% to 50% less than you'd pay retail. For large kitchen appliances such as refrigerators, stoves, and ovens, see "Household Appliances and TVs." For eating utensils, glassware, and china, see "Tableware—Flatware, Glassware, and China" in this chapter, page 364. For tablecloths, place mats, and napkins, see the "Bed, Bath, and Table Linens" section of this chapter, page 302. And be sure to check out "Related Products/Companies" after the company listings in this section for other firms that carry kitchen- and cooking-related items.

FIND IT FAST

CLEANING SUPPLIES • *Colonial Garden Kitchens*
COOKWARE AND BAKEWARE • *Broadway Panhandler, ChuckWagon Outfitters, Colonial Garden Kitchens, Kitchen Etc., Peerless, Professional Cutlery, Zabar's*
CUTLERY • *Broadway Panhandler, Kitchen Etc., Peerless, Professional Cutlery*
FOOD STORAGE AND KITCHEN ORGANIZERS • *Colonial Garden Kitchens, Peerless*
KITCHEN GADGETS AND UTENSILS • *Broadway Panhandler, Colonial Garden Kitchens, Peerless, Professional Cutlery*
LARGE KITCHEN APPLIANCES • *Peerless*

BROADWAY PANHANDLER

477 BROOME ST.
NEW YORK, NY 10013
212–966–3434
FAX: 212–966–9017

Information: price quote
Pay: check, MO, MC, V, AE, Discover
Sells: cookware, cutlery, kitchenware, bakeware, and tabletop accessories
Store: same address; Monday to Friday 10:30–7, Saturday 11–7, Sunday 11–6

Broadway Panhandler is located just blocks from the Bowery, New York City's commercial kitchenware district, but it draws a steady stream of trade from those who like the firm's mix of high-end home cookware and well-chosen professional equipment. Broadway Panhandler doesn't publish a catalog, but you can call or write for prices on appliances and equipment by All-Clad, Bodum, Bourgeat, Braun, Calphalon, Chicago Metallic, Le Creuset, Cuisinart (machines), Kaiser, KitchenAid, Krups, Omega, Pavoni, Pelouze, and Vollrath. Broadway Panhandler's knife department includes Global, Lamson & Goodnow, Sabatier, and Wüsthof-Trident (price lists and manufacturers' brochures may be available for the cutlery). If you're able to visit the store, you'll also find cookbooks, serving pieces, kitchen linens, candy molds, baking supplies, and lots of baskets and gadgets. Savings vary by brand and season, but open-stock cutlery is about 30% off at this writing, and selected cookware lines are discounted up to 35% off list.

Special Factors: Price quote by phone or letter.

CHUCKWAGON OUTFITTERS

250 AVILA BEACH DR.
SAN LUIS OBISPO, CA
  93405
800–543–2359
805–595–2434
FAX: 805–595–7914

Catalog: free (see text)
Pay: check, MO, MC, V, AE, Discover
Sells: cast-iron cookware, accessories
Store: same address
E-mail: cwo@fix.net

Whether you like cast-iron cookware for its down-home good looks or its serviceability, you'll appreciate ChuckWagon Outfitters for bringing so much of it your way. This family-run firm, established in 1992, features the Lodge brand of ironware that includes the Dutch oven that's the "official cookware of the Boy Scouts of America," as well as other lines. True to its affiliations, ChuckWagon's 20-page catalog shows a wide range of fryers, skillets, kettles, muffin tins, trivets and stands, and related camp gear, all at savings of up to 40% on comparable retail. The Dutch ovens that inspired the business are available in flat-bottomed styles for stovetop use, and footed for campfires. The MACA extra-deep ovens can accommodate whole turkeys, and you can order them with lids that are personalized with "your name or your ranch name." (Considering the fact that they look as if they could double for manhole covers with handles, it's hard to imagine them walking away, but al fresco dining makes its own rules.) Those who are unfamiliar with the Dutch oven culture and cooking methods should see the dozens of histories and cookbooks in the catalog for help. (Hint: The Dutch oven appears to be a precursor of the Crock-Pot.)

If you've been searching for square skillets, cast-iron woks, flat griddles, perch-shaped muffin tins, or a cast-iron teakettle or bundt pan, you've found the source. There are a number of classic "catalog curiosities," including ranch chimes (triangles), sad irons (replicas of the non-electric irons that were heated on top of a woodstove), cast-iron trout andirons, enamelware chamber pots, and Volcano cookers, among others. The catalog, regularly $2, is free to readers of this book, so be sure to mention BWBM when you call or write for it.

Wholesale buyers, please note: The minimum opening order is $300, subsequent order minimum is $75. For a price list and terms of sale, call 805–595–2434.

COLONIAL GARDEN KITCHENS

DEPT. CGZ4182
HANOVER, PA 17333–0066
800–323–6000

Catalog: $2
Pay: check, MO, MC, V, AE, CB, DC, Discover
Sells: kitchen equipment and household helps
Store: mail order only

Colonial Garden Kitchens is one of the Hanover Direct, Inc., companies offering moderately priced gadgets, as well as name-brand appliances, at a discount. A third or more of the goods in the color catalog are usually on "sale" at 20% to 40% below their regular prices. And every catalog features the latest in kitchen appliances, specialty cookware and utensils, work units and food storage containers, serving and entertaining equipment, hard-to-find cleaners, bed and bath organizers, and lots of other things that are handy to have around the house. Bread makers, tabletop grills, deep fryers, commercial oven mitts, microwave bacon crispers, and cast-iron muffin tins are among the popular products that have appeared in past catalogs. Everything is backed by CGK's guarantee of satisfaction.

Special Factors: Satisfaction is guaranteed; returns in new or like-new condition are accepted for exchange, refund, or credit.

KITCHEN ETC.

32 INDUSTRIAL DR., DEPT.
 WBM99
EXETER, NH 03833–4557
603–773–0020
FAX: 603–778–9328

Catalog: free
Pay: check, MO, MC, V, Discover
Sells: tableware and kitchenware
Store: locations in CT, MA, NH, and VT; see catalog for locations

Kitchen Etc. has put together a great catalog of fine and everyday china, cookware, cutlery, and serving pieces that brings you helpful buying information, as well as prices that usually run from 20% to 40% below regular retail, with even deeper discounts on some items. The firm has been doing business since 1983 and has eight stores throughout New England at this writing, with more reportedly on the way.

Kitchen Etc. features fine and casual dinnerware patterns from Denby, Franciscan, Johnson Brothers, Lenox, Mikasa, Nikko, Noritake, Pfaltzgraff, Portmeirion, Royal Doulton, Royal Worcester, Studio Nova, Waterford, Wedgwood, and many more. The available patterns are listed, as well as a guide to the shape of each piece, present and future availability (if known), and suggested retail and discount prices. Stemware from Gorham, Lenox, Marquis by Waterford, Mikasa, Noritake, and Royal Doulton is sold. Stainless steel and silverplate flatware is available from Gorham, Mikasa, Oneida, Pfaltzgraff, Reed & Barton, Wallace, and Yamazaki.

The catalog offers cookware and serving pieces from All-Clad, Calphalon, Circulon, Le Creuset, Revere, and T-Fal. If you're looking for cutlery, check the prices on knives from Chicago Cutlery, J.A. Henckels, and Wüsthof-Trident. Selected small kitchen appliances are also available, as well as pasta bowl sets, woks, pizza stones, glassware, and other hard-to-find items. Special orders are accepted on some goods, so if you don't see what you're looking for in the catalog, call to see whether the firm can get it. Kitchen Etc. also maintains a bridal registry service.

Special Factors: Satisfaction is guaranteed; price quote by phone, fax, or letter.

PEERLESS RESTAURANT SUPPLIES

1124 S. GRAND BLVD.,
   DEPT. WBMC
ST. LOUIS, MO 63104
800–255–3663
314–664–0400
FAX: 314–664–8102

Catalog: $10
Pay: check, MO, MC, V
Sells: commercial cookware and restaurant equipment
Store: same address; Monday to Friday 8–5
E-mail: peerless@prls.com
Online: http://www.prls.com

The hefty Peerless catalog—yours for $10—has everything you need to set up a professional kitchen or restaurant dining room, except the food. Since so many of the appliances and utensils can do double duty in home kitchens, the catalog makes a good resource and investment if you're planning any significant kitchenware purchases.

Peerless represents over 2,000 manufacturers of everything from diner sugar shakers to walk-in refrigerators: tableware, trays and carts, bar accessories, restaurant seating, table linens and kitchen textiles, cookware, ranges and ovens, refrigerators, sinks, worktables, cleaning supplies and equipment, ice machines, dishwashers, and much more. Sample offerings include Libbey glassware, Hall and Buffalo china, cutlery by Dexter Russell, WearEver pots and pans, Vollrath stainless steel stockpots and chafing dishes, Rubbermaid's professional line of janitorial storage and food-service containers, Pelouze food scales, Waring professional bar appliances, Peerless' own commercial cleaners and polishes, Metro wire shelves, Market Forge steamers, and Robot Coupe food processors. Peerless also sells cooking equipment by Castle, Dean, Frymaster, Garland, Southbend, and Vulcan; commercial microwave ovens from MenuMaster and Panasonic; refrigeration from Delfield, Ice-O-Matic, Kelvinator, Victory, Scotsman, Traulsen, and True; Eagle sinks; In-Sink-Erator commercial disposers; ventilation equipment; and much more. Peerless offers UL-approved zero-clearance ranges for home kitchens, from Garland, Imperial, Viking, and Wolf.

If you know what you want by manufacturer and model number, you can call or write for a price quote—but the catalog is worth the $10 fee if you're buying more than a couple of items. Food-service professionals should note the services Peerless can provide, including facility design, installation, construction supervision, concept development, and equipment leasing. Used kitchenware is available at big savings, and if you get to St. Louis, stop in and check out the "Bargain Room," which features close-outs.

Special Factors: Quantity discounts are available; authorized returns are accepted within 30 days for exchange, refund, or credit (a 10% restocking fee may be charged, or 20% on special orders); minimum order is $50.

PROFESSIONAL CUTLERY DIRECT

DEPT. WBM9
170 BOSTON POST RD.,
SUITE 135
MADISON, CT 06443
800–859–6994
203–458–5015
FAX: 203–458–5019

Catalog: $3, refundable
Pay: check, MO, MC, V
Sells: kitchen cutlery, cookware, cookbooks, etc.
Store: mail order only
E-mail: wbm9@p-c-d.com
Online: http://www.p-c-d.com

Serious cooks require commercial-quality equipment, which is what you'll find in the 68-page catalog from Professional Cutlery Direct. It's geared to cooks who know the merits of high-carbon stainless steel (it resists corrosion and can be sharpened), or why wood cutting boards are better than plastic (the latter actually promote the breeding of bacteria!). No matter what your experience level, you'll warm to everyday discounts of 20% to 30%, with specials reaching as much as 45% off list.

PCD's stock includes several lines by Cuisine de France Sabatier, F. Dick, Forschner/Victorinox, Global, Kyocera Ceramics, Lamson Sharp, and Wüsthof-Trident: boxed sets, sharpeners and steels, blocks with and without knife sets, wall-mounted knife holders and magnetic strips, professional roll-packs (used by teachers and caterers), and knife attaché cases from a variety of manufacturers, filled with "any professional's dream of knives." Hardwood cutting boards are available in several sizes and styles, as well as the entire All-Clad line, Sitrum, and Chaudier cookware, whisks, pastry tools, mandolines, mortar-and-pestle sets, Bourgeat professional copper cookware, Enclume pot racks, professional cookbooks, and even chef's attire.

The PCD catalog includes product information to help you choose the cutlery that's best for your needs, as well as details on special offers and the volume discount plan for commercial cookware. And there's a cap on shipping—$14.95 at this writing, no matter how much you buy!

Special Factors: Price quote by phone or letter; quantity discounts are available on selected items; returns of most items are accepted within 30 days for exchange, refund, or credit; minimum order is $10.

WESTON BOWL MILL

P.O. BOX 218-WBMC
WESTON, VT 05161–0218
802–824–6219
FAX: 802–824–4215

Catalog: $1, $2 outside U.S.
Pay: check, MO, MC, V, Discover
Sells: woodenware and wooden household items
Store: Main St. (Rt. 100), Weston, VT; daily 9–5

Weston Bowl Mill has been known since 1960 for its wooden salad bowls, but the Mill produces hundreds of other wooden items for use throughout the home and sells them factory-direct to you. Prices of many of the goods run about 30% below comparable retail, and savings are even better on selected goods. Almost everything is available with and without finish (oil or lacquer). The popular salad bowls, thick curves milled from a solid piece of maple or birch, are offered in sizes from 6" to 20" across. You can save by buying the seconds (when available), but note that sales are final on seconds—no returns.

What a great catalog! There's something in here for everyone. Weston sells much more for the dining table and kitchen, including birch plates and trays, maple lazy Susans, meat tenderizers, cheese plates, knife racks, towel racks, tongs, a great selection of carving and cutting boards, and carbon steel knives. The 16-page catalog offers a wide variety of other home items, including hat/coat/mug racks, towel and tissue holders, spoon racks, a large selection of wooden boxes, quilt racks, benches, knickknack shelves, sconces, light-switch plates, chairs, park benches, stools, candleholders, recipe holders, bread loaf slicers, wooden fruits and vegetables, baskets, and on and on. Weston's bird feeders and whirligigs are well priced; likewise the delightful group of wooden toys—vehicles, blocks, tops, puzzles, rocking horses, game boards, cradles, and other classics—that are oil-finished.

Special Factors: Minimum order is $5, $20 with credit cards.

ZABAR'S

**2245 BROADWAY
NEW YORK, NY 10024
212–496–1234
FAX: 212–580–4477**

Catalog: free
Pay: check, MO, MC, V, AE
Sells: gourmet food, cookware, and house-wares
Store: same address; Monday to Friday 8–7:30, Saturday 8–8, Sunday 9–6; house-wares mezzanine Monday to Saturday 9–7, Sunday 9–6
E-mail: info@zabars.com

¡Sí!

Zabar's, thought of by many as New York City's ultimate deli, offers the better part of North America a sampling from its famed counters and housewares mezzanine via a 64-page color catalog. Zabar's has been around since 1934 and offers savings of up to 50% on name-brand kitchenware and competitive prices on foodstuffs.

Past catalogs have offered smoked Scottish, Norwegian, and Irish salmon, plum pudding, peppercorns, Bahlsen cookies and confections, pâtés, mustards, crackers, escargot, Lindt and Droste chocolate, Tiptree preserves, Dresden stollen, olive oil, prosciutto and other deli meats, and similar gourmet fare. (Perishables are packed in ice and shipped via next-day air.) The cookware section features the finest names in pots and pans of every kind, coffee- and espresso makers, and baking accessories. The housewares section has more cookery, small appliances such as toasters and food processors, steam presses and irons, sewing machines, vacuum cleaners and sweepers, blenders and mixers, and more. Zabar's distinguishes itself among kitchenware vendors for the enormous selection of goods and the substantial discounts. The catalog features a representative selection from the store, and price quotes are given over the phone—if you don't see it in the catalog, just call. With any catalog order over $25, receive a pound of Zabar's coffee for $3 ($3.50 for decaf).

Special Factors: Minimum order is $15; minimum shipping fee is $5.50; no orders are shipped to APO/FPO addresses, Canada, or Puerto Rico; orders shipped to Alaska and Hawaii must go second-day air; phone orders are accepted Monday to Saturday 9–5.

RELATED PRODUCTS/COMPANIES

Acrylic wine racks, kitchen organizers • *Plexi-Craft*

Aprons, kitchen towels • *Clothcrafters, Marshall Domestics*

Cake-decorating equipment • *The Party Wholesaler*

Cheese-making kits • *New England Cheesemaking Supply*

Cleaning supplies • *The Cleaning Center, Marshall Domestics, EDGE Distributing, Fuller Brush Independent Distributor, Cal Ben*

Cookware • *Bennett Brothers*

Cutlery • *Bennett Brothers, Lanac, Cutlery Shoppe*

Food and spice containers • *Brushy Mountain Bee Farm, Rafal Spice, Spices Etc.*

Household and homemaking tips • *Reader's Digest, Storey Communications*

Japanese cooking utensils and equipment • *Mountain Ark Trading*

Kitchen accents and knickknacks • *Caprilands Herb Farm, Terry's Village, Lanac*

Kitchen scales • *Triner Scale*

Kitchen tools for persons with limited eyesight or mobility • *Comfort House, The New Vision Store, Independent Living Aids*

Kitchen tools, utensils, and gadgets • *Gurney's, Johnny's Selected Seeds, Pinetree Garden, Rafal Spice, Pendery's, Spices Etc., Grandma's Spice Shop, Clothcrafters*

Mexican cooking utensils • *The CMC Company*

Picnic, wine-toting, pie, bread, and other baskets • *West Rindge Baskets*

Professional-size boxes of aluminum foil and plastic wrap • *The Party Wholesaler*

Small kitchen appliances • *Bernie's Discount, Percy's, S&S Sound City, LVT Price Quote Hotline, Bennett Brothers, American Health Food, Lanac*

Wine-, beer-, mead-, liqueur-making supplies • *E.C. Kraus, Brushy Mountain Bee Farm*

Lighting

Indoor and outdoor lighting fixtures, lamp shades, related goods

The artful use of lighting ranks with color in the success of a room, but it's also one of the biggest design challenges. None of the firms listed here can tell you how to light your home, but you'll find the basics in interior design textbooks and decorating manuals. You'll find another authority in your own observations of lighting that pleases you—whether it's good general illumination, glare-free task lighting for reading or needlework, a combination of the two in a kitchen, subdued but reader-friendly lamps in a bedroom or library, or outdoor lighting that improves security while highlighting the architecture. Note how effects are created, and work with the fixtures you have to try out new ideas—raise or lower the wattage, alter the shading, change the location of the lamp, use tinted bulbs, etc. Study the optimal placement and height of light fixtures, which have distilled to rules of measurement in interior design textbooks. You can do so much with lamps (floor, table, swag, desk, etc.) and conventional ceiling fixtures (canopy and chandelier) that you might not think of retrofitting high-hats, eyeballs, or other recessed fixtures when you review your home lighting. Consider them when you want to update a track system, increase hallway lighting discreetly, or create a special effect with a spotlight or wall-washer.

The firms listed here sell lighting for the home—lamps, ceiling fixtures, bathroom and kitchen fixtures, patio and walkway lighting, building lanterns, etc.—and related electrical accessories, shades, and replacement parts. Some also sell ceiling fans and attachments. Discounts average about 30% to 40% on name-brand goods, and the firms that manufacture their own fixtures sell at competitive prices.

FIND IT FAST

CEILING FANS • Golden Valley, Main Lamp
CHANDELIERS • Brass Light Gallery, King's Chandelier, Luigi Crystal
LAMPS, LIGHT FIXTURES, SCONCES • Brass Light Gallery, Golden Valley, Main Lamp
OUTDOOR LANTERNS AND PENDANTS • Brass Light Gallery, Golden Valley

---

BRASS LIGHT GALLERY

131 S. 1ST ST., DEPT.
  WBMC
MILWAUKEE, WI 53204
800–243–9595
FAX: 414–271–7755

Catalog: $6, refundable (see text)
Pay: check, MO, MC, V
Sells: lighting fixtures
Store: same address; Monday to Friday 9–5, Saturday 10–4

After you've seen the fixtures from Brass Light Gallery, you'll know why you've held off buying from other sources. Not only are the materials and workmanship here of superior quality, but the designs have that satisfyingly "right" quality that's so often lacking in lighting fixtures. The Goldenrod and Continental Collections showcase classic architectural styles for kitchens, bathrooms, bedrooms, and other interior spaces. The Alabaster Collection offers timeless chandeliers, sconces, and table lamps in natural alabaster, at prices often lower than those charged for the originals from the '20s and '30s—when you can find them, intact and unchipped, in antique stores. The Prismatic Collection features authentic vintage glass pendants (ribbed glass), suitable for kitchen and loft spaces. The Arts & Crafts Collection has interior and exterior lanterns and pendants to complement the architecture and design of homes and furniture styled after that eponymous movement in America. There's also a Prairie School Collection, à la Frank Lloyd Wright, with table lamps, ceiling fixtures, and lanterns, and the Classic Exteriors Collection, with great items to enhance your exteriors and landscape. Most of the fixtures are offered in a choice of metal finishes and/or choices of glass shade color or style, allowing you to customize each fixture to your room's decor.

The Brass Light Gallery's catalog—over 100 pages of lighting, plus technical specifications—has been designed for use by homeowners, interior designers, and architects. (The catalog costs $6, refundable with purchase, but a 12-page color brochure is free on request.) Prices here average 20% below retail, but the fixtures are better quality than those being sold by many of Brass Light Gallery's competitors.

Special Factors: Satisfaction is guaranteed.

GOLDEN VALLEY LIGHTING

274 EASTCHESTER DR.,
#117A
HIGH POINT, NC 27262
800–735–3377, EXT. 280
336–882–7330
FAX: 800–760–6678
FAX: 336–882–2262

Catalog: free to BWBM readers (see text)
Pay: check, MO, MC, V, Discover
Sells: lighting fixtures and ceiling fans
Store: mail order only
Online: http://www.gvlight.com

 ¡Si! ★

Golden Valley, whose parent company was founded in 1926, is run by veterans of the lighting industry who offer savings of up to 50% on lighting fixtures and ceiling fans. BWBM readers can call at extension 280 and Golden Valley will send a free 76-page catalog (normally $2) illuminated with gorgeous color photographs, pricing, and descriptions of chandeliers and other hanging fixtures, sconces, bathroom and vanity strip lighting, ceiling fans, standing and table lamps, outdoor lighting, and more. You can also request a price quote by phone or mail; see "Special Factors," below. (Call when you've decided what you want, and have the manufacturer's name, model number, color, finish, and any other details at hand.) When you're ready to order, you can make a deposit of 50% of the cost of the fixture and pay the balance before shipment, or prepay the entire amount and expedite the order. Undecided and need some assistance? Visit Golden Valley's website, where you'll find tips on lighting, selecting fixtures, conserving energy, and making the most of your home lighting.

Special Factors: Price quote by phone or letter with self-addressed, stamped envelope.

KING'S CHANDELIER CO.

P.O. BOX 667, DEPT.
   WBM99
EDEN, NC 27289–0667
336–623–6188
FAX: 336–627–9935

Catalog: $5, $8 outside U.S.
Pay: check, MO, MC, V
Sells: Czech, Venetian, and Strass crystal chandeliers
Store: 729 S. Van Buren Rd. (Hwy. 14), Eden, NC; Monday to Saturday 10–4:30
E-mail: crystal@vnet.net
Online: http://www.chandelier.com

The Kings have been designing and producing chandeliers since 1935 and offer their designs through their catalog of light fixtures to suit every taste, at prices for every budget. There are chandeliers, candelabras, and wall sconces in a range of styles. They offer Victorian gas light reproductions made of hand-polished brass and Venetian crystal trimmings, as well as many variations on the classic chandelier dripping with pendants and ropes of crystal buttons. Many of the models use the brilliant Swarovski Strass trimmings. Prices begin at about $200 for a small chandelier and go up to $12,500 for the palatial Strass Royal Belvedere. Because each fixture is made to order, options are available. Replacement parts for these lighting fixtures are stocked as well.

Since even the 40-page catalog can't show the chandeliers to their best advantage, King's will create a videotape of the lighting fixtures that interest you—preferably not more than six models. The VHS tapes are available for $20.

Wholesale buyers, please note: King's Chandelier extends a 15% discount (on regular catalog prices) to designers, decorators, and contractors.

Special Factors: Satisfaction is guaranteed; returns are accepted within 15 days for refund or credit.

LUIGI CRYSTAL

7332 FRANKFORD AVE.
PHILADELPHIA, PA 19136
215–338–2978

Catalog: $2, refundable
Pay: check, MO, MC, V, AE, Discover
Sells: crystal lighting fixtures
Store: same address; Monday to Friday
9–5:30, Saturday 10–4

Luigi Crystal may be located in the land of Main Liners, but its heart belongs to Tara. Luigi has been creating crystal lighting fixtures since 1935, and the prices are surprisingly low—under $200 for a full-sized chandelier, for example. The 44-page catalog shows each candelabra, chandelier, sconce, and hurricane lamp in black-and-white photographs. Many of the styles are formal and ornate, heavily hung with prisms and pendalogues and set in marble or faceted crystal bases. Several lamps feature globe shades, gold cupid bases, "Aurora" crystal prism shades, and even stained glass. At the other end of the spectrum are simple "Williamsburg chimney lamps" for under $50 a pair and several graceful five-arm chandeliers.

If you're searching for replacement parts for your own fixtures, see the catalog for glass chimneys, bobeches, strung button prisms, drop prisms in several styles (3" to 8" long), and pendalogues. In addition to those models, Luigi's workshops can produce designs to your specifications; call or write to discuss details and prices.

Special Factors: The minimum order on goods sent outside the United States and Canada is $1,000.

MAIN LAMP/LAMP WAREHOUSE

1073 39TH ST.
BROOKLYN, NY 11219
718–436–8500
FAX: 718–438–6836

Information: price quote
Pay: check, MO, MC, V, AE, Discover
Sells: lighting fixtures and ceiling fans
Store: same address; Monday, Tuesday, and Friday 9–5:30, Thursday 9–8, Saturday and Sunday 10–5

Main Lamp/Lamp Warehouse, established in 1954, is noted for its comprehensive inventory of better-quality lamps, lighting fixtures, and ceiling fans, all sold at everyday discounts of up to 50%. Call, fax, or write for prices on lighting fixtures by Corbett, Framburg, Kichler, Nulco, and World Imports. Fredrick Cooper, Crystal Clear, George Kovacs, Lenox, and Stiffel are among the premium lines available. Ceiling fans by Casablanca, Craftmade, Emerson, and other firms are also stocked.

Please note: There is no catalog.

Special Factors: Price quote by phone or letter with a stamped, self-addressed envelope; store is closed Wednesdays; minimum order is $100.

RELATED PRODUCTS/COMPANIES

Kerosene lanterns • West Marine, Campmor
Lamp parts and lamp-making supplies • Warner-Crivellaro, Axner Pottery, Aftosa, Bailey Ceramic, Texas Art Supply, Circle Craft, Glass Crafters
Lamp switch enlargers • Comfort House
Lamps and lighting • The Furniture Patch of Calabash, Clegg's Handyman Supply, Blackwelder's, Carolina Interiors, Priba, Southland, Wicker Warehouse, Tender Heart Treasures, Fran's Wicker & Rattan, Heirloom Reproductions
Lava lamps • Sportsman's Guide
Lighting and electrical supplies • Clegg's Handyman Supply, All Electronics
Magnifying lamps and special lamps for the visually impaired • Damark, Comfort House, Independent Living Aids
Party lights and lights on a string • La Piñata, Sally Distributors
Soccer-themed lamps • Soccer International
Themed lamps for pool and billiards game rooms • Mueller Sporting Goods

Tableware—Flatware, Glassware, and China

Silverware and stainless steel flatware, everyday glasses and crystal, fine and everyday china, serving pieces, and related goods

Buying active patterns of tableware is as easy as picking up the phone and calling one of the discounters listed here. But if your china, crystal, or silver pattern is discontinued, you'll need a replacement specialist. Several firms listed here sell discontinued silver flatware (also called "estate" silver). If you're missing pieces of a china or crystal pattern, write to Replacements, Ltd., 302 Gallimore Dairy Rd., Greensboro, NC 27400–9723, or call 910–275–7224. Replacements has over 250,000 pieces in stock and can help you identify your pattern if you're not sure of the name. The China Connection is another source for discontinued china patterns, by such manufacturers as Castleton, Haviland, Lenox, and Noritake. Send details on the maker, pattern, and piece you're trying to match to The China Connection, 329 Main St., P.O. Box 972, Pineville, NC 28134; or call 704–889–8197.

FIND IT FAST

CHINA AND OTHER DISHWARE • Barrons, Michael C. Fina, Jamar, Lanac, Marks China and Glass, Mikasa Outlet, Rogers & Rosenthal, Rudi's Pottery, Nat Schwartz, Albert S. Smyth
CREAMWARE • Alberene Royal Mail
CRYSTAL • Alberene Royal Mail, Michael C. Fina, Jamar, Marks China and Glass,

Mikasa Outlet, Rogers & Rosenthal, Nat Schwartz, Albert S. Smyth
CUSTOM ENGRAVING • Michael C. Fina, Lanac, Nat Schwartz
ESTATE STERLING • Beverly Bremer, Coinways, Meierotto's MidweSterling, The Silver Queen
FLATWARE • Barrons, Beverly Bremer, Coinways, Michael C. Fina, Jamar, Kaiser Crow, Lanac, Meierotto's MidweSterling, Mikasa Outlet, Rogers & Rosenthal, Rudi's Pottery, Nat Schwartz, The Silver Queen

---

ALBERENE ROYAL MAIL

P.O. BOX 902, CENTER VILLAGE
HARRISVILLE, NH 03450
800–843–9078
603–827–5512

Price List: free
Pay: check, MO, MC, V, AE, Discover
Sells: Creamware, Edinburgh crystal, misc. Scottish foods, videos, music, etc.
Store: showroom at 435 Fifth Ave., 3rd Floor, New York, NY (between 38th & 39th Streets)

Perhaps this company should be called "Everything Scottish." You'll find terrific deals on wonderful Creamware here, that ivory-colored earthenware that looks as though it's been crocheted around the edges, popularized by Wedgwood a century ago and more recently by such upscale yard-salers as Martha Stewart. Alberene pares up to 35% off the going rate, making these pretty pieces affordable. They also carry Edinburgh crystal—the largest selection of Thistle outside of Britain—at 25% to 35% lower than elsewhere. There's more, although for the following items you'll pay about what you would in a store (if you could find them!): teas by Brodies of Edinburgh, Wallace Scotch Whisky Cake, preserves, honey, fudge (all Scottish, of course), Scottish pub glasses, Scottish books, videos, music CDs and cassettes, and even fantastic true-to-life miniatures of European architectural treasures by Fraser Creations, including Stonehenge, Westminster Abbey, and the Anne Hathaway Cottage. Best of all, Alberene doesn't charge shipping to addresses within the U.S., which saves you even more.

Special Factors: Satisfaction is guaranteed; returns are accepted for exchange, refund, or credit.

BARRONS

P.O. BOX 994
NOVI, MI 48376–0994
800–538–6340
FAX: 800–523–4456

Catalog: free
Pay: check, MO, MC, V, Discover
Sells: dinnerware, giftware, and home accessories
Store: mail order only
E-mail: barronsdw@aol.com

Barrons has been selling fine tableware since 1975 and offers savings of up to 65% on the list prices of china, crystal, flatware, and gifts, and stocks over 1,500 patterns. Past catalogs have showcased popular lines of china from Block, Fitz & Floyd, Franciscan, Gorham, Hutschenreuther, Johnson Brothers, Lenox, Mikasa, Minton, Nikko, Noritake, Royal Albert, Royal Doulton, Royal Worcester, Spode, Waterford, and Wedgwood. Crystal from Atlantis, Gorham, Lenox, and Mikasa is offered, and you can save on stainless steel, silverplate, and sterling flatware from Dansk, Gorham, International, Kirk-Stieff, Lunt, Mikasa, Oneida, Reed & Barton, Towle, Wallace, and Yamazaki. Royal Doulton figurines, Gorham crystal gifts, Towle silver serving pieces, and other collectibles and accessories are also sold at a discount.

Special Factors: Satisfaction is guaranteed; returns are accepted within 30 days for exchange, refund, or credit.

BEVERLY BREMER SILVER SHOP

3164 PEACHTREE RD., NE,
   DEPT. WBMC
ATLANTA, GA 30305
800–270–4009
404–261–4009
FAX: 404–261–9708

Information: inquire (see text)
Pay: check, MO, MC, V, Discover
Sells: new and estate sterling flatware, hollowware, gifts, etc.
Store: same address; Monday to Saturday 10–5

Beverly Bremer herself presides over this shop, which has an astounding inventory of American and Continental sterling, from new flatware to old loving cups. "The store with the silver lining," which opened in

1975, is worth a detour if you're traveling anywhere around Atlanta. But if you can't get there, call or write with your needs—Beverly Bremer does nearly half her business by mail and is now completely computerized (request a current list of your flatware pattern).

The briskest trade here is done in supplying missing pieces of sterling silverware in new, discontinued, and hard-to-find patterns. The brands represented include Buccellati, Gorham, International, Jensen, Kirk-Stieff, Lunt, Odiot, Old Newbury Crafters, Oneida, Reed & Barton, Schofield, Frank Smith, State House, Tiffany, Towle, Tuttle, Wallace, Westmoreland, and other firms. If you know the pattern name, call to see whether the piece you want is in stock; you can also send a photocopy of both sides of a sample piece if you're unsure of the pattern. Beverly Bremer will send you a printout of the available pieces in your pattern and a brochure profiling that company.

Although the shop's specialty is flatware, the shelves and cases sparkle with vases, epergnes, picture frames, candlesticks, jewelry, christening cups, thimbles, and other treasures. Silver collectors should note that over 1,000 patterns are carried in stock here, "beautiful as new," and Ms. Bremer says that, unless noted, there are no monograms on the old silver. (She doesn't sell silver on which monograms have been removed, either.) She recommends against resilvering old silverplate as "not a wise use of your money," and she notes that sterling holds its value over time. How many other investments can do that—and enhance your dinner table as well!

Special Factors: Sterling silver pieces are bought; appraisals are performed; complete customer satisfaction guaranteed.

COINWAYS/ANTIQUES LTD.

**475 CENTRAL AVE.
CEDARHURST, NY 11516
800–645–2102
516–374–1970
FAX: 516–374–3218**

Information: price quote
Pay: check, MO, MC, V, AE, Discover
Sells: new and used sterling flatware
Store: same address; Monday to Friday 10:30–5:30, Wednesday 10:30–7:30, Saturday 11–5

Coinways/Antiques Ltd. should be on your list of firms to call when the garbage disposal claims one of your good teaspoons—especially if it's one from an old set or a discontinued pattern. Coinways, which has been in business since 1979, sells both new and used ("estate") sterling flatware, by the piece or in full sets.

You'll save up to 75% on the suggested retail or market prices of silver manufactured by Alvin, Amston, Dominick & Haff, Durgin, Easterling, Gorham, International, Kirk-Stieff, Lunt, Manchester, National, Oneida, Reed & Barton, Royal Crest, State House, Tiffany, Towle, Tuttle, Wallace, Westmoreland, F.M. Whiting, and other firms. If you're replacing a piece in an old pattern that's still active, try to find a piece of the same vintage. (Over the years, some manufacturers have reduced the amount of silver they use in each piece, so that a fork made today will be lighter and feel less substantial than the same piece, circa 1930.) If you write to Coinways for a quote, note the name of the piece, its length and shape, and include a photocopy of the design if you don't know the pattern name.

Special Factors: Orders are shipped worldwide.

MICHAEL C. FINA

545 FIFTH AVE.
NEW YORK, NY 10017
800–BUY–FINA
718–937–8484
FAX: 718–937–7193

Catalog: free
Pay: check, MO, MC, V, AE, Discover
Sells: jewelry, tableware, and giftware
Store: 3 W. 47th St., New York, NY; Monday to Friday 9:30–6, Thursday 9:30–7, Saturday 10:30–6

 ¡Si!

Michael C. Fina, which has been in business since 1935, is known to New Yorkers for great prices on jewelry. Fina also offers an impressive line of tableware, including china by Aynsley, Ceralene Raynaud Limoges, Lynn Chase, Christofle, Dansk, Denby, Phillippe Deshoulieres, Franciscan, Richard Ginori, Gorham, Haviland Limoges, Johnson Brothers, Lalique, Lenox, Mikasa, Minton, Mottahedeh, Noritake, Pickard, Portmeirion, Rosenthal, Royal Copenhagen, Royal Crown Derby, Royal Doulton, Royal Worcester, Sasaki, Spode, Thomas, Versace, Villeroy & Boch, and Wedgwood. Crystal stemware from Atlantis, Baccarat, Christofle, Gorham, Kosta Boda, Lalique, Lenox, Miller Rogaska, Noritake, Orrefors, Riedel, Royal Doulton, St. Louis, Sasaki, Stuart, and Waterford (including Marquis) is available. Fina also sells flatware from Christofle, Jean Couzon, Cuisinart, Dansk, Gorham, International, Georg Jensen, Kirk-Stieff, Ralph Lauren, Lunt, Mikasa, Oneida, Puiforcat, Reed & Barton, Retroneau, Towle, Wallace, and Yamazaki. Sterling silver baby gifts, picture frames, stainless steel and silverplate giftware, and estate pieces are usually available. Fina maintains a bridal registry and employs sales reps fluent in French, Italian, and Russian, as well as Spanish.

Special Factors: Satisfaction is guaranteed; returns (except engraved or personalized items) are accepted within three weeks for exchange, refund, or credit.

JAMAR SILVERWARE AND CHINA

1714 SHEEPSHEAD BAY
  RD.
BROOKLYN, NY 11235
888–722–2238
718–615–2222
FAX: 718–615–2224

Information: price quote
Pay: check, MO, MC, V, Discover
Sells: china, silver, crystal
Store: same address; Tuesday to Saturday 11–5:30

Jamar has been in business since 1952 and offers the best names in china, crystal, and silver, as well as gifts and collectibles. If you know the patterns and pieces you're looking for, you can call for a quote; Jamar doesn't have a catalog but will beat any other advertised price.

Special Factors: Price quote by phone or letter; store is closed Mondays.

KAISER CROW, INC.

14998 W. SIXTH AVE., #500
GOLDEN, CO 80401
800–468–2769
303–215–1111
FAX: 303–215–1115

Brochure: free
Pay: check, MO, MC, V, AE, Discover
Sells: Oneida stainless flatware
Store: mail order only

Kaiser Crow has been in business since 1985 and sells Oneida stainless-steel flatware at discounts of up to 57%. They guarantee that their price is lowest. The brochure illustrates the choices, and all of the goods are first-quality. Call or write for a price quote if you don't see what you're looking for. Details of the Oneida warranty are available upon request.

Special Factors: Satisfaction is guaranteed; returns are accepted within 60 days.

LANAC SALES COMPANY

500 DRIGGS AVENUE
BROOKLYN, NY 11211
718–782–7200
FAX: 718–782–1313

Catalog: free
Pay: check, MO, MC, V, AE, Discover
Sells: fine tableware, home accents, jewelry, and engraving
Store: call for new location

You can send for the 40-page catalog from Lanac Sales to see the selection of gifts and home accents: Limoges hinged boxes, MontBlanc pens, art-glass perfume bottles, fine jewelry, and figurines and collectibles by Guiseppe Armani, Belleek, Fitz & Floyd, Lenox, Lladró, and Royal Doulton, among others. There's a nice collection of home accents and entertaining accessories in the current issue—barware, snifters, decanters, vases, crystal giftware, silver tea services—and even select kitchen equipment, such as Cuisinart coffeemakers and food processors, Omega juicers, Henckels knives, cappuccino machines, and more—all sold at a discount.

But Lanac Sales has built four decades of business on the fundamentals of the formal dining table: china, crystal, and silver. Lanac offers everything from stoneware to porcelain by Aynsley, Bernardaud Limoges, Ceralene Limoges, Fitz & Floyd, Richard Ginori, Gorham, Haviland Limoges, Hutschenreuther, Ralph Lauren, Lenox, Mikasa, Muirfield, Nikko, Noritake, Packard, Swid Powell, Rosenthal, Royal Albert, Royal Doulton, Royal Worcester, Spode, Villeroy & Boch, and Wedgwood. Browse the catalog or call for prices on stainless, plate, and sterling silver from Jean Couzon, Cuisinart, Dansk, W.M. Fraser, Gorham, International, Kirk-Stieff, Lenox, Lunt, Reed & Barton, Retroneau, Sasaki, Towle, Tuttle, and Wallace. And crystal stemware is available from Atlantis, Baccarat, Ceska, Edinburgh, Gorham, Kosta Boda, Ralph Lauren, Lenox, Mikasa, Miller Rogaska, Orrefors, Swid Powell, Rosenthal, Royal Doulton, St. Louis, Stuart, Villeroy & Boch, and Waterford. Savings run up to 65% on suggested retail, and Lanac provides bridal registry services and sells a full line of storage cases to protect your service when it's not in use.

Special Factors: Satisfaction is guaranteed; price quote by phone or letter; custom engraving available.

MARKS CHINA AND GLASS

315 FRANKLIN AVE.
WYCKOFF, NJ 07481–2053
800–862–7578
201–891–0422

Information: price quote
Pay: check, MO, MC, V, Discover
Sells: tableware and giftware
Store: same address; Monday to Thursday 11–8, Friday 10–4, Sunday 11–5, closed Saturday

Set your table for less at Marks, where open stock china is sold at good prices, and "satisfaction is a must." Marks carries the major names, including Aynsley, Bernardaud Limoges, Block Gorham, Hutschenreuther, Lenox, Mikasa, Noritake, Oneida, Pickard, Reed & Barton, Royal Doulton, Sasaki, Spode, Towle, Villeroy & Boch, Wallace, Wedgwood, and Yamazaki, among others. Call the store during business hours with the name of the pattern and the piece you need for a price quote. Marks maintains a bridal registry and can special order settings not in stock, so inquire if you need these services.

Special Factors: Satisfaction is guaranteed; price quote by phone or letter with self-addressed, stamped envelope only; returns (except special orders) are accepted within 14 days for exchange, refund, or credit.

MEIEROTTO'S MIDWESTERLING

4311 NE VIVION RD.,
DEPT. WBMC
KANSAS CITY, MO
64119–2890
816–454–1990
FAX: 816–454–1605

Information: inquire
Pay: check, MO, MC, V
Sells: replacement sterling flatware
Store: same address; Monday to Saturday 10–6 (closed Wednesday and Sunday)
E-mail: sterling@kcnet.com
Online: http://www.kcnet.com/sterling

Meierotto's MidweSterling is home to over half a million pieces of silverware, in both discontinued and current patterns. (Dirilyte, new silverplate and stainless flatware, china, crystal, and giftware are also sold.) Meierotto's offers a lowest-price guarantee on the flatware, maintains a bridal registry, and accepts layaways (20% down). Send a long, stamped, self-addressed envelope for a price-quote form, which includes a guide to standard flatware shapes and sizes. If what you want isn't in stock, Meierotto's will search for it. The firm also buys used silver (inquire for information) and performs silverware repairs and knife reblading. And if you're in the Kansas City vicinity, be sure to drop in—Meierotto's runs "the busiest jewelry store" in the city, doing a big trade in everything from diamonds to watches (Bertolucci, Charriol, Concord, Movado, Omega, Patek Philippe, Piaget, Rado, Sector, Tissot, Raymond Weil, etc.).

Special Factors: Satisfaction is guaranteed; price quote by phone, fax, or letter; layaway orders are accepted (20% deposit).

MIKASA OUTLET STORE

25 ENTERPRISE AVE.
SECAUCUS, NJ 07096
201–867–3517

Information: inquire (see text)
Pay: check, MO, MC, V, AE, Discover
Sells: Mikasa tableware and gifts
Store: same address; Monday to Saturday 10–6, Thursday 10–9, Sunday 11–6

¡Si!

Mikasa strikes the balance between fashion-forward style and affordability in china, crystal, flatware, and gifts. Although some of Mikasa's most popular china patterns feature flowers and abstract geometrics rimming the plates and banding the cups, the full range includes much more sedate, traditional designs. The flatware and crystal patterns complement the selection and are also mid-priced for upper-end table settings.

The Mikasa store sells both first-quality Mikasa tableware at a discount and has a clearance room with seconds and discontinued patterns. If you can't visit, call with the pattern name, name of the piece (white wine goblet, dinner knife, dessert plate, etc.), and the quantity you'd like to buy. If it's in stock or can be obtained, you'll receive a price quote and shipping estimate. Don't delay in ordering, especially if the pattern or piece has been discontinued, because stock moves quickly here.

Special Factors: Authorized returns are accepted for exchange, refund, or credit.

ROGERS & ROSENTHAL, INC.

**Information:** price quote
**Pay:** check or MO
**Sells:** tableware
**Store:** mail order only

2337 LEMOINE AVE.,
   SUITE 101
FORT LEE, NJ 07024–0212
201–346–1862
FAX: 201–947–5812

Rogers and Rosenthal, two old names in the silver and china trade, represent the business of this firm: the best in table settings at up to 60% below list prices. Rogers & Rosenthal has been in business since 1930, selling flatware (stainless, plate, and sterling) by top manufacturers. The brands include Fraser, Gerber, Gorham, International, Jensen, Kirk-Stieff, Lauffer, Lunt, Oneida, Reed & Barton, Sasaki, Frank Smith, Supreme, Towle, Tuttle, Wallace, and Yamazaki. There are china and crystal lines by Aynsley, Bernardaud Limoges, Block, Coalport, Franciscan, Gorham, Hutschenreuther, Lauffer, Lenox, Mikasa, Noritake, Pickard, Portmeirion, Rosenthal, Royal Copenhagen, Royal Doulton, Royal Worcester, Spode, and Wedgwood. Silver baby gifts, Lladró and other figurines, and pewter hollowware are also stocked. Please write or call for a price quote—there is no catalog.

Canadian readers, please note: Only special orders are shipped to Canada.

**Special Factors:** Price quote by phone or letter with self-addressed, stamped envelope; returns are accepted for exchange.

RUDI'S POTTERY, SILVER & CHINA

180 RT. 17 NORTH
PARAMUS, NJ 07652
800–631–2526
201–265–6096
FAX: 201–265–2086

Information: price quote
Pay: check, MO, MC, V, Discover
Sells: tableware
Store: same address and 357 Rt. 9 S., Manalapan, NJ; Monday to Saturday 10–5:30

Rudi's has been in business since 1968 and, in the intervening years, has expanded the firm's stock to include some of the finest goods available at savings of up to 60% on list. China, crystal, and flatware are stocked here; the silverware brands include Gorham, International, Kirk-Stieff, Lunt, Reed & Barton, Towle, Tuttle, and Wallace. Rudi's china dinnerware and crystal stemware lines include Arzberg, Baccarat, Belleek, Bernardaud Limoges, Coalport, Fitz & Floyd, Galway, Gorham, Kosta Boda, Lalique, Lenox, Mikasa, Minton, Noritake, Orrefors, Rosenthal, Royal Copenhagen, Royal Doulton, Royal Worcester, Sasaki, Spode, Stuart, Wedgwood, and Yamazaki. Rudi's also offers limited-edition Christmas ornaments and collectibles issued by a number of the same manufacturers. Call or write for a price quote on your pattern, suite, or limited-issue collectible.

Special Factors: Price quote by phone or letter with self-addressed, stamped envelope.

NAT SCHWARTZ & CO., INC.

549 BROADWAY, DEPT.
 LIB18
BAYONNE, NJ 07002
800–526–1440
FAX: 201–437–4903

Catalog: free
Pay: check, MO, MC, V, AE, Discover
Sells: tableware, giftware, and housewares
Store: same address; Monday to Friday 9:30–6, Thursday 9:30–8, Saturday 10–5

Nat Schwartz & Co., established in 1967, publishes a 32-page catalog filled with fine china, crystal, flatware, housewares, and gifts that represent just a fraction of the firm's inventory. Schwartz's china and giftware department offers Arzberg, Aynsley, Belleek, Bernardaud, Bing & Grøndahl, Block, Edward Marshall Boehm, A. Raynaud (Ceralene) Limoges, Lynn Chase Designs, Dansk, Denby, Philippe Deshoulieres, Christian Dior, Fabergé, Fitz & Floyd, Franciscan, Gien Limoges, Ginori, Haviland Limoges, Hermes, Hummel, Hutschenreuther, Johnson Brothers, Ralph Lauren, Lenox, Lladró, Mikasa, Minton, Mottahedeh, Muirfield, Nikko, Noritake, Pickard, Portmeirion, Swid Powell, Rosenthal, Royal Copenhagen, Royal Crown Derby, Royal Doulton, Royal Worcester, Sasaki, Spode, Thomas, Villeroy & Boch, Vista Alegre, Wedgwood, and other firms. Crystal suites and gifts by Atlantis, Baccarat, Ceska, Daum, Da Vinci, Christian Dior, Fabergé, Galway, Gorham, Ralph Lauren, Lenox, Miller Rogaska, Noritake, Swid Powell, Rosenthal, Royal Doulton, St. Louis, Sasaki, Stuart, Tipperary, Val. St. Lambert, and Waterford are available, among others. Also featured are flatware and hollowware by Baldwin Brass, Boda Nova, Buccellati, Jean Couzon, Cuisinart, Dansk, Empire, W.M.F. Fraser, Gorham, International, Kirk-Stieff, Ralph Lauren, Lunt, Nambé & Nambé Studio, Oneida, Swid Powell, Reed & Barton, Retroneau, Ricci, Sambonet, Sheffield, Towle, Tuttle, Wallace, Wilton Armetale, and Yamazaki. Among the housewares lines are Braun, Calphalon, Le Creuset, Cuisinart, J.A. Henckels, KitchenAid, Krups, Sabatier, Waring Professional, and Wüsthof-Trident. Schwartz provides a number of valuable services, including coordination of silver, crystal, and china patterns, gift and bridal registry, and a corporate gift program. Gift wrapping is offered at no extra charge, and hand engraving is now available. You can send for the catalog, or call for a price quote.

Special Factors: Satisfaction is guaranteed; price quote by phone, fax, or letter; special orders are accepted with a nonrefundable 20% deposit (unless the order is canceled while still on back order); undamaged returns (except engraved items) are accepted within 30 days (a restocking fee may be charged).

THE SILVER QUEEN INC.

730 N. INDIAN ROCKS RD.
BELLEAIR BLUFFS, FL
  33770
813–581–6827
FAX: 813–586–0822

Brochure: free
Pay: check, MO, MC, V, AE, Discover
Sells: new and estate silver flatware
Store: same address; Monday to Friday 9–5,
Saturday 9:30–5
Online: http://www.silverqueen.com

The Silver Queen publishes a brochure with clear color photos of scores of popular sterling flatware patterns, from manufacturers that include Alvin, Buccellati, Frank Smith, Gorham, International, Georg Jensen, Kirk-Stieff, Lunt, Oneida, Reed & Barton, Towle, Tuttle, Wallace, and Westmoreland. The Silver Queen has been in business since 1972 and will quote prices on the pieces of your choice, at an average of 30% or more off list. You can call without getting the brochure if you're shopping for a pattern still in production, or an exact replacement for an old design (estate silver is available). But do get the brochure if you don't have a guide to your pattern: It has six pages of pictures of specialty pieces—mustard ladles, lemon forks, berry spoons, etc.—and provides an excellent visual guide to the relative shapes and sizes.

Special Factors: Price quote by phone or letter.

ALBERT S. SMYTH CO., INC.

29 GREENMEADOW DR.,
  DEPT. WM99
TIMONIUM, MD 21093
800–638–3333
410–252–6666
FAX: 410–252–2355

Catalog: free
Pay: check, MO, MC, V, AE, Discover
Sells: tableware, giftware, and jewelry
Store: same address; Monday to Saturday
9–5, Thursday 9–9

All that gleams and glitters can be found at Smyth, at savings of up to 50% on comparable retail and list prices. Smyth has been doing business since 1914 and publishes a 24-page color catalog that features a wide range of jewelry. Diamonds, strands of semiprecious beads, colored stone jewelry, and pearls are shown, as well as watches by Concord, Movado, Omega, Rado, Seiko, and Tag Heuer. Pens by MontBlanc, Parker, and Waterman are available, as well as things such as mahogany jewelry chests. Tableware and home decorative accents are sold here at impressive savings, including such items as Baldwin brassware, Waterford giftware, fine picture frames, and gifts from Kirk-Stieff and Virginia Metalcrafters. You'll find pewter candlesticks, coffee sets, punch bowls, and place settings by Aynsley, Gorham, Kirk-Stieff, Lenox, Noritake, Reed & Barton, Royal Doulton, Spode, Towle, Villeroy & Boch, Wallace, Waterford, and Wedgwood among the offerings.

Smyth maintains a bridal registry and provides gift consultations and a gift-forwarding service. The catalog shows a fraction of the inventory, so write or call for a price quote if you don't see what you're looking for.

Special Factors: Satisfaction is guaranteed; returns (except personalized and custom-ordered goods) are accepted within 30 days.

RELATED PRODUCTS/COMPANIES

Acrylic glassware for boating • M & E Marine
Everyday china • Kitchen Etc., Peerless
Fine china • Kitchen Etc., Bennett Brothers
Glassware • Stumps, Peerless
Mexican tableware • Pendery's
Miscellaneous tableware • Broadway Panhandler, Peerless
Pewterware • Bennett Brothers
Plastic and paper tableware for catering and entertaining • U.S. Toy, M&N International, The Party Wholesaler
Serving pieces • Kitchen Etc.
Silverware • Bennett Brothers
Stainless steel flatware • Damark
Stoneware • Caprilands Herb Farm
Wooden tableware • Weston Bowl Mill

Wall and Window Treatments, Decorator Fabrics

Wallpaper, wall stencils, wall fabrics;

curtains, shades, blinds, and window

accessories; upholstery, drapery, and other

interior decorating fabric

The companies in this section carry all the fabrics and materials to create ruffles, patterns, and pleats to decorate interior windows and walls, furniture, and other accessories in your home—at savings that reach 75%. If you're handy with needle and thread, or have a creative eye for designing interiors and pulling a room together, take advantage of the products and materials here and get busy!

FIND IT FAST

DECORATOR FABRICS AND TRIM • BMI Home Decorating, The Fabric Center, Hancock's of Paducah, Hang-It-Now Wallpaper, Harmony Supply, Homespun Fabrics & Draperies, Marlene's, Robinson's Wallpaper, Shama Imports, Silk Surplus
DECORATOR STENCILS • Stencil House of N.H.
HAND-EMBROIDERED CREWEL FABRICS • Shama Imports
WALL COVERINGS AND RELATED SUPPLIES • BMI Home Decorating, Hang-It-Now Wallpaper, Harmony Supply, Robinson's Wallpaper
WINDOW TREATMENTS AND HARDWARE • BMI Home Decorating, Harmony Supply, Homespun Fabrics & Draperies, Wells Interiors

BMI HOME DECORATING

Information: price quote
Pay: check, MO, MC, V, AE
Sells: decorator fabric, wall coverings, window treatments, etc.
Store: mail order only

6917 CATALPA CT.
SPRING GROVE, IL 60081
815–675–3703
FAX: 815–675–3603

BMI Home Decorating can give you access to "almost all fabrics," from names that are "too many to list" but number over 200, including many that are usually limited to the trade. In addition to fabric, BMI offers wall coverings and drapery hardware and can fabricate pillows, bedspreads, and headboards to order. The firm has been in business since 1978 and can offer customers savings of 35% or more on suggested list prices, depending on the item, amount ordered, and other criteria. When you call for a price quote, be sure you know the brand name, style and/or number, and book name (for wall coverings).

Special Factors: Price quote by phone or letter.

THE FABRIC CENTER

Catalog: $3
Pay: check, MO, MC, V, Discover
Sells: interior decorator fabrics
Store: mail order only

485 ELECTRIC AVE.,
DEPT. WBMC
FITCHBURG, MA 01420
978–343–4402
FAX: 978–343–8139

 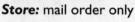

The Fabric Center has been in business since 1932, selling fine fabrics for home decorating at savings of up to 50% on suggested list prices. Fabrics for upholstery and window treatments are available, including lines from Robert Allen, American Textile, Paul Barrow, Covington, George Harrington, Kravet, Peachtree, Waverly, and many others. The firm's splendid 164-page color catalog shows more fabrics than you'd find in most stores—thousands from a wide range of manufacturers, photographed in room settings and grouped with complementary patterns and colorways. The catalog descriptions include fiber content, width, vertical repeat, and a usage code to help you determine if the material is appropriate for draperies, home accessories, or upholstery. And The Fabric Center's "Sampling Service" allows you to try the fabric in your home before you order. The 3" by 4" samples cost 15 cents, the 8" by 10" pieces are 50 cents, and 24" by 27" samples cost $3.95 each. (The price of each $3.95 sample can be credited to each $50 in goods ordered.) Don't miss the scores of trim—tassels, bullion fringe, cording, brush fringe, tiebacks, and more—in colors chosen to complement the widest decorative range.

Special Factors: Minimum order is 1 yard.

HANCOCK'S OF PADUCAH

3841 HINKLEVILLE RD.,
    DEPT. WBMC
PADUCAH, KY 42001
800–845–8723
502–443–4410
FAX: 502–442–2164, 3152

Catalog: $2, refundable (see text)
Pay: check, MO, MC, V, Discover
Sells: home-decorating fabrics, quilting fabrics, pillow forms, quilting supplies, etc.
Store: same address; Monday to Friday 9:30–7, Saturday 10–6, Sunday 1–5
E-mail: hanpad@sunsix.infi.net
Online: http://www.hancocks-paducah.com

You might not expect "America's Largest Fabric Store" to be in Paducah, Kentucky, but the folks at Hancock's will enlighten you. They've pulled together a 64-page color catalog of the best-sellers on the retail floor there, hundreds of upholstery and drapery fabrics that represent the most popular looks in decorating today, from traditional to eclectic design. And they sell them at prices 50% to 70% below suggested retail.

The catalog includes a color shot of the fabric, the name of the design (but not the maker), and the price per yard; width, fiber content, and repeat information are not given consistently. But if you've been going through the shelter magazines and swatch books, you'll recognize much of what you see—except the prices. To be sure, avail yourself of Hancock's sampling service: 12" squares for 75 cents, or 2" by 4" cuttings free upon request. If you're looking for a good selection of solid colors, see the choice of chintzes, warped sateen, jacquards, and other offerings. You'll also find bedding ensembles, cords, tassels, fringes, drapery hardware, fusible backing for roller shades, heavy felt—in short, everything you'll need to transform your rooms into stylish masterpieces. Hancock's will do custom lamination for under $6 a yard (great for patio furniture and tablecloths).

Hancock's separate catalog for quilters ($1) is 76 pages of notions, tools and equipment, materials, a variety of quilt batts, thread, and more. You'll find quilters' collections of fabric by Benartex, Moda, Hoffman, Pat Campbell, Jennifer Sampou, and others; a broad selection of interfacing; basic fabrics (from bridal satin to heavy canvas); and sewing and quilting products by the top-name companies.

Savings on list average 60% plus, and you can join the Hancock's swatch club for quilting or home fabrics, and receive a batch of snippets of Hancock's newest fabrics every month (see the catalogs for details).

Special Factors: Price quote by phone or letter; all goods are first quality; special orders are accepted.

HANG-IT-NOW WALLPAPER STORE

304 TRINDALE RD.
ARCHDALE, NC 27263
336–431–6341
FAX: 336–431–0449

Information: price quote
Pay: check, MO, MC, V, AE, Discover
Sells: wall coverings and decorator fabrics
Store: same address; also 4620 W. Market St., Greensboro, NC; Monday to Friday 9–6, Saturday 9–3, both locations

Hang-It-Now Wallpaper, established in 1981, sells wall coverings at savings of 30% to 65% on list prices. A limited selection of decorator fabrics is also available, at discounts of up to 40%. All major brands of wall coverings (plus strings, grass cloth, and borders) are offered here, including Color House, Crutchfield, Eisenhart, Fashion, Imperial, Katzenbach and Warren, Carey Lind, Sanitas, Seabrook, Sunworthy, United, Van Luit, Warner, and York, among others. Hang-It-Now specializes in providing wall coverings to retail establishments and has done numerous installations for furniture retailers and decorators.

Special Factors: Only first-quality goods are sold.

HARMONY SUPPLY INC.

P.O. BOX 313
MEDFORD, MA 02155
781–395–2600
FAX: 781–396–8218

Information: price quote
Pay: check, MO, MC, V, Discover
Sells: wall coverings, window treatments, and decorator fabrics
Store: 18 High St., Medford, MA; Monday to Saturday 8–5:30, Thursday 8–9

Harmony Supply, in business since 1949, can give your home a face-lift at a discount with savings of up to 70% on wallpaper, coordinating fabrics, and window treatments. Harmony carries over 2,500 designs and patterns of wallpaper, grass cloth, and string cloth, including Laura Ashley, Imperial, Katzenbach and Warren, Ralph Lauren, Sunworthy, Van Luit, and many others. Harmony Supply also sells window treatments—made-to-measure mini, micro, and vertical blinds, including wood, and pleated shades and blinds (Duette, Crystal Pleat, Silhouette, etc.) manufactured by Graber, HunterDouglas, and others. You'll save the most on goods that are currently in stock, but even special orders are discounted up to 70%, and everything Harmony sells is first quality. Call or write for a price quote, since there's no catalog or price list.

Special Factors: Satisfaction is guaranteed; returns (except custom blinds and fabrics) are accepted within 30 days (a 25% restocking fee is charged on special-order goods).

HOMESPUN FABRICS & DRAPERIES

P.O. BOX 4315-WBM
THOUSAND OAKS, CA
91359
FAX: 888–543–2998

Price List and Samples: $2
Pay: check, MO, MC, V, AE
Sells: 10' wide fabrics, custom-made draperies, etc.
Store: mail order only
E-mail: widefabric@aol.com

Homespun "10-Foot Wide" Fabrics & Draperies has a solution to some of the biggest drapery headaches—bulkiness, sun rot, the expense of dry cleaning, and the hassle of pleater hooks among them. Homespun Fabrics sells all-cotton material that's 10 feet wide, or about 105" to 109" after shrinkage. The fabric includes homespun, hobnail, barley, and monkscloth weaves, in white and natural. The width makes the fabric perfect for "seamless draperies," and even eliminates some of the finishing work. Homespun Fabrics manufactures all styles of draperies (suitable to the fabric) and can also custom-make "Fan Pleat" draperies. These operate on a track system that's hung from the ceiling or mounted on the wall, with a buckram header tape with nylon tabs that engage the track. The drapery folds are 4" or 5" deep, so the stackback (the area covered by the curtain when it's drawn back) that would be 37" deep with conventional pinch-pleat draperies is only 11" deep with the Fan Pleat system. Made in Homespun Fabrics' heavyweight cottons, this system produces handsome, neutral window coverings that give you maximum glass exposure. They have a crisp, tailored appearance that's ideal for modern decor and office settings, and are machine washable and dryable and guaranteed against sun rot for seven years. An added bonus: The fabric can be tolerated by people with chemical sensitivities, as one such customer enthused in a letter to the company.

In addition to draperies, Homespun also carries bedcovers and throws, roman shades, tablecloths and napkins, bedskirts, and more, not to mention the hardware for accessorizing your drapes (fanwood poles and decorative ends of all kinds). Some of the fabrics even lend themselves nicely to labor-saving and attractive wall coverings, hiding ugly plaster, old wallpaper, even old electrical outlets. In addition to the heavy cottons, Homespun Fabrics offers open-weave casement fabric, wide muslin, and both regular-width and ultra-wide semi-sheers—batiste, voile, and bouclé slub, in lots of colors. Homespun can create the draperies, or you can do it yourself—and you'll find helpful books on home decorating and guides to making fan pleat draperies, slipcovers, bedspreads, table linens, and accessories.

Special Factors: Returns are accepted within 10 days for exchange, refund, or credit; $5 cutting fee on orders of five or fewer yards.

MARLENE'S DECORATOR FABRICS

■■■■■■■■■■■■■■■

301 BEACH ST., DEPT. 2J
HACKENSACK, NJ 07601
201–843–0844

Flyer: free with SASE
Pay: check, MO, MC, V
Sells: decorator fabrics
Store: mail order only; phone hours Monday to Friday 9:30–6

Marlene's Decorator Fabrics has been selling upholstery, slipcover, and drapery goods since 1946 and can save you up to 60% on the list prices of fabrics by Amerex, Artmark, Barrow, Blautex, Carleton V, Duralee, Elco, Fabricut, Kasmir, Maenline, Ralph Lauren, Sanderson, Stout, Stroheim & Romann, Waverly, Wesco, and many others. Write or call for a price quote, or send a self-addressed, stamped envelope with a sample if you're not sure of the manufacturer or pattern, or to request a brochure. Specify the yardage needed and whether you're interested in upholstery, drapery, or other decorator fabric.

Special Factors: Minimum order is 5 yards retail, 15 to 30 yards wholesale; no returns unless damaged by UPS or the manufacturer.

ROBINSON'S WALL-PAPER INTERIORS

■■■■■■■■■■■■■■■

225 W. SPRING ST., 8LY
P.O. BOX 427
TITUSVILLE, PA
*   16354–0427*
800–458–2426
814–827–1893
FAX: 814–827–1693

Catalog: $2
Pay: check, MC, V, AE, Discover
Sells: wallpaper, borders, decorator fabrics, and accessories
Store: same address; also 3506 Liberty Center, Erie, PA, and 1720 Wilmington Rd., Rt. 18, New Castle, PA
E-mail: rwallcover@mail.usachoice.net
Online: http://www.robinsonswallpaper.com

Robinson's has been in business since 1919 and sells both vinyl-coated and solid vinyl wallpaper, coordinating borders, and fabrics that are suitable for use throughout the home. The 40-page catalog also offers tools and supplies for installation, as well as decorating accents to complement your scheme. Robinson's provides color photographs that show how different designs look when they're installed—a very helpful feature. Free samples of any wall coverings shown in the catalog are available. Prices are up to 60% below suggested retail prices.

Patterns not shown in the catalog are available through Robinson's Custom Order Department at savings of 35% to 60% off book price. See the catalog for details, or call with manufacturer's name, book name, pattern number, price code, and suggested retail price, to receive a quote.

Overseas customers, please note: Robinson's ships orders overseas only to APO/FPO addresses and Japan.

Special Factors: Satisfaction is guaranteed; returns are accepted within 30 days for exchange or refund; excess unopened rolls are also returnable; minimum order is $15 with credit cards.

SHAMA IMPORTS, INC.

P.O. BOX 2900, DEPT.
   WBM–99
FARMINGTON HILLS, MI
   48333–2900
248–478–7740

Brochure: free
Pay: check, MO, MC, V
Sells: hand-embroidered crewel fabrics and accessories
Store: mail order only

Shama Imports, which began business in 1982, offers good prices on hand-embroidered crewel fabrics from Kashmir, India. Since Shama directly imports these fabrics, there is no middleman, which saves you, according to Shama, up to 50%. Crewel is excellent for upholstery, draperies, bedspreads, slipcovers, tablecloths, wall coverings, and apparel. The designs featured in the eight-page color brochure present traditional serpentine flower-and-vine motifs and other distinctive designs, in a range of colors. Background (unembroidered) fabric is also available by the yard, and Shama stocks ready-made crewel chair and cushion covers, tote bags, bedspreads, and tablecloths as well. The fabric is 52" wide, hand-loomed 100% cotton with 100% pure wool embroidery, and can be washed by hand or dry-cleaned. Samples are available for $1 each; those showing one-fourth of the complete pattern cost $5 (refundable). The brochure lists the pattern repeats for all of the designs.

Special Factors: Satisfaction is guaranteed; uncut, undamaged returns are accepted within 30 days for refund or credit; C.O.D. orders are accepted.

SILK SURPLUS

300 TRADE ZONE DR.,
   DEPT. 55
RONKONKOMA, NY 11779
516–467–8800
FAX: 516–467–8909

Information: price quote
Pay: check, MO, MC, V, AE
Sells: discontinued decorator fabric and trim
Store: same address; Monday to Saturday 10–6; two other NY locations, call for directions

Silk Surplus is well known to budget-minded New Yorkers who covet luxurious upholstery and drapery fabrics, because it's where they can save up to 75% (and sometimes even more) on sumptuous Scalamandré and Boris Kroll close-outs and fabrics from other mills. Silks, cottons, velvets, woolens, chintzes, brocades, damasks, and other weaves and finishes are usually available from Silk Surplus, which opened its doors in 1962. Walk-in customers can select from among the bolts in any of the Silk Surplus shops. But if you're buying by mail, you must know exactly which Scalamandré or Boris Kroll fabric you want, and in which color. If it's there, you're in luck. You may also send the store a fabric sample with a query. This is a great shopping stop on a trip to New York City, but only serious searchers for Scalamandré or Boris Kroll close-out fabrics should contact the store intending to buy by mail. If you're a design professional, you may ask for an additional trade discount.

   Special Factors: Price quote by phone or letter with self-addressed, stamped envelope; sample cuttings are free; all sales are final; minimum order is three yards.

STENCIL HOUSE OF N.H., INC.

P.O. BOX 16109, DEPT.
   WBM
HOOKSETT, NH 03106
800–622–9416
603–625–1716

Catalog: $4, refundable with first order
Pay: check, MO, MC, V
Sells: decorator stencils
Store: mail order only
Online: http://www.isystems.com/stencil

Jan Gordon's husband is afraid to turn his back on his wife, president of Stencil House of N.H. "If I see a plain surface, I want to stencil it," she says. The 20-page color catalog from Stencil House offers a dazzling array of decorator-quality stencil designs at craft-store prices. While common craft stencils are one-piece designs, Stencil House's designs are multilayered to allow for two or more colors. The current catalog has over 230 different designs appropriate for walls, floors, stair risers, fireboards, wooden furniture, fabric, and more.

The stencils come precut or "uncut"; you can save an average of $2 to $3 on each by cutting out the designs yourself. Most of the stencils are under $10, and all are one-of-a-kind items, designed by Gordon, although the starred items in the catalog are modeled after authentic stencil designs found in museums and old homesteads. There are quaint country motifs, such as a bird with birdhouse and a laundry line; Shaker-inspired designs; Penn-Dutch stylized vines, flowerpots, hearts, birds, and flowers; themes for children, such as Teddy bears, animals, and alphabets; berries, fruits, and flowers galore; and much more. Stencil House can also custom-design stencils to go with your wallpaper and fabric. If you send in a fabric sample, they'll help you match the paint color and give other color and design advice for free.

Stencil House sells various stencil supplies, including paints (two different paint charts are offered), stencil brushes, brush cleaner, stencil adhesive that won't damage the surface when the stencil is removed; varnish; floor cloth; and unprinted Mylar sheets (for making your own stencils). Stencil House has a "frequent stenciler's plan"—when you've ordered five stencils (no time limit) you get one stencil for free. See catalog for details.

Wholesale customers: Please inquire about wholesale prices and policies.

Special Factors: All payments in U.S. funds. Custom designing and sizing available; no returns on custom orders.

WELLS INTERIORS INC.

███████████

7171 AMADOR PLAZA DR.
DUBLIN, CA 94568
800–547–8982
FAX: 510–829–1374

Catalog: free
Pay: check, MO, MC, V
Sells: window treatments and accessories
Store: 19 locations in CA, NV, and OR; see catalog for locations

Wells Interiors has been in business since 1980, guarantees "the lowest prices" on its goods, and will beat any other dealer's price down to cost on a wide range of top brands. Discounts can run up to 85% on retail prices on Levolor's mini-blinds, verticals, wood blinds, and similar styles by other manufacturers, such as Bali, Del Mar, Graber, Designer Express, HunterDouglas, Jennifer Lynn, Louver Drape, M&B, Westwood, and Windsor. Kirsch woven woods, pleated shades, decorator roller shades, verticals, and mini-blinds are also available, as well as a line of "value-priced" verticals from Wells.

The catalog includes a guide to the lines currently available and includes instructions on measuring your windows and installing the blinds. Details of the firm's warranty are given in the catalog as well.

Special Factors: Written confirmation is required on phone orders.

RELATED PRODUCTS/COMPANIES

Cowhide pillows and cowhides for wall hangings • Steerhides
Custom embroidery • Harris Levy
Decorator fabrics • Priba Furniture, The Furniture Patch of Calabash, Quality Furniture Market
Interior house shutters • Shuttercraft
Interior wall paint • Pearl Paint
Leather • Weaver Leather
Supplies and tools for marbleizing, faux finishes, and gilding • Pearl Paint, Jerry's Artarama
Upholstery books • Frank's Cane and Rush
Upholstery stuffing • Buffalo Batt & Felt
Upholstery supplies • The Button Shop, Frank's Cane and Rush, The Caning Shop, Home-Sew, Newark Dressmaker Supply
Upholstery-weight silk fabric • Utex Trading, Thai Silks
Vintage product labels for papering walls • Original Paper Collectibles
Wall coverings • Priba Furniture
Wall, floor, and fabric stencils • Texas Art Supply, Glass Crafters, Vanguard Crafts
Window screens • Coppa Woodworking
Window textiles • Eldridge Textile

JEWELRY AND GEMS

Fine, fashion, and costume jewelry; loose stones and jewelry-making equipment and supplies

You'll find everything from inexpensive neck chains to investment-grade gems here, at savings of 20% to 75%, from firms that sell to amateur and professional jewelry makers and sometimes supply pieces in finished form.

There are lots of other firms in different chapters of the book that sell jewelry, jewels, and jewelry-making tools and supplies, so be sure to see the "Related Products/Companies" section at the end of this chapter.

Before making a financial commitment of any magnitude, make sure you know what you're buying. *Jewelry & Gems: The Buying Guide— How to Buy Diamonds, Colored Gemstones, Pearls, Gold & Jewelry with Confidence and Knowledge,* by Matlins and Bonanno (Gemstone Press), covers precious and semiprecious stones, pearls, metals, and other materials used in jewelry. Another good title is *Gems and Jewelry: All Color Guide,* by Joel E. Arem. This portable book full of color photographs is a classic consumer guide to precious stones and their settings. Both of these books are available at any number of mail-order and online bookstores in the "Books, Audiobooks, and Periodicals" chapter.

The Federal Trade Commission (FTC) has established guidelines for the jewelry trade and publishes consumer pamphlets that discuss the meanings of terms, stamps and quality marks, and related matters. Request "Gold Jewelry," "Bargain Jewelry," and "Guidelines for the Jewelry Industry" from the Federal Trade Commission, Public Reference Office, Washington, DC 20580.

If you need help in finding an appraiser, contact the American Society of Appraisers at 212–687–6305. The Society will locate an appraiser in your area and have that person contact you, at no charge. (The Society's senior members have at least five years of experience and are required to pass an exam; they handle all "appraisables," not just jewelry.)

The Gemological Institute of America (GIA) can tell you what should appear on a GIA report and confirm whether an appraiser has been trained by the organization. For more information, call or write the Gemological Institute of America, Inc., 580 Fifth Avenue, New York, NY 10036, 212–944–5900. There is also a GIA office in California, at P.O. Box 2110, 1660 Stewart St., Santa Monica, CA 90406.

The Jewelers' Vigilance Committee can tell you whether your dealer is among the good, the bad, or the ugly. This trade association monitors the industry and promotes ethical business practices. For more information call or write the Jewelers' Vigilance Committee, 401 E. 34th St., Ste. N13A, New York, NY 10016, 212–532–1919.

FIND IT FAST

LOOSE STONES AND JEWELRY-MAKING SUPPLIES • Eloxite Corporation, Hong Kong Lapidaries, House of Onyx
MEN'S JEWELRY • Simply Diamonds
PRECIOUS GEM JEWELRY • Diamonds by Rennie Ellen, Eastern Jewelry, House of Onyx, Simply Diamonds
THEMED JEWELRY • Eastern Jewelry, House of Onyx, Nature's Jewelry
WEDDING/ENGAGEMENT RINGS • Diamonds by Rennie Ellen, Simply Diamonds, Wedding Ring Hotline

---

DIAMONDS BY RENNIE ELLEN

Catalog: $2
Pay: check, MO, teller's check, bank draft
Sells: stock and custom-made jewelry
Factory: visits by appointment only

15 W. 47TH ST., RM. 401
NEW YORK, NY 10036
212–869–5525

It's hard to believe that you can buy diamond engagement rings wholesale, but that's Rennie Ellen's business. You can save up to 75% on the price of similar jewelry sold elsewhere by buying here. Rennie Ellen is honest, reputable, and personable, and she's been cutting gems since 1966.

Rennie Ellen sells diamonds of all shapes, sizes, and qualities, set to order in platinum or gold. The color catalog shows samples of Ms. Ellen's design work, including rings, pendants, and earrings set with diamonds. Engagement and wedding rings are a specialty, and the cards and notes from grateful young marrieds that line her office walls testify to her success. The factory is open to customers by appointment only.

Special Factors: Price quote by phone or letter; a detailed bill of sale is included with each purchase; returns are accepted within five working days; minimum shipping, handling, and insurance charge is $15 (sent by registered mail); orders can also be shipped overnight by Federal Express for an extra charge.

EASTERN JEWELRY, INC.

2545 CHANDLER AVE., SUITE #2, DEPT. BBS
LAS VEGAS, NV 89120
702–736–3525
FAX: 702–736–2347

Loose-leaf folder or CD-ROM: free (see text)
Pay: check, MO, MC, V, AE, DC
Sells: jewelry
Store: mail order only
E-mail: jelazer@worldnet.att.net

Anyone who loves the elegant look and feel of gold and jewels in classic, distinctive designs is going to flip over this company. All of the earrings, brooches, bracelets, necklaces, pendants, and rings in Eastern Jewelry's collection are made with 14-karat gold over sterling silver, and most of the jewels are genuine. Eastern is really a jewelry wholesaler but will sell to individuals, too (there's no minimum, but orders under $100 are charged a $5 surcharge); the prices here reflect radical discounts from the usual retail price.

You could go to a Fifth Avenue jeweler and buy a bracelet dripping with diamonds set in 14-karat gold for thousands—or you could buy the same design from Eastern, albeit in gold over sterling silver with smaller diamonds, for $46 (retails for $189). You get the same effect as the movie stars and princesses without the cost or the worry. When you call for information, you'll receive a pack of about 70 loose-leaf pages in a folder with prices, descriptions, and pictures. Color sheets are extra. By press time, Eastern should have CD-ROMs to send out to customers as well.

Among the hundreds of pieces here, you'll find diamond circle brooches made with green agate, amethyst, sapphires, blue topaz, garnets, and mixed-color gems ranging from $14 to $26. There are dozens of bracelet designs to choose from, including bangles with inset jewels and continuous-link designs with a single jewel set in each link. The earrings range from the classic dangling rows of rubies, diamonds, garnets, etc., to tasteful flowers, hearts, and geometric designs; most of the earrings are under $20 a pair, and many are closer to $10. The rings, necklaces, and pendants reflect the same tasteful aesthetic and good value. If you're looking for Judaica or crosses, you'll find them here, too. Don't just stop with one piece; you can buy dazzling jeweled necklace-and-earring sets for much less than you'd pay for a single piece elsewhere (starting as low as $22 per set), and you'll look like you're ready for a night at the Oscars. All jewelry comes in a gift box and has a certificate of authenticity. The owner speaks Hebrew, Bulgarian, Russian, Romanian, and Spanish, but understands many other languages as well!

Wholesalers, corporate/promotional gift buyers: Eastern Jewelry offers attractive quantity discounts.

Special Factors: Quantity discounts available; $5 handling charge added to orders under $100; returns accepted on manufacturer-damaged goods only.

ELOXITE CORPORATION

P.O. BOX 729, DEPT. 4
WHEATLAND, WY 82201
307–322–3050
FAX: 307–322–3055

Catalog: $1
Pay: check, MO, MC, V, Discover
Sells: jewelry craft supplies
Store: 806 Tenth St., Wheatland, WY; Monday to Friday 8:30–4, Saturday 8:30–3
Online: http://www.eloxite.com

Eloxite has been selling wholesale jewelry findings, cabochons, beads, and other lapidary supplies since 1955. Prices here are up to 75% below those charged by other crafts sources for findings and jewelry components. Jewelry findings with a Western flair are featured in the 88-page catalog: bola ties and slide medallions, belt buckles and inserts, and coin jewelry are prominent offerings. Also shown are pendants, rings, earrings, lockets, tie tacks, jewelry boxes, money clips, barrettes, pins and more, made to be set with cabochons or cut stones, as well as jump rings, chains, pillboxes, screw eyes, and ear wires. The stones themselves are sold—cut cubic zirconia and synthetic gemstones and oval cabochons of abalone, agate, black onyx, garnet, opal, obsidian, jasper, and malachite. There's also a full range of jewelry supplies and equipment, including tumblers, soldering tools, grinding wheels, and more.

Sandwiched between the pages of jewelry components are quartz clock movements and blanks for clock faces, clock hands, and ballpoint pens and letter openers for desk sets. Discounts are available on most items, and specials are usually offered with orders of specified amounts.

Special Factors: Wholesale orders only; quantity discounts are available; undamaged returns are accepted within 15 days for exchange or refund (a $2 restocking fee may be charged); minimum order is $15; C.O.D. orders are accepted.

HONG KONG LAPIDARIES, INC.

2801 UNIVERSITY DR.
CORAL SPRINGS, FL 33065
954–755–8777
FAX: 954–755–8780

Catalog: $3, $5 outside U.S.
Pay: check, MO, MC, V
Sells: jewelry supplies, beads, cabochons, and loose stones
Store: mail order only

Hong Kong Lapidaries, established in 1979, sells a wide range of precious and semiprecious stones in a variety of forms. The 58-page catalog lists items of interest to hobbyists as well, and the prices run as much as 70% below comparable retail.

Thousands of cabochons, beads, loose-faceted and cut stones—heart shapes and charms, flowers and leaves, rings, donuts, and more—mosaic stones, and strung chips of pearl, garnet, amethyst, onyx, abalone, and other kinds of semiprecious stones are offered through the catalog, which comes with a separate 12-page color brochure that shows representative pieces. Egyptian clay scarabs, coral, cameos, cubic zirconia, yellow jade, cloisonné jewelry and objets d'art, 14K gold-filled and sterling silver beads, and ball earrings are available. Hobbyists should note the necklace thread—100% silk or nylon—in a score of colors and 16 sizes, as well as stringing needles.

Special Factors: Satisfaction is guaranteed; price quote by fax; quantity discounts are available; returns are accepted within 12 days; minimum order is $50; C.O.D. orders are accepted.

HOUSE OF ONYX

120 N. MAIN ST.
GREENVILLE, KY
42345–0261
800–844–3100
502–338–2363
FAX: 502–338–9605

Catalog: free
Pay: check, MO, MC, V, Discover
Sells: investment-grade stones, jewelry, and gifts
Store: same address; Monday to Friday 9–4
E-mail: onyx@muhlon.com
Online: http://www.houseofonyx.com

Can a gem dealership be down-homey? This one is! The House of Onyx publishes a large tabloid catalog filled with reports on the gem industry and listings of diamonds and other precious stones, as well as specials on gifts and jewelry. Right on the front cover is a photo of owners Shirley and Fred Rowe III, with the caption "Come see us!" Imported gifts and jewelry from Mexico, China, and India have been offered in the past, including Aztec onyx chess sets, ashtrays, bookends, vases, statuettes (including dinosaurs), and candlesticks. Cloisonné and vermeil beads, jewelry, and artware, and carvings of soapstone, rose quartz, tiger's eye, Burmese jadeite, lapis lazuli, carnelian, turquoise, and agate are usually available. The jewelry includes semiprecious bead necklaces, freshwater and cultured pearls, cameos, diamond and gemstone rings, gold and jeweled watches, earrings, and pendants, from department-store grade to fine one-of-a-kind pieces. Collectors of crystals and mineral specimens should check here for amethyst, fluorite, quartz, pyrite, and other geodes and samples. House of Onyx also offers Jim Kaufmann's unusual semiprecious intarsia and can supply solid-gold mountings as well.

House of Onyx has been in business since 1967 and offers a wide range of investment-quality stones, with discounts of 50% and 60% offered on parcels of $1,000 and up. The investment stones account for much of the business here, and the catalog is packed with useful articles and commentary on gems and investing, including colorful and sometimes humorous commentary by owner Fred Rowe and others. In fact, the catalog itself makes wonderful reading, and the summer "information" issue has become a much-requested reference for fans.

Special Factors: Satisfaction is guaranteed; investment gemstones are sold with an unlimited time return guarantee and a "100% purchase price refund" pledge; other returns are accepted within 30 days; minimum order is $25.

NATURE'S JEWELRY

222 MILL RD.
CHELMSFORD, MA
01824–3692
800–333–3235
FAX: 800–866–3235

Catalog: free
Pay: check, MO, MC, V, AE, Discover
Sells: fashion and novelty jewelry
Store: mail order only
Online: http://www.netplaza.com/
naturesjewelry

No matter what your personal style, taste, or budget, you'll find a bauble to suit your fancy in the Nature's Jewelry catalog. Each issue has nearly 100 pages of classic, theme, and holiday jewelry and accessories, including strands of semiprecious stones, preserved wildflower jewelry, pins and watches with environmental themes, jewelry for the season— from "star" bow earrings in red and green for Christmas to a cuff of enameled hearts for Valentine's Day—and much more, at very affordable prices. Many of the designs are exclusives, so they're hard to compare with other jewelry, but prices on items at Nature's Jewelry are up to 50% lower than those charged elsewhere for similar pieces. Many of the pierced earrings are priced under $10, and a large number of the other pieces cost under $20.

If you'd like to be able to wear fresh flowers every day, you'll love the collection of handmade, hand-painted stone-and-resin buds and blossoms. Past catalogs have shown lilacs, roses, irises, pansies, poppies, and other flowers, and there's even a line of preserved blossoms in earrings, pins, and pendants. Love pigs? They've shown up here, as adornments for dress or person, as have cows, sheep, lots of cats, horses, dinosaurs, dolphins, whales, pandas, fish, birds, dragonflies, coyotes, frogs, and many other animals. Inexpensive tennis bracelets, golf-motif jewelry, "pieces of nature" (real parsley, four-leaf clovers, maple leaves, etc.) dipped in 24K gold, and chunks of "beach glass" made into beautiful, jewel-like necklaces and earrings have also appeared. Every catalog features lots of new offerings in each issue, as well as sale pages with dozens of pieces at 50% off. For really big savings, check out the website for 35% to 70% off close-outs.

Special Factors: Satisfaction is guaranteed; returns are accepted for exchange, refund, or credit.

SIMPLY DIAMONDS

Information: inquire
Pay: check, MO, MC, V, AE, Discover
Sells: diamond jewelry
Store: mail order only
E-mail: 75224.1032@compuserve.com

P.O. BOX 682, DEPT. A
ARDSLEY, NY 10502–0682
800–552–2728
914–693–2370
FAX: 914–693–2446

Thanks to family affiliations with merchants who've been doing business in New York City's diamond district for decades, Simply Diamonds can offer both stock and custom jewelry at excellent prices. Simply Diamonds features a lovely line of jewelry, including diamond name bracelets and charms—wonderful gifts for birthdays, Mother's Day, graduations, anniversaries, and on and on. Simply Diamonds has access to thousands of settings for rings, pendants, men's rings, and other pieces, and can provide color pictures on request. The firm also executes individual commissions—including engagement rings—at a discount. The custom division will work with you from concept to execution, or you may send ad photos or other depictions of the piece you want replicated. (Color postcards and brochures of some of the custom pieces are available.)

Simply Diamonds wants its customers to understand what they're buying, and would be pleased to discuss grade, size, color, and clarity—all factors that affect the price and value of the stones. As the proprietors themselves say, "Buying diamond products is a very confusing and mysterious subject to most. Anyone is welcome to call, and we will be glad to answer any diamond-related question." Pieces are backed by GIA, EGL, and IGI certificates (available on request), and satisfaction is guaranteed on every purchase.

Special Factors: Satisfaction is guaranteed; returns are accepted within seven days for exchange, refund, or credit; C.O.D. orders are not accepted.

WEDDING RING HOTLINE

172 RT. 9
ENGLISHTOWN, NJ 07726
732–972–7777
FAX: 732–972–0720

Brochure: free
Pay: check, MO, MC, V, AE, Discover
Sells: wedding bands, diamonds, and engagement rings
Store: same address (by appointment)
E-mail: diamondmjs@aol.com
Online: http://www.weddingringhotline.com

Why pay a fortune for your wedding rings when you can save from 30% to 70% through Wedding Ring Hotline? This firm, a division of Bride & Groom's West, manufactures its own line of classic styles in solid white, pink, and yellow 14K gold. All sizes are available, in 2 mm to 12 mm widths, with plain and milgrain (tiny beading) edges. Wedding Ring Hotline can also produce the rings in 10K and 18K gold, and platinum. Engraving services are available, and the firm also sells diamond wedding and engagement rings, nationally advertised lines of wedding rings, and can make other jewelry to order; inquire for information, or call for a price quote on any name-brand engagement or wedding ring.

Special Factors: Satisfaction is guaranteed; price quote by phone or letter; returns are accepted within 30 days for exchange, refund, or credit; engraving is free on all orders over $200.

RELATED PRODUCTS/COMPANIES

Costume jewelry • Beauty Boutique, Gold Medal Hair Products, J. Tiras, DesignerOutlet, Ebay, The Ultimate Outlet
Extra-size bangle bracelets • Amplestuff
Fine jewelry • Bennett Brothers, Albert S. Smyth, Beverly Bremer, Michael C. Fina, Lanac, Ebay, DesignerOutlet, The Ultimate Outlet, Nat Schwartz, Meierotto's MidweSterling
Jewelry boxes • Airline International
Jewelry-making supplies • Axner Pottery, Bailey Ceramic, Ceramic Supply, The Artist's Club, Circle Craft, Craft Catalog, National Artcraft, Sunshine Discount
Silver belt buckles, conchos, and saddle decorations • Weaver Leather
Watches • M & E Marine, Bennett Brothers, Albert S. Smyth, Professional Cutlery Direct, Ace Luggage, Airline International, Meierotto's MidweSterling

LUGGAGE AND LEATHER ACCESSORIES

Leather luggage, briefcases, attaché cases, computer bags, handbags, backpacks, desk accessories, manicure sets, etc.; leather-care products and services

The firms listed here stock everything you should need to tote your effects around town, to the office, and farther afield. In addition to handbags, briefcases, suitcases, trunks, and small leather goods, some of the firms also sell cases for musical instruments and portfolios for models and artists.

If you're buying luggage, consider the pros and cons of different luggage materials: Waterproof, puncture-proof materials and lockable closures are good considerations. Wheeled suitcases help bridge the distances in mammoth hub airports, and built-in, partly recessed wheels that are designed to avoid jamming in conveyor belts are the best bets.

For other companies that sell leather goods, see "Related Products/Companies" at the end of this chapter.

FIND IT FAST

BRIEFCASES AND LUGGAGE • Ace Luggage, Airline International, Al's Luggage, Jobson's, Leather Unlimited, The Luggage Center, Santa Maria
HANDBAGS • Ace Luggage, Al's Luggage, Leather Unlimited, J. Tiras
LEATHER DESK ACCESSORIES AND GIFT ITEMS • Ace Luggage, Airline International, Jobson's
LUGGAGE REPAIR • Airline International, Santa Maria

ACE LUGGAGE AND GIFTS

Catalog: $2, refundable with first order
Pay: check, MO, MC, V, AE, Discover
Sells: luggage and leather goods, fine pens, etc.
Store: same address; Monday to Saturday 10–6, Thursday 10–7 (extended hours in December), Sunday 12–5
E-mail: aceluggage@aol.com

2122 AVE. U
BROOKLYN, NY 11229
800–DIAL–ACE
718–891–9713
FAX: 718–891–3878

Ace, which was established in 1961, sells luggage by Andiamo, French, Lark, Lexi, Lucas, Metro Dakota, Samsonite, LeSport Sac, Ricardo, Travelpro (Rollaboard), and Zero Halliburton, at discounts of up to 40%. Briefcases and attaché cases by Eagle Creek, Jack Georges, Jansport, Lodis, National, and Sacoche are available, as well as handbags and small leather goods by Etienne Aigner, Bosca, Filofax, Garys, and Rolfs. You'll find leather desk accessories, travel alarms, Victorinox Swiss Army knives and watches, lighters, pens, and other small luxuries. The 36-page catalog that's published during the holiday season features gift merchandise, but catalogs and price quotes on the luggage and leather goods are available throughout the year, and special discounts are available for corporate and quantity orders.

Readers in Canada, please note: Orders are shipped via UPS.

Special Factors: Price quote by phone (please have brand and model number before calling).

AIRLINE INTER-NATIONAL LUGGAGE & GIFTS, INC.

8701 MONTANA AVE.
EL PASO, TX 79925
800–592–1234
915–778–1234
FAX: 915–778–1533

Catalog: free
Pay: check, MO, MC, V, AE, Discover
Sells: luggage and leather goods, gifts, etc.
Store: same address; Monday to Saturday 9:30–6, Thursday 9:30–7, Sunday 11–5; also Sunland Park Mall, El Paso, TX; Monday to Saturday 10–9, Sunday 12–6
E-mail: airint@whc.net
Online: http://www.airint.com

Airline International began its life in 1978 as a luggage-repair business serving airlines in the El Paso area and began selling new luggage when the airlines needed replacements for suitcases too badly damaged to be fixed. The firm has expanded over the years to offer luggage from every major manufacturer, as well as other small leather goods and gifts. The 36-page color catalog shows attaché cases, briefcases, overnighters and suitcases, laptop cases, backpacks, and other pieces by Andiamo, Atlantic, Hugo Bosca, Kenneth Cole, Dakota, Dilana, Dopp, Jack Georges, Hartmann, High Sierra, Kipling, Mundi, Outta Here, Rolfs, St. Thomas, Travelpro (Rollaboard), and other firms. Airline International also sells leather desk sets and agendas, travel accessories, and a broad selection of well-chosen executive gifts, such as Seth Thomas weather stations, Howard Miller clocks, calculators, globes, jewelry boxes, collapsible umbrellas, Swiss watches, Cross and Waterman pens, banks, puzzles, and games. Savings on the luggage shown in the review catalog averaged 25% on list prices, but Airline International says that some prices are as low as 50% off suggested retail. And if your suitcase was mauled on your last business trip, you'll appreciate the fact that you can still get your luggage or handbag fixed here.

Special Factors: Price quote by phone or letter; returns are accepted for exchange, refund, or credit.

AL'S LUGGAGE

2134 LARIMER ST.
DENVER, CO 80205
303–295–9009
303–294–9045
FAX: 303–296–8769

Catalog: $2, refundable
Pay: check, MO, MC, V, AE, Discover
Sells: leather goods and luggage
Store: same address; Monday to Friday
9–5:30, Saturday 9–5

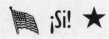 ¡Si! ★

The $2 catalog fee brings you a sheaf of photocopied materials from Samsonite, including price lists, brochures, ordering instructions, and shipping rate charts. Al's Luggage has been selling leather goods and luggage since 1948 and carries Diane Von Furstenberg, Jordache, Lion Leather, London Fog Luggage, Members Only, Platt, Stebco, Winn, and WK. In addition to current lines of suitcases, overnight bags, cosmetics cases, totes, wardrobes, duffels, and garment bags, Al's offers business cases, portfolios, and even camcorder carrying cases. The catalog shows only Samsonite models, which are sold here for 30% to 50% below list prices. If you're shopping for an item by another manufacturer, call or write for a price quote.

Special Factors: Price quote by phone or letter with self-addressed, stamped envelope; C.O.D. orders are accepted.

JOBSON'S LUGGAGE WAREHOUSE

666 LEXINGTON AVE.
NEW YORK, NY 10022
800–221–5238
212–355–6846
FAX: 212–753–3295

Catalog: free
Pay: check, MO, MC, V, AE, DC, Discover
Sells: luggage, leather goods, and accessories
Store: same address; Monday to Saturday
9–6, Sunday 11–5

 ¡Si! ★

Jobson's Luggage Warehouse has served New York City since 1949 and makes its "warehouse-priced" inventory available to customers world-wide through a very clear, 32-page catalog. Jobson's sells luggage, attaché cases, backpacks, laptop cases, and accessories by Air Express, American Tourister, Atlas, Boyt, Delsey, Eastpack, Eiffel, Perry Ellis,

Hartmann, Jansport, Lark, Lion, Lucas, Paolo Marino, Samsonite, Schlesinger, Skyway, Travelpro, Zero Halliburton, and other manufacturers. Jobson's has a great selection of business cases, choice small leather goods, desk and travel accessories, manicure sets, pens by Cross and MontBlanc, and gifts. You can send for the catalog, which shows just a fifth of Jobson's inventory, or if you have the model and color information for anything from any of the firms mentioned, call or write for a price quote.

Special Factors: Satisfaction is guaranteed; price quote by phone or letter; unused returns are accepted within 30 days for exchange, refund, or credit.

LEATHER UNLIMITED CORP.

7155 CTY. HWY. B, DEPT. WBMC99
BELGIUM, WI 53004–9990
920–994–9464
FAX: 920–994–4099

Catalog: $2, refundable
Pay: check, MO, MC, V, AE, Discover
Sells: leather-crafting supplies and equipment and finished products
Store: same address; Monday to Friday 7–4

Here's a catalog for the beginner, the seasoned leather worker, and the rest of us. It offers all sorts of leather-crafting supplies, from kits to raw materials, as well as leather cleaners and conditioners, a line of bags, business cases, small leather goods, and even black-powder (shooting) supplies. Leather Unlimited has been in business since 1970 and offers substantial savings on crafts supplies, beginning with leather—sold by the hide or in pieces. The weights run from fine lining grade to heavy belting leather, in a variety of finishes and colors. There are laces, belt blanks, key tabs, and dozens of undyed embossed belt strips; these are matched by hundreds of belt buckles, which run from embossed leather buckles to a line with organization logos and sporting themes. The 92-page catalog features dozens of kits for making all sorts of finished goods, plus stamping tools, punches, carvers, rivets, screws, snaps, zippers, lacing needles, sundry findings, leather-care products and dyes by Fiebing's, and Missouri River patterns for making authentic Native American and frontier-style clothing.

Among the finished products available here are sheepskin rugs, slippers, mittens, hats, and purses made of sheepskin and deerskin, duffels and sports bags, leather totes, and wineskins. Leather Unlimited also manufactures leather motorcycle accessories and sells top-grain belt leather business cases, portfolios, wallets, and other small leather goods. And the firm recently added a line of books on Indian lore, crafts, and related topics. The prices are outstandingly low—up to 50% below comparable retail on some items—and extra discounts are given on quantity or volume purchases.

Special Factors: Satisfaction is guaranteed; authorized returns are accepted within 30 days; minimum order is $40.

THE LUGGAGE CENTER

960 REMILLARD CT.
SAN JOSE, CA 95122
800–450–2400
408–288–5363
FAX: 408–998–2536

Information: price quote
Pay: MO, MC, V, AE, Discover
Sells: luggage, business cases, and travel accessories
Store: call for 30 locations in California

The Luggage Center can save you up to 50% off the manufacturers' suggested list prices on the top names in luggage, and even more when the firm is running a sale. The latest lines from well-known makers are available, including Andiamo, Briggs & Riley, Delsey, Eagle Creek, Lark, Lifestyles International, Ricardo, Samsonite, and Skyway. Business cases, garment bags, and travel accessories are carried as well; call or write for a price quote.

Canadian readers, please note: Orders to Canada are shipped via UPS.

Special Factors: Returns are accepted within 30 days.

SANTA MARIA DISCOUNT LUGGAGE

125-F E. BETTERAVIA
SANTA MARIA, CA 93454
TEL/FAX: 805–928–2252

Information: price quote
Pay: check, MO, MC, V, AE, Discover
Sells: luggage and travel accessories
Store: same address; Tuesday to Friday 10–6, Saturday 10–5; also San Luis Luggage, 1135 Chorro St., San Luis Obispo, CA
Online: http://www.luggageman.com

Santa Maria Discount Luggage offers everything from backpacks to three-suiters, at discounts of up to 60% on list. This family-run firm has been in business since 1971 and sells only first-quality goods. The available brands include American Valise, Atlantic, Briggs & Riley, Eagle Creek, Jansport, Samsonite, Travelpro (Rollaboard), Zero Halliburton, and other manufacturers. You can call or write with a model name and number for prices on suitcases, business cases, garment bags, backpacks, duffels, and anything else made by these firms. Or you can visit the Discount Luggage website, which has an online catalog and ordering information. If you're in the Santa Maria area or are near the San Luis Obispo store, drop in—and bring any luggage that needs fixing, because both shops do repairs.

Special Factors: Satisfaction is guaranteed; returns are accepted within 30 days for exchange, refund, or credit.

J. TIRAS CLASSIC HANDBAGS, INC.

6101 ROYALTON, #106
HOUSTON, TX 77081
800–460–1999
713–660–0090
FAX: 713–660–0095

Brochure: free with long SASE
Pay: check, MO, MC, V, AE
Sells: designer handbag look-alikes
Store: The Centre at Post Oak, 5000 Westheimer, Houston, TX; Monday to Saturday 10–7, Sunday 12–5

Great design, fine workmanship, and top-notch materials are what justify paying hundreds of dollars for bags by Bottega Venetta, Louis Vuitton, Salvatore Ferragamo, Bally, Donna Karan, Judith Leiber, and other designers. But if you had the chance to buy a look-alike for up to 80% less, would you insist on the real thing?

Jerome and Jeannie Tiras have been building their business since 1989 on the obvious answer, with a great lineup of copies of handbags by well-known designers, sans trademarks, logos, etc. If you know the originals, you'll recognize the copies—but not the prices, which average $80 to $160 for the leather copies, and begin at $75 for a gold evening bag and run to $750 for a leopard-patterned mini-audiere done completely in rhinestones and crystals. (The inspirations for many of the evening bags are Judith Leiber's creations, which routinely fetch $950 to thousands of dollars for jewel-encrusted specimens. The "everyday" bags are copies of designer originals selling for $300 to $2,000.) Tiras' color brochure shows a selection of handbags, totes, change purses, wallets, purse accessories, and other little luxuries, as well as a collection of fashion jewelry.

Special Factors: Unused returns (except sale items) are accepted within 10 days for exchange, refund, or credit; minimum order is $50.

RELATED PRODUCTS/COMPANIES

Cowhides • Steerhides
Deerskin goods • The Deerskin Place
Leather-care products • Dairy Association, Justin Discount Boots, UPCO, Weaver Leather, Bailey's
Luggage • Bennett Brothers, Damark
Luggage carts • Bennett Brothers
Replacement luggage-weight zippers • A. Feibusch
Sheepskin goods • Arctic Sheepskin
Small leather goods • Bennett Brothers, Huntington Clothiers

──MUSIC, AUDIO, AND VIDEO──
Audiocassettes, CDs, LPs, and Videotapes

Music, instructional, and entertainment audio and video media

The companies in this section sell music of all types, in all forms—from old-fashioned vinyl LPs to high-tech CDs—and audio selections that include radio dramas and music instruction. (For books on cassette, see the "Books, Audiobooks, and Periodicals" chapter.) You'll also find movie, stand-up comedy, and educational videos in every conceivable category, including vintage, alternative, and hard-to-find selections.

If you're a web surfer, check out CDnow's website (http://www.cdnow.com) for an all-purpose music information site (also see company listing, this section). CDnow has one of the best collections of music-related links to other internet sites.

FIND IT FAST

EDUCATIONAL AND INSTRUCTIONAL VIDEOS • Homespun Tapes, Video Yesteryear
LPs • Berkshire Record Outlet, CDnow, Harvard Square, Record-Rama, Upstairs Records
MUSIC AND ENTERTAINMENT VIDEOS • CDnow, Harvard Square, Video Yesteryear
MUSIC CDs AND AUDIOCASSETTES • Adventures in Cassettes, CDnow, Upstairs Records

USED CDs AND AUDIOCASSETTES • Audio House, Berkshire Record Outlet, Harvard Square, Record-Rama
VINTAGE RADIO AUDIOCASSETTES • Adventures in Cassettes
VINTAGE TV/CINEMA VIDEOS • Video Yesteryear

ADVENTURES IN CASSETTES

A DIVISION OF META-COM, INC.
5353 NATHAN LANE,
DEPT. WO99
PLYMOUTH, MN 55442
800–328–0108
FAX: 612–553–0424

Catalog: free
Pay: check, MO, MC, V, AE, Discover
Sells: audiotapes and music CDs
Store: mail order only
E-mail: aic4radio@aol.com
Online: http://www.aic-radio.com

Adventures in Cassettes offers hundreds of audiotapes featuring vintage radio classics, for those of us who long for the days of being entertained with the radio, our hands busy, or having a story told to us with the lights out. The selection includes such comedy greats as Amos 'n Andy, Abbott and Costello, Baby Snooks, The Great Gildersleeve, The Bickersons, Fibber McGee and Molly, Burns and Allen, Jack Benny, Fred Allen, and Our Miss Brooks. If mysteries, thrillers, and adventure are more your line, see the selection of *New Adventures of Sherlock Holmes, Crime Classics, Dark Fantasy, Weird Circle,* and *Murder at Midnight.* And the Western classics are here as well: *Have Gun, Will Travel; Gunsmoke;* and *Sergeant Preston of the Yukon* among them.

Special Factors: Satisfaction is guaranteed; returns are accepted within 30 days for exchange, refund, or credit.

AUDIO HOUSE

P.O. BOX 531-G
GRAND BLANC, MI
  48439–0531
810–695–3415
FAX: 810–695–1753

Catalog: $3, refundable (see text)
Pay: check, MO, MC, V, AE, DC, Discover
Sells: used music CDs
Store: mail order only
E-mail: ahcd@tir.com
Online: http://audiohousecd.com

Audio House has been brokering used CDs to individuals since 1983 and provides you with a great market and great prices—whether you're buying or selling. Audio House publishes a master catalog of CD listings every two months and releases a 10-page supplement in the off months. A sample costs $3 (refundable with purchase), and a year's subscription is $10 ($12 to Canada)—but it's a free download from the website. There's something for everyone here, from world music to Better Than Ezra to Andy Williams. Audio House makes its stock of 15,000 titles available through the catalog or website only—there is no membership fee. A number of the selections are on obscure labels, and locating them here at an average of about $8, guaranteed to play like new, is an audiophile's dream. On the website you can search, order, and download the catalog for instant gratification. If you want to cull your own collection, see the catalog for details on selling your used CDs to Audio House. Audio House also offers an interesting fund-raiser: If you are trying to raise money for band uniforms or your church needs a new roof, your group can donate a few of their unwanted CDs for cash.

Wholesale buyers, please note: Contact Audio House for details on resale terms and pricing.

Canadian readers, please note: Only U.S. funds are accepted, or payment should be made by credit card.

Special Factors: Satisfaction is guaranteed; returns are accepted within 30 days for exchange, refund, or credit; phone hours are Monday to Friday 10–6.

BERKSHIRE RECORD OUTLET

R.R. 1, RTE. 102 PLEASANT
 ST.
LEE, MA 01238–9804
413–243–4080
FAX: 413–243–4340

Catalog: $2 cash; $5 check or credit card
Pay: check, MO, MC, V
Sells: classical recordings
Store: same address; Saturday 10–5:30
Online: http://www.berkshirecoutlet.com

If you're an LP holdout who loves classical music, Berkshire is your source: 220 pages of thousands of classical overstocked and remaindered recordings—LPs, tapes, and compact discs—at savings of 33%-plus on the release prices. The catalog is organized alphabetically by label—from Abbey to Xenophone—and by price within those groupings. Each entry is coded to indicate whether the recording is offered in stereo, mono, quadraphonic, or reprocessed stereo mode (or in digital or analog CD), and the country of origin is noted if the recording is an import. Berkshire has been in business since 1974 and is a gold mine for lovers of classical music, but note that sound tracks, ethnic music, folk songs, and poetry readings also appear. Several pages of remaindered books on classical music and musicians round out the collection.

Japanese customers, please note: The website includes a Japanese-language version.

Special Factors: Minimum order is $15, inclusive of shipping.

CDNOW

JENKINS COURT, STE. 300
610 OLD YORK RD.
JENKINTOWN, PA 19046
800–595–6874
215–885–8471
FAX: 800–461–9232

Information: internet website, no catalog
Pay: check, MO, MC, V, AE, Discover
Sells: music CDs, movies, and music videos
Store: online only
Online: http://www.cdnow.com

CDnow carries almost every album currently in print in the United States. Their prices are 30% and more below other CD stores—as a "cyberstore" they don't have to pay for floor space. This site is laid out for maximum usability. The music inventory at CDnow is separated into Music (Rock, Jazz, Country, etc.) and Classical. In Music you can search by artist (when you do, you'll be able to see everything he or she has recorded that's still in print, as well as a listing of "Not Available" titles), by album, or by song title. There's lots here for the browser—in-depth reviews, ratings, and biographical information written by well-known freelance music writers, discussion groups, sound samples, and music-related links galore. The Classical section allows you to search by composer, title of album or composition, performer or soloist, conductor, record label, primary instrument, genre, and several other elements. The site at the time of writing featured American Music Awards titles at $8.49—50% off list. This site also sells vinyl LPs and CD imports, as well as movies, music videos, Japanese import videos, DVDs (digital video discs), music-related books, tee shirts, and more.

Special Factors: Any item can be returned within 30 days of delivery for full refund, except Japanese imports, vinyl, and tee shirts (unless defective); see website for details.

HARVARD SQUARE RECORDS, INC.

P.O. BOX 381975-W9
CAMBRIDGE, MA 02238
617–868–3385
FAX: 617–547–2838

Catalog: $2–$5 (see text)
Pay: check, MO, MC, V
Sells: out-of-print LPs, audiotapes, and videotapes
Store: mail order only
E-mail: hsrecord@user1.channel1.com
Online: http://www.lpnow.com

Harvard Square has been doing business since 1985 selling sealed, current-issue, and out-of-print LPs, and it offers a large selection of imports and cutouts. (Cutouts are discontinued records, equivalent to remaindered books; they're often so marked by notching or cutting out a small piece of the corner of the jacket or cover—hence the name.) Harvard Square has separate catalogs devoted to vinyl, cassettes, and video. The current "Sealed Vinyl" catalog runs from Jon Anderson to the Vienna Boys Choir, and many of the LPs cost just $4 to $6. The music is listed alphabetically within category: Rock and Pop, R&B and Dance, Blues, Jazz and Easy Listening, Country and Gospel, World and Traditional, Spoken Word, Sound Effects, Soundtracks, Classical, and others.

When you send your catalog fee ($2 to the U.S., $3 to Canada, $5 to international addresses), specify LPs, videos, or audiotapes (cassettes), and you'll receive the appropriate catalog. Please note that stock cannot be held, so order promptly; if the item is sold out, you'll receive a refund check or a merchandise credit—you can indicate which you'd prefer on the order form.

Special Factors: Returns of defective (unplayable) goods are accepted within 14 days for replacement or merchandise credit. There is no minimum order.

HOMESPUN TAPES

BOX 340, DEPT. WH
WOODSTOCK, NY 12498
800–338–2737
914–246–2550
FAX: 914–246–5282

Catalog: free
Pay: check, MO, MC, V, Discover
Sells: music instruction videos, audiocassettes, CDs, and books; and miscellaneous recording and music supplies
Store: mail order only
E-mail: hmspn@aol.com

If the best way to learn is by doing, then pick up that banjo, flute, or accordion collecting dust in your corner and start playing. Have no fear, because Homespun Tapes, founded in 1981 by Jane and Happy Traum (the latter of the folk/blues duo Happy and Artie Traum), will guide you through the learning or mastering process with their unique instructional music tapes. If you've been wanting to take lessons but have been too busy or broke, these tapes will restore your confidence and save you money at the same time.

Homespun's 72-page catalog features instructional videotapes, audiocassettes, and CDs by the very best musicians in their fields. You can learn guitar arrangement from Patty Larkin; jazz piano from Warren Bernhardt; singing techniques from Maria Muldaur; fingerpicking and flatpicking from Doc Watson; banjo from Pete Seeger; Appalachian dulcimer from Lorraine Lee; and on and on. There are instructional tapes for children and tapes for musicians at all levels of expertise. The tapes are created with close-ups and split-screen imaging techniques, three-camera systems, good studios, and top camera operators to present the clearest possible angles. There are about 250 titles in the current catalog, spanning accordions to whistling, averaging in price from about $15 to $40. Homespun Tapes also has a small selection of musician supplies, such as study recorders, Keith tuners, and slides and strings, as well as scores of books. But the real bargain here is the time and money you'll save by taking lessons from a pro right in your own home.

Special to readers of this book: If you mention BWBM, Homespun Tapes will take 20% off your initial instructional videotape, audiocassette, or CD order.

Special Factors: Overseas customers can wire money directly into Homespun's bank account or pay by credit card or in U.S. funds; returns are accepted, but see catalog for more details; wholesale orders are available (call Hal Leonard at 800–554–0626).

RECORD-RAMA
SOUND ARCHIVES

4981 MCKNIGHT RD.
PITTSBURGH, PA
   15237–3407
412–367–7330
FAX: 412–367–7388

Information: price quote
Pay: check, MO, MC, V, AE, Discover
Sells: vintage 45s, LPs, and CDs
Store: same address; Tuesday to Saturday
10–6, closed Sunday and Monday
E-mail: record-rama@musicmaster.com
Online: http://www.musicmaster.com

When word reached the Library of Congress that a retired paper goods salesman was claiming to have the country's largest known collection of 45s, a curator was sent over to check it out. Sure enough: Record-Rama Sound Archives, which shares a building with the local post office, holds the record with 1.5 million oldies on 45s, plus a million LPs. Paul C. Mawhinney's collection began with his youthful purchase of Frankie Lane's "Jezebel," and an obsession was born.

Mr. Mawhinney isn't sitting on this national treasure; he has created the MusicMaster: The 45 RPM Singles Directory, the ultimate reference on 45s produced from 1948 to 1996. The MusicMaster, organized by artist and title, is now the most-used reference in the New York Public Library, and a must-have for any library or serious collector. Record-Rama offers the MusicMaster Database, and other directories—the CD–5 Singles Directory and the 45 RPM Christmas Singles Directory, both by artist/title. (Call for current directory prices.) Mr. Mawhinney's CD collection currently numbers over 300,000, and he has amassed a large selection of CD-ROMs as well. If you're looking for a title, he probably has it—just call and ask, or use his WORLDSEARCH LP and CD locating service. Maintenance products for LPs and CDs are available, as well as over 10,000 phonograph needles and other supplies for DJs. By press time, Record-Rama promises to have the world's largest online database on the history of American music. Check it out!

Please note: Just mention BWBM and get an additional 10% discount on any record and any single disc CD (multiple discs and boxed sets are excluded).

Special Factors: Calls are not accepted on the weekends; phone quotes are limited to two requests per call.

UPSTAIRS RECORDS

140 58TH ST., DEPT. WBM,
STE. 6W
BROOKLYN, NY
11220–2521
800–487–7824
718–567–3333
FAX: 888–666–8778
FAX: 718–567–2310

Catalog: free
Pay: check, MO, MC, V, AE, Discover
Sells: DJ equipment, sound, lighting, and recordings
Store: 2968 Avenue X, Brooklyn, NY; Monday to Thursday 9–7, Friday 9–5, Sunday 10–5, closed Saturdays
E-mail: sales@upstairsrecords.com
Online: http://www.upstairsrecords.com

Whether you're just looking for a classic copy of Boogie Down Productions on wax or are buying the lighting and equipment for a club, Upstairs Records is your source. This Brooklyn-based music emporium specializes in DJ equipment, club gear, and hip hop music, much of which is produced by small independent labels—hard to find at all in some parts of the country, and rarely at savings of up to 35% (see the catalog for the "low price guarantee"). Upstairs Records offers a "Vinyl Record Pool," a standing-order service for new releases in "hard-core rap, R&B, hip hop, dance, or reggae" and a "Vinyl Fax Club," which entitles you to receive a monthly list of 12" singles and vinyl LPs in stock, and includes special discounts and giveaways. (Current terms and order forms for these services can be found in the catalog.)

Upstairs Records has two catalogs, one with equipment, the other with music only. The 75-page equipment catalog has everything to turn you into a mixing, sampling, scratching fool—or at least that's what the neighbors will think. Turn here for discount prices on 4-track recorders, CD players, DAT recorders, digital samplers, DJ videos, lighting—including strobe, special effects, and others—microphones, mixers of all types, studio monitors, vinyl accessories, and much more from top-name manufacturers. Upstairs Records can also help you design a sound system for your restaurant, club, or bar—just fax the blueprints with your sound and lighting ideas. The 64-page music catalog is a deejay's dream, with hundreds of CDs and cassettes ranging from big band to comedy to gospel to Latin to rap to soundtracks, and everything in between. There's more of everything on the website, which is updated daily and offers new-release information, top-selling music charts, special deals and close-outs, write-ups, and a section for vinyl and breakbeats. You can order directly online.

Special Factors: Authorized returns are accepted within 30 days with some limitations and restrictions; see the catalog for sales terms and price protection policy.

VIDEO YESTERYEAR

BOX C, DEPT. WBM 99
SANDY HOOK, CT 06482
800–243–0987
FAX: 203–797–0819

Catalog: $4.95 and $3.95 (see text)
Pay: check, MO, MC, V, AE, CB, DC, Discover
Sells: ancient and obscure cinema videotapes
Store: mail order only
E-mail: video@yesteryear.com
Online: http://www.yesteryear.com

"Why would anyone in his right mind buy video cassettes by mail?" So begins the introduction in Video Yesteryear's 362-page catalog. Here's why: Video Yesteryear offers hard-to-find videos—including many foreign films, nostalgia movies, silent films, and old TV shows—at great prices. If you're a movie or old TV buff, you know that very few video stores carry these titles. The phonebook-sized, black-and-white catalog is filled with thousands of titles in categories that include comedy/cartoons, music, drama, adventures, crime/mystery/horror, westerns, serials, sword and sandal, documentary/exploitation/avant-garde/ propaganda, and golden age of TV. This company even has films dating back to 1896! Whether you're a teacher looking for an illuminating documentary on the U.S. government's campaign to kindle the fires of patriotism among Negroes during World War II (*The Negro Soldier,* produced by Frank Capra in 1944), a parent wishing to introduce her child to 1930s cartoon classics, or a hostess throwing a silent movie party for friends, this is a great source.

So vast is Video Yesteryear's inventory that they've produced two catalogs, Volume 1 ($4.95) and Volume 2 ($3.95). Each catalog has an index that covers the entire Video Yesteryear inventory. The website will give you a sampling from which you can order online, but it's not as extensive as the catalogs. (You can also request a shorter, abbreviated catalog that's free.) The prices at Video Yesteryear are very reasonable when you take advantage of the "buy three and get one free" offer, as well as the discounted videos listed in a separate section of the large catalog. If you order 13, you'll get an additional 10% off. Videotapes are available in VHS, BETA, and 8mm formats, as well as European formats.

Wholesalers: Please inquire about resale prices and minimums.

Special Factors: Wholesale orders available; online ordering available; products guaranteed to be free of manufacturing defects or defective merchandise replaced (company will not exchange one title for another); internet customers: call or see website for special ordering instructions.

RELATED PRODUCTS/COMPANIES

Alternative and underground culture videos • *Essential Media*

Animal-care and training videos • *KV Vet, Drs. Foster & Smith, Kennel Vet, That Fish Place/That Pet Place, Valley Vet*

Art-related videos • *Jerry's Artarama, Ceramic Supply of New York & New Jersey, Art Express, The Potters Shop*

Craft and hobby instructional videos • *Brushy Mountain Bee Farm, Sewin' in Vermont, Baron Barclay Bridge Supplies, Woodworkers' Discount Books, Glass Crafters, Axner Pottery Supply, Weaver Leather*

Documentary and educational videos • *The Scholar's Bookshelf, Essential Media, Shar Products*

Do-it-yourself instructional videos • *Woodworkers' Discount Books, Reader's Digest*

Entertainment videos • *Barnes & Noble, Bear Mountain Books, Gold Medal Hair Products*

Exercise videos • *Reader's Digest, Amplestuff*

IMAX videotapes • *The Astronomical Society*

Language audiotapes • *Dover Publications*

Music CDs and audiotapes • *Damark, Shar Products, Daedalus, Barnes & Noble, Essential Media, Bear Mountain Books, Reader's Digest, Gold Medal Hair Products, Anyone Can Whistle*

Music-related instructional videos • *Shar Products, Musician's Friend, Elderly Instruments, American Musical Supply*

Sports-related videos • *The House*

Survival and hunting videos • *Cutlery Shoppe, Deer Shack*

Audio and Video Equipment and Supplies

Stereo and speaker systems, CD players, radios, VCRs, camcorders, home entertainment systems, etc.

Whether you're a regular Joe wanting a pair of good speakers for your car or a sound nut who can't stand to listen to R&B CDs without a subwoofer, the firms in this section will please you with audio supplies and equipment up to 80% off regular retail. Some of these companies also sell video equipment such as camcorders, VCRs, and all-around home-entertainment systems. Between the price of technology going down and the good discounts offered by these companies, you'll find some amazing deals here.

For firms that sell related goods, particularly equipment for stage, studio, and deejay, as well as electronic instruments and supplies, see the section following this one, "Musical Instruments, Accessories, and Sound Equipment," page 426. And refer to "Related Products/Companies" at the end of this section for other firms that sell audio, sound, and recording equipment as well as video-related goods.

FIND IT FAST

AUDIO EQUIPMENT • CAM Audio, Crutchfield, J&R Music World, S&S Sound City
BLANK AUDIO- AND VIDEOTAPES • CAM Audio, Wholesale Tape and Supply
DUPLICATING SERVICES FOR AUDIO- AND VIDEOTAPES • Wholesale Tape and Supply

PHONOGRAPH PARTS AND SUPPLIES • Lyle Cartridges
SPEAKER KITS • Gold Sound
SPEAKERS • Audio Concepts, Crutchfield, J&R Music World
USED, DEMO, AND CLOSE-OUT AUDIO AND VIDEO EQUIPMENT • Gold Sound,
Westcoast Discount Video
VIDEO EQUIPMENT • CAM Audio, Crutchfield, J&R Music World, S&S Sound City,
Westcoast Discount Video

AUDIO CONCEPTS, INC.

901 S. 4TH ST., DEPT. WBMC
LA CROSSE, WI 54601
608–784–4570
FAX: 608–784–6367

Brochure: free
Pay: check, MO, MC, V
Sells: ACI speakers
Store: mail order only
E-mail: aci@lse.fullfeed.com
Online: http://www.audioc.com

If you'd like to assemble a good audio system but don't think you can afford it, here's one way to save on the thing that seems to cost the most—the speakers. Audio Concepts, Inc., (ACI) has been manufacturing and selling speakers factory-direct since 1977 and suggests that you can save up to 50% over the cost of comparable speakers. ACI's models are sold in pairs and individually, and a home theater package is available. ACI sells everything from satellites to three-ways, in-wall speakers to subwoofers, center channels to rear speakers. The cabinets, made with furniture-grade wood veneers, are offered in a number of finishes. A recent sale had a pair of wall speakers for $139 and a package featuring a pair of Sapphire III's with a Titan subwoofer for $1,699. The website and brochure show the speakers and a range of accessories—stands, cables, wall brackets, etc.

Special Factors: Satisfaction is guaranteed; authorized returns in new condition sent in the original packaging are accepted within 15 days for exchange, refund, or credit.

CAM AUDIO, INC.

MISSIONARY TAPE AND EQUIPMENT SUPPLY
2210 EXECUTIVE DR.
GARLAND, TX 75041
800–527–3458
972–271–0006
FAX: 972–271–1555

Catalog: free
Pay: check, MO, MC, V, Discover
Sells: audio and video components, blank tapes, etc.
Store: same address; Monday to Friday 8:30–5
Online: http://www.camaudio.com

CAM Audio, in business for nearly 30 years, was recommended by a reader for excellent service and prices on audio and video products. The audio line includes tapes, labels, albums, and storage units; in video, you'll find cameras, decks and monitors, and a full line of blank videotape. The sound equipment includes microphones, speakers, mixers, and amps. Available brands include Ampex, Anchor Audio, Apollo, Ashley, Bogen, Crown, Draper, Electro-Voice, Elmo, JVC, Marantz, Maxell, Motorola, Panasonic, Phonic, Sanyo, Sharp, Shure, Sony, TDK, Teac, Telex, 3M, Ultimate Support, University Sound, and Videonics. See the catalog for current offerings, and if you're pricing anything in the audio or video line from the firms mentioned here, you can call or write with the model number for a price quote. CAM is also a leading supplier of discount-priced church equipment through its Missionary Tape division.

Special Factors: Price quote by phone or letter.

CRUTCHFIELD

1 CRUTCHFIELD PARK,
DEPT. WH
CHARLOTTESVILLE, VA
22911–9097
800–955–9009
FAX: 804–817–1010
TDD: 800–388–9753

Catalog: free (see text)
Pay: check, MO, MC, V, AE, CB, Discover
Sells: audio and video components, home theater, car stereos, telephones and pagers, and digital satellite systems
Store: Rio Hill Shopping Center, Charlottesville, and Market Square East Shopping Center, Harrisonburg, VA
E-mail: webmaster@crutchfield.com
Online: http://www.crutchfield.com

Crutchfield publishes an informative, 120-plus-page catalog of home and car stereo components, home theater and digital satellite systems, video equipment, telephones, and car alarms. The catalog is loaded with buying tips and product specifications on featured goods, which are priced from 10% to 55% below list. Good prices are just one of the pluses here—you may find the Crutchfield catalog more helpful when you're comparing product features than the articles in industry magazines. Crutchfield backs everything it sells with a guarantee of satisfaction, and the staff can provide extensive support. Installation walk- throughs over the phone, custom installation kits and wiring harnesses for car stereos, and informative consumer service guides are among the available benefits. Crutchfield, which was established in 1974, is a factory-authorized repair station for most of the brands it sells and does not sell gray-market goods.

Crutchfield's car stereo components line, which includes equipment for pickup trucks and hatchbacks, features goods by Blaupunkt, Cerwin-Vega, Clarion, Clarion ProAudio, Infinity, JBL, Jensen, JVC, Kenwood, Kenwood Excelon, Kicker, MTX, Panasonic, Pioneer, Polk Audio, Profile, Pyle, Sanyo, Sony, Sony ES, and USAcoustics. Crutchfield also sells radar detectors by BEL and Whistler, as well as dozens of types of car antennas, and Crimestopper alarm systems to protect your investment.

The home audio portion of the catalog includes pages of features and comparisons of current models of receivers, CD players, cassette decks, speakers, and shelf systems, and shows digital satellite systems and accessories, portable and personal audio, home theater systems, remote controls, CD cabinets, and other accessories. The brands include AR, Bose, Carver, Harman-Kardon, Infinity, JVC, Kenwood, NHT, Pioneer,

Polk Audio, Sony, Sony ES, Technics, and Yamaha. You'll also find camcorders, DVD players, TVs, and VCRs from JVC, Panasonic, Pioneer, and Sony offered here.

Please note: The catalog is free to readers of this book, but be sure to identify yourself as a BWBM reader when you request your copy.

If you're online, be sure to check out Crutchfield's website, which is always being favorably reviewed by web critics and consumers alike for its selection, user-friendly format, and forward-thinking attitude.

Special Factors: Satisfaction is guaranteed; returns are accepted within 30 days.

GOLD SOUND

4285 S. BROADWAY,
   DEPT. WBM
ENGLEWOOD, CO 80110
303–761–3652
FAX: 303–762–0527

Catalog: free
Pay: check, MO, MC, V, AE, Discover
Sells: high-end speaker kits; used, demo, and close-out home and professional audio equipment
Store: same address; Monday to Friday 10–6, Saturday 11–5

If you thought you had to spend thousands to get high-end speakers, think again. Gold Sound has designed and sold quality speaker kits for home and professional use since 1976. Speaker kit advantages include: (1) better sound, deeper bass, greater clarity; (2) lower cost (up to 80% savings!); (3) greater flexibility in size, wood finish, and appearance, plus space-saving units you can build into walls, ceilings, and furniture; (4) easy upgrades for newer technologies (you can dramatically improve your existing 25-year-old speakers); and (5) they're educational and fun! *Stereo Review* has praised Gold Sound speakers as the high end of the high end; they've won the International Consumer Electronics Show's Innovation Design Award; and they're used by NASA, Boeing, and scores of institutions and corporations.

In prebuilt speakers, you pay mainly for labor, advertising, overhead, and store markup. Use your time and only pay for what makes sound: the working parts. A Gold Sound $299 kit has better parts and sound, says owner/designer Ron Gold, than $1,000 assembled units. All kits use high-quality European- and U.S.-made components, yet several cost under $200. The kits include detailed, easy-to-follow plans. Kits with completely built cabinets need as little as one evening to assemble. The kits are also available without cabinets, for people who prefer to make their own. Home kits for stereo or home theater use include sub-woofers, satellites, bookshelves, towers, centers, surrounds, and in-wall models. Pro models are popular for clubs, musicians, deejays, schools, and churches. The catalog lists and describes in detail each Gold Sound Kit, and also has some amazing deals (up to 70% off retail) on close-outs, demos, and used units, including receivers, amplifiers, CD players, turntables, tuners, tape decks, mixers, microphones, and pro equipment from well-respected makers. If you're in the area, stop by Gold Sound's Denver showroom, where you can hear many assembled kits.

Special Factors: Speaker kits have a 30-day money-back guarantee and a 2-year replacement warranty; quantity discounts are available.

J&R MUSIC WORLD

59–50 QUEENS-MIDTOWN
EXPRESSWAY, DEPT.
WLO99
MASPETH, NY 11378–9896
800–221–8180
FAX: 800–232–4432

Catalog: free
Pay: check, MO, MC, V, AE, Discover
Sells: audio, video, computers, music, small appliances, etc.
Store: Park Row, New York, NY; Monday to Saturday 9–6:30, Sunday 10–6
Online: http://www.jandr.com

J&R enjoys top billing among New York City electronics and computer discounters for its depth of saving and selection, especially in the audio, video, and computer departments. You can call for the 216-page catalog or to get price quotes on current lines of TVs, VCRs and video equipment, audio components and equipment, computers and peripherals, phones, fax machines, radar detectors, cameras, and personal appliances. J&R also sells tapes, music CDs, and software, as well as exercise equipment, vacuum cleaners and microwave ovens, and even cigar humidors, pens, and watches. All major brand names, from Advent to Yamaha, are represented here, and everything sold by J&R is guaranteed to be brand-new and factory fresh.

Special Factors: Satisfaction is guaranteed.

LYLE CARTRIDGES

115 S. CORONA AVE.,
  DEPT. WBMC
VALLEY STREAM, NY 11582
800–221–0906
516–599–1112
FAX: 516–599–2027

Catalog: free with SASE
Pay: check, MO, MC, V, AE, Discover
Sells: phono cartridges, replacement styli, turntables, tone arms, and phono-related accessories
Store: same address; Monday to Friday 9–5, Saturday 10–1 (October to May)
E-mail: lylemax@aol.com

Lyle Cartridges has been in business since 1952 and is a great source for the cartridges and replacement styli (factory original) that bring your LP music to life. If you're sticking by your LPs despite music CDs, you'll really appreciate this reliable, well-informed source. As the proprietors put it, "We specialize in phono-related products, and have the largest stock of 78 RPM replacement styli in the country. As LPs have become harder to find, so too have our products and services."

Lyle sells phono cartridges and replacement styli by Audioquest, Audio-Technica, Bang & Olufsen, Blue Oasis, Clearaudio, Grado, Ortofon, Pickering, Shure, Stanton, and Sumiko. Record-care products by Discwasher, LAST, Techniclean, and VPI are stocked. Lyle also sells Grado headphones, turntables by Rotel and VPI, and other accessories including record-cleaning machines, parts, phono-alignment tools, record sleeves, and more. This is the first source to consult if you have to replace arm parts, since you may be able to save on both labor and material costs—parts prices are up to 60% less than list or comparable retail.

Special Factors: Authorized returns are accepted; defective goods are replaced; minimum order is $15, $25 with credit cards.

S&S SOUND CITY

58 W. 45TH ST.,
DEPT. WBMC
NEW YORK, NY
10036–4280
800–326–1677
212–575–0210
FAX: 212–221–7907

Information: price quote
Pay: check, MO, MC, V, AE, Discover
Sells: audio and video, home-office products, air conditioners
Store: same address; Monday to Friday 8:30–7, Saturday 9–6

S&S Sound City has been in business since 1975, selling TVs and video equipment, audio components, radios, telephones, microwave ovens, air conditioners, DVD, closed-circuit TV systems, and video surveillance systems. The inventory includes goods from Air Temp, Carrier, Denon, Friedrich, General Electric, Harman-Kardon, JBL, JVC, Mitsubishi, Motorola, Onkyo, Panasonic, ProScan, Quasar, RCA, Sharp, Sony, Southwestern Bell, and Technics. Call or write for a price quote.

Special Factors: Returns are accepted within seven days; special orders are accepted.

WESTCOAST DISCOUNT VIDEO

5201 EASTERN AVE.
BALTIMORE, MD 21224
410–633–0508
410–633–8171
FAX: 410–633–7888

Pay: check, MO, MC, V, AE, Discover
Sells: video equipment and accessories
Store: Monday to Friday 9–6, Wednesday and Saturday 9–1 ET

Westcoast Discount Video is a specialty firm dealing with a wide variety of video equipment and accessories for all analog formats—i.e., VHS, SVHS, 8mm, Hi-8, VHS-C, and SVHS-C, as well as the new digital. This is an excellent source for auxiliary lenses, filters, lighting equipment, batteries, battery chargers, power packs, microphones, tripods, and other equipment on both current and not-so-current models at a savings of up to 50%. They can also custom-design a video system that's just right for individual needs and preferences—free of charge.

Special Factors: Price quote by phone; shipping not charged on orders over $75; C.O.D. orders accepted.

WHOLESALE TAPE AND SUPPLY COMPANY

2841 HICKORY VALLEY RD.
CHATTANOOGA, TN
  34714
800–251–7228
FAX: 423–894–7281

Catalog: free
Pay: check, MO, MC, V, AE, Discover
Sells: audio and video duplicating services, CD replication, blank tapes, etc.
Store: same address; call for hours
Online: http://www.wts-tape.com

Wholesale Tape, which has been selling audiovisual supplies and services worldwide since 1977, publishes a catalog featuring blank audio- and videocassettes, AV accessories, high-speed audio duplicating equipment, and duplication services for CD, audio, and video. Wholesale Tape produces audiotapes for professional duplication; different types of cassettes are available in clear, white, and black shells (housing) and standard tape lengths (12 to 122 minutes); custom tape lengths and colors can be provided. Wholesale Tape also sells audio- and videotape from Ampex, Fuji, and Maxell.

If you need an audiotape or videotape copied or distributed but don't have the necessary equipment, consider Wholesale Tape's duplicating and fulfillment services. Custom labels and shell imprinting can be produced, and cassette boxes, albums, shipping envelopes, and storage units are also sold.

Special Factors: Satisfaction is guaranteed; quantity discounts are offered; C.O.D. orders are accepted; minimum order is $30.

RELATED PRODUCTS/COMPANIES

Car audio systems • *Percy's, Bernie's Discount, Crutchfield*
CD players and other audio components • *American Musical Supply, Damark, Bernie's Discount, Percy's, Beach Sales, Upstairs Records, Crutchfield, EBA Wholesale, B & H Photo-Video–Pro Audio*
Digital recording equipment • *American Musical Supply, Wray's Music House*

Radios • Defender Industries
Sound systems • Sam Ash
Surplus audio/video parts • H&R Company, All Electronics
Video equipment • Percy's, Bernie's Discount, Damark, Beach Sales, Crutchfield, EBA Wholesale, LVT Price Quote Hotline, Cole's Appliance, Porter's Camera Store, B & H Photo-Video—Pro Audio
Video imaging kits • MacWarehouse

Musical Instruments, Accessories, and Sound Equipment

New and used musical instruments; sheet music, instrument stands, parts, and other musician supplies; sound and recording equipment for stage, studio, and deejay

Whereas the firms in the previous section carry goods primarily for people who listen to music, this section features companies that cater to those who play or produce music. The firms listed here sell top-quality instruments—everything from school band recorders to grand pianos. Professional musicians rarely pay full price for their instruments, and if you buy from the same sources they use, neither will you. You'll also find electronic equipment and supplies for professional or at-home studio recording, as well as stage electronics, deejay equipment, and even karaoke machines.

FIND IT FAST

ACCORDIONS AND CONCERTINAS • Accordion-O-Rama
BAND INSTRUMENTS • Giardinelli Band Instrument, Interstate Music Supply, National Educational Music Co., Swords Music Companies, West Manor
BRASS AND WOODWINDS AND ACCESSORIES • Discount Reed, JAYNEL Instrument Stands, Kennelly Keys
CHILDREN'S MUSICAL INSTRUMENTS AND MUSIC-RELATED TOYS • Anyone Can Whistle

ELECTRONIC KEYBOARD • Interstate Music Supply, Kennelly Keys, Musician's Friend

GENERAL MUSICAL INSTRUMENTS • American Musical Supply, Anyone Can Whistle, Sam Ash, Elderly Instruments, Giardinelli Band Instrument, Interstate Music Supply, National Educational Music Co., Swords Music Companies, Thoroughbred Music, West Manor

GUITARS, STRINGED INSTRUMENTS, AND ACCESSORIES • Carvin Corp., Interstate Music Supply, Kennelly Keys, Mandolin Brothers, Metropolitan Music, Musician's Friend, Shar Products, Weinkrantz

MUSICAL CHIMES • American Musical Supply, Anyone Can Whistle

PERCUSSION INSTRUMENTS • Anyone Can Whistle, Interstate Music Supply, Kennelly Keys

PIANOS AND ORGANS • Altenburg Piano House

SONGBOOKS AND SHEET MUSIC • Elderly Instruments, Patti Music Company, Shar Products, Wray's Music House

STAGE AND STUDIO ELECTRONICS AND EQUIPMENT • Sam Ash, Carvin Corp., Interstate Music Supply, Musician's Friend, Thoroughbred Music, Wray's Music House

USED INSTRUMENTS • Altenburg Piano House, Elderly Instruments, Mandolin Brothers, Wray's Music House

---

ACCORDION-O-RAMA

307 SEVENTH AVE., 20TH FL., DEPT. WBMC
NEW YORK, NY 10001
212–675–9089
FAX: 212–206–8344

Catalog: $1
Pay: check, MO, MC, V
Sells: accordions, accessories, and services
Store: same address; Tuesday to Friday 10–5, Saturday 11–3 (may be open longer; call)

Accordion-O-Rama, in business since 1950, has an extensive inventory of new and rebuilt accordions and concertinas that are all sold at a discount. Accordion-O-Rama is an authorized dealer and factory-service center for several leading brands. They can tune and repair your instrument and will customize your instrument to meet your requirements—including MIDI. Concertinas and accordions—electronic, chromatic, diatonic, and piano—are offered here at considerable savings. Accordion-O-Rama carries its own line, as well as instruments by Arpeggio, Avanti, Cordovox, Crumar, Dallape, Elka, Excelsior, Farfisa, Ferrari, Gabbanelli, Galanti, Guerrini, Hohner, Polytone, Sano, Scandalli, Solton, Sonola, Paolo

Soprani, Vox, and other firms. The catalog features color photos of individual models with specifications. New and reconditioned models are stocked, and accordion synthesizers, amps, speakers, generators, organ-accordions, and accordion stands are available.

When you write for information, be sure to describe the type of accordion that interests you. In addition to the color catalog ($1), you can request the black-and-white catalog, which is free, or order a video: The "Demonstration" video provides a tour of Accordion-O-Rama, and the "Basics of MIDI" tape gives an introduction to MIDI. Either tape can be purchased for $25 or both for $45 (postpaid in the United States).

Special Factors: Trade-ins are welcomed; wholesale prices are based on volume.

ALTENBURG PIANO HOUSE, INC.

1150 E. JERSEY ST.
ELIZABETH, NJ 07201
908–351–2000
FAX: 908–527–9210

Brochure: free
Pay: check, MO, MC, V, AE, Discover
Sells: pianos and organs
Store: same address; Monday to Friday 8–7, Saturday 8–5, Sunday 12–5; also Asbury Park and Trenton, NJ

The Altenburg Piano House has been doing business since 1847, and it is still run today by the Altenburg family. Altenburg sells pianos and organs by "almost all" manufacturers, including lines by Hammond, Petrof, Mason & Hamlin, Bechstein, Bluthner, used Baldwin, and various one-of-a-kind pianos, as well as Altenburg's own models. Prices are at least 35% below list or suggested retail. If you call for literature, you'll receive information and specifications on Altenburg's line of upright, grand, and console models, including details on encasing, action, workmanship, and warranty. If you're in the area of Elizabeth, New Jersey, drop by the Art Deco showroom and hear an Altenburg—they've been recommended by no less than Franz Liszt.

Special Factors: Inquire for information.

AMERICAN MUSICAL SUPPLY

**600 INDUSTRIAL AVE.
PARAMUS, NJ 07652–3607
800–458–4076
320–796–2088
FAX: 201–262–3332**

Catalog: free
Pay: check, MO, MC, V, AE, Discover
Sells: musical instruments and recording equipment
Store: Victor's House of Music, 762 Rt. 17 N, Paramus, NJ; Monday to Thursday 10–8, Friday and Saturday 10–6
E-mail: victorshom@aol.com
Online: http://www.victors.com (store) and http://www.americanmusical.com (catalog)

 ¡Sí!

Forget the brass and woodwinds—American Musical Supply is rock and roll all the way. The 132-page catalog opens with Audio-Technica mikes and ends with Roland keyboards and MIDI peripherals. Recorders, speakers, amps, headsets, signal processors, monitors, digital audiotape and CD players and recorders, equalizers, mastering decks, pedals and effects boxes, cables, pickups, tuners, and other accessories are offered. Guitars are featured as well—the latest acoustic and electric models from Gibson, Ibanez, Martin, and others. The percussion section includes drums by Pearl and Tama, as well as cymbals, chimes, cowbells, and other esoteric instruments. American Musical Supply sells electronic keyboards and accessories, books, manuals, and videos on technique, making music with MIDI, Recorded Versions Guitar transcriptions, and much more. Prices run up to 70% below list, although discounts vary from item to item. AMS is the mail-order division of Victor's House of Music, a third-generation family business. If you need advice on the best equipment for your music, they should be able to help. Call for "dent and scratch" deals and close-outs. And be sure to check out both websites for great deals.

Special Factors: Minimum order is $10; C.O.D. orders are accepted.

ANYONE CAN WHISTLE

323 WALL ST.
KINGSTON, NY
  12401–4407
800–435–8863
914–331–7728
FAX: 914–339–3301

Catalog: free
Pay: check, MO, MC, V, AE, Discover
Sells: Woodstock Chimes, exotic and novelty musical instruments, gifts, music CDs, etc.
Store: same address; Monday to Saturday 10–6
E-mail: anyone@chimes.com

Anyone Can Whistle was founded in 1991 by the creator of the famous Woodstock Chimes. The philosophy behind the store and mail-order business is that anyone, regardless of training or past experience, can enjoy the act of creativity. The current mini-catalog gives you just a taste of what Anyone Can Whistle carries. (If there's an exotic instrument you're seeking, just call and ask; chances are, they'll have it or can get it.) Here you'll find unusual instruments such as a German concertina (selling for $135, regularly $195), a Calypso steel drum, and a waterfall pentatonic bamboo xylophone from Southeast Asia. There are also children's instruments, such as a "Kiddy Keys" Baby Grand piano (for children 3 and up, with color-coded keys for that emerging Mozart), "lollipop" drums, and a children's accordion. You'll find party favors and unique, creative gifts that you and your children will love, including puppets, world music CDs, juggling sets, and tiny whistles that do things when you blow: an alligator's jaws pop open, a caged canary flutters before a cat, race cars zoom around a tiny track. And, of course, Anyone Can Whistle sells Woodstock Chimes, from tiny magnetic refrigerator chimes to the 56" baritone "Gregorian Chimes." Don't miss this store if you're visiting Kingston, New York. You and your children won't ever want to leave.

Special to BWBM readers: Anyone Can Whistle has a specific selection of goods that they'll offer to you for 20% to 40% off if you mention that you're a BWBM reader.

Special Factors: For Canadian and international shipping rates, please inquire; no C.O.D. orders accepted.

SAM ASH MUSIC CORP.

P.O. BOX 9047, DEPT.
   WBMC
HICKSVILLE, NY 11802
800–472–6274
908–572–0263
FAX: 908–572–7138

Information: inquire
Pay: check, MC, V, AE, Discover
Sells: instruments and electronics
Store: 19 locations in CT, FL, NY, NJ, OH,
PA, and CA; call main number for addresses

In 1924, violinist and bandleader Sam Ash opened a musical-instrument shop in Brooklyn. The company is still family-run, but now boasts 19 stores and patronage by superstars, schools and institutions, and recording studios, as well as the music-making general public. Regular half-off specials are a feature here, so don't buy anywhere else until you've given Sam Ash a call.

Musical instruments, musical electronics, karaoke, music software, sound systems, electronic keyboards, recording equipment, disk jockey equipment, digital home pianos, specialized lighting, and accessories are available from hundreds of manufacturers, including Akai, AKG, Audio-Technica, Bach, Bose, Buffet, Bundy, Casio, Cerwin-Vega, Charvel, dbx, DigiTech, DOD, Electro-Voice, E-Mu, Ensoniq, Epiphone, Fender, Fostex, Gemeinhardt, Gibson, Guild, Ibanez, Jackson, JBL, JVC, Karaoke (sing-along machines), Kawai, Kurzweil, Leblanc, Ludwig, Mackie, Marshall, Martin, Mesa-Boogie, Noble & Cooley, Ovation, Paiste, Pearl, Rickenbacker, Roland, Sabian, Schilke, Selmer, Sennheiser, Shure, Paul Reed Smith, Sony, Suzuki, SWR, Takamine, Tama, Tascam, Technics, Toa, Yamaha, and Zildjian. Sheet music is stocked, repairs and service are performed, and trade-ins are accepted at the stores.

Please note: For a Spanish-speaking sales representative, call 212–719–2299 (NY) or 305–628–3510 (FL).

Special Factors: Minimum order is $25.

CARVIN CORP.

12340 WORLD TRADE DR.
SAN DIEGO, CA 92128
800–854–2235
619–487–1600
FAX: 619–487–8160

Catalog: free
Pay: check, MO, MC, V, AE, Discover
Sells: Carvin instruments and accessories
Store: same address; Monday to Friday 9:30–6, Saturday 10–4; also 7414 Sunset Blvd., Hollywood, and 1907 N. Main St., Santa Ana, CA; Monday to Friday 10–7, Saturday 10–6, both latter locations
Online: http://www.carvin.com

Carvin "Guitars & Pro Sound" manufactures its own line of instruments and equipment to exacting standards. You'll find the specifications, features, and individual guarantees of each instrument noted in the 48-page color catalog; prices are 50% off list. You'll also find luminaries of the music world shown throughout the catalog alongside Carvin equipment—Greg Allman, Chet Atkins, Larry Carlton, and Stanley Clarke are a few who've appeared in past catalogs.

Mixers, amps, mikes, monitor systems, and electric guitars are offered here, as well as professional-quality guitars designed for the requirements of professional musicians. All of Carvin's instruments and equipment are sold under a 10-day "in your hands" trial arrangement. Servicing and performance testing is done free of charge during the warranty period, and warranties range from one to five years, depending on the item.

Please note: The toll-free line is staffed Monday to Friday 7–6 and Saturday 10–4 PT.

Special Factors: Satisfaction is guaranteed; returns are accepted for refund; minimum order is $25 with credit cards.

DISCOUNT REED CO.

24307 MAGIC MOUNTAIN
   PKWY., #181
VALENCIA, CA 91355
800–428–5993
805–294–9437
FAX: 805–294–9762

Price List: free
Pay: check, MO, MC, V, Discover
Sells: reeds for musical instruments
Store: mail order only
Online: http://www.discountreed.com

Discount Reed sells just that—"mail-order reeds at fantastic savings"—through the eight-page price list. The firm, which began business in 1980, sells woodwind reeds by the box, priced up to 50% less than the list prices—which represents really big savings if you're used to buying reeds one at a time. Both natural and synthetic reeds for all types of clarinets and saxophones are stocked, as well as reeds for oboes and bassoons, in strengths from 1 to 5½ (soft to hard). The names include Bari, Fibracell, Grand Concert, Dave Guardala, Fred Hemke, Java, Jones (double reeds), Marca, Mitchell Lurie, Olivieri, Peter Ponzol, Queen, Rico, RKM, Eugene Rosseau, V–12, V–16, Vandoren, La Voz, and Zonda. (If you're looking for a reed not listed in the flyer, call or write, since it may be available.) In addition, Discount Reed sells Harrison and Vandoren reed cases, reed trimmers, La Voz reed guards, Blue Note sax straps, swabs, metronomes, and other accessories.

Special Factors: Satisfaction is guaranteed; institutional accounts are available (purchase orders from schools accepted, 30 days net); minimum order is $20 with credit cards.

ELDERLY INSTRUMENTS

P.O. BOX 14249-WM99
LANSING, MI 48901
517-372-7890, EXT. 123
FAX: 517-372-5155

Catalog: free (see text)
Pay: check, MO, MC, V, Discover
Sells: new and vintage musical instruments, books, audio- and videotapes, and music CDs
Store: 1100 North Washington, Lansing, MI; Monday to Wednesday 11–7, Thursday 11–9, Friday and Saturday 10–6; mail order hours Monday to Saturday 9–5
E-mail: web@elderly.com
Online: http://www.elderly.com

 ¡Si!

Elderly Instruments has an extraordinary selection of in-print, hard-to-find recordings of all types of music, from folk and bluegrass to jazz and classical, listed in the closely printed 128-page "Recordings" catalog. (For a sample of Elderly's picks, call "Dial-a-Ditty-a-Day," several minutes of an Elderly selection: 517–372–1212, Touch-Tone required.) Elderly Instruments also sells books on dance, repair and construction of instruments, music history, folklore, and even songbooks and videotapes (request the "Books and Videos" catalog).

Despite the impressive publication department, this firm has built 25 years of business on vintage instruments. Epiphones, Fenders, Martins, Dobros, Gibsons, Rickenbackers, and other electric and acoustic guitars have been offered in the past, as well as banjos, violins, mandolins, and other fretted instruments. (There are two additional catalogs: "Electric" and "Acoustic," for new guitars and effects of each type. Request the catalog that better answers your needs.) Elderly Instruments also sells new instruments, lays claim to the title of world's largest dealer of new Martin guitars, and is among the top 20 Gibson dealers. You'll find a good selection of equipment here by Alvarez-Yairi, Boss, Collings, Crate, DiMarzio, Dobro, DOD, E.S.P., Fender, Gibson, Guild, Martin, Sigma, Steinberger, Stelling, Taylor, and Yamaha, among other names. The monthly "vintage used instruments list" is sent free with catalog orders or on request ($2 if sent outside the U.S.), or you may subscribe for $15 ($30 outside the U.S. and Canada). Prices are as low as 50% off list, and everything is covered by the Elderly Instruments guarantee of satisfaction (see the catalog for details).

Please note: Phone hours are Monday to Saturday, 9–5.

Special Factors: Satisfaction is guaranteed; unused, authorized returns are accepted within five days for exchange, refund, or credit; minimum order is $10.

GIARDINELLI BAND INSTRUMENT CO., INC.

**7845 MALTLAGE DR.
LIVERPOOL, NY 13090
800–288–2334
315–652–4792
FAX: 800–652–4535
FAX: 315–652–4534**

Catalog: free, $7 outside U.S.
Pay: check, MO, MC, V, AE, Discover
Sells: brasses, woodwinds, string, percussion, and accessories
Store: same address; Monday to Friday 8:30–5, Saturday 9–1
E-mail: music@giardinelli.com
Online: http://www.giardinelli.com

Giardinelli has been selling fine brasses and woodwinds since 1947 and publishes a 200-page catalog with an exhaustive listing of brass, woodwind, percussion, and string instruments. Trumpets, flugelhorns, trombones, French horns, euphoniums, tubas, clarinets, flutes, piccolos, saxophones, oboes, bassoons, guitars, violins, violas, cellos, congas, drum sets, keyboard percussion, and more are all available, as well as a full line of accessories. The newest catalog features an expanded selection of guitars and amps, orchestral instruments, and even more percussion. The brands include Bach, Besson, Buffet, Bundy, Courtois, DEG, Emerson, Farkas, Gemeinhardt, Getzen, Glaesel Strings, Holton, Humes & Berg, Leblanc, Ross Percussion, Schilke, K. Schiller Strings, Selmer, Signet, Denis Wick, Yamaha, Yanagisawa, and others. Mouthpieces, mutes, reeds, metronomes, tuners, cases, stands, cleaning supplies, repair and tool kits, and books round out the catalog, and Giardinelli features its own line of fine stock and custom mouthpieces for brasses. Savings run up to 50%, and the customer service department can assist you if you have questions or need advice. If you're a new shopper, check out their website. You can now order online.

Please note: If you're contacting Giardinelli online, please use the e-mail address given above.

Special Factors: Satisfaction is guaranteed; returns are accepted for exchange, refund, or credit; institutional accounts are available.

INTERSTATE MUSIC SUPPLY

P.O. BOX 510865
13819 W. NATIONAL AVE.
NEW BERLIN, WI 53151
800–982–BAND
FAX: 414–786–6840

Catalog: free (see text)
Pay: check, MO, MC, V, Discover
Sells: instruments, electronics, and accessories
Store: Cascio Music Co., same address; Monday to Friday 8–8, Saturday 8:30–5 CT; also 11010 North Port Washington Rd., Mequon, WI; Monday to Thursday 10–8, Friday 10–5:30, Saturday 10–4
E-mail: ims@execpc.com
Online: http://www.execpc.com/~ims

Interstate Music Supply is a division of Cascio Music Company, which has been in business since 1946. IMS serves everyone's musical needs, beginning with schools and music teachers. The 370-page "School Discount Catalog" lists a wide range of equipment, at savings of up to 60%. Everything from woodwind reeds and corks to full lines of brass, woodwind, percussion, and stringed instruments is available, including repair kits and parts, cleaning supplies, neck straps, cases, storage units, music stands, stage lighting, sound systems, piano labs, and even riser setups for bands and orchestras. There are great buys on goods from Anvil, Bach, Blessing, Buffet, Bundy, Dynamic, Emerson, Engelhardt, Fender, Fostex, Franz, Gemeinhardt, Gibson, Holton, Korg, Kramer, Leblanc, Ludwig, Mesa-Boogie, Orff, Ovation, Pearl, Roland, Sansui, Schilke, Seiko, Selmer, Trace-Elliot, Vandoren, Vito, Yamaha, and Zildjian. Be sure to check the back of the catalog for "close-outs and blow-outs"—special best buys on everything from computer products to elementary music instruments to oils and polishes.

Interstate Music also produces three other 132-page catalogs: "Guitars" (guitar/bass instruments); "MIDI, Keyboard, and Recording" (including keyboards and computer software); and "Drums" (percussion instruments and accessories). But if you don't see what you want, call or write—it may be available.

Special Factors: Satisfaction is guaranteed; price quote by phone or letter with SASE; returns are accepted within 10 days for exchange, refund, or credit; institutional accounts are available; minimum order is $25.

JAYNEL INSTRUMENT STANDS

Brochure: free
Pay: certified check or MO
Sells: woodwind instrument stands
Store: mail order only

TRIANGLE TECHNOLO-
GIES, INC.
P.O. BOX 1219, DEPT.
WBM
WOODSTOCK, NY 12498
914–679–6906
FAX: 914–679–2482

JAYNEL Instrument Stands were the brainchild of an accomplished flutist who found herself in a tricky performance situation. She was required to play several woodwind instruments in a difficult live piece in which the composer hadn't written in rests between the instrument changes. Not only did she have to come up with a design that would be sturdy, functional, and easy-to-use—and did—but she added a surprise for those who practice in sunlit studios: Her stand doubles as a prism, sending lustrous rainbows everywhere.

The JAYNEL Instrument Stand, which is a clear, triangular block of polished acrylic with legs, is stable, space-saving (important in cramped performance situations), and portable (it comes with a nylon carrying case). The principal flutist of the New York Philharmonic, the West Point Academy band, music teachers at major academies, jazz recording artists, and others use and rave about these functional little rainbow-makers.

The company, Triangle Technologies, Inc., offers the stands in eight different configurations, in different sizes and with various pegs to accommodate flutes, alto flutes, clarinets, oboes, English horns, soprano saxophones, piccolos, trumpets, and flugelhorns, in any combination. They can also custom-design a stand to meet your special needs. A discount of about 40% off the factory-direct price applies when you order five or more JAYNEL stands.

Special to BWBM readers: Triangle Technologies is offering the readers of this book 20% off when you mention this listing.

Special Factors: Quantity discounts available; no credit cards accepted at this time; custom orders available.

KENNELLY KEYS MUSIC, INC.

20505 HWY. 99
LYNNWOOD, WA 98036
425–771–7020
FAX: 425–670–6713

Information: price quote
Pay: check, MO, MC, V, AE, Discover
Sells: musical instruments and accessories
Store: same address
E-mail: kennelly@seanet.com
Online: http://www.musicconnect.com

Kennelly Keys Music, in business since 1960, offers discounts of up to 40% on the retail prices of instruments and accessories. The brass and woodwind names represented here include Altus, Blessing, Buffet, Burbank, Canadian Brass, Getzen, Holton, Keilworth, Leblanc, Powell, Schilke, and Yanagisawa. The guitar, keyboard, percussion, and combo departments carry EV, Gibson, Godin, Hamer, Heritage, LP, Mackie, Marshall, Martin, Ovation, Pearl, Seagull, Sonor, Soundtech, and Takamine. Kennelly Keys Music offers a full-line service department for repairs, tune-ups, and questions, and provides "dealer prep" on all instruments it sells. There is no catalog, so see the website, or call or fax with inquiries and for price quotes; product literature is available on specific models or lines.

Special Factors: Institutional accounts are available; authorized returns are accepted; minimum order is $25.

MANDOLIN BROTHERS, LTD.

629 FOREST AVE.
STATEN ISLAND, NY
10310–2576
718–981–8585, 3226
FAX: 718–816–4416

Catalog: free
Pay: check, MO, MC, V, AE, Discover
Sells: new and vintage fretted string instruments and accessories
Store: same address; Monday to Saturday 10–6
E-mail: mandolin@mandoweb.com
Online: http://www.mandoweb.com

Mandolin Brothers has been selling vintage fretted instruments at good prices since 1971, and it offers select new instruments at a standard discount of 35% from list prices. The 75-page catalog is packed with listings of vintage guitars, mandolins, mandolas, banjos, electric basses, ukuleles, and other stringed instruments. Part of the catalog is devoted to new equipment—guitars, mandolins, banjos, electronics, and accessories. The instruments carried include Benedetto, Bourgeois, Breedlove, Buscarino, Campellone, Collings, D'Angelico, D'Aquisto, Deering, Dobro, Everett, Flatiron, Gibson, James Goodall, Guild, Heritage, Hofner Basses, Kentucky, Lowden, Martin, National Reso-Phonic, Ovation, Parker Fly, Jose Ramirez, Bart Reiter, Rich & Taylor (banjos), Rickenbacker, Santa Cruz, Paul Reed Smith, Steinberger, Stelling, Taylor, Ted Thompson, Trace (acoustic amps), Trinity College, and Wildwood. There are pickups by DiMarzio, EMG, and Seymour Duncan, travel guitars, acoustic basses, cables, strings, straps, frets, mutes, capos, books, videos, and more. Written instrument appraisals and repairs are available, and if you're a collector or vintage instrument enthusiast, be sure to visit the website: Mandolin Brothers publishes its comprehensive listing of instruments in *Vintage News,* which may be read online, or you can subscribe (see the catalog or website for current rates). The site also has an excellent collection of links. Mandolin Brothers ships in-stock instruments on a three-day approval basis—and that includes vintage equipment. If you're in the Staten Island area, be sure to visit the well-stocked showroom, an official site on the "New York Music Trail," and try out the instruments.

Special Factors: Satisfaction is guaranteed; returns are accepted within three days.

METROPOLITAN MUSIC CO.

Catalog: $1.25
Pay: check or MO
Sells: stringed instruments and accessories
Store: mail order only

P.O. BOX 1415
STOWE, VT 05672
802–253–4814
FAX: 802–253–9834

Metropolitan Music Co., in business since 1928, sells stringed instruments and accessories through the 40-page catalog and maintains a workshop for repairs and adjustments. There are some "student" quality instruments here, but most of the models are chosen for professional musicians. Metropolitan carries John Juzek violins, violas, cellos, and basses, and bows by F.N. Voirin, Glasser, and Emile Dupree. Bridges, pegs by Taperfit and other firms, bow hair and parts, fingerboards, necks, chin rests, Resonans shoulder rests, Ibex tools, strings, cases, and bags are all stocked. This is an excellent source for the experienced musician who is familiar with the instruments and accessories. Books on instrument repair and construction are available, as well as a fine selection of wood, parts, and tools. The prices listed in the catalog are subject to discounts of 30% to 50%.

International readers, please note: Metropolitan Music can supply a list of worldwide distributors upon request but does not handle overseas shipments.

Special Factors: Price quote by phone or letter with a self-addressed, stamped envelope; minimum order is $15.

MUSICIAN'S FRIEND

P.O. BOX 4520
MEDFORD, OR 97501
800–776–5173
FAX: 541–776–1370

Catalog: free
Pay: check, MO, MC, V, Discover
Sells: guitar, bass, and keyboard electronics, stage and studio gear, etc.
Store: five locations in Medford and Eugene, OR; Kirkland and Tukwila, WA; and Las Vegas, NV; call main number for addresses
Online: http://www.musiciansfriend.com

 ¡Si!

Musician's Friend garnered a ringing endorsement from a New York City performer who found the firm's service and selection preferable to the music emporiums of the city. Musician's Friend has been supplying the pros with recording equipment and electronics, including keyboards, guitars, bass, and recording gear, since 1981. (The catalogs are customized to your interest, so specify the instrument you play when you call or write.) Musician's Friend offers a double guarantee that you'll get the best prices with them: first, by pledging to beat the lowest price out there; and second, by guaranteeing the lowest price for 45 days after you purchase your equipment (they'll refund the difference).

The catalog copy includes specs, list and discount prices, and equipment features; the brands include Alesis, ART, Boss, Charvel, DigiTech, DiMarzio, Epiphone, Fatar, Gibson, Ibanez, Jackson, Kawai, Korg, Kurzweil, Marantz, Marshall, Martin, Pignose, QSC, Rocktron, Roland, SansAmp, SKB, Sony, VOX, Washburn, Zoom, and many others. You can send for the catalog, or call the toll-free line with the manufacturer's name and the model number of the equipment you want for a price quote. And don't miss the books and videos, which include guides to home recording, writing better lyrics, and designing sound systems for worship.

If you can get to the website, you'll find the catalog, and then some: product reviews, music software downloads, a free electronic newsletter, a directory of manufacturers' support numbers, a great page of links, and even a page for tracking your order.

Special Factors: Satisfaction is guaranteed; price quote by phone; authorized returns are accepted within 45 days for exchange, refund, or credit.

NATIONAL EDUCATIONAL MUSIC CO., LTD.

1181 RTE. 22, DEPT.
  WBMC
MOUNTAINSIDE, NJ 07092
908–232–6700
FAX: 908–789–3025

Catalog: free
Pay: check, MO, MC, V, AE
Sells: instruments and accessories
Store: mail order only
Online: http://www.nemc.com

NEMC has been supplying schools with new band and orchestra instruments since 1957, at savings of up to 60% off the manufacturers' suggested list prices. NEMC sells brass, woodwind, stringed, and percussion instruments by Alpine, Amati, Blessing, Buffet, Decatur, DEG, Fox, Gemeinhardt, Getzen, Holton, International Strings, John Juzek, Korg, Larilee, Leblanc, Lewis, Ludwig, Meisel, Mirafone, F.E. Olds, Pearl, F.A. Reynolds, Ross, Schreiber, Vito, Zildjian, and other makers. The 64-page catalog also offers imported master violins and violas, as well as cases, stands, strings, bows, and other accessories. NEMC provides "the longest warranty in the industry" on woodwinds, drums, and brass and stringed (except fretted) instruments.

Please note: Only U.S. funds are accepted.

Special Factors: Returns (of instruments) are accepted within seven days (a restocking fee may be charged); minimum order is $50.

PATTI MUSIC
COMPANY

P.O. BOX 1514, DEPT. 39
MADISON, WI 53701–1514
800–777–2884
FAX: 608–257–5847

Catalog: $2
Pay: check, MO, MC, V, Discover, JCB
Sells: sheet music, music books, teaching methods and aids, metronomes, etc.
Store: 414 State St., Madison, WI; Monday to Friday 9:30–5:30, Saturday 9:30–5
E-mail: ajsmadsn@aol.com
Online: http://www.pattimusic.com

One of the hardest items to find at a discount is sheet music, but that's the raison d'être of Patti Music Company's mail-order department. Patti Music has been in business since 1936 and publishes a 192-page catalog of sheet music and books and teaching methods for piano and organ, including 10 pages of metronomes, tuners, and related products. Savings on the sheet music run around 15%, and the other goods are discounted up to 33%.

Piano methods, teaching solos, and ensembles are among the 17,000 titles featured in the catalog, representing music publishers from Alfred to Zimmermann. The catalog also lists repertoire and methods for organ, books and dictionaries for musicians and teachers, Christmas music, New Age music, music from movies and Broadway shows, plus manuscript paper, theory books, flash cards, and other teaching aids. The proficiency levels of the music and instructional material run from beginner to advanced. In addition to sheet music, there are metronomes from Franz, Matrix, Seiko, and Wittner, tuners from Korg and Seiko, piano and music furniture, music stands, and musical award and gift ideas.

Please note: The $2 catalog fee is waived for teachers or music professionals.

Special Factors: Discounts are available through the catalog only, not in the store.

SHAR PRODUCTS COMPANY

P.O. BOX 1411
ANN ARBOR, MI 48106
800–248–7427
313–665–7711
FAX: 800–997–8723

Catalog: free
Pay: check, MO, MC, V, Discover
Sells: sheet music, stringed instruments, videos, accessories
Store: 2465 S. Industrial Hwy., Ann Arbor, MI; Tuesday to Friday 9–6, Saturday 9–5
Online: http://www.sharmusic.com

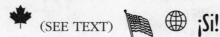 (SEE TEXT)   ¡Si!

"Shar is managed by knowledgeable string players and teachers, who are sympathetic to the needs of the string community," states the firm, which has been in business since 1962 and sets prices up to 50% below list or full retail. The 64-page general catalog gives equal time to stringed instruments and to the firm's extensive collection of music-related accessories and classical music videos (instructional and documentary), CD-ROMs, and audiocassettes, for adults and children. If you play violin, viola, cello, or bass, see the catalog for the cases, bows, chin and shoulder rests, strings, bridges, tailpieces, pegs, music stands, humidifying tubes, endpins, metronomes, tuners, and other supplies and equipment. Student violins are available, as well as a large collection of new, old, and rare violins by master violin makers.

The 88-page "Sheet Music" catalog features hundreds of sheet music titles for string and chamber music players, including Broadway music, fiddle music, Walt Disney selections, wedding music, sacred and cultural music, and much more. (You can also see the selections online and order directly from the website.) The "Sheet Music" catalog also offers manuscript paper, educational materials, music games, and more. Not all goods are discounted, but savings overall average 30%, and selected lines are offered at further savings periodically.

Canadian readers, please note: Personal checks are not accepted at the Ann Arbor location. Most of the products available in the U.S. store are also offered at Shar of Toronto, at 26 Cumberland St., Toronto, Ontario M4W 1J5, Canada; for current hours and stock availability, call 416–960–8494.

Special Factors: Satisfaction is guaranteed; C.O.D. orders are accepted; sheet music not in catalog can be special-ordered.

SWORDS MUSIC COMPANIES, INC.

4300 E. LANCASTER AVE.
FORT WORTH, TX
76103–3225
800–522–3028
817–536–8742
FAX: 817–536–4293

Information: price quote
Pay: check, MO, MC, V
Sells: electronic and band instruments
Store: same address; Monday to Saturday
10:30–7 CT

Swords Music Companies has been selling music equipment and accessories since 1969 and offers savings of up to 50% on suggested list. You can call or write for availability and prices on guitars, drums, keyboards, amps, and band equipment from Akai, Alesis, Blessing, Crate, DigiTech, DOD, Electro-Voice, E-Mu, Epiphone, Fender, Gibson, Hamer, Ibanez, Jackson, Korg, Leblanc, Ludwig, Marshall, Martin, Ovation, Pearl, RCA, Roland, Sabian, Sigma, Takamine, Tama, Tascam, and Yorkville, among others. When you call for a quote, ask about Swords' "meet-or-beat" pricing and for details on the returns policy.

Special Factors: Price quote by phone or letter with a self-addressed, stamped envelope; returns are accepted within 14 days for exchange or credit; minimum order is $50.

THOROUGHBRED MUSIC, INC.

7726 CHERI CT.
TAMPA, FL 33634
800–800–4654
FAX: 800–818–9050
FAX: 813–881–1896

Catalog: free
Pay: check, MO, MC, V, AE, Discover
Sells: musical instruments, music electronics, and accessories
Store: 5 locations in Tampa, Orlando, Clearwater, Sarasota, and Bradenton, FL; call for addresses and hours
Online: http://www.tbred-music.com

  ¡Si!

If they don't know about it already, serious rock musicians and studio engineers should see the 146-page color catalog from Thoroughbred Music, which showcases amps, CD and digital audiotape players and recorders, drum machines and effects boxes, MIDI equipment, special-effect lighting, matador timbales, and hundreds of other electronics and instruments (guitars and bass, banjos, keyboards, mandolins, drums, etc.). The top-name manufacturers are represented here, and Thoroughbred backs up their great prices with a "lowest price guarantee." Suggested retail and Thoroughbred's prices are listed side by side, the latter averaging 20% to 25% less. The catalog includes a number of pages of instructional books, tapes, and videos.

If you don't see what you're looking for, call—it may be available. And be sure to visit the website, with over 150 pages featuring online ordering, giveaways, music resources, information, contests, and over 600 links.

Special Factors: Satisfaction is guaranteed; price quote by phone or letter.

WEINKRANTZ MUSICAL SUPPLY CO., INC.

870 MARKET ST., SUITE
1265
SAN FRANCISCO, CA
94102–2907
800–736–8742
FAX: 415–399–1705

Catalog: free
Pay: check, MO, MC, V
Sells: stringed instruments and accessories
Store: same address; Monday to Friday 9–5, PST

Stringed instruments are the whole of Weinkrantz's business—violins, violas, cellos, and basses. Weinkrantz, founded in 1975, prices the instruments and accessories 30% to 50% below suggested retail. The 40-page catalog lists the available instruments and outfits, cases, music stands, metronomes, bows, strings, and other supplies. There are several pages of strings alone, including Jargar, Larsen, Pirastro, Prim, and Thomastik. Weinkrantz carries violins and violas by T.G. Pfretzschner, Roma, Ernst Heinrich Roth, and Roman Teller. Cellos by these firms and Karl Hauser, Wenzel Kohler, Lothar Semmlinger, and Anton Stohr are cataloged, as well as basses from Roth and Emanuel Wilfer. Instruments from well-known smaller workshops are also in stock but not cataloged because of limited production. Call or write with specific requests.

If you don't want to buy an outfit, you can order the bow, case or bag, rosin, string adjusters, and other equipment à la carte. Strings, bow hair, chin rests, bridges, metronomes, and tuners are all sold at a discount. Instrument bags and cases by Gewa, Gordge, Jaeger, Reunion Blues, and Winter are also available.

Special Factors: Satisfaction guaranteed (see the catalog for the policy on strings).

WEST MANOR MUSIC

831 E. GUNHILL RD.
BRONX, NY 10467–6109
718–655–5400
FAX: 718–655–1115

Price List: free
Pay: check, MO, MC, V
Sells: musical instruments
Store: same address; call for hours

West Manor Music has been supplying schools and institutions with musical instruments since 1956, and it offers a wide range of equipment at average discounts of 45%. The 16-page catalog lists clarinets, flutes, piccolos, saxophones, oboes, English horns, cornets, trumpets, flugelhorns, trombones, French horns, euphoniums, tubas, violins, violas, cellos, string-bass, electric and acoustic guitars, snare drums, drum sets, cymbals, xylophones, timbales, marimbas, orchestra chimes, congas, tambourines, bongos, and other instruments. Drum stands and heads, strings, reeds, cases, music stands, metronomes, mouthpieces, amplifiers, music books, manuscript pads, cases, and other supplies and accessories are sold. All of the instruments are new and guaranteed for one year. West Manor also offers an "overhaul" service for popular woodwinds and brasses, and it can perform repairs as well.

Special Factors: Quantity discounts are available; minimum order is $25, $100 with credit cards.

WRAY'S MUSIC HOUSE

326 MARKET ST.
LEMOYNE, PA 17043
888–761–8222
717–761–8222
FAX: 717–731–0568

Information: price quote
Pay: check, MO, MC, V, AE, Discover
Sells: musical instruments and electronics
Store: same address; Monday to Friday
10–7, Saturday 10–5
Online: http://www.wrays.com

Wray's has brought the sound of music to central Pennsylvania since 1955, and it runs a very busy showroom serving area musicians. You can enjoy the store's selection, if not the ambiance, by visiting Wray's website, where you'll find both lists and pictures of the new and vintage equipment sold here—new and used guitars, amps, effects, synths, keyboards and pianos, percussion, MIDI, pro-audio gear, digital audiotape, and recording equipment. The names include AKG, Alesis, Audio-Technica, Behringer, Beyer, Crest, Crown, dbx, Drum, DigiTech, Seymour Duncan, Electro-Voice, Epiphone, E.T.A., Fatar, Fender, Gibson, Guild, Hafler, Hart Dynamics, Kawai, Korg, Kurzweil, Latin Percussion, Lexicon, Mackie, Marshall, Mesa-Boogie, Ness, Numark, Ovation, Peavey, Premier, PRS, Roland, Rolls, Sabian, Shure, Slingerland, Paul Reed Smith, Studio Master, Takamine, Tascam, Taylor, Telex, Toca, Yamaha, Zildjian, and Zoom. Wray's also offers an extensive selection of sheet music and lighting equipment—call with your needs.

Savings at Wray's can reach 50% on list, and the firm is run by seasoned musicians who know the equipment. If you can't get to the store or the website, you can call or write for prices on new equipment. And if you live in the greater Harrisburg area, you can visit both Wray's Music House and Do Wray Mi Pianos, which offers both acoustic and electronic models.

Special Factors: Satisfaction is guaranteed; returns are accepted for exchange, refund, or credit.

RELATED PRODUCTS/COMPANIES

Deejay equipment • Upstairs Records
Duplication for audiotapes, videotapes, and CDs • Wholesale Tape and Supply
Miscellaneous musician supplies • Homespun Tapes
Stage and recording studio equipment • Upstairs Records, B & H Photo-Video—Pro Audio, MacWarehouse

━ OFFICE, BUSINESS, PROFESSIONAL ━
Computer Hardware and Software

PC and Macintosh computers and

peripherals, software, computer

supplies and accessories

Donate your old Underwood to the local museum (does anyone type on a manual anymore?), because the companies here offer everything you'll need to equip your home office or business with the latest high-tech computer equipment—at a fraction of the cost you'd pay from a retail store. Two factors are in the consumer's favor: (1) Competition in the computer world is fierce; and (2) technology keeps getting cheaper. Computers are one item for which you definitely should not pay full price. The firms here, as well as some of the firms in other parts of the book (see "Related Products/Companies"), sell hardware and software to fit every need and task. For computer workstations and other computer furniture, see the firms listed in the next section, "Office Furnishings."

COMPUTER DISCOUNT WAREHOUSE

CDW COMPUTER
CENTERS, INC.
200 NORTH MILWAUKEE
AVE.
VERNON HILLS, IL 60061
847–465–6000
FAX: 847–465–6800

Catalog: free
Pay: check, MO, MC, V, Discover
Sells: computer hardware and software, peripherals, etc.
Store: showrooms in Chicago and Vernon Hills, IL; call for hours and addresses
Online: http://www.cdw.com

CDW is a major "direct channel reseller" of more than 30,000 computer hardware, software, and peripheral items at discount prices. CDW is the number-one direct reseller of Compac, IBM, Microsoft, Toshiba, and ViewSonic products, and it sells other top name brands including 3Com, Apple, Hewlett-Packard, Simple Technology, and Sony. The company has been in business since 1982 and publishes a comprehensive 104-page PC catalog, in addition to seven specialty catalogs.

If you're a net shopper, be sure to check out CDW's outstanding website, after which you may never want to look anywhere else. There you'll see the entire inventory with search, browse, and compare options that allow you to find the most deeply discounted products. This site has a "coupons" page that lists manufacturer rebates for many different products, helping you get even better deals. CDW won five 1997 *Computer Shopper* "Best Buy" awards, including "Best Vendor Website." Secure online ordering is available at the website, where prices, product specifications, and availability are updated daily.

Please note: A $25 handling fee is charged on orders shipped outside the United States.

Special Factors: C.O.D. orders must be paid with cashier's check or money order; 30-day return policy with some limitations and restrictions (see website or catalog for details).

DARTEK COMPUTER SUPPLY CORP.

175 AMBASSADOR DR.,
   DEPT. WBMC
NAPERVILLE, IL 60540
800–832–7835
630–355–3000
FAX: 800–808–1106

Catalog: free
Pay: check, MO, MC, V, AE, Discover
Sells: PC and Macintosh supplies and equipment
Store: mail order only
E-mail: info@dartek.com
Online: http://www.dartek.com

Dartek and MacWholesale (800–531–4MAC) can save you up to 60% on the equipment you need to make the most of your PC or Mac. Dartek has been serving the industry since 1978 and offers everything from software to workstations through its catalogs, and a selection is shown on the website. Both the Dartek (PC) and MacWholesale catalogs show a full range of hardware, components, software, and accessories, by Adobe, Brother, Hayes, Hewlett-Packard, IBM, Iomega, Magnavox, Maxell, Microsoft, Novell, O'Sullivan, Seagate, Sony, Syquest, 3M, and Verbatim, among others. Dartek sells a wide range of software, including desktop publishing, word processing, PIMs and contact management, accounting and spreadsheet, legal, mailing list management and databases, virus detection and other utilities, disk management, communication, information/reference, programming, tutorials, and more. And you'll find the supplies you'll need to stay productive—cables, power conditioners, data storage, toner cartridges, ribbons, paper, labels, binding equipment, computer care and maintenance supplies, security devices, and telephony devices, also at savings.

Special Factors: Satisfaction is guaranteed; quantity discounts are available; authorized returns are accepted (a restocking fee may be charged) within 45 days for exchange, refund, or credit; institutional accounts are available; minimum order is $25; C.O.D. orders are accepted.

EDUCORP DIRECT

7434 TRADE ST.
SAN DIEGO, CA
  92121–2410
800–843–9497
619–536–9999
FAX: 619–536–2345

Catalog: free
Pay: check, MO, MC, V, AE, Discover
Sells: CD-ROM software and Macintosh shareware
Store: mail order only
Online: http://www.educorp.com

EDUCORP Direct offers thousands of CD-ROM software titles for Macintosh, Windows, and DOS platforms—games, entertainment, general interest, education, multimedia tools, and desktop publishing clip art, fonts, and photos. EDUCORP also carries hard-to-find titles, so check here if you can't locate a program elsewhere.

Special Factors: Quantity discounts are available for dealers; authorized returns are accepted within 30 days (a 25% restocking fee may be charged); institutional discounts are available.

LYBEN COMPUTER SYSTEMS, INC.

5545 BRIDGEWOOD
STERLING HEIGHTS, MI
  48310
800–493–5777
810–268–8100
FAX: 810–268–8899

Catalog: free
Pay: check, MO, MC, V, AE
Sells: computers and hardware, software, and accessories
Store: mail order only
Online: http://www.lyben.com

Lyben Computer Systems, Inc., has been in business since 1982 and offers a full range of computer accessories, supplies, and peripherals. Lyben can save you up to 70% on the suggested retail price on goods from such companies as American Power, GVC, Panasonic, Sony, and 3M, to name a few. Lyben's 242-page full-line catalog runs from batteries to workstations and wrist pads, with all of your computer needs in between—magnetic media, storage units, cleaning tools and products, shredders, binding systems, memory upgrades, cables, switches, game cards, modems, buffers, network products, software and CD-ROMs, printers, and much more. The promotional 48-page catalogs give you a sample of the 3,000-plus items Lyben sells—if you don't see what you're looking for, call for the big book. If you're online, visit the website—you'll find a sample of the products there, as well as the "Internet Specials."

Special Factors: Minimum order is $15; C.O.D. orders are accepted.

MACWAREHOUSE

P.O. BOX 3013, DEPT.
WBM99
1720 OAK ST.
LAKEWOOD, NJ
08701–3013
800–397–8508
FAX: 732–905–9279

Catalog: free
Pay: check, MO, MC, V, AE, Discover
Sells: Macintosh software and peripherals
Store: mail order only
Online: http://www.warehouse.com

Whether you're a dedicated Macintosh user or are toying with making a cross-platform leap, you'll want to see the 204-page catalog from MacWarehouse. More than a roundup of current releases and enhancements, MacWarehouse offers upgrades for a wide range of programs, an extensive line of enhancements and memory upgrades, network media, monitors, video cards, online service packages, and a broad range of accessories, tools, cables, hardware, and little things to make your Mac sing—including MIDI connections, video imaging kits, and sound-recording systems. MacWarehouse has an equally impressive selection of software: word processing, databases, utilities, accounting, graphics, desktop publishing, project managers and PIMs, spreadsheets, multimedia packages, security systems, and much more. The products run from Access PC to Zephyr, and the discounts are a satisfying 25% to 50%—and even more on specials and bundled software.

Special Factors: Price quote by phone or letter; authorized returns are accepted; institutional accounts are available; C.O.D. orders are accepted.

THE MAC ZONE

---

707 S. GRADY WAY, #3
RENTON, WA 98055–3233
800–248–9948
FAX: 425–430–3525

Catalog: free
Pay: check, MO, MC, V, AE, Discover
Sells: Mac-compatible hardware, software, accessories, and peripherals
Store: mail order only
Online: http://www.zones.com

Like its counterpart for PCs (see The PC Zone, this section), the Mac Zone catalog delivers 140 pages of hardware and software for your system. Look here for the most recent releases in communications, productivity, databases, word processing, desktop publishing, graphics, multimedia, voice-recognition software, spreadsheets and financial programs, system tools and utilities, entertainment, games, reference works, training software and tapes, and much more. The hardware runs from memory to monitors; scanners, digital cameras, printers, video and sound cards, drives (hard, optical, CD-ROM, removable, etc.), input devices, modems, power managers, and entire systems are all available. Prices run up to 50% below manufacturers' suggested list or comparable retail, and if you don't see what you're looking for in the catalog, call—chances are, it's available.

Please note: The Zone has separate, dedicated phone lines for international sales (by country) and corporate, education, and government buyers—see the catalog for information.

Special Factors: Authorized returns are accepted; corporate and business accounts are available.

MEI-MICRO CENTER

1100 STEELWOOD RD.
COLUMBUS, OH
    43212–9972
800–634–3478
614–481–4417
FAX: 614–486–6417

Catalog: free
Pay: check, MO, MC, V, AE, Discover
Sells: computer media, computer and printer accessories, computer hardware and software
Store: mail order only; phone hours Monday to Friday 8–11, Saturday 9–7 ET
Online: http://www.mei-microcenter.com

MEI-Micro Center founded its business in 1986 on great buys on magnetic media, which are still here, in the 96-page catalogs—diskettes, tape cartridges, CD-ROMs, etc. You'll also find media storage units, backup units, sound cards, surge suppressers, printer supplies (ribbons, toner cartridges, inkjet modules, paper, etc.), computers (PowerSpec COMPAC, HP, and more), hardware (printers, scanners, networking products, keyboards, etc.), and software. The prices are excellent, and MEI-Micro Center has a good website where you can browse and order online.

Please note: MEI-Micro Center doesn't ship goods outside the United States and Canada.

Special Factors: Satisfaction is assured; returns are accepted.

MICROWAREHOUSE, INC.

P.O. BOX 3014,
    DEPT. WBM99
1720 OAK ST.
LAKEWOOD, NJ
    08701–3014
800–397–8508
FAX: 732–905–9279

Catalog: free
Pay: check, MO, MC, V, Discover
Sells: computers, components, software, and accessories
Store: mail order only
Online: http://www.warehouse.com

There's one way to keep up with the new releases, upgrades, innovations in peripherals, and other developments in computing—find a source to do it for you. MicroWarehouse not only leads with the latest releases, but it also gives you great prices on everything it sells. The 164-page catalog is packed with software for current operating systems, as well as modems, fax machines, scanners, disk drives, expansion devices, printers, monitors, memory upgrades, and much more. The software runs the gamut from word processing and integrated communications to databases, utilities, graphics, and contact management. The Upgrade Warehouse division can handle both live and competitive upgrades, and detailed product information is available through a fax-back service. All of this, and savings of up to 50%, have helped establish MicroWarehouse as a leading supplier. The "MicroSystems Warehouse" catalog gives you another 78 pages of hardware—systems from makers that run from AST to Zenith. The "Data Comm Warehouse" catalog provides networking solutions specialties, and MacWarehouse handles the needs of Macintosh users. Be sure to request the catalog that best serves your needs.

Special Factors: Authorized returns of defective items are accepted within 120 days for exchange, refund, or credit; institutional accounts are available; C.O.D. orders are accepted.

NECX

FOUR TECHNOLOGY DR.
PEABODY, MA 01960
978–538–8356
FAX: 978–538–8751

Information: internet site only, no catalog
Pay: check, MO, MC, V, AE, Discover
Sells: computers and peripherals
Store: online, phone, and fax orders only
E-mail: callman@necx.com
Online: http://www.necx.com

Ask your favorite computer wiz what's his or her favorite source for computer hardware and peripherals, and she or he is apt to say NECX. When my own computer guy highly recommended this site, I took him seriously; that recommendation couldn't come from anyone more discerning, persnickety, and impatient when it comes to efficiency, service, and quality. NECX is the oldest and largest website for computer shoppers, and the company guarantees the lowest prices and fast shipping. NECX was ranked second on the BizRate 1997 Best in Overall Customer Satisfaction survey (see BizRate listing, page 260).

NECX sells a wide array of computer parts and components, from high-end graphics accelerators to complete computer systems, motherboards, and modems. A combination of complete product descriptions, specifications, and product reviews allows you to make informed decisions. Departments include home and office computer center, memory express, and an area for corporate accounts. There's also a "Bargains and Rebates" page, where NECX searches the web for all current manufacturer rebates on products they carry, then lists them for consumers. You either receive the rebate with your product or can print out the rebate coupon from your own computer. Be sure to check out the "Outlet Center," where end-of-line, open-boxed, demonstration models or special deals will net you even more savings. (To keep processing costs—and therefore customer costs—low, Outlet Center purchases may only be made online—not over the phone.) You can order off the website, or by phone or fax.

Special Factors: Institutional accounts are available; satisfaction guaranteed; unopened, original purchases may be returned for a refund; see website for complete returns policy.

THE PC ZONE

707 S. GRADY WAY
RENTON, WA 98055–3233
800–408–9663
FAX: 425–430–3525

Catalog: free
Pay: check, MO, MC, V, AE, Discover
Sells: PC and Mac components, software, hardware, and accessories
Store: mail order only
Online: http://www.zones.com

The Zone catalogs—PC and Mac—give you 140 pages of software and hardware for your system and platform. You'll find the latest releases in personal productivity, communications, databases, desktop publishing, utilities, spreadsheets, word processing, graphics, multimedia, and more. PC and Mac Zone also offer entertainment and games packages, reference works, training tapes and tutorials, and laptop luggage, and the catalogs list memory upgrades, CD-ROM drives, OCR devices and scanners, bar-coding equipment, monitors, mice, modems, UPSs and power managers, voice-recognition software and equipment, backup devices, printers, other peripherals and accessories, and much more. Request the PC or Mac catalog, and if you don't see what you're looking for, call—it may be available, just not listed. You can also search the website's online catalog for specific products and check for current specials.

Please note: The Zone has separate, dedicated phone lines for international sales (by country) and corporate, education, and government buyers—see the catalog for information.

Special Factors: Authorized returns are accepted; institutional accounts are available; C.O.D. orders are accepted.

RECYCLED SOFTWARE, INC.

P.O. BOX 33999
LAS VEGAS, NV 89133
800–851–2425
702–655–5666
FAX: 702–655–5662

Price List: free
Pay: check, MO, MC, V, AE, Discover
Sells: used computer software
Store: mail order only; phone hours Monday to Friday 7–4 PT
E-mail: recycledsw@aol.com
Online: http://members.aol.com/recycledsw/

Recycled Software markets complete, original, pre-owned software for IBM-compatible systems (DOS, Windows 3.1 and 95, OS/2, etc.), at prices 50% and more off original list. The software comes from individuals and firms and may be resold legally (if a manufacturer prohibits resale, Recycled Software won't offer that software). For information about selling your software, refer to the flyer that comes with the price list. Both current and earlier versions of programs are available, including popular titles of all kinds—antivirus and backup, business/contact managers, computer-aided design, communication, databases, desktop organizers, desktop publishing, financial and statistical, flowcharting tools, graphics and design, integrated packages, online/web utilities, operating systems, print utilities, and much, much more. The earlier versions are a great way to take advantage of a version or competitive upgrade discount, or for use on older machines that can't handle the new software.

Recycled Software sells only fully documented, non-OEM software, English-version as sold in the United States, guaranteed free of viruses or defects (checked with two virus-detection programs). At this writing, the price list includes the version number, list price, media size (CD or disk sizes), the date (for games), and the Recycled Software price—one if the materials include a blank registration form, a lower one if the form is not included. The price list from Recycled Software includes complete ordering instructions and answers to several FAQs. The price list is updated weekly on the website. Recycled also sells computer-related books at great prices.

Wholesale buyers, please note: 15% discount available to resellers.

Readers outside the United States, please note: Recycled Software honors publisher prohibitions on sale of programs outside the United States when such restrictions are imposed.

Special Factors: Satisfaction is guaranteed; price quote by phone; returns are accepted within 30 days for exchange, refund, or credit.

RELATED PRODUCTS/COMPANIES

Computer software for the visually impaired • *Independent Living Aids*
Computer supplies • *Viking Office Products, Quill, Reliable Corp.*
Computers and computer accessories • *Damark, J&R Music, Defender Industries*
Desktop publishing and computer arts tools and supplies • *Fidelity Products*
Digital imaging components • *B & H Photo-Video–Pro Audio*
Leather laptop-computer cases • *Airline International Luggage, Jobson's Luggage*
Software • *J&R Music, Bear Mountain Books, Reader's Digest*
Surplus computer components • *H&R Company*
Vinyl pages, pockets, and binders for storing CDs • *20th Century Plastics, University Products, Store Smart*

Office Furnishings

Functional furniture and furnishing accessories for home offices, professional settings, reception rooms, storerooms, hospitals, churches, schools, day-care facilities, etc.

Whether you're looking for an inexpensive, ergonomic desk chair for home or computer workstations for two dozen employees, these companies will have what you need. Many of the firms here carry furnishings for institutional settings—church pews, stacking cafeteria chairs, gymnasium bleachers, chalkboards—while others are more focused on the needs of small businesses. Every company listed here will save you significant amounts of money.

For companies that carry office machines and other office accessories, see the listings in the next section, "Office and Shipping Supplies, and Office Machines."

FIND IT FAST

CHILDREN'S INSTITUTIONAL FURNITURE • Alfax, Business & Institutional Furniture, Dallas Midwest
INSTITUTIONAL FURNITURE • Alfax, Business & Institutional Furniture, Dallas Midwest, Factory Direct Furniture, Frank Eastern
OFFICE FURNITURE • Alfax, Business & Institutional Furniture, Dallas Midwest, Factory Direct Furniture, Frank Eastern, K-Log, National Business Furniture
SAFES FOR HOME AND OFFICE • Safe Specialties, Value-tique

ALFAX WHOLESALE FURNITURE

Catalog: free
Pay: check, MO, MC, V, AE
Sells: office and institutional furniture
Store: mail order only

DEPT. C–1501
370 SEVENTH AVE., STE.
1101
NEW YORK, NY
10001–3981
800–221–5710
212–947–9560
FAX: 800–638–6445
FAX: 212–947–4734

 ¡Si!

Alfax has been selling office furnishings since 1946 and does a brisk business with institutional and commercial buyers, especially schools and churches. The best discounts are given on quantity purchases, but even individual items are reasonably priced.

The 100-page color catalog shows furnishings for offices, cafeterias, libraries, conference rooms, and even religious institutions. Tables and chairs are offered in several styles, as well as a range of files and literature storage systems. There are several pages of institutional nursery and child-care furnishings, play centers, cots, and accessories. Pulpits and lecterns, stackable padded pews, PA systems, trophy cases, carpet mats, lockers, hat racks, park benches, heavy steel shelving, prefabricated office and computer stations and workstations are just a few of the institutional furnishings and fixtures available. Many products have home applications, and all of the equipment is designed for years of heavy use.

Special Factors: Satisfaction is guaranteed; institutional accounts and leasing are available.

BUSINESS & INSTITUTIONAL FURNITURE COMPANY

BOX 92039
MILWAUKEE, WI
   53202–0039
800–558–8662
414–272–6080
FAX: 800–468–1526
FAX: 414–272–0248

Catalog: free
Pay: check, MO, MC, V, AE, Discover
Sells: office and institutional furnishings
Store: mail order only; phone hours Monday to Friday 7–6, Saturday 8–12 CT
E-mail: bi@bi-furniture.com
Online: http://www.bi-furniture.com

Although the best prices at B&I are found on quantity purchases, even individual pieces of furniture and office equipment are competitively priced. The 116-page "business" catalog is devoted to office furnishing basics and includes a range of items appropriate for waiting and reception rooms, home offices, and studies. B&I has been in business since 1960.

The office furniture includes desks, files, bookcases, credenzas, and panels and panel systems (for office partitioning). The seating runs from stacking lunchroom chairs to leather-upholstered ergonomic executive chairs—reception, clerical, specialty, folding—they're all here. There are data- and literature-storage units, computer workstations, locking cabinets, waste cans, mats, announcement boards, and much more. Over 250 brands are represented, and B&I can provide space planning and design services.

B&I also publishes a "school" catalog of everything from auditorium seating to audio-visual/TV caddies to overhead projectors, all at a discount. You can call for a free copy of either catalog, or order them online from the website.

Special Factors: "15-year, no-risk warranty"; volume discounts are available.

DALLAS MIDWEST

4100 ALPHA RD., STE. 111
DALLAS, TX 75244
972–866–0101
FAX: 972–866–9433

Catalog: free
Pay: check, MO, MC, V, AE
Sells: office and institutional furniture
Store: mail order only

The Dallas Midwest catalog runs fewer than 100 pages but showcases furnishings and fixtures for hospitals, schools, nurseries, and churches, as well as offices. In addition to executive desks and chairs, Dallas Midwest sells conference furniture, partitions and dividers for cubicles, computer and AV carts and workstations, wooden and metal files, and all sorts of folding and adjustable worktables. There's a good selection of stacking chairs—padded, molded, and wooden—and heavy-duty folding chairs in metal and wood. Many of these items can be used in institutional settings, as well as the indoor and outdoor sign boards, crowd-control post and rope systems, mobile stages and risers, lecterns, and shelving.

If you're purchasing for a school or day-care center or need sturdy, child-size equipment, see the pages of classroom desks and chairs, stools, maple plywood storage units for toys and books, canvas sling cots and map mats, easels, play sinks and stoves made of birch, activity tables in various shapes, oak tables and chairs, and even a sandbox, slide, seesaws, and a wooden playground set. The church furnishings include pulpits, kneelers, credence tables, communion tables, and stands, and include a well-priced line of unfinished pieces in solid oak. (A separate catalog devoted to unfinished furnishings for school and church is available upon request.)

Dallas Midwest also sells heavy-duty library shelving and book carts, park benches, picnic tables, bike racks, and such useful things as folding lecterns and the "Lightning" boards that can be used with markers, chalk, crayons, slides, and magnetic and adhesive products. Dallas Midwest discounts 30% to 50% on list prices and offers special savings on orders over $1,000. All products carry a 15-year warranty against defects in material and workmanship.

Institutions, please note: Terms are net 30 days for qualifying institutions, and a 2% discount is given for orders paid by check.

Special Factors: Price quote by phone; quantity discounts are available; authorized returns are accepted for exchange, refund, or credit; institutional accounts are available.

FACTORY DIRECT FURNITURE

P.O. BOX 92967
MILWAUKEE, WI 53202
800–972–6570
414–289–9770
FAX: 414–289–9946

Catalog: free
Pay: check, MO, MC, V, AE
Sells: office furniture and institutional equipment
Store: mail order only
Online:
http://www.factorydirectfurniture.com

The 80-page catalog from Factory Direct Furniture features some of the best buys around on office furniture, filing cabinets, bookcases, seating, workstations, storage units, office panel systems, and institutional furnishings. Factory Direct Furniture has been in business since 1974 and carries ergonomic seating for the executive as well as support staff, a full range of files, panel systems, computer workstations and work centers, bulletin and announcement boards, reception furniture, lockers, stacking chairs, and conference furniture. Savings of 40% are routine, and a number of items are tagged 70% below manufacturers' list prices.

Please note: Factory Direct Furniture offers a 10-year guarantee on everything it sells, normal wear and tear excepted. See the catalog for details on the warranty and the firm's "meet or beat" pricing policy.

Special Factors: Satisfaction is guaranteed; quantity discounts are available.

FRANK EASTERN CO.

599 BROADWAY
NEW YORK, NY
10012–3258
800–221–4914
212–219–0007
FAX: 212–219–0722

Catalog: $1
Pay: check, MO, MC, V
Sells: office, institutional, and computer furniture
Store: same address; Monday to Friday 9–5

 ¡Si!

Frank Eastern, in business since 1946, offers furnishings and equipment for business and home offices at discounts of up to 60% on list and comparable retail. Specials are run in every 80-page catalog. Frank Eastern's offerings include desks, chairs, filing cabinets, bookcases, storage units, computer workstations, and wall systems and panels. Seating is especially well represented: ergonomic, executive, clerical, drafting, waiting room, conference, folding, and stacking models in wood, leather, chrome, and plastic are shown in the catalog. Ergonomic seating is a Frank Eastern specialty, and the prices here are a good 25% less than those listed in two comparable office-supply catalogs. There's an ergonomic task chair with air-lift seat adjustment and adjustable backrest for only $49, as well as the hard-to-find Hag balans vital chair—a stool/knee-rest combo that helps to align your spine. Don't overlook good buys on solid oak bookcases, wall organizers, lateral filing cabinets, and mobile computer workstations.

Special Factors: Satisfaction is guaranteed; quantity discounts are available; minimum order is $75 with credit cards.

K-LOG

P.O. BOX 5
ZION, IL 60099–0005
800–872–6611
847–872–6611
FAX: 847–872–3728

Catalog: free
Pay: check, MO, MC, V
Sells: office, A/V, and computer furniture and equipment
Store: mail order only
E-mail: info@k-log.com
Online: http://www.k-log.com

K-Log can outfit every department in the company, from the executive suite to the shipping room. The office furniture, much of which is suitable for schools, includes desks and tables, a wide range of seating, filing cabinets, literature racks, shelving, wall-panel systems, easels, bulletin boards, and display systems. The AV section includes projectors and screens, PA systems, electronic presentation systems and components, and equipment carts and tables. And over a third of the catalog shows computer furniture—components and space-saving workstations, including models that position the monitor below the desktop (it's viewed through a glare-shielded cutout), computer workstations, carrels, and computer-study units designed for wheelchair access. K-Log pledges to "sell lower than any competitor's published price" for identical products. Check out their internet site for "Internet-Only Super Specials."

Please note: Unless the catalog copy states otherwise, all goods are shipped unassembled.

Special Factors: Price quote by phone or letter; quantity discounts are available; authorized returns are accepted (a restocking fee may be charged) for exchange, refund, or credit; institutional accounts are available.

NATIONAL BUSINESS FURNITURE INC.

735 N. WATER ST.
P.O. BOX 92952
MILWAUKEE, WI 53202
414–276–8511
FAX: 414–276–8371

Catalog: free
Pay: check, MO, MC, V, AE
Sells: office and computer furnishings
Store: mail order and outside sales staff (see text)

 ¡Si!

You can furnish your office for less through the 184-page catalog from National Business Furniture, which offers everything from announcement boards to portable offices at savings of up to 64%. NBF has been in business since 1975 and sells office systems, desks and tables for every purpose, credenzas, bookcases, shelving, computer workstations, desk organizers, literature racks, service carts, lockers, floor mats, reception furniture, and much more. The selection is super: There's a range of filing cabinets and an extensive line of seating, including executive, clerical, luxury, ergonomic, conference, folding, stacking, and reception chairs. NBF has an outside sales staff that will come to your office, help you think about your space and organization needs, and then help you design the most comfortable and efficient workspace.

Special Factors: Price quote by phone or letter with a self-addressed, stamped envelope; quantity discounts are available.

SAFE SPECIALTIES, INC.

**10932 MURDOCK RD.,
STE. 104–105A
KNOXVILLE, TN 37932
800–695–2815
423–675–2815
FAX: 423–675–2850**

Catalog: $2
Pay: check, MO, MC, V, AE, Discover
Sells: home and office safes
Store: same address (Exit 374, off I–40);
Monday to Friday 10–6, Saturday 10–2
Online: http://www.imagesbuilder.com/
safespec.1.html

Safe Specialties has been selling home and office safes since 1989 and offers popular home and office models at an average of 30% off list prices. If you're shopping for a depository safe, pistol box, gun safe, secured box for your RV or truck, a data or diskette safe, in-wall or in-floor safe, fire-resistant file cabinet, or hotel safe, try Safe Specialties. Models from Amsec, Cannon, FireKing, Ft. Knox, Hayman, Homak, Liberty, Meilink, and other firms are available, at competitive prices. Money-handling equipment—cash drawers, coin counters, money bags, and related products—are also offered, as well as mailroom supplies and mailboxes.

Special Factors: Inquire for information on shipping rates and methods.

VALUE-TIQUE, INC.

**P.O. BOX 67, DEPT. WBM
LEONIA, NJ 07605
888–444–2135**

Catalog: $1 (in cash, see text)
Pay: check, MO, MC, V, AE, DC, Discover
Sells: Sentry safes, fireproof files, media safes and storage chests
Store: Discount Safe Outlet, 117 Grand Ave., Palisades Park, NJ; Monday to Friday 9–5, Saturday 9–1
Online: http://www.cwn.com/discountsafe

Value-tique has been selling home and office safes since 1968 and offers a range of well-known brands at discounts of 25% and more. Your savings are actually greater because Value-tique also pays for shipping. And the $1 catalog fee (cash is requested) buys a $5 credit certificate, good on any purchase. Value-tique sells Sentry Safes, the EDP Media-Safe and media chests for computer disk storage, a standard home and office safe, and different wall safes. Elsafe, Gardall, Knight, Meilink, and Star safes are also available, as well as Pro-Steel gun safes. Models include wall and in-floor safes, cash-drop safes, styles with digital keypad push-button locks, and many others for home and business use. If you're not sure of the best type for your security purposes, call Value-tique to discuss your needs. Before ordering, measure to be sure the safe will fit the intended location.

Special Factors: Shipping is free in the continental United States.

RELATED PRODUCTS/COMPANIES

Acrylic literature stands and acrylic office accessories • *Plexi-Craft*

Bookends • *Barnes & Noble Books by Mail*

Computer and graphic-design furniture • *Fidelity Products, A.I. Friedman, Pearl Paint, Daniel Smith*

Executive desk accessories • *Bennett Brothers, Ace Luggage, Jobson's Luggage, Fountain Pen Hospital*

Home office furniture • *Bennett Brothers, Damark, Reliable Corp.*

Office furniture and accessories • *Sobol House, Blackwelder's, Fran's Wicker & Rattan, Eastern Butcher Block, Genada Imports, Shaw Furniture, Quality Furniture, Penny-Wise Office Products, Viking Office Products, Quill, Reliable Corp., Dartek, The Furniture Patch of Calabash, Sunrise Business Products*

Shelving for computer workstations • *Woodworker's Hardware*

Wooden woven wastebaskets and magazine baskets • *West Rindge*

Office and Shipping Supplies, and Office Machines

General office supplies; fax, phone, copy, and other office machines; boxes, packaging materials, and other shipping products

If you're still using a single source for your office needs, send for catalogs from a few of the vendors listed here, then pull your last few supply invoices. Compare prices—especially on items your firm uses in bulk. You're probably paying more than you should, and the perks you get from a dedicated supplier are also available from the discounters: open accounts, quick shipment, special orders, and custom services are now routine. The firms listed here sell the countless products needed to run a business.

For firms specializing in computers, computer-related hardware, such as printers and modems, and computer software, see "Computer Hardware and Software," page 448. For office and business furnishings, such as desks, workstations, chairs, shelving, and the like, see "Office Furnishings," page 459. The section following this one, "Printing Services," features companies that can custom-print logos, payroll checks, business cards, invoices, rubber stamps, letterhead, and other items for you and your business. And if you're looking for promotional items or clothing with your company's logo, see the last section of this chapter, "Professional Uniforms and Promotional Products," page 494.

Other companies that sell furniture, supplies, and services of use to small businesses and home offices are listed in "Related Products/Companies" at the end of this section.

FIND IT FAST

BAGS • Associated Bag, Plastic BagMart, U.S. Box
BINDERS AND ORGANIZERS FOR BUSINESS AND PHOTOS • Store Smart, 20th
Century Plastics, University Products
CARDS AND STATIONERY • Current
CASH REGISTERS • Business Technologies
COMMERCIAL ARTS SUPPLIES • Fidelity
GENERAL OFFICE SUPPLIES AND OFFICE MACHINES • Fidelity, OfficeMax,
Penny-Wise Office Products, Quill Corp., Reliable Corp., Sunrise Business Products
PRESENTATIONS MATERIALS AND SERVICES • Visual Horizons
PRINTER/COMPUTER/COPY MACHINE SUPPLIES • DCS, Viking
RESALE PACKAGING AND PRESENTATION DISPLAYS • U.S. Box
SCALES • Triner Scale
SHIPPING SUPPLIES • Associated Bag, Fidelity, ULINE, Yazoo Mills
WRITING IMPLEMENTS • Fountain Pen Hospital

ASSOCIATED BAG COMPANY

400 W. BODEN ST.
MILWAUKEE, WI
  53207-7120
800-926-6100
800-926-4600 (SPANISH)
FAX: 800-926-4610
TDD: 800-926-4611

Catalog: free
Pay: check, MO, MC, V, AE
Sells: poly bags, shipping and packaging supplies
Store: mail order only

 ¡Sí! Ⓒ

Bags, boxes, bubble pack—that's just the beginning of what's available from Associated Bag Company, a container specialist that's been in business since 1938. The well-designed catalog features over 100 pages of plastic bags and packaging materials for a range of purposes: zipper-lock bags, flat poly bags, rolls and envelopes of bubble material, foam sheeting, corrugated boxes and rolls, cloth drawstring bags, mailing tubes and envelopes, sealing tape, stretch wrap, shrink wrap, packing peanuts, antistatic bags, giant covers and liners, and much more. They even have a section on safety and clean-up with items such as poly gloves and boots, nylon handcuffs, medical specimen and syringe containers, even cadaver bags! Recycled products are noted throughout the catalog, and dispensers for tape and paper, shrink guns, and other equipment are also available. Prices are good, and savings are greater on quantity buys.

In addition to the customary commercial uses, these products are suited to a number of household tasks, including one very costly undertaking—moving. Get the containers locally, but handle the packing yourself with wrapping materials from Associated Bag, and you can save several hundreds of dollars in materials and labor. Just make sure your homeowner policy, or the moving company, will still provide coverage if there's breakage.

Special Factors: Satisfaction is guaranteed; price quotes on custom orders; competitive bidding; quantity discounts are available; free test samples available; same-day shipping; returns are accepted.

BUSINESS TECHNOLOGIES

3350 CENTER GROVE DR.
DUBUQUE, IA 52003–5225
800–451–0399
319–556–7994
FAX: 319–556–2512

Catalog: free
Pay: company check, MO, MC, V
Sells: cash registers and related supplies
Store: same address; Monday to Friday 8:30–5

Business Technologies sells Sharp cash registers and supplies for just about every other cash register brand. Upon inquiry, you'll receive manufacturers' brochures, a selection guide, and a roster of optional accessories that can customize the register to the needs of your business. Even the "simple" machines have programmable tax and percentage capabilities, and the top-of-the-line models are built-in bookkeepers and gofers: One system allows a restaurant to track employees' tips and guests' balances and even transmit orders to a printer in the kitchen. Other features include management reports, credit authorization, currency conversion, and scanner functions, among others (depending on the model). Prices at Business Technologies average 30% below list, and the firm provides technical support, a one-year warranty, and free programming.

Special Factors: Price quote by phone, fax, or letter; minimum order is $25.

CURRENT

1005 E. WOODMAN RD.,
 KEYCODE DM24
COLORADO SPRINGS, CO
 80941
800–525–7170
FAX: 719–593–5900

Catalog: free
Pay: check, MO, MC, V, AE, Discover
Sells: stationery, gifts, wrapping paper, cards, etc.
Store: outlets in CA, CO, and OR

Current, in business since 1950, publishes a monthly, 68-page color catalog of stationery, gifts, and household items in appealing designs, many exclusive to Current, ranging from animal and nature scenes to quilt motifs and other Americana. All-occasion and holiday cards are available, as well as notepads, personal cards and stationery, gift wrapping, ribbon, stickers, recipe cards and files, toys, games, organizers, kitchen helps, calendars, memo boards, mugs, and other gifts. Current's "Expressions of Faith" line features Christian-oriented cards, gifts, and products for children. Prices are very reasonable, and discounts are given based on the number of items ordered.

Special Factors: Satisfaction is guaranteed; sliding discounts of 20% and more are offered on orders of eight or more items; returns are accepted.

DCS

6501 STATE RTE. 123 N.
FRANKLIN, OH 45005
800–735–3272
513–743–4060
FAX: 513–743–4056

Catalog: $3, refundable
Pay: MC, V, Discover
Sells: toner cartridges, diskettes, cables, printer ribbons, etc.
Store: same address; Monday to Friday 8–5

DCS, formerly known as Dayton Computer Supply, offers a comprehensive selection of supplies for computers, printers, copiers, and other office machines. If you're looking for buys on magnetic media, see the firm's own bulk-pack computer disks, which meet or exceed ANSI standards and are backed by the DCS guarantee. DCS also sells diskettes and other data storage media by BASF, Dysan, KAO, Maxell, Sony, 3M, and Verbatim. There's a full line of cabling supplies and various accessories, including switch boxes, gender changers and adapters, surge protection devices, mice and mouse supplies, printer stands, and disk storage boxes.

In business since 1979, DCS is one of the top 50 toner cartridge remanufacturers in the nation, producing cartridges for hundreds of laser printers and copiers. (New cartridges from the original manufacturers—Apple, Canon, Epson, Hewlett-Packard, IBM, Okidata, Panasonic, Toshiba, and Xerox—are also available.) And DCS is a major ribbon distributor, so if you're having trouble locating replacements, try here. "If we can't find it, it probably cannot be found," say the management.

Please note: Orders are shipped to Canada via UPS only, and shipped to APO/FPO addresses by U.S. mail.

Special Factors: Satisfaction is guaranteed; price quote by phone; quantity discounts are available; C.O.D. orders are accepted; institutional accounts are available.

FIDELITY PRODUCTS CO.

5601 INTERNATIONAL PKWY.

P.O. BOX 155

MINNEAPOLIS, MN 55440–0155

800–328–3034 (OFFICE SUPPLIES)

800–326–7555 (GRAPHICS SUPPLIES)

FAX: 800–842–2725

Catalog: free
Pay: check, MO, MC, V, AE, Discover
Sells: office and shipping supplies, graphics products, builders/engineers/architects supplies
Store: mail order only
E-mail: bwagner@libertydiversified.com
Online: http://www.fidelityproducts.com

Fidelity, established in 1961, is one of the country's biggest suppliers of corrugated storage and general business products. There are three catalogs to peruse from Fidelity. The 68-page "Direct" catalog features a broad selection of heavy-duty file units, as well as shipping supplies, scales, parts bins, industrial shelving, lockers, and much more. The prices represent average savings of 40% on list prices, and quantity discounts are offered on many items. Moreover, this and the "Graphics"

catalog have a lowest price guarantee, which means they'll refund the difference and give you an additional 10% off your original price if you find a competitor's ad with a current lower price.

The 68-page "Graphics" catalog offers tools and supplies for architects, engineers, contractors, and anyone doing desktop publishing and computer-aided design. Here are drawing boards and tables, computer furniture, light boxes and projection equipment, Pantone color charts, Brother and Kroy lettering equipment, a wide range of writing instruments and markers, paper and production supplies, portfolios, flat files, and more. Spot checks showed that prices are an average 30% below list, and quantity pricing is offered as well.

The 48-page "Bear" catalog is for builders, engineers, and architects, and there is some overlap with the above catalog. Here you'll find sonic distance measuring devices, magnetic locators, hard hats, Polaroid cameras, tool bags, books on such subjects as land development, a contractor's field guide, electrical references, and more. The "Bear" prices average from 15% to 20% below retail.

Special Factors: Satisfaction is guaranteed; price quote by phone; quantity discounts are available; returns (in original packing) are accepted within 30 days for exchange, refund, or credit.

FOUNTAIN PEN HOSPITAL

10 WARREN ST.
NEW YORK, NY 10007
800–253–PENS
212–964–0580
FAX: 212–227–5916

Catalog: free
Pay: check, MO, MC, V, AE, Discover
Sells: fountain pens, writing instruments, and repair services
Store: same address; Monday to Friday 8–5:45
Online: http://www.fountainpenhospital.com

The Fountain Pen Hospital has been restoring fine fountain pens to health since 1946, and it does a brisk business in vintage pens and new models—at a routine 20% off list, to 40% on some lines and models. The 64-page pen catalog shows writing instruments from Aurora, Caran d'Ache, Eversharp, Mont Blanc, Namiki, OMAS, Parker, Pelikan, Rotring, Stipula, Visconti, Waterman, and scores of other top-brand pen makers. There are handsome leather pen cases, satin-lined chests that can accommodate up to 52 pens and pencils, refills (ink cartridges, leads, erasers, etc.), Filofax agendas, books on pen collecting, and desk accessories. The 10-page current price list that accompanies the annual catalog will clue you in on best buys and additional savings offers.

For the serious investor and vintage collector, check out *Vintage Pen Quarterly,* their publication that comes out four to six times a year and has money-saving coupons for new pens, parts, and accessories, as well as a roundup of the current selection of rare and vintage pens and pencils ($10 for a year's subscription). You can also call or write to inquire about the availability of specific old or new models, or ask about the procedure for sending in a pen for repair.

Special Factors: Satisfaction is guaranteed; price quote by phone or letter; returns are accepted within seven days for exchange, refund, or credit; minimum order is $10.

OFFICEMAX INC.

3605 WARRENSVILLE
   CENTER RD.
SHAKER HEIGHTS, OH
   44122–5203
800–788–8080

Catalog: free
Pay: check, MO, MC, V, AE, Discover
Sells: office supplies and equipment
Store: stores nationwide (call for nearest location)
Online: http://www.officemax.com

OfficeMax, with over 700 locations, is the country's largest office products superstore chain. The stores themselves offer discounts of up to 70% on thousands of office and computer products, while the color catalog showcases the best-selling items—from paper clips to computers—and includes list prices, the OfficeMax discount prices, and your savings. If you don't see what you want in the catalog, it can probably be special-ordered from the master catalog at all OfficeMax stores.

Special Factors: Satisfaction is guaranteed; shipping is free on orders of $50 or more within designated store areas. Call for locations.

PENNY-WISE OFFICE PRODUCTS

6911 LAUREL BOWIE RD.,
   SUITE 209
BOWIE, MD 20715
800–942–3311
301–699–1000
FAX: 301–277–6700

Catalog: free
Pay: check, MO, MC, V, AE, Discover
Sells: office supplies, equipment, and furniture
Store: mail order only
Online: http://www.penny-wise.com

Penny-Wise has been in the discount office supply arena for over a decade and uses a time-honored formula: guaranteed lowest prices on everyday office needs, and free shipping on qualifying orders. Place an order from the 64-page catalog of specials and you'll receive the "big book" that showcases over 20,000 products. The Penny-Wise discount prices are listed next to the retail list prices, and a number of items that are usually sold by the box are available here by the piece. In addition to supplies, Penny-Wise sells office furniture, electronics, some peripherals, and business services—rubber stamps, business cards and stationery, printed envelopes and binders, embossing stamps, imprinted pens and gifts, and more. Orders of $25 or more (with some exceptions) are delivered free within the United States, and open accounts are available.

Wholesale buyers, please note: Penny-Wise does not sell goods for resale.

Special Factors: Satisfaction is guaranteed; shipping is not charged.

PLASTIC BAGMART

900 OLD COUNTRY RD.
WESTBURY, NY 11590
800–343–BAGS
516–997–3355
FAX: 516–997–1836

Catalog: free with SASE
Pay: check, MO, MC, V
Sells: plastic bags
Store: same address; Monday to Friday 9–5, Saturday 9–3

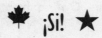 ¡Si! ★

Plastic BagMart, established in 1980, offers plastic bags in sizes most frequently used in homes, offices, and industry. Prices are up to 60% lower than those charged by supermarkets and variety stores for smaller lots. The BagMart stocks plastic bags in sizes from 2" square to 50" by 48", one to four mils thick. Garbage and trash cleanup bags, kitchen and office waste-can bags, food-storage bags, recycling bags, large industrial-type bags, zip-top styles, plastic shopping bags, compactor, garment, and other types are available. The bags are sold in case lots only (100 to 1,000 bags per case, depending on the size). BagMart offers quantity discounts, too, and you can mix and match cases to earn them. The little 8-page catalog features the most popular lines, but if you don't see what you need, write with particulars.

Canadian readers, please note: Orders are shipped by UPS only.

Special Factors: Satisfaction is guaranteed; price quote by letter with a self-addressed, stamped envelope; returns are accepted within 10 days; minimum order is one case; prices include shipping.

QUILL CORPORATION

100 SCHELTER RD.
LINCOLNSHIRE, IL
60069–3621
800–789–1331
FAX: 800–789–8955

Catalog: free (see text)
Pay: check, MO, MC, V, AE
Sells: office supplies and equipment
Store: mail order only
Online: http://www.quillcorp.com

Quill, founded in 1956, offers businesses, institutions, and professionals savings of up to 80% on a wide range of office supplies and equipment. There are real buys on Quill's house brand of office and computer supplies, which are comparable in performance and quality to name brands costing much more. Quill's semiannual 600-plus-page "big book" is augmented with monthly 72-page catalogs featuring specials and general office supplies and equipment, including files, envelopes, mailers, supplies for typewriters, word processors, and printers. In addition to everyday needs—labels, scissors, paper trimmers, pens and pencils, etc.—Quill sells copiers and supplies, word processors, telephones, fax machines, binders and machines, dictating machines, accounting supplies, office furnishings, and much more. Quill's custom department offers competitive prices on custom-imprinted letterhead, labels, mailers, forms, cards, signs, and stamps.

In addition to the general editions, Quill publishes specialty catalogs of accounting supplies, legal supplies, medical office supplies, computer products, business furniture, school supplies, industrial office supplies, government office supplies, and holiday cards and stationery. You can order any of the specialty catalogs (as well as products) by phone or from the website, and learn about special offers and promotions.

Please note: Quill does business with companies and professionals. Terms (30 days net) are available to qualified businesses. Goods are not shipped outside the U.S.

Special Factors: Satisfaction is guaranteed; institutional accounts are available; returns are accepted; minimum order is $25.

RELIABLE CORP.

P.O. BOX 1502

OTTAWA, IL 61350–9914

800–359–5000

FAX: 800–326–3233

Catalog: free
Pay: check, MO, MC, V, AE, Discover
Sells: office supplies and equipment
Store: mail order only
Online: http://www.reliable.com

Reliable's commitment to giving deep discounts to small businesses has been its strong suit since 1918. The firm's big catalog, published twice a year, features thousands of products from nationally known manufacturers—from Ampad legal tablets to Xerox copier cartridges. Discounts run to 80% on list prices, and you don't have to buy in huge quantities to save. Reliable augments the general book with a slew of specialty catalogs: business furniture, computer supplies and accessories, home office, desktop printing, shipping and warehouse supplies, and seasonal items. You'll receive separate catalogs based on what you order from the big book and general sales catalogs, or you can request them—by phone or the website. And

Reliable backs everything it sells with an unconditional assurance of satisfaction.

Special Factors: Satisfaction is guaranteed; institutional accounts are available; minimum order is $25.

STORE SMART

**180 METRO PARK
ROCHESTER, NY 14623
800–424–1011
716–424–5300
FAX: 800–424–5411
FAX: 716–424–5313**

Catalog: free
Pay: check, MO, MC, V, AE
Sells: clear vinyl adhesive-backed pockets
Store: same address; Monday to Thursday 9–5:30, Saturday 9–5
Online: http://www.storesmart.com

Store Smart is a sister company of Visual Horizons, also listed in this section. Click onto the website, or order the free 8-page catalog, and you'll be greeted with a selection of about 250 different-sized vinyl, adhesive-backed pockets. Business is booming at Store Smart as customers discover that these pockets have hundreds of uses. Stick them onto proposals, bulletin boards, telephones, computers, file cabinets, and more. You'll find sizes to fit business cards, CD-ROMs and $3^1/2''$ computer disks, coins and slides, $8^1/2''$ by 11" pages, all the way up to $26^3/8''$ by $38^5/8''$. You can customize just about anything with Store Smart pockets. They act as a permanent protector of the material, yet the material can easily be removed and replaced. The prices are excellent if you can order in large qualities. Order online, over the telephone, or by fax or mail.

Special Factors: Satisfaction is guaranteed; rush service available.

SUNRISE BUSINESS PRODUCTS

43 ROYALSTON LN.
CENTEREACH, NY
11720–1414
800–222–PENS
516–698–0700
FAX: 516–698–0837
FAX: 718–937–3171

Catalog: free (see text)
Pay: check, MO, MC, V, AE, Discover
Sells: office supplies and equipment
Store: mail order only
E-mail: sunrise1@mail.idt.net
Online: http://www.sun-rise.com

When you send for a catalog from Sunrise you'll receive the 36-page roundup of best-selling office supplies; order from that and you'll receive the mammoth office supply catalog. Sunrise is using the techniques of the superstores but going them better on price on some items, and on product selection and delivery ($35 is the floor for free delivery, not the $75 customarily set). The stock is what you'd expect from a firm that can offer over 60,000 items, deliver furniture free and set it up (with some limits), and perform document printing and binding, check printing, and "print-on-demand" services (no prepress or Veloxing required). Sunrise has been in business since 1953 and commits to next-day delivery on orders placed by 5 P.M. ET. If you don't see what you're looking for in the catalog you receive, just call for availability and pricing—it may be in the warehouse.

Special Factors: Satisfaction is guaranteed; price quote by phone or letter; shipping is included on orders over $35; quantity discounts are available; returns in original packaging are accepted within one week of delivery for exchange, refund, or credit (a restocking fee of 20% applies after 7 days, and no returns are accepted after 30 days).

TRINER SCALE

2482 SANDERWOOD
MEMPHIS, TN 38118
901–363–7040
FAX: 901–363–3114

Flyer: free
Pay: check, MO, MC, V, Discover
Sells: manual and electronic scales
Store: same address; Monday to Friday
8–4:30
E-mail: triner@mem.net
Online: http://www.trinerscale.com

Triner Scale, which was founded in 1897, sells a full line of mechanical and electronic scales. Triner also sells a pocket scale, a precision instrument that weighs things up to 4 ounces. A finger ring permits the scale to hang while measurements are taken; the item to be weighed is secured with an alligator clip. Suggested uses include postage determination (a rate chart is included), food measurement, lab use, craft and hobby use, and weighing herbs. It's a useful item to have on hand, and it can give you accurate readings of postage costs. The pocket scale costs under $10, and the electronic miniscales, $125; inquire for information.

Wholesale buyers: Quantity pricing begins at $6.50 for 1 to 20 units.
Special Factors: Shipping is not charged.

20TH CENTURY PLASTICS, INC.

P.O. BOX 2376
BREA, CA 92822–2376
800–767–0777
FAX: 800–786–7939

Catalog: free
Pay: check, MO, MC, V, AE, Discover
Sells: photo albums and accessories, binders, organizers, scrapbooks, etc.
Store: mail order only
Online: http://www.20thcenturydirect.com

¡Sí!

20th Century Plastics helps you save your memories with a wide selection of archival photo and slide storage sheets and albums, as well as safekeepers for your collections of stamps, baseball cards, recipes, and periodicals. The 48-page color catalog also features a variety of binders and report covers, as well as photo albums, video- and audiocassette portfolios, static-proof floppy disk storage, CD-ROM storage, and business-card files. The prices of the archival-quality photo storage products are excellent, and there are especially good prices on the albums.

Whether you're organizing snapshots at home or creating a storage and filing system for a large office, you'll find solutions here.

Please note: Specify the "photo" or "business" catalog when you call or write.

Special Factors: Satisfaction is guaranteed; returns are accepted within 30 days for exchange, refund, or credit.

ULINE

2200 S. LAKESIDE DR.
WAUKEGAN, IL 60085
800–295–5510
FAX: 800–295–5571

Catalog: free
Pay: check, MO, MC, V, AE, DC, Discover
Sells: shipping supplies
Store: mail order only
E-mail: ulinecs@uline.com
Online: http://www.uline.com

Whether you're running a mom-and-pop business out of your home or are in charge of a warehouse, ULINE is the source for every kind of packing need. This family-run, reader-recommended business has warehouses in Illinois, Minnesota, New Jersey, and California; orders are shipped from the location nearest you to ensure the quickest and most cost-effective service. The 208-page catalog features anti-static products, bags and bag sealers, boxes, bubble and cushioning material, tape and tape dispensers, envelopes, foam, labels, mailers, packing list envelopes, strapping, stretch wrap, tags, tubes—everything from aerosol products to vermiculite. And ULINE has over 500 different box types in stock—one of their biggest advantages over other shipping-supply houses. At ULINE, the more you buy, the more you save—there are quantity price breaks on all items. If you wish to see a sampling of ULINE's inventory, check out the website.

Special Factors: Satisfaction guaranteed 100%; returns must be made within 30 days; C.O.D. orders not accepted.

UNIVERSITY PRODUCTS, INC.

517 MAIN ST.
HOLYOKE, MA 01041–0101
800–628–1912
FAX: 800–532–9281

Catalog: free
Pay: check, MO, MC, V, AE, DC, Discover
Sells: archival-quality materials for conservation, restoration, and preservation
Store: mail order only
Online: http://www.universityproducts.com

You may not know it, but anarchy reigns on your bookshelves, in the pages of your photo albums, and among the works of art on your walls. It's sad, but true: Most of us store and display our precious belongings in materials and under conditions that damage them, sometimes irreparably.

Help is available from University Products, which publishes the comprehensive "Archival Quality Materials" catalog. University Products has been selling conservation and library supplies to institutions since 1968 and does business with preservation-minded individuals and institutions who want to protect their collectibles and other treasures. Both the materials used in display and storage and the conditions under which we keep them affect the long-term "health" of many collectibles. Problems with spotting, discoloration, and damage may be seen in stamps, antique textiles, comic books, baseball trading cards, postcards, scrapbooks, photographs, sheet music, and even currency. To meet the need for safe storage of these goods, University Products sells acid-free manuscript boxes and interleaving pages, files, photo albums and Mylar page protectors, archival storage tubes, slide and microfiche storage materials, mounting materials and adhesives, an extensive selection of acid-free papers of all types, storage cases and cabinets, dry-mount and framing equipment, and related tools and supplies. The catalog includes valuable information on conservation basics for a range of materials and collectibles and offers discount coupons and quantity discounts on most items. Since a "basic retouching" of an old photograph can cost over $100, each dollar spent in preservation can save a hundred in restoration—if restoration is possible. You can also check the website to view the products.

Special Factors: Satisfaction is guaranteed; quantity discounts are available; institutional accounts are available.

U.S. BOX CORP.

1296 MCCARTER HWY.
NEWARK, NJ 07104
800–221–0999
973–481–2000
FAX: 973–481–2002

Catalog: free
Pay: check, MO, MC, V, AE
Sells: resale packaging
Store: mail order only
E-mail: sales@usbox.com
Online: http://www.usbox.com

U.S. Box Corp. has been selling retail and gift packaging since 1948. This is primarily a business-to-business firm, but it offers products that consumers use routinely: wrapping paper, tape, gift boxes, ribbon, and mailing bags, for example. Prices are as much as 60% lower here than those charged for comparable items in variety and stationery stores. Additional discounts of 5% apply to orders over $500, and up to 15% on totals of $2,500 plus. Samples of the goods may be purchased at unit cost plus $2 shipping; this is recommended, since returns are not accepted.

U.S. Box Corp.'s 148-page color catalog showcases their dizzying inventory, beginning with every conceivable type of box: cotton-filled jewelry boxes from plain gold or silver to leopard and other designs, as well as velvet-lined suede and leatherette jewelry boxes; custom plastic boxes; wooden-slat boxes; boxes designed for watches, ties, apparel, breakables, plates, cakes, candy, etc.; gift boxes shaped like rabbits, houses, and sleighs; heavy-duty shipping boxes and mailers. You'll also find paper bags, gift bags, party bags, net bags, shopping bags, tins, drawstring bags; labels of every size, shape, and description, from functional to fancy; bows, ribbons, and other box decorations, such as bells, roses, animals, and metallic elastic; packing and decorative fillers, such as shredded mylar and plastic in every color; tissue sheets and gift wrap in indescribable choices; poly/cello bags and rolls—patterned, colored, and clear; plastic storage containers for anything you could think of; jewelry displays, plastic tray liners for small items of every shape and size, and more. Consolidate your packaging needs and you'll easily meet the $150 minimum order.

Special Factors: Returns are not accepted; minimum order is $150.

VIKING OFFICE PRODUCTS

950 W. 190TH ST.
TORRANCE, CA 90502
310–225–4500
FAX: 310–327–2376

Catalog: free
Pay: check, MO, MC, V, AE
Sells: office supplies, furniture, computer supplies, stationery
Store: mail order only
Online: http://www.viking.com

 ¡Sí!

Viking Office Products began business in 1960 and sells office supplies, furnishings, and computer supplies at discounts of up to 69%. The semi-annual 550-page general catalog features daily office needs, from pens and markers to ergonomic seating and filing cabinets, all of which are sold at a discount. The brands represented include most of the major brands, as well as Viking's own label. Once you place an order, you'll receive the monthly sale catalogs, with extra-deep discounts on every-day office needs. Viking covers every purchase with a 30-day free trial and a one-year unconditional guarantee of satisfaction, and expedited delivery service is routine.

Special Factors: Satisfaction is guaranteed; institutional accounts are available; shipping is free on orders over $25 within the 48 contiguous United States.

VISUAL HORIZONS

180 METRO PARK
ROCHESTER, NY 14623
800–424–1011
716–424–5300
FAX: 800–424–5411
FAX: 716–424–5313

Catalogs and Samples: free
Pay: check, MO, MC, V, AE
Sells: business presentations material, equipment, and services
Store: same address; Monday to Thursday 9–5:30, Saturday 9–5
Online: http://www.visualhorizons.com

Visual Horizons is a company devoted to helping you make the best business presentation possible, with services and products to help you create, deliver, or publish memorable, eye-catching presentations at less cost than you'd incur if you hired a PR consultant and a graphic designer. Their "Powerful Presentations Source Book" is a 56-page color catalog peppered throughout with testimonials from happy customers, and well-designed photo layouts and descriptions of the products and services that made them that way. Presentation formats the company supports are LCD panels and screen shows, slides and overheads, computer disks and CD-ROMs, video, and flip charts. You'll find imaging equipment, slide projectors, slide scanners, wall screens, light tables, overhead projectors, communication boards, audiovisual furniture, label printers, and much more. In business for 25 years, Visual Horizons has a staff of people who can provide all kinds of services, from slide duplicating to designing logos to creating your entire presentation. They have 300 dynamic graphic images you can choose from—with or without words, in many languages—if you don't want to design your own, or they can custom-design graphics for you. Their free imaging software enables you to send computer files through your modem, and their host computer will transform those images into slides. The prices get good when you order in quantity, and there are special deals on certain services. Visit the website for more details, or call. "Advice is free," they say.

Special Factors: Satisfaction is guaranteed "110%."

YAZOO MILLS, INC.

---

305 COMMERCE ST.
P.O. BOX 369
NEW OXFORD, PA 17350
800–242–5216
717–624–8993
FAX: 717–624–4420

Catalog: free
Pay: check, MO, MC, V, AE, Discover
Sells: shipping tubes
Store: mail order only

Yazoo Mills takes its name from the Mississippi town where it was founded in 1902, but since moving to Pennsylvania in 1936, Yazoo has run the plant from New Oxford. The firm manufactures paper tubes for shipping and industry—carpet "cores," cable reels, fax paper tubes, even heavy blast casings for the mining industry—Yazoo makes them all. Yazoo also offers shipping tubes in the sizes most popular among artists: lengths from 12" to 85", in diameters of 2" to 12" (the larger sizes are "heavy duty" or "extra heavy duty"). The tubes are sold by the case—48 in a carton of 2" by 1" tubes, to one of the 12" by 85"—with plastic plug inserts for the ends. The prices, which include shipping, are so low that even if all you need are two mid-size tubes, it's probably worth buying from Yazoo—they're priced up to 80% below art-supply houses!

The tubes can be used for storage as well as shipping art and other objects; note that they're made of recycled paperboard and may be made in acid-free stock. Yazoo does much of its manufacturing to job specifications and can give you quotes on custom sizes or colors. Incidentally, tubes are a great way to store your tablecloths and table linens. Just unroll them and set your table—no ironing necessary!

Special Factors: Shipping is not charged; minimum order is one carton of stock tubes; C.O.D. orders are accepted.

RELATED PRODUCTS/COMPANIES

Antique telephones • Phoneco
Attaché cases, briefcases, leather portfolios • Bennett Brothers, Airline International Luggage, Ace Luggage, Jobson's Luggage, Al's Luggage
Books on the graphic arts • Print Bookstore
Calendars • Books.com, Barnes & Noble Books by Mail
Commercial artist/design supplies • A.I. Friedman, Pearl Paint, Daniel Smith
Fax machines • Bernie's Discount, Damark, J&R Music, LVT Price Quote Hotline
General office supplies • Texas Art Supply, MEI-Micro Center
Information relevant to small businesses • Consumer Information Center, U.S. Gov't Superintendent of Documents
Office and shipping supplies and desk accessories for the visually impaired • The New Vision Store, Independent Living Aids
Office cleaning supplies • The Cleaning Center
Overhead projectors • Cheap Joe's Art Stuff, A.I. Friedman
Power generators • Harbor Freight Tools, Northern Hydraulics
Shredders, calculators, and other small office machines • Damark, LVT Price Quote Hotline
"Talking" clocks, calculators, and other office machines for the visually impaired • The New Vision Store, Independent Living Aids
Telephones • Crutchfield, S&S Sound City, EBA Wholesale, J&R Music, LVT Price Quote Hotline
Typewriters, word processors • LVT Price Quote Hotline
Writing implements • Jobson's Luggage, J&R Music, Pearl Paint, Albert S. Smyth

Printing Services

Stationery, invitations, letterhead,

logo design, personal and business checks,

business cards, bills of lading, invoices, and

other business forms

Jazz up your company image with some new letterhead and business cards. Increase efficiency and save time and money with preprinted business checks, invoices, and shipping forms that you can feed through your printer. Need a rubber stamp to identify your child's books, some monogrammed stationery, or customized invitations? Some of the firms here can do that, too. Don't pay full price for printing services! All of the companies in this section can save you lots of money. For other firms that offer discount custom stationery and other printing services, see "Related Products/Companies" at the end of this section.

FIND IT FAST

BUSINESS CARDS AND ADDRESS LABELS • *American Stationery, Brown Print, Invitation Hotline, Lighthouse Colorprint, Moore Business Solutions, Mr. Z's*
CHECK-PRINTING SERVICES • *Checks in the Mail, Moore Business Solutions*
GENERAL PRINTING SERVICES • *Mr. Z's*
INVOICES, STATEMENTS, AND OTHER BUSINESS FORMS • *Moore Business Solutions, Mr. Z's*
PERSONALIZED CARDS AND STATIONERY • *American Stationery, Invitation Hotline*
WEDDING INVITATIONS • *American Stationery, Invitation Hotline*

AMERICAN STATIONERY CO., INC.

Catalog: free
Pay: check, MO, MC, V, AE, Discover
Sells: personalized stationery
Store: mail order only

P.O. BOX 207, DEPT. W
PERU, IN 46970
800–822–2577
FAX: 317–472–5901

American Stationery offers an excellent selection of personalized stationery, at prices up to 45% below those charged by other firms for comparable goods and printing. The company has been in business since 1919 and also produces "The American Wedding Album," a 64-page color catalog with a wide range of wedding invitations and accessories.

The correspondence selections include embossed sheets and notes in four colors, deckle-edged and plain sheets and envelopes in white and pastels, and heavyweight Monarch sheets, business envelopes, and "executive" stationery. The styles range from traditional to casual, for both business and personal correspondence. There are great buys here, including the "Typewriter Box" of 100 printed sheets and the same number of printed envelopes for $25, as well as informals and notes in contemporary and calligraphic typefaces, notepads in spiffy designs, and a choice of ink colors—navy, teal, and gray, as well as the standard range. Stationery for children, personalized memo pads, bill-paying envelopes, bordered postcards, a good selection of gummed and self-sticking return-address labels, desk accessories, and related goods are shown in the 32-page color catalog.

Special Factors: Satisfaction is guaranteed; returns are accepted for replacement or refund.

BROWN PRINT & CO.

P.O. BOX 935
TEMPLE CITY, CA 91780
626–286–2106

Price List and Samples: $2
Pay: check or MO
Sells: custom-designed business cards
Store: mail order only

Brown Print & Co. has been designing and printing business cards and stationery since 1966. For the person looking for something different, Brown offers just that. Mr. Brown, the proprietor, will send you a generous assortment of actual samples, ranging from black glossy stock and gold foil with iridescent metallic colors to standard black-and-white cards with raised inks and artwork. Fold-overs and other unusual formats are also available. Mr. Brown's talents would be wasted on someone who wanted a conventional card; his specialty is unusual design, and he enjoys working with his customers to create "the amusing, the novel, and other effective visual concepts."

Special Factors: Quantity discounts are available; minimum order is 250 or 500 cards.

CHECKS IN THE MAIL, INC.

2345 GOODWIN LN.
NEW BRAUNFELS, TX
78135–0001
800–733–4443
FAX: 800–822–0005

Brochure: free
Pay: check, MO, MC, V, Discover
Sells: check-printing services
Store: mail order only, phone hours Monday to Friday 7–7 CT
Online: http://www.checksinthemail.com

  ¡Si!

The designs offered by Checks in the Mail are among the liveliest available from the big check-printing firms. The Anne Geddes line, for example, features those now-famous photos of real babies as potted sunflowers, pea pods, cabbages, and others. Why you'd want these on your checks is one question. Why not? is another. There are scores of designs for personal checks, offered in wallet and carbonless duplicate styles, and in three-to-a-page desk sets. Other options such as logos, designer typestyles, and message lines are also available. Business checks are available in a choice of formats and designs, in continuous-feed and laser-printer styles.

Prices begin at $5.99 for 200 wallet-style personal checks and run up to $30.99 for a desk set of 300 duplicate checks. The checks are guaranteed to be printed to your bank's standard, and confidentiality of your bank data is assured. You'll also find personalized address labels and business cards offered here. See brochure or website for details.

Special Factors: Satisfaction is guaranteed.

INVITATION HOTLINE

68 HAWKINS RD.
MANALAPAN, NJ 07726
800–800–4355, EXT. 921
732–536–9115
FAX: 732–972–4875

Information: price quote
Pay: check, MO, MC, V, AE, Discover
Sells: printed wedding invitations, business and social stationery, favors, holiday cards, etc.
Store: by appointment only; phone hours Monday to Friday 9–5
E-mail: invhotline@aol.com

When you're budgeting your wedding, every chance to save money helps. Invitation Hotline can cut the cost of invitations, reply cards, wedding stationery, favors, programs, and the other printed goods you may need by 25% (save more on volume and multiple orders). Invitation Hotline offers the products you've probably seen in the big books of samples at the local stationery or print shop and can also provide envelopes laser-printed in calligraphic script at 25% below rates commonly charged by print shops. Nearly two dozen manufacturers and scores of lines are available at this writing, but Invitation Hotline stresses customer service over price and selection as its greatest asset. The proprietors understand everything about the selection process—including your state of mind—and help you work toward the best choice for your tastes, needs, and budget. They can help you to compose the wording on invitations and other printed matter and are experienced in custom design work and processing foreign-language orders.

Invitation Hotline can also supply other goods that are shown in the stationery books—general invitations, personal and business stationery, business cards, birth announcements, and notices of Bar and Bat Mitzvahs, anniversaries, and other red-letter days. If you don't have access to the sample books, call Invitation Hotline to discuss your needs.

Special Factors: Accuracy is guaranteed; price quote by phone or letter.

LIGHTHOUSE COLORPRINT

P.O. BOX 465, DEPT.
  WBMC
SAINT JOSEPH, MI
  49085–0465
616–428–7062, EXT. 2
FAX: 616–428–0847

Order Kit and Samples: $5, refundable (see text)
Pay: check or MO
Sells: color printing services
Store: mail order only
Online:
http://www.lighthousecolorprint.com

If you're looking for an understated business card on engraved stock, keep dialing. Lighthouse Colorprint produces calling cards that won't disappear in anyone's wallet—they feature a full-color photograph of you, or your building, your delivery van, your product line—in short, whatever image you want clients to associate with your firm. Lighthouse cites its own marketing studies that show full-color business cards are held longer and generate more sales than any other medium. The pricing includes typesetting, layout, photo scanning, color separations, and full color proofs. The resolution of 200 lines per inch—up to 50% higher than the industry standard—helps to preserve the quality of the image.

Lighthouse Colorprint believes that it can meet your best price, if not beat it, and "the larger the order, the lower the price per piece." For example, a standard photographic business card job goes from 22 cents each for 1,000 to 4 cents on orders of 15,000 or more; 4" by 6" postcards drop from 33 cents each at 1,000 to 6 cents at 15,000. (Making fair comparisons can be difficult, since no two jobs are identical—from the prep to the specs to the time frame—but customers have reported savings of up to 75%.) The $5 fee Lighthouse charges for the "Custom Order Kit" brings you price lists, order forms, samples of business cards, postcards, and brochures, and a $25 certificate that "may be redeemed on any order," says the firm. The samples demonstrate the print quality, typography, and paper stock and finish, and the price lists detail extra options and charges. Anticipate some back-and-forth on type specs and color, options, proofs, and other details—just as you would with a walk-in print house.

Wholesale buyers, please note: A resale number is required for the wholesale discount of 20% on regular rates.

Special Factors: Price quote by phone, e-mail, or letter; quantity discounts are available; minimum order is 1,000 pieces.

MOORE BUSINESS SOLUTIONS DIRECT

111 BARCLAY BLVD.
LINCOLNSHIRE, IL 60069
800–323–6230
847–913–3200
FAX: 800–329–6667

Catalog: free
Pay: check, MO, MC, V, AE, Discover
Sells: business forms, desktop publishing and presentation forms
Store: mail order only
Online: http://www.moorebsd.com

The "Moore Business Products" catalog features continuous forms (single and multiple) and checks, preprinted and ready to run through your accounting, payroll, or other software program. The list of compatible software covers hundreds of titles; the forms can be produced for manual or typewriter use; and other customizing options allow you to tailor the forms to your needs and have a logo imprinted. The prices are lower than those charged by local print shops, even on small orders of 250 pieces, and 50%-plus on quantities of 2,000 or more. Invoices, statements, payroll vouchers, checks, self-mailers, letterhead, envelopes, labels, and related forms are offered, as well as blank and lined printout paper, postcards, business cards, and rotary cards.

Moore's separate "Image Street" catalog shows laser stationery suites —coordinated sets of letterhead, envelopes, mailing labels, business cards, announcement cards, brochure forms, and other items—designed to reflect different business personalities. "Image Street" also sells formatted newsletters, heavy-coated laser papers, bordered cards and invitations, certificates and awards forms, presentation folders, placards, die-cut tent cards, and place cards. The bookshelf includes desktop publishing classics, primers on writing copy, publicity handbooks, and even label-formatting and forms software. "Image Street" can also provide printing services in conjunction with selected software programs (also available), which can reportedly cut your printing costs by half and reduce the turnaround time by as much as two-thirds. It's a great way to upgrade your business image without breaking the budget. Moore also publishes a catalog for the health-care professional, with forms and other office needs created expressly for the needs of a medical practice.

Special Factors: Satisfaction is guaranteed; request catalog by type or order from the website; quantity discounts are available; returns are accepted for exchange, refund, or credit; institutional accounts are available; minimum order is $30.

MR. Z'S PRINT SERVICES

P.O. BOX 3368
SPRING HILL, FL 34611
352–683–5683
FAX: 352–688–3922

Information Pack With Samples: free
Pay: check, MO, MC, V
Sells: business card and other printing services
Store: 12549 Spring Hill Dr., Spring Hill, FL; Monday to Thursday 8–4, Friday 9–12

I love this company. There's nothing hidden or phony about what they do and how they charge. Mr. Z's is an actual family-run printer—not a printer broker—that has been serving mail-order clients since 1984. The company specializes in raised-print business cards, but they also print letterheads, envelopes, flyers, tickets, invoices, statements, carbonless forms, menus, Rolodex cards, memo pads, postcards, door hangers, and all other types of promotional materials at wholesale prices—which means savings of 50% or more to you. Basic bright-white raised business cards start at $13.95 for 500 (the normal retail price is close to $23). When you request information, you'll get tiny strips of actual card stock in different colors and textures as well as samples of business cards. You can either provide a current business card sample for Mr. Z to match, or choose one of the typefaces provided and follow the enclosed instructions as to color, design, and layout. If something is unclear, Mr. Z's will call you; they won't print your order without contacting you first if it appears to have an error or poor artwork. To sweeten the deal, shipping is free.

Special Factors: Orders to Alaska, Hawaii, and Puerto Rico, add $6.50; free shipping within the continental U.S.

RELATED PRODUCTS/COMPANIES

Braille embossing services • *The New Vision Store*
General printing services • *Penny-Wise, Quill Corp., Sunrise Business Products*
Logo design services • *Visual Horizons*
Logo screen-printing on mugs, pens, and other corporate gifts • *Nelson Marketing, Best Impressions*
Logo silk-screening and embroidery for clothing and uniforms • *Tafford Manufacturing, Cotton Scrubs, Cheap Aprons/Allstates Uniform*

Professional Uniforms and Promotional Products

Institutional and professional workwear and miscellaneous promotional goods—with and without custom logos

The firms listed in this section specialize in clothing and other products screen-printed, embroidered, or embossed with your company's name or logo. Some of the clothing is quite specialized, for people in the restaurant, catering, or medical professions. Other clothing is more all-purpose—janitorial jumpsuits, polo-style shirts, and baseball caps, to name a few. If you're looking for corporate gifts, this section has them—from golf balls, totes, and key rings to pens and clocks—all custom-printed with your company's name, of course, so that your clients will be thinking of you.

FIND IT FAST

CUSTOM LOGO DESIGN SERVICES • Cheap Aprons/Allstates Uniform, Tafford
FOOD INDUSTRY CLOTHING • Cheap Aprons/Allstates Uniform
GENERAL WORK CLOTHING AND CASUAL APPAREL • Cheap Aprons/Allstates Uniform, Nelson Marketing
MEDICAL INDUSTRY CLOTHING • Cotton Scrubs, Tafford
MISCELLANEOUS PROMOTIONAL PRODUCTS • Best Impressions, Nelson Marketing

BEST IMPRESSIONS PROMOTIONAL PRODUCTS CATALOG

Catalog: free
Pay: check, MO, MC, V, AE, Discover
Sells: business-promotion products
Store: mail order only
Online: http://bestimpressions.com

P.O. BOX 802
LASALLE, IL 61301
800–635–2378
FAX: 815–883–8346

This catalog won't overwhelm you with choices. Instead, it features the most popular items currently appearing at seminars and conventions and—hopefully—your clients' desks in the near future. Most of the products are in the $1 to $5 price range—pens, pocket calculators, rulers, wipe-off boards, mouse pads, memo cubes, key rings, and similar items lead the 32-page catalog. There are novelties (stress balloons, stuffed toys, etc.), "giveaways" (sunglasses, playing cards, fortune cookies, lapel pins, magnets, buttons, etc.), and the classics—ceramic mugs and sports bottles, measuring tapes, flashlights, golf balls, fanny packs, caps, tote bags, and calendars. The small collection of executive gifts includes travel alarms, desk clocks, portfolios, and mugs with matching tile coasters. Savings can run up to 50%, depending on the item and quantity ordered, and prices include execution of your design in one color in one imprint area (additional colors are extra). Camera-ready artwork is required, or it can be produced by the firm's art department for $30 per item. Each product has a minimum order—250 Bic Clics, 100 mouse pads, and 1,000 balsa gliders are typical examples—but many minimums can be lowered (surcharges apply). And selected products are available for accelerated shipment, at no extra charge—see the catalog or website for details.

Special Factors: Price quote by phone; quantity discounts are available; institutional accounts are available; minimum orders vary by item.

CHEAP APRONS/ ALLSTATES UNIFORM

CATALOG SALES, 599 CANAL ST. LAWRENCE, MA 01840
800–367–2374
FAX: 978–689–2483

Catalog: free (see text)
Pay: check, MO, MC, V, AE
Sells: monogrammed or screen-printed apparel, uniforms, hats, etc.
Store: same address for showroom; Monday to Friday 9–5, Saturday 9–1
Online: http://www.cheapaprons.com

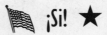 ¡Sí! ★

If you own a restaurant, are a caterer, run a business, or even have a weekend bowling team that needs a morale booster, you should know about Cheap Aprons and Allstates Uniforms, sister companies supplying workwear and casual apparel that's custom-monogrammed or screen-printed with your logo. Cheap Apron's 32-page color catalog offers aprons of every kind (wrap, café, bib, full-length bistro, waist, etc.), button-down shirts in plain and patterned, bow ties and neckties, polo shirts and tee shirts, tuxedo shirts, chef's apparel, table linens, baseball-style caps, sweatshirts, and more—all at reasonable prices that include a one-color screen-printed logo. Cheap Aprons offers quantity discounts on every item, and there are additional deals in the catalog as well as website-only specials.

In Allstates Uniform's 16-page catalog you'll find other types of workwear—work jackets, coveralls, waterproof rain suits, utility smocks, tee shirts, caps, and tank tops among them. The screen-printing is included in the good prices, and quantity discounts are listed here as well.

Special Factors: Satisfaction guaranteed; see catalogs for returns policy; custom logo design is available; specify which catalog you want when you request it.

COTTON SCRUBS & CO.

104 PARK DR.
P.O. BOX 1014
MONTGOMERYVILLE, PA
  18936–1014
888–225–7160

Catalog: free
Pay: check, MO, MC, V, AE, Discover
Sells: all-cotton scrubs for medical professionals
Store: three locations in Pennsylvania; call for addresses and hours

Doctors, nurses, veterinarians, techs—these and other medical professionals spend their time and energy helping us and our loved ones feel better. Cotton Scrubs & Co. is a new venture by Tafford (see listing this section) dedicated to helping the caregivers feel comfortable as well. Imagine a surgeon dressed in a gaily decorated cartoon alligator print being the first person your child sees when he comes out of anesthesia. The styles, colors, and prints offered here make the whole experience more human. And medical professionals will jump for joy at the all-cotton fabric that breathes and is easy to care for, in cuts that provide a soft, natural fit. Since these items come directly to the consumer from the manufacturer, you'll save an average of 20% (retail prices and Cotton Scrubs' prices are listed side by side, so you can calculate the discounts). In addition to the good selection of scrubs (drawstrings and tops, tunics, skorts, scrub dresses, etc.) there are a number of amusing and useful items here: themed and matching earrings, pendants, and pins, comfort shoes and socks, color-coordinated stethoscopes, and more. Sizes run from XS to 4X.

Special Factors: Custom embroidering available; unworn garments may be returned within 30 days for refund or exchange.

NELSON MARKETING

P.O. BOX 320
OSHKOSH, WI 54902–0320
800–722–5203
FAX: 800–355–5043
TDD: 800–642–2076

Catalog: free
Pay: check, MO, MC, V, AE, Discover
Sells: business-promotion products and apparel
Store: mail order only
Online: http://www.nelsonmarketing.com

Nelson Marketing offers businesses hundreds of proven imprinted promotional or corporate identity products, and backs up their lowest price guarantee with a "double the difference" promise—they'll double the difference between their prices and a lower one if you find a lower-priced item within 30 days of purchase. Nelson puts out two catalogs, one for miscellaneous items, the other for corporate apparel and sportswear.

The 64-page products catalog features pens and pencils, plaques and awards, folios, totes and duffels, sport towels, hats, golf accessories, sweatshirts, printed note cubes and "stickies," mouse pads, magnets, first-aid kits and safety devices, flying disks and novelties, flashlights and tools, clocks, mugs, squeeze bottles, umbrellas, and more. The catalog descriptions include notes on surcharges for setup, dies, screens, cuts, logos, etc., making it easy to calculate the delivered price. Items that can be expedited through production are flagged with a "quick ship" symbol, and product samples are available.

The 24-page apparel and sportswear catalog offers polo shirts for men and women, ties, vests, crew-neck sweaters, button-down shirts, rugby shirts, sweatsuits, jackets, hats, and more—all embroidered with your company's logo at no "extra" charge (the logos are included in the price). Naturally, the more you buy, the more the unit price goes down.

Special Factors: Goods are guaranteed to be delivered exactly as ordered, or the order will be rerun, refunded, or credited; quantity discounts are available; institutional accounts are available.

TAFFORD MANU-FACTURING, INC.

104 PARK DR.
P.O. BOX 1001
MONTGOMERYVILLE, PA
 18936
800–283–0065
215–643–9666
FAX: 215–643–4922

Catalog: free
Pay: check, MO, MC, V, AE, Discover
Sells: uniforms, shoes, and accessories for the medical professional
Store: three retail locations in PA; call for addresses and hours

Compared to the average catalog of uniforms for health-care professionals, Tafford has the best fashion buys for the dollar around. The firm manufactures its own uniforms, which means you beat at least one markup, and the size selection is great—from XS to 6X, petite to tall. The 80-page color catalog shows mostly women's clothing, although most of the scrubs and warm-ups are unisex. Say good-bye to the intimidating doctor or nurse dressed in clinical white. You'll find many colors, prints, and styles here—even jumpsuits and matching baseball-style caps—designed to suit every figure type, including maternity styles. The catalog also shows cardigans, jackets, shoes (from traditional "nurse" styles to clogs and Birkenstocks), emblem pins, reference books, and brightly colored basic equipment—stethoscopes, blood pressure kits, scissors, otoscopes, etc. Both the retail and the discount prices of the clothing are given, so you see how much you're saving—usually 20% or 30% on the regular retail. Consult your colleagues before ordering, because if you buy as part of a group, Tafford also offers special services such as swatches and samples, volume discounts, and custom embroidery and logo silk-screening.

Special Factors: Satisfaction is guaranteed; unworn, undamaged, unwashed returns are accepted within 30 days for exchange, refund, or credit.

RELATED PRODUCTS/COMPANIES

Barber's capes, aprons, chef's hats and kitchen whites • Clothcrafters, Marshall Domestics, Professional Cutlery Direct
Party goods and events decor with your logo • M&N International
Scrubs and lab coats • Marshall Domestics
Work clothing • Marshall Domestics, Cahall's Work Wear

SPECIAL NEEDS

Clothing, tools, gadgets, and home and office accessories for children and adults with special physical or medical requirements

If you're fortunate enough to be youngish, of average size, in excellent health, with no disabilities, then you probably take for granted, as I often do, all the little activities and pleasures in life that come easily and naturally. The companies in this chapter provide all kinds of products to restore dignity, help out, and make life more fun for people who are extra large, are visually impaired, have limited strength or mobility, or have physical conditions requiring special clothing, furniture, or personal accessories. From seat belt extenders to chair-lift seats, Braille playing cards to all-cotton children's clothing, you'll find a lot here that you and your loved ones will appreciate.

FIND IT FAST

CLOTHING FOR DISABLED CHILDREN • Special Clothes
POST–BREAST SURGERY PRODUCTS • B&B Company
PRODUCTS FOR EXTRA-LARGE PEOPLE • Amplestuff
PRODUCTS FOR MISCELLANEOUS POST-OPERATIVE OR MEDICAL CONDITIONS • Comfort House, Special Clothes, Support Plus
PRODUCTS FOR THE ALLERGY-SENSITIVE • National Allergy Supply
PRODUCTS FOR THE ELDERLY OR THOSE WITH LIMITED MOBILITY • Amplestuff, Comfort House, Support Plus
PRODUCTS FOR THE VISUALLY IMPAIRED • Independent Living Aids, The New Vision Store

AMPLESTUFF

P.O. BOX 116
BEARSVILLE, NY 12409
914–679–3316
FAX: 914–679–1206

Catalog: free
Pay: check, MO, MC, V
Sells: products and books for plus-size and supersize people
Store: mail order only
E-mail: amplestuff@aol.com

One evening Amplestuff president Bill Fabrey received a call from a 540-pound man across the country in the hospital for an emergency appendectomy. His most serious suffering was caused by humiliation for lack of a hospital gown that fit him. Bill made sure the very next morning there were four hospital gowns waiting for the grateful patient when he woke up. There aren't many businesses with this kind of concern and personal rapport with their customers. Amplestuff's motto is "make your world fit you," and its 34-page catalog is devoted to products that big people all over the world will surely appreciate, many of them appropriate for anybody with movement restrictions. Items such as airline seat belt extenders, fanny packs ("you shouldn't have to be slender to wear a fanny pack"), large-size socks, silver- and gold-plated bangles in 8", 9", or 10" sizes, extra-large clothes hangers, extra-large bath towels, reach extenders, a portable bidet, 10" car steering wheels (for more leg and stomach room), blood pressure kits, personal fans, and more are offered, with photographs and descriptions of each. There are also size-friendly videos and books, including exercise videos, art books, and a resource guide to the best books related to the larger-size population.

Bill Fabrey says half of his business dealings are in communications, since there are very few sources out there knowledgeable about improving the lives of ample-size people. You can also subscribe to the *Ample Shopper,* a 12-page newsletter chock full of news, reviews, ratings, information, how-to articles, Q&A, consumer activism, and more. The review issue at the time of this writing spoke to the hazards of automobile airbags for larger-size people. The newsletter is $15 for a year, U.S. and Canada ($22 elsewhere). Amplestuff's voicemail is often on, but the staff always returns calls promptly.

Wholesalers: Inquire for terms.

Special Factors: U.S. funds only; quantity discounts on some items; satisfaction is guaranteed; orders by phone, fax, and mail—no e-mail orders.

B&B COMPANY, INC.

2417 BANK DR., DEPT.
 WCO1
P.O. BOX 5731
BOISE, ID 83705–0731
800–262–2789
208–343–9696
FAX: 208–343–9266

Brochure: free
Pay: check, MO, MC, V, Discover
Sells: Bosom Buddy breast prostheses
Store: mail order only

B&B has been producing the "Bosom Buddy Breast Form," a comfortable, reasonably priced external breast prosthesis, since 1976. The form is weighted and shaped to ideal dimensions with cushioned pillows, each of which contains $1\frac{1}{2}$ ounces of tiny glass beads. (The weight may be adjusted by adding or removing pillows.) The form itself is all-fabric (no silicone or plastic is used), made of nylon softened with fiberfill, with an all-cotton backing that rests next to your skin. Bosom Buddy is interchangeable (fits both left and right sides), available in sizes from 32AAA to 46DDD, and it costs $60 for sizes AAA and AA, $65 for sizes A through D, and $70 for sizes DD and DDD. These prices are about 50% below silicone models. The breast forms are available in a choice of three colors to best blend with your own skin tone. The brochure gives complete details, and B&B's staff can answer any questions you may have by phone.

Wholesale customers: The minimum order is three breast forms, or $100.

Special Factors: Satisfaction is guaranteed; returns are accepted.

COMFORT HOUSE

189-WM FRELINGHUYSEN AVE.

NEWARK, NJ 07114–1595

973–242–8080

FAX: 973–242–0131

Catalog: $2, refundable
Pay: check, MO, MC, V, AE, Discover
Sells: all-around helpful tools and gadgets
Store: mail order only
E-mail: wbm@comforthouse.com
Online: http://www.comforthouse.com

Here are 24 pages of products designed to make the little things easier for everyone, beginning with the catalog itself, which is printed in a big, clear typeface. Comfort House, in business since 1991, sells things such as cleaning tools with extension poles that anyone might find useful, as well as electric vegetable peelers, lamp switch enlargers, zipper pulls, and seat-lift chairs, designed specifically for those with limited strength and mobility. There are doorknob turners, dressing aids, various gripping devices, exercisers, sleeping and bathing aids, travel accessories, gardening tools, and much more. Comfort House is not a discount catalog, although a couple of price checks showed savings of over 30% on some of the body-care products; this is simply a great collection of products that can help people perform everyday tasks more easily and more safely, as well as coping with changed conditions.

In addition to what's shown in the catalog, Comfort House accepts special orders for any of thousands of products for general personal care, incontinence, mobility assistance, or needs associated with orthopedics, ostomy, laryngectomy, mobility, and urology.

Wholesale terms are available to drug, medical, and surgical-supply stores only. Inquire on company letterhead for terms and pricing.

Special Factors: Satisfaction is guaranteed; returns in unused condition are accepted within 30 days.

INDEPENDENT LIVING AIDS

27 EAST MALL
PLAINVIEW, NY 11805
800–537–2118
516–752–8080
FAX: 516–752–3135

Catalog: $1
Pay: check, MO, MC, V, Discover
Sells: aids for the visually impaired
Store: mail order only
E-mail: indlivaids@aol.com
Online: http://www.independentliving.com

For twenty years ILA has been distributing unique and hard-to-find aids to people who are visually handicapped. The 72-page color catalog features hundreds of items to help individuals with special needs live more comfortably and safely. A sampling of their products includes large-face watches and desk clocks, magnifiers (handheld and clip-ons for eyeglasses), desk lamps, floor lamps, and other lighting to enhance visibility, recorders, calculators, and all kinds of "talking" items—from clocks, telephones, and bathroom scales to thermometers and money identifiers. You'll find canes and walkers, writing guides for checks and envelopes, large-face playing cards and other games in Braille, including bingo and Trivial Pursuit, and much more. There are personal care items (mirrors, e.g.), cooking aids such as tactile meat thermometers, bath and shower items such as the Gentle Jet Bidet that attaches easily to any toilet seat, a whole section on accessories for diabetic care, books about and for the visually impaired (such as large-print cookbooks), and computer software that adapts to any computer. The prices on most items are very reasonable, but Independent Living Aids also runs specials and has a wholesale division, where savings generally run over 20%. The real plus with this company is that they offer hard-to-find items, many of which would be useful for the rest of us and our aging parents as well. The website is really terrific, too.

Special Factors: Wholesale customers must have a resale number; returns must be made within 30 days.

NATIONAL ALLERGY SUPPLY, INC.

4400 ABBOTT'S BRIDGE ROAD
DULUTH, GA 33096
800–522–1448
FAX: 770–623–5568

Catalog: free
Pay: check, MO, MC, V, AE, Discover
Sells: nondrug products to avoid allergens
Store: mail order only
Online: http://www.natlallergy.com

 ¡Si!

National Allergy Supply is the nation's largest discount allergy products supplier. The "Allergy Relief Catalog" is a 24-page color catalog designed for people who suffer from sneezing, runny nose, swollen and itchy eyes, coughing, wheezing, post nasal drip, and many other allergy and asthma symptoms. Ryner Wittgens started this company nine years ago as a result of his daughter's being diagnosed with six different airborne allergies. He made it his goal to find the best products out there for people like his daughter, for whom ordinary household environments full of pet dander, dust mite allergen, dust mold, chemical gassing of carpets, and toxins from household cleaners make life difficult if not dangerous. Even if you're not allergy-prone, there are lots of ways to make your environment cleaner and healthier. You'll find all-cotton bedding, nondown comforters, air cleaners, carpet treatments, vinyl and cotton gloves for people with chemically sensitive skin, household cleaners, skin- and hair-care products, floor dusters, vacuum cleaners specially designed to eliminate 99.97% of allergens, in-home asthma treatments, respiratory masks, breathing and sleeping aids, window fans, and much more.

The catalog is not overwhelming. One gets the sense that the company has selected only the best one or two manufacturers in each category, and explanatory text accompanies each product with descriptions about its benefit to allergy-sensitive people. There are plenty of testimonials from happy customers, and the company offers a 100% satisfaction guarantee on all their products. National Allergy Supply keeps a staff of highly trained reps who are available to answer all of your questions.

Special to BWBM readers: Identify yourself as a reader of this book and National Allergy will send you a free video about allergen avoidance in your home, a $9 value. Mention offer FVID when calling.

Special Factors: Satisfaction guaranteed; Canadian customers must pay by credit card; phone hours are 24 hours a day, Monday through Saturday.

THE NEW VISION STORE

Product List: free
Pay: check, MO, MC, V, Discover
Sells: products to aid the visually impaired
Store: same address; Monday to Friday 10–4

919 WALNUT ST., 1ST FL.
PHILADELPHIA, PA 19107
215–629–2990

Bill Ankenbrant understands the challenges faced by visually impaired persons. Visually impaired himself, he launched his store and mail order company to "provide products that promote hope and independence for every customer wherever possible." The 8-page typewritten product list, which also comes out in Braille twice a year, presents a variety of necessary but hard-to-find items, some of which are discounted, others discounted 20% if you buy in small quantity, but all at reasonable prices. The New Vision Store offers such products as canes (auto-fold, rigid fiberglass, folding support canes, and others); flame-retardant oven mitts; raised-number timers, clocks, and calculators, as well as large-print, talking, and Braille versions; magnifiers of all kinds; labeling supplies, such as kits, labeling guns, Braille-embossing guns, as well as tapes for clothing, magnetized tapes, and labels of every kind; bill organizers; talking thermometers; a variety of sunglasses; small electronics such as Walkmans, desk recorders, and desk radios; mailing supplies including free-matter-for-the-blind labels and two- and four-cassette mailers; a variety of user-friendly watches; desk accessories such as rulers and pens, as well as signature guides and slates of different sizes for note-writing; and much more. Send in a greeting card to New Vision and they'll emboss it for you in Braille for $3.

Special Factors: If you have a product not found in the catalog, The New Vision Store will find it for you; mail-order hours are the same as store hours; request in writing for shipping Free Matter for the Blind; see company literature for other shipping fees and policies.

SPECIAL CLOTHES, INC.

P.O. BOX 333
EAST HARWICH, MA 02645
TEL/FAX: 508–896–5172

Catalog: $1
Pay: check, MO, MC, V
Sells: clothing for children and adults with disabilities
Store: mail order only
E-mail: specialclo@aol.com
Online: http://www.special-clothes.com

Special Clothes, Inc., was founded in 1987 by Judith Sweeney, whose interest in developing adaptive designs was inspired by her experiences as an educator involved with children with special needs. Special Clothes has two catalogs—one for children, one for adults—to help people for whom dressing is a daily struggle. Because the company prices the clothing by size, pricing is not inflated, and there are quantity discounts that enable you to cut costs further. All garments of knit, fleece, or denim are 100% cotton, most garments are latex-free, and functional features such as snap crotches, bib fronts, and G-tube access are inconspicuous. The 40-page children's catalog is for toddlers to size–18 teens. (There's a handy sizing chart included that helps you choose the right size for your child.) Among the clothing and accessories offered are all-cotton bodysuits with snap crotches and optional gastrostomy-tube access (Special Clothes will conceal the access opening with a stitched-on pocket), available in solid colors and a variety of styles; snap-on bodysuit extenders that add four inches to the torso length; a travel bag to carry catheterization items safely, easily, and discreetly; all-cotton absorbent briefs and nylon protective pull-ons; feeding bibs; knit jumpsuits; denim and chambray overalls; jeans, trousers, and dress pants; shirts and skirted leggings; heavyweight flannel diapers; swimwear, socks, slippers, mittens, and more. All clothing is available in a variety of colors, closure options, G-tube access, length, etc. Special Clothes' Birthday Club will give your child a greeting card and a 15%-off coupon when you send in your child's name and birth date.

The adult catalog offers bodysuits, sleepers, jumpsuits, knit pants, and wheelchair jackets and ponchos, and includes a sizing chart to accommodate small to extra-large adults. The catalogs include some helpful incontinence and parent resources, as well as lists for sale ($1 each) of other manufacturers of adaptive clothing for adults, health-care supplies, special needs publications, and service organizations.

Wholesale buyers and institutions: Please inquire about Special Clothes' terms and pricing.

Special Factors: See catalog for returns policy; custom orders are available (but not returnable).

SUPPORT PLUS

99 WEST ST., DEPT.
  WBM99
BOX 500
MEDFIELD, MA 02052
800–229–2910
508–359–2910
FAX: 508–359–0139

Catalog: free
Pay: check, MO, MC, V, AE, Discover
Sells: support hosiery, therapeutic apparel, foot products, comfort footwear
Store: mail order only
E-mail: supportplu@aol.com

Support Plus has been in business since 1972 and offers an extensive selection of supportive hosiery and undergarments for men and women, as well as comfortable leather footwear. Discounts average about 15%, but some items are priced 30% less than regular retail.

If your physician recommends or prescribes support (elastic) hosiery, you'll find this catalog a helpful guide to what's available. Support Plus offers panty hose, stockings, knee-highs, and men's dress socks in different support strengths. (The compression rating for each style is given in the catalog descriptions.) Among the brands sold here are Bauer & Black, Berkshire, Futuro, Hanes, T.E.D., and Support Plus' own line. Maternity, cotton-soled, control-top, open-toe, and irregular styles are available.

Support Plus also sells posture pads for chairs and beds, joint "wraps" for applications of heat and cold, Dale abdominal and lumbosacral supports, Futuro braces and joint supports, and personal-care products and bathing aids—eating and dressing implements, bedding, underpads and disposable pants, bath seats and rails, and toilet guard rails. The catalog also features a collection of comfort-styled shoes and slippers for women by Barefoot Freedom, Clinic Shoe, Foot Saver, Daniel Green, Munro, and Soft Spots, in standard and hard-to-fit sizes, and a line of women's underwear and foundation garments.

Special Factors: Price quote by phone for quantities in excess of 12 pairs; unworn returns are accepted.

RELATED PRODUCTS/COMPANIES

Audiobooks • Blackstone, Books.com, Bargain Book Warehouse, The Family Travel Guides Catalogue

Bathroom fixtures for disabled persons • The Faucet Outlet

Blood-pressure and other health-monitoring equipment • Creative Health Products, Tafford Manufacturing, Cotton Scrubs, Essentials

Braille spice labels • Grandma's Spice Shop

Closed-caption decoders • S&S Sound City

Cookbooks for diabetics, allergy sufferers, and dieters • Jessica's Biscuit

Custom-made nonallergenic comforters • J. Schachter

Incontinence supplies, hospital gowns, hospital sheets • Marshall Domestics

Mail-order catalogs in Braille and/or audio • Essentials (prescription and OTC drugstore items), Grandma's Spice Shop (herbs, spices, coffee, tea, etc.)

Mastectomy bras • The Smart Saver, Lady Grace

Office workstations with wheelchair access • Dallas Midwest, K-Log

Post-mastectomy swimwear • World Wide Aquatics

Snap-up-the-back nightgowns • Chock Catalog

Wigs • Paula Young, Beauty by Spector, Gold Medal Hair Products, Especially Yours

SPORTS, FITNESS, AND RECREATION

Clothing, equipment, and supplies for sports, recreation, hunting, and camping

Organized sports and outdoor recreational pursuits—from camping to golf to volleyball—are supplied here, and discounts of 30% are routine. These suppliers sell clothing and equipment for boating, cycling, running, golfing, skiing, aerobics, racquet sports, skin and scuba diving, camping, hunting, hiking, basketball, soccer, and other endeavors. Custom services, such as racquet stringing and club repairs, are usually priced competitively as well. Buying your gear by mail may be the only sport that repays a nominal expenditure of energy with such an enhanced sense of well-being.

For firms that offer foul-weather gear, swimwear, and other clothing for athletes and nature lovers, see the "Clothing, Hats, Furs, and Accessories" chapter, page 83. For companies that offer other sports- and recreation-related items, see the listings at the end of this chapter under "Related Products/Companies."

FIND IT FAST

ARCHERY • Bowhunters Warehouse
BILLIARDS, TABLE TENNIS, DARTS • Mueller Sporting Goods
BOATS AND WATER SPORTS • Bart's Water Sports, Berry Scuba, Central Skindivers, The House, Mohawk Canoes, Overton's, Performance Diver, SOAR Inflatables, Water Warehouse, World Wide Aquatics
CAMPING AND SURVIVAL • Campmor, Cutlery Shoppe, Don Gleason's, Sierra Trading Post, The Sportsman's Guide, Wiley
CYCLING • Bike Nashbar, Performance Bicycle

DANCE AND TUMBLING • Better Health Fitness
GOLF • Discount Golf Superstore, Golf Haus, Virtual Fairway
HUNTING • Bowhunters Warehouse, Cheap Shot, Deer Shack, The Sportsman's Guide, Wiley
KITES • BFK Sports
PLAYGROUND EQUIPMENT • Better Health Fitness
RACQUET SPORTS • Holabird
SKIING AND SNOWBOARDING • Al's Ski Barn, The House
SOCCER • Acme Soccer, Soccer International
VOLLEYBALL • Spike Nashbar
WEIGHTLIFTING, FITNESS, AND SPA • Better Health Fitness, Creative Health Products, Fitness Factory Outlet, Fitness Systems

---

ACME SOCCER AND WIDGET WORKS

P.O. BOX 811
CARRBORO, NC
27510–0811
800–333–4625
FAX: 919–644–6808

Catalog: free
Pay: check, MO, MC, V, AE, Discover
Sells: soccer gear
Store: mail order only

  ¡Si!

Soccer moms: Stop despairing at the coming of spring. Sure, your kid has outgrown her shin guards and needs some new cleats. But Acme Soccer knows this, and that's why the company purchases manufacturers' overstocks of soccer gear and can sell it to you at prices that are 50% to 60% off the regular retail price. The 32-page color catalog has items for kids and adults, including soccer shorts; tee shirts with cool slogans and pictures, as well as plain ones and the designer logos the kids flip for; soccer shoes of every type and style, designed for indoor courts as well as muddy fields; socks; knit hats and visor caps; gloves; shin guards; equipment bags; single-color team shirts; nylon windbreakers and other jackets; and soccer accessories and gifts.

Note to Spanish-speaking customers: Acme welcomes your calls and has Spanish-speaking reps to assist you.

Special Factors: Acme recommends that you call before placing your order, since some of the items are stocked in limited quantities; returns accepted on clean, unused, or defective merchandise (see catalog for details); no C.O.D. orders.

AL'S SKI BARN

BOX 59 COTTONWOOD
*   PARK*
JACKSON, WY 83001
FAX: 307–734–8824

Information: internet site only, no catalog
Pay: MO, MC, V
Sells: ski equipment
Store: online only
E-mail: info@untracked.com
Online: http://untracked.com

Skiing is an expensive sport, but it just got cheaper. Al's Ski Barn is a virtual ski shop that acquires surplus ski equipment or equipment from outfits that are going out of business, and then sells it directly to you off their website—at savings that reach up to 60% and more. All equipment is still warrantied by the manufacturer, but it may be last year's stock. (Next year your brand-new equipment will be last year's model anyway!) When you visit Al's user-friendly, uncomplicated website, you'll see what they currently have in stock. The stock changes periodically when new equipment comes in, so if you don't find what you're looking for right away, check back. Next to each item is the retail price and then Al's Ski Barn price. The savings are significant. For example, the current selection as of this writing included K2 Four skis, 178 and 183 cm, regularly $600, Al's price $449. A pair of '96 Atomic Premiere skis were regularly $525, but $199 at Al's. Bindings that were normally $300 ('96 Marker MSI Graphite EPS 99 mm) were being sold by Al's at $149. Al's carries top-name skis and bindings, including Atomic, Blizzard, Dynastar, Head, K2, Kastle, Look, Marker, Salomon, Tyrolia, and Volkl. Don't forget to check out the "Bargain Stall," where the drastically marked down sale items will blow your boots off. If you don't find what you're looking for right away, check back or join Al's Ski Barn's e-mailing list to receive e-mail when new inventory is added.

Special Factors: Returns are negotiable; all equipment warrantied by manufacturer; all items shipped from MN warehouse.

BART'S WATER SPORTS

P.O. BOX 294-WBM
NORTH WEBSTER, IN
  46555
800–348–5016
219–834–7666
FAX: 219–834–4246

Catalog: free, $5 outside U.S.
Pay: check, MO, MC, V, AE, Discover
Sells: water sports, marine/boating, and personal watercraft goods
Store: Hwy. 13, North Webster, IN; Monday to Saturday 9–6
E-mail: bartsports@kconline.com
Online: http://www.bartsports.com

The thrills of water sports are cheaper at Bart's, where wet suits, skis, and marine products cost up to 40% below list, and clearance items are offered at even greater savings. Bart's has been in business since 1972 and backs every sale with a guarantee of satisfaction. The 72-page color catalog features name-brand water skis, personal watercraft accessories, and marine equipment for boats. Wakeboarders can choose from pages of boards and accessories, and there's a large selection of floats, tubes, and other inflatables. Ski vests and wet suits for men, women, and children are offered, in addition to wet-suit accessories, swimwear for men and women, tee shirts, sunglasses, gloves, boat lifts, and boat/PWC covers.

Special Factors: Satisfaction is guaranteed; quantity discounts are available; returns are accepted within 60 days; minimum order is $250 on shipments overseas.

BERRY SCUBA CO.

6674 N. NORTHWEST
  HWY., DEPT. W–99
CHICAGO, IL 60631
800–621–6019
773–763–1626
FAX: 773–775–1815

Catalog: free
Pay: check, MO, MC, V, AE, Discover
Sells: scuba-diving gear
Store: same address; also Lombard and Palatine, IL, and Atlanta, GA

Berry Scuba, "the oldest, largest, and best-known direct-mail scuba firm in the country," carries a wide range of equipment and accessories for diving and related activities. Shop here for regulators, masks, wet suits, fins, tanks, diving lights, strobes, underwater cameras and housings, diving watches, pole spears, and other gear and accessories for underwater use. Berry has been in business since 1960 and sells on a price-quote basis, but will send you the free catalog on request.

Special Factors: Orders are shipped worldwide.

BETTER HEALTH FITNESS

5302 NEW UTRECHT AVE.
BROOKLYN, NY 11219
718–436–4693
718–436–4801
FAX: 718–854–3381

Information: inquire
Pay: check, MO, MC, V, AE
Sells: exercise and playground equipment
Store: same address; Monday to Wednesday 10–6, Thursday 10–8, Sunday 12–5 (closed Friday and Saturday)

Whether you're buying a stationary bicycle for rainy-day workouts or outfitting an entire gym, you'll get it for less at Better Health. The firm has been selling top-of-the-line equipment and gear since 1977, including Alva (ballet barres), Apex Mats, Barracuda (swim gear), Century, Cybex (strength equipment), Everlast, EverYoung, Healthometer, Impex, K-Swiss (footwear), Landice, Life Fitness (massage equipment), Monark (cycles), Pacemaster (treadmills), Park Structures (commercial playground equipment), Sacro Ease (car seat supports), Schwinn, Trimline (treadmills), Trotter (treadmills), Tuff Stuff, and Vision Fitness. You can save up to 20% on the regular prices of equipment by these and other manufacturers. Fax them for quotes on treadmills, ski machines, dual-action exercise cycles, multistation units, free weights, benches, aerobic and tumbling mats, dance studio equipment, saunas, massage equipment, locker room equipment, boxing equipment, indoor/outdoor resilient flooring, and related goods. If you're within the New York/New Jersey/Connecticut area, Better Health can design and install a wooden, metal, or Plastisol-coated steel home or commercial playground set, or provide you with gym layout and related design services. Treadmills and weights are available on a regional basis.

Special Factors: Satisfaction is guaranteed; price quote by fax; authorized returns are accepted within 15 days for exchange, refund, or credit; minimum order is $50.

BFK SPORTS, INC.

Catalog: free
Pay: check, MO, MC, V, AE, Discover, JCB
Sells: kites and kiting supplies
Store: same address; Monday to Saturday
11–6, Sunday 12–5
E-mail: bfk@gte.net
Online: http://www.kitestore.com

2500 E. IMPERIAL HWY.
  #122
BREA, CA 92821
714–529–6589
FAX: 714–529–6152

If the last kite you flew was cut from a surplus shopping bag and sported a tail made from strips of an old sheet, you'll find BFK Sports a revelation. Here are "sport" kites, used for recreation and in kiting competitions, which are flown using two, three, or even four lines. Beyond sport kiting lies the world of stunt flying and "buggy" kiting, in which the operator navigates a "high traction" kite from a three-wheeled buggy platform on the ground. BFK carries the kites and equipment for all levels of kiting, from top-name manufacturers. You'll find all types of kite line, winders, carbon spars, kite bags, windsocks and wind meters, and books, magazines, and videos. BFK also offers other "flying toys"— boomerangs, rubber-band gliders, rockets, and yo-yos. Even custom-made land sailers are available—no kiting experience required.

BFK's website and catalog showcase the current stock and include details on the firm's "lowest price" policy. And you can visit the website or the stores to find discontinued and close-out items at up to 50% off list price.

Special Factors: Satisfaction is guaranteed; new, unused returns (with some exceptions) are accepted within 15 days for exchange, refund, or credit; C.O.D. orders are accepted.

BIKE NASHBAR

**4111 SIMON RD., DEPT.
WBM9
YOUNGSTOWN, OH
44512–1343
800–NASHBAR
FAX: 800–456–1223**

Catalog: free
Pay: check, MO, MC, V, Discover
Sells: bicycles, accessories, apparel and equipment
Store: same address; call for hours
Online: http://www.nashbar.com

Bike Nashbar, one of the country's top sources for casual and serious cyclists, publishes a 70-plus-page catalog that runs from rain parkas to panniers, sold at "guaranteed lowest prices." Bike Nashbar has been in business since 1973 and sells its own line of road, touring, and ATB bikes, which have features usually found on more expensive models. There are full lines of parts and accessories, including saddles from Avocet, San Marco, Selle Italia, TRICO, and Vetta, gears, brakes, chain wheels, hubs, pedals, derailleurs, handlebars, and other parts by Campagnolo, Control Tech, Shimano, and other firms. Panniers and bags, racks, helmets, protective eyewear, gloves, tires and tubes, wheels, toe clips, locks (Nashbar, Kryptonite, and Specialized), handlebar tape, grips, tire pumps, lights, and other accessories are offered. Bike Nashbar also features a large selection of cycling clothing—its own label and Cannondale, Inmotion, and Insport—as well as shoes by Duegi, Look, Scott, Sidi, Specialized, Time, and Vittoria. The catalog includes a good bit of technical information, and if you need more assistance, just call.

Special Factors: Satisfaction is guaranteed; technical advice is available.

BOWHUNTERS WAREHOUSE, INC.

1045 ZIEGLER RD.
P.O. BOX 158
WELLSVILLE, PA 17365
800–735–2697
717–432–8611
FAX: 717–432–2683

Catalog: free
Pay: check, MO, MC, V, Discover
Sells: equipment for bow hunting, hunting, and archery
Store: same address; Monday, Wednesday, and Friday 10–8, Tuesday and Thursday 10–6, Saturday 10–4

You can save up to 40% on a complete range of supplies for bow hunting, bow fishing, archery, and hunting through the 144-page catalog from Bowhunters Warehouse, which has been in business since 1974. The catalog features a large selection of bows and arrows, as well as points, feathers, bow sights, rests, quivers, targets, bow-hunting books and videotapes, game calls, camouflage clothing and supplies, shooting equipment, and other gear for outdoor sports. Bowhunters Warehouse also builds arrows to order, and the catalog includes a complete description of the features and available options for custom arrows. Specifications are included with the information on the hunting equipment, making this a good reference as well as a source for real savings.

Special Factors: Authorized returns are accepted; minimum order is $15; C.O.D. orders are accepted.

CAMPMOR

P.O. BOX 700
SADDLE RIVER, NJ
07458–0700
800–230–2151
201–445–5000

Catalog: free
Pay: check, MO, MC, V, AE, Discover
Sells: camping gear and supplies
Store: 810 Rt. 17 N., Paramus, NJ; Monday to Friday 9:30–9:30, Saturday 9:30–6, closed Sunday
E-mail: catalog-request@campmor.com
Online: http://www.campmor.com

Campmor's 144-page catalog is full of great buys on camping goods, bike touring accessories, and clothing. You'll save up to 50% on clothing by Borglite Pile, Columbia Interchange System, Sierra Designs, Thinsulate, and Woolrich, as well as duofold and Polypro underwear, Sorel and Timberland boots, and other outerwear. Swiss Victorinox knives are offered at 30% off list, and Buck knives, Coleman cooking equipment, Sherpa snowshoes, Silva compasses, Edelrid climbing ropes, and books and manuals on camping and survival are available. You'll also find tents and sleeping bags by Coleman, Eureka, Moonstone, The North Face, Sierra Designs, Slumberjack, Wenzel, and Campmor's own lines, as well as backpacks by JanSport, Kelly Camp Trails, and Peak. Campmor has been in business since 1946 and is worth a trip if you're in the Paramus area—or check the website, which includes complete ordering information and numbers, shipping rates, and other details for overseas customers.

Special Factors: Returns are accepted for exchange, refund, or credit; minimum order is $20 on phone orders.

CENTRAL SKINDIVERS

160–09 JAMAICA AVE.
JAMAICA, NY 11432–6111
718–739–5772
FAX: 718–739–3679

Catalog: free
Pay: check, MO, MC, V, AE, Discover
Sells: scuba-diving equipment
Store: same address; Monday to Saturday
10–6:30

Central Skindivers, in business since 1952, sells diving gear at savings of up to 40%, including tanks from Dacor, Sherwood, and U.S. Divers, and a full range of regulators, masks, fins, gauges, computers, suits, and other gear. There are buoyancy jackets from Dacor, Seaquest, Sherwood, U.S. Divers, and Zeagle, and watches and timers from Chronosport, Citizen, Heuer, and Seiko. Call for the catalog or a price quote.

Special Factors: Shipping is not charged; minimum order is $50.

CHEAP SHOT, INC.

P.O. BOX 685
1797 RT. 980
CANONSBURG, PA 15317
412-745-2658
FAX: 412-745-4265

Catalog: free
Pay: check or MO
Sells: ammunition
Store: Gun Runner, 950 S. Central Ave., Canonsburg, PA; Monday to Friday 8–8, Saturday 8–5, Sunday 10–4

Cheap Shot, "shooters serving shooters since 1976," offers savings of 33% and more on the usual prices of ammo and reloading components from CCI, Federal, Hornady, Remington, and Winchester. The 12-page catalog also offers a "reloading library," with several manuals on the subject. Because Cheap Shot specializes in ammo and buys in volume, the discounts are better than those offered by many hunting catalogs.

Please note: Federal regulations on age and identification requirements are stated in the catalog, and you must provide a signature and driver's license number in order to purchase ammunition.

Special Factors: Authorized returns are accepted; C.O.D. orders are accepted (a 25% deposit is required).

CREATIVE HEALTH PRODUCTS

5148 SADDLE RIDGE RD.,
   DEPT. WBM
PLYMOUTH, MI 48170
313-996-5900
FAX: 313-996-4650

Catalog: $2
Pay: check, MO, MC, V, AE, Discover
Sells: fitness testing equipment, health-monitoring products
Store: mail order only (see text)

Creative Health Products has been selling health, fitness, and exercise equipment since 1976 and carries some of the best product lines available. Savings vary from item to item but average 30% on list or regular retail prices. The company guarantees that their prices are lowest, so you really can't go wrong here (see catalog for details.) The 20-page catalog lists current models of stationary bicycles, ergometers, and stair climbers by Cateye and Monark. There are heart-rate/pulse monitors, fitness measuring equipment, strength and flexibility testers, blood pressure testers, stethoscopes, body-fat calipers, bio-impedance body-fat analyzers, scales, and other measurement tools, as well as rehabilitation devices. Creative Health Products also carries an impressive line of health and fitness books, videos, and training software, and the catalog includes extensive guides and articles on buying different types of devices. Please note that this is professional equipment and, even with discounts, the prices are not low. Creative Health welcomes questions about any of the products and can help you find the best equipment for your needs. Although primarily a mail-order firm, Creative Health welcomes visitors (weekdays, 9–4), so drop by if you're in the area (call first for directions).

Special Factors: Exercise equipment is not refundable; quantity discounts are available; institutional accounts are available; C.O.D. orders are accepted.

CUTLERY SHOPPE

390 E. CORPORATE DR.
P.O. BOX 610
MERIDIAN, ID 83706–0610
800–231–1272
208–884–7500
FAX: 208–884–7575

Catalog: free
Pay: check, MO, MC, V, AE, Discover
Sells: cutlery, knives, sharpeners, etc.
Store: same address

If you enjoy great knives and cutting tools—or know someone who does—this is the place to shop. Cutlery Shoppe's 64-page catalog offers knives of every kind imaginable at prices that average 35% off list on many items. For the outdoorsman, there are "hawks" (to use as camp axes or for throwing), knives for multipurpose camping chores, spearing, hunting, fishing, and underwater use, general-use survival knives, folding knives, combat knives, police models, Swiss Army knives in every conceivable permutation, Leatherman Super Tools, and many more. Cutlery Shoppe also sells tools—for example, the compact Cool Tool for bikers that comes with a wrench, tire lever, chain breaker, Allens of every needed dimension, socket heads, and a bottle opener—a great gift for your favorite biking fanatic. Or the nifty "Credit Card Companion," which is a tool kit that fits together like a puzzle and fits in your wallet!

There is a fine and extensive selection of kitchen cutlery and accessories here as well, including chef's knives of every shape and size, wonderful kitchen tools such as a cylindrical cheese grater on a handle, spatulas, poultry shears, chef steels, and more. There's a section of videos and books about survival, and plenty of survival gear, including such items as tick pliers, emergency candles that create heat and light for 22 hours, flashlights, and all kinds of handgun concealers. The manufacturers represented here are top names.

Please note: Consult your local ordinances regarding the purchase, possession, and use of weaponry and personal-protection devices.

Special Factors: Satisfaction is guaranteed; volume discounts are available; returns are accepted within 30 days for exchange, refund, or credit.

DEER SHACK

DEPT. WBMC–99
P.O. BOX E, 7155 CTY.
  HWY. B
BELGIUM, WI 53004–0905
800–443–3337
920–994–9818
FAX: 920–994–4099

Catalog: $2
Pay: check, MO, MC, V, Discover
Sells: deer-related and hunting products
Store: mail order only
Online: http://www.deershack.com

This catalog is devoted to the culture of the deer hunter, where a camo gun sock is listed under "Great Stocking Stuffers" and the audiotapes include *Vocabulary of Deer*. Much of the 64-page color catalog shows handsome gifts—limited-edition prints of hunting scenes, hand-painted bronzes, mirrors and home accents adorned with shed antlers, and signs, mats, plaques, desk accessories, belt buckles, mugs, and humorous literature. The hunting gear includes bow and gun accessories, decoy and scent supplies, game transport and processing supplies, Hatchbag vehicle liners, camo wear and blinds, tree stands, maps, and books and tapes covering everything from locating game to tanning hides.

Special Factors: Satisfaction is guaranteed; returns (except personalized goods) are accepted for exchange, refund, or credit.

DISCOUNT GOLF SUPERSTORE

888–394–4653
425–778–3777
FAX: 425–778–2679

Information: internet only, no catalog
Pay: cashier's check, MO, MC, V, AE, Discover, JCB
Sells: golf equipment
Store: online only; phone hours are Monday to Friday 8–6, Saturday 9–4, Sunday 10–4 (PT)
E-mail: golfsales@golfdiscount.com
Online: http://www.golfdiscount.com

If you love to surf (the internet, that is) as well as to golf, then Discount Golf Superstore is the place for you. Discount Golf Superstore—"your internet source to the lowest prices on the best names in golf!"—brings 20 years experience in the golf retail business to golf enthusiasts looking to pay about 20% less than they would at retail. There's a page of fan e-mail from satisfied customers (quite a few of whom were left-handed golfers ecstatic to have found southpaw-friendly clubs), which is always heartening to see. This site carries clubs by the top-name manufacturers, including at the time of this writing Top Flite, Cleveland Golf, Ping, Taylor Made, Callaway, Power Bilt, La Jolla, Mitsushiba, and many others, as well as putters, bags, travel covers, and even golf shoes by Dunlop, Etonic, Reebok, Foot-Joy, and Bite.

Straightforward and easy to use, this site has something too many other online shops lack: customer service. If you have questions, you can call and speak to a helpful sales rep who will even find the clubs you're looking for if DGS doesn't happen to be showing them at present on their site. The site is changed and updated frequently, so the selection will vary. All merchandise comes with the manufacturer's warranty.

Corporate clients: DSB provides imprinting. You can have your corporate logo on golf balls, caps, shirts, and other items. Call toll-free 888–394–4653 for more information.

Special Factors: Satisfaction guaranteed; returns accepted within 30 days, but customer pays shipping; no personal checks accepted.

FITNESS FACTORY OUTLET

2875 S. 25TH AVE.
BROADVIEW, IL 60153
800–383–9300
708–345–9000
FAX: 708–345–9772

Catalog: free
Pay: check, MO, MC, V, AE, Discover
Sells: fitness and exercise equipment
Store: same address; Monday to Friday 11–7, Saturday 10–5 CT
Online: http://www.fitnessfactory.com

Fitness Factory Outlet has been supplying homes, schools, and gyms with fitness equipment since 1988 and offers a full range of machines and accessories at discounts averaging 40%. Home-use equipment and gyms begin at under $100, and the featured "Body-Solid" line offers a lifetime warranty on frames, pads, pulleys, cables, hardware, and all of the parts. The 48-page color catalog also shows rubber flooring, dumbbells, cable attachment bars, boxing and aerobic-conditioning equipment (treadmills, steppers, stationary bicycles, etc.), at good savings. You can call or write for the catalog, or request one from the website, which showcases most of the current product offerings.

Special Factors: Satisfaction is guaranteed; authorized returns in like-new condition are accepted for return within 31 days for exchange, refund, or credit (shipping and handling charges are not refundable).

FITNESS SYSTEMS MFG. CORP.

104 EVANS AVE.
SINKING SPRING, PA
 19608
888–255–2130 (CATALOG)
800–967–1827,
 800–822–9995 (ORDERS)
FAX: 610–670–0135

Catalog: free
Pay: check, MO, MC, V, Discover, AE
Sells: food and vitamin supplements for exercise enthusiasts and athletes
Store: mail order only
E-mail: vitaminout@aol.com
Online: http://www.jerron.com/fitness/fsmc

I have to confess that after looking through the catalog from Fitness Systems, I felt intimidated and puny. This is a company for athletes and exercisers who are majorly devoted to their physiques, strength, and performance. If you're looking for vitamin C, this is not your best source. However, you beefcake bodybuilders will love Fitness Systems' discounts—to the tune of 40% to 50% off list—on Sports Edge supplements that you're not apt to find anywhere else, such as Cymaltex (natural testosterone booster); Maximum Strength and Power Blend; Creatine Monohydrate (an ergogenic aid for maximizing physical power and endurance); anabolic amino formulae; daily vitamin packs; muscular weight gain formulae; 100% egg protein; and many more products designed to enhance your every muscle and movement. The closely printed black-and-white catalog has explanatory text, testimonials, ingredient listings, and other useful information that's not only helpful but necessary. The website contains the same information and products as the catalog, if you prefer to shop online. The manager assures us that all ingredients are herbs or other components you'd find at your local nutrition center. These products, claim the company, are scientifically designed, of the highest purity, are 100% natural, and contain no sugar, starch, artificial colors, flavors, or preservatives. It's always a good idea, however, to consult your physician and trainer before taking these or any other nutritional and vitamin supplements.

Special Factors: Free shipping on orders of $150 or more; special shipping fees apply to international orders; foreign orders: minimum purchase is $100, payable in U.S. funds.

DON GLEASON'S CAMPERS SUPPLY, INC.

9 PEARL ST., P.O. BOX 87
NORTHAMPTON, MA
  01061–0087
413–584–4895
FAX: 413–586–8770

Catalog: free
Pay: check, MO, MC, V, Discover
Sells: camping supplies and equipment
Store: same address; Monday to Friday 9–5:30, Thursday 9–8:30, Saturday 9–5
E-mail: cat96@gleasoncamping.com

Don Gleason has been helping America hit the trail since 1957, with everything from tents to trowels. The firm's 64-page catalog is packed with good buys on equipment—tents and screen houses by Eureka, The North Face, and Sierra Designs, sleeping bags by The North Face and Slumberjack, air mattresses, tarps, blankets, primus stoves and cookware, Coleman coolers, first aid kits, Buck knives, duffles, and back-packs and rucksacks by Camp Trails, Eagle Creek, JanSport, and The North Face. Don Gleason has an excellent selection of tent stakes and grommet kits, seals and other tent-mending supplies, hook-and-loop fastening, bungee cords and bungee-by-the-yard, camp toilets, cots, compasses, flashlights, insect repellents, axes, picks, and even gold-panning equipment. Savings run up to 50%, and there are volume dis-counts of 10% and 15% on the freeze-dried food from Mountain House. See the catalog for details of the no-hassle warranty.

Special Factors: Satisfaction is guaranteed; quantity discounts are available; returns are accepted for exchange, refund, or credit; mini-mum order is $10 with credit cards.

GOLF HAUS

700 N. PENNSYLVANIA
LANSING, MI 48906
517–482–8842
FAX: 517–482–8843

Price List: free
Pay: check, MO, MC, V
Sells: golf clubs, apparel, and accessories
Store: same address; Monday to Saturday 9–5:30

Golf Haus has "the absolute lowest prices on pro golf clubs" any-where—up to 70% below list—and stocks goods by every major manu-facturer. All of the models sold here are available nationwide, which means that, unlike the "exclusive models" offered by a number of dis-counters, the goods at Golf Haus can be price-shopped fairly. There are clubs, bags, putters, balls, and other golf equipment and supplies by Cobra (including the "King Cobra" line), Hogan, Kunnan, Lynx, Mac-Gregor, Maxfli, Mizuno, Ping, PowerBilt, Ram, Spalding, Taylormade, Tiger Shark, Titleist, Wilson, and other firms. There are shoes by Dexter, Etonic, Footjoy, and Reebok, as well as Bag Boy carts, gloves, umbrel-las, spikes, scorekeepers, visors, rain suits, tote bags, socks, and much more.

Please note: Golf Haus is offering a free set of head covers with an order of a complete set of clubs (woods and irons) to readers who mention BWBM.

Special Factors: Free shipping and insurance on orders shipped within the continental United States; minimum order is $50.

HOLABIRD SPORTS

9220 PULASKI HWY.
BALTIMORE, MD 21220
410–687–6400
FAX: 410–687–7311

Brochure: free
Pay: check, MO, MC, V, AE, Discover
Sells: racquet sports equipment and athletic footwear
Store: same address; Monday to Friday 9–5, Saturday 9–3
Online: http://www.holabirdsports.com

Buy here and get the "Holabird Advantage": equipment and footwear for racquet sports at up to 40% below list prices, service on manufacturers' warranties, and free stringing with tournament nylon on all racquets. If you're in the Baltimore area, drop by and try out a racquet on Holabird's indoor court.

Holabird has been in business since 1981 and carries tennis racquets by scores of firms, including Donnay, Dunlop, Estusa, Fischer, Fox, Head, Kneissl, Mizuno, Prince, Pro-Kennex, Rossignol, Slazenger, Spalding, Volkl, Wavex, Wilson, Wimbledon, Yamaha, and Yonex. There are tennis balls by Dunlop, Penn, and Wilson, ball machines by Lobster, and footwear by Adidas, Asics, Avia, Converse, Diadora, Fila, Head, K-Swiss, New Balance, Nike, Prince, Reebok, Wilson, and others.

Racquetball players should check the prices on racquets by E-Force, Ektelon, Head, Pro-Kennex, Spalding, and Wilson. The squash department features racquets by Black Knight, Dunlop, Ektelon, Fox, Head, Pro-Kennex, Prince, Slazenger, Spalding, and Wilson, and eye guards by Black Knight, Ektelon, Leader, and Pro-Kennex. Pros can save their clubs sizable sums on court equipment and maintenance supplies, such as court dryers, tennis nets, ball hoppers, and stringing machines.

Holabird also stocks a full line of running, basketball, cross-training, aerobic, walking, and hiking shoes, as well as sandals, tee shirts, socks, caps, sunglasses from Ray-Ban, and Timex sport watches. See the monthly eight-page catalog for specials, or call or write for a price quote.

Special Factors: Authorized returns (except used items) are accepted within seven days; shipping is $3.99 on all orders, no matter how large.

THE HOUSE

Catalog: free
Pay: check, MO, MC, V, AE, Discover
Sells: windsurfing, snowboarding, in-line skating, and kayaking equipment
Store: same address; Monday to Friday, 10–7, Saturday 9–2
Online: http://www.the-house.com

300 S. OWASSO BLVD.,
DEPT. WBMC
ST. PAUL, MN 55117
612–482–9995
FAX: 612–482–1353

Put wind and water together and you have the prime ingredients for the thrilling sport of windsurfing, also known as sailboarding. The right equipment helps, which is what you'll find at The House—at discounts that average 25% but run much deeper on sale items and special purchases (for example, the after-Christmas clearance catalog offered items at as much as 70% off list). The House has been in business since 1982, selling light to heavy wind sailboards, sails, masts, harnesses, fins, and a broad selection of windsurfing apparel. The 40-plus-page catalogs feature equipment by BIC, Chinook, DaKine, Fanatic, Fiberspar, Maui Magic, Mistral, NeilPryde, O'Brien, SeaTrend, Simmer, Tiga, Topsails, Windsurfing Hawaii, and other manufacturers. The boards run from entry-level to custom models for pros, and the catalog includes numerous informative sidebars on choosing equipment and evaluating construction and materials. Car racks by Automaxi, Barrecrafters, and Thule are offered, as well as windsurfing books and videos, wet suits, dry suits, harnesses, and other accessories by Bare, Body Glove, O'Neill, and Ronny.

The House also answers your winter sports needs with a full line of snowboards from Aggression, Apocalypse, H-Ride, Heavy Tools, Joyride, Kemper, Kingpin, Limited, Liquid, Original Sin, Pyramid, and Rad Air; boots by Alpina, Airwalk, Grunge, and Vans; and related equipment.

Please note: Phone hours are Monday to Friday 8–7, Saturday 9–1 CT.

Special Factors: Satisfaction is guaranteed; authorized returns are accepted within 20 days for exchange, refund, or credit.

MOHAWK CANOES

**963 NORTH C.R. 427
LONGWOOD, FL 32750
800–686–6429
407–834–3233
FAX: 407–834–0292**

Catalog: free
Pay: check, MO
Sells: canoes and canoe accessories
Store: same address; Monday to Friday
8:30–4:30, 9–noon Saturday
E-mail: mohawk@magicnet.net
Online: http://www.mohawkcanoes.com

Canoes are not inexpensive, but if you take care of them right they'll last a lifetime. Mohawk Canoes, in the manufacturing business for 35 years, builds quality canoes and offers them factory direct to paddlers at 30% below suggested retail price. This company has a fully functioning website, which you can browse for the models, prices, and company policies rather than requesting a catalog. One of the reasons Mohawk can sell their canoes at these discount prices is that they don't spend a lot of money on advertising, fancy catalogs, and PR. These gorgeous canoes are made of Royalite and Royalex, a lightweight, durable material, and come in beautiful colors with high-quality webbed or caned ash seats and yokes. There are solo models, tandem models, and short white-water play-boats designed for river rodeos and extremely challenging rivers. You can buy a solo version for as little as $486.75 (suggested list price on this canoe is $649), and the tandem models start at $656.25 (suggested retail: $875). Mohawk also sells accessories such as paddles, life jackets, canoe hardware, seat cushions, car racks, and more. The literature has helpful charts that compare Mohawk canoes with other manufacturer's models, as well as ratings compiled by *Backpacker Magazine,* so you can see how Mohawk stacks up next to the leading competitors when it comes to stability, tracking and turning, speed, portaging, and construction quality. For wholesale rates, the minimum order is six canoes.

Special Factors: No credit cards accepted; due to packing and shipping requirements, Mohawk cannot accept returns.

MUELLER SPORTING GOODS, INC.

**4825 SO. 16TH ST.,
DEPT. 60
LINCOLN, NE 68512
800–925–7665
FAX: 402–423–5964**

Catalog: free
Pay: check, MO, MC, V, Discover
Sells: billiards, table tennis, and darts equipment
Store: 20th and Highway 2, Lincoln, NE; also 5705 Hickman Rd., Des Moines, IA; Monday to Saturday 9–6, Sunday 1–5
E-mail: msginfo@inetnebr.com
Online: http://www.mueller-sporting-goods.com

Whether you've a basement rec room for the kids or own a billiards parlor, Mueller Sporting Goods is the place to shop for a full selection of pool cues and accessories, dart boards and darts, table tennis accessories, and other indoor games. An even greater selection and better prices than before can be found here; Mueller's color catalog has been expanded to 180 pages, and now they have a "lowest-price" policy. The catalog offers an extensive selection of pool cues from the top manufacturers, including limited editions and collectors' models, as well as carrying cases, racks, bridges, balls, chalk, replacement felt and table bumpers, and a complete selection of cue-repair materials. (Repair services are available; prices for replacing tips, ferrules, shafts, collars, and joints, and for rewrapping the staff, are listed.) Mueller also sells products designed to give you an edge—wood conditioners, tip shavers, burnishers, and waxers—and books and videos on every aspect of the game.

Mueller serves other interests—table tennis, the British pub favorite, darts, and a variety of other games such as foosball, shuffleboard, and craps and blackjack. There are tournament-grade dart boards and page after page of darts, annotated with copy that reads more like Defense Department announcements of stealth weapons than descriptions of equipment for a bar game. The darts can be customized with a choice of shafts and "flights" (the feather element); bar stools, posters, and dart-related gifts are also available. Mueller's carries a roll-away, fold-up table tennis table by Rollomat, as well as balls, paddles, and all kinds of accessories and paddle-repair supplies. If you're a real fanatic of one of these indoor sports, check out the extensive selection of tee shirts, plaques, and themed decor that Mueller's offers. Both list and discount prices are given, and savings average 40% but reach 55% on some items. You won't get these items cheaper anywhere else.

Special Factors: Price quote by phone or letter; quantity discounts are available; returns (except personalized and custom-made goods) are accepted within 30 days for exchange, refund, or credit; lowest price guaranteed (see catalog for details.)

OVERTON'S SPORTS CENTER, INC.

P.O. BOX 8228,
   DEPT. 57612
GREENVILLE, NC 27835
800–334–6541
919–355–7600
FAX: 919–355–2923

Catalog: free
Pay: check, MO, MC, V, AE, Discover, JCB
Sells: boating accessories and water sports goods
Store: 5343 S. Boulevard, Charlotte; 111 Red Banks Rd., Greenville; and 3062 Wake Forest Rd., Raleigh, NC
E-mail: custserv@overtonsonline.com
Online: http://www.overtons.com

Overton's lays claim to the title of "World's Largest Water Sports Dealer," selling a wide range of equipment for boating, waterskiing, snorkeling, and other avocations at up to 40% off list. Overton's was established in 1975 and publishes three catalogs. The 132-page color "Water Sports" catalog features skis and accessories ranging from junior trainers to experts' tricks, jumpers, and slaloms by Connelly, EP, Jobe, Kidder, O'Brien, and other firms. Wet suits, apparel, knee boards, water toys, inflatables, snorkeling accessories, boating accessories, books, videotapes, and personal watercraft accessories are also offered. The 48-page swimwear and apparel catalog, "Kristi's," features such names as De La Mer, Bendigo, Venus, Solar Tan Thru, Point Conception, OP, O'Neill, Take Cover, and many more. The look is California young, with eye-popping prints dominating the collection.

The 200-page "Discount Boating Accessories" answers your boating needs with a wide range of products: boat seats and covers, safety equipment, instruments, electronics, hardware, cleaners, fishing equipment, clothing, fuel tanks, and performance accessories. The brands include Apelco, Aqua Meter, Brinkman, Eagle, Interphase, Ray Jefferson, Maxxima, Newmar, PowerWinch, Shakespeare, and Si-Tex, among others. The equipment catalogs give both the list or comparable retail and Overton's discount prices. If you're online, don't miss the terrific website—products, sports information, special buys, and much more.

Canadian readers, please note: Only U.S. funds are accepted.

Special Factors: Satisfaction is guaranteed; quantity discounts are available; unused returns are accepted within 30 days for exchange, refund, or credit; C.O.D. orders are accepted.

PERFORMANCE BICYCLE SHOP

P.O. BOX 2741
CHAPEL HILL, NC 27514
800–727–2453
FAX: 800–727–3291

Catalog: free
Pay: check, MO, MC, V, Discover
Sells: bicycle parts and cycling apparel
Store: 35 stores in CA, CO, IL, MD, NC, OR, PA, VA, and WA
Online: http://www.performancebike.com

Serious cyclists are familiar with Performance Bicycle Shop for the company's line of bicycling parts, accessories, and clothing. The firm's parts department is well stocked with tubes, tires, pumps, bars and stems, saddles, and all other components from derailleurs to brake accessories. Performance has been in business since 1981 and offers a large selection of cycling clothing, as well as helmets, cycling shoes, gloves, panniers, outerwear, bras and briefs, and hundreds of products to enhance performance. Most of the top-name brands are represented in the 80-page color catalog. In-line skates (Rollerblades) and camping gear are also available. This company often features specials, and the end-of-year sale catalog offers up to 70% off on many products.

Special Factors: Satisfaction is guaranteed.

PERFORMANCE DIVER

P.O. BOX 2741,
  DEPT. WBMC
CHAPEL HILL, NC 27514
800–933–3299
FAX: 800–727–3291

Catalog: free
Pay: check, MO, MC, V, Discover
Sells: scuba equipment and apparel
Store: mail order only
E-mail: catalog@performancediver.com

Performance Diver, established in 1990, sells a full line of scuba equipment, apparel, regulators, gauges, BDCs, wet suits, and a wide variety of accessories. Although many of the items are manufactured by the same companies that sell under well-known labels in dive shops, they're available here under the Performance name at savings of up to 50% on comparable retail. The catalog emphasizes technologically advanced design, with the latest construction methods used to maximize performance, comfort, and safety. You don't have to dive to appreciate the good selection of Citizen watches, tee shirts, Lycra suits, or duffel bags.

Special Factors: Satisfaction is guaranteed; returns are accepted for exchange, refund, or credit.

SIERRA TRADING POST

5025 CAMPSTOOL RD.,
  DEPT. WBMC–99
CHEYENNE, WY
  82007–1802
800–713–4534
307–775–8000
FAX: 800–378–8946
FAX: 307–775–8088

Catalog: free
Pay: check, MO, MC, V, Discover
Sells: outdoor clothing and equipment
Store: same address; Monday to Saturday 9–6, Sunday 12–6; also 2000 Harvard Way, Reno, NV; Monday to Saturday 10–7, Sunday 11–5
Online: http://www.sierratradingpost.com

Sierra Trading Post, established in 1986, offers casual and outdoor clothing and camping gear in a charming 56-page catalog. Sierra is essentially a mail-order outlet store that sells close-outs, overruns, and special purchases at savings of up to 70%. Rugged clothing and outerwear, shoes for hiking and running, great pants and shorts, socks, sweaters, underwear, wool felt clogs, and even comfortable dresses are among the offerings. Name brands pepper the catalog—The North Face, Marmot, Lowe, Pearl Izumi, Nike, Teva, Sportif USA, and Gregory among them. Sleeping bags, backpacks, tents, flannel sheets, and down and wool comforters are also available.

Non-U.S. readers, please note: Orders are shipped outside the United States (via USPS) to APO/FPO destinations, Canada, and Japan only.

Special Factors: Satisfaction is guaranteed; returns are accepted for exchange, refund, or credit.

SOAR INFLATABLES

Catalog: free
Pay: check, MO, MC, V
Sells: inflatable boats and accessories
Store: mail order only
Online: http://www.soar1.com

20 HEALDSBURG AVE.
HEALDSBURG, CA 95488
707–433–5599
FAX: 707–433–4499

There are only three other companies in the world, according to SOAR Inflatables owner Larry Laba, who make inflatable canoes, and his are less expensive because he manufactures and sells them factory-direct to the consumer. The boats are 12' ($1,300), 14' ($1,425), and 16' ($1,550). Why spend that much when a regular canoe could cost as little as $500 (or up to $3,000)? Because, says Laba, his boats can be rolled up to fit into a backpack, a car trunk, an RV, and any airline storage unit. You can't do that with a rigid canoe. For regular (noncommercial) use, your SOAR Inflatable will last a lifetime. And these canoes handle virtually any condition a rigid canoe can, including Class 3 white water—this, from a customer who did it. (Incidentally, Outward Bound of Colorado uses SOAR Inflatables and hasn't had any complaints as of this writing.) SOAR Inflatables are fun and reliable, as witness the dozen or more testimonials from happy customers in the flyer that comes with the 8-page color catalog. These customers range from urban apartment dwellers to families with children to professional river guides, and they all echo the same themes: easy maneuverability, extreme ruggedness, versatility, and convenience.

Rolled up, the canoes weigh between 52 and 67 pounds, and they come with two seats, a double-action hand pump, straps to keep your inflatable tightly rolled, and a repair kit. Other items available in the catalog include collapsible paddles (and kayak paddle converters), duffel bags, padded seats with backs, a pump that hooks up to your car battery, and more. The catalog provides details for canoe aficionados, such as abrasion resistance, buoyancy, and drag. For more about these remarkable boats, visit the website. SOAR Inflatables offer quantity discounts to businesses, ranging from 10% to 30% off, depending on the numbers purchased.

Special to BWBM readers: Mention that you're a reader of this book and SOAR will take 20% off your boat.

Special Factors: Satisfaction guaranteed, with a 30-day trial; limited 5-year warranty.

SOCCER INTERNATIONAL

Catalog: $2
Pay: check or MO
Sells: soccer gear, accessories, books, videos, and gifts
Store: mail order only
E-mail: sdobson@cais.com
Online:
http://www.soccerinternational.com/soccerintl

P.O. BOX 7222, DEPT.
WBM–99
ARLINGTON, VA
22207–7222
703–524–4333

Soccer International, founded in 1976 by a rabid soccer buff, publishes an 18-page color catalog of game-related items ranging from professional equipment to novelties. The savings run up to 30% on some goods, compared to the prices charged by other firms, but generally average about 20% less. Quantity discounts are also available. The catalog is a must-see for any soccer enthusiast or friend of one, since it's a great resource for gifts as well as gear.

You'll find a number of balls, plus a variety of jerseys and tee shirts. PVC leg shields and ankle guards, a ball inflator, nets and goals, practice aids, and a great selection of books and videotapes on coaching, game strategy, and soccer rules are available. If you're a mom used to shivering at soccer practice, you'll want Lava Buns, the stadium cushion. Pop it in the microwave for a few minutes and it will keep your bottom warm for hours! Soccer International also sells soccer-theme games, radios, doormats, mugs, cloisonné pins, bumper stickers, doorknobs, and lamps. This is where you'll find the World Cup 1994 video highlights (of most of the games), as well as a large selection of other videos, and many soccer books—great for coaches at all levels of expertise. They also carry posters, ties, and playing cards, as well as replica team jerseys of four of the top soccer-playing countries. Soccer-loving puzzle buffs will enjoy the challenge of Mordillo jigsaw puzzles from Germany, which run from 500 to 2,000 pieces.

Canadian readers, please note: Orders must be paid in U.S. funds, drawn on the Canadian postal service or on a U.S. bank.

APO/FPO readers, please note: Orders are not shipped to APO/FPO addresses during November or December.

Institutional buyers, please note: Catalog prices are mainly for single items, but Soccer International's specialty is sales to teams, leagues, clubs, and schools. If you're buying in multiples for a group, let the company know when you request the catalog.

Special Factors: Minimum order is $15; shipping is not charged on orders over $35 sent within the contiguous United States; quantity pricing available.

SPIKE NASHBAR, INC.

4111 SIMON RD., DEPT.
 WBM9
YOUNGSTOWN, OH 44512
800–SPIKE–IT
FAX: 800–456–1223

Catalog: free
Pay: check, MO, MC, V, Discover
Sells: volleyball gear and apparel
Store: same address (Nashbar Outlet Store); call 330–782–2244 for hours
E-mail: mail@spike.nashbar.com
Online: http://www.nashbar.com/

Spike Nashbar, established in 1990, offers competition volleyball gear, clothing, and accessories. The 32-page color catalog offers over two dozen balls for indoor and outdoor play, from Brine, Mikasa, Molten, Spalding, Tachikara, and Wilson. Over two dozen lines of clothing are offered, and several nets and net systems are available, including one from Park and Sun for under $90 and "the best portable net system available," the Spectrum series, which costs about $226. There are volleyball shoes for men and women by Asics, Kaepa, Mizuno, Power, and Reebok. Sport bras, socks, tee shirts, shorts, duffels, sport watches, and sunglasses from Bausch & Lomb are also sold, as well as vital knee protection from Asics and Body Glove. If you've ever watched or played serious volleyball, you'll know why they're part of the standard uniform of the game. Spike Nashbar has a "guaranteed lowest price" policy; see the catalog for details. And don't miss the website—you can order a print catalog, look at the online catalog, or check the close-outs and bargains while you're there.

Canadian readers, please note: Only U.S. funds are accepted.

Special Factors: Satisfaction is guaranteed; quantity discounts are available; returns are accepted for exchange, refund, or credit.

THE SPORTSMAN'S GUIDE

411 FARWELL AVE.,
 DEPT. WBM9
SO. ST. PAUL, MN
 55075–0239
800–888–3006,
 DEPT. WBM9
FAX: 800–333–6933

Catalog: free
Pay: check, MO, MC, V, AE, Discover
Sells: outdoor clothing and footwear, hunting and camping gear, military surplus, etc.
Store: mail order only
Online: http://www.sportsmansguide.com

The Sportsman's Guide is a potpourri of gear and goodies for the rough-and-ready set, over 200 pages that begin with thermal underwear and end with insulated gloves. In between are work boots and athletic footwear, parkas and Australian-style dusters, flannel shirts, work jackets, and much more, from well-known manufacturers. The catalog shows gear for camping (tents and sleeping bags) and hunting (rifle optics and ammo), as well as auto accessories, watches, power tools, cookery and cutlery, telescopes, boat covers, and hunting-related gifts. Prices run from reasonable to great, and devotees of The Sportsman's Guide can join the firm's Buyer's Club (about $30 annually at this writing) for a 10% discount on regular catalog prices and "Members Only" specials at up to 75% off. Even if you're not the hunting type, you may find that membership pays off—any catalog that offers lava lamps, snowshoes, and abdominal exercisers is aiming for the broadest possible appeal!

Special Factors: Satisfaction is guaranteed; see catalog order form for information and shipping restrictions on certain goods; returns are accepted for exchange, refund, or credit.

VIRTUAL FAIRWAY

MISSION VIEJO, CA
TEL/FAX: 714–348–6947

Pay: check, MO, MC, V
Sells: used golf balls
Store: internet only
Online: http://www.virtual-fairway.com

Sometimes the simplest, least complicated things in life are the best. Virtual Fairway is just such a company. Three years ago Cindy Carpino and her husband started a business so that Cindy could be a working mom at home with their children. Her husband, a golf fanatic, came up with the idea of a company that would sell nothing but used golf balls over the web, and the rest of the story is a happy one for both the Carpinos and their satisfied customers.

Golf balls are expensive. Period. And quality, high-grade, used golf balls at 50% less than they cost brand new is the solution. For low handicap and scratch golfers, used golf balls are great for practice. For mid and high handicap golfers as well as beginners, used golf balls will save money as you perfect your stroke. The inventory changes at Virtual Fairway, but at this writing the monthly special was featuring Titleist HP2 Distance balls at $10 a dozen. Among the selections were Top Flight Strata Tour (90 or 100) for $18/dozen, Wilson Titanium Spin (90 or 100) at $16/dozen, Titleist Professional (90 or 100) for $16/dozen, all the way down to Top Flite Hot XL ($8), AA Grade ($6), and A Grade ($3). The selection featured six top brands and 24 choices. At the site you can read e-letters from happy Virtual Fairway customers from all over the world. Whether you're golf-obsessed or merely a novice, this is an address you'll want to visit. Virtual Fairway offers 10% off if you order 200 dozen, but the prices are already deeply discounted. You can order by phone, fax, or right on the site.

Special Factors: Satisfaction is guaranTEED.

WATER WAREHOUSE

Catalog: $2
Pay: check, MO, MC, V, Discover
Sells: swimming pool supplies and equipment
Store: mail order only

6950 51ST ST.
KENOSHA, WI 53144–1740
800–574–7665
FAX: 414–605–1080

Swimming pools have two lives—summer and winter—and Water Warehouse sells supplies and equipment for both seasons, at savings of up to 50% on list or comparable retail. Here are all the chemicals you need to keep the water safe and cut down on maintenance: Monarc chlorinating tabs, oxidizers (shocks), rust and scale preventers, algaecides, pH balancers, and other agents. You'll also find water-testing kits, pool skimmers, vacuums, thermometers, filters, and brushes, and the tools for enjoying the fruits of your labor—inflatable loungers, sport tubes, kiddie "riders," flippers, water balls, and diving games. When the weather turns cool, Water Warehouse helps out with high-speed pool pumps (for quick draining), repair kits for vinyl liners, winterizing plugs (to save the skimmer), covers for all pool shapes and sizes, and water sleeves to hold the covers down. The 52-page color catalog features these products and more from top-name manufacturers, and there are seasonal sales that lower the discount prices even further.

Special Factors: Satisfaction is guaranteed; returns are accepted within 30 days for exchange, refund, or credit.

WILEY OUTDOOR SPORTS, INC.

P.O. BOX 99, DEPT. WBMC
DECATUR, AL 35602
800–494–5397
FAX: 205–351–8743

Catalog: free
Pay: check, MO, MC, V, Discover
Sells: hunting, camping, and outdoor gear and equipment
Store: 1808 Sportsman Lane, Huntsville, AL; Monday to Friday 9–6, Saturday 9–4:30
Online: http://www.fyeo.com

This family-run business has been outfitting hunters with a full range of equipment and gear since 1953 and offers savings that average 30% but can run as high as 50% on certain items and lines. Wiley specializes in hunting, reloading, camping, and optical equipment, and serves the dedicated outdoors enthusiast. The catalog includes a good selection of tents, backpacks, knives, binoculars, and clothing, as well as the hunting equipment. The firm prides itself on its commitment to good service and lifelong customer relationships, and it invites serious inquiries only about its goods.

Special Factors: Satisfaction is guaranteed; unused returns are accepted within 10 days for exchange, refund, or credit; minimum order is $25; C.O.D. orders (via UPS only) are accepted.

WORLD WIDE AQUATICS

Catalog: free, $2 outside U.S.
Pay: check, MO, MC, V, AE, Discover
Sells: swimwear and accessories
Store: mail order only

DEPT. WBMC
10500 UNIVERSITY CEN-
TER DR., STE. 295
TAMPA, FL 33612–6462
800–726–1530
813–972–0818
FAX: 813–972–0905

Buying a swimsuit is one of the top ten Most Dreaded Shopping Activities, in part because of the convergence of large expanses of skin, fluorescent lights, and endless mirrors. Swimsuit styles are also problematic —they're often cut to reveal more than comfort and reputation allow. World Wide Aquatics solves all of these problems and offers savings of up to 50% on selected suits as well.

The firm's 52-page color catalogs show swimsuits, trunks, shorts, and cover-ups for men, women, and children from Aquajogger, Dolfin, Hind, Hydro-Fit, Ocean, Quintana Roo, Speedo, and Tyr. The styles run from racing-sleek to skirted, full-coverage models, including a line designed for post-mastectomy wear. The sizes run from children's 4 to women's size 24, men's to a 40-inch waist. "Aqueous" shoes for use in the pool and water-exercise equipment are also available. World Wide Aquatics sells workout wear by Dolfin and Speedo (including triathlon clothing that goes from bike to beach), wet suits, swimming goggles, bathing caps, and competition equipment and books.

World Wide Aquatics has been in business since 1972 and offers deep discounts on multiples of 6 on selected suits—ideal for schools and swim clubs. See the catalog for details, or if you know the style you want from one of the manufacturers listed here, call for availability and a quote.

Special Factors: Satisfaction is guaranteed; new, unused returns (except books and videos) with hangtags and labels are accepted in the original packaging for exchange, refund, or credit.

RELATED PRODUCTS/COMPANIES

Auto-racing safety equipment and gear • Racer Wholesale

Black powder supplies • Leather Unlimited

Boats, boat clothing and shoes, and boating supplies • M & E Marine, Defender Industries, West Marine, Freeport Marine

Car racks for kayaks, canoes, skis, surfboards, etc. • Car Racks Direct

Child-friendly outdoor recreation and vacation guides • The Family Travel Guides Catalogue

Exercise equipment • J&R Music, Damark

Extra-large fanny packs • Amplestuff

Fishing gear • M & E Marine, Bennett Brothers

Folding bicycles • Aircraft Spruce

Gymnastics shoes and dancewear • Dance Distributors

Hunting and camping gear • Mass. Army & Navy, RV Direct, Ruvel, Chuck-Wagon Outfitters

Leather duffels and sports bags • Al's Luggage, Leather Unlimited

Miscellaneous sporting equipment • Bennett Brothers

Mosquito netting, gun-cleaning cloths, sleeping bag liners • Clothcrafters

Rifle scopes • Mardiron

RV equipment • RV Direct

Saddlery supplies • Weaver Leather

Snowmobiles and ATVs • Manufacturer's Supply

Sports bras • The Smart Saver

Sport-themed belt buckles • Leather Unlimited

Swimming pool and spa items • CISCO

Swimwear • Lady Grace, The Ultimate Outlet

Swiss Army knives • Ace Luggage, Lens Express

Tarps and tent-floor liners • Bob's Superstrong Greenhouse Plastic

Telescopes, binoculars, spotting scopes, etc. • Orion Telescope

Wineskins • Leather Unlimited

Zippers for tents and sleeping bags • The Button Shop, A. Feibusch, Newark Dressmaker Supply

TOOLS, HARDWARE, SHOP MACHINES

Hand, power, and machine-shop tools, machine parts, and hardware

This chapter offers the do-it-yourselfer, woodworker, hobbyist, wood-cutter, and small-time mechanic a wealth of tools and hardware, some of it at rock-bottom prices. Replacement parts for lawnmowers, trimmers, garden tractors, snowmobiles, snow throwers, blowers, go-carts, minibikes, and even plumbing and electrical systems are available from these companies. The tools run from hex wrenches and fine wood chisels to complete workbenches and professional machinery, and the hardware includes hard-to-find specialty items as well as nuts and bolts.

See "Related Products/Companies" at chapter's end for other firms that also carry tools and various hardware-store items.

FIND IT FAST

ABRASIVES AND RELATED TOOLS • Econ-Abrasives, Red Hill Corporation
HARDWARE, TOOLS, AND MACHINES • William Alden, Camelot Enterprises, Coastal Tool, Enco Manufacturing, Harbor Freight Tools, Holz Tool, Northern Hydraulics, Surplus Center, Tool Crib of the North, Tool Hauz, Tools on Sale, Wholesale Tool, Woodworker's Hardware
HOBBYIST TOOLS • Micro-Mark, Tool Crib of the North, Wholesale Tool
MACHINE PARTS • Manufacturer's Supply, Surplus Center
SURPLUS ELECTRONICS COMPONENTS, TOOLS • All Electronics, H&R Company, Surplus Center
TOOL-BUILDING MANUALS • Poor Man's Catalog
WOODCUTTER/LOGGER EQUIPMENT AND SUPPLIES • Bailey's, H&H Manufacturing, Northern Hydraulics

WILLIAM ALDEN COMPANY

27 STUART ST.
BOSTON, MA 02116
TEL/FAX: 800–249–8665
TEL/FAX: 617–426–3430

Catalog: free
Pay: check, MO, MC, V, AE, Discover
Sells: tools for contractors, woodworkers, general handy work
Store: mail order only; phone hours Monday to Friday 8–9, Saturday 9–5 ET; fax anytime
Online: http://www.williamalden.com

The 152-page color catalog from William Alden Company showcases the hand and power tools most in demand from do-it-yourselfers, contractors, and woodworkers. Equipment from Bosch, DeWalt, Freud, Hitachi, Irwin, Jet, Makita, Milwaukee, Porter-Cable, and Ryobi is available, as well as clamps and vises from American Tool, Gross Stabil, Jorgensen, Pony, Stanley, and Vise-Grip; Fuller countersinks; Lenox hole saws; and Stanley measuring tapes and hand tools. You'll find gauges, gouges, levels, chisels, saws, nippers, snips, hammers, mallets, cabinet hardware and drawer slides from Amerock and Knape & Vogt, and a good basic selection of furniture pulls and knobs. The discounts run up to 50%, and there are excellent prices on items that are often sold closer to list price—like the Goldblatt tool bags, face masks and breathing filters, and Maglite flashlights. Past catalogs have included a "Bulk Buy Page" with extra savings on things you may use regularly: multiples of sanding belts, wood glue, dust masks, paint rollers, drill bits, and masking tape. Everything is covered by the William Alden pledge that "We sell only new, first-quality products—no seconds!"

Special Factors: Satisfaction is guaranteed; price quote by phone or letter; returns are accepted within 30 days for exchange, refund, or credit.

ALL ELECTRONICS CORP.

P.O. BOX 567,
  DEPT. WBMC
VAN NUYS, CA 91408–0567
800–826–5432
818–904–0524
FAX: 818–781–2653

Catalog: free, $5 outside the U.S.
Pay: check, MO, MC, V, AE, Discover
Sells: surplus electronics and tools
Store: 905 S. Vermont Ave., Los Angeles,
CA; Monday to Friday 9–5, Saturday 9–4;
also 14928 Oxnard St., Van Nuys, CA; Monday to Friday 9–6:30, Saturday 9–5
Online: http://www.allcorp.com

  ¡Si!

Electronics hobbyists will appreciate the 96-page catalog from All Electronics, which has been in business since 1967. Every issue features a huge number of surplus parts, hardware items, and tools. Semiconductors, transducers, heat sinks, sockets, cables and adapters, fans, plugs, switches, solenoids, relays, capacitors, piezoelectric elements, fuses, resistors, transformers, potentiometers, keyboards, computer fans, PC boards, and hard-to-find and one-of-a-kind items are typical offerings. While much of the stock is for electronics hobbyists, the catalogs usually offer such items as telephone cords and jacks, TV and video accessories, screwdrivers, soldering irons, hemostats, and rechargeable batteries.

Special Factors: All parts are guaranteed to be in working order; returns are accepted within 30 days.

BAILEY'S

44650 HWY. 101
P.O. BOX 550
LAYTONVILLE, CA 95454
800–322–4539
FAX: 707–984–8115

Catalog: free, $6 outside U.S.
Pay: check, MO, MC, V, AE, Discover
Sells: "woodsman" supplies
Store: same address; Monday to Friday 7–6, Saturday 8–1; also 196 Edwards Dr., Jackson, TN; Monday to Friday 7–6, Saturday 8–1
E-mail: baileys@bbaileys.com
Online: http://www.bbaileys.com

Bailey's, one of the country's best sources for "mail-order woodsman supplies, at discount prices," stocks a large number of goods everyone will find useful—specialty boots, leather conditioners, outdoor clothing, and safety gear. Campers and even urbanites will appreciate the well-priced outerwear (Filson jackets and pants, flannel shirts, rain slickers, etc.) and the first-aid kits and portable fire extinguishers. In addition, there are boot dryers, E.A.R. plugs and headset noise mufflers, and work gloves.

The 100-page color catalog features wood-cutting equipment (including chain saws) and lists Oregon and Bailey brand chain reels and bars for saws by Echo, Homelite, Husqvarna, McCulloch, Pioneer, and Stihl. Silvey chain grinders, spark plugs, automatic measuring tapes, guide bars, bar and chain oil, bar wrenches and files, and other tools are available. Bailey's carries a full line of heavy-duty calked leather, rubber, and PAK-insulated boots, as well as Vibram and Air Bob boots, all available with and without steel toes. There are log splitters, Alaskan sawmills, Woodbug and the new Lucas portable small-log sawmills, chain-saw-powered winches, fire-fighting equipment, climbing gear, and reforestation supplies (including seedlings). Bailey's is the place to call if you have questions about your chain saw. Savings run as high as 60% on goods in the general catalog—and even more on items offered in the sales flyers. If you're nuts about wood and logging, check out Bailey's wood business cards made of aspen, bird's eye maple, eastern red cedar, curly maple, and cherry.

Special Factors: Bailey's NRI number is 23079956.

CAMELOT ENTERPRISES

P.O. BOX 65, DEPT. W
BRISTOL, WI 53104–0065
414–857–2698

Catalog: $2, refundable
Pay: check, MO, MC, V
Sells: fasteners, tools, and hardware
Store: 8234 199 Ave. (facing 83rd St.), Bristol, WI; Tuesday to Friday 8–6, Saturday 8–12; other hours by appointment only

Camelot, founded in 1983, sells "quality fasteners, hardware, and tools direct to the craftsman" at savings of up to 60%, through a 32-page catalog that's jam-packed with garage and workshop necessities. Camelot carries a full range of nuts (hex, K-lock, wing, stop, etc.), bolts (hex-head, machine, carriage), screws (wood, lag, drywall, machine), washers, grease fittings, turnbuckles, eyebolts, solderless electrical terminals, cotter pins, anchors, and other hardware. And you don't have to buy by the pound to get wholesale prices—Camelot packages the hardware in counts of 10, 25, 50, 100, etc. Camelot's tools include screwdrivers, punches, air tools, pliers, snips, rasps, and other hand and power tools for hobbyists and machinists by Astro, Best Tool, Cal-Van, Camelot, Chicago Pneumatic, Excalibur, General, Ingersoll-Rand, Lisle, Milton, Milwaukee, and Truecraft, among others. Shop equipment, Excalibur fastener sets, Marson pop rivets, and Camelot's own twist drills and fasteners are also sold at competitive prices.

Wholesale buyers, please note: If your business is in Illinois, Indiana, or Wisconsin, you must provide a copy of your resale certificate to buy wholesale from Camelot.

Special Factors: Satisfaction is guaranteed; price quote by letter only; returns are accepted within 10 days for replacement, refund, or credit; no collect calls are accepted.

COASTAL TOOL & SUPPLY

248 SISSON AVE.
HARTFORD, CT 06105
860–233–8213
FAX: 860–233–6295

Catalog: free
Pay: check, MO, MC, V, AE, Discover
Sells: hand, power, and air tools
Store: same address (Exit 46 off I–84); Monday to Friday 8–5, Saturday 8–4
E-mail: sales@coastaltool.com
Online: http://www.coastaltool.com

Coastal Tool offers the top names in tools at discounts of up to 50% on list price. Neither the catalog nor the website shows all of the thousands of products Coastal offers, but you can call or write if you don't see what you're looking for. The brands include Bosch, Delta, DeWalt, Dremel, Eklind, Emglo, Fein, Hitachi, Klein, Leatherman, Makita, Milton, Milwaukee, Porter-Cable, Roto-Zip, Senco, Skil, Stanley, Vise-Grip, Wilton, and Wiss, among others. Coastal's customers run from Saturday do-it-yourselfers to contracting firms and institutions, so the sales staff is used to fielding a wide range of questions and requests. If you can't visit, you can tap their collective wisdom through the website. Log on and send the "Tool Doctor" your toughest questions about power tools, or subscribe to Coastal's tip-filled e-mail newsletter. If you're not handy but know someone who is, see the "Gift List"—it's a great source for ideas when you're shopping for your handiest man or woman.

Special Factors: Satisfaction is guaranteed; returns (in condition received) are accepted for exchange, refund, or credit.

ECON-ABRASIVES

Catalog: free
Pay: check, MO, MC, V, Discover
Sells: abrasives and related products
Store: mail order only

P.O. BOX 1628,
  DEPT. WBMC
FRISCO, TX 75034
800–367–4101
972–335–9234
FAX: 972–377–2248

Econ-Abrasives has been in the business for over 30 years, and the company began selling sandpaper by mail in 1987. As a manufacturer of industrial-grade abrasives, Econ-Abrasives applies the same high standards to the products it makes for the home shop hobbyist and the professional woodworker: The belts are resin-bonded aluminum-oxide grit, seamed with a butt joint that allows them to be run bidirectionally, offered in open or closed coat. (Silicon carbide and aluminum zirconia grits are available as well.) The grits run from 24 to 400, sizes from 1" by 30" to 6" by 200" to 53" by 103"—and if yours isn't on the list, Econ-Abrasives can make it up.

And that's what's on just 3 of the 32 pages of the catalog. Econ-Abrasives offers comparably diverse options in sanding sheets, adhesive-backed discs and rolls, sanding blocks and disc bases, flap wheels and sanding drums, and specially shaped forms for difficult sanding jobs (crevices, recesses, turnings, etc.). Other sanding-related goods are available, including sanding mitts, steel wool, rigid steel hand scrapers, belt-cleaning tools, glues and fillers, router and drill bits, wood chisels, buffing wheels, grinding wheels, and safety gear.

Prices are competitive with discount tools stores on small quantities, but volume purchases are where you'll really save. The catalog includes a glossary of abrasives terms and recommendations for different jobs, so you don't have to be a pro to shop here.

Special Factors: Price quote by phone or letter; minimum order is $25 with credit cards.

ENCO MANU-FACTURING COMPANY

5000 W. BLOOMINGDALE AVE., DEPT. WBMC
CHICAGO, IL 60639
800–860–3400
773–745–1500
FAX: 800–860–3500
FAX: 773–745–1118

Catalog: free
Pay: check, MO, MC, V, Discover
Sells: machining tools and hardware
Store: same address; also 12 locations in AZ, CA, FL, GA, IL, MN, OH, TX, and WA (see catalog for locations or call 800–873–3626)
E-mail: encomfg@aol.com

If the notion of saving big on lathes and mills has you riveted, read on. Enco, in business since 1940, is one of the country's biggest suppliers of machine shop equipment. The 500-page catalog lists lathes, mills, grinders, cutting tools, woodworking equipment, fabricating equipment, hand tools, air compressors, measuring tools, and more, including 10 pages of books, manuals, and software. You'll also find abrasives, safety equipment, tool storage units and chests, and even janitorial supplies here. Prices are routinely 30% to 50% below list or comparable retail, and volume discounts are available. In addition, Enco says they'll do their "best to meet or beat the price" on any of their same merchandise offered at a lower price elsewhere (see catalog for details). The catalog includes full terms of sale and the locations and hours of Enco's 13 branches around the country.

Special Factors: Quantity discounts are available; institutional accounts are available; minimum order is $25; C.O.D. orders are accepted.

H&H MANUFACTURING & SUPPLY CO.

P.O. BOX 692
SELMA, AL 36701–0692
334–872–6067
FAX: 334–872–0813

Catalog: free
Pay: check or MO
Sells: chain-saw parts and logging equipment
Store: 111 Hwy. 80 E., Selma, AL; Monday to Friday 7–5, Wednesday 8–12 noon

H&H Manufacturing runs a mail-order firm known as "Saw Chain" that's been offering savings of up to 60% on saw chain and other logging needs since 1964. You can buy the chain, guide bars, and sprockets here for chain saws by Craftsman, John Deere, Echo, Homelite, Husqvarna, Jonsered, Lombard, McCulloch, Olympic, Pioneer, Poulan, Remington, Stihl, and other firms. The chain is sold in a range of pitches and gauges, and both gear-drive and direct-drive sprockets to fit all models are stocked. Swedish double-cut files, Esco rigging products, Windsor and Tilton saw chain and bars, wire rope, logging chokers, slings, and other logging equipment are also available. Remember to include all requested information when ordering chain and sprockets—make and model, chain pitch, gauge, number of drive links, type of bar, and length.

Special Factors: Chains, bars, files, and sprockets are guaranteed to last as long as or longer than any other make; returns are accepted for replacement; C.O.D. orders are accepted.

H&R COMPANY

16 ROLAND AVE.
MOUNT LAUREL, NJ
08054–1012
609–802–0422
FAX: 609–802–0465

Catalog: $5/year's subscription, refundable
Pay: check, MO, MC, V, Discover
Sells: new and surplus electromechanical, robotic, and optical components
Store: mail order only
E-mail: sale@herbach.com
Online: http://www.herbach.com

Herbach & Rademan Co., aka H&R Company, was established in 1934 and offers surplus bargains—chiefly electronics, robotics, optics, and intriguing mechanical devices. The 112-page catalogs feature capacitors, lasers, power supplies, compressors, fans, stepping and gearhead motors, test equipment, relays, resistors, air and hydraulic cylinders, solenoids, transformers, and similar equipment. Computer components, including monitors, keyboards, cables, and power line filters, are usually available. H&R also sells goods that nearly anyone, electromechanically inclined or not, can use: security equipment, microscopes, wire strippers, educational kits, phone accessories, digital scales, heavy-duty outlet strips and surge suppressers, model trains and cars, closed-circuit TV components, goggles, robotics components, compasses, cabinet slides, parts bins, tool cases and cabinets, magnets, weather balloons, and reference books on technical topics. Product specifications are given in the catalog. H&R also runs close-out and "grab bag" sales—and will purchase large quantities of your surplus current, quality electromechanical components, optics, relays, computer peripheral devices, and other similar items. Smaller quantities of special items are also purchased. Call to inquire.

Special Factors: Satisfaction is guaranteed; price quote by phone, fax, or letter; returns with original packing materials are accepted within 30 days; minimum order is $25, $50 on open account, $100 on orders outside the United States and Canada.

HARBOR FREIGHT TOOLS

■■■■■■

3491 MISSION OAKS BLVD.
P.O. BOX 6010
CAMARILLO, CA 93011
800–423–2567
FAX: 805–388–0760

Catalog: free
Pay: check, MO, MC, V, AE, Discover
Sells: tools, hardware, industrial equipment, machinery
Store: same address; also 40 other locations in AZ, CA, KY, NV, OR, and UT
Online: http://www.harborfreight.com

You'll find great prices on everything from air compressors to woodworking equipment in the 60-page catalog from Harbor Freight Tools, which offers workshop necessities at savings of up to 80% on list and comparable retail. Specials are run frequently, making this a valuable source for the hobbyist and do-it-yourselfer.

The typical catalog offers air tools; compressors; hand tools for all kinds of work; automotive repair and maintenance equipment; shop equipment; power tools and supplies; metalworking, welding, and plasma cutting tools; woodworking machines and tools; generators; engines; pumps; and even a roundup of useful things for home and garden—posthole diggers, stud sensors, push brooms, ladders, paint sprayers, and more.

Special Factors: Shipping is free on orders over $50 delivered within the continental United States.

HOLZ TOOL SUPPLY

819 BROADWAY, DEPT. WBMC

MT. VERNON, IL 62864

800–233–4676

618–242–4676

FAX: 618–242–4679

Catalog: $1, refundable
Pay: check, MO, MC, V, AE, Discover
Sells: professional-quality tools
Store: same address; Monday to Friday 7:30–5, Saturday 8–12
E-mail: holztool@accessus.net

Contractors, woodworkers, and serious do-it-yourselfers have been buying better for less from Holz Tool since 1985. Among the most popular lines are the Porter-Cable nailers and staplers, Amana router bits, Compass drywall and tek screws, Delta woodworking machinery, Bessey clamps, Elco tapcon concrete screws, Knaack jobsite tool chests, fiberglass ladders and equipment from Blue Ribbon Ladder, Performax power drum sanders, Sait grinding wheels and abrasives, Weather Guard truck boxes and van equipment, Wej-it concrete anchors, David White surveying equipment, and power tools by Makita, Milwaukee, Porter-Cable, Skil, and other firms. The current 34-page catalog offers a wide selection of shop tools and blades and bits, but you can also send for manufacturers' catalogs, or call directly with model information for a price quote. Holz is an authorized service center for Delta, Milwaukee, and Porter-Cable power tools, and assures us that "courteous people answer the phones and will help you find the proper tool for the job." If what you want is not in stock, Holz will be happy to order it.

Special Factors: Price quote by phone or letter; authorized returns are accepted for exchange, refund, or credit (a 15% restocking fee may be charged).

MANUFACTURER'S SUPPLY

P.O. BOX 167, DEPT.
WBMC–99
DORCHESTER, WI
54425–0167
800–826–8563
FAX: 800–294–4144

Catalog: free
Pay: check, MO, MC, V, Discover
Sells: replacement parts for chain saws, lawnmowers, snowmobiles, ATVs, minibikes, etc.
Store: mail order only
Online: http://www.mfgsupply.com

Manufacturer's Supply is the source for the parts you'll need to get snowmobiles, ATVs, and all kinds of other motorized vehicles and power implements functioning again, at prices up to 50% below list or comparable retail. Consult the 216-page catalog for original replacement parts for snowmobiles by Arctic Cat, Polaris, Scorpion, Ski-Doo, Yamaha, Suzuki, Skiroule, John Deere, and others. Logging safety equipment (hard-hats, chaps, and boots), as well as sprockets and nose assemblies, chains, grinders, files, air filters, T-wrenches, starter springs, carburetor parts, and guide bars (for dozens of chain saw brands) are available.

In addition, Manufacturer's sells parts for standard and riding lawnmowers, as well as semi-pneumatic tires for mowers and shopping carts, wheelbarrows, and hand trucks. The firm stocks wheels, hubs, bearing kits, roller chains, sprockets, clutches, belts, and other goods for trailers, minibikes, go-carts, riding mowers, snow throwers, rototillers, garden tractors, and ATVs. The snowmobile parts include everything from lubricants to windshields—carburetors, fuel filters, cleats, tracks, studs, pistons, gaskets, drive belts, wear rods, slides, suspension springs, and engines, among other items. Also available are wood-chopping tools, Woodchuck wood-burning furnaces, Magic Heat waste heat reclaimers, and chimney-cleaning brushes. Manufacturer's Supply has been in business since 1960 and welcomes inquiries on products not shown in the catalog. You can order a copy on the website, or view everything Manufacturer's stocks in the online version.

Special Factors: Authorized, unused returns are accepted within 30 days (a 20% restocking fee may be charged); shipping is $4.99 per order to destinations in the contiguous United States; minimum order is $10; C.O.D. orders are accepted.

MICRO-MARK

340–2314 SNYDER AVE.
BERKELEY HEIGHTS, NJ
   07922–1595
908–464–6764
FAX: 908–665–9383

Catalog: $1
Pay: check, MO, MC, V, AE, Discover
Sells: model-building tools and supplies
Store: mail order only
E-mail: micromark@worldnet.att.net
Online: http://www.micromark.com

Micro-Mark's 80-page color catalog offers a complete line of miniature, specialty, and hard-to-find tools and supplies for hobbyists, miniaturists, craftspeople, jewelers, and anyone else who loves to tinker with small objects and models. Most of their 2,500 items are at discount prices, including miniature versions of power tools, which make difficult tasks easy. The catalog is not indexed, unfortunately, but the large selection makes up for that. A sampling of the products they carry includes soldering irons; foot switches for power tools; mini disc/belt sanders; landscaping accessories for dollhouses, model railroads, architectural models, and dioramas; knife and tool sets; goggle-style magnifiers; lathe and milling machine accessories; a miniature lumber shop; paints, finishes, and brushes of all types; a large selection of tweezers and other holders; accessories for rotary tools; precision cutting knives; a miniature metal shop; and carving tools. Readers will be happy to see the savings; retail-store prices are listed next to Micro-Mark's, and savings range from 20% to 40% and more. Be sure to look for Micro-Mark's summer sale, where items are discounted up to 70%.

Special Factors: Wholesale rates to qualified individuals and businesses; satisfaction guaranteed or full refund or credit of items returned within 30 days.

NORTHERN HYDRAULICS, INC.

P.O. BOX 1499, DEPT.
24619
BURNSVILLE, MN
55337–1499
800–533–5545
FAX: 612–894–0083

Catalog: free
Pay: check, MO, MC, V, Discover
Sells: do-it-yourself items, power tools, etc.
Store: same address and 31 other outlets in FL, GA, IA, MN, NC, SC, TN, TX, VA, and WI
Online: http://www.northern-online.com

Northern Hydraulics makes it easy to save up to 50% on gas engines, pressure washers, generators, trailer parts, painting and welding equipment, tarps, air tools and compressors, winches, power tools, farm and garden and RV equipment, and much more. The 148-page catalog and the smaller sale catalogs offer a good selection of tools and equipment for home and commercial workshop, for farm, garage, rental store, construction firms, warehouses, and light industrial operations. You'll find tow hoes, shop hoists and presses, parts washers, log splitters, Homelite and McCulloch chain saws, hydraulic pumps and parts by J.S. Barnes and Parker. Vertical- and horizontal-shaft replacement gas engines from Briggs & Stratton, Honda, Kohler, and Tecumseh are offered, for tillers, mowers, and lawn tractors. Air compressors by American IMC and Campbell-Hausfeld are offered, as well as air tools from Chicago Pneumatic, Ingersoll-Rand, and Northern Hydraulics' own line.

Northern also sells go-carts and parts, tires, casters and wheels, RV equipment, tractor lamps and seats, sandblasting and painting equipment, trailer parts, hand and power tools by Black & Decker, Bosch, Makita, Skil, and others. The lawn and garden equipment includes gas trimmers, cultivators, garden carts, ag pumps, mower tires, blowers, sprayers, tillers, and much more. Georgia Boots, gloves, and other protective items are also available. And you'll find boating accessories, personal security devices such as lights and alarms, cordless phones, solar fences, and electronic fences, all at discount prices.

Special Factors: Authorized returns are accepted for exchange, refund, or credit.

POOR MAN'S CATALOG

Catalog: $1
Pay: check, MO
Sells: U-Build plans for power tools
Store: mail order only

7000 20TH ST., #930
VERO BEACH, FL
32966–8878
561–778–1807

Every once in a while you discover someone out there offering something totally unique that's a real find. Poor Man's Catalog is just such a company. Johnny Blackwell, a mechanical wizard, has written scores of books and handbooks on low-cost tool-building and has been written up and praised by national media luminaries. The 28-page catalog is mind-boggling and made this Baby Boomer wish she were retired or had more time to tinker. Machinists and metal workers take note: Building your own machines and power tools saves you between 50% and 90% off what the purchased item would cost! Every U-Build plan is designed for low-cost building in the home shop using mostly recycled materials. Among the eclectic selection of U-Build plans in the current review catalog at the time of this writing were a sheet metal brake, a vacuum dust collector for routers, a micrometer work holder for a bench grinder, an ARC-welding gun, an emergency power generator, air coolers, power saws, power sanders, wood-turning lathes, floodlights, photographic enlargers, a mulcher, a lawn trimmer, a fruit press—even a lie detector! There are also fun projects for the hobbyist, including a model boiler for any model steam engine, a replica of the 1832 Atlantic locomotive that runs under the power of a tiny permanent-magnet located in the boiler, and a Civil War Parrott rifle model.

The single-tool plans are inexpensive, ranging from $8 to $14. But you can order three for $19.95, six for $37.95, or ten for $56.95 (wonderful for educational institutions). There's also a six-page catalog of book offerings on subjects devoted to photographic equipment ("build everything from your own simple coffee-can camera that develops its own pictures, to a precision telephoto lens made from a piece of plumbing, and loads in between"), lawn and garden tools, woodworking tools and accessories, power sanders and accessories, and more. These subject books are more expensive than the U-Build plans ($34.95 for *Photographic Equipment,* for example), but very reasonable when you think of the alternative: taking an extension class or buying the equipment new.

Special Factors: Satisfaction guaranteed. Quantity discounts available. Extra postage applies on Canadian and overseas orders.

RED HILL CORPORATION

P.O. BOX 4234
GETTYSBURG, PA 17325
800–822–4003
717–337–3038
FAX: 717–337–3936

Catalog: free
Pay: check, MO, MC, V
Sells: abrasives and refinishing products
Store: Supergrit Abrasives, 1540 Biglerville Rd., Gettysburg, PA
E-mail: info@supergrit.com
Online: http://www.supergrit.com

Red Hill's business is the rough stuff that gets things smooth—abrasives. The company was founded in 1978 and offers a wide range of abrasives and refinishing products at prices up to 50% below regular retail. The 28-page catalog includes belts (aluminum oxide, silicone carbide, and zirconia on cloth backing) in 19 sizes; plain-back, hook-and-loop, and pressure-sensitive sanding disks; paper disks for orbital sanders; sheets; sleeve and drums; sanding screens; rolls; graphite cloth to reduce friction between the sanding belt and the sander; and foam-core sanding blocks. In addition, the catalog offers abrasives for vibrating hand sanders, RAKSO's paper-backed steel wool sheets (to mount on sanders, for finishing work), felt-backed sanding disks that work with a hook-and-loop fastening system, and abrasive cords and tapes (for getting into crevices). Triangles for Bosch, Fein, and Ryobi triangular sanders are sold in bags of 25 for 20 cents to 35 cents each, about half the price of regular retail. The catalog also lists auto-body refinishing products, masking tape, tack cloths, and a stick for cleaning sanding belts when the grit gets clogged— a money saver in itself.

Red Hill has introduced NicSand Sanding Gel in grits 3,000, 5,000, and 10,000, which is sold in a kit with a pad that attaches to electric drills (under $10). The gel is great for polishing marble or glass tabletops or your car, or for deglossing surfaces between finishes. And you'll find glue guns and glue sticks here—and at $5 a pound for five pounds of sticks (white clear, amber clear, and super amber), they cost just a third of the going rate at the typical hardware store, and the savings increase on larger quantities.

Special Factors: Price quote by phone or letter on special order sizes; quantity discounts are available; minimum order is $25; C.O.D. orders are accepted.

SURPLUS CENTER

P.O. BOX 82209
LINCOLN, NE 68501–2209
800–488–3407
FAX: 402–474–5198

Catalog: free
Pay: check, MO, MC, V, AE, Discover
Sells: new and surplus industrial goods, hardware, etc.
Store: 1015 W. "O" St., Lincoln, NE; Monday to Friday 8–5, Saturday 8–12

Surplus Center, established in 1933, publishes a 180-page catalog that's a treasury of parts for the "build-it-yourselfer." One-third of the catalog features hydraulic equipment of all types, including cylinders, valves, pumps, and motors, as well as hoses, filters, and tanks. Also featured are pressure washers, blowers, winches, electrical motors of all kinds, electrical generators, air compressors, surveying equipment, spray pumps, vacuum pumps, gearboxes, gas engines, and more. Heavy-duty 400-amp DC welders are available, as well as sandblasters, inverters, multimeters, battery chargers, and a full line of residential and commercial burglar alarms. Some of the goods are real government surplus, but most are brand-new bargains. If you have any questions about an item, you can call Surplus Center's staff technicians for information.

Special Factors: Authorized returns are accepted (a restocking fee may be charged); C.O.D. orders are accepted.

TOOL CRIB OF THE NORTH

P.O. BOX 14040
GRAND FORKS, ND 58208
800–358–3096
FAX: 800–343–4205

Catalog: free
Pay: check, MO, MC, V, Discover
Sells: tools and hardware
Store: Duluth, MN, and Fargo, Grand Forks, and Minot, ND; see catalog for locations
Online: http://www.toolcribofthenorth.com

For 50 years Tool Crib of the North has provided a wide selection of top-quality tools for do-it-yourselfers, hobbyists, contractors, and industrial buyers. The company offers a broad range of tools, industrial and shop equipment, and supplies—ladders, pumps, generators, motors, woodworking equipment, saws, compressors, abrasives, concrete handling equipment, trailers, and much more. You can send for the 108-

page quarterly catalog, or call or write for price quotes on items by DeWalt, Black & Decker, Bosch, Delta, Hitachi, Jet, Makita, Milwaukee, Freud, Porter-Cable, Powermatic, Ryobi, David White, Emglo, and other major manufacturers. You'll find that the prices here are up to 40% below the regular retail prices (listed next to discounted prices), and the catalog includes helpful line drawings and product specifications. Canadian readers: Only U.S. funds are accepted.

Special Factors: Shipping is free on orders over $500.

TOOL HAUZ, INC.

122 E. GROVE ST.
MIDDLEBORO, MA
  02346–1288
800–533–6135
508–946–4800
FAX: 508–947–7050

Brochure: free
Pay: check, MO, MC, V
Sells: tools and hardware
Store: same address and 57 Crawford St., Needham, MA

The "bargain list" from Tool Hauz, Inc., features the best names in woodworking and power tools, at discounts that sometimes beat even those of the "wholesale" sources. You'll find everything from Barco Rocket hammers and Stabila levels to Bauer ladders and RMC saw stands—routers, drills, screw guns, disc sanders, and power saws; all types, by Black & Decker, Bosch, Hitachi, Homelite, Makita, Metabo, Milwaukee, Porter-Cable, Sioux, and Skil. Supplies and hardware, including abrasives, saw blades, hole saws, Jet screws, drill bits, tarps, tool aprons, glue, and related goods, are stocked as well. Call for the price list, or a price quote if you know the model you're looking for.

Special Factors: C.O.D. orders are accepted.

TOOLS ON SALE

SEVEN CORNERS HARD-
WARE, INC.
216 W. SEVENTH ST.
ST. PAUL, MN 55102
800–328–0457
FAX: 612–224–8263

Catalog: free
Pay: check, MO, MC, V, AE, Discover
Sells: tools for contractors, masons, and woodworkers
Store: same address; Monday to Friday 7–5:30, Saturday 8–1 CT
Online: http://www.7cornershdwe.com

If you can't get to St. Paul to visit Seven Corners Hardware, where there are "over 40,000 items on the floor," you can do business with the firm's mail-order division, Tools on Sale. The parent company was founded in 1933 and specializes in tools for contractors and woodworkers.

The Tools on Sale catalog is one of the last great freebies in America—520 pages of name-brand tools, at discounts of up to 50%. You'll find everything from air compressors to workbenches here, from manufacturers that include Black & Decker, Bosch, Delta, Dewalt, Dremel, Elu, Freud, Hitachi, Jorgensen, Maglite, Makita, Milwaukee, Porter-Cable, Rigid, Ryobi, Senco, Skil, Stanley (including contractor-grade tools), 3M, and David White, among others. If you're looking for carpet-installing tools, professional vacuum cleaners, laser levels, stair templates, Werner ladders and scaffolding, demolition hammers, moisture meters, water stones, or mechanics' cabinets, or just want to see 16 pages of construction aprons and nail bags, look no farther. And there are a dozen pages of books, videos, and manuals on everything from making a hobbyhorse to building a home. Free freight on orders shipped to the United States (except Alaska and Hawaii) is an added bonus.

Special Factors: Shipping is not charged on orders shipped within the 48 contiguous United States; authorized returns are accepted for exchange, refund, or credit; institutional and government accounts are available.

WHOLESALE TOOL CO., INC.

P.O. BOX 68, DEPT. WBMC

12155 STEPHENS DR.

WARREN, MI 48089–3962

800–521–3420

810–754–9270

FAX: 800–521–3661

FAX: 810–754–8652

Catalog: free

Pay: check, MO, MC, V, Discover

Sells: tools, hardware, and machinery

Store: same address; also 6 other locations in FL, IN, MA, NC, OK, and TX; see catalog for locations

E-mail: wtmich@aol.com

Wholesale Tool has been bringing good prices and a great tool selection to hobbyists and industry since 1960, through the 790-page "Full-Line Catalog." This hefty tome runs from Toyota forklifts to Crescent wrenches and is a treasury for do-it-yourselfers as well as woodworkers, machinists, contractors, and surveyors. Wholesale Tool is geared to the professional, as you can see from the collection of reference works—no Sunset guides to building decks, but *Die Design Fundamentals,* the 25th edition of *The Machinery Handbook,* a guide to world screw threads, and *Creep Feed Grinding* are here, among others. Wholesale Tool represents both popular commercial brands and industrial suppliers: Black & Decker, Brown & Sharpe, Brubaker Tool, Chicago Pneumatic, Desmond, Dorian Tool, Dremel, Florida Pneumatic, Fowler, General, General Electric, Hanson, Heinrich, Jorgensen, Lufkin, Master Lock, Merit, Milwaukee, Minute Man, Mitutoyo, Norton, Porter-Cable, Rigid, Ryobi, Shop-Vac, Starrett, 3M, Vise-Grip, Wesco, and Yuasa, among others. The comprehensive product descriptions include model number, technical specifications, Wholesale Tool's price, and sometimes the list price. Savings average 30%, and the catalog features several pages of clearance and odd-lot items, which are sold below cost.

Special Factors: Authorized returns are accepted within 30 days (a 10% restocking fee may be charged); minimum order is $25.

WOODWORKER'S HARDWARE

P.O. BOX 180
SAUK RAPIDS, MN 56379
800–383–0130
FAX: 800–207–0180

Catalog: $3, refundable (see text)
Pay: check, MO, MC, V, Discover
Sells: cabinet and furniture hardware
Store: mail order only; phone hours September to April: Monday to Friday 8–8, Saturday 8–noon; May to August: Monday to Friday 8–5, closed Saturday

Cupboards, drawers, cabinets, doors—they all require hardware, which is what you'll find at Woodworker's Hardware: 216 pages of hinges, knobs, pulls, slides, catches, latches, supports, and a variety of bits and other woodworking supplies. The current edition of the catalog showcases over 4,500 items, and you can order the catalog over the phone—the $3 is offset by a $5 coupon that can be applied to your first order.

The collection of specialty hinges, slides, mounts, and fixtures will be appreciated by anyone who's designing an entertainment center, curio or display cabinet, computer workstation, bookcase, or built-ins. The catalog features an extensive selection of specialty shelving and bins for kitchen cabinets—"white wire" and plastic lazy Susans that make use of inaccessible space in corner cabinets, trays that conceal the steel wool and sponge behind the fixed panel in front of the sink, and heavy-duty drawer and cupboard organizers and caddies for all kinds of storage and shelving. Several models of the built-in ironing closets are offered, as well as folding step stools designed to be fitted in behind a pull-out panel or fascia, and things like breadboards, swing-up shelves for heavy appliances, tambour doors, brass rail fittings and brackets, oak moldings, and TV and video mounts for wall or ceiling. Look here for cord grommets and paper slots for printer stands, mini-halogen cans and strip lighting, keyboard trays and slides, and more. Fasteners, drive screws, bits, levelers and glides, abrasives, respirators, glue, putties, and lubricants are all available. If you're looking for hardware from a specific firm, you can call for a price quote, or see the catalog.

Special Factors: Satisfaction is guaranteed; price quote by phone or letter; quantity discounts are available; authorized returns of unused, undamaged goods are accepted within 30 days for exchange, refund, or credit.

RELATED PRODUCTS/COMPANIES

Books and videos on woodworking • Woodworkers' Discount Books
Do-it-yourself books and free online information • Reader's Digest
Electrical surplus and miscellaneous tools • American Science & Surplus
General hardware and handyman supplies • Clegg's Handyman Supply
Marine hardware • Defender Industries
Musical instrument-making tools • Metropolitan Music
Peel-and-stick floor plans • Design Works
Plumbing supplies, hardware, and fixtures • CISCO, Baths from the Past
Power tools • Damark
Screen-door, shutter, and window hardware • Coppa Woodworking, Shutter-craft
Shop aprons and tool belts • Clothcrafters
Storage equipment • Fidelity
Woodworking tools • Hot Tools, Woodworker's Supply

TOYS, GAMES, AND PARTY SUPPLIES

Enjoyable diversions for children and adults;

party and event supplies and decorations

Parents know that one of the biggest annual expenses is the Birthday Party. Somehow the guest list keeps getting bigger, the party favors more elaborate. If you're throwing a kid's party, you'll find great sources here: companies that supply piñatas, balloons, penny candy, party favors, and more at tremendous savings compared with your local mall superstore. Likewise, if you're hosting an event, say, a fund-raiser, retirement party, or a Super Bowl get-together, you'll want to check out the party suppliers here for themed decor, custom-imprinted items such as napkins and matchbooks, and great catering supplies. This chapter also features firms that sell discounted games and toys for children from one to one hundred. Be sure to see the listings under "Related Products/Companies" at the end of the chapter for relevant items found in other parts of this book.

FIND IT FAST

BRIDGE SUPPLIES • Baron Barclay, C&T Bridge
CHILDREN'S PARTY FAVORS AND DECOR • Kaye's Holiday, La Piñata, Oriental Trading Company, Sally Distributors, U.S. Toy
HOLIDAY DECORATIONS • Kaye's Holiday
PARTY AND EVENT DECOR AND SUPPLIES • M&N International, Oriental Trading Company, Paradise Products, The Party Wholesaler, Sally Distributors, Stumps, U.S. Toy
STICKERS • Stickers 'N' Stuff
TOYS • Constructive Playthings

BARON BARCLAY BRIDGE SUPPLIES

3600 CHAMBERLAIN
LANE, SUITE 230
LOUISVILLE, KY
40241–1989
800–274–2221
502–426–0410
FAX: 502–426–2044

Catalog: free
Pay: check, MO, MC, V
Sells: bridge playing and teaching materials
Store: mail order only
E-mail: baronbarclay@baronbarclay.com
Online: http://www.baronbarclay.com

Baron Barclay Bridge Supplies carries materials and equipment for every kind of bridge player, from novice to old hand. Established in 1946, Baron Barclay stocks hundreds of books on bridge and sells them at quantity discounts of up to 50%. Over half of the 64-page color catalog is devoted to teaching manuals and texts, books on strategy and bidding, bridge history and reference texts, and complete courses in bridge. Videotapes and instructional software are also available, as well as a great choice of playing cards, scoring cards and club forms, recap sheets, and a variety of gifts and equipment—bridge-motif china, scarves, jackets, magnetic card sets, games, jewelry, watches, pens and pencils, and even electronic bridge games.

Special Factors: Satisfaction is guaranteed; quantity discounts are available; returns are accepted within 30 days for exchange, refund, or credit (videotapes and software for exchange only).

C&T BRIDGE SUPPLIES

3838 CATALINA ST.
LOS ALAMITOS, CA 90720
800–525–4718
562–598–7010
FAX: 562–430–8309

Catalog: free
Pay: check, MO, MC, V, AE, ACBL scrip, Discover
Sells: bridge books and supplies
Store: same address; Monday to Friday 8–5
E-mail: tedinlosal@aol.com

The card game of bridge originated from the English game of whist about a century ago, but it is often associated with the leisure pursuits of Eisenhower-era suburbanites. In reality, bridge is a demanding engagement whose challenge has survived fad and fashion. There are several variations on the game, each of which alters the ratio of luck to skilled bidding in the player's success. C&T Bridge offers the serious hand a great source for books on strategies, theory, play, bidding, self-tests and aids to mastering inner bridge, and even that great equalizer, playing bridge with your spouse. Several series of pamphlets are available, most on strategy and bidding methods. Bridge videos, computer programs, and handheld games are available, as well as playing cards (by the single deck or dozen), timers, guide cards, boards, score slips, recap sheets, and card holders and shufflers. Pricing is competitive, and quantity discounts of up to 25% apply to the books and autobridge practice sets. Bridge teachers are extended an extra 10% off multiples of selected titles.

Special Factors: Quantity discounts are available.

CONSTRUCTIVE PLAYTHINGS

U.S. TOY COMPANY, INC.
1227 E. 119TH ST.
GRANDVIEW, MO
** 64030–1178**
816–761–5900
FAX: 816–761–9295

Catalog: free (see text)
Pay: check, MO, MC, V
Sells: toys and educational products
Store: CA, CO, FL, IL, KS, PA, TX; call for address
E-mail: ustoy@ustoyco.com
Online: http://www.ustoyco.com

 ¡Si!

Constructive Playthings sells wholesome, growth-oriented diversions for children and makes a "lowest price guarantee" on everything it carries (see the catalog for details). Constructive Playthings has been in business since 1953 and features brightly colored, washable, durable toys, from musical play mats for infants to classic painted wood blocks to real steel tool sets, as well as kid-friendly furniture and outdoor playthings such as teepees, sand diggers, and giant tumble balls. All items are made to withstand lots of play; in fact, Constructive Playthings also sells directly to schools and child-care institutions (the school edition of the catalog costs $3). Before giving in to this year's movie character, see if you can't get your children interested in these games and diversions instead—they'll outlast seasonal fads and are easier on your budget.

Please note: If you represent an educational institution, write on letterhead and request the school edition of the catalog (minimum order, $25).

Special Factors: Satisfaction is guaranteed; returns are accepted for exchange, refund, or credit; institutional accounts are available.

KAYE'S HOLIDAY

6N021 MEREDITH RD.,

DEPT. WBMC99

MAPLE PARK, IL 60151

630–365–2224

FAX: 630–365–2223

Catalog: $1 for 2 issues
Pay: check, MO, MC, V
Sells: holiday ornaments and decorations
Store: mail order only
Online: http://www.cookeee.com/kaye

Tired of missing those post-Christmas clearances with the half-price buys on ornaments? Here's a sale that never stops: Kaye's Holiday, where decorations for Christmas, Easter, Halloween, and other holidays are priced from 20% to 75% below regular retail (and sometimes well below wholesale) every day. Kaye has been in business since 1982 and sends out a little eight-page, black-and-white catalog showing handmade ornaments of blown glass, fabric, straw, and wood, tagged at $1 and up. These are the same ornaments—from Poland, Germany, Czechoslovakia, and all over the globe—that can be found in import shops and gift catalogs selling for three times as much. Ornaments make wonderful gifts and keepsakes, and they're great to give when you're dropping in on people during the holidays. As a special offer for BWBM customers, Kaye's is offering two ornaments and a catalog for $2.50.

Wholesale buyers, please note: The minimum order for wholesale pricing is $500.

Special Factors: Order as early as possible for the best choice.

LA PIÑATA

NO. 2 PATIO MARKET,
OLD TOWN
ALBUQUERQUE, NM
87104
TEL/FAX: 505–242–2400

Brochure: $2, refundable
Pay: check, MO, MC, V, Discover
Sells: piñatas, paper flowers, and porcelain dolls
Store: same address; Monday to Saturday 10–5:30, Sunday 11–5:30

La Piñata, established in 1955, is a marvelous source for piñatas—the hollow papier-mâché animals and characters that are traditionally filled with candy and broken by a blindfolded party guest. Prices here are low, most between $2.50 and $12. The stock includes superheroes such as Batman, Superman, and Spiderman, and Sesame Street characters, pumpkins, Santas, snowmen, witches, stars, reindeer, footballs, and other seasonal themes. And there are all sorts of animals, including bears, burros, bulls, elephants, unicorns, tigers, pigs, kangaroos, and cows—as well as a piñata bat your guests can use to smash your selection to bits. La Piñata also offers a spectacular but inexpensive line of brilliantly colored paper flowers and dozens of handsome porcelain collector dolls in Native American costume. These dolls are reproduced in authentic dress, with beadwork and hand-painted designs.

Special Factors: Price quote by phone or letter; C.O.D. orders are accepted.

M&N INTERNATIONAL, INC.

P.O. BOX 64784, DEPT.
WBMC99
ST. PAUL, MN 55164–0784
800–479–2043
FAX: 800–479–3863

Catalog: free, $6 outside U.S.
Pay: check, MO, MC, V, Discover
Sells: party supplies
Store: same address; Monday to Friday 9–4

You can turn your next get-together into an event with a little help from M&N International, where it's always time to party. The firm's 160-page color catalog is published in spring and fall, and each edition features seasonal themes as well as year-round party staples. The spring/summer catalog includes St. Valentine's Day, Easter, St. Patrick's Day, Mardi Gras, the Chinese New Year, Mother's Day, Father's Day, Bastille Day, graduation themes, Independence Day, and weddings, anniversaries, and showers. M&N sells the streamers, balloons, banners, cutouts and posters, table props, and hats and favors for the holidays, as well as classic themes such as Casino Night, the playoffs (football, baseball, basketball, and hockey), Hawaiian luaus, rock and nostalgia, Oktoberfest, and "Western Chuckwagon Roundup," to name a few. The depth of the stock is impressive—there are six pages of props for Mardi Gras events alone—and parents, office managers, and teachers will appreciate the great selection of basics for all kinds of celebrations, promotional events, and entertaining. For example, the "Caterer's Corner" features a number of large-capacity crystal-cut acrylic trays and bowls—perfect for serving crowds at home or at the office—as well as tablecloths and skirts, ice molds, cutlery and tableware, candles, disposable buffet-warming pans, specialty carryout and meal service containers (including several styles perfect for catering children's parties), doilies, tissue paper and curling ribbon, confetti and streamers, party hats of all types, message banners, backdrop paper, and more.

If you're planning a promotional event, you can also order a number of items imprinted with your logo and message, including paper shopping bags, sport bottles and insulated mugs, flying disks, pens and pencils, lollipops, key rings, magnets, sun visors, buttons, napkins, wrapped mints, buckets, balloons, and even "wrist ticket" armbands used for admission management at concerts and sports events. M&N International has been in business since 1961, will meet or beat the competition's prices, and charges a reasonable 6% shipping on orders over $200 (at this writing).

Special Factors: Satisfaction is guaranteed; quantity discounts are available; authorized returns are accepted for exchange, refund, or credit; institutional accounts are available; C.O.D. orders are accepted.

ORIENTAL TRADING COMPANY, INC.

P.O. BOX 3407, DEPT. 868
OMAHA, NE 68103
800–228–2269
FAX: 800–327–8904
TDD: 800–833–7352

Catalog: free
Pay: check, MO, MC, V, AE, Discover
Sells: party goods, novelties, etc.
Store: mail order only
Online: http://www.oriental.com

  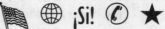

Before you throw another party or plan a single fund-raising event, consult "The World's Biggest Toy Box," from Oriental Trading. It's a novelty shop in 156 pages, crammed with everything from balloons and stickers to spun-glass bridal favors, resin animals and figurines, party favors, tickets, bingo supplies, penny candies, ribbon, inflatables, stuffed toys, masks, glow-in-the-dark jewelry, tropical drink stirrers, costumes, and lots more. Most of the products are sold by the dozen, gross, pound, or other multiple, at prices that are easily 50% below what individual items cost in party goods stores—and often even cheaper. Oriental Trading has been in business since 1932 and releases seasonal catalogs with special holiday selections regularly.

Special Factors: Quantity discounts are available; authorized returns (except food, candy, and costumes) are accepted after contacting customer service within five days of receipt of goods.

PARADISE PRODUCTS, INC.

P.O. BOX 568, DEPT.
WBMC
EL CERRITO, CA
94530–0568
510–524–8300
FAX: 510–524–8165

Catalog: free bulk mail, $3 first class
Pay: check, MO, MC, V
Sells: party paraphernalia
Store: mail order only
E-mail: paradise-party@worldnet.att.net

Paradise Products has been sponsoring bashes, wingdings, and festive events since 1952, when it began selling party products by mail. The

100-page catalog is a must-see for anyone throwing a theme event. The firm sells materials and supplies for over 60 different kinds of events, including celebrations of Oktoberfest, the '50/'60s, the Gold Rush, Presidents' Day, St. Patrick's Day, fiestas, "Las Vegas Night," Hawaiian luaus, pirate parties, Super Bowl celebrations, weddings, graduations, Fourth of July parties, and back-to-school festivities. Balloons, streamers, tissue balls and fans, party hats, banquet table coverings, crepe paper, pennants, garlands, and novelties are among the items available. Paradise's prices are as much as 50% below those charged by other party-supply stores, depending on the item and the quantity ordered.

Canadian readers, please note: Paradise requires payment for the catalog and orders in U.S. funds drawn on U.S. banks only, or by MasterCard or VISA.

Special Factors: Goods are guaranteed to be as represented in the catalog; shipments are guaranteed to arrive in time for the party date specified (terms are stated in catalog); minimum order is $20 or a $3 service charge applies.

THE PARTY WHOLESALER

2638 SW 28TH LANE
COCONUT GROVE, FL
33133
305–443–0042
FAX: 305–442–2689

Catalog: $3
Pay: check, MO, MC, V, AE, Discover
Sells: party supplies, restaurant disposables
Store: (warehouses) same address; also call for four other warehouse locations in FL

The Party Wholesaler, in business since 1983, sells restaurant and party and entertaining supplies and related goods in case lots and "retail packs," at discounts of up to 40% on the regular prices. The 32-page color catalog is full of table goods, decorations, and the little things that add fun to festive occasions: paper plates and napkins in vibrant colors and snappy designs, including ensembles for children's birthdays, wedding parties, and showers; plastic cutlery and cups; tablecloths; doilies; balloons; crepe paper; party hats; streamers and pennants; favors; and other novelties. Guest towels and toilet paper are sold here, as well as a good selection of candles, hors d'oeuvre picks and drink stirrers, cocktail napkins with amusing slogans, wrapping paper, gift bags, bows and ribbon, and invitations in upbeat designs and colors.

The Party Wholesaler has a "serious" section for restaurateurs and caterers, which includes a selection of cake-decorating supplies, cake pans, deli and bakery containers, commercial-size rolls of foil and poly film, and aluminum and foil take-out containers. The catalog includes tips on party planning, and the order form even features shopping lists so that you don't overlook anything.

Special Factors: Satisfaction is guaranteed; returns of unopened, unused goods are accepted within 30 days for exchange, refund, or credit.

SALLY DISTRIBUTORS, INC.

4100 QUEBEC AVE. N.
MINNEAPOLIS, MN 55427
800–472–5597
612–533–7100
FAX: 800–575–1453
FAX: 612–533–0141

Catalog: free, $5 outside U.S.
Pay: check, MO, MC, V, Discover
Sells: party goods, toys, novelties, seasonal items, etc.
Store: same address; Monday to Friday 8–5, Saturday 8–12
E-mail: sallydist@sallydist.com

Sally Distributors can help your church, organization, or school make merry on a budget, or serve as your own personal source for well-priced decorations for holidays and celebrations. The 96-page color catalogs feature the season's strong sellers—Fourth of July themes, Valentine's Day, Easter, St. Patrick's Day, Halloween, etc.—with table and room decorations, favors, games, banners, novelties, and a wide selection of stuffed toys. Every edition shows latex and Mylar balloons and inflation equipment (custom printing services are available, minimum 1,000 balloons), garlands and streamers, decorative light sets, greeting cards, gift wrap and ribbon, flags and pennants, toys and novelties, and all sorts of prizes and treats—feather masks, party classics such as woven finger traps and kazoos, "wedding bubbles" (a fun alternative to rice), and even piñatas and the candy to go in them are a few examples.

Most of the products are packed in multiples—balloons are sold by the dozen (30" metallics) or gross (11" latex in 42 colors), bandannas by the dozen, and things such as plastic bird warblers and bead necklaces by the gross. Prices are easily 40% less than usual retail, and savings are even greater on quantities of certain items. Sally Distributors passes on the actual shipping costs only, a welcome departure from the inflated fees asked by many vendors. It's that kind of thinking that has kept the company going since 1921!

Please note: The products are not intended for use by children under three years of age.

Special Factors: Quantity discounts are available; only authorized returns are accepted for exchange, refund, or credit; institutional accounts are available; a $2 surcharge is imposed on orders under $30.

STICKERS 'N' STUFF, INC.

**P.O. BOX 430, DEPT. WBM
LOUISVILLE, CO
80027–0430
303–604–0422
FAX: 303–665–8779**

Catalog and Samples: $2
Pay: check, MO, MC, V
Sells: novelty stickers
Store: mail order only

Stickers 'N' Stuff, founded in 1980, sells a wide variety of adorable stickers: prism (rainbow effect), chrome (foil background), hologram (like the emblem on your credit card), fuzzies, and neon stickers. The designs include lots of Teddy bears, cats, unicorns, butterflies, angels, balloons, rainbows, wild animals, holiday themes (Christmas, Thanksgiving, Valentine's Day, etc.), and the American flag. In addition, Stickers 'N' Stuff sells striped adhesive bandages in heart shapes, sticker collecting books, "liquid crystal" jewelry, sticker "earrings," endangered species stickers, and even scratch-and-sniff stickers. Parents, teachers, and day-care workers may derive the most benefit from a stash of assorted stickers, skillfully deployed on a rainy day. Thanks to this firm, stickers that cost 25 cents in the toy store cost as little as 6 cents here, or an average of 8 cents for the Sampler Assortment of 366 stickers. You can save even more on half or full cases, which are usually bought for resale. And you can try them out before you order: $2 brings you the catalog and a generous batch of stickers, enough to last a couple of Saturday afternoons!

Special Factors: Satisfaction is guaranteed; quantity discounts are available; returns are accepted for exchange, refund, or credit.

STUMPS

ONE PARTY PLACE
P.O. BOX 305
SOUTH WHITLEY, IN
   46787–0305
800–348–5084
219–723–5171
FAX: 219–723–6976

Catalog: free
Pay: check, MO, MC, V, AE, Discover
Sells: party goods, display items, etc.
Store: mail order only; phone hours Monday to Friday 7–9, Saturday 8–3 CT
Online: http://www.stumpsparty.com

Stumps, in business since 1926, specializes in "the latest and the most innovative ways to make any event glamorous and fun." According to the company, schools and theaters are partial to Stumps' wide range of theme decorations ranging from Celestial to Mardi Gras to Hollywood to elegant balloons and romantic gardens. The kits include magnificent lighted archways, shooting stars, gigantic moons and suns, and larger-than-life movie cameras and awards.

Stumps also offers everything required to brighten a room for a holiday, reunion, or wedding, including 150 different balloons, thousands of holiday decorations, gossamer, streamers, parade materials, and a variety of tableware—much of which is priced up to 50% below retail. And if you're looking for real savings, check the quantity pricing on imprinted favors—glassware, frames, key rings, invitations, noisemakers, and even clothing are available. You'll find most of the imprintables in the 425-page "Prom" catalog, and other festive imprinted items and decorations in the other specialty catalogs.

Special Factors: All prices listed are wholesale; satisfaction is guaranteed; price quote by phone or letter; quantity discounts are available; authorized returns (except worn clothing and personalized/customized products) are accepted within 15 days for exchange, refund, or credit (a 15% restocking fee may apply); institutional accounts are available; minimum order is $15.

U.S. TOY CO., INC.

1227 E. 119TH ST.
GRANDVIEW, MO
   64030–1117
800–255–6124
816–761–5900
FAX: 816–761–9295

Catalog: $3
Pay: check, MO, MC, V
Sells: novelties and fund-raising items
Store: Garden Grove, CA; Englewood, CO; Apoka, FL; Skokie, IL; Leawood, KS; North Wales, PA; and Carrollton, TX; see catalog for locations
Online: http://www.ustoyco.com/

It's always party time at U.S. Toy Company, where masks, costumes, favors, festive tableware, streamers and decorations, games, grab-bag prizes, little toys and novelties, penny candy, jewelry, stuffed animals, inflatables, balloons, hats, crowns, and other fun things are available at discounts of up to 70% on regular retail. In addition to party goods grouped by theme—Halloween, St. Patrick's Day, Easter, Mardi Gras, etc.—the 160-page U.S. Toy catalog has everything you need for your fund-raiser. Some products are sold in cases or large lots, but much is available in small quantities—making this a great source for parents, teachers, camp directors, and anyone else looking for inexpensive party materials.

Special Factors: Institutional accounts are available; minimum order is $25.

RELATED PRODUCTS/COMPANIES

Adult puzzles and games • Airline International Luggage & Gifts
Astronomy-themed games and puzzles • Astronomical Society of the Pacific
Baby toys • Chock Catalog, Baby Bunz, After the Stork, The Natural Baby
Candle- and soap-making kits • Brushy Mountain Bee Farm
Casino-game computers • Mardiron
Children's bee-themed games and activities • Brushy Mountain Bee Farm
Children's musical instruments, toys, party favors, and sheet music •
Anyone Can Whistle, Shar Products
Children's travel games • Family Travel Guides Catalog
Craft kits • Craft Resources, Vanguard, The Artist's Club, The Caning Shop, CR's Bear and Doll Supply, Frank's Cane and Rush, Gramma's Graphics, Warner-Crivellaro Stained Glass

Craps, blackjack, shuffleboard, darts, foosball, and other rec-room games • Mueller Sporting Goods

Doll buggies • Wicker Warehouse

Dollhouse plans • Woodworker's Supply

Dolls and toy-making supplies and parts • CR's Bear and Doll Supply

Game books, stickers, cut-and-assemble projects • Dover Publications

Grow-your-own-butterfly and other educational kits • American Science & Surplus

Kid's bath foam • Fuller Brush Independent Distributor

Kid's pedal plane • Aircraft Spruce & Specialty

Kites and kite-building kits • BFK Sports

Miniatures • Wicker Warehouse

Old-fashioned games • Gohn Bros.

Onyx chess sets • House of Onyx

Penny candies • Bates Bros., Bulkfoods.com, Durey-Libby

Playground equipment • Better Health Fitness

Sleds, toboggans, go-carts • RV Direct, Northern Hydraulics

Toy chests • Fran's Wicker & Rattan, Eastern Butcher Block

Water toys • Overton's

Wooden toys, blocks, puzzles • Weston Bowl Mill, The Natural Baby

TRAVEL

Money-saving travel and moving services
of various kinds

This section includes a handful of companies that in one way or another could save you money on your next move, airline ticket, cruise, or European trip. Travel is a big industry, so there's a lot of information out there, as well as a mind-boggling number of choices. If you have the creativity—and in some cases, flexibility—to nail down your itinerary in a slightly unconventional way, there are lots of ways to save. In addition to the company listings, here are some basics to get you started.

CONSOLIDATORS/BUCKET SHOPS

Consolidators, also known as bucket shops, are travel wholesalers who buy cruise slots, blocks of rooms, and plane seats from airlines, hotels, and charter agents, and resell them for less than the hotels, airlines, or often the charter operators themselves are willing to accept for individual tickets or rooms. Travel agents are big customers of consolidators, but individuals may buy from them, too, which will often save them 20% to 30% on APEX fares and much more on full economy tickets.

Unitravel III Corporation, one of the oldest consolidators in the business, books flights in the United States and Europe and sells directly to individuals. Contact Unitravel at least a month before you anticipate traveling, and allow for some uncertainty, because tickets might not be available until shortly before the day of departure. The toll-free number is 800–325–2222 for more information, or write to 11737 Administrative Dr., Ste. 120, St. Louis, MO 63146.

Council Travel, a leader in student, youth, and low-priced airfares, has offices in over 27 states and districts. Council can also issue student IDs, get you Eurorail passes, and set you up in a language program for work or study abroad. This student-friendly company also has information on youth hostels, home stays, and other economical, youth-oriented accommodations. For more information, call toll-free 800–2COUNCIL, or visit the website at http://www.counciltravel.com/.

STA Travel has a number of offices in major California cities, as well as in the District of Columbia, Chicago, Boston and Cambridge, New York City, Philadelphia, and Seattle; call 800–777–0112 for the location nearest you.

Nouvelle Frontiers is an off-price travel broker that sells to consumers as well as to travel agencies. For information, call 212–779–0600 or 800–366–6387.

You can also try *Travac Tours and Charters,* at 212–563–3303 or 800–872–8800.

HOTEL BROKERS

If you have a credit card, belong to an automobile club, use a discount telephone long-distance service, or are otherwise listed somewhere on the American information grid, you've no doubt been solicited to join a dining and travel club. Depending on how frequently you travel, the annual membership, if there is one, might be worth it for the discounts.

Another way to save on your hotel stays, however, is to book through a broker, who may work like a consolidator or an independent agent, providing reservations and confirmations, often at a discount, but sometimes when space is otherwise unavailable. Many of these services require prepayment to the service for the room and stay, for which you'll receive a voucher that can be used when you check in. The services listed below act as agents and allow you to pay the hotel in the customary way:

Quikbook has connections with good mid-priced hotels in New York, Boston, Atlanta, San Francisco, Washington, DC, Chicago, and Los Angeles, and can be reached at 800–789–9887 or 212–532–1660; or fax to 212–532–1556; or write to Quikbook, 381 Park Ave. South, New York, NY 10016.

Central Reservation Service handles reservations in the following cities: New York, Chicago, Boston, Atlanta, New Orleans, San Francisco, Miami, and Orlando. If you book through them, you'll save from 10% to 40%. The staff speaks both Spanish and English. Call 800–548–3311 or 407–740–6442; the address is Central Reservation Service, 220 Lookout Pl., Ste. 200, Maitland, FL 32751.

HOME EXCHANGES

One of the cheapest ways to save on hotel bills, especially if you're quartering a family, is to billet in someone else's home. *International*

Home Exchange Service/Intervac is an organization that compiles three directories a year listing over 9,000 homes worldwide (most are outside the United States). The apartments and houses in this directory are available for exchange and rent, so you don't necessarily have to exchange your own home to take advantage of a good deal. For more information, write to International Home Exchange Service/Intervac, 30 Corte San Ferrando, Belvedere Tiburon, CA 94920, or call 415–435–3497.

In a city such as New York, where every single hotel room may be booked for the weekend, it's nice to know that there are thousands of vacant apartments available for less than a hotel would cost—with a number of advantages, namely more space, use of a full kitchen, and no doubt better ambiance. These are listed under "Bed and Breakfasts" in the yellow pages of the local phone directory or weekly entertainment newspaper classifieds. Just about every major city has companies that make their business out of connecting owners with overnight guests.

NEWSLETTERS

If you travel frequently or would like to be able to afford to, you'll find the following newsletters of interest:

Consumer Reports Travel Letter, produced by Consumers Union, is a well-regarded "consumerist" publication for both business and recreational travelers. *CRTL* conducts in-depth comparisons of accommodations and prices in the United States and abroad, scrutinizes airline food, investigates travel scams, recommends methods of screening travel agents, and has probed the mare's nest of airline booking systems. Each monthly issue of *CRTL* runs around 24 pages; a year's subscription costs $39 at this writing, or $59 for two years. Call 800–234–1970, or write to Circulation Department, *Consumer Reports Travel Letter,* P.O. Box 53600, Boulder, CO 80322 for information. Single copies of back issues are available for $5 each. For a summary of current information, see *Consumer Reports Best Travel Deals: How to Get Big Discounts on Airfares, Hotels, Car Rentals, and More.* Published by Consumer Reports Books, it summarizes recent newsletter articles of note and is the best $9 you'll spend on travel this year.

Travel Smart is another newsletter that stays current with travel opportunities of all types, including discount fares and rates (including specials for seniors). Subscribers are offered deals on car rentals, cruises, accommodations, and air travel. And *Travel Smart* is full of great tips especially valuable to frequent travelers: A recent issue offered tips on how to see Israel on the cheap, listed a number of airline price drops, recommended restaurants in several cities for their moderately priced meals, and featured a guide to taking a break in the

Caribbean at "affordable prices." A year of monthly issues costs $37; for more information, write to *Travel Smart,* 40 Beechdale Rd., Dobbs Ferry, NY 10522–9989, or call 914–693–8300.

OTHER RESOURCES

Whether your travels are confined to your armchair or you actually get up and go, you'll find travel guides a great help in planning your trip. The best-known series are Fodor's, Fielding's, Frommer's, and Birnbaum's. These are reliable, general-purpose guide books to whole countries and major cities. The Frommer "$-A-Day" series is especially helpful if you're pinching pennies, but don't overlook the other books. If you're traveling abroad and want an informed guide to culturally and historically significant sites, see the Blue Guide series, which is highly recommended. Zagat offers *Zagat Survey Hotels, Resorts and Spas 1998;* it's widely available in bookstores across the country.

Many of the firms listed in "Books, Audiobooks, and Periodicals" sell travel guides and related literature, but specialty bookstores have far better stock and selection, and the staff can usually provide personal assistance in selecting the right book for your needs, even by mail.

The Complete Traveller Bookstore does a brisk mail-order trade through its 52-page catalog, which lists all the major guides, as well as Insider's Guides, the Michelin green and red guides, the fascinating Lonely Planet books, and scores of specialty guides that cover everything from Alaskan hideaways to shopping in Seoul. Maps, foreign language tapes, and travel accessories are sold through the catalog as well. Store shoppers can peruse the collection of antiquarian travel books, including some early Baedekers, which are perched at the tops of the bookcases. For a copy of the catalog, send $1 to The Complete Traveller Bookstore, 199 Madison Ave., New York, NY 10016. The phone number is 212–685–9007. Please note: This is not a discount bookseller.

FIND IT FAST

AUTOMOBILE TRANSPORTING SERVICES • A2B Automobile Moving
DISCOUNT CRUISE PACKAGES • Vacations to Go
LOWEST-PRICE TRAVEL BIDS • TravelBids
LOW-FARE, UNBOOKED AIRLINE SEATS • Airhitch
ONLINE TRAVEL SERVICES • Microsoft Expedia
SENIORS' LOW-COST LEARNING/TRAVEL PACKAGES • Elderhostel
UP-TO-DATE, COMPREHENSIVE COURIER TRAVEL INFORMATION • International Association of Air Travel Couriers

A2B AUTOMOBILE MOVING

888–274–4722
FAX: 562–691–7650

Information: internet website only, no catalog
Pay: bank check, MO, MC, V, AE
Sells: automobile, pickup, and van transport services
Store: online and telephone only
E-mail: shipacar@pobox.com
Online: http://www.choicemall.com/shipacar

Moving? Save time, money, and mileage—and reduce your overall stress by having A2B Automobile Moving transport your car, van, or truck to your new home. A2B is an internet-only company that can save you 20% to 40% over moving van rates. They usually pick up your vehicle at your door and promptly deliver it to your new location anywhere in the continental U.S. This company, founded in 1995, has specially designed trucks and licensed, insured carriers. Major corporations recommend A2B for relocating employees, as do individuals, whose letters pepper the website with tried-and-true testimonials. You can get a free quote right on the website, or call or send e-mail with your questions.

Special Factors: Vehicle transportation within the continental U.S.; for Canadian destinations, inquire; member of the Better Business Bureau.

AIRHITCH

2641 BROADWAY, 3RD FL.
NEW YORK, NY 10025
212–864–2000
800–326–2009

Information Packet: free
Pay: MC, V
Sells: low-fare, unbooked airline seats
Store: same address; Monday to Friday, 10–5; Saturday noon–3; also offices in Paris, El Segundo and San Francisco, CA; reps worldwide
E-mail: airhitch@netcom.com
Online: http://www.airhitch.org

On any given day, hundreds of seats go empty between the U.S. and Europe, as well as on domestic flights. Airhitch takes advantage of these empty seats by putting people in them for low fares. "The Airhitch system was created for the free-spirited, independent, and resourceful traveler who does not have a rigorous schedule, and enjoys seeing different places even when en route to his/her final destination." Here's how it works, in brief. When you call Airhitch you'll be given an information packet and will then be asked to register. The staff will fax you a form to fill out and fax back, ask you to register online, or if the former two options are not available to you, they will mail you an information packet and registration form. Once registered, you let Airhitch know your target date of departure and your destination (including a region of departure and three destination options). The "date range" for your departure must be a span of 5 days minimum, and you must be prepared to leave on any flight, on any day within your date range. (A "call-in" date is assigned for you slightly before the beginning of your date range.) Airhitch staff will help you make a strategy for prioritizing from among available flight alternatives to maximize the chances of getting you as close as possible to where you want to go, when you want to go.

Note that this is a one-way transaction only. You need to go through the procedure again for the return flight. There are reps overseas who can assist you. Sound complicated? Ponder this: You can go across the Atlantic for $175, and from the East Coast to the West Coast for about $119. If you're not rigid about travel times and dates, this is definitely a great bargain way to travel.

Special Factors: Pay by credit card only.

ELDERHOSTEL

75 FEDERAL ST.
BOSTON, MA 02110–1941
617–426–8056
FAX: 617–426–8351
TDD: 617–426–5437

Catalog: free (see text)
Pay: varies (see text)
Sells: inexpensive travel/learning packages for seniors
Office: same address; Monday to Friday 9–9
Online: http://www.elderhostel.org

"I can't imagine an Elderhostel-free retirement"—so says one of the many happy clients whose life has been enriched by this wonderful organization. If you're 55 years or older and you want to see the world without spending your children's inheritance, Elderhostel is the way to travel. Imagine studying the literature of Jane Austen in the White Mountains of New Hampshire; traveling to Greece to explore the spectacular art and architecture; or conducting field research in Belize to save the endangered dolphin population. Elderhostel was started in 1975 with 200 participants and a few programs; now it offers 10,000 programs in 70 countries every year plus 300 service programs that bring volunteer energy to worthy causes around the world. The cost for programs is low, ranging from $390 for a weeklong program in the U.S., which includes meals, rooms, instruction, and field trips, to $2,600 for two-and-a-half weeks in Europe, which includes airfare. And since Elderhostel is a 501(c)(3) organization, expenses incurred to participants are generally tax-deductible! When you call Elderhostel or visit the website, you'll be asked to choose which of four catalogs you want: "U.S.," "Canada," "International," or "Service."

Special Factors: Specify which catalog you want when ordering; forms of payment accepted vary depending on which travel program you book.

INTERNATIONAL ASSOCIATION OF AIR TRAVEL COURIERS

P.O. BOX 1349
LAKE WORTH, FL 33460
561–582–8320
FAX: 561–582–1581

Information packet: free
Membership: $45 for one year (see text)
Pay: check, MO, MC, V
Sells: up-to-the-minute courier travel information
Office: same address, Monday to Friday, 9–5; also office in England
E-mail: iaatc@courier.org
Online: http://www.courier.org

IAATC is the premier clearinghouse for consumers who wish to travel as couriers to foreign destinations. Being a courier is a superdiscount way to travel, but it's not easy to find out about whom to book with, and how to do it. After speaking with a company representative, I learned some of the many pitfalls of the courier industry, and it became clear to me why one would want and need to join IAATC. For one thing, courier companies (of which there are hundreds) come and go, sometimes weekly. You could book with a company and find yourself out of luck come travel day. For another thing, new flights and opportunities spring up hourly, and some of these last-minute deals are unbelievably cheap. You won't be able to get this hard-to-find information from anyone as accurately as from IAATC, which specializes in customer service. The IAATC "does not sell tickets or profit in any way from your courier flight. Its mission is to provide up-to-date information on all courier travel opportunities available to couriers, while working to support air courier travel as a way to see the world on a shoestring."

Courier flights work like this, in short: Companies need to send packages overseas. If they send them cargo, the packages might spend two to three days in customs before even getting on the plane. If companies want to send packages on regular flights (getting overseas in a few hours), airline regulations require that they be accompanied by a live body. That's where you enter in. You take the packages as your check-in luggage, and hand over the package to the waiting representative when you arrive at the destination airport. You might have to give up some of your carry-on luggage allotment, which is the downside. The upside is that your fare will be up to 85% less than you'd pay otherwise!

A one-year membership to IAATC is $45, which entitles you to telephone support, 24-hour access to their fax-on-demand system, IAATC's online access system for couriers, and a bimonthly subscription to both *The Shoestring Traveler* and the *Air Courier Bulletin*.

Special Factors: Information is for foreign destinations only; no domestic travel service; customers must pay in U.S. funds or British pounds.

MICROSOFT EXPEDIA

Information: internet website only, no catalog
Pay: MC, V, AE, CB, DC, Discover
Sells: travel information and services
Store: online only
Online: http://www.expedia.com

I tried out quite a few travel sites before I hit upon Expedia. As the name suggests, it's fast and easy to use. Some of the virtual travel agents have quick fare-finders that only work if you happen to be traveling between two of the major cities they've included in their calculations. Others allow you to go to the trouble of entering in all the information about your trip, only to inform you that no such flight exists. At Expedia, you sign up (for free), then you're off on a fun-filled adventure in finding (and booking, if you wish) your own flight. You choose the departure and destination cities or airports and the times and dates on both ends of your trip. Expedia's "Travel Wizard" will search any or all airlines, sort them by price or by schedule (those that fall closest to your specifications), and then list them, complete with connecting flights if applicable, exact times of departure/arrival, price, airline, and any restrictions that apply. You don't have to reserve the flight in order to get the full details. (How many times have you asked an airline rep to give you a quote, only to have her go through the whole booking routine?) Further, you can list your itinerary in "Fare Tracker" to receive weekly updates of the lowest fares available between those cities.

Other features that make Expedia a good travel site include the Expedia "Travel Network," which informs you about cruises, vacation packages, resorts, special interest vacations, and more; loads of travel news and feature articles; listings of hotels worldwide; a currency converter; maps, driving directions, weather updates, and much more. Will Expedia find you cheaper fares than other travel sites? A recent survey done by Internet Shopper of online travel bookers compared the top ten sites. Expedia produced the second cheapest fare out of the ten, but it definitely ranked best in terms of user-friendliness.

Special Factors: Ticketing and travel restrictions may apply; refer to your particular itinerary for details.

TRAVELBIDS TRAVEL DISCOUNT AUCTION

━━━━━━━

4800 RIVERBEND ROAD
BOULDER, CO 80301
FAX: 303–443–4705

Information: $5 per bid; internet website only, no catalog
Pay: MC, V, AE
Offers: lowest-price bids on travel reservations
Store: online only
Online: http://www.travelbids.com

TravelBids is an online auction that allows travelers to save money by having many different travel agents bid for their business. Here's how it works: The customer makes a reservation (but not a purchase) for a flight, cruise, hotel room, etc., and then registers it on the TravelBids site. The registration is a one-time fee of $5, and the first listing is free. After that, each additional listing is $5, presumably to keep nonserious travelers from posting trips that they're not really going to take, thus taking up the time of the travel agent bidders. The travel agents then have a specified amount of time to make bids on that listing, from one to 72 hours (specified by the customer). You are guaranteed at least a 6% discount, because TravelBids has already negotiated with a travel agent who will give that discount—but it is typically a higher percentage off. Travel agents are willing to give up all or part of their commission, because the consumer has done 99% of the work in making the travel arrangements. A quick look at the most recent bids showed two customers on a six-day trip to Peter's Island saving $255 off their $3,826 ticket price; a flight from Victoria, BC, to Chicago was $25 less than the original $409 price tag; and a cruise that was $6,668 had been bid down by $465. (You can view the last 50 trip auction results at the site.) In essence, this is a "lowest price guarantee" type of deal—you find the lowest-priced tickets, and TravelBids will shave even more off.

Special Factors: Guaranteed at least 6% off your ticket price; registration requires a signed fax sheet from the consumer.

VACATIONS TO GO

1502 AUGUSTA DRIVE,
  STE. 415
HOUSTON, TX 77057
800–338–4962
713–974–2121
FAX: 713–974–0445

Catalog: free
Pay: major credit cards (see text)
Sells: cruises
Store: same address; Monday to Friday 8:30–5:30

There's a lot of fierce competition out there between travel agents looking to book your dream vacation. Vacations to Go calls themselves "America's premier discount cruise specialist," and I was impressed with their no-nonsense approach. They claim to offer the lowest prices available on cruises 99% of the time, which they accomplish by being one of the largest sellers. This means that they have access to discounts and special fare programs that aren't available to the rest of the nation's travel agents. If the prices go down after you've booked your trip, they'll refund the difference (see catalog for details). Besides their regular low fares, here are some tips on how to save even more with Vacations to Go: (1) Book your trip in the fall; fall departures are traditionally less popular, and you'll get some great deals. (2) Take advantage of their group discounting program. You'll get a group rate (great for small family reunions) that's anywhere from 25% to 60% off the regular price, and if you book 15 full-fare people, the sixteenth gets to go for free—this on top of the group discount. (3) Take advantage of last-minute specials. Luckily, "last minute" to a cruise line means three months from departure, so that's plenty of time to plan. Vacations to Go has been in business since 1984, and their "cruise counselors" are easy and pleasant to talk to. Details on booking, cancellations, paying, etc., are in the catalog, or you can call for more information.

Special Factors: The type of credit cards accepted is determined by the cruise line on which you'll be traveling; quantity discounts available; smoke-free cruises available.

RELATED PRODUCTS/COMPANIES

Airline animal carriers • Kennel Vet
Car racks and strapping for transporting large items • Car Racks Direct
Coffee travel kit • Grandma's Spice Shop
Family- and children-oriented travel guides • The Family Travel Guides Catalogue
Luggage and travel accessories • Ace Luggage, Airline International Luggage, Al's Luggage, Jobson's Luggage Warehouse, Santa Maria Discount Luggage, The Luggage Center
Packing materials and bags of every size and description • Associated Bag
RV accessories • RV Direct
Travel tips brochures • Consumer Information Center, U.S. Gov't Superintendent of Documents

THE COMPLETE GUIDE TO BUYING BY MAIL

CATALOGS AND PRICE QUOTES

CATALOGS

Most of the companies in this book publish catalogs, which usually cost between $1 and $5. Firms sometimes ask for an SASE, which is a long (#10), self-addressed envelope with one first-class stamp. If an SASE is requested and you don't send one, don't expect a response.

You can order the stamps to mail all those catalog requests directly from the U.S. Postal Service. Both stamps and stamped envelopes are available; ask your postmaster or carrier for the "Stamps by Mail" form, or call 800–STAMP–24. The stamps are usually delivered within a few days.

"Refundable" Catalogs. Catalog fees that are "refundable" can be recouped when you place an order. Please note: If you don't place an order, you won't get the refund. Procedures for reimbursement vary; some firms send a coupon with instructions to enclose it with your order and deduct the amount from the total. (The coupon may be dated, forcing you to order within a limited time to recoup the fee.) If there's no coupon in the catalog, deduct the amount from the order total after adding tax, shipping, and other surcharges, and note the reason for the deduction on the order form. If there's no time limit on deducting the fee, assume a six-month limit.

Sending for Catalogs. Unless the listing states otherwise, you can call first and make sure the catalog is available. Sometimes the customer service rep will process a request right then, saving you the time it takes to write a letter, and possibly the catalog fee as well. If you write for the catalog, you can send a postcard for any that are free and a letter for any requiring payment. The correspondence should note the catalog you want (some firms have several), mention enclosures, include your return address, and refer to BWBM as your source. If the catalog costs up to $1, you can send a dollar bill or coins taped between thick pieces of cardboard. For catalogs costing over a dollar, send a check. (If the check is lost and never cashed, you're not out any money, but if you use a money order, you may have to pay a stop-payment fee in excess of the face value of the order to get reimbursed—a loss no matter what.) Tip: When writing the check, jot down the address and phone number of the firm in the memo field and in your check register. This way, you're sure to be able to get in touch with the firm if you don't receive the catalog. (Do this if you order and pay by check, too, since you may inadvertently toss the catalog and later regret it.) Don't send stamps unless they're requested, and don't assume you can pay for a catalog by credit card—call and ask first.

Receiving Catalogs. Catalog publication schedules vary, and when firms run out of catalogs, are between printings, or issue catalogs seasonally, there can be a delay of weeks or months before you receive one. Some firms notify customers of delays; most don't. Consequently, please allow six to eight weeks to receive your catalog.

PRICE QUOTES

Some mail-order firms don't publish catalogs, but sell their goods on a price-quote basis. Their name-brand goods can be identified by manufacturer's name, stock or model number, and color or pattern name or code. Cameras, appliances, audio and TV/video components, tableware, furniture, and sporting goods are commonly sold by discounters on a price-quote basis.

A price quote is simply the statement of the cost of that item from that firm. The company may guarantee that price for a limited period of time or until stock is depleted. Some firms include tax, shipping charges, insurance, and handling in their price quotes, giving you one figure for the final cost.

Finding the Information. Before writing or calling for a price quote, have the manufacturer's name, product code (model or style number or pattern name), and size and color information, if applicable. You'll find this information on the factory cartons or tags of goods in stores and in manufacturers' brochures. If you're pricing an item you found in a catalog, remember to look for the manufacturer's data, not the vendor's catalog code numbers. If you're using a buying guide or magazine as a source for information, verify the information before requesting a price quote—the reference may be out of date or contain typos.

Price Quotes by Letter. Most of the firms listed in this book will give quotes over the phone—in fact, many prefer it. When you write requesting price quotes, include all of the available information about the item or items. Leave blanks next to each item so that the person giving the quote can enter the price, shipping cost or estimate, and related charges. Ask the firm to note how long it will honor the given prices, and ask for prices of no more than three items at a time. Note: You must include an SASE with your request if you want a response.

Price Quotes by Phone. Have all of the information in front of you when you call. Don't make collect calls, and to avoid problems later, take down the salesperson's name, and make notes of the conversation.

HOW TO ORDER

Before ordering, make sure you're getting the best deal.

COST COMPARISONS

Your chief consideration is the delivered price of the product. Compute this from your price quotes and/or catalogs, then compare the figure to the delivered cost of the item if purchased from a local supplier. Consider mileage costs if you must drive to the local source, parking fees, sales and use tax, shipping and trucking, installation, etc. If you're buying a gift, compare the costs of having the mail-order firm wrap and send the item for you to the value of your own time, and materials and mailing costs. Finally, weigh the intangibles—return policies, the prospect of waiting for a mail delivery versus getting the item immediately, the guarantees offered by the retailer and mail-order firm, etc. After contemplating costs and variables, you'll reach the bottom line and best buying option.

Before ordering any large item, measure all of the doorways through which the article must pass, allowing for narrow hallways, stairs, and the like.

ORDERING

If the catalog is more than six months old and unless it's an annual, verify stock availability and prices by phone, or request a new edition and order from that. (You may find yourself billed for the difference between the old price and the new if you order from an out-of-date catalog.) Use the catalog order form, along with the self-sticking address label on the catalog. If there's no order blank, use one from another catalog as a guide. Transcribe the code numbers, names of items, number of items ordered, units, prices, tax, and shipping charges onto a separate piece of paper. Include your name, address, and phone number, the firm's name and address, and appropriate information if you're having the order sent to another address. Note any minimum-order requirements. Make a copy of the order, and file it with the catalog.

Second Choices and Substitutions. When the firm advises it and you're willing to accept them, give second choices. These usually refer to differences in color, not product. If you'll accept substitutions, which may be different products that the firm considers comparable to what you ordered, you must give permission in writing on the order form. It's unlawful for a firm to make substitutions without written authorization from the buyer. If you don't want second choices and want to be sure the firm knows this, write "NO SECOND CHOICES OR SUBSTITUTIONS ACCEPTED" in red on the order form.

PHONE ORDERS

Phone orders have a number of advantages over mail orders. They're usually processed more quickly and, when the phone operator has stock information, you'll know right away whether an item is available. Before picking up the phone to place your order, follow this procedure:

1. Have your credit card ready.
2. Make sure the card is one that's accepted by the firm, has not expired, and has a credit line sufficient for the purchase.
3. Have the delivery name, address, and ZIP code available.
4. Fill out the order form to use as a guide and as a record of the transaction. Include the catalog code numbers, units, colors, sizes, etc.
5. Have the catalog from which you're ordering at hand—the operator may ask for encoded information on the address label.
6. When you place the call, ask the operator the following:
7. What is your name or operator number?
8. What are the terms of the return policy (unless they're clearly stated in the catalog)?
9. Are any of the items you're ordering out of stock? If yes, when is new stock expected?
10. When will the order be shipped?
11. Will any of the items be shipped separately?
12. What is the total, including shipping and tax, that will be charged to my account?
13. What is my order number?

Many operators are required to ask for your home phone number, and sometimes your office number as well. This is done so that they can verify that you are the person placing the order, not a criminal who has obtained your card information illegally. Since the firm may be stuck with the bill if the charge is fraudulent, it may refuse your order if you won't divulge your number, especially if you're buying certain types of goods and your order total is high.

While you're on the phone, the operator may try to "upsell" you, or get you to buy more goods. Beware of such unplanned purchases if you're trying to stick to a budget, but listen—you may be offered a real bargain on goods the firm wants to clear out. When this happens, the company's loss is your gain. Just make sure you really want the item, since a bargain you'll never use is no bargain at all.

Once the transaction is completed and you've noted the operator's name or number, recorded the order number, checked off the items you ordered, struck off those you didn't, entered the billing amount, and noted the date of the call, put this record in your file with the catalog. They may prove valuable later if you have problems with your order.

BUYING AT WHOLESALE

Buying at true wholesale assumes that you're operating as a business, which intends to resell what you're buying, whether in its purchased state or in another form. You can buy at wholesale from those firms listed in this book that have a star in the row of symbols—but only if you and/or your order qualify. At least one of the following special sales terms will apply to your order:

Letterhead or Business Card Required. This provides evidence that you're doing business as a company, not as an individual.

Resale Number or Business Certificate Required. This proves that you're registered with local authorities as a business entity. Resale numbers are usually required for sales tax exemption.

Bank and Credit References Required. These are not usually necessary unless you want to open an account or have the order invoiced instead of paying when you place it.

Limitation of Payment Methods. Some firms allow you to charge a wholesale order to a credit card, and some require a check or money order—especially with the first order.

Minimum Order Requirements. Minimums almost invariably apply to wholesale orders; they're usually stated in dollars, although they may be in number of items or multiples, and sometimes a combination of the two.

Many of the firms listed in this book that sell at wholesale will send you the same catalog that consumers receive, with a discount schedule or a separate price list. Some have completely separate retail and wholesale catalogs, with different product lines. Wholesale catalogs often have much less descriptive information than their consumer equivalents, making "sample orders" quite valuable. Because return policies are customarily strict—restocking fees of 10% to 25% are often charged—be sure you know what you're buying before you order. (It's not wise to buy anything that's marked "final sale, no returns accepted.") On the positive side, the shipping costs are usually charged as a fraction of the order value, or are the actual shipping costs, paid C.O.D. to the carrier. In several comparisons to the rates charged to consumers, they worked out to much less—which should surprise no one who has bought by mail recently.

Be sure to check the listing before contacting the company as a wholesale buyer, since wholesale sales terms may be noted in the text. And please don't ask the company to accept your order if you won't meet their terms.

PAYMENT

There are two basic ways to pay for your order: now or later. You can prepay, using a check, money order, or debit card, or buy on credit. The distinction between these types of payments is based on the rules that apply to refunds under the FTC Mail or Telephone Order Rule, but some methods have characteristics of both categories.

Prepaid Orders. Payments made by check or money order are sometimes called "cash" by catalogers, since the firm receives dollars instead of extending credit on the basis of a promise to pay.

Personal checks, accepted by most firms, are inexpensive and can be sent without going to the bank or post office. Since some firms wait until your check has cleared before sending your order, shipment may be delayed by as much as two weeks. Checks do provide you with a receipt (the canceled check), which is returned with your monthly statement. (If your bank is dropping this service, or charging extra for it, consider using another bank or paying by credit card.) Use the "memo" space on your checks to jot down the firm's address, so if you lose track of the company in the future, you'll have a way to find it again.

Certified checks are guaranteed personal checks. You bring your check to the bank on which it's drawn and pay a fee of about $5 to $9. The bank marks the check "certified" and freezes that sum in your account. Every company that accepts personal checks will accept a certified check, and the guarantee of funds should obviate the delay for clearance. The canceled certified check is returned with the other canceled checks in your statement. Firms that request certified checks for payment will usually accept a bank check, a teller's check, or a cashier's check as well.

Bank money orders are issued by banks for a fee, usually $1 to $3. Ask the teller for a money order in the desired amount and fill in the firm's name and your name and address. If the order isn't dated mechanically, insert the date. Most come with a carbon receipt; some have stubs that should be filled in on the spot before you forget the information.

Bank money orders are generally treated as certified checks (i.e., no waiting for clearance). If necessary, you can have the order traced, payment stopped, and a refund issued. You'll find this vital if your order is lost in the mail, since there's always a chance it has been intercepted.

Postal money orders, sold at the post office, are available in amounts up to $700 and cost 75 cents. They're self-receipting and dated, and can be replaced if the order is lost or stolen. Copies of the cashed money order can be obtained through the post office for up to two years after it's paid. This can prove helpful in settling disputes with firms that claim nonreceipt of payment. And, like stamped envelopes and stamps, money orders can be bought from postal carriers by customers who live on rural routes or who have limited access to the post office.

Credit, Charge, and Debit Cards. Those wafers of plastic in your wallet have been important factors in the mail-order boom, and the pairing of 800 lines and credit cards has proven an irresistible combination for millions of consumers, creating phenomenal growth in phone orders.

Paying for an order with a credit card is simplicity itself—use a card accepted by the firm, make out the order form, and provide your account number, card expiration date, phone number, and signature in the blanks. If you're ordering from a catalog without a form, supply the same information on a sheet of paper. Using credit cards can make life easier if the shipping costs aren't given or are difficult to calculate—they'll be added to the order total, and the order won't be held up as it might be if you paid by check or with a money order. Always check the minimum-order requirements when using a card, since they're often higher than those imposed on prepaid orders.

"Debit" cards deserve a special mention because they may *look* like regular credit cards, but when the issuing bank receives the invoices for purchases, it deducts those amounts from your checking, savings, or money management account. This makes the debit card an electronic, instantly debited check, not a credit card, and it's important to know that the FTC views debit-card payments as cash payments. See the discussion of the FTC Mail or Telephone Order Rule for more information on the debit-card issue.

RETURN POLICIES

Most catalog firms guarantee satisfaction and will accept returns within 10, 14, or 30 days after you've received the order. Firms selling on a price-quote basis usually accept returns only if the product is defective.

Some goods—personalized or monogrammed, custom-made, surplus, and sale items—are routinely exempted from full return policies. (If a firm has to special-order an item for you, it may refuse to accept returns on that item—and may require you to buy a minimum number or amount.) Health regulations usually prohibit returns of intimate apparel and bathing suits, but some companies will accept them. For more information, see "Returns," page 602.

Check the company's return policy before ordering. If you're shopping for a big-ticket item that carries a manufacturer's warranty, ask the mail-order firm for a copy of the warranty before you buy, and see "Evaluating Warranties," page 607, for determining its value.

CANCELING YOUR ORDER

When you order goods or services from a firm, whether by phone or mail, you enter into a contract of sale. You don't have the right to call the firm and rescind an order, nor do you have the right to stop payment on a check or money order on the basis of what an FTC staffer describes as "buyer's remorse." (This term seems almost poetic in an industry that thrives on impulse purchases.) State laws vary on matters of contract, but, strictly speaking, your second thoughts might give the firm cause to bring legal action against you. This is especially true if the company has undertaken action on an order, in what is termed "constructive acceptance of payment."

But if, after placing an order, you learn that the firm is in financial trouble or has a bad business record, stopping payment would seem worth the risk. If you're considering canceling an order, check the terms of the offer first. Magazine and book subscriptions are often sent on an approval basis, giving you a cancellation option anyway. Goods offered with an unconditional guarantee of satisfaction can be sent back when they arrive. If these terms aren't offered and you're determined to cancel, contact the firm to discuss the matter.

SHIPPING, HANDLING, INSURANCE, AND SALES TAX

When comparison shopping, consider shipping, insurance, tax, and handling as part of the total. (See "Cost Comparisons," page 588, for more information.)

SHIPPING

This section addresses the concerns of consumers buying from U.S. firms who are having goods delivered to addresses in the United States.

Shipping Computations. The largest ancillary cost of an order is usually shipping, which is calculated in a variety of methods described below.

Postpaid item prices, which include shipping charges, are popular because there's no math for customers to do—although the shipping and packing costs are passed along in the item price.

Itemized shipping costs are often seen as amounts in parentheses after the product price or code number. If you compare the UPS or USPS tape on the delivered parcel, you may find that the shipping fee you paid the firm is higher than what it really cost. But your fee may include the cost of packing and materials, or it may be prorated. (A California firm might compute all shipping charges based on the price of sending goods to Kansas, midway across the country, making up on local deliveries what it loses on shipments to the East Coast.) And there are some firms that, quite simply, seem to be gouging the consumer with shipping charges that are far higher than their real costs. If you feel charges are exorbitant, contact the company and protest—or take your business elsewhere.

Numeric charges are based on the number of items you're ordering, as in "$2.50 for the first item; 75 cents each additional item." Companies often limit these kinds of charges, so additional purchases made after you reach a certain number of items are exempted from shipping charges entirely.

Flat order fees are simple dollar amounts charged on all orders, usually regardless of the number of items or weight. (Extra charges may apply if part of the order is shipped to another address.) A flat fee may represent a bargain if you're placing a large order, but note that some firms selling this way will charge extra for heavy, outsized, or fragile items. Check the catalog carefully before ordering.

Free shipping is offered, often by smaller companies, on large orders. Customarily, orders under a certain dollar or item amount are charged shipping on some basis, but if your order exceeds a certain amount, no shipping is charged. The fact is often noted on the order blank—"on orders $100 and over, WE pay postage" or "free shipping on three dozen pairs or more same size, style, and color"—usually with the proviso that the order must be sent to one address.

Sliding scales, tied to the cost of the order, are used by many companies. For example, if the goods total $15.00, you pay $2.75 for shipping; from $15.01 to $30.00, the charge is $3.50, etc. This is great if you're ordering many inexpensive, heavy items, but it seems unfair when you're buying one expensive thing. Some firms remedy this by using itemized shipping charges for small, high-ticket goods, and most limit the shipping charges to a maximum dollar amount, usually $7 to $12.

Tables, based on the weight and sometimes delivery distance of the order, require the most work on your part: You must tally the shipping weights given with the item prices, find your zone or area on the rate chart, and then compute the shipping charges. Outsized goods will have to be shipped by truck; their catalog code numbers often have a suffix letter indicating this. Some firms include in their catalogs all the rate charts you'll need to figure exact costs; others state at the bottom of the order form, "Add enough for postage and insurance. We will refund overpayment." In this case, the best solution is to pay by credit card, or call the firm itself and ask the shipping department to give you a quick calculation over the phone. If you're paying by check, you could send in the order without adding anything for shipping and ask the firm to bill you, but this may delay delivery.

Saving on Shipping Costs. When you have a chance to save on shipping by placing a large order, consult friends and coworkers to see whether they want to combine orders with you. But count the time spent conferring, consolidating orders, and distributing the goods as part of the cost of the order.

Carriers. No matter which method a firm uses to calculate shipping, it will usually send your goods by USPS, UPS, truck, or an overnight delivery service.

United Parcel Service (UPS): UPS is the delivery system many businesses prefer for mail order. UPS is cheaper, all costs considered, than USPS; it automatically insures each package for up to $100.

United States Postal Service (USPS)—Parcel Post (PP): The costs for Parcel Post, or fourth-class mail, are somewhat higher than UPS charges, but Parcel Post offers one distinct advantage: Only packages sent by the U.S. Postal Service can be delivered to a post-office box. (UPS must have a street address to deliver goods, although carriers will usually deliver to rural routes.) If you're having a package sent to a post-office box, write "DELIVERY BY PARCEL POST ONLY; UPS NOT ACCEPTABLE" in bold red letters on the order form, unless there's a box to check to indicate your preference. On your check, write "GOODS TO BE DELIVERED BY PARCEL POST ONLY." When the firm cashes the check, it's agreeing implicitly to this arrangement and should send the goods by Parcel Post.

Truck: When the firm specifies that an item must be sent by truck, or if you've ordered both mailable and nonmailable (outsized) goods, the entire order may be sent by truck. Sometimes firms indicate that goods are to be trucked with the term "FOB" or "freight," followed by the word "warehouse," "manufacturer," or the name of the city from which the goods are trucked. "FOB" stands for "free on board," and it means that the trucking charges will be billed from that point. When "manufacturer" follows FOB in the catalog, it means that the mail-order firm is probably having that item "drop-shipped," or sent from the manufacturer, instead of maintaining its own warehouse inventories of the product. If you're ordering nonmailable goods that you think will be drop-shipped, ask for the location of the manufacturer's warehouse so that you can estimate the trucking costs. If you want the item quickly, ask the mail-order company to verify that the manufacturer has the product in stock before placing the order, and whether the manufacturer can ship it by an overnight service.

Truck charges are usually collected in cash or certified check upon delivery, and the additional expense is a real factor to consider when ordering very heavy items from a firm that's located far away. Truckers usually make "dump deliveries," meaning they unload the goods on the sidewalk in front of your home or business. For an additional fee (usually $10 to $20), you can usually have the goods delivered inside your house or apartment. Additional fees may be incurred if your order happens to be the only one the trucker is picking up from the firm that day or if the driver has to notify you of delivery. Before ordering an item you know will have to be trucked, get the price plus trucking charges and compare it to the cost of the same item if locally bought and delivered.

HANDLING

Some firms charge an extra fee for processing or packing your order (usually $1 to $5), which is often waived on orders over a certain dollar amount. The handling fee helps to cover the costs of labor and materials used in processing your order, and it, like the shipping fee, may be taxed in certain states.

INSURANCE

Packages shipped by UPS are automatically insured for up to $100; you shouldn't have to pay extra insurance on those orders. (If you're buying from a firm that delivers via UPS but has a preprinted charge for insurance on the order form, don't pay it.) UPS charges an additional fee for each additional $100 in value on the same package, the cost of which is usually covered in the shipping charge. The USPS doesn't insure automatically, so if you're having your package delivered by mail, not UPS, be sure to request insurance. Charges for postal insurance range from 70 cents for goods worth up to $50, to $5.00 for package contents worth from $400.01 to $500.00. Goods valued at more than $500 but under $25,000 must be registered as well as insured, and some goods can't be insured. If the item you're buying is uninsurable, have the firm arrange shipping with a carrier that will insure it. If you're not sure whether the firm will insure your goods, ask—before you order. The small fee is a worthwhile expense, something you know if you've ever had an uninsured order go awry. (See "Accepting Deliveries," page 599, for more information.)

Most insurance claims arise as a result of damage to or loss of goods.

Procedures for claiming and reimbursement vary according to the carrier's rules and the firm's policy, but contact the firm as soon as you discover any damage to your shipment and ask the customer service department what to do. If there is documentation (signature of receipt on the UPS carrier's log or USPS insurance receipt), the claim can be verified and processed, and eventually you should be reimbursed or receive replacement goods. If there is no documentation and the worst happens—the goods never arrive—the firm may absorb the loss and send a replacement order. (If you paid with a credit card, you should be able to get a charge-back. See "The Fair Credit Billing Act," page 612, for more information.) But if repeated entreaties for a refund or duplicate order meet resistance, state your case to the agencies listed in "Obtaining Help," page 610. And be sure to tell BWBM—see "Feedback," page 615, for more information.

SALES TAX

You're supposed to pay sales tax on an order if you're having goods delivered to an address in the same state in which the mail-order firm, a branch office, or representative is located, and when the goods ordered are taxable under the laws prevailing in the area. Most states require payment of sales tax on handling, packing, and shipping charges, as well as the goods.

Those are the general rules. The right of a state to create its own definition of "doing business" in that state, or "establishing nexus," rankles consumers who have to pay tax on what they perceive as out-of-state orders, and businesses that have to be tax collectors for 50 states. The issue of nexus is no stranger to the U.S. Supreme Court; one energetic individual took on both Sears and Montgomery Ward over 40 years ago and lost, and other mail-order firms have done battle with state governments and lost as well.

State governments are trying to collect tax on all mail-order purchases delivered to residents of their states, calling such a tax a "use" tax. Mail-order companies envision an accounting nightmare, and consumers stand to lose one of the traditional benefits of shopping out-of-state: not paying sales tax on their purchases (unless nexus exists). The court cases now being decided are running in favor of the tax department, which means we're seeing changes—more firms are collecting taxes from more customers. And regardless of the practices of the company, your personal obligations are never waived—if your state requires you to pay sales tax on purchases from out-of-state firms, you're required to do so. The common perception of actual compliance with such a law is "I'd have to have rocks in my head to pay tax if I don't *have* to." If you have questions, and especially if your purchases include business deductions and involve depreciation, you'd be smart to consult an accountant or the local tax authority for guidance.

SHIPMENTS ABROAD

Shipments to and from Canada. Since the North American Free Trade Agreement (NAFTA) was passed, commerce between the U.S. and Canada is much more fluid, although not all tariff problems have been eliminated. Mail-order companies that will ship to Canada are indicated by the maple leaf icon. If you're living in Canada, the best way to determine the tariffs, shipping, and payment policies is to ask the vendor. He or she will be well versed on serving customers like you.

Shipments to APO/FPO Addresses. Most of the firms listed in this book will send goods to APO and FPO addresses. Finding out which is easy: Look for an American flag symbol above the company description.

Mail-order firms generally ship orders via the USPS's PAL (parcel airlift) to the military mail dispatch center, where they are shipped overseas via SAM (space available mail). The size restrictions are the same as those for regular first-class mail, or 108" combined length and girth, and 70 pounds maximum. Firms sometimes charge additional handling fees for shipping to APO/FPO addresses, so read the catalog carefully and write for a shipping estimate before ordering if instructions aren't clear. Please note that neither UPS nor Federal Express makes APO/FPO deliveries, and that the USPS does not offer C.O.D. service to APO/FPO addresses.

Shipments Worldwide. Many of the companies that ship to Canada and U.S. military personnel also ship orders worldwide—indicated by the globe symbol. If you're planning to have goods delivered to Japan, Israel, Europe, or any other address not in the United States or Canada, see the catalog for details (if available) on the firm's shipping policy. If it's not clear, or if the firm sells on a price-quote basis, write or call the company and request a shipping quote before sending any funds. Since the employees of firms listed in this book are unlikely to be familiar with import restrictions and duty rates in other countries, check before placing your order to avoid unpleasant surprises. Most firms request payment in U.S. funds; this may be most easily handled by charging your purchase to your credit card, but before ordering, check with your issuing bank for rates and charges that may apply to converting funds.

RECEIVING YOUR ORDER

What do you do when your order arrives? And if it doesn't? The following section details your basic rights and responsibilities.

ACCEPTING DELIVERIES

When the postal or UPS carrier or trucker delivers your order, inspect the carton, bag, or crate before signing for it. If you're having someone else accept the package, ask that person to do the same. If the packaging is extensively damaged, you can refuse to sign for or accept the goods. See "Returns," in this section, for caveats on this practice.

If the box, bag, or carton is in good condition, accept it and open it as soon as possible. Unpack the goods carefully, putting aside the packing materials and any inserts until you've examined the contents. Most firms include a copy of your order form or a computerized invoice itemizing the order. If it's a printout or there's no invoice at all, get your copy of the order and check to make sure you got what you requested. Check the outside of the box, since some firms insert the invoice with the packing slip in a plastic envelope affixed to the top or side of the carton.

Check your order for the following: damaged goods; short shipments; unauthorized substitutions; wrong sizes, colors, styles, or models; warranty forms if the products carry manufacturers' warranties; missing parts; and instruction sheets if a product requires assembly. Make sure ensembles are complete—that scarves, belts, hats, vests, ties, ascots, and other components have been included. Test electronic goods as soon as possible to make sure they function properly, and do not fill out the warranty card until you've tried the product and are satisfied that it's not defective. (Check the product itself for signs that it has been used. If you've been sold a demonstration model, reconditioned unit, or someone else's return as new and unused goods, you should seriously consider returning it—or negotiating a lower price.) Try on clothing and shoes to make sure they fit. Check printed, engraved, or monogrammed goods for accuracy. If you decide to return a product, see "Returns" for more information.

If the goods are damaged, contact the seller immediately. Describe the condition of the goods and what you'd like done to correct the problem. If the firm asks you to file a complaint with the delivery service, request shipping information from the seller (the seller's shipping address, day of shipment, seller's account number, applicable shipment codes, and other relevant data). File the complaint with the delivery service, documenting your claim with photographs, if it seems necessary, and send a copy of the complaint to the seller. If you charged the purchase on a card with an extended warranty program, contact the issuer about the matter. Be persistent but reasonable.

If you receive a short shipment (one or more items you ordered are not included in the package), the firm may have inserted a notice that the item is being shipped separately or an option notice if it's out of stock. (See "The Option Notice," page 601, for more information.) Some companies don't back order and will include a refund check with the order or under separate cover when a product is out of stock, or bill your account with the adjusted total if you used a credit card. If your shipment is short and there's no explanation, first check the catalog from which you ordered to see whether that item is shipped from the manufacturer or shipped separately by the firm. If there's no mention of special shipping conditions or delays in shipment in the catalog, contact the firm immediately.

DELAYED SHIPMENTS

What constitutes a real delay in receiving an order? What should you expect from the company if it has to delay shipping your order? The following section details your basic rights and responsibilities in this event.

The FTC Mail or Telephone Order Rule. The Federal Trade Commission's "Mail or Telephone Order Rule" addresses one of the biggest problems in the mail-order industry: late delivery. Mail-order shoppers should understand the principles of the Rule, know what types of transactions are exempt from its protection, and understand what actions they're obliged to take to ensure protection under the regulations.

Please note: When a state or county has enacted laws similar in purpose to the functions of the FTC Mail or Telephone Order Rule, the law that gives the consumer the most protection takes precedence.

General terms of the Rule: The Rule specifies that a firm, or "seller," must ship goods within 30 days of receipt of a properly completed order, unless the firm asks for more time in its catalog, advertisement, or promotional literature. The operative term here is "ship"—the firm does not have to have delivered the goods within 30 days under the terms of the Rule. And it must have received a properly completed order: Your check or money order must be good, your credit must be good if you're charging the order, and the firm must have all the information necessary to process the order. The 30-day clock begins ticking when the firm gets your check or money order made out in the proper amount, but stops if it is dishonored. If you're paying with a credit card, it begins when the firm receives valid account data—*not* when it charges the card.

If your check or money order is insufficient to cover the order total or is dishonored by the bank, if your credit card payment is refused authorization, or if you neglect to include data necessary to the processing of your order (which could include size or color information, your address, etc.), the 30-day clock will not start until the problems are remedied—the firm receives complete payment, payment is honored by the bank, the credit card purchase is authorized, or you supply the missing data.

Exceptions to the Rule: The 30-day limit applies only when a firm does not ask you to allow more time for shipment. (Most qualifiers request extra time for delivery, which only confuses the issue.) Certain kinds of goods and purchases are not protected by the Rule. These include seeds and growing plants; C.O.D. orders; purchases made under negative-option plans (such as book and record clubs); and magazine subscriptions and other "serial deliveries," except for the first issue. Genuinely "free" items don't fall under the Rule, but catalogs for which payment or compensation is requested are protected.

Assuming your order is covered under the Rule, the firm from which you're ordering must follow a specific procedure if it is unable to ship your order within 30 days. You must respond under the terms of the Rule if you want to retain all of your rights. Read on.

The Option Notice: If a firm is unable to ship within 30 days of receiving your properly completed order, or by the deadline given in its literature, it must send you an option notice. An option notice written in compliance with the Rule will tell you that there is a delay in shipping the item and may include a revised shipping date. If it does, and that date is up to 30 days later than the original deadline (either 30 days or a date specified by the firm), it should offer you the option of consenting to the delay or canceling the order and receiving a refund. The option notice must also state that lack of response on your part is implied consent to the delay. If you decide to cancel the order, the firm must receive the cancellation before it ships the order.

If the new shipping deadline is over 30 days after the original date, or the firm can't provide a revised shipping date, the option notice must say so. The notice should also state that your order will be automatically canceled unless the firm receives consent to the delay from you within 30 days of the original shipping date, and unless it is able to ship the order within 30 days after the original deadline and has not received an order cancellation from you as of the time of shipping.

The firm is required to send notices by first-class mail and to provide you with a cost-free means of response—a prepaid business-reply envelope or postcard. If you want to cancel an order, get the response back to the firm as quickly as possible after you receive the option notice. Photocopy the card, form, or letter, and send it "return receipt requested" if you want absolute proof of the date it was received. (If the firm ships your order the day after it received your cancellation, and you can prove it, you have the right to refuse delivery, have the order returned to the firm at its expense, and claim a prompt refund or credit.)

The Renewed Option Notice: When a firm is unable to meet its revised shipping deadline, it must send you a renewed option notice in advance of the revised deadline. Unlike the first notice, second and subsequent notices must state that if you don't agree in writing to a new shipping date or indefinite delay, the order will be canceled. And the consent to a second delay must be received before the first delay period ends, or the order must be canceled, according to the Rule.

If you consent to an indefinite delay, you retain the right to cancel the order at any time before the goods are shipped. And the firm itself may cancel the order if it is unable to ship the goods within the delay period, and must cancel the order under a variety of circumstances.

The Rule and Refunds: Under the terms of the Rule, when you or the firm cancel the order, you're entitled to a prompt refund. If your order was prepaid, the firm must send you a refund check or money order by first-class mail within seven working days after the cancellation. If you paid with a debit card, inform the firm when you cancel or when it notifies you that it's canceling the order that it must treat the payment as if it were cash, a check, or a money order, and reimburse your account within seven working days or send you a refund check. If you used a credit card, the Rule states that refunds must be made within one billing cycle. (We assume that these "refunds" are credits to your account, which will void the charge made for the goods.) The firm is not permitted to substitute credit vouchers for its own goods instead of making a reimbursement.

RETURNS, GUARANTEES, AND WARRANTIES

Your right to return goods is determined by the policy of the firm, the problem with the order, the conditions under which you make the return, and state and federal laws. See "Return Policies" and "Accepting Deliveries" for general information. Product warranties, whether written or implied, apply to many goods bought by mail. "Guarantees and Warranties," page 604, provides a comprehensive discussion of all types of warranties.

RETURNS

Return policies are often extensions of a firm's pledge of satisfaction. The policy determines how quickly you must return the product after receipt (if there's a time limit), acceptable causes for return, and what the firm will do to remedy the problem. Some companies will take anything back, but most exclude custom-made goods, personalized items, special orders, intimate apparel, bathing suits, and hats. Some also exempt sale items. Even a no-frills policy usually makes provisions for exchanges when the firm has erred or if the product is defective. It's important to read "Implied Warranties" for information on laws concerning product performance and rights you may have that are not stated in the catalog.

Obtaining Authorization. Before returning a product for any reason, check the inserts that may have been packed with the order, as well as the catalog, for instructions on return procedures. If there are no instructions, contact the firm for authorization to return the item. This is easiest handled by phone; you'll usually receive an "RMA," or authorization number, which you must use on all correspondence concerning that return, and on the package when you send it back. The reverse side of the statement that was enclosed with your order may be printed as a return form; if so, complete it. If it's not, write a letter: State the reason for the return, the item price and order number, date of delivery, and what you'd like done. Depending on the firm's policy, you may request repairs or replacement of the item, an exchange, a refund check, a credit to your charge account, or store credit for future purchases from the firm. Keep a photocopy of the letter or notes of your phone conversation for your files.

Restocking Fees. Some firms impose a charge on returned goods, to offset the labor and incidental costs of returning the item to inventory. Restocking fees, usually 10% to 15% of the price of the item, are most commonly charged by firms selling furniture, appliances, and electronics. Restocking fees are not usually charged when you're returning defective goods, or if the item was shipped incorrectly.

Sending the Item. Follow the mailing procedure outlined in the catalog, order insert, or authorization notice from the firm. When you send the goods back, include the return form or a dated letter with your name and address, the order number, the authorization number or name of the person approving the return (if applicable), and a statement of what you want—repair, exchange, refund, or credit. Keep file copies of your letter and invoices.

Pack the item in the original box and padding materials if requested, and insure it for the full value. Allow the firm at least 30 days to process the return or respond before writing or calling again, unless you were promised a more speedy resolution.

Refunds and Credits. If you want your charge account credited for the return, provide the relevant data. Not every firm will issue a refund check or credit your account; some offer replacement or repair of the product, an exchange, or catalog credit only.

Exchanges. If you're exchanging the product for something entirely different, state the catalog code number, size, color, price, unit, etc., of the item you want in the letter you enclose with the return or on the authorization form.

Postage Reimbursement. Some firms send UPS to pick up a return free; accept returns sent postage-collect; or will reimburse you for the shipping and insurance charges on a return. Lots will not. Businesses are not required by federal law to refund the cost of returning goods, even when the return is a result of the firm's error. State and local laws, however, may make provisions for this; check to see whether they do.

GUARANTEES AND WARRANTIES

Although the terms "guarantee" and "warranty" are virtually synonymous, they're distinguished here for the sake of clarity. In this book, a "guarantee" is the general pledge of satisfaction or service a firm offers on the sales it makes. Guarantees and related matters are discussed in "Return Policies," "Returns," and "Implied Warranties." A "warranty" is used to mean the written policy covering the performance of a particular product. Both guarantees and warranties are free; paid policies (including "extended warranties") are service contracts.

Warranties are regulated by state and federal law. Understanding policy terms will help you shop for the best product/warranty value; knowing your rights may mean the difference between paying for repairs or a replacement and having the firm or manufacturer do it.

The Warranty Act. The Magnuson-Moss Warranty—Federal Trade Commission Improvement Act, also known as the Warranty Act, is a 1975 law that regulates printed warranties. Oral "warranties"—the salesperson's assurance of product performance and pledge of satisfaction—are worthless unless they're in writing.

The Warranty Act requires that warranties be written in "simple and readily understood language" that states all terms and conditions. If the product costs more than $15, a copy of the warranty must be available before purchase. In a store, it should be posted on or near the product, or filed in a catalog of warranties kept on the premises with a notice posted concerning its location. Mail-order firms comply with the law by making copies of warranties available upon request.

The Warranty Act requires the warrantor to use the term "full" or "limited" in describing the policy. A single product can have several warranties covering different parts, and each can be labeled separately as "full" or "limited." For example, a TV set may have a full one-year policy on the set and a limited 90-day policy on the picture tube. Generally speaking, the conditions stated here apply to warranties on goods costing over $15.

Full warranties provide for repair or replacement of the product at no cost to you, including the removal and reinstallation of the item, if necessary. The warranty may be limited to a certain length of time and must state the period of coverage. Full warranties can't be limited to the original purchaser—the warrantor must honor the policy for the full term even if the item has changed hands. Implied warranties (see page 606) may not be limited in duration by the terms of the full warranty and, in some states, may last up to four years.

The item should be repaired within a "reasonable" length of time after you've notified the firm of the problem. If, after a "reasonable" number of attempts to repair, the product is still not functioning properly, you may invoke the "lemon provision." This entitles you to a replacement or refund for the product.

Registering your product with the warrantor under a full warranty is voluntary, a fact that must be stated clearly in the terms. You can send the registration card to the firm, but this is at your discretion and not necessary to maintain the protection of the warranty. You certainly have no obligation to provide any firm with the intimate details of your life—income, age, home-ownership status, purchasing and reading habits, dependents, pets, etc.—often solicited with such forms.

Limited warranties provide less coverage than full warranties. Under them, you can be required to remove, transport, and reinstall a product; to pay for labor if repairs are made; and to return the warranty card to the firm in order to validate the policy. The warrantor can also limit the warranty to the original purchaser and give you prorated refunds or credits for the product. (The "lemon provision" doesn't apply to a limited warranty.)

Warrantors may also limit implied warranties (see the following section) to the length of time their policies run, but no less. If they limit the implied-warranty time, they must also state: "Some states do not allow limitations on how long an implied warranty lasts, so the above limitation may not apply to you." The warrantor, however, may not limit the extent of protection you have under implied warranties.

Other provisions of the Warranty Act include the following:

- If you complain within the warranty period, the firm must act to remedy the problem within the terms of the warranty.
- If a written warranty is provided with the product, the warrantor can't exclude it from protection under implied warranties.
- A warrantor can exclude or limit consequential damages (see the following section) from coverage under both full and limited policies as long as the warranty states: "Some states do not allow the exclusion or limitation of incidental or consequential damages, so the above limitation or exclusion may not apply to you."
- All warranties must include information on whom to contact, where

to bring or mail the product, and the name, address, or toll-free phone number of the warrantor.

- All warranties, full and limited, must state: "This warranty gives you specific legal rights, and you may have other rights that vary from state to state."

Implied Warranties. Implied warranties are state laws that offer protection against major hidden defects in products. Every state has these laws, which cover every sale unless the seller states that no warranties or guarantees are offered—that goods are sold "as is." But if a particular product sold by a firm with a no-guarantee policy carries a written warranty, the implied warranty of the state is also valid on that item. The terms of implied warranties differ from state to state, but many have similar sorts of provisions.

The warranty of merchantability is a common implied warranty. It means that the product must function properly for conventional use—a freezer must freeze, a knife must cut, etc. If the product does not function properly and your state has a warranty of merchantability, you're probably entitled to a refund for that item.

The warranty of fitness for a particular purpose covers cases in which the seller cites or recommends special uses for the product. For example, if a seller says that a coat is "all-weather," it should offer protection in rain and snow. If it claims that a glue will "bond any two materials together," the glue should be able to do that. When a salesperson makes these assurances, check the printed product information to verify the recommendation or call the manufacturer. While the salesperson may have a direct incentive—commissions—to inveigle you into buying a product, the manufacturer should be more committed to your satisfaction and return business.

Consequential Damages. Incidental or consequential damages occur when a product malfunction causes damage to or loss of other property. The FTC uses the example of an engine block cracking when the antifreeze is faulty. Less extreme is the food spoilage caused by a refrigerator breakdown or the damage resulting from a leaky waterbed mattress.

Written warranties usually entitle you to consequential damages, but warrantors are allowed to exempt this coverage under both full and limited warranties. If the warrantor excludes consequential damages from coverage, the warranty must state: "Some states do not allow exclusion or limitation of incidental or consequential damages, so the above limitation or exclusion may not apply to you."

Provisions for consequential damages entitle you to compensation for the property damage or loss, as well as repair or replacement of the defective product. In the engine block example, the exemption of damages must be considered as a definite disadvantage when evaluating the product/warranty value.

Evaluating Warranties. Appraise the written warranty as thoroughly as you do the product's other features before you buy. In reading the warranty, bear in mind past experiences with products and warranty service from that manufacturer or seller, experiences with similar products, and your actual needs. Don't rush to buy the first model of a new product if you can wait. Later models are sure to be cheaper and better—just consider VCRs, CD players, and computers.

In evaluating a warranty, ask yourself the following questions:

- Is the warranty full or limited?
- Does it cover the whole product, or specific parts?
- How long is the warranty period?
- Do you contact the manufacturer, seller, or a service center for repairs?
- Will you have to remove, deliver, and reinstall the product yourself?
- Do you have to have repairs done by an authorized service center or representative? If so, how close is the nearest facility?
- Will the warrantor provide a temporary replacement for use while your product is being serviced?
- Are consequential damages excluded? If the product turns out to be defective, could the consequential damages result in a significant loss?
- If reimbursement is offered on a pro rata basis, is it computed on a time, use, or price schedule?
- Do you have the choice of a refund or replacement if the item can't be repaired?

Envision a worst-case scenario in which the product breaks down or malfunctions completely. What expenses could be incurred in consequential damages, supplying a substitute product or service, transporting the product to the service center or seller, and repair bills? Will returning the product be troublesome, and living without it while it's being repaired inconvenient? Your answers determine the value the warranty has for you. Consider that quotient along with the price and features of the product when comparison shopping to find your best buy.

Complying with Warranty Terms. Understanding and fulfilling the conditions of a warranty should be simple, but we've outlined a few tips that may make it easier:

- Read the warranty card as requested.
- Read the instructions or operations manual before using the product, and follow directions for use.

- Keep the warranty and dated receipt or proof of payment in a designated place.
- If the manufacturer offers a rebate on the product that requires sending the proof of payment, photocopy the receipt and keep the copy with the warranty.
- Abuse, neglect, and mishandling usually void the warranty. Other practices that may invalidate the policy include improper installation, repair or service by an unauthorized person or agency, use of the product on the wrong voltage, and commercial use. If others will be using the product, be sure they know how to operate it.
- Perform routine maintenance (cleaning, oiling, dusting, replacement of worn components, etc.) as required by the manual, but don't attempt repairs or maintenance that isn't required or permitted in the warranty or guide.

If you have a question about maintenance or use, contact the manufacturer or service center. If you void the warranty by violating its terms, you'll probably have to absorb the costs of repairs or replacement.

Obtaining Service. If the product breaks down or malfunctions, you'll find that you can expedite resolution if you follow these guidelines:

- Read the operating manual or instructions. The problem may be covered in a troubleshooting section, or you may find that you expected the product to do something for which it wasn't designed.
- Contact the warrantor, whose name, address, and/or phone number appear on the warranty, unless the seller offers service under warranty.
- Call, write, or visit as appropriate. State the nature of the problem, the date it occurred, and whether you want a repair, replacement, refund, and/or consequential damages. Bring a copy of the warranty and proof of payment when you visit, and include copies if you write. (Remember that your rights in respect to the nature and extent of compensation depend upon the terms of the warranty and laws prevailing in your area.)
- If you leave the product for repairs or have it picked up, get a signed receipt that includes the date on which it should be ready, an estimate of the bill if you have to pay for repairs, and the serial number of the product, if one is given.
- If you send the product, insure it for the full value. Include a letter describing the problem, the date on which it occurred, and how you'd like it resolved.
- After a call or visit, the FTC recommends sending a follow-up letter reiterating the conversation. Keep a photocopy, and send it by certi-

fied mail to the person or agency with which you spoke.

- Keep a log of all actions you take in having the warranty honored, including dates on which actions, visits, and calls were made, and keep a record of the expenses you incur in the process.
- If you've written to the seller or manufacturer concerning the problem and received no response after three to four weeks, write again. Include a photocopy of the first letter, ask for an answer within four weeks, and send the second letter by certified mail (keep a photocopy). Direct the letter to the head of customer relations or the warranty department, unless you've been dealing with an individual.
- If you've written to the manufacturer, it may help to contact the seller (or vice versa). A reputable firm doesn't want to merchandise through a seller who won't maintain good customer relations, and a responsible seller knows that marketing shoddy goods is bad for business. Bilateral appeals should be made after you've given the responsible party an opportunity to resolve the problem.
- If you have repairs done, ask to see the product demonstrated before you accept it, especially if you're paying for repairs. If there are indications that the problem may recur (e.g., it exhibits the same "symptoms" it had before it broke or malfunctioned), tell the service representative—it may be due to something that wasn't noticed during the repair.
- If you're paying for repairs, ask for a guarantee on parts and/or labor, so you won't face another bill if the product breaks down shortly after you begin using it again.
- If the product keeps malfunctioning after it is repaired and it is under full warranty, you can probably get a replacement or refund under the "lemon provision." Write to the manufacturer or seller, provide a history of the problems and repairs, plus a copy of the warranty, and ask for a replacement or refund. If the warranty is limited, the terms may entitle you to a replacement or refund. Write to the manufacturer or seller with the product history and a copy of the warranty, and ask for a new product or compensation.
- Explore your rights under your state's implied-warranty and consequential-damages laws. They may offer you protections not given in the product warranty.
- If you've been injured by a malfunctioning product, contact an attorney.
- If, after acting in good faith and allowing the manufacturer or seller time to resolve the problem, you are still dissatisfied, contact your local consumer-protection agency for advice.
- You may also report problems to other agencies and organizations. For more information, see "Obtaining Help," page 610.

COMPLAINTS

COMPLAINT PROCEDURES

A formal complaint is justified if you've notified the firm of a problem and asked for resolution, following procedures outlined in the catalog, warranty, or this guide, with unsatisfactory results. Give the firm one last chance to remedy the situation before asking for help from outside agencies. If your problem concerns nondelivery or dissatisfaction with a product and you paid with a credit card, you may be able to withhold payment or ask for a charge-back under the Fair Credit Billing Act. See "The Federal Trade Commission," page 612, for more information.

The Complaint Letter. State your complaint clearly and concisely with a history of the problem and all the appropriate documentation: photocopies of previous letters, proof of payment, the warranty, repair receipts, etc. Don't send original documents—use photocopies and keep the originals in your file. Make sure your letter includes your name and address, the order or product number or code and descriptive information about the product, and the method of payment you used. Type or print the letter, and please don't be abusive. Tell the firm exactly what you want done. Give a deadline of 30 days for a reply or resolution, and note that if you don't receive a response by that time, you'll report the firm to the U.S. Postal Service, Better Business Bureau, Direct Marketing Association, Federal Trade Commission, or other appropriate agency. (See "Obtaining Help," following, for information.)

If the firm doesn't acknowledge the request or you're not satisfied by the response, take action.

OBTAINING HELP

Several agencies and organizations can help you with different types of problems related to mail order. Some undertake investigations on a case-by-case basis, and others compile files on firms and act when the volume of complaints reaches a certain level.

When you seek help, provide a copy of your final complaint letter to the firm, as well as the documentation described in "The Complaint Letter."

Consumer Action Panels (CAPs). CAPs are third-party dispute resolution programs established by the industries they represent. They investigate consumer complaints, provide service information to consumers, and give their members suggestions on improving service to consumers.

MACAP helps with problems concerning major appliances. Write to Major Appliance Consumer Action Program, 20 N. Wacker Dr., Ste. 1231, Chicago, IL 60606, or call 800–621–0477 for information.

Better Business Bureaus (BBBs). Better Business Bureaus are self-regulatory agencies, funded by businesses and professional firms, that monitor advertising and selling practices, maintain files on firms, help resolve consumer complaints, and disseminate service information to consumers. BBBs also perform the vital service of responding to inquiries about a firm's selling history, although they can't make recommendations. Most BBBs have mediation and arbitration programs and are empowered to make awards (binding arbitration).

Whether you want to check a firm's record before ordering or file a complaint, you must contact the BBB nearest the company, not the office in your area. You can obtain a directory of BBB offices by calling 703–276–0100, or by sending your request and a self-addressed, stamped envelope to the Council of Better Business Bureaus, Inc., 4200 Wilson Blvd., Suite 800, Arlington, VA 22203–1804. Write to the appropriate office, and ask for a "consumer complaint" or "consumer inquiry" form, depending on your purpose. The Better Business Bureau also has a good website, which you can visit at http://www.bbb.org/.

Direct Marketing Association (DMA). The DMA is the largest and oldest trade organization of direct marketers and mail-order companies in existence. Over half of its members are non-U.S. firms; this gives it some clout in dealing with problematical foreign orders placed with member firms.

The DMA's Mail Order Action Line (MOAL) helps to resolve nondelivery problems with any direct-marketing firm, not just members. Upon receiving your written complaint, the DMA contacts the firm, attempts to resolve the problem, notifies you that it is involved, and asks you to allow 30 days for the firm to solve or act on the problem. To get help, send a copy of your complaint letter and documentation to Mail Order Action Line, DMA, 1111 19th St. NW, Ste. 1100, Washington, DC 20030–3606.

A consumer may also use the DMA's "Telephone Preference Service" and "Mail Preference Service" to reduce the number of solicitation calls and/or mailings he or she receives. The DMA will keep your name on a list for five years; marketers who want to avoid mailing or calling unreceptive consumers can consult the list before launching a sales campaign. Remember: This is a service that's used by marketers, but unless every firm from which you're receiving solicitations consults it, it will not stop all contacts (although most reputable firms do use it). To reduce mail, write your name and address with your request, clearly mark it "HOME" (this service does not work for business addresses), and send to Mail Preference Service, Direct Marketing Association, P.O. Box 9008, Farmingdale, NY 11735–9008. To reduce the number of solicitation calls you receive, write your name, address, and *home* phone number (again, mark it "HOME") and mail to Telephone Preference Service, Direct Marketing Association, P.O. Box 9014, Farmingdale, NY 11735–9014. If, after a few months, you're still receiving calls and/or mail, try dealing with the marketer directly. And there is nothing wrong with politely saying "good-bye" to a complete stranger who intrudes in your home via the phone line, and hanging up. You have no obligation to have a conversation; moreover, you should be suspect of any person calling from one firm saying they "represent" another, such as your phone company or credit-card firm. Request the person's name, phone number, and the name of the firm they work for, and hang up. Then contact the "referring" firm and make a complaint. Unscrupulous companies trying to induce you to switch phone service or otherwise garner your business may misrepresent themselves, and this helps to identify and stop such activity. And even if the referring firm authorized the contact, you can make it clear that you don't want your data shared with third parties.

The Federal Trade Commission (FTC). The FTC is a law-enforcement agency that protects the public against anticompetitive, unfair, and deceptive business practices. While it doesn't act on "individual" complaints, it does use your complaint letters to build files on firms. When the volume or nature of problems indicates an investigation is justified, the FTC will act. Several levels of action are possible, including court injunctions and fines of up to $10,000 for each day the violation is occurring. Report deviations from FTC regulations; your letter may be the one that prompts an investigation.

The Fair Credit Billing Act (FCBA). Passed in 1975 under the FTC's Consumer Credit Protection Act, this act offers mail-order shoppers who use credit cards as payment some real leverage if they have a problem with nondelivery. The Act established a settlement procedure for billing errors that include, among other discrepancies, charges for goods or services not accepted or not delivered as agreed. The procedure works as follows:

1. You must write to the creditor (phoning will not trigger FCBA protection) at the "billing error" address given on the bill.
2. The letter must include your name and account number, the dollar amount of the error, and a statement of why you believe the error exists.
3. The letter must be received by the creditor within 60 days after the first bill with the error was mailed to you. The FTC recommends sending it by certified mail, return receipt requested.
4. The creditor has to acknowledge your letter, in writing, within 30 days of receipt, unless the problem is resolved within that time.

5. You do not have to pay the disputed amount, the related portion of the minimum payment, or the related finance charges while it is being disputed.
6. If an error is found, the creditor must write to you, explaining the correction. The disputed amount must be credited to your account and related finance charges must be removed. If the creditor finds that you owe part of the amount, it must be explained in writing.
7. If the creditor finds that the bill is correct, the reasons must be explained in writing and the amount owed stated. You will be liable for finance charges accrued during the dispute and missed minimum payments.
8. You may continue to dispute at this point, but only if your state's laws give you the right to take action against the seller rather than the creditor. Write to the creditor within 10 days of receiving the justification of the charge and state that you still refuse to pay the disputed amount. If you continue to challenge, contact your local consumer protection agency, since the creditor can begin collection proceedings against you and the agency may be able to recommend other means of handling the problem that don't jeopardize your credit rating.

Disputes over the quality of goods or services are covered under the FCBA if state law permits you to withhold payment from a seller. This applies to credit-card purchases over $50 that are made in your home state or within 100 miles of your mailing address. (The limits do not apply if the seller is also the card issuer, as is often the case with department stores.) Contact your local consumer protection agency for advice before taking action.

The United States Postal Service (USPS). The USPS takes action on complaints and resolves about 85% of the problems. This may be because, under provisions of the U.S. Code, it can go to court, get a restraining order, and withhold mail delivery to a company. (This is a very serious action and is never undertaken simply at a private citizen's request.) A number of readers have reported that the USPS acts more swiftly, with better results, than do any of the other agencies we've cited here. You can send a copy of your final complaint letter and documentation to the Chief Postal Inspector, U.S. Postal Service, Washington, DC 20260—but readers have told us that writing directly to the Postmaster of the post office nearest the firm is what does the trick.

Bankruptcy Courts. Bankruptcy courts may offer information, if no actual compensation, on errant orders and refunds. If you've written to the company and received no response and its phone has been disconnected, contact the U.S. Bankruptcy Court nearest the firm. Tell the clerk why you're calling, and ask whether the company has filed for reorganization under Chapter 11. If it has, get the case number and information on filing a claim. Chapter 11 protects a business against the claims of its creditors; all you can do is file as one of them, and hope. As a customer, your claim comes after those of the firm's suppliers, utilities, banks, etc. The "take a ticket" approach is no guarantee that you'll get anything back, but if it's your only shot, take the trouble to file.

The editor of BWBM would like to know whether you are particularly unhappy (or happy) with the service you've been receiving from one of the companies listed in this book. See "Feedback," following, for more information.

FEEDBACK

Your suggestions, complaints, and comments help to shape each edition of *Buy Wholesale by Mail*. When you write, please use the guidelines that follow.

Firms If you'd like your company considered for inclusion, have your marketing director send The Print Project a copy of your current catalog or literature with prices and background information on your firm. Companies are listed at the discretion of the editor and must meet the established criteria to qualify for inclusion.

Consumers If you wish to make suggestions for the next edition, send your postcard or letter to:

The Print Project, BWBM
P.O. Box 703
Bearsville, NY 12409

COMPANY INDEX

J. Schachter Corp., 304
John Scheepers, Inc., 238
Scholar's Bookshelf, 65
Nat Schwartz & Co., Inc., 374
Scope City, Inc., 81
Sewin' in Vermont, 298
Sewing Machine Super Store, 299
Seymour's Selected Seeds, 239
Shama Imports, Inc., 385
Shar Products Company, 443
Shaw Furniture Galleries, Inc., 339
R.H. Shumway Seedsman, 240
Shuttercraft, Inc., 315
Sierra Trading Post, 532
Silk Surplus, 386
Silver Queen, Inc., 376
Simply Diamonds, 396
Smart Saver, 104
Smiley's Yarns, 164
Daniel Smith, 183
Albert S. Smyth Co., Inc., 376
Snugglebundle, 115
SOAR Inflatables, 533
Sobol House, 340
Soccer International, 534
Solar Cine Products, Inc., 82
Solo Slide Fasteners, Inc., 164
Southland Furniture Galleries, 341
Special Clothes, Inc., 507
Spices Etc., 211
Spike Nashbar, Inc., 535
Sportsman's Guide, 536
Sportswear Clearinghouse, 104
Steerhides, 341
Stencil House of N.H., Inc., 386
Stickers 'N' Stuff, Inc., 571
Store Smart, 478
Storey Communications, Inc., 66
Strand Book Store, 67
Stu-Art, 184
Stumps, 572
Suburban Sew 'N Sweep, Inc., 300
Sultan's Delight, 203
Sunglasses U.S.A., Inc., 287
Sunrise Business Products, 479
Sunshine Discount Crafts, 136
Support Plus, 508
Surplus Center, 556
Swords Music Companies, Inc., 444

Tafford Manufacturing, Inc., 499
Tartan Book Sales, 68
Taylor's Cutaways and Stuff, 165
Tender Heart Treasures, Ltd., 342
Terry's Village, 343
Texas Art Supply, 185
Thai Silks, 166
That Fish Place/That Pet Place, 12
Think Ink, 137
Thoroughbred Music, Inc., 444
Thread Discount Sales, 167
J. Tiras Classic Handbags, Inc., 404
Tire Rack, 38
Tom Thumb Workshops, 149
Tomahawk Live Trap Co., 13
Tool Crib of the North, 556
Tool Hauz, Inc., 557
Tools on Sale, 558
TravelBids Travel Discount Auction, 583
Marion Travis, 344
Triner Scale, 480
Bonnie Triola Yarns, 168
Turncraft Clocks, Inc., 138
Turner Greenhouses, 241
20th Century Plastics, Inc., 480

ULINE, 481
Ultimate Outlet, 105
University Products, Inc., 482
UPCO, 14
Upstairs Records, 413
U.S. Box Corp., 483
U.S. Gov't Superintendent of Documents, 69
U.S. Toy Co., Inc., 573
Utex Trading Enterprises, 169
Utrecht, 186

Vacations to Go, 584
Valley Vet Supply, 15
Value-tique, Inc., 466
Van Bourgondien Bros., 242
Van Dyck's, 243
Van Engelen, Inc., 243
Vanguard Crafts, 138
Video Yesteryear, 414
Viking Office Products, 484
Village Carpet & Interiors, 322

Virtual Fairway, 536
Visual Horizons, 484

Wag-Aero Group of Aircraft Services,
39
Wall Rug & Carpets, 323
Warehouse Carpets, Inc., 323
Warner-Crivellaro Stained Glass Sup-
plies, Inc., 139
Water Warehouse, 537
WearGuard Corp., 106
Weaver Leather, 140
Webs, 169
Wedding Ring Hotline, 397
Weinkrantz Musical Supply Co., Inc.,
445
Wells Interiors, Inc., 387
West Manor Music, 446
West Marine, 40
West Rindge Baskets, Inc., 345
Westcoast Discount Video, 423

Weston Bowl Mill, 355
Wholesale Tape and Supply Company,
424
Wholesale Tool Co., Inc., 559
Wicker Warehouse, Inc., 346
Wiley Outdoor Sports, Inc., 538
Willow Ridge/Bedford Fair Lifestyles,
107
Wood's Cider Mill, 211
Woodworkers' Discount Books, 70
Woodworker's Hardware, 560
Woodworker's Supply, Inc., 315
World Wide Aquatics, 539
WorldWide Auto Parts, 41
Wray's Music House, 447

Yazoo Mills, Inc., 485
Paula Young Fashion Wigs, 279

Zabar's, 356